new testament theology

new
testament
theology

Leon Morris

Academie
Books Grand Rapids,
Michigan
Zondervan Publishing House

NEW TESTAMENT THEOLOGY

Copyright © 1986 by Leon Morris

ACADEMIE BOOKS
is an imprint of
Zondervan Publishing House
1415 Lake Drive S.E.
Grand Rapids, Michigan 49506

Library of Congress Cataloging in Publication Data

Morris, Leon, 1914–
    New Testament theology.

    Includes bibliographical references.
    1. Bible. N.T.–Theology. I. Title.

BS2397.M64   1985   225.6   85–29441

ISBN   0–310–45570–7

All Old Testament Scripture quotations, unless otherwise noted, are taken from the *Holy Bible: New International Version* (North American Edition), copyright © 1973, 1978, 1984 by the International Bible Society, used by permission of Zondervan Bible Publishers. New Testament Scripture selections, unless otherwise noted, are the author's own translations.

Designed by Louise Bauer

Edited by Gerard Terpstra

Printed in the United States of America

87 88 89 90 91 92 93 94 95 / AK / 10 9 8 7 6 5 4 3

contents

abbreviations

BAGD	Walter Bauer, *A Greek-English Lexicon of the New Testament and Other Early Christian Literature,* ed. William F. Arndt and F. Wilbur Gingrich, 2d ed., rev. F. Wilbur Gingrich and Frederick W. Danker (Chicago, 1979)
CBQ	*Catholic Biblical Quarterly*
Chmn	*The Churchman*
ExpT	*The Expository Times*
HTR	*The Harvard Theological Review*
IB	*The Interpreter's Bible,* ed. George A. Buttrick, 12 vols. (Nashville, 1952–57)
IBD	*The Illustrated Bible Dictionary,* 3 vols. (Leicester, 1980)
IBNTG	C. F. D. Moule, *An Idiom Book of New Testament Greek* (Cambridge, 1953)
IDB	*The Interpreter's Dictionary of the Bible,* ed. George A. Buttrick and Keith R. Crim, 6 vols. (Nashville, 1976)
Int	*Interpretation*
MM	James Hope Moulton and George Milligan: *The Vocabulary of the Greek Testament* (London, 1914–29)
NIDNTT	*The New International Dictionary of New Testament Theology,* ed. Colin Brown, 3 vols. (Grand Rapids, 1975–78)
NTS	*New Testament Studies*
RTR	*The Reformed Theological Review*
SBK	Hermann L. Strack und Paul Billerbeck: *Kommentar zum Neuen Testament aus Talmud und Midrasch,* 4 vols. (München, 1922–28)
SJT	*The Scottish Journal of Theology*
TDNT	Gerhard Kittel and Gerhard Friedrich, eds., *Theological Dictionary of the New Testament,* 10 vols. (Grand Rapids, 1964–76)
Theol	*Theology*
TynBul	*Tyndale Bulletin*
WTJ	*The Westminster Theological Journal*

preface

The aim of this book is to provide a compact introduction to the theology of the New Testament. The subject is a big one, as the existence of several massive volumes testify, but I have not sought to add yet another large work. Rather I have tried to steer a middle course between being unhelpfully brief and being too long and technical for the student or the interested layman. If such readers are stimulated to tackle the larger works, I will be well rewarded. In pursuing my aim I have not gone deeply into the controversies that interest the scholarly world, though I hope I have written with reasonable awareness of what scholars are saying. I have simply tried to set out the principal theological teachings of the books of the canonical New Testament as I see them, without trying to interact with scholarly theories. I would prefer to have provided more adequate documentation, but that too would have lengthened the book unduly.

Unless otherwise noted, I have used the New International Version for quotations from the Old Testament. I have made my own translation for quotations from the New Testament; this gives the reader the advantage of seeing what I understand the meaning of the Greek to be and, of course, the disadvantage of the limitations of a personal translation. I encourage the reader to check my readings against the standard translations.

I express my gratitude to ANZEA, the publishers of the forthcoming *Festschrift* for D. Broughton Knox, for permission to use my contribution to that work, "The Apostle Paul and His God."

Leon Morris

introduction

Although *New Testament Theology* is the title of a large number of books, its precise meaning is far from obvious. Part of the problem stems from different ways of using the word *theology*. Thus Rudolf Bultmann has a notable two-volume work entitled *Theology of the New Testament* in which he discusses a good deal of the New Testament. Two of his major sections are entitled "The Theology of Paul" and "The Theology of the Gospel of John and the Johannine Epistles," but his other major divisions are "Presuppositions and Motifs of New Testament Theology" (in which he includes the chapters "The Message of Jesus," "The Kerygma of the Earliest Church," and "The Kerygma of the Hellenistic Church Aside From Paul") and "The Development Toward the Ancient Church." This appears to mean that, although his book title refers to theology "of the New Testament," he finds theology in only two places, the Pauline and the Johannine writings. He expressly differentiates the teaching of Jesus from theology, for his opening sentence reads, "*The message of Jesus* is a presupposition for the theology of the New Testament rather than a part of that theology itself."[1] It would seem from this classification that most of the New Testament is not theology, and in any case it seems that there are two theologies, and not one.

W. G. Kümmel, by contrast, has a book whose full title is *The Theology of the New Testament According to Its Major Witnesses: Jesus—Paul—John*. This appears to mean that there is such a thing as the "the" theology of the New Testament, though a doubt remains because, while there is a chapter called "The Theology of Paul," the other chapter headings lack this key word ("The Proclamation of Jesus According to the First Three Gospels," "The Faith of the Primitive Community," etc.). In any case he disenfranchises most of the writers. It cannot be said that Kümmel deals with the theology "of the New Testament."

A similar comment can be made about Hans Conzelmann's *Outline of the Theology of the New Testament*. The table of contents indicates that the treatment is in five parts: The Kerygma of the Primitive Community and the Hellenistic Community, The Synoptic Kerygma, The Theology of Paul, The Development After Paul, and John. If we take this outline seriously, only one part deals specifically with theology.

Donald Guthrie approaches the subject thematically. He takes the great subjects dealt with in the New Testament and surveys the contributions made by all the writers to each of his themes.[2] We could continue this survey indefinitely. It

---

[1] Rudolf Bultmann, *Theology of the New Testament* (New York, 1951), 3. By contrast S. Neill says, "Every theology of the New Testament must be a theology of Jesus—or it is nothing at all" (*Jesus Through Many Eyes* [Philadelphia, 1976], 10). In marked contrast to Bultmann, J. Jeremias devotes the whole of vol. 1 of his *New Testament Theology* (London, 1971) to "The Proclamation of Jesus."

[2] *New Testament Theology* (London, 1981).

seems that almost every New Testament theologian sees his task differently from the way it appears to other practitioners of the art. Gerhard Hasel points out that of the eleven who produced New Testament theologies between 1967 and 1976 no two "agree on the nature, function, method, and scope of NT theology."[3]

It is clear that "theology" may be understood in more ways than one. Geoffrey W. Bromiley defines it briefly in this way: "Strictly, theology is that which is thought and said concerning God."[4] *The Shorter Oxford English Dictionary* sees it as "The study or science which treats of God, His nature and attributes, and His relations with man and the universe." Clearly it refers to disciplined thinking about God, and we might understand it in this sense: "A coherent system of ideas that interpret in logical fashion matters relating to God." Perhaps it would be better to say, ". . . that in principle is capable of interpreting . . . ," for our theologies are not always as coherent and effective as we would wish. But they do represent our attempt at setting out in orderly fashion our understanding of God and his revelation in Christ, and of what all this means for his worshipers. "New Testament theology" will then be that understanding of matters relating to God that is expressed by, or underlies, or may be deduced from, the New Testament. It will not necessarily always be expressed in set terms by the New Testament writers, but it will be implied in what they have said, for what they say always has as its basis their understanding of the ways of God. It we take the term "New Testament" seriously, we will resist the temptation to discard passages or books that we see as of inferior importance or even unauthentic. Everything in the New Testament is part of the thinking of the early church, whether it goes back to Jesus himself or to one of his followers.

The question inevitably arises concerning how far we are to repeat what the New Testament writers have said and how far we are to interpret it. Is our primary concern with "what they meant" or with "what they mean"? There is no substitute for pursuing the former question. We must make a sincere attempt to find the meaning the authors conveyed when they wrote their books in their own historical situations. But, of course, as we do so some element of interpretation is inevitable. We read these writings across a barrier of many centuries and from a standpoint of a very different culture. We make every effort to allow for this, but we never succeed perfectly. In this book I am striving hard to find out what the New Testament authors meant, and this not as an academic exercise, but as the necessary prelude to our understanding of what their writings mean for us today.

We must bear in mind that the writers of the New Testament books were not writing set theological pieces. They were concerned with the needs of the churches for which they wrote. Those churches already had the Old Testament, but these new writings became in time the most significant part of the Scriptures of the believing community. As such, they should be studied in their own right, and these questions should be asked: What do these writings mean? What is the theology they express or imply? What is of permanent validity in them?[5]

---

[3] *New Testament Theology* (Grand Rapids, 1978), 9–10. Leonhard Goppelt has a useful summary of the history and problems of New Testament theology in his *Theology of the New Testament*, i (Grand Rapids, 1981): 251–81. Interestingly neither there nor in vol. 2 does he treat Mark, Ephesians, the Pastoral Epistles, or the minor Catholic Epistles.

[4] Everett F. Harrison, Geoffrey W. Bromiley, and Carl F. H. Henry, eds., *Baker's Dictionary of Theology* (Grand Rapids, 1960), 518.

[5] Hendrikus Boers speaks of a "theological, that is, systematic presentation of the unchanging religious teaching contained in the Bible" (*What Is New Testament Theology?* [Philadelphia, 1979], 32). Charles C. Ryrie differentiates biblical theology from systematic theology and from exegesis: "It is a

It is with questions like these that this book is concerned. This work is not a history of New Testament times, nor an account of New Testament religion. Nor does it proceed from a view that the New Testament was written as theology. As I have just said, the New Testament writers wrote to meet the needs of the churches of their day as they saw them. But what they wrote should not be understood as a series of random reflections. Behind all these books is the deep conviction, the deep theological conviction, that God has acted in Christ. In other words, there is theology behind all the New Testament writings. We cannot write a theology of Peter or James or even of Paul, for in no case do we have sufficient material, or even an indication that the writer is giving us what he sees as most important for Christian theology. They are all occasional writings. But these writings are theologically informed, and we do well to take seriously the ideas expressed or implied in them.

Another problem arises from the very nature of the project. William Wrede long ago maintained that "the name New Testament theology is wrong in both its terms,"[6] and many scholars since his time would agree. Wrede argues that we should take into consideration the whole of early Christian literature, not simply the books in the canon, and further that the New Testament is concerned with religion rather than with theology. Indeed, he thinks that the subject would be better called "early Christian history of religion" or "the history of early Christian religion and theology."[7]

But is the title really wrong in either aspect? It is, of course, possible to write a theology of the early church, taking into consideration all the early literature available. But the church has always given the canonical writings a special place,[8] and there seems no real reason why these writings should not be studied together,[9] with no more than passing references to other early literature. The church has always regarded the canonical books as "inspired" (however the term has been understood). It is to these books and no others that Christians refer when they wish to establish authentic Christian teaching.[10] Wrede puts little difference between the canonical writings and other early Christian literature: "No New Testament writing was born with the predicate 'canonical' attached. The statement that a writing is canonical signifies in the first place only that it was pronounced canonical afterwards by the authorities of the second- to fourth-century church, in some cases only after all kinds of hesitation and disagree-

---

combination which is partly historical, partly exegetical, partly critical, partly theological, and thereby totally distinctive" (*Biblical Theology of the New Testament* [Chicago, 1982], 11).

[6] Cited from his essay, "The Task and Methods of 'New Testament Theology' " reprinted in Robert Morgan, *The Nature of New Testament Theology* (London, 1973), 116.

[7] Ibid.

[8] Cf. F. F. Bruce, "The New Testament comprises all the writings which have any reasonable claim to be regarded as the foundation documents or primary sources of the Christian faith" (*The Message of the New Testament* [Grand Rapids, 1983], 11).

[9] Cf. Norman Perrin, "The fact remains that the New Testament is an entity, which as an entity, has played and does play an enormous role in Christian history, and I am not prepared to dissolve it into something else without much stronger grounds than the historical ambiguities of the process of the formation of the canon" (cited in Hasel, *New Testament Theology*, 135–36.)

[10] James D. G. Dunn finds a good deal of diversity in the New Testament, but he sees the canon as important. It "marks out the limits of acceptable diversity" (*Unity and Diversity in the New Testament* [Philadelphia, 1977], 378); "The traditions of the NT have a normative authority which cannot be accorded to later church traditions" (p. 383); "The NT is canonical . . . because the interlocking character of so many of its component parts hold the whole together in the unity of a diversity which acknowledges a common loyalty" (p. 387).

ment. . . . Anyone who accepts without question the idea of the canon places himself under the authority of the bishops and theologians of those centuries."[11] But this is too simple. Specifically it overlooks the fact that no bishop and no theologian (or even council) seems ever to have assumed the right to make any book canonical or, for that matter, uncanonical.

What seems to have happened was something like this: Some of the faithful are perplexed. They are finding that in some churches books like 2 and 3 John are not read as sacred Scripture, whereas in others they are. Some are reading books like 1 Clement. What is the right course? What should they do? The question is referred to an authority, a bishop or a theologian or a council. When the decision is given, it is in some such statement as this: "These are the books that have been recognized in the church." For example, when Athanasius gave his well-known list of the books of the New Testament (the first official list that has our twenty-seven books, no more and no fewer), he referred to the authentic books as those "delivered to the fathers," and he went on to list them as those "handed down, and accredited as Divine."[12] He did not decree that henceforth they were to be canonical; he said that they had been received as such, and the formula was always something like that. No Christian or group of Christians seems ever to have taken upon himself or itself the authority to add any book to the accepted list or to delete any book from it.[13] If we take seriously the idea that God guides his church, we must see in this an indication that these are the books that he means his people to have. It is a striking fact that, at a time when there was no machinery for imposing a decision on the world-wide church, exactly the same twenty-seven books were practically universally accepted.[14] We should not see the canon as an arbitrary arrangement brought about by some bishops and theologians. It holds a special place in the Christian scheme of things,[15] and there is not the slightest reason why it should not be studied by itself for that reason.

---

[11] Morgan, *Nature of New Testament Theology*, 70–71. The idea that no New Testament writing was written as canonical is perhaps not quite as certain as Wrede maintains. Revelation opens with a benediction on him who reads it and those who hear it (Rev. 1:3). Where would they hear it read other than in the gathering of Christians for worship? It is possible that this book was meant to be read in church as canonical from the first. H. B. Swete holds that the writer "claims for his book that it shall take rank with the prophetic books of the O.T." (*The Apocalypse of St. John* [London, 1906], 1). So also Robert H. Mounce, *The Book of Revelation* (Grand Rapids, 1977), 66.

[12] *Nicene and Post-Nicene Fathers*, Second Series, iv (Grand Rapids, 1957): 551–52.

[13] This is not to deny that certain church leaders (Irenaeus, for example) played important roles in discussions about the canon nor that in time criteria such as "apostolicity" were used as tests. But all the evidence points not to a deliberate "canon making," but to the whole church as proceeding at varying speeds and at differing times to similar conclusions. Denis M. Farkasfalvy follows a question about the canonicity of Revelation with this statement: "It seems that the Church knew how to identify as 'apostolic books' those it needed. And, of course, it did all this on the basis of its convictions that it possessed in its apostolic foundations all that was needed to build upon" (William R. Farmer and Denis M. Farkasfalvy, *The Formation of the New Testament Canon* [New York, 1983], 156). I refer to this more or less subconscious process.

[14] The Peshitta, a Syriac version of the New Testament dating from about the fifth century, does not contain 2 Peter, 2 John, 3 John, Jude, and Revelation. Alfred Wikenhauser says that the eastern half of the Syrian church still holds this canon; the western half (the Jacobites) have the full twenty-seven books, but "so far as is known, these five writings are not used in their liturgy" (*New Testament Introduction*, [New York, 1958], 57). But overwhelmingly Christendom agreed on the twenty-seven–book canon. There was, of course, a good deal of discussion and for a long time there was uncertainty in some places about certain books such as Hebrews and Revelation. But in the end these twenty-seven books were recognized, not because some bishop or theologian gave them canonical status, but because the church in general came to see in them part of the revelation God had given.

[15] Cf. B. F. Westcott, "As if by some providential instinct, each one of those teachers who stood nearest to the writers of the New Testament plainly contrasted his writings with theirs, and definitely

Wrede's second point is that "theology" is the wrong word; he insists strongly on a historical approach (cf. Morgan's reference to "the theological method of interpreting the tradition by historical methods").[16] It is, of course, possible to study the New Testament in this way, but I cannot agree that it is the only way. I simply do not know enough about the history of the early church to attempt it,[17] and I marvel at the confidence with which some approach the task. The historical approach is a very uncertain approach, because our *knowledge* of the history of the early church (as opposed to our conjectures and deductions) is so meager. The Gospels are not concerned to give us a history of the life and times of Jesus of Nazareth. They tell us what is important for our salvation, and the history is more or less incidental.[18] With the information at present at our disposal it is simply not possible to give anything like an accurate historical account of the life of Jesus of Nazareth and of the first days of the church that resulted from his life and death and resurrection. Scholars dispute about how much of the Gospels goes back to Jesus; there are endless discussions about the authenticity of this or that saying and about that or this incident. If we are to insist on accurate history before we can speak of theology, we are in sad case indeed.[19]

We see Wrede's concern for history in his contention that "in the last resort, we at least want to know *what was believed, thought, taught, hoped, required and striven for* in the earliest period of Christianity; not what certain writings say about faith, doctrine, hope, etc."[20] I share Wrede's desire for information about what was believed and thought and so on (though I do not see how that desire is to be gratified without some startling new source of information), but I strongly dissent when he declines to take an interest in what the New Testament says about faith and doctrine and hope. I do very much want to know what it says about such things. Those whose area of expertise is history are certainly free to pursue history. But theology is a distinct discipline, and it may be pursued even when we are not

---

placed himself on a lower level. The fact is most significant; for it shows in what way the formation of the Canon was an act of the institution of the Church, derived from no reasoning, but realized in the course of its natural growth" (*A General Survey of the History of the Canon of the New Testament* [Cambridge, 1855], 65–66).

[16] Morgan, *Nature of New Testament Theology*, 59. Morgan argues for the separation of historical and theological studies in an article entitled, "A Straussian Question to 'New Testament Theology'" (*NTS* 23 [1976–77]: 243–65). *Inter alia* he points out that "it was precisely Baur's tight-knit unity of the course of history with its metaphysical theological interpretation which made his theology extremely vulnerable and open to falsification through his historical picture being corrected" (p. 256); "Historians and theologians can be seen to obey different rules" (p. 259). He is not, of course, arguing that the two disciplines can be pursued completely separately: "What is historically false cannot be theologically true" (p. 265). But Wrede's position cannot be sustained.

[17] It is comforting that Hans Conzelmann has no section in his *Theology of the New Testament* on the "problem of the historical Jesus," and that he says, "I find this problem a baffling one." He says further, "I must nevertheless insist that the 'historical Jesus' is not a theme of New Testament theology" (*An Outline of the Theology of the New Testament* [London, 1969], xvii).

[18] Cf. J. Bonsirven, "Since I am writing a work on theology, it is no business of mine to trace back the history of primitive Christianity, to unravel the problems which are raised by the gaps in the documents at our disposal" (*Theology of the New Testament* [London, 1963], 157).

[19] Rudolf Schnackenburg objects to the historical approach on three principal grounds: (1) the chronology is uncertain and the "development" very disputable; (2) this kind of theology "seems to be indistinguishable from comparative religion"; and (3) it destroys the "unity of New Testament theology" (*New Testament Theology Today* [New York, 1963], 24).

[20] Morgan, *Nature of New Testament Theology*, 84–85 (Wrede's italics).

certain of the historical details surrounding the documents in which it is enshrined.[21] To go into the precise times at which given doctrines emerged and the exact early Christians who first enunciated them would be interesting, but it is not what I see as biblical theology. As Bernard Weiss put it long ago, "Biblical theology cannot concern itself with the critical and specialized investigations regarding the origin of NT writings, because it is only a historical-descriptive science and not a historical-critical one."[22] Theology is concerned rather with faith and hope and love, with sin and salvation, with life here and now, with our hopes for the hereafter, and above all with God and with what God has done in Christ.[23] The approach that insists on a close historical study of the way the New Testament writings reached their present form is inadequate.

This is not to deny that there is development of thought in the New Testament. There is certainly development, even if we are not in a position to trace that development with any exactness. But in any case the task of theology is descriptive, rather than historical. It is concerned to say what the theological teachings of the various writings are, not to explain when and how their various authors got them. Christians are concerned primarily with a group of books in their canonical form, rather than with how they got into that form.[24] The theologian, of course, must have some concern for history. The New Testament documents emerged at a given time and in a given culture, neither of which is ours. We must go back to that time and ask our questions in the light of that given culture if we are to make sense of the documents. What I am eschewing is the attempt to trace in detail the sequence of events in the early church and the way the documents came to be in their present form as the necessary prelude to theology.

Because New Testament theology is basically occupied with the final product, not with working out the steps along the way, it seeks out what is distinctive of the early Christians over against what Judaism or Hellenism or first-century

---

[21] Indeed, Adolf Schlatter sees New Testament theology as "an indispensable tool which critical introduction constantly uses in its own work" (Morgan, *Nature of New Testament Theology*, 159). Hendrikus Boers says that the outcome of the work of the *Religions-geschichtliche* school "was that the presentation of such a history [i.e., the history of a living religion, not a history of doctrines] became separated not only from the New Testament canon but also from usefulness for contemporary Christianity" (*What Is New Testament Theology?* [Philadelphia, 1979], 66). We do a disservice to the church if we do not recognize that theology has a place of its own, a place quite distinct from that of history.

[22] Cited in Hasel, *New Testament Theology,* 36.

[23] We must not overlook the point made by Floyd V. Filson in his article "How I Interpret the Bible": "I work with the conviction that the only really objective method of study takes the reality of God and his working into account, and that any other point of view is loaded with presuppositions which actually, even if very subtly, contain an implicit denial of the full Christian faith" (*Int* 4 [1950]: 186).

[24] Hans Conzelmann makes this point with respect to Luke's writings: "This study of St. Luke's theology is, by its approach to the problems, for the most part not dependent on any particular literary theories about St. Luke's Gospel and the Acts of the Apostles, for it is concerned with the whole of Luke's writings as they stand. If these form a self-contained scheme, then for our purpose literary critical analysis is only of secondary importance." He agrees that this secondary importance is not to be despised and then proceeds, "We must make it plain, however, that our aim is to elucidate Luke's work in its present form, not to enquire into possible sources or into the historical facts which provide the material" (*The Theology of St Luke* [London, 1961], 9). Similarly Joseph A. Fitzmyer says, "It is the theology of the end product that has to be synthesized. This, in the long run, is more important than what can be ferreted out in the twentieth century as the theology of 'Q' or of the teaching of Jesus" (*The Gospel According to Luke [I–IX])*, [New York, 1983], 144).

society in general believed. It is reasonable to expect that the Christian community had some things in common with each of these others and some things peculiar to itself. Individual Christians surely had their own personal emphases (just as they do today). It is important to see what is distinctive of Christians, both as a group and as individuals. In this study I will attempt something of an overview of the thought of each—that is, of Christians as a whole and as individuals—and attempt to discover both what is distinctive and what is common to all. The great Christian affirmations should emerge.

I am more respectful of Wrede's insistence on the concern of the New Testament writers for religion. But as I see it, religion and theology go together, or should do so. Each is impoverished without the other. A purely pragmatic religion, with no considered theology behind it, is unsatisfying. At the same time a theology that does not issue in right religious practices is not worth much. Theology, as the New Testament writers see it, necessarily issues in right attitudes and right practices, and that toward both God and other people. But where the theology and the religion with which it is so closely bound up can be distinguished, this book is concerned with the former.

The Christian theologian, accordingly, becomes involved in his subject. Morgan points out that "a theologian does not have the same freedom as a historian. He cannot say that this was how the tradition understood Christianity, but that it is not a live option for him. If he is to remain a *Christian* theologian, he *must* be able to claim continuity with the tradition, and that means weaving the pattern of his own position with threads received from the past."[25] In some measure all Christians are involved in this task of identifying the threads in the New Testament and weaving them into a pattern. It may be that none of us will be completely successful; we are not big enough and our grasp is not comprehensive enough to accomplish the task. It may even be that some will see the task as an effort to reconcile the irreconcilable.[26] But at least what we are trying to do in a study like this is to come to grips with the teaching of the whole New Testament. We are trying to be, not Paulinists or followers of John or of the Synoptic theologians, but theologians of the New Testament.

This leads to a further problem confronting anyone who would write a theology of the New Testament these days—namely, a widespread recognition that there are considerable differences among the writers of the various New Testament books. Some argue that there can be no such thing as a theology "of the New Testament"; they prefer to think of a number of "theologies."[27] They see the differences among the writers as so considerable that they can talk only of contradictions, and, of course, if there are contradictions, it is useless to seek a common theology.

---

[25] Morgan, *Nature of New Testament Theology,* p. 41.

[26] It is out of some such conviction that many these days prefer to work with a "canon within the canon"; they see some canonical book or books as basically reliable and relegate the others to a secondary place or even ignore them altogether. Hans Küng points out that this "demands nothing but to be more biblical than the Bible" (*Structures of the Church* [New York, 1964], 164). In any case all such approaches are hopelessly subjective; there is no compelling reason for singling out one part of the New Testament over against the rest. Everything depends on the personal choices of the individual and, whatever the selection, it inevitably results in a theology that is impoverished by the omission of important parts of Scripture. Hasel has a useful discussion of "the canon within the canon" with references to the literature (*New Testament Theology,* 164–70).

[27] Cf. Schlatter, "New Testament theology must be divided into as many theologies as there are New Testament authors" (Morgan, *Nature of New Testament Theology,* 140).

But, while we recognize the differences, we must also recognize that there is a unity. If there had not been some kind of unity, the various books would not all have been accepted into the one canon. For all their differences the writers of the New Testament books were all recognized as Christians, as were the many other believers who did not write books. There was something that marked Christians off from other people, and that something was recognized by both the Christians themselves and the outsiders who viewed them. There was a recognition among the Christians that God had acted in Jesus of Nazareth, especially in his death and resurrection. There was a recognition that what God had done demanded from them an attitude of trust (their word was "faith") and a resulting life of service— service to their God and and service to other people.

A good deal depends on what we are looking for. In bringing out his thought of unity in the diversity of the New Testament, A. M. Hunter draws attention to the use of a variety of phrases: in the Synoptic Gospels, "the kingdom of God"; in Paul, "being in Christ"; and in John, "the Logos becoming incarnate." He proceeds, "Now isolate each of these phrases, and observe what is likely to happen. Your study of the Kingdom of God may take you back through Judaism to the Old Testament and perhaps even (as it did Otto) to primitive Aryan religion. Your study of the Pauline formula 'in Christ' may take you back to Hellenistic mysticism (as it did Deissmann). Your study of the *Logos* may take you back through Philo to Plato and the Stoics."[28] There is no real connection between primitive Aryan religion, Hellenistic mysticism, and Philo, Plato, and the Stoics. It would be easy to conclude that the three expressions quoted have nothing to do with each other. But that would be too hasty a conclusion. As Hunter goes on, "When Jesus said, 'The Kingdom of God has come upon you' (Luke x.9) and Paul 'If any man is in Christ, there is a new creation' (2 Cor. v.17) and John 'The *Logos* became flesh and dwelt among us' (John i.14), they were not making utterly different and unrelated announcements; on the contrary, they were using different idioms, different categories of thought, to express their common conviction that the living God had spoken and acted through his Messiah for the salvation of his people."[29]

This means that we should not hastily assume that different forms of expression necessarily point to irreconcilable contradictions. There is such a thing as "unity in diversity," and where it exists we should seek it out. I do not mean, of course, that Hunter's example proves that all the diversities in the New Testament will, on examination, resolve themselves into a satisfying unity. We are at the beginning of the enterprise. We do not know where it will lead. All I am saying is that what Hunter has done shows plainly that there can be a basic unity when some of the New Testament writers are using their natural thought forms to express ideas that on the surface are not closely related. We must not pass over the diversities, but it is important also that we do not neglect the unity.

We could perhaps draw an illustration from our own experience. In a congregation of like-minded Christian people we commonly find differences. Some members are better informed and are more profound thinkers than others. Some of the others may express themselves in ways that the former would not choose, ways that are open to legitimate objection. But are they necessarily saying

---

[28] *The Unity of the New Testament* (London, 1943), 14.

[29] Ibid., 14–15. Hunter finds a basic unity in the New Testament in teaching about the *kerygma*, Jesus as Lord, the church, and salvation.

things that are incompatible with the way the better informed would express them? There may be a deep and moving unity in a congregation, no matter what the forms of expression of individual members are. There may also, of course, be perversity of spirit and the holding of opinions that the congregation at large would not accept. We must look at the New Testament and see what the teaching of the various writers means and whether or not the differences point to irreconcilable contradictions.

At this point I am saying no more than that in modern congregations we sometimes find widely differing forms of expression used by people whose basic beliefs are much the same and that in the same way there may be a New Testament equivalent. There are outstanding thinkers and writers in the New Testament, but, however great their differences, we must be clear that they were members of the same community of faith; they did not emerge from some wilderness, barren of religious convictions. They were all shaped by their contact with Christ, but also to some extent by the community to which they belonged. What they wrote is *Christian* teaching, however individual their expression. And they all wrote under the tutelage of the same Holy Spirit.

This does not mean that all ways of expressing the Christian position are acceptable. Paul complained of "another gospel—that is not another" (Gal. 1:6–7), and through all the centuries the church has known of people who claimed to be Christians but who were so far from the distinctive Christian faith that they were labeled heretics. We must look at the differences in the New Testament as well as the unity to see whether we are confronted with incompatible opinions or not. One big difference is that the preaching of Jesus, with its emphasis on the kingdom of God, is some distance removed from the preaching of the early church with its emphasis on the death and resurrection of Jesus. Nothing in the Epistles leads us to think that the first Christians made any attempt simply to pass on what Jesus had said. They did, of course, remember it and they passed it on as its preservation in the Gospels shows.

But for the early Christians there was no going back on the cross and the resurrection. These events constituted the central part of God's great saving acts, and in one way or another the New Testament writers all express it. Paul could speak of "a new creation" (2 Cor. 5:17), which Acts shows plainly had happened in Paul's own case (Acts containing three accounts of his conversion). There is an emphasis on life in Acts, John, and Paul, and with that goes a stress on the importance of believing and living in newness of life. And throughout the New Testament there is a strong emphasis on the Cross and the Resurrection; the Gospels lead up to it as their climax, and the other books look back to it as their basis. In other words Christianity points us to a great act of God that centers on the Cross (this is crucial in the literal sense of that word) and challenges us to embrace "salvation," which means abandoning an old way of life and proceeding in a new one. The New Testament writers do not all express this in the same way, nor do they all emphasize identical aspects. It was the case from the first, as it has been the case through the centuries, that one aspect of the faith is more congenial to one Christian, another to another. But these writers are all writing about authentic Christian experience and specifically about what God has done for our salvation. It will be our task to look for the theological truth behind the various ways of expressing it.

This subject could be approached in any one of a number of ways. We could begin with the Gospels, proceed to Acts, and take the Epistles in chronological order. Or we could tackle everything in chronological order—at least this could be done if the chronological order were known. There are other possibilities, as the variety of New Testament theologies amply attests. In the lack of any generally accepted procedure, we will start with the Pauline writings, for there can be little doubt that these are the oldest part of the New Testament. After that, dates are hazardous, but we will proceed to Jesus as he is depicted by Mark, Matthew, the Lucan writings, and John—in that order. This does not mean that the teaching of Jesus is either uncertain or unattainable. On the contrary, the Gospels give us reliable accounts of Jesus, and his words and deeds are of fundamental importance. But there is no denying that the accounts are later than the writings of Paul and they thus may well be looked at after we have studied Paul. Hebrews will follow, and after that the remaining writings. If the reader protests that there are objections to this order, I quite agree. But then there are objections to any order. And in any case here, as some wit once remarked about systematic theology, it does not matter much where you start, you must go through it all before you come out. With this stimulating thought before us, let us proceed to look at the New Testament books.

part one

the pauline
WRITINGS

aul was a very gifted man, and his wide and effective ministry[1] was helped by the fact that he was equally at home in two worlds, the world of Judaism and the world of Hellenism (perhaps we should add a third—the world of Rome). He was "an Israelite, of the seed of Abraham, of the tribe of Benjamin" (Rom. 11:1; cf. 2 Cor. 11:22), a fact in which he clearly gloried. Of fleshly descent and achievement he could write, "If any other man has confidence in the flesh, I have more; circumcised the eighth day, of the nation Israel, of the tribe of Benjamin, a Hebrew of the Hebrews; with regard to the law, a Pharisee, with

regard to zeal, persecuting the church, with regard to righteousness in the law, blameless" (Phil. 3:4–6). His manner of life accorded with his deep conviction that the way to God was not that of obedience to the law, yet on occasion his practice could be Judaic; for example, Luke tells us that at Cenchrea he had his hair cut off because of a vow (Acts 18:18), evidently a Nazirite vow.[2] Although he became a fervent believer in Christ and, indeed, gave his entire life over to living for Christ and preaching Christ, he did not go back on his Judaism. He could ask, "What, then, is the advantage of the Jew? or what is the profit of circumcision?" and

---

[1] Edgar J. Goodspeed said, "Certainly Paul has dominated Christian theology ever since the first century, and he is still revealing new moral values in the mid-twentieth" (*Paul* [Philadelphia, 1947], 221). Cf. Michael Grant, "Without the spiritual earthquake that he brought about, Christianity would probably never have survived at all. Yet his importance also extends very widely beyond and right outside the religious field. For he has also exercised a gigantic influence, for generation after generation, upon non-religious events and ways of thinking—upon politics and sociology and war and philosophy and that whole intangible area in which the thought-processes of successive epochs become formed"; he goes on to call Paul "one of the outstanding makers of the history of mankind" (*Saint Paul* [New York, 1976], 1).

[2] Some hold that this could not have been a Nazirite vow on the grounds that the hair could be shaved off only in Jerusalem. But I. Howard Marshall cites evidence that, while the sacrifice had to be offered in Jerusalem, the hair could be shaved elsewhere (*The Acts of the Apostles* [Leicester, 1980], 300).

though the logic of his argument leads us to expect the answer "Nothing," his answer is "Much in every way . . ." (Rom. 3:1–2). Throughout his writings he makes constant appeal to the Jewish Scriptures, and it is clear that to the end of his days it mattered to him that God had given such a treasure to his nation.

There is a marked difference in the way he handled Greek writings. It is clear from Paul's grasp of the Greek language that all the treasures of Greek literature were open to him, but in all his writings he quotes from a Greek author only twice (1 Cor. 15:33; Titus 1:12; Luke tells of another quotation, this one in a sermon, Acts 17:28). Paul's interest was in the Old Testament; he quotes from it constantly, and, interestingly, he quotes mostly from the Septuagint (Greek) rather than from the Hebrew.

Paul identified with Israel. Even in writing to Gentiles he calls Abraham "our forefather" and Isaac "our father" (Rom. 4:1; 9:10), and he refers to "all our fathers" (1 Cor. 10:1). He looks for peace on "the Israel of God" (Gal. 6:16).[3] Perhaps this identification is nowhere as poignant as in his emotional treatment of the problem of Israel's rejection of the Messiah. Christ meant everything to him (Phil. 3:8), but he could wish himself accursed from Christ if only that would avail for his fellow Israelites (Rom. 9:3). It is plain from all he wrote that Paul valued his Jewish heritage highly. Even though it could not compare with the Christian way (2 Cor. 3:11), he still saw it as having "glory" (Rom. 9:4; 2 Cor. 3:7). He was unlike many converts to a new religion who become very bitter against the faith they have forsaken. Paul was a Christian through and through, but he was also an Israelite through and through, and we will not make sense of his writings unless we bear this mind.[4]

But, although he was so thoroughly Jewish and apparently at first thought his ministry would be among Jews (Acts 22:17–20), his work turned out to be largely among Gentiles. He was equipped for this in that he was a citizen of Tarsus, where he had had a good education and became thoroughly familiar with the way of life in

[3]The precise meaning of this expression is disputed. Many agree with RSV: "Peace and mercy be upon all who walk by this rule, upon the Israel of God," which equates the Israel of God with the church. But such a way of referring to the church is not found elsewhere, and some see a reference to non-Christian Israel. In the nineteenth added to the Eighteen Benedictions there is a prayer for peace and other blessings "upon us and upon all Israel thy people." If Paul had a view like this he "now prays for his fellow countrymen who have not yet accepted Christ" (Raymond T. Stamm, *IB*, 10:591). F. F. Bruce is reminded that Paul looks for the salvation of "all Israel" (Rom. 11:26), and sees "an eschatological perspective" here (*The Epistle to the Galatians* [Grand Rapids, 1982], 275). N. Herman Ridderbos, however, supports the first view: "In view of what has gone before (*cf.* 3:29; 4:28, 29) we can hardly doubt that this *Israel of God* does not refer to the empirical, national Israel as an equally authorized partner *alongside of* the believers in Christ ('they who walk by this rule'), neither only to the believing part of the national Israel, but to all the believers as the new Israel. In this benediction, then, the apostle has the readers of his letter, in so far as they walk by the new rule, in mind, but from them its scope goes out to include in the widest sense all believers whatsoever, the new people of God" (*The Epistle of Paul to the Churches of Galatia* [London, 1954], 227). And, while he does not specifically call the church Israel elsewhere, he clearly regarded it as the true Israel (Rom 2:28–29; 9:6; Phil. 3:3).

[4]W. D. Davies has made out a convincing case for Paul's essential Jewishness in *Paul and Rabbinic Judaism* [London, 1948]. In his conclusion he writes, "It appears that for the Apostle the Christian Faith was the full flowering of Judaism, the outcome of the latter and its fulfilment; in being obedient to the Gospel he was merely being obedient to the true form of Judaism. The Gospel for Paul was not the annulling of Judaism but its completion" (p. 323). David Daube shows the Jewishness of Paul's usage in a number of points in his *New Testament and Rabbinic Judaism* (London, 1956); for example, in his missionary practice (pp. 336ff.).

the world of Hellenistic culture. He was a Roman citizen (Acts 16:37; 22:25–28), in which capacity he made his well-known appeal to Caesar (Acts 25:11). It accords with this citizenship that he urges the Romans to be subject to the governing authoritics (Rom. 13:1–7) and says that prayer should be made for kings and all in authority (1 Tim. 2:1–3). Clearly he valued his heritage, both Greek and Roman.

Jew though he was, Paul made it clear that the work to which he was called was largely to be done among the other nations of the world. He was the apostle to the Gentiles (Rom. 11:13), "a minister of Christ Jesus to the Gentiles" (Rom. 15:16); his call was to preach Christ among the Gentiles (Gal. 1:16; Eph. 3:8). He spoke of an agreement with the Jerusalem apostles whereby he and Barnabas were to go to the Gentiles, while James, Peter, and John went to Jews (Gal. 2:9). He called himself "the prisoner of Christ Jesus on behalf of . . . the Gentiles" (Eph. 3:1), and "a teacher of Gentiles" (1 Tim. 2:7; also, in some MSS, 2 Tim. 1:11).

This complex background complicates our study of Paul's writings. So does the apostle's literary style. He rushes on, often leaving out words he expected his readers to supply (and which they hope they are supplying correctly!). He is an original thinker, sometimes struggling with language to say things that no one had said before. This increases our difficulty and at the same time makes our quest the more rewarding.[5]

There is, of course, considerable dispute about which writings are Paul's. These days many scholars hold that the Pastoral Epistles do not come from this great apostle (though he may have written some fragments that are embedded in these letters). Not a few have their doubts about Ephesians and/or Colossians, while 2 Thessalonians is also rejected by some. To go into discussions about the authenticity of all these writings would involve a major digression from my main theological purpose. So let me simply say that I propose to include them all as belonging within the scope of this study. Good reasons have been urged for accepting all of them as Pauline,[6] and, while many remain unconvinced, at least there is something about them all that in the judgment of the church led them to be accepted as products of

---

[5] Cf. Stephen Neill, "A great thinker, Paul can be and often is abominably difficult. But he is not intentionally difficult. Again and again he is trying to say things that had never been said before and for which he has no vocabulary to hand. . . . It often happens that when Paul is most difficult, he is also most original" (*Jesus Through Many Eyes* [Philadelphia, 1976], 42).

[6] For Ephesians, see, for example, Markus Barth, *Ephesians 1–3* (New York, 1974), 41; for Colossians, Reginald H. Fuller, *A Critical Introduction to the New Testament* (London, 1966), 59–64; Ralph P. Martin, *Colossians and Philemon* (London, 1974), 32–40; for 2 Thessalonians, Ernest Best, *A Commentary on the First and Second Epistles to the Thessalonians* (London, 1977), 50–58; for the Pastorals, Donald Guthrie, *The Pastoral Epistles and the Mind of Paul* (Leicester, 1977); Ronald A. Ward, *A Commentary on 1 and 2 Timothy and Titus* (Waco, 1974), 9–13; J. N. D. Kelly, *A Commentary on the Pastoral Epistles* (New York, 1963), 30–34. Donald J. Selby thinks that as time went on Paul probably "tended to allow his amanuenses, who were also his fellow workers and traveling companions, more and more freedom in composing the letters." Their involvement in the work and their increasing familiarity with what Paul taught "would make such sharing in the composition of the letters not only feasible but inevitable" (*Introduction to the New Testament* [New York, 1971], 323). E. Earle Ellis points to the importance of the work of amanuenses and also of the inclusion of "pre-formed pieces—hymns, biblical expositions and other literary forms that are self-contained and that differ from the language, style and theological expression elsewhere in the same and in other letters." He thinks that "any conclusions about the authorship of the letters on the basis of their language, style and theological idiom are questionable at best" (*NTS* 26 [1979–80]: 498–99).

Paul. In the broad sense of the term they are "Pauline";[7] they stand apart from writings like those of John or the Synoptics. We may well consider them together.

Some scholars trace development in Paul's thought from the earlier to the later letters, but this is probably a vain pursuit. The letters all come from a comparatively short period of time toward the end of Paul's life. But Paul had been a Christian and a preacher for seventeen or more years before writing the first of his extant letters. His essential position must have been established well before he wrote his letters. The differences in the letters are to be accounted for by the different circumstances of the apostle and the different situations that called them forth, rather than by some supposed development in his thinking.

We must bear in mind the fact that Paul's writings are real letters, letters written to real people who had real problems. He never attempts to set out in order a summary of his theology. Because of the way some themes keep coming up, and because of the way Paul treats them, we can deduce that they are important. But where there was no controversy he said little, and this includes important topics like the authority of Scripture or the personality of God. All Paul's letters are occasional writings, not chapters in a systematic theology, and we must be on

our guard against thinking that we can set out in orderly fashion a summary of all the theological topics he saw as important. But all that he writes is theologically informed, and this enables us to say things with confidence. We may not be able to set forth systematically "the theology of St. Paul," but we can certainly say that Paul gave expression to some important theological ideas. Whether these ideas present a complete theology or not, they make a rewarding study.

We should not overlook the fact that these writings were produced early. While there is uncertainty about some of the dating, Paul's first extant letter must have been written within about twenty years of the Crucifixion, and the main body of his writings was completed within a very few years. Thus it did not take long for the essentials of Christian doctrine to appear in their Pauline formulation. This fact is significant especially in a day when some critics give the impression that for many years the early church was busy evolving and shaping what came to be Christian orthodoxy.

There are those who hold that Paul took over a good deal from the primitive church,[8] but this raises the question, "What primitive church?" There is no reason to doubt Martin Hengel's estimate that Paul was converted "somewhere between 32 and 34."[9] There were certainly some Christians

---

[7]Thus, A. M. Hunter holds that, while the Pastorals contain no more than fragments of Paul's writings (as P. N. Harrison argued), "in their present form they are the work of a Paulinist" (*Introducing New Testament Theology* [London, 1969], 87n.1). Similarly Nils Alstrup Dahl says of Ephesians, Colossians, and the Pastoral Epistles, that they "represent Pauline catechetical traditions even if not written by Paul" (*Studies in Paul* [Minneapolis, 1977], 22n.1).

[8]A. M. Hunter, for example, lists seven points that Paul took over: "(1) the apostolic *kerygma* . . . ; (2) the confession of Jesus as Messiah, Lord and Son of God; (3) the doctrine of the Holy Spirit as the divine dynamic of the new life; (4) the conception of the Church as the New Israel; (5) the sacraments of Baptism and the Lord's Supper; (6) 'the Words of the Lord' which Paul quotes or echoes in his letters; and (7) the hope of the *Parousia*—or Christ's coming in glory" (*The Gospel According to St. Paul* [Philadelphia, 1966], 12).

[9]*Between Jesus and Paul* (Philadelphia, 1983), 11. Reasoning from the inscriptions giving the date of Gallio's proconsulate in Achaia, Paul's stay in Corinth (Acts 18:11ff.) and the time notes in Gal. 1:18,

before Paul, but not many. If anyone belonged to the "early" church Paul did; and when Christian tradition was established, he played a part in establishing it.[10] Let me say with the utmost plainness that there is no reason at all for holding that there was significant growth in Christian theology before Paul became a Christian. His theology is very full and very profound—and very early. But Paul's writing is solid evidence that the basic Christian position was firmly established before the middle of the first century, less than twenty years after Jesus' death. Later writers add much, but Paul's theology is rich and full, and its early date is significant.

---

21 he arrives at a date of A.D. 32–34 for Paul's conversion; he sees the Crucifixion as having taken place in A.D. 30 (pp. 30–31). George Ogg dates the Resurrection in A.D. 33 and Paul's conversion A.D. 34 or 35 (*The Chronology of the Life of Paul* [London, 1968], 30). Nils A. Dahl puts Paul's conversion "only a couple of years after Christ's death" (*Studies in Paul* [Minneapolis, 1977], 2).

[10] Even when we allow for the time he spent in Arabia (Gal. 1:17), which cannot have been a lengthy stay, for it is included in a period of three years in which he did other things as well (Gal. 1:18), there was not a long period when Paul was cut off from the life of the church. He was for an unknown length of time at Tarsus (Acts 9:30; 11:25), but there is no reason for believing that he was out of touch with the church. The man who had been through the experience on the Damascus road and the vigorous personality revealed in the Pauline correspondence was not the person to stand aloof from the life of the church. We cannot but think of him as active from the first. Beker's view that Paul received "not *the* tradition but a *variety* of traditions" (*Paul the Apostle,* 118–19), like other such verdicts, overlooks Paul's early involvement with the church. He refers to "the variety and multiplicity of pre-Pauline traditions in the early church" (p. 127). Really! Dahl likewise sees Paul as dependent on "previously existing traditions" (*Studies in Paul,* 10), but he also refers to Paul's "decisive impact on the church in its formative years" (p. 19), and says further, "Here I use the common term 'pre-Pauline' Christianity to refer to teachings *which Paul is likely to have had* in common with other early Christian teachers and preachers" (p. 96; my italics).

1

God at the Center

Paul's great interest is in God.[1] We usually take it for granted that a New Testament writer will be writing about God, and this assumption is not unjustified. But we usually do not notice the fact that Paul uses the name of God with astonishing frequency.[2] His usage is distinctly exceptional. He refers to God far more often than does anyone else in the New Testament. He has more than 40 percent of all the New Testament references to God (548 out of 1,314)—a very high proportion. It is really extraordinary that one writer, whose writings total about a quarter of the New Testament, should have nearly half the total number of references to God. In Romans[3] he uses the word *God*

153 times, an average of once in every 46 words. It is not easy to use any word as often as that.[4] Paul does not keep up this rate throughout his correspondence, but in all his letters he speaks of God often.

Paul was a God-intoxicated man, and he spoke constantly about the One who was central in his thinking.[5] Everything he dealt with he related to God. He taught that God is sovereign over life in all of its aspects, so that there is no part of our experience of which we can say that God is irrelevant to that. Paul saw God as important everywhere in the present time and he looked forward to a time when God would be "all in all" (1 Cor. 15:28).

[1] Cf. Dean S. Gilliland, "The first factor that conditioned Paul's thinking was his Jewish conception of God. . . . God is the only, the living and altogether righteous One, working out his purposes in the world, entering into fellowship with people, and creating a family for himself here on earth. God at the center made Paul's religion personal, ethical, historical, and officially monotheistic" (*Pauline Theology & Mission Practice* [Grand Rapids, 1983], 20).

[2] It is interesting to notice, for example, that Rudolf Bultmann, in his great work *Theology of the New Testament,* begins his treatment of Paul's theology with a discussion of *sōma,* "body"; he never does get around to a systematic discussion of the central concept in Paul's theology.

[3] I have examined Paul's usage in Romans in W. Ward Gasque and Ralph P. Martin, eds., *Apostolic History and the Gospel* (Exeter, 1970), ch. 17, "The Theme of Romans."

[4] In Romans the only words Paul uses more frequently than "God" are the definite article, καί ("and"), ἐν ("in"), and αὐτός ("he"). Even very common words like δέ ("but" or "and") and the verb "to be" are used less frequently. Of the important theological concepts in this letter, the next most frequent is "law" 72 times, which is a long way back. Then come "Christ" (65 times), "sin" (48), "Lord" (43), and "faith" (40). Statistics do not mean everything, but we should be aware that Paul uses the word "God" with unusual frequency.

[5] Charles C. Ryrie wrote, "Basic to Pauline theology is the concept of God" and "The doctrine of God is the central doctrine of Pauline theology" (*Biblical Theology of the New Testament* [Chicago, 1982], 167, 203).

ONE GLORIOUS GOD

Like any good Jew, Paul is a strict monotheist; there is and can be only one God (Rom. 3:30; 1 Cor. 8:4, 6; Gal. 3:20; Eph. 4:6; 1 Tim. 1:17; 2:5). That one God he sees as the Father of his people (Rom. 1:7; 1 Cor. 1:3; 2 Cor. 1:2–3; Gal. 1:3–4; Eph. 4:6; 5:20; Phil. 1:2; 1 Tim. 1:2; 2 Tim. 1:2; Titus 1:4), and the Father is clearly a great God. All the depths of riches, wisdom, and knowledge are his (Rom. 11:33); Paul may sometimes prefer to link the power and the wisdom with Christ, but it is still the power and the wisdom of God (1 Cor. 1:24; cf. 2:5, 7). The power by which Christ lives is from God (2 Cor. 13:4), and the Christian's abundant power for living comes from God (2 Cor. 4:7; 6:7; 13:4; 2 Tim. 1:8). From another point of view all power and authority in the civil state derive from God (Rom. 13:1–7). Paul is interested in different kinds of power and in the fact that in the end it is only God who gives it (whatever kind it may be).

Akin to this is Paul's interest in glory (he uses the word 77 times, nearly 47 percent of its New Testament occurrences). Once he complains that sinners come short of God's glory (Rom. 3:23; cf. 1:23), and he can refer to a human "hope of the glory of God" (Rom. 5:2). But more often he delights in God's glory (2 Cor. 4:6, 15; Phil. 2:11) or sees it as a motive for conduct: we should, like Abraham, "give glory to God" (Rom. 4:20; cf. 15:7; 1 Cor. 10:31; 2 Cor. 1:20; Phil. 1:11). Frequently he speaks of "glorifying" God (Rom. 15:6, 9; 1 Cor. 6:20; 2 Cor.

9:13: Gal. 1:24). The God who is so central to Paul is a glorious God.

Sometimes Paul refers to divine qualities. He sees God as "living" (1 Tim. 3:15; 4:10), as "faithful" (1 Cor. 1:9; 10:13; 2 Cor. 1:18), as "living and true" (1 Thess. 1:9). God "cannot lie" (Titus 1:2). The apostle speaks of the God "of endurance and encouragement" (Rom. 15:5), of "the God of hope" (Rom. 15:13), and of "the God of all encouragement [or consolation]" (2 Cor. 1:3; cf. 1:4; 7:6). God is "the God of love and peace" (2 Cor. 13:11), "the God of peace" (Rom. 15:33; cf. 1 Cor. 14:33; Phil. 4:9; 1 Thess. 5:23). Paul also assures us that the God of peace "will crush Satan under [our] feet" (Rom. 16:20); this statement shows God as active and gives a new dimension to our understanding of peace. Peace is certainly not a quiescent state; it is compatible with militant opposition to evil. Paul, then, can speak of God's qualities, but it is characteristic of his writings that he more commonly refers to what God is doing than to his nature and state.

PREDESTINATION

Paul is insistent that the will of God is being done; he speaks of this repeatedly (e.g., Rom. 1:10; 12:2; 1 Cor. 1:1; 4:19; Eph. 1:1, 4–5, 11; Col. 1:1; 4:12; 1 Thess. 5:18). The central truth of Christianity is that Christ "gave himself for our sins," and he did this "according to the will of our God and Father" (Gal. 1:4),[6] a thought that Paul repeats in a variety of ways. Thus there is made known "through the church, the manifold wisdom of God

---

[6]Cf. George S. Duncan: "It [i.e., the cross] was not merely something which God had *permitted*, it was something which God the Father had *willed;* and His purpose behind it was the redemption of His children from the present evil world" (*The Epistle of Paul to the Galatians* [London, 1939], 14). Similarly, M. A. C. Warren remarks that in the Cross "we are to see not an attempt to change God's mind but the very expression of that mind" (*The Gospel of Victory* [London, 1955], 21).

according to the eternal purpose which he worked out in Christ Jesus our Lord, in whom we have boldness . . ." (Eph. 3:10–12).[7] Paul speaks of this wisdom as hidden and that which "God foreordained before the ages for our glory" (1 Cor. 2:7; cf. Rom. 16:25–27). It has now been made known to the saints "to whom God willed to make known what is the richness of the glory of this mystery among the Gentiles" (Col. 1:26–27). There is a strong argument for predestination in the opening chapter of Ephesians, where we read that believers were chosen in Christ before the foundation of the world (v. 4) and were predestined for adoption through Jesus Christ (v. 5). God's "good pleasure" was purposed in Christ (v. 9), and believers were predestined according to the plan of him "who works all things according to the purpose of his will" (v. 11).

Predestination as Paul saw it gives assurance: "Those whom he foreknew, he also predestined to be conformed to the image of his Son . . . and those whom he predestined, these he also called, and those whom he called, these he also justified; and those whom he justified, these he also glorified" (Rom. 8:29–30). Moffatt translates Romans 11:29 in this way: "God never goes back upon his gifts and call." Left to ourselves, we would never be certain that we had done what was necessary for our salvation. But we are not left to ourselves: God has predestined and called his own. This is a way of saying that our entire salvation, from first to last, is of God. We have the assurance that God chose us before the foundation of the world and that he does not go back on his calling. Nothing can give us assurance like that.

We should also notice that God predestines people for ethical achievement. Paul does not see this doctrine as a magnificent incentive to laziness. Rather, we are "created in Christ Jesus for good works, which God prepared beforehand that we might walk in them" (Eph. 2:10). Because we are God's elect, we are to "put on a heart of compassion, goodness, humility, gentleness, longsuffering" (Col. 3:12). Predestination is not for privilege, but for service. It is a reminder that good works are not optional for the believer, but the very object for which we are predestined.

GOD WILL JUDGE[8]

Now if God intends us to do good works it follows that he is not indifferent to the way we live. One day he will call on us to give account of ourselves (Rom. 3:19). Paul refers often to the fact that evil deeds register before God. For example, people who boast in the law and yet break it are not simply making themselves into hypocrites and treating the law lightly, but they are dishonoring God (Rom. 2:23); they are causing his name to be blasphemed (v. 24). When Paul quotes from Scripture to show that people are evil, the passages he cites relate this to God: "no one searches for God"; "there is no fear of God before their eyes" (Rom. 3:11, 18). Again, the trouble with "the mind of the flesh" is that it is hostile to God; it does not and cannot submit to God's law; it cannot please God (Rom. 8:7–8). Therein lies the tragedy of the natural man. People may talk back to God (Rom. 9:20) and disobey him (Rom. 11:30). Even religious people,

---

[7] For the authorship of Ephesians, see 21n.6 above.

[8] D. B. Knox has a thoughtful article entitled "Punishment as Retribution: A Criticism of the Humanist Attitude to Justice" (*Interchange* 1 [1967]: 5–8) in which he emphasizes that sin *deserves* punishment, a fact that is, of course, very relevant to the subject of judgment.

those zealous for God, may be bereft of knowledge in spiritual things; they may not perceive that saving righteousness is "the righteousness of God" and accordingly do what is quite wrong; they may try to establish their own righteousness (Rom. 10:3). There are those who use the Word of God for their own profit (2 Cor. 2:17) or handle it craftily (2 Cor. 4:2). Paul knows of people who are without God (Eph. 2:12) or are alienated from the life of God (Eph. 4:18)—people who do not please God (1 Thess. 2:15) or who do not know him (1 Thess. 4:5; 2 Thess. 1:8) or who despise him (1 Thess. 4:8; cf. 2 Cor. 10:5).

Paul, then, does not see evil in all its varied forms simply as so many ethical misdemeanors. He relates it all to God. It is a dishonoring of God, a failure to fear God, a hostility to God, and more. And God takes knowledge of it. People are responsible for their actions. We will be called on to give an account of ourselves, and we will be liable to punishment for those deeds in which we come short of what we should have accomplished. This has been so from the beginning, for "the judgment came from one sin [or one man] issuing in condemnation" (Rom. 5:16). It matters little whether we read "one sin" or "one man," for both Adam and his sin are in mind. That sin resulted in a condemnation that affects the whole human race.

Paul sees God as active in judgment right now. For believers this is a merciful provision of God in which "we are disciplined by the Lord in order that we may not be condemned with the world" (1 Cor. 11:32). The sufferings we encounter are an evidence of God's love. His discipline is to prevent us from suffering the fate of the worldly. We should bear in mind that judgment is part of the gospel (Rom. 2:16); we may not easily adjust to the thought that judgment belongs to the good news, but if we are to understand Paul's view of judgment, we must make the attempt.

Sin reaps its own harvest, for sinners receive "in themselves the fitting recompense of their going astray" (Rom. 1:27). It would be easy to see this as a natural process of cause and effect, by which the inevitable consequences of sin are themselves the punishment of sin. But although Paul recognizes that there is truth in this, he insists that the hand of God is in it all. Three times he says of Gentile sinners that "God gave them up" to the unpleasant consequences of their sin (Rom. 1:24, 26, 28). God is never neutral; he is always opposed to evil. Paul can even say of sinners who "did not receive the love of the truth so that they should be saved" that "God sends them strong delusion" (2 Thess. 2:10–11).

In such passages it would have been easy to express the thought impersonally. But Paul is not envisaging a process in which a helpless God stands by and watches. God is an active God, a God who participates in the process,[9] a God who has made this a moral universe so that people who reject "the love of the truth" end up believing a lie. That is part of his judgment. The inevitable

---

[9] A. L. Moore rejects as "an intolerable dualism" the view that some are drawn by God and others by Satan: "It could not for a moment be contemplated. Therefore, while in verses 13f. God is shown to be responsible for the whole process of salvation, he is also, in verses 11f., not excluded from activity in the process of unbelief leading to condemnation" (*1 and 2 Thessalonians* [London, 1969], 105). F. F. Bruce puts it this way: "To be misled by falsehood is the divine judgment inevitably incurred in a moral universe by those who close their eyes to the truth" (*Word Biblical Commentary: 1 & 2 Thessalonians* [Waco, 1982], 174).

result of rejecting God's salvation is delusion, but again Paul does not leave this to the operation of natural causes. God is in it.[10] In the same spirit he quotes from Isaiah words that speak of God's giving sinners "a spirit of stupor" (Rom. 11:8). Sinners cut themselves off from real life and reduce themselves to unremitting dullness and a horrifying inability to see God's good gifts for what they are. And the hand of God is in that too. Paul knows nothing whatever of an absentee God.

From another point of view God's judgment is shown in the persecutions and afflictions the Thessalonian Christians endured (2 Thess. 1:5). These troubles were sent to them as God's loving discipline, and it is because God's hand is in such discipline, and because they are aware of it, that Christians are enabled to bear the troubles so well.

But, although present judgment is a stern reality, more significant for Paul is the future judgment, the judgment that will take place at the end of the age. "God will judge men's secrets" (Rom. 2:16), he writes, and clearly this truth is basic; nothing can be hidden from God, and no one will escape scrutiny (Rom. 2:3; 14:12). Judgment will be universal, and those outside the church are specifically mentioned (1 Cor. 5:13). Not only will God judge everybody, but he will judge with perfect justice, without partiality (Rom. 2:11) and with "righteous judgment" (Rom. 2:5; 2 Thess. 1:5–6), with a judgment according to truth (Rom. 2:2). Those who love law are warned that hearing

the law is not enough; to be just before God means obeying the law (Rom. 2:13). This seems to be a reference to Jewish discussions. Some of the rabbis thought that all that was necessary was to hear the law, and that all Israelites would be saved.[11] Paul insists that law must not only be heard but also obeyed if one is to be just before God. The judgment of God is a much more serious business than many of his fellow countrymen thought. They had no easy out.

Paul has an interesting argument when he speaks of an objection to his view of the salvation of sinners. Some apparently asked, "If God saves sinners freely, then is he not unjust if he brings his wrath on the lost?" The apostle does not rebut the objection directly, but asks a question in his turn, "If that were so, how will God judge the world?" (Rom. 3:5–6). That God will judge the world is so certain that it does not need to be demonstrated; it can be assumed as beyond doubt. Anything that does not square with the fact that God will judge must be unhesitatingly dismissed.

Now and then Paul speaks of people as receiving praise from God in the judgment (Rom. 2:29; 1 Cor. 4:5), but mostly he is concerned with the truth that when we think of judgment we think of those with whom God is not well pleased (1 Cor. 10:5), those who face eternal destruction (1 Cor. 3:17; 6:13). Nevertheless, however judgment is viewed, for the apostle the

---

[10] "God does not deceive. Deception is the work of the lawless one (v. 10). What he sends is error-and-its-moral-consequences, its outworking" (Ronald A. Ward, *Commentary on 1 & 2 Thessalonians* [Waco, 1973], 162).

[11] Eleazar of Modiim said, "'If you will hear' (Ex. 15:26) is the most universal rule (the fundamental principle), in which the (whole) Law is contained" (*SBK*, 3:87). As to the salvation of all Israel, there is no shortage of statements like this one from R. Levi: "In the Hereafter Abraham will sit at the entrance to Gehenna, and permit no circumcised Israelite to descend therein" (Gen. Rab. 48.8).

basic thing is that God is active in bringing it about.[12]

THE LOVE OF GOD

From all this it would be easy to deduce that Paul thinks of God as a supremely great God, One who created all things, is working out his purposes in creation, and is ruthless in punishing those who try to hinder that purpose. But this would be wrong. Paul's great interest in God centers not so much in his power and his majesty and the judgment he brings to bear, as in his love and concern for his people. For his people! Interestingly Paul does not often say that God loves Christ, though this thought does occur: Christ is "the beloved" (Eph. 1:6). But his emphasis is on the totally unexpected thought that God, who is so good and so great, regards the human race, sinners as we all are, not simply with tolerance and magnanimity, but with love. It is significant that Paul so often calls God "Father"; indeed he speaks of him in this way in every one of his letters. The combination of the ideas of God's power and his fatherhood means, as William Barclay says, that "we get the full, rounded idea of God, as a God whose power is always motivated by His love, and whose love is always backed by His power."[13]

In a very important passage Paul tells us that "God demonstrates his own love for us in this: While we were still sinners, Christ died for us" (Rom. 5:8). This is totally alien to human experience. We know that occasionally someone will lay down his life for someone else, but he does this incredibly noble deed for a good person or for one closely tied to him in some way, or perhaps in a good cause. People do not voluntarily die for those they do not esteem. Yet while people were still sinners and thus worthless in God's sight, Christ died for them. This is a key thought in Paul and it underlies much of what he writes. God gives his love unstintingly; he has poured it out into our hearts by the Holy Spirit (Rom. 5:5).

And his love is all-powerful. In a magnificently rhetorical passage Paul comes to his climax with the thought that nothing in this whole earth or beyond can separate God's people from God's love (Rom. 8:38–39). "The love of God" quite naturally forms part of the benediction (2 Cor. 13:14), and Christians are God's "beloved children" (Eph. 5:1). God does things for his people. We may translate Romans 8:28 as "he [i.e., God] works all things together for good . . ." or "all things work together. . . ."[14] But, however we translate it, the thought is that God brings good gifts to his people ("things" do not work together of themselves). The love of God is at work in us and for us (cf. the similar thought in 1 Cor. 2:9). God is indeed "rich in mercy" and thus loved us with a great love despite our sinfulness (Eph. 2:4). He gives generously to those who love

---

[12] I have dealt with the subject of judgment at rather fuller length in my *Biblical Doctrine of Judgment* [London, 1960]. John A. T. Robinson speaks of "our basic conception of judgment as encountering God." He further remarks that "judgment means the justification of God, the manifest and final vindication of love's design. And God is not finished till that is accomplished—till he is all in all" (*On Being the Church in the World* [London, 1960], 139–40).

[13] *The Mind of St. Paul* [New York, 1958], 33.

[14] Translations like NIV, RSV, JB, GNB accept some variant of "God works together. . . ," while NEB takes "the Spirit" (the subject of the preceding verb, v. 27) as the subject. C. K. Barrett and C. E. B. Cranfield favor "all things work. . . ," whereas C. H. Dodd and F. J. Leenhardt argue for "God works. . . ."

him, and they are expected to respond in giving to others. When they do they find that "God loves a merry giver" (2 Cor. 9:7). We should not miss Paul's emphasis on the divine love and on God's constant care for those he has made. So characteristic is the divine love that Paul speaks quite naturally of believers as "loved by God and called to be saints" (Rom. 1:7; cf. 2 Thess. 3:5; Titus 3:4).

The above verses show that love and election belong together, and this link is found elsewhere (e.g., Rom. 9:25; 11:28; Col. 3:12; 1 Thess. 1:4; 2 Thess. 2:13).[15] People do not always notice this, and some see election as a grim process whereby God arbitrarily predestined certain people to be damned eternally. But, as Paul understood it, God's election is a device for rescuing people, not for condemning them. It is the outworking of God's love. And it is effective. No one can bring a charge against God's elect (Rom. 8:33). Paul sees the principle at work in the history of Israel, wherein "God's purpose in election" is clear (Rom. 9:11). It is true that in this passage we are told of Esau's rejection as well as of Jacob's election, but Paul decisively and emphatically dismisses the charge that God is unjust. His argument is complex, but what is plain is that throughout it all he insists that God's purpose is mercy (Rom. 9:15).[16]

Everything depends on that mercy (Rom. 9:16), and Paul brings it all to a climax with the statement that God has shut up all people to disobedience "so that he may have mercy on them all" (Rom. 11:32). Subsequently he makes his appeal to the Roman Christians on the basis of God's mercies (Rom. 12:1). Elsewhere he argues that it is "according to his mercy" that God saved us (Titus 3:5; cf. 1 Cor. 7:25; 2 Cor. 4:1; 1 Tim. 1:13, 16). He sees God's gifts and his call as irrevocable (Rom. 11:29); God does not go back on his call. Paul can speak of "the prize of the high calling of God in Christ Jesus" (Phil. 3:14), and he prays that his converts may prove worthy of that call (2 Thess. 1:11).

An interesting aspect of the call, and one that obviously meant much to Paul, is that God did not choose the attractive and promising among this world's people, but the foolish, the weak, and the lowly, even "the things that are not" (1 Cor. 1:28). God does not proceed along the lines of wisdom as this world knows it, and in any case that kind of wisdom cannot bring us to God (1 Cor. 1:20–21; 3:19). We should not miss the point that, though God in his wisdom calls unpromising people, he does not leave them as they were. He makes something special out of them, for he calls them to holiness (1 Thess. 4:7).[17]

---

[15] We should probably include here this quotation from Malachi: "I loved Jacob, but hated Esau" (Rom. 9:13). The words are best taken as referring to nations rather than to individuals and as pointing to election. C. E. B. Cranfield takes the words in this way and adds, "But, again, it must be stressed that, as in the case of Ishmael, so also with Esau, the rejected one is still, according to the testimony of Scripture, an object of God's merciful care" (*A Critical and Exegetical Commentary on the Epistle to the Romans,* ii [Edinburgh, 1979]: 480). Cf. Genesis 27:39–40; Deuteronomy 23:7.

[16] Rudolf Bultmann points out that Stoicism regarded ἔλεος "as a sickness of the soul . . . it is unworthy of the sage." It was seen as an emotion, and thus "in judicial practice ἔλεος entails partiality" (*TDNT*, 2:478). He also says, "Mention of God's ἔλεος does not always have express reference to the Christ event. It may simply denote the grace of God, with a stronger or weaker suggestion that this grace has come through Christ" (p. 484). Thus, from another point of view we see that God is at work, mercy is always God's mercy.

[17] Ernest Best points out that "they are 'the saints', the sanctified, they belong to the domain of God." He further comments that, while the slave or the free man called to be a Christian remains a

God, then, is active, in unpromising people. And because he is the kind of God he is, a God "rich in mercy," he reaches out to the undeserving, the sinful and the helpless. His self-revelation is one example of how this takes place. All revelation, however it be understood, is an outworking of God's love. D. B. Knox makes the point that God is ceaselessly active: He "controlled the migrations of the Syrians from Kir and the Philistines from Caphtor as completely as He brought up the Israelites out of Egypt (Amos 9:7)." But we do not regard the movements of the Syrians and the Philistines as revelation. God has not interpreted them to us. "For an event to be revelational, it must be interpreted by God Himself."[18] It is God who makes plain to people what can be known of him (Rom. 1:19–20).

We should understand here also the references to the "oracles" of God (Rom. 3:2) and to the Word of God (e.g., Rom. 9:6; 1 Cor. 14:36; Eph. 6:17; Col. 1:25; 1 Thess. 2:13; 1 Tim. 4:5). In such ways, God is active in revealing. God's servant Paul might be a prisoner and find his activities curtailed, but the Word of God "is not bound" (2 Tim. 2:9). It is active, infallibly accomplishing the purpose of God.

Another way of referring to revelation is to ascribe it to God's Spirit (1 Cor. 2:10). Again, all Scripture is "God-breathed," the utterance of God, and thus profitable (2 Tim. 3:16). Some New Testament Epistles contain the thought that God would make clear to the early church what was needful for individual Christians; this knowledge was not definitive like Scripture but constituted guidance for daily living (Phil. 3:15; cf. 1 Cor. 14:26). In all this, God is active. He provides what sinners need so that they may experience salvation.

And God reaches out with more than knowledge. He reaches out with the gospel, which Paul sees as "the gospel of God" (Rom. 1:1; 15:16; 2 Cor. 11:7; 1 Thess. 2:2, 8–9) and "the gospel of the glory of blessed God" (1 Tim. 1:11). The good news of salvation for sinful people originated with God. In his gospel his power finds expression, for the gospel *is* power; it does not just tell about power (Rom. 1:16; 1 Cor. 1:18; cf. 2:5). It is through the gospel that God brings us into his family: we can call him "Father" (Rom. 8:15; Gal. 4:6–7; 2 Thess. 1:1–2; 2:16; Philem. 3), and we are "sons" (Rom. 8:14, 19; Gal. 3:26), "children" (Rom. 8:16; 9:8; Phil. 2:15), "heirs of God" (Rom. 8:17). It is as children of God that we know what it is to enter into the glory of liberty (Rom. 8:21).

THE SALVATION OF GOD

The God who loves so deeply will not leave sinners to perish, and Paul's whole theology and religious experience are based squarely on what God has done in Christ for our salvation. He began it, for the Incarnation is due to God; he sent his Son (Rom. 8:3; Gal. 4:4). We usually think of Christ as dying for us, and it is right that we should. But we should not overlook the fact that God "did not spare his own

---

slave or free man, "the impure man called to be a Christian cannot remain impure but must seek sanctification" (*A Commentary on the First and Second Epistles to the Thessalonians* [London, 1977], 168).

[18]*RTR* 19 [1960]: 5–6.

Son but delivered him up for us all" (Rom. 8:32).[19] The Father was active in the work of atonement and, of course, the Resurrection is characteristically ascribed to God (e.g., Rom. 4:24; 8:11; 10:9). It is important to see that for Paul the Incarnation, Jesus' atoning death, and the Resurrection are all to be understood as the outworking of God's love, bringing about our salvation. God is not passive, doing no more than acquiescing in a salvation won·by Christ. He is active. He effects it all.

Repentance is God's gift (2 Tim. 2:25), as is the eternal life that follows (Rom. 6:23). Salvation is due to "the righteousness of God," an expression that recurs (Rom. 1:17; 3:5, 21–22, 25–26; 10:3; 2 Cor. 5:21; Phil. 3:9; cf. Rom. 8:33; note that Paul does not say "the righteousness of Christ," though that phrase has a long and honorable history among Christians). The expression must be understood carefully. We usually use the term *righteousness* to denote an ethical virtue, as the Greeks did. But the Hebrews saw the term as pointing to a legal standing, as can be seen, for example, from the woe pronounced on those who "take away the righteousness of the righteous from him" (Isa. 5:23 KJV, ASV; the NIV paraphrases this clause like this: "who . . . deny justice to the innocent."). In the sense of an ethical virtue, righteousness cannot be taken away from anyone. The prophet means that unjust judges are taking away the "right standing" from people who were entitled to

it; they were asserting that people were guilty when in fact they were in the right.[20]

Sometimes in the Old Testament righteousness and salvation are linked, as when God says, "My salvation will last forever, my righteousness will never fail" (Isa. 51:6) and when the psalmist writes, "The Lord has made his salvation known and revealed his righteousness to the nations" (Ps. 98:2). God will not forsake his people. It is right that he should deliver them, and he will. That God acts in accordance with right does not mean that there is a law or norm set over him that he must obey. In the Bible, God is revealed as great, and there is no one and no thing set over him. He acts in accordance with right because he is a righteous God. It is natural for him to act rightly.

It is important to grasp Paul's point that when God saves, he saves in a way that accords with right. This is an aspect of salvation that appealed to the Reformers but is lost in much modern writing, where the emphasis tends to be on deliverance from the power of evil and the like.

For example, Ernst Käsemann sums up his discussion of " 'the righteousness of God' in Paul" in this way: "His doctrine of the δικαιοσύνη θεοῦ demonstrates this: God's power reaches out for the world, and the world's salvation lies in its being recaptured for the sovereignty of God. For this very reason it is the gift of God and also the salvation of the individual human being

---

[19] Cf. D. Martyn Lloyd-Jones: "It is God who acted on Calvary. *He!* He who acted there is the One who is going to give us all these other things. And I know and am certain of this, because of what He has already done there! God acted through men, through the instrumentality of men, but the action was the action of God" (*Romans: An Exposition of Chapter 8:17–39* [Grand Rapids, 1980], 383–84).

[20] George Buchanan Gray pointed out that the word for "righteous" retains its "original forensic sense" (*A Critical and Exegetical Commentary on the Book of Isaiah* [Edinburgh, 1912], 1:94). More recently John Mauchline explains the expression as withholding "from the innocent the acquittal to which he is entitled" (*Isaiah 1–39* [London, 1962], 86).

when we become obedient to the divine righteousness."[21] Elsewhere Käsemann refers to forensic aspects of justification and includes righteousness in his discussion, but here, as he sums up what Paul means by "the righteousness of God," he speaks of nothing but power and sovereignty. It goes without saying that both power and sovereignty are important (also for Paul), but neither of these concepts helps us understand what the Bible means by *righteousness*. Certainly its connection with right is fundamental.

Sometimes Paul uses the expression to reveal a quality in God, as when he says, "If our unrighteousness brings out God's righteousness . . ." (Rom. 3:5); God is inherently righteous and can be relied on to act in righteousness. But more characteristically the expression means a right standing that comes from God and is the gift of God. It is "the righteousness from God" that "comes through faith" (Rom. 3:22). It is important to see that "righteousness" is "a free gift" (*dōrea*) (Rom. 5:17). In the sense in which we usually use the word, the sense of an ethical virtue, righteousness cannot be given (just as we saw earlier that it cannot be taken away). It must be earned by ethical achievement. That it is a gift points to a forensic activity. God gives the status of being "right." He credits righteousness apart from works (Rom. 4:6).

There are other ways of considering salvation than as a legal standing, and Paul uses a number of them. For example, God sets forth Christ as a "propitiation" (Rom. 3:25). Some people do not use the King James Version these days, partly because such terms as *propitiation* are not widely understood, but more because modern scholars do not see the concept of "the wrath of God" as an important one. But we should be clear that Paul sees God as being angry with sinners.

That is the thrust of his massive argument in Romans 1:18–3:20. The passage is introduced with the statement that the wrath of God is revealed from heaven against every form of evil (Rom. 1:18), and the term *wrath* occurs three more times (2:5, 8; 3:5). In a passage where Paul could very easily have said that sin brings its own fearful consequences, he declares instead that "God gave them up" to those consequences (Rom. 1:24, 26, 28). What is this but the wrath of God in action? Indeed, Paul implies as much by including the words in the development of his theme that God's wrath is revealed against all unrighteousness (v. 18). The apostle is clear that "wrath and anger" are stored up for sinners (Rom. 2:5, 8) and that it is God who brings his wrath to bear on sinners (Rom. 3:5; 9:22).

The concept of the wrath of God is by no means confined to the opening chapters of Romans. Paul refers to it often. Thus he tells us that the wrath of God comes on the disobedient (Eph. 5:6; Col. 3:6); people are by nature "children of wrath" (Eph. 2:3). For those who continue in sin there is no end to this wrath (1 Thess. 2:16).

The word *propitiation* signifies "the turning away of anger," usually by an offering. If it does not have this meaning in Romans 3:25, what has become of the wrath that Paul has made so clear in the earlier discussion? How are sinners saved from it? I am not arguing that we should stake everything on the use of one word rather than another; we may prefer some other word than

---

[21] Ernst Käsemann, *New Testament Questions of Today* (London, 1969), 181–82.

propitiation. It is the concept that matters, and in Romans 3 the argument demands some expression that includes the idea of removing from sinners the wrath that Paul has shown so convincingly is all that they can expect.

The Bible says that it is through what Christ has done that we are saved from that wrath (Rom. 5:9; 1 Thess. 1:10). God has "not appointed us for wrath but for the obtaining of salvation through our Lord Jesus Christ" (1 Thess. 5:9). Paradoxically, the removal of that wrath is God's own doing (cf. Ps. 78:38, "Many a time turned he his anger away, and did not stir up all his wrath" KJV). To find the paradox difficult or even to reject it is not to get rid of Paul's argument.[22] Paul sees God as active in dealing with the situation that is posed by his wrath, which, in essence, is his strong and vigorous opposition to everything that is evil.[23]

God is seen as active in other ways in the saving work of Christ, mostly as initiating them. Thus reconciliation is reconciliation to God (Rom. 5:10; 2 Cor. 5:20), a reconciliation that God effects (2 Cor. 5:18–19). God confirmed the covenant (Gal. 3:17), he forgave sinners (Eph. 4:32), he reckoned Abraham as righteous, justifying him (Gal. 3:6; the verb for "reckon" is passive, with no subject stated, but the passage clearly shows that it is God who does the reckoning). He "made sin on our behalf" the Christ who "knew no sin" (2 Cor. 5:21).

The thought that salvation is by grace runs through the New Testament, and this grace is "the grace of God" (Rom. 5:15; 1 Cor. 1:4; 3:10; 15:10; 2 Cor. 1:12; 6:1; 8:1; 9:14; Gal. 2:21; Eph. 3:2, 7; Col. 1:6). "The grace of our Lord Jesus Christ" comes easily to our lips and is, of course, scriptural. But we should bear in mind that in the New Testament grace is as likely to be linked with God as with Christ.

THE CHRISTIAN LIFE

God's activity is seen in various aspects of the corporate life of the saved. The church is the church of God (1 Cor. 1:2; 10:32; 11:22; 15:9; 2 Cor. 1:1; Gal. 1:13; 1 Tim. 3:5, 15; cf. the plural "churches of God," 1 Cor. 11:16; 1 Thess. 2:14; 2 Thess. 1:4). So too Paul speaks of "the Israel of God" (Gal. 6:16),[24] "a habitation of God" (Eph. 2:22), and "members of God's household" (Eph. 2:19). Akin to this is the thought that believers are God's temple, and the fact that the

---

[22] C. F. D. Moule notes that there are those "who still adhere to the translation 'propitiate,' " but he holds that "they are driven to the *reductio ad absurdum* of God's propitiating himself" (Michael Goulder, ed., *Incarnation and Myth: The Debate Continued* [London, 1979], 86n.). Perhaps. But those who reject "propitiate" are not taking Paul's words with full seriousness. The apostle has described God's opposition to sin as "the wrath of God" (Rom. 1:18) and he has ascribed the removal of that wrath to God himself. What other word means the removal *of wrath*? Moule apparently favors "expiate," but this has nothing to do with wrath. Those who use "propitiate" are not trying to be difficult or absurd. They are trying to preserve two scriptural truths: that the wrath of God is exercised against all sin, and that his wrath is no longer exercised against believers because of Christ's atoning death. Those who reject it can scarcely fail to see that Paul referred to God's wrath; apparently they see salvation as doing nothing about that wrath.

[23] See further my articles in *ExpT* 62 (1950–51): 227–33; lxiii (1951–52): 142–45; *NTS* 2 (1955–56): 33–43, and the fuller treatment in my *Apostolic Preaching of the Cross* (London, 1965), chs. 5–6; *The Atonement* (Leicester, 1983), ch. 7. See also David Hill, *Greek Words and Hebrew Meanings* (Cambridge, 1967), ch. 2; George E. Ladd, *A Theology of the New Testament* (Grand Rapids, 1975), 429–33.

[24] For this expression, see 20n.3 above.

temple is sacred (1 Cor. 3:16–17) tells us something about the relationship of believers to God.[25] Not only does the church belong to God, but it is a group in which he is active. He has "set" some people in it, notably the apostles but also others (1 Cor. 4:9; 12:28); he has "blended" the members of the body (1 Cor. 12:24).

Paul sees God as interested also in individuals. God gives some good gift to each of his people; he gives each a "charisma" (1 Cor. 7:7), assigns to each a place in life (1 Cor. 7:17), works in all of them (1 Cor. 12:6), and gives them prosperity (1 Cor. 16:2). He gives a spirit "of power and love and sober-mindedness" (2 Tim. 1:7). When he gives the gift of prophecy, even the person who is not a church member will be compelled to say, "God is really among you!" (1 Cor. 14:25). Believers will, of course, know that presence for themselves, but it is a presence that on occasion can thus be made manifest to outsiders. When the body of Christ grows, it is God who makes it grow (Col. 2:19). God's activity even extends beyond his work in and for people. An interesting sidelight in Paul's discussion of the resurrection is his affirmation that God gives to each seed "a body" (1 Cor. 15:38); even one small seed does not grow independently of him.

God made us for his own specific purpose and gave us the Spirit (2 Cor. 5:5). He establishes us and anoints us (2 Cor. 1:21), the anointing being another reference to his giving of the Spirit. Similarly he can make all grace abound for us (2 Cor. 9:8). He teaches us (1 Thess. 4:9) and supplies all our need (Phil. 4:19). The armor with which we are equipped is "the armor of God" (Eph. 6:11, 13), and in this armor we are mighty to demolish the positions of the enemy (2 Cor. 10:4). Believers do not trust in their own abilities, but in such equipment from God, and Paul can say, "Our sufficiency is of God" (2 Cor. 3:5). God is in the beginning of Christian life, for he "appointed" us to the getting of salvation, not to wrath (1 Thess. 5:9). Paul says that God "separated" him from his mother's womb and called him (Gal. 1:15) and that he assigns fields of work to his people (2 Cor. 10:13). He speaks of God as opening the door for service (Col. 4:3) and of clearing the way (1 Thess. 3:11). It is plain that Paul sees the Christian life as dependent on God and his call, not on some bright idea of the believer. And he sees Christian service as carried out at God's direction and with the equipment God supplies. God is in it all.

Paul has a good deal to say about the service of God, and here we notice first that it is God whom believers are expected to serve. Salvation is not only a privilege, but also a responsibility— specifically a responsibility to God. In discussing service we should emphasize what God does in the servant rather than what the servant does in serving. Thus God works in his people (Phil. 2:13); and when the servants do well, it is God who gives the increase, not they (1 Cor. 3:6–7). God works with them so that they may be called "God's fellow workers" (1 Cor. 3:9).[26] In the proclamation of the gospel of reconcili-

---

[25] William F. Orr and James Arthur Walther comment on "holy" as applied to the church: "It partakes of the numen of God himself" (*1 Corinthians* [New York, 1976], 174).

[26] The passage can also be understood to mean fellow workers with one another and belonging to God ("partners working together for God" GNB). But it seems more likely that the Greek means "fellow workers with God" (as RSV, NIV, NEB). Hans Conzelmann comments, "The accent lies on θεοῦ, 'God's'" (*1 Corinthians* [Philadelphia, 1975], 74).

ation it is God who beseeches sinners to be reconciled (though he does it through the preachers [2 Cor. 5:20]).

On the other hand, Paul exhorted the Romans to offer themselves to God (Rom. 6:13; cf. 12:1); they are God's slaves (Rom. 6:22; 12:11; cf. 1:1; 1 Thess. 1:9). We should understand this to mean, not that they are menials, but that they are wholeheartedly God's; it is the language of utter devotion.[27] It is important that they be pleasing to God (Rom. 14:18) and that they worship him (1 Cor. 14:25), and in this connection we should not overlook the references to prayer (Rom. 10:1; 15:30; 1 Cor. 11:13; Eph. 6:18–19). Believers must bear in mind that there are "commandments of God" (1 Cor. 7:19; Titus 1:3) and that even the freedom of Christians does not mean that they are "free from God's law" (1 Cor. 9:21).[28] "Commandments" and "law" in these verses are not to be understood in the sense of burdensome restrictions, but as God's gracious provision whereby he gives guidance for his people so that they will know the right way.

THE KINGDOM OF GOD

The Synoptics have much to say about "the kingdom of God." This is not Paul's favorite topic, but it does occur in his writings. He says that this kingdom is not a matter of food and drink, but that it is concerned rather with righteousness and the like (Rom. 14:17; cf. 1 Cor. 8:8); in other words, it is with qualities God approves rather than with human desires. The kingdom involves power more than talk (1 Cor. 4:20); the power of God (not human effort) is primary. This does not mean that human effort has no place (Col. 4:11), but that it is not the most significant thing. Again, it is God who will reckon the Thessalonians worthy of the kingdom (2 Thess. 1:5).

There is a present aspect to the kingdom, but there is also a marked eschatological emphasis to which Paul often gives expression. It reflects his conviction that God will be active in the last times. So he tells us that evildoers of various kinds will not inherit the kingdom (Gal. 5:21) and, again, that flesh and blood cannot inherit it (1 Cor. 15:50). In its final form this physical, earthly body has no place in it (bodily values are conserved in the resurrection, but that is another matter). It is "at the end" that all earthly authority will be brought to an end, the kingdom will be handed over to God, and God will be "all in all" (1 Cor. 15:24–28).

Resurrection belongs to God. It is God who raised Christ from the dead (e.g., Rom. 10:9; Col. 2:12; 1 Thess. 1:10); usually the Bible describes the

---

[27] Sometimes it is suggested that Paul's use of "slave" in reference to himself has nothing humble about it, nor is he putting himself on a level with other Christians when he uses it. "Rather, he is using the honorific title of the OT men of God" (Ernst Käsemann, *Commentary on Romans* [Grand Rapids, 1980], 5). There may be a glance at Old Testament usage, but this overlooks Paul's application of the concept to believers in general as well as to himself. In addition to the passages cited in the text, see 1 Corinthians 7:22, Ephesians 6:6, and 2 Timothy 2:24; δουλεύω ("serve as a slave") is used of believers several times (Rom. 7:6; 12:11; 14:18; Eph. 6:7; Phil. 2:22; Col. 3:24; 1 Thess. 1:9).

[28] C. K. Barrett thinks it quite possible to take the genitive to refer to the implied νόμος, thus giving the meaning "not subject to the law *of God*," a view supported by Moule, Blass-Debrunner, and Dodd. But he prefers to see the genitive as referring to Paul, who is then saying that he is not "God's lawless one" (*A Commentary on the First Epistle to the Corinthians* [London, 1978], 213–14). The former way of taking the expression seems preferable, but either way Paul is saying that the believer is subject to God's law.

Resurrection in terms of Jesus having been raised,[29] though sometimes Jesus is said to have risen (e.g., Rom. 14:9; 1 Thess. 4:14). And at the end of time it is God who will raise the dead (1 Cor. 6:14). Death is too strong for us to ever overcome. But it is not too strong for God, and in the end he will overthrow it decisively (1 Cor. 15:50–57).

Even when not using the "kingdom" terminology, Paul is strongly conscious of the fact that God is sovereign in all of life. He often calls God to witness that what he is saying is true (e.g., Gal. 1:20; Phil. 1:8; 1 Thess. 2:5, 10; 2 Tim. 4:1). He appeals to God's knowledge of situations (2 Cor. 11:31; 12:2–3; Gal. 4:8–9). The things Christians speak, they speak before God (2 Cor. 2:17; 12:19; 1 Thess. 2:2). Paul's setting forth of the truth in such a way as to commend himself to people's consciences is done "before God" (2 Cor. 4:2); he is manifest to God (2 Cor. 5:11), and his care for the Corinthians is "before God" (2 Cor. 7:12). If his conduct is unrestrained, that too is before God (2 Cor. 5:13). He looks to the Lord to give holiness to the Thessalonian converts (1 Thess. 3:13; this looks forward to the parousia; it is an eschatological holiness). He reminds the Colossians that they have died to an old way of life and that now their life is "hidden with Christ in God" (Col. 3:3).

More could be added; it is clear that Paul thinks of God as present with the believer at all times and in all he does. God is a caring and watching God. It is not that he is waiting to see if we do evil so that he can pounce when we do. Paul's thought is rather that God is concerned with the way his people live and, accordingly, is with them at all times, ready to give them the help and the guidance they need.

God is a God who delights to bless. He has called his people in peace (1 Cor. 7:15), and in whatever calling the believer may be he can "abide with God" (1 Cor. 7:24). God works all things for good for those who love him (Rom. 8:28). Paul finds in Scripture a reference to the wonderful things that God freely bestows on us now (1 Cor. 2:12). "The peace of God" is with God's people (Phil. 4:7; Col. 3:15). Salvation is from God (Phil. 1:28), and so is mercy (2:27).

And what more shall I say? This brief survey has by no means exhausted Paul's understanding of God's unceasing activity, but is enough to indicate a point all too frequently overlooked: that Paul is a man in the presence of God. More than anything, he is preoccupied with the fact that the great God, the only God, has taken action for the salvation of sinners and that this action has many facets. It centers on the Cross, but it is also manifest in an extraordinary variety of ways. Wherever he looks, Paul sees God.

---

[29]A. W. Argyle says that only eight out of sixty-four New Testament references to Christ's resurrection say that he arose; all the rest say that the Father raised him. This emphasis shows "that the victory over the grave was an achievement, not of human nature, not even of Christ's perfect human nature, but of the Godhead. God was in Christ, and it was God who raised Him" (*ExpT* 61 [1949–50]: 187).

2

JESUS CHRIST OUR LORD

Many Christians habitually refer to our Savior as "Christ," but most of us are quite unaware that this is a habit that we owe to Paul. Unlike the other New Testament writers, Paul uses the title "Christ" frequently. Out of 529 occurrences in the New Testament, 379 are found in the Pauline Epistles; thus, he has the extraordinary proportion of just under 72 percent. The highest total in any non-Pauline writing in the New Testament is 25 in Acts (Paul has 65 in Romans, which is much shorter). It is clear that Paul's usage is very different from that of any of the other New Testament writers.

The word "Christ" is, of course, a transliteration of a Greek word meaning "anointed," just as "Messiah" is a transliteration of a Hebrew word with the same meaning. In the Old Testament a number of people were anointed, notably kings, who were known as "the Lord's anointed" (1 Sam. 16:6; 2 Sam. 1:14). We also read of priests being anointed (Exod. 30:30; Lev. 4:5), and, though less often, prophets (1 Kings 19:16). In each case the action signified that the person in question was solemnly set apart for the service of God.

But in time the idea arose that one day there would appear not simply *an* anointed one, but *the* anointed one, one who would do the will of God in a specially significant way. The actual expression "Messiah" is found but rarely in the Old Testament (Dan. 9:25–26), but the idea is present much more often and at some times in the history of Israel, notably the New Testament period, there was widespread expectation that the Messiah would come.

The title was not much used of Jesus during his earthly life (17 times in Matthew; 7 in Mark; 12 in Luke, and 19 in John). But the early Christians recognized that Jesus was this one chosen by God, as is clearly shown by Paul's free use of the expression and the more occasional use of it by other writers. There is a question whether Paul saw it as a title ("the Messiah") or as a proper name. C. E. B. Cranfield argues that the apostle's frequent word order of "Christ Jesus" shows that he saw it as a title,[1] but this scarcely seems an adequate reason. More convincing is Vincent Taylor's argument that, in the Gentile world, "Christ" would be a

[1] *A Critical and Exegetical Commentary on the Epistle to the Romans* (Edinburgh, 1975), 1:51. See also Oscar Cullmann, *The Christology of the New Testament* (London, 1959), 134.

meaningless title (whereas something like "Lord" would be very significant).[2] To accept this view is not to be oblivious of the fact that Paul sometimes does use the word in the sense of "Messiah." He was well aware of what it meant. But usually we cannot insist on the meaning in a Pauline writing.[3]

Interestingly, Paul also uses the human name "Jesus" quite often. He has it 214 times—more than anyone else except John (who has it 237 times). It is intriguing that, while Paul refers to so few incidents in Jesus' earthly life, he so often uses the name that recalls that earthly life. It may be that he is bringing out the truth that the humanity of Jesus was real and important. When he combines the two names, as he frequently does, Paul prefers the order "Christ Jesus" (83 times) to "Jesus Christ" (26 times).[4] But if he includes the title "Lord," the order is normally the other way around; he says "our Lord Jesus Christ" more often (54 times) than "Christ Jesus our Lord" (8 times). The full title occurs 62 times in Paul's writings, whereas in the rest of the New Testament it is found only 19 times.

Paul uses the title "Lord" 275 times, which is 38 percent of the New Testament total of 718. This term, like the English word "sir," may be used as an ordinary form of address in polite society or, more strictly, as referring to an exalted person such as a noble. The word is used in the former sense in the parable in which Jesus speaks of the son who said to his father, "I go, sir" (Matt. 21:30). But we must bear in mind that Paul's letters were mostly addressed to people in the contemporary Greek world, where "Lord" was quite often used not only of a noble, but of an even more exalted being—a deity. A well-known invitation to dinner reads: "Antonius son of Ptolemaeus invites you to dine with him at the table of the lord Sarapis. . . ."[5] This is an invitation to a meal in an idol temple (cf. 1 Cor. 8:10); eating such meals in such places apparently was a widespread practice. To proclaim Jesus as Lord would be very meaningful in the Greek world of the day.[6] It would also be significant for Jewish readers, for when the Old Testament was translated into Greek, this word was used to render the divine name "Yahweh." Those who were familiar with that translation were familiar with "Lord" as a way of referring to God (a usage we see in the KJV and several modern versions, where LORD [in capitals and small capitals] is the normal way of translating "Yahweh").[7]

[2] *The Names of Jesus* (London, 1953), 18–23.

[3] Martin Hengel sees the title "Christ" as taken over by Paul from "the pre-Pauline Hellenistic community in Jerusalem." He thinks that "it expressed the fact that the crucified Jesus and no other is the eschatological bringer of salvation. *yešūaʿ mešīhā* was already the most important missionary confession in the earliest Palestinian community" (*Between Jesus and Paul* [Philadelphia, 1983], 77).

[4] These figures must be regarded as approximate, as the order in the MSS often differs.

[5] Bernard P. Grenfell and Arthur S. Hunt, eds., *The Oxyrhyncus Papyri*, part 3 (London, 1903), 260.

[6] Cf. W. Foerster: "[Paul] does not make any distinction between θεός and κύριος as though κύριος were an intermediary god; there are no instances of any such usage in the world contemporary with primitive Christianity" (*TDNT*, 3:1091).

[7] Maurice Casey argues that there is "pre-Pauline material embedded in the epistles," showing that "Lord" and "Christ" "both originated in their full sense much less than twenty years after the death and resurrection of Jesus" (M. D. Hooker and S. G. Wilson, eds., *Paul and Paulinism* [London, 1982], 124). I am a little skeptical about there being much "pre-Pauline" material, but if there is such, Casey's position seems eminently reasonable. A very high christology goes back at least to about fifteen years after the Crucifixion. Indeed the use of "Lord" probably indicates an earlier date still. There is some evidence that when the scribes copied the LXX, they wrote the divine name in Hebrew (out of

Paul calls Jesus "God's Son" 4 times, and another 13 times he writes "his Son," "his own Son," or the like. This is a title that can mean much or little; thus, it is used of believers in general (Rom. 8:14) but also of Jesus, in this respect having the maximum meaning. Thus, he says that the Resurrection shows Jesus to be the "Son of God in power" (Rom. 1:4). He speaks of God's revealing him (Gal. 1:16) and sending him (Rom. 8:3; Gal. 4:4). God did not spare his own Son (Rom. 8:32), a statement that points us to "the death of his Son" (Rom. 5:10) and to the gospel of the Son (Rom. 1:9). Paul lived his life by faith in the Son of God (Gal. 2:20), and God predestined believers to be conformed to the "image" of his Son (Rom. 8:29). In keeping with this, the Son is preached (2 Cor. 1:19), and those who respond are called "into the fellowship" of the Son (1 Cor. 1:9); they are "transferred into the kingdom of [God's] beloved Son" (Col. 1:13).[8] The full knowledge of the Son is yet future (Eph. 4:13), and, indeed, we await the Son from heaven (1 Thess. 1:10). The Spirit is the Spirit of God's Son (Gal. 4:6). It is clear that when Paul thinks of Jesus as the Son of God, he thinks of him as occupying the highest place.[9] In Paul's writings we should give this term the maximum meaning, not the minimum.

Paul uses other terms also. Now and then he speaks of Jesus as Savior (Eph. 5:23; Phil. 3:20; 2 Tim. 1:10; Titus 1:4; 2:13), though perhaps not as often as we might have expected . But this is clearly an exalted title, for we also read of "God our Savior" (1 Tim. 1:1; 2:3; 4:10; Titus 1:3; 2:10; 3:4). An interesting expression Paul uses for Christ in 1 Corinthians 15:45 is "the last Adam" (cf. Rom. 5:12–21). There are other expressions, but I will consider them in the context of the general exposition.

JESUS THE MAN

Even this brief look at Paul's terminology is enough to show that he had a very high view of the person of Christ. But we must not overlook the fact that he was also certain of the genuine humanity of Jesus. It is true that in common with the epistolary tradition throughout the New Testament he does not refer to many incidents in Jesus' earthly life. But he says more than is sometimes realized. Thus he tells us that Jesus was a man (1 Cor. 15:21), born of a woman (Gal. 4:4), a descendant of David (Rom. 1:3), and, despite his royal lineage, a poor man (2 Cor. 8:9). He had brothers (1 Cor.

reverence). Joseph A. Fitzmyer, however, has examined the evidence and concluded that Palestinian Jews did use "Lord" in referring to Yahweh. He argues that "the transfer of that title to Jesus undoubtedly took place on Palestinian soil itself. It would thus mean that the primitive confession 'Jesus is Lord' (1 Cor. 12:3; Rom. 10:9) was a response to the early kerygma itself and was not then a product of missionary activity during the evangelization of the eastern Mediterranean" (*The Gospel According to Luke (I–IX)* [New York, 1983], 202).

[8] The expression reminds us of "the kingdom of God." P. T. O'Brien sees it as "an interim period between the resurrection of Jesus and the final coming of the kingdom of God" (*Word Biblical Commentary: Colossians, Philemon* [Waco, 1982], 28). Eduard Schweizer points out that "Son of his love" (τοῦ υἱοῦ τῆς ἀγάπης αὐτοῦ) "is a Semitic formulation and means little more than 'beloved Son'"; but he adds, "although presumably in Greek greater stress is laid on love" (*The Letter to the Colossians* [Minneapolis, 1982], 53).

[9] Graham Stanton sees Jesus as "'Son of God' in a *unique* sense." He says further, "Did Paul consider Jesus to be 'divine'? The answer would appear to be clear: Jesus stood in the closest possible relationship to God, for his favourite phrase 'his Son' points to the similarity, as it were, of God and Jesus, rather than to their 'difference'" (M. Goulder, ed., *Incarnation and Myth: The Debate Continued* [London, 1979], 154, 157 [Stanton's italics]).

9:5), so he knew what family life was like. He was meek and gentle (2 Cor. 10:1), obedient to the Father (Phil. 2:8), and without sin (2 Cor. 5:21). He had a ministry among the Jews ("became a servant of the circumcision for the truth of God" [Rom. 15:8]). He had apostles (including Cephas and John [Gal. 2:9]), who were called "the Twelve" (1 Cor. 15:5). He instituted the Holy Communion (1 Cor. 11:23–25). He was killed by the Jews (1 Thess. 2:15), by the method of crucifixion (Gal. 6:14), was buried, and then raised on the third day (1 Cor. 15:4).

Paul knew enough about the teaching of Jesus to be able to quote some of his sayings (1 Cor. 7:10; 9:14). He also knew that there were some matters on which he had no saying of Jesus (1 Cor. 7:12, a statement that implies that he had a good stock of such sayings). He has some echoes of Jesus' teachings, things he expresses in his own way but clearly derived from his Master (e.g., Rom. 12:14; 13:9–10; 16:19; 1 Cor. 13:2). Clearly his knowledge of Jesus was not slight. The fact that two of the Evangelists were with him when he wrote Colossians and Philemon (Col. 4:10, 14; Philem. 24) shows that he had access to good sources of information. And through all that he says it is clear that Paul saw Jesus as truly a man. There is no suggestion here of a docetic Christ, one who looked human but was not. For Paul, Jesus was very much "one of us."

CHRIST AND GOD

Paul, then, is clear on the genuine humanity of Jesus. But his deep interest is not there. His entire life had been revolutionized by his meeting with Jesus on the Damascus road. That confrontation meant that a whole way of life passed away and a new life began, a new life full of spiritual power that Paul attributed to Jesus. Of this new life he could say, "To me to live is Christ" (Phil. 1:21) and "I live in faith in the Son of God who loved me and gave himself up for me" (Gal. 2:20). This involved him in becoming a preacher of the gospel (1 Cor. 1:17), "a preacher and an apostle" (1 Tim. 2:7), and in this capacity he saw the power of Christ at work in the lives of his converts. His letters are the product of a vigorous, dynamic personality, ceaselessly occupied in pursuing the divine calling that he had received and in giving expression to his deep convictions regarding the One who had done so much for him and through him.

In a variety of ways, Paul brings out the more-than-human aspect of Christ. One is his habit of classing his Savior with God, referring to him in the same breath as God the Father. Thus he normally begins his letters with a greeting: "Grace to you and peace from God our Father and the Lord Jesus Christ" (Rom. 1:7; 1 Cor. 1:3; 2 Cor. 1:2; Gal. 1:3; Eph. 1:2; Phil. 1:2; 2 Thess. 1:2; 1 Tim. 1:2; 2 Tim. 1:2; Titus 1:4; Philem. 3).[10] Occasionally he links the Father and Christ in prayer: "May God our Father himself and our Lord Jesus direct our way to you" (1 Thess. 3:11; cf. 2 Thess. 2:16–17). He can speak of God as "the God and Father of our Lord Jesus Christ" (Rom. 15:6; 2 Cor. 1:3; 11:31; Eph. 1:3; cf. Eph. 1:17; Col. 1:3). This relationship may

---

[10] It is possible that Colossians and 1 Thessalonians begin in the same way, for in each case some MSS have these words. But most scholars agree that in these two letters the greeting mentions the Father only.

be understood as one of subordination; that is, that God is the God of Jesus. But it may also be understood in the sense that we know God only to the extent that Jesus has made him known. He is not some abstract, remote deity, but the Father of Jesus Christ.[11] In this spirit it is through Christ that Paul offers thanksgiving to God (Rom. 1:8; 7:25; Eph. 5:20), or again that he offers thanks to Christ himself for the power he gave him and for putting him into the ministry (1 Tim. 1:12). Christ is "God's power and God's wisdom" (1 Cor. 1:24), and this is not so very different from seeing Christ as being himself the source of power (1 Cor. 5:4; 2 Cor. 12:9).

Paul has a good deal to say about the Holy Spirit, who is clearly a very exalted personage. And he is "the Spirit of Christ" (Rom. 8:9; Phil. 1:19). People may call on the name of Christ in much the same fashion as they call on the name of God (1 Cor. 1:2; cf. 5:4); they can "beseech through the name of our Lord Jesus Christ" (1 Cor. 1:10), or "command" in that name (2 Thess. 3:6), or look for that name to be glorified in the lives of believers (2 Thess. 1:12).

There are some important passages in which Paul dwells on the relationship of Christ to God. Philippians 2:5–11 is one such passage; it is often understood as an early hymn that Paul took over. This may well be the case; in it there is some unusual vocabulary, and a number of scholars have arranged the material as poetry. There is no reason why Paul should not either have composed a hymn himself or taken over a hymn that someone else had written. If the latter, he has certainly made it his own (those who see it as poetry usually see some prose insertions they think Paul made to express his own views more clearly).

Many modern scholars insist that the passage is to be understood soteriologically; that is, it tells us about what Christ did for our salvation, not about his essential nature. Paul is certainly emphasizing what Christ did for us, but that does not mean that what he says does not help us understand Christ's essential nature.[12] Paul says that Christ, "in the form of God," "did not esteem it something to be grasped at to be equal with God" (v. 6). These two expressions surely indicate deity.[13] It is not easy to see being "in the form of God" as meaning anything less.[14] Could this be said of any other human or of an angel? The second expression

[11] J. C. O'Neill comments on the Romans passage: "In the present context God is assumed to be already clearly known, and the blessing asks that the congregation may now unite with one voice to praise him, as 'Father of our Lord Jesus Christ' " (*Paul's Letter to the Romans* [Harmondsworth, 1975], 237).

[12] Cullmann emphasizes Christ's saving work and can say, "Functional Christology is the only kind which exists." But he also says, "We can neither simply speak of the person apart from the work nor of the work apart from the person" (*The Christology of the New Testament*, 326).

[13] Ralph P. Martin's *Carmen Christi* (Cambridge, 1967) is an exhaustive study of this passage. In summing up his discussion of v. 6*b*, *c*, he says, "The preincarnate Christ had as His personal possession the unique dignity of His place within the Godhead as the εἰκών or μορφή of God. . . . He possessed the divine equality, we may say, *de jure* because He existed eternally in the 'form of God' " (p. 148). Johannes Behm sees a reference to "the image of sovereign divine majesty"; the "specific outward sign" of Christ's "essential divine likeness" is "the μορφή θεοῦ" (*TDNT*, 4:751).

[14] Martin comments that the expression "looks back to our Lord's pre-temporal existence as the Second Person of the Trinity" (*The Epistle of Paul to the Philippians* [Grand Rapids, 1969], 96). F. W. Beare hesitates to take the expression as meaning "being God" but holds that it "is . . . not to be conceived as a mere appearance, but as a form of existence which in some sense exhibits Christ's true nature" (*A Commentary on the Epistle to the Philippians* [London, 1969], 78–79).

sees equality with God as no advance on Christ's position.[15] If this is the case what position could he have other than that of God?

Paul goes on to speak of Christ's coming to be "in the likeness of men" and of his humbling himself[16] and becoming obedient to death, the death of the Cross (vv. 7–8). We should not miss the point that even this statement of lowliness has implications of deity. Death for us is not a matter of choice, but a necessity; for him it was the result of obedience, and therefore it points to something more than humanity in him. But his lowly position was not final. God "highly exalted him" and, further, "freely gave him the name that is above every name, in order that in the name of Jesus every knee should bow, of those in heaven and earth, and below the earth, and every tongue confess that Jesus Christ is Lord, to the glory of God the Father" (vv. 9–11). This is not to be understood in the sense that, as a reward for his voluntary submission, God gave him a higher station than the one he had before (there is no higher station than being "in the form of God"); the contrast is with the lowliness to which he descended. If he has the name that is above every name, and if all creation bows to him and

confesses him as Lord, then this means deity.[17] Paul is not setting Jesus up as a rival God or as someone who in any way detracts from the Father's special place, for it is all "to the glory of God the Father." There is no opposition and no rivalry, but a profound and perfect unity.

It cannot be said that the passage is easy to understand. There are exegetes who consider that it pictures Jesus as being greater than created beings but less than God. Does not God exalt him and *give* him the name above every name? James D. G. Dunn explains this passage in terms of Adam typology. The meaning is "that every choice of any consequence made by Christ was the antithesis of Adam's, that every stage of Christ's life and ministry had the character of a fallen lot freely embraced."[18] But this is not doing justice to the language Paul uses: "being in the form of God," "emptied himself," "having come to be in the likeness of men," "having been found in the shape of a man." This is more than Adam typology.[19] Some things are perhaps not expressed as we might have expected Paul to express them. But if he was adopting and adapting a previously written hymn, he was limited to some extent by the words he took

---

[15] G. Stählin explains ἴσα εἶναι θεῷ in this way: "Christ was and is equal to God by nature. This equality is a possession which He can neither renounce nor lose" (*TDNT*, 3:353).

[16] Karl Barth insists that this does not mean that he ceased to be God: "He humbled Himself, but He did not do it by ceasing to be who He is" (*Church Dogmatics*, iv, i [Edinburgh, 1956]: 180).

[17] Cf. Martin: "The glorified Jesus is the object of worship in the same way as the Jews invoked their covenant God" (*Carmen Christi*, 252).

[18] *Christology in the Making* (London, 1980), 121.

[19] Cullmann can say, "All the statements of Phil. 2:6ff. are to be understood from the standpoint of the Old Testament history of Adam." But he draws a very different conclusion from that of Dunn: "Unlike Adam, the Heavenly Man, who in his pre-existence represented the true image of God, humbled himself in obedience and now receives the equality with God he did not grasp as a 'robbery' " (*Christology*, 181). Dunn also draws attention to C. K. Barrett: "With this we must compare the story of Adam: at every point there is negative correspondence" (*From First Adam to Last* [London, 1962], 16). But Barrett later says of the same passage, with reference to equality with God: "As the eternal Son of God, he had it; yet emptied himself and became obedient" (p. 72). J. L. Houlden finds the Adam typology inadequate; the author "speaks of Christ as personally existent before his entry into this world. . . . This notion of Christ's pre-existence, arising so quickly in the history of the Church, here finds perhaps its earliest statement" (*Paul's Letters From Prison* [London, 1977], 75).

over. In any case the strength of the language remains. The thrust of the whole is to put Christ with God, not with created beings.

Another significant passage is Colossians 1:15–20.[20] This refers to "the Son of his love" (v. 13) as "the image of the invisible God" (v. 15). "Image" (*eikōn*) can mean a copy; e.g., the image of the emperor on a coin. But it can also be used to indicate, not dissimilarity (an image, not the real thing), but similarity (the image is exactly the same, not different). It is this second meaning that is required here. Paul is saying, not that the Son is different from the Father, but that he is exactly like him.[21] He is, further, the "firstborn of all creation." This does not mean that he was the first to be created;[22] rather it signifies that he stands in relation to the entire creation in the relationship the firstborn son has to his father's estate. In antiquity a great property involved a host of people—dependents, hired servants, and slaves—among whom there were varying orders of importance. But the father's firstborn, the son who was his heir, was the most important of all. The term *firstborn* marked a significant rela-

tion, and that is its meaning here. The Son is the most significant of all there is, because he stands in such a relationship to the Father as does no one and nothing else in all creation.[23]

Indeed, creation took place "in him" (v. 16); this may mean that he was God's agent in bringing it about (cf. 1 Cor. 8:6), or it may be akin to Paul's thought elsewhere of being "in Christ" (cf. Acts 17:28 for the thought of being "in" God); all that exists is caught up in his creative activity.[24] The apostle proceeds to spell this out in terms of location (in heaven or on earth), visibility (visible or invisible), and authority (thrones, lordships, etc.); nothing is exempted. And not only was all this mighty creation brought about "through" him, it was also created "for" him (which is also said of the Father [Rom. 11:36; 1 Cor. 8:6]). He is the end and aim of it all; everything moves toward him as its ultimate goal. He is the Alpha and the Omega of all creation, its beginning and its end. He is "before all things" (v. 17).[25] The reference is primarily to time; he existed before everything, and this carries with it the thought that he was accordingly preeminent above all things. A further

---

[20] This passage, like Philippians 2:5–11, is widely regarded as a pre-Pauline hymn that the apostle had taken over and adapted with additions of his own. A useful account of discussions of the passage may be found in R. P. Martin, *Colossians and Philemon* (London, 1981), 61–66.

[21] Cf. H. Kleinknecht: "Image is not to be understood as a magnitude which is alien to the reality and present only in the consciousness. It has a share in the reality. Indeed, it is the reality" (*TDNT*, 2:389). Martin says, "The term 'image of God' is not fully understood by the meaning of 'representative of God', however perfect that representation may be thought to be. The phrase must include the thought that God Himself is personally present, *Deus manifestus*, in His Son" (*Carmen Christi*, 112–13).

[22] J. B. Lightfoot reminds us that the fourth-century church fathers drew attention to the fact that the word is not πρωτόκτιστος ("first created"), but πρωτότοκος ("first born") (*Saint Paul's Epistles to the Colossians and Philemon* [London, 1927 edn.], 145). He sees the word as indicating sovereignty as well as priority.

[23] "He is Lord of creation and has no rival in the created order" (Martin, *Colossians*, 58).

[24] Dunn comments, "This may simply be *the writer's way of saying that Christ now reveals the character of the power behind the world*" (*Christology in the Making*), 190 (Dunn's italics). But this is not what Paul says. It is not taking seriously the plain meaning of the words used.

[25] On ἔστιν Lightfoot comments, "The imperfect ἦν might have sufficed (comp. Joh. i:1), but the present ἔστιν declares that this pre-existence is absolute existence" (*Colossians*, 153).

thought is that he not only created all things, but he sustains them; it is in him that "all things hold together (*synestēken*)." Creation does not function without his sustaining hand.

Paul proceeds to the point that this supreme person is head of the body that is the church (v. 18) and goes on to say that he is the "beginning" (*archē*); the term probably combines the meanings of priority in time and source (cf. Heb. 2:10). He is "the firstborn from the dead," clearly a reference to the Resurrection. Ralph P. Martin cites Lohse for the point that the combination of "beginning" and "firstborn" suggests that he is the founder of a new people (cf. Rom. 8:29; is there a link between creation and the new creation?).[26] The purpose (*hina*) of this is that "in all things he might be preeminent." We are not allowed to lose sight of the fact that Paul is ascribing to Christ the highest place that can be imagined. There is something of the same thought in his further statement that all the "fullness" dwelt in him, this term denoting the full total of divine powers.[27] For Paul the divine powers are, of course, not spread over a multiplicity of deities, but concentrated in one God, and that God in all his fullness dwells in Christ.[28] To

this is added the information that his reconciling activity not only brought deliverance to people on earth but is also effective in heaven (v. 20).

This is a staggering collection of descriptions and it makes it abundantly clear that Paul saw Christ not only as the man from Nazareth, but also as a being with cosmic significance.[29] He is supreme over the church, but he is much more than that. He was God's agent in bringing creation into being, and he is supreme over every authority, celestial as well as terrestrial, however it is conceived. The passage is a breathtaking expression of the supreme grandeur of the person of Christ.

DIVINE FUNCTIONS

It is in keeping with all this, even if not expressed in such lofty terms, that Paul sees Christ as existing before the Incarnation. Of the rock the Israelites encountered in the wilderness, he says, "The rock was Christ" (1 Cor. 10:4). There are problems here, but what is beyond doubt is that Paul was sure of Christ's preexistence (cf. 2 Cor. 8:9; Gal. 4:4; Phil. 2:6).[30]

Further, he assigns a number of functions indifferently to God and to

---

[26] Martin, *Colossians*, 59.

[27] Lightfoot sees this as "a recognised technical term in theology, denoting the totality of the Divine powers and attributes" (*Colossians*, 157; see also his Detached Note, 255–71). The word was certainly used by the later Gnostics to denote the totality of the divine powers. If such teaching was as early as this, Paul is denying that Christ was part only of the πλήρωμα; all the divine power dwelt in him.

[28] C. H. Dodd sees the πλήρωμα as "God himself regarded in his attributes rather than in his personal identity" (*Abingdon Bible Commentary* [New York, 1929], 1255).

[29] Markus Barth argues against the tendency he sees in such writers as A. Vögtle, E. Schweizer, and J. Murphy-O'Connor to restrict Christ's saving work to the salvation of people ("Christ and All Things," in *Paul and Paulinism*, ed. M. D. Hooker and S. G. Wilson [London, 1982], 160–72). He says, "In the New Testament the Messiah or Son of Man is in person the sign and guarantee, the mediator and the sum of the salvation and renewal of all things as well as persons from all nations" (p. 170). Cf. Paul Beasley-Murray: "As the image of the invisible God, he has dominion over the whole creation. As the first-born he is sovereign lord over all creation. All things owe their origin to him. All things find their focal point in him. He is lord of all!" (*Pauline Studies*, ed. Donald A. Hagner and Murray J. Harris [Exeter and Grand Rapids, 1980], 179).

[30] Cf. John Knox: "Paul not only speaks of the pre-existence of Christ but obviously takes for granted that the conception was a familiar one to his readers and that they did not need to be convinced of its truth. He never explains it or argues for it. He never makes a point of it. This means

Christ. Thus, he refers to the kingdom of God (Rom. 14:17) and the kingdom of Christ (1 Cor. 15:24–25; Col. 1:13); it is the kingdom of both in Ephesians 5:5. The day of God in the Old Testament becomes "the day of our Lord Jesus Christ" (1 Cor. 1:8). He speaks of the grace of God (1 Cor. 1:4) and the grace of Christ (Rom. 16:20), "the gospel of God" (Rom. 1:1) and "the gospel of Christ" (Rom. 15:19), "the church of God" (1 Cor. 10:32) and "the churches of Christ" (Rom. 16:16), "the Spirit of God" (1 Cor. 2:11) and "the Spirit of Christ" (Rom. 8:9), the peace of God (Phil. 4:7) and the peace of Christ (Col. 3:15), the judgment seat of God (Rom. 14:10) and the judgment seat of Christ (2 Cor. 5:10). He also says that God will judge the secrets of men through Christ (Rom. 2:16). Sin is normally sin against God, but it is also sin against Christ (1 Cor. 8:12). Paul looks for God to be all in all (1 Cor. 15:28) as Christ is all in all (Col. 3:11).

In the same general category are passages in which Paul speaks of such things as the will of God in Christ (1 Thess. 5:18), of testifying before God and Christ (and "the elect angels" [1 Tim. 5:21]), and of seeing the glory of God in the face of Christ (2 Cor. 4:6). To be without Christ is much the same as to be without God (Eph. 2:12). Sometimes Paul applies to Christ words that refer to God in the Old Testament (e.g., Rom. 10:13; 1 Cor. 1:2; 2:16; Eph. 4:8; Phil. 2:10–11; Col. 1:16). The Septuagint word for Yahweh, "Lord," he uses freely of Christ.[31]

There is a reference to "the mystery of God, namely, Christ" (Col. 2:2), as well as to "the mystery of Christ" (Col. 4:3; again in Eph. 3:4). Now the Greek word *mystērion,* which we translate "mystery," is not exactly equivalent to the English word. It does not mean something difficult to work out but which we may solve if we are diligent and concentrate on the correct clues. Rather, it means something impossible to work out, something like "secret," but commonly a secret that has been made known.

It is frequently used of the gospel, and this is a splendid illustration of the term. Who could ever have worked it out that our salvation is not in any sense the product of our own effort? Not our good works, not our prayers, not our study of God's Word and God's ways, nothing of human striving at all. Who would have guessed that this required the coming of the Son of God in lowliness as the baby of Bethlehem, one who would live in relative obscurity and die in rejection? These truths had to be made known. They constitute a divine mystery, the gospel.

To speak of Christ as "God's mystery" is to place him in the forefront of this work of salvation; he is the very center and heart of it all. And to speak of the mystery as Christ's is to place him with God. This is reinforced by passages that associate revelation with Christ, as Paul does when he speaks of the "revelation of Jesus Christ" that taught him (Gal. 1:12). This surely is the significance also of "the word of Christ" (Col. 3:16) or his "words" (1 Tim. 6:3). The preaching, the *kērygma,* is "of Christ," and there are many references to preaching Christ

---

that, among his own churches at least, and presumably elsewhere, the idea was well established when his major letters were written, within fifteen or twenty years of Jesus' crucifixion" (*The Humanity and Divinity of Christ* [Cambridge, 1967], 10–11). John A. T. Robinson similarly holds that the concept of Christ's preexistence is very early (*Twelve New Testament Studies* [London, 1962], 143n.12).

[31] For the view that the use of "Lord" for Yahweh is post-Christian, see 40n.7 above.

(1 Cor. 15:12; 2 Cor. 1:19; 4:5; Phil. 1:15–18). The gospel is, of course, "the gospel of Christ" (e.g., Rom. 15:19; 1 Cor. 9:12; 2 Cor. 4:4; 9:13; Gal. 1:7).

The Jews prided themselves on the revelation God had given through Moses, but Paul holds that they do not understand Moses. When the writings of the old covenant are read, there is "a veil" that prevents them from seeing the true meaning. But that veil is done away "in Christ" (2 Cor. 3:14–16). In other words the key to revelation, even in the Old Testament, is Christ. In common with the other New Testament writers, Paul holds that the Old Testament, rightly read, leads to Christ (Gal. 3:24).

Clearly all this means that Christ is the center of the message that Paul proclaimed. And clearly this message is derived from Christ. This is not saying in express words that Christ is divine, but it comes very close to living it out. It was what Christ did, specifically in his atoning death, and what Christ revealed to Paul that formed the heart and center, not only of his preaching but also of all his thinking and living. And what is at the center is Christ.

IS CHRIST GOD?

Does Paul ever in clear terms refer to Christ as God? It is possible to interpret certain passages in this way. The most noteworthy is Romans 9:5, where the NIV translates, "Christ, who is God over all, forever praised!" and the RSV reads, "God who is over all be blessed for ever." Some weighty considerations support the former translation: (1) The structure of the sentence supports it, for "who is" would be expected to refer to "the Christ" (which precedes it), rather than to "God" (which comes later). The construction is similar to that in 2 Corinthians 11:31, where there is no doubt that "who is" refers to what precedes.[32] (2) If the words do not refer to Christ, they form a benediction praising God and such a benediction normally begins, "Blessed be God. . . ." The word order does not support the RSV reading. (3) The reference to Christ "after the flesh" looks for a further statement by way of contrast. The expression should not be left hanging as it would be if the RSV translation is accepted. (4) A joyful doxology praising God scarcely fits the context with its generally sad tone, whereas it is understandable immediately after the mention of Christ, as it brings out his greatness and consequently stresses the magnitude of the gift made to Israel. (5) The ascription of the benediction to God requires an abrupt change of subject.

The most important argument for "God be blessed . . ." is that Paul does not elsewhere unambiguously call Christ "God." This is a strong point. With all his statements about the greatness of Christ, Paul so often uses terms other than "God." But the fact that he does not do this elsewhere does not mean that he does not do it here. In the light of all this we should take the natural sense of the Greek seriously and refer the words to Christ.[33]

---

[32] The participle ὤν does not often occur in the New Testament with both a prepositional phrase and the noun to which it refers, so it is unlikely that ὁ ὢν ἐπὶ πάντων refers to θεός. A further point is that the punctuation in our texts is, of course, not original, so that we cannot be sure whether Paul would have had a full stop after σάρκα (as RSV) or a comma (as NIV).

[33] This view is supported by C. E. B. Cranfield, *Romans*, 2:464–70. He says, "The superiority of the case for taking v.5b to refer to Christ is so overwhelming as to warrant the assertion that it is very

We should notice some other passages. Thus, Paul writes of "the grace of our God and Lord Jesus Christ" (2 Thess. 1:12) and of "the great God and our Savior Jesus Christ" (Titus 2:13).[34] In both cases it is easy to understand the Greek sentence as referring to one person only, a person who is styled as both "God" and "Christ." In each case the definite article occurs before "God" and is not repeated before "Lord [Savior] Jesus Christ," a construction that most naturally is taken to indicate that one person is meant. This is not quite certain, for the New Testament writers did not invariably apply grammar so rigidly. In any case "Lord" is often definite even without the article; it may be translated and may mean "the Lord."[35] We can say, however, that in both cases there is the possibility that Jesus Christ is being called "God."[36]

THE LOVE OF CHRIST

Since Christ is so closely connected with God, and since Paul has so much to say about the love of God, it is not surprising that he also writes of the love of Christ. This is especially true because he sees the cross of Christ as of central importance, the cross where Christ in love died for sinful humanity.

In what is perhaps the most moving passage in all his writings he applies Christ's sacrifice personally to himself: ". . . the Son of God who loved me and gave himself for me" (Gal. 2:20). In a similar statement in which Paul links himself with other believers, the Ephesians are urged to walk in love "even as Christ also loved us and gave himself for us . . ." (Eph. 5:2). We see the same link between Christ's love and his giving of himself up to death in the way his love for the church works out (Eph. 5:25). The love of the Son is clearly

nearly certain that it ought to be accepted" (p. 468). See also Oscar Cullmann, *Christology*, 306–14; Bruce M. Metzger in *Christ and Spirit in the New Testament*, ed. B. Lindars and S. S. Smalley (Cambridge, 1973), 95–112; D. E. H. Whiteley, *The Theology of St. Paul* (Philadelphia, 1964), 118–20; W. L. Lorimer, *NTS* 13 (1966–67): 385–86; O. Michel, *Der Brief an die Römer* (Göttingen, 1966), 228–29. Maurice F. Wiles says that Romans 9:5 "is invariably and unhesitatingly applied to the Son rather than to the Father by all patristic writers" (*The Divine Apostle* [Cambridge, 1967], 83). The fact that Greek was the native language of many of them makes this all the more important.

[34] Ronald A. Ward cites the words in Titus 2:13 from the RSV: "our great God and Savior Jesus Christ," and comments, "There can be little doubt that this is the correct translation" (*1 and 2 Timothy & Titus,* 261). William Hendriksen finds the single Greek article impressive and sees this interpretation supported by the fact that nowhere in the New Testament is ἐπιφάνεια ("appearing") applied to more than one person, and that one person is always Christ (*New Testament Commentary, Exposition of the Pastoral Epistles* [Grand Rapids, 1957], 373–75). On the other hand, J. N. D. Kelly, while respectful of the reference to Christ, decides against it, for Paul nowhere else (with the possible exception of Rom. 9:5) says that Christ is God, and in the Pastorals Christ is normally set side by side with God as two persons. In these epistles Kelly thinks that Christ's relationship to God is one of dependence (*The Pastoral Epistles,* 246).

[35] I have pointed this out in my book *The First and Second Epistles to the Thessalonians* (Grand Rapids, 1959), 212. I added, "At the same time we should not overlook the fact that Paul does link them very closely indeed. The fact that there can be this doubt as to whether one or both is meant is itself indicative of the closeness of their connection in the mind of Paul. He makes no great distinction between them."

[36] In some quarters the concept that Jesus Christ was God incarnate is seriously doubted or even rejected by Christian writers, as in John Hick, ed., *The Myth of God Incarnate* (London, 1977); Michael Goulder, ed., *Incarnation and Myth: The Debate Continued* (London, 1979). This view is opposed in writings such as Michael Green, ed., *The Truth of God Incarnate* (London, 1977). In this book I cannot discuss the controversy in detail, but it does seems that the language of Paul is incarnational; whatever be the verdict on the precise meaning of an individual passage, his overall position is that Christ is God.

related to the love of the Father, and Paul can link the two in a prayer that begins, "Now may our Lord Jesus Christ himself, and God our Father, who loved us and gave us eternal comfort . . ." (2 Thess. 2:16).[37] The two are, of course, linked inseparably in a lyrical passage in Romans 8. After asking "Who will separate us from the love of Christ?"[38] Paul speaks of being "made more than conquerors through him who loved us" and then expresses his profound conviction that nothing whatever "will be able to separate us from the love of God that is in Christ Jesus our Lord" (Rom. 8:35–39). In another lyrical passage he prays that his readers, "being rooted and founded in love [their love for Christ? his love for them?] . . . may be strong to comprehend with all the saints what is the breadth and length and height and depth, and to know the love of Christ that passes knowledge" (Eph. 3:17–19). "The love of Christ constrains us" (2 Cor. 5:14), so that that love is effective through all our Christian service.[39]

From all this it is plain that the love of Christ is linked closely with the love of the Father and that this is a dominant conception. Paul's emphasis on love is sometimes strangely overlooked. He is seen as a rather quarrelsome type, always ready to engage in vigorous dispute, and as being much more remarkable for pugnacity than for any tenderness of feeling. But Paul is absolutely clear on the wonder of God's great love for us, a love that issued in the Cross and brought us salvation. We will see later that this love evokes an answering love in believers. Here we notice that love is characteristic of both God the Father and Christ. It is not too much to say that Paul comes to understand what love is when he stands before the Cross, a love that is the love of God as it is the love of Christ; it is the love of God in Christ. Everything else pales into insignificance beside this great love.[40]

SALVATION AND CHRIST

We will look more closely at Paul's understanding of salvation in chapter 3. Here we are concerned simply with the fact that, however it is understood, salvation is brought about by Christ. It is a mark of the greatness of Christ in Paul's eyes that he accomplished the salvation of the world. Christ is the Savior we await from heaven (Phil.

---

[37] Though we have the double subject "our Lord Jesus Christ" and "God our Father" the verbs are singular, an interesting indication that Paul viewed the two as closely related, possibly even as in some sense one. Perhaps this passage should be added to those in the previous section that may indicate that Christ is God.

[38] There is a textual problem. While most agree that we should read "Christ," some good MSS read "God," and one or two have the same reading as in v. 39: "the love of God which is in Christ Jesus." But the whole passage interweaves the love of Christ and the love of God.

[39] C. K. Barrett notes the possibility of reading the text as meaning our love for Christ and further H. Lietzmann's view that there is "a mystical double meaning." But he says firmly, "The fundamental thought here must be that of Christ's love for us, since this alone can provide a suitable introduction to what follows" (A Commentary on the Second Epistle to the Corinthians [New York, 1973], 167). So also Philip Hughes says that Paul's conduct "is dictated by the love of Christ (not so much his love for Christ—though that inevitably is involved—as Christ's love for him, which is prior to and the explanation of his love for Christ . . .)" (Paul's Second Epistle to the Corinthians [Grand Rapids, 1962], 192).

[40] Paul uses the verb ἀγαπάω 33 times, the noun ἀγάπη 75 times, and the adjective ἀγαπητός 27 times, a total of 135 of the 318 occurrences of the words in the New Testament. He uses these words more than anyone else does. John, who is usually regarded as "the apostle of love," has them 44 times in his Gospel and 62 times in the epistles, a total of 106.

3:20; cf. Titus 3:6), and salvation is through him (1 Thess. 5:9; 2 Tim. 2:10). There are general terms, like "Christ died for ungodly people" (Rom. 5:6; cf. v. 8), and there is emphasis on the fact of his death (Rom. 8:34; 14:9, 15; 1 Cor. 8:11; 15:3; Gal. 2:21). That death may be seen as effecting reconciliation (Rom. 5:10–11; 2 Cor. 5:18–20; Eph. 2:16; Col. 1:20), which is much the same as making peace (Eph. 2:14–15; cf. Phil. 4:7).

Paul speaks of redemption as being "in Christ Jesus" (Rom. 3:24). Elsewhere he declares that Christ "redeemed us from the curse of the law," which leads him to the other thought that he has "become a curse for us" (Gal. 3:13). Christ is linked with our justification (Gal. 2:17), forgiveness (Col. 3:13), and victory (1 Cor. 15:57). He brought peace (Rom. 5:1), hope (Eph. 1:12; Col. 1:27; 1 Thess. 1:3; 1 Tim. 1:1), sonship (Eph. 1:5), the promise of life (2 Tim. 1:1), eternal life (Rom. 5:21; 6:23), light (Eph. 5:14), and riches in glory (Phil. 4:19; cf. "the unsearchable riches of Christ" [Eph. 3:8]). The "free gift" that brings justification is from Christ (Rom. 5:15ff.), and believers are "joint heirs with Christ" (Rom. 8:17).

From another point of view, Christ is the one foundation on which Christians build (1 Cor. 3:11), and, again, he is the cornerstone (Eph. 2:20). He offered himself for us as a sacrifice (Eph. 5:2); Paul can speak of a specific sacrifice and call Christ "our Passover" (1 Cor. 5:7). Christ received us "to the glory of God" (Rom. 15:7), which says that his saving work is operative where it counts.

Negatively, the way of the law has been ended by Christ (Rom. 10:4). The same point may be made by referring to circumcision. The man who submits to this rite thereby places himself under an obligation to keep the whole law; anyone who follows this path thereby rejects what Christ is offering and gains nothing (Gal. 5:2–4). In Christ what matters is not circumcision nor, for that matter, the lack of it. It is "faith working through love" (Gal. 5:6; cf. 6:15). The whole function of the law is to bring people to Christ.

"IN CHRIST" AND "WITH CHRIST"

One of Paul's favorite expressions is "in Christ," with variations like "in the Lord," "in Christ Jesus," and "in him."[41] It occurs in every one of Paul's letters except his letter to Titus. Interestingly, Paul never says "in Jesus"; this may indicate that he had the risen Lord in mind. He applies the expression to himself quite freely, but he is not referring to a state in any way peculiar to himself or to leading Christians. All believers, regardless of their social standing or their educational disadvantages, are "in Christ." The words apply to individuals (2 Cor. 12:2) and also to churches (Gal. 1:22).

Sometimes the expression means simply "Christian." For example, when Paul speaks of Andronicus and Junia as being "in Christ" before he was (Rom. 16:7), he means that they were Christians before he was converted. "The faithful in Christ Jesus" (Eph. 1:1) are just as clearly the Christians, and so are "the brothers in the Lord" (Phil. 1:14;

---

[41] A. M. Hunter says that in one of its forms the expression is found "some 200 times" (*The Gospel According to St Paul* [London, 1966], 33). Adolf Deissmann puts the total at 164 (*The Religion of Jesus and the Faith of Paul* [London, 1926], 171; apparently this does not include the Pastorals).

cf. 1 Cor. 1:30; Philem. 16). The phrase may be connected with the beginnings of the Christian life, as when we read of Rufus that he was "elect in the Lord" (Rom. 16:13) and of the slave who was "called in the Lord" (1 Cor. 7:22). It may refer to the bringing about of the Christian salvation, for if anyone is "in Christ," there is a new creation (2 Cor. 5:17), and, again, those who were once far off have in Christ been made near (Eph. 2:13; the verse refers to "the blood of Christ," which brought this about). In Christ Jesus, Paul fathered the Christians at Corinth "through the gospel" (1 Cor. 4:15).

Furthermore, we should probably understand God's "eternal purpose in Christ Jesus our Lord" (Eph. 3:11) to refer to his purpose of salvation, and this is clearly intended when Paul says that there is "no condemnation for those in Christ Jesus" (Rom. 8:1). This is also the case when he tells us that "the blessing of Abraham comes to the Gentiles in Christ Jesus" (Gal. 3:14) and when we read of God's "promise in Christ Jesus" (Eph. 3:6).

The expression can bring out the attitudes that should characterize Christians. They are to be "of the same mind in the Lord" (Phil. 4:2); quarreling is no part of being in Christ. And they should "stand fast in the Lord" (Phil. 4:1; 1 Thess. 3:8; cf. Eph. 6:10), for giving way to opposition is also no part of being in Christ. Timothy was "faithful in the Lord" (1 Cor. 4:17). Paul was "confident in the Lord" (Gal. 5:10; Phil. 2:24; 2 Thess. 3:4). He cites Scripture to show that a believer who glories should glory in the Lord (1 Cor. 1:31); it is a pride that centers on what Christ has done in the converts. Christians are free people, with a liberty in Christ Jesus (Gal. 2:4); Christ has freed them "for freedom" (Gal. 5:1—a verse that puts a strong stress on our liberty). Or there may be emphasis on the emotions. Believers have "consolation" in Christ (Phil. 2:1). They rejoice in the Lord (Phil. 3:1; 4:4, 10). And Paul speaks of his love for the Corinthians as a love "in Christ Jesus" (1 Cor. 16:24) and of Ampliatus as his "beloved in the Lord" (Rom. 16:8).

There are many ways of bringing out the truth that truly Christian work is work done "in Christ." Thus, those who work in the Lord's service are "fellow workers in Christ Jesus" (Rom. 16:3, 9), and "the ministry" that Archippus received he received "in the Lord" (Col. 4:17). Paul writes to the Thessalonians about people "who are over [them] in the Lord" (1 Thess. 5:12)—evidently the office bearers in the local church. He labors at presenting "every man perfect in Christ" (Col. 1:28; cf. Apelles "approved[42] in Christ" [Rom. 16:10]). The Corinthians are Paul's "work in the Lord" and "the seal" of his apostleship in the Lord (1 Cor. 9:1–2). There are many "instructors in Christ" (1 Cor. 4:15), and Paul himself "speaks in Christ" (2 Cor. 2:17; 12:19). Christians labor in the Lord (Rom. 16:12) and abound in the work of the Lord (1 Cor. 15:58). The opening of a door in the Lord (2 Cor. 2:12) is an opportunity for further service. Tychicus was "a faithful servant in the Lord" (Eph. 6:21, a statement repeated in Col. 4:7). When Paul became "the prisoner in the Lord" (Eph. 4:1), he evidently saw his imprison-

---

[42] Δόκιμος means "approved, having passed the test." Here Cranfield thinks the word is used "possibly because Paul happened to know that under some particular serious trial he had proved himself a faithful Christian," or perhaps that Paul wanted no more than simply to vary his commendation (*Romans*, 2:791). The former seems more likely in this place.

ment not as unmitigated disaster, but as an opportunity for greater Christian service.

An interesting verse in this connection is Romans 16:22. Tertius may have written simply a greeting in the Lord, but "in the Lord" is at the opposite end of the sentence from "greet" and right after "wrote this letter." If he meant that he wrote the letter in the Lord, there is a teasing little question as to precisely what "writing in the Lord" means. Presumably it would signify that Tertius saw his writing as a piece of Christian service.[43]

For Paul, all of life is lived in Christ. He speaks of his "ways in Christ Jesus" (1 Cor. 4:17), and instructs the Colossians to "walk in him" (Col. 2:6). Phoebe was to be received "in the Lord" (Rom. 16:2); she was to be given a proper Christian welcome. Marriage is an important part of life that Paul relates to this concept when he urges widows to marry "in the Lord" (1 Cor. 7:39). Christians are "a holy temple in the Lord" (Eph. 2:21); they are "sanctified in Christ Jesus" (1 Cor. 1:2). And at a somewhat lower level Paul passes on a friendly greeting "in the Lord" (1 Cor. 16:19). No part of life is too great or too small to be unrelated to the Lord. Paul instructs children to obey their parents "in the Lord" (Eph. 6:1).[44] And, at the other end of life, believers who die "fall asleep in Christ" (1 Cor. 15:18). This means that they have hope in Christ; their hope is not only for this life (1 Cor. 15:19).

Believers are "all one in Christ Jesus" (Gal. 3:28); there is a strong bond of unity that ties them all together. Many hold that Paul's expression should be understood in terms of the Hebrew concept of corporate personality, "a conception which enabled him to think of the community in terms of its representative head."[45] It points at one and the same time to the life Christians share with one another and to Christ, who alone makes this quality of life possible. While "in Christ" is rightly applied to individuals, we should not overlook the strongly corporate character of the state to which it points.[46] It is a strong expression for the unity of all Christians. We who are believers belong together, but we are primarily not in this or that church, but "in Christ." There is a genuine and close unity with Christ.

Sometimes Paul puts this the other way around. Just as it is true that the believer is "in" Christ, so it is true that Christ is "in" the believer. Paul can say simply, "Christ lives in me" (Gal. 2:20). He is most anxious that this should be the experience of others, for he speaks of his travail (the word is used of birth pains) "until Christ be formed in" the Galatians (Gal. 4:19). Christ is "in" the Corinthians (2 Cor. 13:5) and the Romans (Rom. 8:10). Paul wants Christ to be magnified in his (Paul's) body (Phil. 1:20) and says that there is proof that Christ speaks "in" him (2 Cor. 13:3). He prays that Christ may dwell in the hearts of the Ephesians (Eph. 3:17).

---

[43] Cranfield favors the view that Tertius speaks of "greeting in the Lord"; if, however, it is "writing in the Lord," "one might understand Tertius to be expressing by ἐν κυρίῳ a certain awareness of the importance of that in which he had played a vital part, or simply indicating that he had done what he had done as a Christian as part of his service of his Lord" (*Romans*, 2:806).

[44] Some good MSS (including B D) omit "in the Lord," but it seems that the words should be read.

[45] A. M. Hunter, *The Gospel According to St Paul* (Philadelphia, 1966), 34.

[46] "To be 'in Christ' is to be a member of the ultimate, eschatological order, the divine community of love, proleptically present and partially realized in the church, whose spirit is the very Spirit of God and the very presence of the risen Christ" (John Knox, *Chapters in a Life of Paul* [London, 1954], 158).

This flexibility underlines Paul's certainty of the close bond that unites Christ to his people. They are in him; he is in them. While the apostle prefers the former way of putting it, he is not averse to the latter. Either way, the wonder of Christ's presence motivates the servant of God.

Paul also has a good deal to say about being "with" Christ. He brings out the centrality of the Cross for our salvation by saying that the believer "has died with Christ" (Rom. 6:8; Col. 2:20; 2 Tim. 2:11). He makes this a little more specific by saying that he has been "crucified with Christ" (Gal. 2:19) and that "our old man was crucified with him" (Rom. 6:6). Clearly Paul sees it as important that we identify with the death of Christ. He goes on to the thought that we were buried with him in baptism (Rom. 6:4; Col. 2:12). There is a rich symbolism in that sacrament. But Paul does not stop with death. He goes on to the thought that we have been raised with Christ (Col. 2:12; 3:1); that is, we have been made alive with him (Eph. 2:5; Col. 2:13).

All such expressions vividly bring out the deep spiritual experience of the Christian. The death of Christ has dealt with the sin of believers and has brought them a whole new way of life. They have died to their unregenerate past and have risen to a completely new way of life, a life in which Christ is everything: "To me to live is Christ" (Phil. 1:21). Believers' lives are "hidden with Christ in God" (Col. 3:3); they will live by the power of God (2 Cor. 13:4). The death leads on to the resurrection: "If we died with Christ, we believe that we will live with him" (Rom. 6:8). Christ "died for us so that, whether we wake or whether we sleep, we shall live with him" (1 Thess. 5:10). Paul is so sure of the wonderful thing that Christ has done for us that he sees believers associated with Christ now, in all the newness that life in Christ has come to mean.

But, wonderful though that is, it does not exhaust the riches of the life Christ has made available. Paul looks for the day when the God who raised Jesus "will raise us also with Jesus" (2 Cor. 4:14). He wants "to depart and be with Christ," which he sees as "far better" (Phil. 1:23), for then the believer "will be always with the Lord" (1 Thess. 4:17; cf. 2 Tim. 2:11–12).

Suffering is an inevitable part of the believer's lot here and now, but if we suffer with Christ now, we will be glorified with him in the hereafter (Rom. 8:17; cf. Col. 3:4).[47] Paul sums up much when he asks, "He who did not spare his own Son but gave him up for us all, how will he not with him freely give us all things?" (Rom. 8:32). Paul is not proceeding from some abstract, theoretical basis, but from what God has already done. The Cross is eloquent evidence of God's love and care for his people. And if God has done all that already, it is inconceivable to Paul that he is going to quit now. We may be absolutely sure that the God who has done so much will see the work of salvation through to its end.

Much more could easily be added. Paul sees all things in the light of Christ. Believers are called into the fellowship of God's Son (1 Cor. 1:9) and are to live in the light of this fact.

---

[47] Adolf Deissmann holds that the formula "with Christ" "nearly always means the fellowship of the faithful with Christ after their death or after His coming" (*Light from the Ancient East* [London, 1927], 303n.1). He may mean that this is the case in the early church; as we have seen, while this use occurs in the New Testament, there are also significant passages which apply "with Christ" to the present experience of the Christian.

The churches to which they belong are churches of Christ (Gal. 1:22). All of life is Christ's and the end of all things is "the day of our Lord Jesus Christ" (1 Cor. 1:8). But enough has been said to show that for Paul Christ is supreme. He is Lord of everything and everyone. His lordship extends beyond this world and this life. It extends to heaven and it includes all eternity.[48]

---

[48] There is no significant development in christology throughout the epistles, so that this rich and full theology must have been developed before A.D. 50. Moreover Paul clearly expects his readers to understand the christological titles and concepts, and this tells us that they are older still. Martin Hengel asks what picture of Christ Paul had after his encounter on the Damascus road "so as to become the foundation of his gospel apart from the law" and proceeds to a second question: "Do we have any reason to suppose that Paul's christology changed in essential points during his activity in Syria and Cilicia in the years which now followed?" (*Between Jesus and Paul* [Philadelphia, 1983], 31; cf. also 39–40). If his essential christology was formed on the Damascus road, it was very early indeed.

3

GOD'S SAVING WORK
IN CHRIST

What happened on the Damascus road had decisive significance for Paul. His vision of Jesus turned his whole world upside down. From that moment he was certain that Jesus Christ is the supremely great One and, as we saw in chapter 2, cannot be thought of as less than God. Now if such a great Person came to this earth to bring salvation, some things follow inevitably. One is that the human race must have been in a very serious plight indeed. Another is that the work of saving the race was too great to be brought about with human resources; it needed something far more than we sinners can possibly bring to the task.

This does not mean that Paul reasoned it all out in a vacuum. He was no doctrinaire theorist, and in his earlier, pre-Christian days he had been well content with his position (Phil. 3:4–6). He did not start with the idea that we are all sinners, look around for a solution, and finally fix on Christ. It was meeting with Christ that changed everything. That meeting started him off on a completely new track. Jesus' entry into this world was in order to deal with our need, and Jesus' death was central to it all (1 Cor. 1:23). A great cost implies a great cause: we are all sinners in need of redemption. We have failed to live up to the highest and best that we know, and this spells ultimate disaster. The God of whom Paul wrote will not treat sin as of no consequence; and, therefore, the evil we do now will necessarily follow us into the hereafter. The coming of Jesus taught Paul some important things about the meaning of salvation. If we are to understand salvation, it is perhaps best to start with the catastrophe in which the human race involved itself when it fell into sin.

SLAVES TO SIN

Sin is many-sided, and Paul uses a variety of terms to bring this out.[1] He has no simplistic idea of what sin

Note: The subject matter of this section is treated at greater length in my book *The Cross in the New Testament* (Grand Rapids, 1965), chs. 5–6.

[1]The basic word is ἁμαρτία, "missing the mark" (which Paul uses 64 times), with the corresponding nouns ἁμάρτημα (twice), ἁμαρτωλός (8 times) and the verb ἁμαρτάνω (17 times). Sin is also ἀδικία, "unrighteousness" (12 times); cognates are ἄδικος, "unrighteous" (3 times) and ἀδικέω, "to do wrong" (9 times). Sin is also ἀνομία, "lawlessness" (6 times), with ἄνομος, "lawless man" (5 times) and ἀνόμως, "lawlessly" (twice); παρακοή, "disobedience" (twice); ἀσέβεια, "godlessness" (4 times), with ἀσεβής, "godless man" (3 times); παράβασις, "a stepping across,

means. And, although he certainly emphasizes its seriousness, he is not obsessed with it as some of his detractors have claimed. He uses the word for sin (*hamartia*) sixty-four times, of which forty-eight occur in Romans, a letter in which he deals with the subject at some length. Thus, in all his other letters put together the word "sin" occurs only fourteen times.

Paul most often uses the word in the singular: sin is not only an evil we commit, but a power that holds us in bondage. More than once he speaks of people at large as "slaves of sin" (Rom. 6:17, 20), and in a piece of vivid imagery he sees us all as "sold under sin" (Rom. 7:14). Just as a slave is sold to a master (whether we like it or not), so we come under the control of sin (whether we like it or not). Paul speaks of himself as "brought into captivity to[2] the law of sin" (Rom. 7:23), where the imagery is that of the capture of a prisoner of war. It is unexpected to have a reference to "law" in such a connection, but as Cranfield says, "It is a forceful way of making the point that the power which sin has over us is a terrible travesty, a grotesque parody, of that authority over us which belongs by right to God's holy law."[3] Paul is saying two things: (1) sin has no right to control us (made in God's image as we are) and (2) it has nevertheless taken control. So it is that, though we may serve[4] God's law with our minds, yet, as things are, in the flesh we serve sin's law (Rom. 7:25).

The apostle is in no doubt about mankind's subjection to sin. At the beginning of Romans he has a strong argument to show the universality of sin. He begins with the Gentiles who "having come to know God, did not glorify him as God" (Rom. 1:21). They did not have the law that is revealed in the Old Testament, so they cannot be accused of breaking it. But Gentiles "are a law for themselves" (Rom. 2:14); their conduct shows that they know right from wrong (Rom. 2:15). Therefore, when they sin they are "without excuse" (Rom. 1:20), and Paul paints a dismal picture of what this means (Rom. 1:21–32). But not only are the Gentiles sinners, the same is true of the Jews. The Jews prided themselves on their possession of the law, but it is keeping the law that counts, not just listening to it (Rom. 2:13). Being a Jew, a member of the people of God, means being a Jew inwardly, not simply in externals (Rom. 2:28). Paul comes to a climax with a series of quotations from the Old Testament that speak of all people as being sinful (Rom. 3:10–18). The Jew cannot shrug this off, saying that all these statements refer to the Gentiles, for the law speaks to those who have it, the Jews (Rom. 3:19). What the law does is bring the knowledge of sin (Rom. 3:20). Paul goes on to say plainly, "All sinned, and they come short of the glory of God" (Rom. 3:23).

Clearly this refers to the actual evil deeds we all commit, but Paul also has the idea that sin is part of us. He speaks

---

transgression" (5 times), with παραβάτης, "transgressor" (3 times); παράπτωμα, "a fall beside" (16 times); πώρωσις, "hardening" (twice); κακία, "badness" (6 times), with κακός, "bad" (26 times) and κακοῦργος, "evil doer" (once); ἥττημα, "defeat" (twice); πονηρία, "wickedness" (3 times), with πονηρός, "wicked" (13 times); ἔνοχος, "guilty" (once).

[2] It is unexpected to have the preposition ἐν used with "law" (ἐν τῷ νόμῳ), but the meaning does not appear to be in doubt.

[3] *A Critical and Exegetical Commentary on the Epistle to the Romans* (Edinburgh, 1975), 1:364.

[4] Δουλεύω, "to serve as a slave," governs both clauses.

of "the law of sin that is in [our] members" (Rom. 7:23)[5] and says that we are "by nature children of wrath" (Eph. 2:3). Children not sanctified by the faith of a parent are "unclean" (1 Cor. 7:14). Such passages appear to be saying that we sin because of what we are.[6] Our very nature inclines us to do wrong (a fact we can all verify from personal experience; we all find it difficult to be virtuous, whereas we can slip into evil quite easily). There is a solidarity in the human race: "We are members of one another" (Eph. 4:25). In groups we accept low standards, as for example in the foreign policies of the nations, which are dictated by unabashed self-interest. And any "in" group tends to adopt a judgmental attitude to those outside, while it resolutely advances its own causes.[7]

Paul has a good deal more to say on the subject, but this is enough to bring out his point that we all commit sin. Not only so, but we cannot break free. We are caught up in the power and the consequences of the evil we do. We are enslaved.

THE FLESH

"Flesh" is a term Paul uses often and with a bewildering variety of meanings. It is one of his characteristic words, for he uses it 91 times out of 147 in the New Testament. John, by contrast, has it only 13 times, which indicates something of the Pauline character of the term. Strictly it denotes the soft part of the physical human body as in the expression "flesh and blood" (1 Cor. 15:50), from which it comes to be used more or less in the sense of "body," as when Paul refers to an "infirmity of the flesh" (Gal. 4:13; cf. the reference to Christ's body [Col. 1:22]). It comes to signify what is human, as when Paul says, ". . . in me, that is in my flesh" (Rom. 7:18) and again when he asks, "What I plan, do I plan according to the flesh?" i.e., "in a human manner" ("like a worldly man" [2 Cor. 1:17 RSV]). In this sense we are all involved in "the flesh"; we "walk in the flesh" ("we live in the world" [2 Cor. 10:3 GNB]). It is inevitable. If we are human, we are "in the flesh."

But physical flesh is weak, and physical weakness may lead on to the thought of moral weakness; "in a human manner" all too easily comes to mean "human, without God" and thus "human, opposed to God." "Flesh" readily comes to signify that which is connected with life in the body but which is opposed to the things of God.[8] In this sense it is closely related

---

[5] "Sin does not remain an external power outside a man. As Paul saw it, sin takes up its residence within a man, and occupies him as an enemy occupies a conquered country" (William Barclay, *The Mind of St. Paul* [New York, 1958], 190).

[6] "Man sins because he is a sinner in the wrong relationship with God. . . . Sin is something that has somehow got its hold upon the human race as a whole" (William Hordern, *The Case for a New Reformation Theology* [Philadelphia, 1959], 130).

[7] John Burnaby points out that there is an operation of resistance to the will of God that cannot be confined to "the operation of personal freedom." He adds, "The resistance is present already in the many-threaded web by which the individual is bound up with society in which he is placed, and ultimately with the species to which he belongs. . . . One can hardly contemplate the apparently incorrigible self-righteousness, the shameless Pharisaism which is exhibited in the *collective* behaviour of every human group—social, political, national, or ecclesiastical—without being compelled to acknowledge that in human nature as we see it there is a hard core which everywhere opposes itself to the Spirit's persuasion" (*Theol* 62 [1959]: 15).

[8] Günther Bornkamm points out that, while Paul frequently uses the word "flesh" in senses found in the Old Testament, often he has it in a fuller sense: "Then it designates man's being and attitude *as opposed and in contradiction to God and God's Spirit*" (*Paul* [London, 1971], 133; Bornkamm's italics).

to sin. Even though Paul may serve the law of God with the mind, "with the flesh" he serves the law of sin (Rom. 7:25). Small wonder that he refers to "sinful flesh" (Rom. 8:3), to "sinful passions" that worked in our members when we were "in the flesh" (Rom. 7:5), and to "being puffed up by the mind of the flesh" (Col. 2:18)—a warning to us not to take "the flesh" as necessarily pointing to gross sins, especially to sexual sins. It can include these, but "flesh" can also be very cerebral. It is instructive to notice that "the works of the flesh" include "fornication, uncleanness, lasciviousness," but also "idolatry, witchcraft, hatreds, strife, jealousy, angers, discords, divisions, factions, murders, drunkenness, carousings, and the like"' (Gal. 5:19–21). It is plain that from the human standpoint "flesh" can be attractive and highly respectable as well as gross and highly sensual. But wherever people concentrate on the purely human and on promoting the interests of this life only, there is sin.[9]

Paul is clear that the fleshly minded face ultimate disaster: "He who sows to his flesh will from the flesh reap corruption" (Gal. 6:8). "When we were in the flesh, the sinful passions aroused by the law worked in our members to bear fruit for death" (Rom. 7:5). To what else could a concentration on the flesh lead? Paul has a notable passage in which he starts with the point that the law could not do what it aimed at because "it was weak through the flesh" (Rom. 8:3; cf. "You do not do what you want to" [Gal. 5:17]). He goes on to characterize Christians as those who "do not walk according to the flesh, but according to the Spirit" (v. 4). By contrast, there are those "who are according to the flesh," people who "set their minds on the flesh" (v. 5). They are in serious trouble because "the mind of the flesh is death" (v. 6); it is "enmity against God, for it is not subject to God's law, nor can it be" (v. 7). Thus, "those who are in the flesh" simply "cannot please God" (v. 8). Paul does not say that "the mind of the flesh" brings death as its punishment. He says that it *is* death. To set oneself to the gratification of the purely human nature is to enter a living death. We may go through the motions of living, but, cut off from Christ "who is our life" (Col. 3:4) and from "the living and true God" (1 Thess. 1:9), what we have is no more than a travesty of life. It is the tragedy of the worldly minded, those who live on the level of the flesh, that while they claim to have life in abundance ("living it up!"), they do not even understand what "life" is.

Christians have been liberated from bondage to "the flesh." But this took place because of Christ's saving work; before they believed, they were just as much in bondage as anyone else. But they are no longer "in the flesh" (Rom. 8:9); they have put off "the body of the flesh" (Col. 2:11), implying that previously they were involved in it. "Formerly" they lived "in the lusts of the flesh" (Eph. 2:3). To be free of the flesh is not a natural achievement.

THE LAW

One of Paul's important categories is law. He uses the word "law" (*nomos*) 119 times, well over half of its New Testament total of 191 (62 percent). Not only does he use it often, but he

---

[9]"Though the flesh is not itself evil, sin invades man through it, finding the easiest entry there. Sin may then grow strong in the flesh and cause havoc in every department of life. It may create a lower nature in the flesh to war constantly with the divine inspiration and to bring about a state of tension and self-contradiction" (W. David Stacey, *The Pauline View of Man* [London, 1956], 162).

uses it in a variety of ways, some of which are difficult to follow. He can speak of "the law of sin" and "the law of [the] mind" (Rom. 7:23), "the law of the husband" (Rom. 7:2), and "the law of the Spirit of life in Christ Jesus" and "the law of sin and death" (Rom. 8:2), to cite but a few. Mostly he has in mind the law God gave through Moses, seeing it as a good gift of God: "The law is holy, and the commandment holy and righteous and good" (Rom. 7:12); "The law is spiritual" (Rom. 7:14), and it is "good" (Rom. 7:16; 1 Tim. 1:8).[10] The law does not contradict God's promises (Gal. 3:21).[11]

But it is easy to misunderstand the place of law, and it is Paul's contention that by and large his nation has done just that. It is true that there are some beautiful and moving statements about God's grace and God's forgiveness in Jewish writings, but the Jewish writings are not saying the same as Paul is. For them, keeping the law is funda-mental and God's mercy operates within that frame.[12] The Jews rightly welcomed the law as a great good that God had bestowed on them.[13] But they wrongly exalted it into the way of salvation,[14] a mistake Paul himself had made before his conversion (Phil. 3:4–6). Some of them at least held that the possession of the law in itself or the study of it was enough. The great Hillel said, "The more study of the Law the more life."[15] Such views were vigorously opposed by others. Thus Simeon, the son of the Gamaliel under whom Paul studied (Acts 22:3), said, "Not the expounding [of the Law] is the chief thing but the doing [of it]; and he that multiplies words occasions sin."[16] The end of such disputes was not awe at the wonder of God's grace, but a deep respect for the law that all too easily degenerated into legalism.[17]

Paul insists that by "works of law" no one will be justified before God (Rom. 3:20; Gal. 2:16; 3:11); that is not the

---

[10] The word is καλός, which also means "beautiful," whereas elsewhere (Rom. 7:12) he uses ἀγαθός of the commandment.

[11] Cf. W. D. Davies, "The concentration of the new life 'in Christ' is of the essence of Paul's approach to the Law, which comes not to be dismissed by him but transposed to a new key" (M. D. Hooker and S. G. Wilson, eds., *Paul and Paulinism* [London, 1982], 4).

[12] Morna D. Hooker cites a moving statement from the Qumran scrolls beginning, "As for me, my justification is with God. In his hand are the perfection of my way and the uprightness of my heart. He will wipe out my transgression through his righteousness. . . ." She points out that this looks like something that Paul might have written, but there are differences: "The author of the Qumran document thinks of God's righteousness as something which functions within the system of Law; it operates for those who accept God's commands and obey them." She says further that Paul's idea of righteousness *apart from* the law "would surely have shocked the Qumran writer" (*A Preface to Paul* [New York, 1980], 39). Bornkamm makes much the same point (*Paul*, 139).

[13] E. P. Sanders in an important work argues that Christians have not always seen this (*Paul and Palestinian Judaism* [London, 1977]). He stresses the Jewish idea that God had elected the nation and given the law. He sees the emphasis on God's choosing of the people and rejects the idea that Jews held that the keeping of the law merits salvation. Paul's difference from orthodox Jews was his rejection of any way of salvation other than through Christ (p. 550). Sanders calls us to think again about the way Jews regarded grace and law, and this is valuable. But in the end the Jews were very much involved in legal niceties (whether and/or how they had fulfilled their obligation). With all their emphasis on covenant and the like, "legalism" remained an important concept for them. Paul repudiated it.

[14] Bornkamm cites some impressive Jewish statements about God's faithfulness and his mercy. But he goes on to say that the Jewish statements "are always in the context of God's unique relationship to his chosen people and never imply questioning of the law as the means of salvation" (*Paul*, 139).

[15] *Aboth* 2:7, Danby's translation. See the statement of Eleazar of Modiim (29n.11 above).

[16] Mishnah, *Aboth* 1:17, Danby's translation. Cf. also Josephus, *Ant.* xx.44.

[17] It did not invariably do this, and there are some fine statements in rabbinic literature and in the Qumran scrolls welcoming God's forgiving love. But more typical are exhortations to obedience.

purpose of law at all. The function of law was not to do away with sin but to show it up for what it is. It was brought in "in order that the trespass might increase" (Rom. 5:20; cf. 3:20). Paul uses the singular. He is not saying that the law caused more trespasses, but that it brought out clearly what trespass is. A magnifying glass does not increase the number of dirty marks, but it does show up more plainly the ones that are there and it enables us to perceive some that we could not see with the unassisted eye. As Paul sees it, the function of the law is similarly to make clear what sin is. It is not to bring salvation,[18] but to prepare the way for it. The law shows us our sin (and our sins) clearly and thus our need of salvation. The law was there to bring us to Christ "so that we might be justified by faith" (Gal. 3:24).[19]

Paul puts this another way when he speaks of the law as bringing death. He says that he was alive "without law" once, but "when the commandment came sin sprang into life and I died" (Rom. 7:9–10); the commandment brought death (v. 10). The law shows people that they are sinners and thus worthy of death.[20] Paul would not

have known sin had it not been for the law. He found the commandment "You shall not covet" particularly significant (Rom. 7:7). It is comparatively easy to control one's actions, but one's deep-seated desires are another thing. And the law prohibits coveting. It shows coveting as the evil thing it is.

In this way the law becomes an ally of sin. Paul speaks of sin as making the commandment its "base of operations" (Rom. 7:8, 11).[21] The personification of sin brings out the point that the good law, the good commandment, did not prevent sin, but rather served as a means whereby sin made advances. Cranfield points out that "the merciful limitation imposed on man by the commandment and intended to preserve his true freedom and dignity can be misinterpreted and misrepresented as a taking away of his freedom and an attack on his dignity, and so can be made an occasion of resentment and rebellion against the divine Creator, man's true Lord."[22] It would not have been expected that the law would turn into our enemy, but in its alliance with sin that is what has happened.[23] We see this from another angle when we are

---

[18] Nils Alstrup Dahl contests the view of some Jewish scholars that Paul "cannot have been familiar with the classical Jewish doctrine that the Torah is God's life-giving revelation." He goes on to say, "This simply does not follow. Paul knows very well that Jews rejoice at their possession of the Law (Rom. 2:17–20). But he explicitly denies that the Law was able to make alive (Gal. 3:21)" (*Studies in Paul* [Minneapolis, 1977], 134–35).

[19] Actually Paul says that the law was our παιδαγωγός. The term denoted a slave who had special responsibility for looking after the boys in a wealthy household. He taught them good manners, for example, and took them to school. Thus, he saw to it that they got their education, though he was not himself their instructor. "When the young man became of age the π. was no longer needed" (*BAGD*, 603).

[20] Sometimes Judaism recognizes this: "we who have received the Law and sinned will perish, as well as our heart which received it." But the writer goes on to elevate the Law: "the Law, however, does not perish but remains in its glory" (4 Ezra 9:37; cf. v. 32).

[21] Paul's word is ἀφορμή, "lit. the starting-point or base of operations for an expedition, then gener. the resources needed to carry through an undertaking" (*BAGD*).

[22] *Romans,* 1:350.

[23] Cf. G. Aulen, "That the Law is counted as a hostile power does not depend only or chiefly on the fact that the Law inexorably condemns sin. The real reason lies deeper. The way of legal righteousness which the Law recommends, or, rather, demands, can never lead to salvation and life. It leads, like the way of human merit, not to God, but away from God, and deeper and deeper into sin. . . . Thus the Law is an enemy, from whose tyranny Christ has come to save us" (*Christus Victor* [London, 1937], 84).

told that "it stands written, 'Cursed is everyone who does not continue to do all the things that are written in the book of the law'" (Gal. 3:10).[24]

In the light of all this it is not surprising that Paul sees the law as the very opposite of the way of salvation. Christ, he says, "is the end of the law" (Rom. 10:4); he is the end in the sense of the fulfillment of the law, the end to which it points. He is the end also in that the law cannot function to bring about salvation in the light of Christ's saving work. If people could obtain righteousness by the way of law, "then Christ died for nothing" (Gal. 2:21). Paul pays a good deal of attention to the promises of God, but "if the inheritance is from the law it is no longer from the promise" (Gal. 3:18). He contrasts being "under grace" with being "under law" (Rom. 6:14–15; cf. 11:6).

It is clear that Paul is in rebellion against Judaism's insistence on the way of law—the way he had tried and found wanting.[25] Now he knew the way of grace and he could not but see the law as an enemy: so far from bringing salvation, it was an ally of sin. People needed deliverance from law. A legalist mentality is slavery.[26]

DEATH

As we commonly see it, death is inevitable. Bodies like ours must die in due course. But that is not the way it seemed to Paul. When he says, "In Adam all die" (1 Cor. 15:22), he is not saying that mortality is the common human lot. He is saying that the sin of Adam brought death into the world. Because Adam sinned, and we are "in Adam," we die. "The wages of sin is death" (Rom. 6:23); that wage was death for Adam and it is death for us. Sin works death in us (Rom. 7:13); people who sin "are worthy of death" (Rom. 1:32). To give oneself to sin means death (Rom. 6:16); the end result of sinning is death (Rom. 6:21).

We have seen that people may be slaves to sin, and this inevitably leads to death (Rom. 6:16); sin and death go together. It is sin that gives death its sting (1 Cor. 15:56). It is not passing from this life as such, but death as we in fact know it, that is the horror. If we were all sinless, we would doubtless in due time finish our course and have some form of transition into the world to come. But it would not be the horror that death represents; there would be no "sting." The "sting" is the result of sin.

Death is hostile to the very end; it is the "last enemy." But it is the last *enemy,* not the final *victor;* it will be done away with (1 Cor. 15:26). There is hope in these words. Hostile as it is, and strong as it is, death will be overthrown. Decisively. In this view of death Paul and the other Christians

---

[24] Cf. Martin Noth: "On the basis of this law there is only one possibility for man of having his own independent activity: that is transgression, defection, followed by curse and judgment. And so, indeed, 'all those who rely on the works of the law are under a curse'" (cited in Hooker and Wilson, *Paul and Paulinism,* 28–29).

[25] Martin Dibelius points to rabbinic teaching about grace and adds, "It is true that, as a Christian, Paul wrote as if he had never, during his pre-Christian life, known those ideas about God's grace; but it may be that the convert saw the logical conclusions of the religion of the law more sharply and single-mindedly than he could have seen them before" (*Paul* [Philadelphia, 1966], 23).

[26] A distinction has often been made between "the moral law" and "the ceremonial law." The distinction is an ancient one, and Maurice F. Wiles points out that it was universally made by patristic exegetes (*The Divine Apostle,* Cambridge, 1967, p. 68). But it is not a distinction made by Paul, or for that matter any other biblical writer.

contrasted markedly with people of the ancient world in general. For them death was the end of everything, and they could regard it only with deep pessimism. For the believer death has been vanquished.

THE WRATH OF GOD

God does not take sin as a matter of course. Sin inevitably leads to what Paul calls "the wrath of God" or simply "the wrath." This wrath "is revealed from heaven against all impiety and unrighteousness" (Rom. 1:18). Notice that it is something "revealed," not a matter of human observation, and that it is directed against "all" forms of wickedness. A little later, Paul, addressing a hypothetical opponent who judges people who do certain evil things and yet does them himself, declares, "According to your hardness and your impenitent heart you are storing up for yourself wrath, in the day of wrath and revelation of the righteous judgment of God, who will requite each according to his works . . . to those who out of a spirit of faction disobey the truth and obey unrighteousness there will be wrath and anger. There will be trouble and anguish upon every individual who does evil, Jew first and Greek too" (Rom. 2:5–9). Clearly he is referring to the eschatological wrath, as also when he speaks of "the wrath to come" (1 Thess. 1:10). He may be referring to the same thing or to a present activity of God when he says, "The wrath of God comes on the sons of disobedience" (Eph. 5:6; Col. 3:6), or when he pronounces us "by nature children of wrath like all the others" (Eph. 2:3).

What is clear is that God is not passive about sin but is vigorously opposed to it, a truth that Paul brings out in other language when he speaks of people as being "alienated" from God (Eph. 4:18; Col. 1:21) or as "enemies" of God (Rom. 5:10; Phil. 3:18; Col. 1:21). Some of this refers to hostility from the side of evil people, but the characteristic Pauline picture of God is of One who takes action against evil.

There are some who argue that we should understand "the wrath of God" as an impersonal process of cause and effect; that is, "sin always leads to disaster."[27] But that is not the kind of thing Paul says, nor for that matter do the writers of the Old Testament, whose writings he regarded as sacred Scripture. We should not, of course, understand God's wrath as vindictive. It is the other side of his love; it is his love blazing out in fiery indignation against all evil in the beloved. It is the hostility of God's holy nature to every form of sin. Paul does not see God as neutral where any form of evil is concerned, nor as impotent to do anything about it. Paul's God resolutely opposes every form of evil. Perhaps "wrath" is not an ideal word in our culture to designate the divine attitude. But do we have a better? It is important at all costs to preserve the truth that Paul is setting forth when he uses terms like *wrath* and *judgment,* indicating by them that God is actively and diametrically opposed to evil in every shape and form.

---

[27] This was done notably by C. H. Dodd in *The Epistle of Paul to the Romans* (London, 1944), 20–24; *The Johannine Epistles* (London, 1961), 25–27; *The Bible and the Greeks* (London, 1954), ch. 5. A. T. Hanson argued the case in *The Wrath of the Lamb* (London, 1957). Against this view, see Alan Richardson, *An Introduction to the Theology of the New Testament* (London, 1958), 75–79, and my *Apostolic Preaching of the Cross* (London, 1965), chs. 5–6. I have never seen anyone explain the meaning of an impersonal process of wrath in a genuinely theistic universe.

JUDGMENT

We saw earlier that Paul was sure of the judgment of God, a judgment that operates here and now and that will take place on the largest scale at the end of the age. All mankind is subject to the divine judgment and because all are sinners, that is a frightening prospect. We might comfort ourselves with the reflection that death will free us from some of the forces that oppress us—for example, the flesh. But death does not avert judgment. We will all be raised, and we will stand before God's judgment seat.

A significant feature of the judgment is that the Judge will be Christ. He is "the Lord, the righteous judge" who will give the "crown of righteousness" on judgment day (2 Tim. 4:8). In one sense that is reassuring; he has died for us and we can be sure of being judged by One who loves us and is deeply concerned for us. In another sense it is disturbing; when he has been so whole-hearted in his sacrifice of himself for us, we cannot expect that he will countenance tepid and half-hearted service from us. All will be judged, the living and the dead alike (2 Tim. 4:1). We must not think that we can escape (Rom. 2:3). We might face judgment calmly enough if we could be sure that some things would not come out, but the judgment will be searching. "God will judge men's secret things . . . through Christ Jesus" (Rom. 2:16); the Lord "will bring to light the hidden things of darkness and will make manifest the motives of the hearts" (1 Cor. 4:5).

Judgment in Paul's writings is invariably according to works (Rom. 2:6; 1 Cor. 3:8), even though the apostle emphasizes so strongly that salvation is all of grace. Usually Paul, like the other New Testament writers, deals with one of these at a time without relating them. But on one occasion at least he does bring them together. He says plainly, "No one can lay any other foundation than the one that has been laid, and this is Jesus Christ" (1 Cor. 3:11). Christ's saving work (salvation by grace) is the foundation of the whole Christian life. But in our Christian lives we build on that foundation, some with gold, silver, or costly stones; others with wood, hay, or straw (v. 12). Judgment Day will test what we have built; the shoddy will be burnt up in the testing fires and only what is valuable will survive (vv. 13–15). Paul makes it clear that he is referring here only to the saved. Of the person whose work is burnt up he says, "He himself will be saved, but so as through fire" (v. 15). It accords with the evidence to say that whether we will be saved or not depends on the foundation, Christ's saving work. If we have Christ as our foundation, we are saved. But our judgment (and our reward in heaven) depends on what we build, on what we put into Christian living.

Judgment, then, is an important feature of Paul's position. He sees us all, Christian and non-Christian alike, as answerable to God. And he makes it clear that if we have nothing more than our own miserable achievements to plead, we will be in sore trouble on Judgment Day.

"THIS PRESENT EVIL WORLD"

Paul sees a number of other factors that make life difficult for people in what he calls "this present evil world" (Gal. 1:4). It is not that the world is inherently evil. On the contrary, the apostle quotes approvingly the words of Psalm 24:1: "The earth is the Lord's and all that is in it" (1 Cor. 10:26).

But he sees a certain meaninglessness running through all creation: "The creation was subjected to futility. . . . The whole creation groans together and travails together right up till now"; there is such a thing as "the bondage of corruption" (Rom. 8:20–22). Paul does not say it explicitly but his meaning is surely that the Fall affected the whole creation, man, of course, especially, but in some measure everything else as well.

Paul is pessimistic about the world's wise people. He speaks of "the futility of their minds" (Eph. 4:17) and assures us that "the world through wisdom did not know God" (1 Cor. 1:21). Confronted with the Cross, a demonstration of God's power and God's wisdom, the Jewish world saw a stumbling block and the Greek world saw folly (1 Cor. 1:23). Small wonder that Paul warns against the world's philosophy and empty deceit (Col. 2:8) and against being deceived "with empty words" (Eph. 5:6). He holds that "the wisdom of this world is folly before God" (1 Cor. 3:19) and asks, "Did not God make foolish this world's wisdom?" (1 Cor. 1:20). All this speaks to a generation like ours, dazzled as we are by our spectacular technological achievements and depressed beyond measure by our failure to achieve our major goals like peace and justice and the alleviation of poverty. "There is a pointlessness about life for most peo-

ple, an aimlessness, a futility. We may deceive ourselves temporarily by activism or the like, but it is there. Paul felt it, and we feel it, too."[28]

An aspect of Paul's thought that is not congenial to our age in general is his conviction that there are evil forces at work in this world and that these forces work against the best interests of mankind. Thus he refers to "the ruler of the power of the air, the spirit who now works in the sons of disobedience" (Eph. 2:2). This figure is probably to be identified with Satan (Rom. 16:20; 1 Cor. 5:5; 7:5; 2 Cor. 2:11; 11:14; 1 Thess. 2:18; 2 Thess. 2:9; 1 Tim. 5:15). And when he speaks of idol worshipers as offering sacrifice "to demons" (1 Cor. 10:20), he is saying that there is something "demonic" about such worship.

Most exegetes hold that Paul is referring to some such beings when he speaks of being in bondage to "the elemental spirits of the universe" (Gal. 4:3, RSV, NEB; GNB has "the ruling spirits of the universe"),[29] though some prefer the meaning, "the basic principles of the world" (NIV; cf. v. 9).[30] There can be no doubt about "the rulers, the authorities" against whom we wrestle and who are expressly differentiated from "blood and flesh" and who are joined with or identified as "the world-rulers of this darkness" and "the spiritual forces of evil in the heavenlies" (Eph. 6:12). The "rulers and

---

[28] Leon Morris, *The Cross in the New Testament* (Grand Rapids, 1965), 206.

[29] Peter T. O'Brien argues "with the majority of recent commentators, that the phrase denotes 'the elemental spirits of the universe,' the principalities and powers which sought to tyrannize over the lives of men" (*Word Biblical Commentary: Colossians, Philemon* [Waco, 1982], 110; and see 129–32). F. F. Bruce quotes approvingly H. H. Esser, that these words "cover all the things in which man places his trust apart from the living God; they become his gods, and he becomes their slave" (*The Epistle to the Galatians* [Grand Rapids, 1982], 204).

[30] R. A. Cole is aware of the majority view but prefers "the elementary stages of religious experience (whether Jewish or Gentile) through which they have gone in the past, but which are now out-dated by Christ" (*The Epistle of Paul to the Galatians* [London, 1965], 113–14). J. B. Lightfoot accepted the meaning "elementary teaching" (*Saint Paul's Epistle to the Galatians* [London, 1902], 167; *St Paul's Epistles to the Colossians and to Philemon* [London, 1876], 180).

authorities" are expressly said to have been created by Christ (Col. 1:16), and he is, of course, supreme over them (Col. 2:10). These beings are not powerful enough to separate us from the love of God in Christ (Rom. 8:38–39), but the clear implication of the passage is that they are hostile and may be expected to attempt to do so.

The thought of evil spirits is not congenial to our age, though in recent times there is an acceptance of the "demonic" by many. It is undeniable that evil runs through much of modern life. It is a curious but depressing fact that civilized people perpetrate greater horrors than barbarians. The horrors of atomic bombs, chemical warfare, and mass starvation, to say nothing of the trade policies of the rich nations that keep unemployment (and consequent misery) high in the undeveloped nations—these are some of the products of civilized peoples.

Evil is so widespread and so powerful that many feel that puny mankind cannot take all the discredit for it! Whether we accept such a position or not, we should be clear that Paul did. We cannot understand his conception of the meaning of Christ's saving work unless we see it against a background of the evil and the futility in this world, a world populated by evil spirits as well as evil people. The apostle was very conscious that all our resources are inadequate to defeat the forces of evil. Paul was not a pessimist. His writings thrill with the triumph of Christ. But he was certainly realistic about the magnitude of the forces that in one way or another enslave or oppress mankind.

THE CROSS

Paul informs the Corinthians that when he first came to their city, he had resolved "to know nothing among [them] except Jesus Christ and him crucified" (1 Cor. 2:2). He says of himself and his colleagues, "We preach Christ crucified" (1 Cor. 1:23). He reminds the Galatians that when he was among them "Jesus Christ was placarded before your eyes as crucified" (Gal. 3:1). Such passages make it clear that for Paul the Crucifixion was central,[31] and the whole thrust of his correspondence underlines this. Again and again he comes back to the Cross.[32] It was the atoning death of Christ and not his exemplary life that brought salvation to sinners, and Paul never tires of emphasizing this. He has influenced Christian vocabulary to this day. We do not commonly realize, for example, that, apart from the Crucifixion narratives and one reference in Hebrews, Paul is the only New Testament writer to refer to "the cross." He does this repeatedly (1 Cor. 1:17–18; Gal. 5:11; 6:12, 14; Eph. 2:16; Phil. 2:8; 3:18; Col. 1:20; 2:14; the one non-Pauline reference is Heb. 12:2); he refers to the Crucifixion as well (1 Cor. 1:23; 2:2, 8; 2 Cor. 13:4; Gal. 3:1; cf. references to being crucified with Christ, Rom. 6:6; Gal. 2:20). It is Paul more than any other who refers to "the death" of Christ. Others use expressions like "the blood"

---

[31] Cf. A. J. B. Higgins: "The Pauline emphasis is throughout on the Cross and the death of Christ" (*SJT* 6 [1953]: 283); Richard N. Longenecker, "The conclusion is inescapable that the focus of Paul's preaching was on the redemptive significance of Christ's work" (*The Ministry and Message of Paul* [Grand Rapids, 1971], 90).

[32] For Paul the meaning of the cross was such that it solved many problems. Leander E. Keck comments on the factions in the church at Corinth: "Paul confronted all factions alike with the center of his gospel—the cross of Christ. When the logic of the cross is understood, there can be no cliques, because this logic destroys the basis for forming them" (*The New Testament Experience of Faith* [St. Louis, 1976], 85).

(cf. 1 Pet. 1:19), which, of course, Paul uses, too (Rom. 3:25; 5:9; Eph. 1:7 etc.). There cannot be the slightest doubt about the center of the Christian gospel as Paul understood it.

Sometimes Paul seems to indicate that Christ's death is linked with the death that sinners should die. They should die because death is "the wages of sin" (Rom. 6:23). Paul says, "One died for all, therefore all died" (2 Cor. 5:14). It is not easy to see what this means except that Christ died the death of sinners.

Paul goes on to say, "Him who knew no sin, he [i.e., God] made sin on our behalf, so that we might become God's righteousness in him" (2 Cor. 5:21). This is a very difficult verse. But let us notice first that it refers to an act of God. This is often obscured when the verse is misquoted as though it read, "Christ was made sin. . . ." But the verb is not passive; Paul is speaking plainly of what God did. The love of God for sinners is such that he deals with sin even at the cost of making his Son "sin" on their behalf. The meaning appears to be that Christ took the place of sinners and endured what sinners should endure. In the end we must confess to an element of mystery, but the fact that Jesus Christ endured what sinners should have endured seems plain enough.

And this comes out when Paul says, "Christ redeemed us from the curse of the law, having become a curse for us, for it is written, 'Cursed is everyone who is hanged on a tree'" (Gal. 3:13). The reference to the Old Testament (Deut. 21:23) shows that it is the curse

that comes from breaking God's law that is in mind (Deut. 27:26), as indeed Paul expressly says. It is not easy to see what Christ's being made a curse for us means except that he bore the curse that otherwise would have been ours ("our hell itself belongs to him," says Bouttier)[33]. Now we are "redeemed." The curse no longer rests on us. Christ's death has effectively removed it.[34]

Along with Paul's emphasis on the death of Christ we should take his joy in the Resurrection, a mighty act of God that he mentions in every letter to a church except 2 Thessalonians. He sometimes says that God raised Christ (Rom. 8:11; 1 Cor. 15:15; Eph. 1:20; Col. 2:12), more often that Christ "was raised," which amounts to the same thing (Rom. 6:4, 9; 1 Cor. 15:12, 13, 14 etc.), more rarely that Christ "rose" (Rom. 14:9; 1 Thess. 4:14). He may refer to Christ in his exaltation, "seated at the right hand of God" (Col. 3:1; cf. Eph. 1:20–21; Phil. 2:9). We should not separate the death and resurrection as though trying to determine which was the more important. They belong together and form one powerful divine atoning act. Paul does not see the death as a defeat; it was the means whereby God triumphed over every form of evil.

The Resurrection changed everything. It ushered in the new age. This is true because God was so obviously and so powerfully at work in the Resurrection that nothing can be the same again. Death is defeated. There is new life. The Resurrection "first appears as a

---

[33] Michel Bouttier, *Christianity According to Paul* (Naperville, Ill., 1966), 35.

[34] It is possible that when some imperfectly instructed Christian said "Jesus is accursed" (1 Cor. 12:3), he was reflecting the teaching of Gal. 3:13. David E. Aune, however, holds that the exclamation "was not uttered within the Corinthian community, but is a hypothetical Pauline construct created as an antithesis to the distinctively Christian exclamation, 'Jesus is Lord!'" (*Prophecy in Early Christianity and the Ancient Mediterranean World* [Grand Rapids, 1983], 257). The latter view seems less likely.

small part of the future age which has fallen into our world."[35] As such it assures us of the reality of the "future age."

DELIVERANCE

In an earlier section we saw that sinners are in desperate case, and that from several points of view. But, however their plight is viewed, Paul sees the Cross as the answer. For example, the power of sin is broken and our slavery to sin is ended. "We died to sin" (Rom. 6:2) is a thought repeated in other ways—"Our old man was crucified with him in order that the body of sin might be rendered null and void, so that we should no longer be enslaved to sin" (v. 6); "He who has died has been justified from sin" (v. 7); "You, reckon yourselves to be dead to sin" (v. 11); "Sin will not lord it over you" (v. 14); "You were sin's slaves" (vv. 17, 20), where the past tenses refer to a situation that is over; "You have been made free from sin" (vv. 18, 22). The whole chapter is an exultant exposition of the complete defeat of sin that Christ's salvation means. There are other passages where the same point is made, but these are sufficient for our purpose.

It is the same with "the flesh." There is a contrast between "the works of the flesh" and "the fruit of the Spirit" (Gal. 5:19–23); in these verses it is clear that the flesh is no longer in control. How can that be? "Those who are Christ's have crucified the flesh, together with its passions and lusts" (Gal. 5:24). Once Christians were "in the flesh," but that is all past; they are no longer there (Rom. 7:5); they are "not in the flesh"

(Rom. 8:9). But although the power of the flesh has been broken, believers are still called on to oppose it. They are to mortify the flesh (Rom. 8:13; cf. Col. 3:5), to make no provision for it (Rom. 13:14), to cleanse themselves from its defilement (2 Cor. 7:1), and the like. It is a "become what you are" situation.

The death of Christ has released us from our bondage to law; we have "died to that in which we were held fast" and now the law is powerless against us (Rom. 7:6). We "have been made dead to the law through the body of Christ" (Rom. 7:4). For believers Christ is "the end of the law for righteousness" (Rom. 10:4); their righteousness is not brought about by the doing of good works, but by Christ's saving work. Christ came specifically "in order to redeem those under law" (Gal. 4:5). Such vigorous language is a repudiation of all attempts to use keeping the law as a means of acquiring righteousness before God. It is what Christ has done, specifically his death, that delivers from all forms of law.[36]

Paul's triumph song in 1 Corinthians 15 shows that death is no longer a tyrant to be feared. Human weakness is no more able to prevail against death than it was before, but it is not human weakness that counts. It is the power of God in Christ, the power that we see so splendidly manifested when Christ defeated death and rose triumphant. Paul agrees that death is the final enemy, but he is certain of its destruction (1 Cor. 15:26). There is magnificent defiance in his taunt song as he addresses death at the culmination of this chapter: "Death is swallowed up in victory. Where,

---

[35] Lucien Cerfaux, *The Christian in the Theology of St. Paul* (London, 1967), 62.

[36] Wilfred Knox stresses the importance of Paul's attitude to the law: "Apart from the revolutionary attitude to the Law there is nothing in this system which was not a legitimate inference from the beliefs of the older disciples. We hear of no conflict on any other aspect of Pauline teaching. . . . Yet the whole centre of gravity had been shifted" (*St. Paul* [New York, 1932], 50).

death, is your victory? Where, death, is your sting?" (1 Cor. 15:54-55; the words are quoted from Isa. 25:8; Hos. 13:14). He goes on to exclaim, "Thanks be to God who gives us the victory through our Lord Jesus Christ!" (1 Cor. 15:57). In this spirit he says that "Christ, having been raised from the dead, dies no more; death no longer has lordship over him" (Rom. 6:9). He also speaks of believers as having been "risen with Christ" (Col. 3:1) and says that "those who received the abundance of grace and the free gift of righteousness will reign in life through the one, Jesus Christ" (Rom. 5:17); they "are more than conquerors through him" (Rom. 8:37). Death is no longer a powerful tyrant, but a vanquished foe. Christ has won the decisive victory.

The wrath of God no longer rests on believers: "Having been now justified by [or in] his blood, we shall be saved from the wrath through him" (Rom. 5:9). "God did not appoint us to wrath, but to the obtaining of salvation through our Lord Jesus Christ" (1 Thess. 5:9). Paul does not minimize the strong opposition God always has to every form of evil. That is one of the facts of life. But for the believer the significant fact is that Christ's death averts God's wrath; God set forth Christ as "a propitiation" (Rom. 3:25);[37] that is, as a means of turning wrath away.

From yet another angle Paul brings out the truth that Christ's death brings deliverance. Christ delivers from all the other forces that enslave us. "Having disarmed the rulers and the authorities, [he] made a spectacle of them, having triumphed over them in it [the Cross]" (Col. 2:15). Always when Paul mentions such spiritual powers of evil, there is the thought that they have been defeated by Christ and now have no power over the believer. Bondage to the elemental spirits belongs to the past (Gal. 4:3).

Again, God's judgment need not be feared. It is not that it is not a reality and a serious reality at that. It is that Christ has done such a work for us that we need not be afraid of it. Thus "the judgment is from one sin and brought condemnation," but over against that Paul can set "the free gift" that followed many trespasses and issued in justification (Rom. 5:16). So also "the free gift of righteousness" means that believers "will reign in life through the one, Jesus Christ" (Rom. 5:17).

All creation is in bondage to futility, but "it will be set free from the slavery of corruption into the liberty of the glory of God's children" (Rom. 8:21). And Christ "gave himself for our sins, so that he might deliver us from the present evil world, according to the will of our God and Father" (Gal. 1:4). Conceive of our enemy how you will, Paul sees it as beaten by the tremendous saving work God has accomplished in Christ.

JUSTIFICATION

Paul makes a great deal of use of the legal category[38] of justification, especially in Romans and Galatians.[39]

---

[37] For a discussion of this word, see above, pp. 34–35.

[38] T. R. Glover says of Paul, "His relations with God and Christ are quite obviously beyond expression in legal terms" (*Paul of Tarsus* [London, 1925], 92). Taken as a whole, this is, of course, true. But it does not do justice to the fact that Paul chose precisely legal terms to express some of his thought. We will not do justice to him if we overlook this.

[39] Günther Bornkamm is an example of those who see justification by faith as central to Paul's theology. He calls it "the basic theme in his theology," and maintains that "his whole preaching, even

There has been quite a bit of discussion of the term in recent times and justification has been understood in a variety of ways.[40] Let us start by noticing that justification is basically a legal term. Thus, an ancient document directs the judges that when they are settling a case in court, they "shall justify the righteous, and condemn the wicked" (Deut. 25:1). That is to say, they are to give their verdict of acquittal to those who are in the right (and their verdict of condemnation to those who are in the wrong, but that is not our immediate concern). Paul makes it clear that we are all sinners (Rom. 3:23), that we all face judgment (2 Cor. 5:10),[41] and that God is a righteous judge (2 Tim. 4:8). How then is it possible for the sinner to escape?

Paul's answer is that Christ has provided the way. We are "justified by his blood" (Rom. 5:9). We are justified freely "by his grace through the redemption that is in Christ Jesus" (Rom. 3:24). We are justified "by his grace" (Titus 3:7). Paul has many ways of bringing out the truth that we contribute nothing to the process of our justification. For example, our efforts at keeping the law will not do at all (Rom. 3:20; Gal. 2:16; 3:11); in the end we all emerge as guilty. But Paul is equally insistent that God justifies us. "It is God who justifies; who condemns?" (Rom. 8:33–34). He tells the Corinthians, "You were justified in the name of the Lord Jesus Christ and in the Spirit of our God" (1 Cor. 6:11), so that all three Persons of the Trinity are somehow caught up in it. We should immediately add, however, that his emphasis is on what Christ has done, and specifically on his death.

How can the death of Christ change the verdict on sinners from "Guilty" to "Innocent"? Some have said in effect, "It is by changing the guilty, by transforming them so that they are no longer bad people, but good ones." No one will want to minimize the transformation that takes place in a true conversion or to obscure the fact that this is an important part of being a Christian. However, such a transformation does not fit the justification terminology. It is sometimes argued that the verb normally translated "to justify" (*dikaioō*) means "to make righteous" rather than "to declare righteous." But this agrees neither with the word's formation nor with its usage. Verbs ending in *-oō* and referring to moral qualities have a declarative sense;[42] they do not mean "to make—." And the usage is never for the transformation of the accused; it always refers to a declaration of his innocence.

when it says nothing expressly about justification, can be properly understood only when taken in closest connection with that doctrine and related to it" (*Paul* [London, 1971], 116; cf. also 135). He finds no opposition between this and the teaching of Jesus, but rather "Paul's gospel of justification by faith alone matches Jesus' turning to the godless and the lost" (p. 237).

[40]Thus, Joachim Jeremias says, "Justification is forgiveness, nothing but forgiveness, for Christ's sake" (*The Central Message of the New Testament* [London, 1965], 57). Stephen Neill appears to hold that justification essentially means pardon (*Jesus Through Many Eyes* [Philadelphia, 1976], 59–60). T. W. Manson sees it as a regal rather than a judicial act, with the meaning of amnesty or pardon (*On Paul and John* [London, 1963], 57). Bornkamm says it has much the same meaning as reconciliation (*Paul*, 141). Such views fail to do justice to the language Paul chooses to use.

[41]Curiously, Stephen Neill says that Paul teaches "the certainty of judgment, from which, however, the Christian is exempt" (*Jesus Through Many Eyes*, 46). If the Christian were exempt there would be no problem. The trouble is that, according to Paul, Christians do face this prospect. What else does 2 Corinthians 5:10 (to take an example at random) mean?

[42]Thus, ἀξιόω means "to deem worthy," "to reckon as worthy," not "to make worthy"; ὁμοιόω means "to declare to be like."

We noticed earlier when we were looking at the expression "the righteousness of God" that this refers to "a right standing," which is the gift of God to us. That is what justification means—God has given us right standing so that we get the verdict of acquittal when we are judged. He "justifies the ungodly" (Rom. 4:5). And he does this on the basis of Christ's atoning death. Traditionally this has been understood in the sense that Christ's death, viewed from one aspect, means a dealing with the penal consequences of sin. Since the penalty has been paid, there is nothing more for us to pay.[43] Therefore, we are "justified."

This way of looking at the Cross preserves the important truth that God not only saves sinners, but saves them in a manner that accords with right. Some ways of looking at salvation seem almost to proceed along the lines that "might is right"; God is stronger than Satan (or evil), so he puts forth his power and delivers us. There is, of course, an aspect of salvation in which something like this can be said; we have already noticed that Christ won the victory. But that is not the whole story. Salvation is too big to be comprehended wholly by any one of our categories. We need them all, and specifically we need to know that our penalty is paid and our acquittal brought about in a way that is right.

A COMPLEX ATONEMENT

Paul makes use of a variety of vivid pictures to bring out what God's saving work accomplished and to help his readers understand what it means.[44] Sometimes, for example, he speaks of redemption (e.g., Rom. 3:24; 1 Cor. 1:30; Gal. 3:13; 4:5; Eph. 1:7; Col. 1:14),[45] a term we may easily misunderstand since its use concerned activities that we are not familiar with. Its original use was for the practice of buying prisoners of war out of their captivity. Their right place was in their homeland, but a strong enemy had them in its power. They could be restored to freedom only by paying the price (called a "ransom"). Redemption was also used in reference to the release of a slave by the payment of a price, which reminds us of the slaveries that Paul saw as binding sinners. It makes meaningful his exhortation: "For freedom did Christ free us; stand fast therefore and do not again be caught up in the yoke of slavery" (Gal. 5:1). Now and then a ransom was required to release a person from a death sentence (e.g., Exod. 21:28–30), and this makes it important to bear in mind that sinners are under a sentence of death (Rom. 6:23), from which Christ can set them free. Redemption means the paying of a price to set someone free (cf. 1 Cor. 6:20; 7:23). No one in the New Testament ever asks the question,

---

[43] Cf. William Barclay: "It is not possible to take these sayings [i.e., 2 Cor. 5:21; Gal. 3:13] as having any other meaning as Paul saw it, than that what ought to have happened to us did happen to Jesus Christ, and that He bore the suffering and the shame which we rightly should have borne"; "someone must have paid the penalty which was due; and that someone was Jesus Christ. We are, as Paul put it, justified by His blood" (*The Mind of St Paul* [New York, 1958], 104, 106). A. M. Hunter says that the same passages "reveal the holy love of God taking awful issue in the Cross with the sin of man. Christ, by God's will, dies the sinner's death and so removes sin. Is there a simpler way of saying all this than that Christ bore our sins and that his sufferings were what, for lack of a better word, we can only call 'penal'?" (*The Gospel According to St. Paul* [Philadelphia, 1966], 26).

[44] I have examined some of these in my books, *The Apostolic Preaching of the Cross* (London, 1965) and *The Atonement* (Leicester, 1983).

[45] "Redemption through the cross of Christ lies at the heart of Paul's thought" (Rudolf Schnackenburg, *New Testament Theology Today* [New York, 1963], 74).

"To whom was the ransom paid?" The question is illegitimate. The concern of the New Testament writers is with the costly nature of our salvation, not with any recipient of a price.

Again, Paul tells us that in explaining the Last Supper, Jesus said, "This cup is the new covenant in my blood" (1 Cor. 11:25). Central to Jewish life was the fact that God had made a covenant with the nation: he was their God, and they were his people (Exod. 24:4–8; cf. 19:3–6). But the people kept breaking the covenant, and in due course Jeremiah prophesied that there would be a "new covenant" (Jer. 31:31–34). Paul's recording of Jesus' words shows that he recognized that the Savior's death was to be seen as inaugurating a major change, as the making of the new covenant foretold by the prophet. It was a covenant characterized, not by a stress on outward codes of conduct, but on inwardness, on the law written on the heart (Jer. 31:33). And it would be based on forgiveness (Jer. 31:34). Christianity, accordingly, is not to be understood as Judaism with a few minor modifications. It is radically new, with its forgiveness and its inwardness, and it rests on God's firm promises.

Another of Paul's concepts is reconciliation, a way of looking at the Cross that nobody else in the New Testament uses.[46] Many these days see it as the principal constituent in Paul's view of atonement.[47] It is certainly important, but this view is difficult to substantiate. It is far from widespread in the apostle's writings, being found in four

passages only (Rom. 5:10–11; 2 Cor. 5:18–20; Eph. 2:11–16; Col. 1:19–22). Even if we enlarge this by including references to "making peace" and the like, the concept still comes short of being dominant.

But if we should not exaggerate the importance of the concept of reconciliation, neither should we minimize it. Reconciliation is a personal category; it means the making of peace after a quarrel or a state of hostility. Three of the four passages refer to us as "enemies" of God, or speak of "enmity" or "hostility," so that a very real process of reconciliation is envisaged. It is sometimes emphasized that no New Testament passage says that God was reconciled to people, that it is always a process of people being reconciled. But this is too simple. The problem is not any overt hostility of people to God, which God broke down through the Cross. The problem is rather God's demand for righteousness, coupled with the fact that we are all sinners. Reconciliation does not mean such a change in us that we are no longer hostile. It points to a new state of affairs brought about "through the death of his Son" (Rom. 5:10), and by God's "not imputing to them their trespasses" (2 Cor. 5:19). Reconciliation is "through the cross" which killed the enmity (Eph. 2:16); peace was made "through the blood of his cross," reconciliation was effected "in the body of his flesh through death" (Col. 1:20, 22). All these passages point to sin as the cause of the hostility and to Christ's death as having dealt with sin.[48] The

[46] Leonhard Goppelt thinks it unlikely that anyone in the primitive church used this concept before Paul. Indeed, "in all the Christian literature of the 1st century this word is found only in Paul." He adds, "It corresponded to his way of seeing Christ's work of salvation strictly as the work of God" (*Theology of the New Testament* [Grand Rapids, 1982], 2:139).

[47] The case is argued by Ralph P. Martin in *Reconciliation: A Study of Paul's Theology* (Atlanta, 1981).

[48] Cf. Emil Brunner: "It is not primarily the sense of guilt which has to be removed, but the actual stain of guilt itself. Many men have scarcely any sense of guilt at all; it is not aroused in them until they

cause of the hostility being thus removed, reconciliation takes place. But none of these passages would be easy were we to understand reconciliation as essentially a process taking place within sinners.

Most translations these days avoid "propitiation" (Rom. 3:25 KJV), but this does seem to be an important category for Paul (see above, pp. 34–35). The linguistics show that the meaning is "propitiation" rather than "expiation," and Paul takes "the wrath of God" seriously, for he sees it as exercised toward "all impiety and un-righteousness of men" (Rom. 1:18). It is, of course, true that propitiation is a difficult word, and I agree that it would be helpful to replace it. It is the idea, not the word, that is important. But the trouble is that the substitutes so far suggested do not preserve the idea. "Expiation" certainly does not, for all its popularity in some circles, because it is an impersonal word. One expiates a crime or a sin, not a person. But sinners are confronted with the wrath of a divine Person. And one of the things Paul says that Christ's atonement does is to remove that wrath.

In the ancient world the universal religious rite was sacrifice. All over that world people offered animals on their altars, trusting that their gods would accept their sacrifices and that their sins would be forgiven. The Jewish system of sacrifice is set out in Leviticus, and Paul sees Christ as the sacrifice that perfectly fulfills all that is foreshadowed in the Levitical system, the one sacrifice that really removes sin. Usually he uses general terms, as when he says, "Christ loved us and gave himself for us, an offering and a sacrifice to God . . ." (Eph. 5:2), or when he refers to Christ's blood, for the manipulation of blood was a central feature in most sacrifices. Now and then he refers to a specific offering such as the Passover sacrifice (1 Cor. 5:7), and he may refer to a sin offering (Rom. 8:3; cf. NIV). In such passages Paul is saying that all that the sacrifices dimly foreshadowed is perfectly fulfilled in Jesus Christ. Christ did what the sacrifices of animals could never do.

Paul does not make as much use of the category of forgiveness as we might have expected. But he does use it. He says simply, "The Lord forgave you" (Col. 3:13; cf. Eph. 4:32), and he can link this with the Cross, for example, when he refers to Christ "in whom we have redemption through his blood, the forgiveness of trespasses" (Eph. 1:7; cf. Col. 2:13). He also declares: "Blessed are those whose transgressions are forgiven" (Rom. 4:7, quoting Ps. 32:1). Although this is not stressed in Paul, it is one aspect of his thought. We are guilty sinners, but in Christ God has forgiven us. Our sins no longer remain to condemn us.

Adoption is another of Paul's vivid pictures (Rom. 8:15; Gal. 4:5; Eph. 1:5; future, Rom. 8:23). The practice was Roman rather than Jewish; Paul could find an illustration of God's saving activity in any area of life. In adoption a person who did not belong to a given family was brought into that family as a full member, with all the rights and all the obligations that went with family membership. In a similar way, reasons Paul, we who were not part of the heavenly family have been

have come into contact with Christ. And it is in Christ alone that we all come to know what our guilt really is. The first element, therefore, in the act of reconciliation is not the removal of this subjective sense of guilt, but the knowledge that our guilt has been purged" (*The Mediator* [London, 1946], 522).

adopted into it. The death of Christ is involved in this, for he came "in order to redeem those under the law, so that we might receive the adoption" (Gal. 4:5).

Paul uses other figures; I have not tried to be exhaustive. This selection is given simply to indicate something of the richness and complexity of the apostle's thought. For him Christ's salvation was many-sided, and he ransacks his vocabulary to find ways of expressing some little fraction of the great deed God has done in Christ.

LOVE AT WORK

Paul does not put much difference between the love of God and the love of Christ, and indeed he speaks of "the love of God that is in Christ Jesus our Lord" (Rom. 8:39), and again of "love with faith from God the Father and the Lord Jesus Christ" (Eph. 6:23). This love is especially to be seen in Christ's atoning death. It is that death for us, while we were still sinners, that shows us God's love (Rom. 5:8); in v. 5 it is said that that love is "poured into our hearts." God's mercy and God's love are not far apart, for God "being rich in mercy, on account of his great love with which he loved us, gave us life with Christ when we were dead in trespasses" (Eph. 2:4–5). For Paul faith is very important, and he tells us that he lived his whole life "in faith in the Son of God who loved [him] and gave himself for [him]" (Gal. 2:20). Faith is meaningless, it appears, apart from the love of Christ (in the Pastorals love is mentioned ten times, and in nine of them it is linked with faith). Paul also sees Christ's love for all believers, for Christ "loved us and gave himself for us, an offering and a sacrifice to God" (Eph. 5:2).

It is plain from much that Paul writes that the love of God in Christ gripped him. He sees God as "the God of love and peace" (2 Cor. 13:11); love is absolutely central to our understanding of God. So it is that in the well-known benediction he speaks not only of "the grace of our Lord Jesus Christ" but also of "the love of God" (2 Cor. 13:14). In the same spirit he quotes and applies the words of the prophet that God called "her who was not beloved, beloved" (Rom. 9:25, citing Hos. 2:23); it was in love that God brought salvation to people who were sorely in need of love. Paul, of course, sometimes says his correspondents are "beloved" of the Lord (Col. 3:12; 1 Thess. 1:4; 2 Thess. 2:13). It was out of love that the Lord Jesus and God the Father gave us "eternal consolation and good hope in grace" (2 Thess. 2:16).

God's love is all-powerful (Rom. 8:35–39). Nothing can defeat it. It is this great truth that dominates Paul's thinking and is his motivation in Christian service (2 Cor. 5:14). It often finds expression in places where the word "love" is not mentioned. What else are we to make, for example, of the words "by grace you have been saved through faith, and that not of yourselves; it is the gift of God" (Eph. 2:8)? None of the words for love is used here, but the passage is an eloquent expression of the love that brought salvation to people who deserved nothing. Indeed this is the meaning of grace, a word Paul uses 100 times out of its 155 New Testament occurrences. Two out of every 3 occurrences of this great Christian word are in Paul's writings. For him grace was a glorious reality, and he could not go long without referring to it in some way. It is not too much to say that for Paul all God's dealings are done in grace; they are an expression of grace. And how are we to understand grace apart from divine love?

Sometimes Christians have all unwittingly given a picture of a stern and demanding God, who demands uprightness of life and sits in judgment on all who do not produce it. He is the judge of all and in his hands sinners face a dismal prospect. Into this picture comes a loving Son, who died for us and thus delivered us from his inflexible Father. Wherever people got this caricature, it was not from Paul. The apostle does not separate the Father and the Son. They are one, one in love, one in the costly loving action that brings salvation to sinners, one in the constant love lavished on the saved to supply their every need (Phil. 4:19), one in the love that keeps believers in the right way.

Love from first to last is the way Paul sees God in Christ, and it is this love that brought salvation.

4

life in the spirit

The ancient world was not unfamiliar with the thought that from time to time a divine spirit would come into this world and take possession of worshipers. Thus people would understand when the Christians spoke of the Spirit as being "in" believers (e.g., Rom. 8:9, 11; 1 Cor. 3:16). But we should not think of Christians as simply reproducing a commonplace of first-century theology. In fact they confronted their world with a radically new conception.

There were two especially significant differences in the way Christians understood the presence of the Spirit. The first arose from the fact that the ancients in general thought that the divine spirit would come on only a few outstanding people. It would be a most unusual experience, reserved for those who were especially close to the deity. But the Christians insisted that all believers have the Spirit.[1] Thus, Paul says positively, "As many as are led by the Spirit of God, they are the sons of God" (Rom. 8:14), and negatively, "If anyone does not have the Spirit of Christ, this person is not his" (Rom. 8:9). It is nonsense to talk about a Christian who does not have the Spirit. That is a contradiction in terms. It is a distinctive of the Christian way that the lowliest believer enjoys the presence of God's Spirit within him.

In the second place there is a difference in the way the presence of the Spirit is known. The pagan believed that when the spirit came on anyone, there would be curious physical phenomena, perhaps of the "whirling dervish" type (the priests of Cybele with their twirling knives inflicted many an injury), perhaps in ecstatic speech (Plato speaks warmly of the holy women at Dodona and Delphi who conferred many great benefits on Greece when they were mad—i.e., possessed by a divine spirit—but few or none when in their right minds).[2] But Paul says, "The fruit of the Spirit is love, joy, peace, longsuffering, kindness, goodness, faith, meekness, self-control" (Gal. 5:22–23; cf. Eph. 5:9). It is ethical conduct, not ecstatic behavior, that demonstrates the presence of the Spirit. This is to be seen in the name by which the Christians knew him—"the Holy Spirit" (not the powerful Spirit, or the wise Spirit, or the like).

---

[1] Cf. Martin Dibelius: "Paul was able simply to take for granted, as regards both his own and the other churches, that every Christian had received the Spirit as a supernatural gift connected with his conversion" (*Paul* [Philadelphia, 1966], 92). Notice that he assumes this in writing to the Romans, a church not of his founding.

[2] *Phaedrus,* 244B.

Paul was sure that the Spirit is divine; he is "the Spirit of God" (Rom. 8:14; 1 Cor. 2:11; 2 Cor. 3:3; cf. the reference to the Spirit's sword as being "the word of God" [Eph. 6:17]). So, too, he is "the Spirit of Christ" (Rom. 8:9), "the Spirit of Jesus Christ" (Phil. 1:19), and "the Spirit of his [God's] Son" (Gal. 4:6). But he is identical with neither the Father nor the Son, for he can be mentioned side by side with both (2 Cor. 13:14). He is "the Spirit who is from God [*to ek tou theou*]" (1 Cor. 2:12), and God "sent" him (Gal. 4:6). The Spirit searches "the deep things of God" and knows "the things of God" from the inside, just as the spirit of a man knows "the things of the man" (1 Cor. 2:10–11). When Paul says, "You are God's temple and the Spirit of God dwells in you" (1 Cor. 3:16; cf. 6:19), he is saying that the Spirit is divine; he is God dwelling in us.

Many see the Spirit as a force, an influence. But Paul seems rather to have understood the Spirit as a person. The giving of gifts looks like the activity of a person, more particularly since Paul concludes his list by informing his readers that the division is made "according as he wills" (1 Cor. 12:4–11). He speaks of the mind of the Spirit (Rom. 8:6, 27) and urges people not to "grieve" the Spirit (Eph. 4:30). The love of God is poured into our hearts through the Spirit (Rom. 5:5), and the Spirit produces love in us (Gal. 5:22), both activities being evidently personal. The expression "the love of the Spirit" (Rom. 15:30) may be understood as the love that Paul has for the Spirit or the love that the Spirit has for him; either way the Spirit is a person. And this might be said of the fact that the Spirit leads believers (Gal. 5:18). There should be no doubt that for Paul the Spirit is a person, a great divine person indeed, but in fact a person and not simply an impersonal influence.

In the light of all this it is not surprising that Paul sees the Spirit as engaging in significant activities. He can say that believers are "in" the Spirit, just as he has spoken of their being "in" Christ (though he does not do this so often). Believers are not "in the flesh, but in the Spirit" (Rom. 8:9); they may speak "in the Holy Spirit" (1 Cor. 12:3); they are to "walk in the Spirit" (Gal. 5:16); Paul's conscience is at work "in the Holy Spirit" (Rom. 9:1). In a somewhat similar way Paul speaks of "those who are according to the Spirit [*kata pneumatos*]" (Rom. 8:5; Gal. 4:29), and of those who "walk according to the Spirit" (Rom. 8:4; cf. 2 Cor. 12:18), or who "walk in the Spirit" (Gal. 5:16, 25). All such expressions mean that the presence of the Spirit is the dominating factor in the life of the believer. The Christian is indwelt, empowered, guided by God's Spirit.

It is clear that for the apostle the Spirit is a real person, living in believers (1 Cor. 6:19; 2 Tim. 1:14), strengthening them for service (Rom. 8:26; 2 Cor. 3:6; Eph. 3:16), and teaching them what they should say (1 Cor. 2:13). The result is a string of Christian virtues, such as righteousness, peace, and joy (Rom. 14:17; cf. 1 Thess. 1:6), the hope of righteousness (Gal. 5:5), and introduction into the presence of the Father (Eph. 2:18). This is pretty close to "salvation in the sanctifying work of the Spirit" (2 Thess. 2:13; cf. Titus 3:5) and to "the mind of the Spirit," which is "life and peace" (Rom. 8:6). "He who sows to the Spirit" is he who "of the Spirit" will "reap life eternal" (Gal. 6:8).

THE GIFTS OF THE SPIRIT

Paul also speaks of certain "gifts" of the Spirit (*charismata*). Whereas the virtues we noticed in the preceding paragraph were expected to be present in all believers, the gifts were not. Every believer must have righteousness and peace, but not every believer will have, say, the gift of healing. It is the one Spirit who is at work, but there are "diversities of gifts" (1 Cor. 12:4; cf. "to one . . . to another . . . to another" in vv. 8–10). Paul likens the church to a body with many different members (1 Cor. 12:12ff.), and, though this refers to natural endowments, it also has its application to the spiritual gifts. And when he comes to his series of questions beginning "Are all apostles?" (1 Cor. 12:29–30), the only possible answer in each case is "No!"[3]

It is clear from the general tone of Paul's references to the gifts that the Corinthians valued them highly and that the exercise of these gifts gave a magnificent spontaneity to church life in Corinth. But Paul warns this church against being "puffed up" (1 Cor. 4:6 et al.);[4] there may even have been some element of competition among the believers ("My *charisma* is better than yours!"). This may be the point of inserting the wonderful chapter on love (1 Cor. 13) into the middle of the treatment of the gifts; it is apparently a way of pointing the Corinthians to a far better way than that of competing for spectacular evidences of the working of the Spirit. Paul does not minimize the gifts, indeed he tells the Corinthians to be "zealous" for them (1 Cor. 14:1), and he prides himself on speaking in tongues more than all of them (1 Cor. 14:18). But above all, the gifts must be used to edify (1 Cor. 14:12, 26); they are given in order that believers be built up in their spiritual lives and thus are not to be used for personal gratification.

A curious feature of the gifts is that, despite the confident claims of many, it is difficult to discover precisely what they were. Take the list in 1 Corinthians 12:28. Although it is clear that apostles were "sent" people, there is vigorous dispute as to whether the term means a "missionary" generally or whether it should be confined to the Twelve (with a few additions like Paul). It is impossible to be certain. Is a "prophet" someone like the great figures of the Old Testament? Or does he resemble rather the preacher in a modern church? We do not know. With "teachers" we feel that we are on safer ground, but are we? We know of people with a natural aptitude for teaching ("a born teacher"!), and we know of people who are teachers because they have learned to teach through a course of training. But what is a *charisma* for teaching? "Powers" (*dynameis*) apparently were miracles, but what miracles were in distinction from healing (which is another gift) it is not easy to see. And as for healing, the expression is "gifts of healings" (both nouns are plural). Does this mean that one person had a variety of healing gifts? Or that one could heal one kind of ailments and another another? Of *antilēmpseis* we can say only that it is connected in some way with helping, but what form of help required a special *charisma*? We do not know. There is a similar difficulty with *kybernēseis,* a word connected with steering (a *kybernētēs* was a steersman

---

[3] Each question is introduced by μή, which indicates that a negative answer is expected.

[4] The verb is φυσιόω, which is found six times in 1 Corinthians and only once elsewhere in the New Testament.

on a ship). That is plain enough, but precisely what "steering" was done in the early church is a matter on which we have no information.[5] As for "tongues," some see this as meaning an utterance in one of the world's recognized languages—a language that the speaker had not learned, while others hold that it means speaking unintelligible sounds.[6] In view of the difficulties, it is a trifle mystifying that some interpret the gifts so confidently. It is not too much to say that not one of the gifts can be identified with complete confidence.[7]

Today the charismatic gifts are sometimes seen as dispensing with the need (and the possibility) of a regular ministry. The early church was thoroughly charismatic, it is held, and when the Spirit came on a person, that person would exercise some form of ministry (1 Cor. 14:26). But there were no "office-bearers." Paul is usually cited as a prime witness for this position. But it is more than doubtful whether this can be sustained.

There can be no doubt about Paul's enthusiasm for the gifts, but this does not seem to have exhausted his understanding of the ministry of the church. At least in writing to the church at Philippi he referred to "bishops and deacons" (Phil. 1:1; there are of course many references to bishops, elders, and deacons in the Pastorals, but these are regarded as non-Pauline by many, so I will leave them out of the discussion at this point). And surely he has a ministry of some sort in mind in one of his earliest letters when he says, ". . . those who are set over you in the Lord and admonish you" (1 Thess. 5:12; they are also to be highly regarded in love "on account of their work" [v. 13]). It is more than difficult to run any group for any length of time without office-bearers of any sort, and there is sound evidence that the early church did not try. It took some time for the fully developed Christian ministry to appear, but some forms of leadership were there from the first. Paul's interest in apostles (he uses the word thirty-four times of its seventy-nine New Testament occurrences) fits in with this. So does his direction to the Corinthians to be "in subjection" to people like Stephanas (1 Cor. 16:15–16). And, at least in the Pastorals, a *charisma* was given by the laying on of hands (1 Tim. 4:14; 2 Tim. 1:6), an act that most see as a reference to ordination or commissioning for ministry.

The Spirit, then, is active in the life of the believer and of the church. He does things like bearing witness with our spirit (Rom. 8:16), interceding for us (Rom. 8:26–27), and sanctifying us (Rom. 15:16). He has a part in justification (1 Cor. 6:11) and in revelation (1 Cor. 2:10; cf. 1 Tim. 4:1). When we believed, we were "sealed" with the Spirit (Eph. 1:13; 4:30); that is to say,

---

[5] A standard work like *BAGD* gives no indication of the uncertainty connoted by the word when it says: "*administration;* the pl. indicates proofs of ability to hold a leading position in the church." A similar understanding is found in NIV, NASV. But what evidence is there that the early church was sufficiently organized to have places for people with gifts of "administration"? A charismatic administration is almost a contradiction in terms.

[6] Charles C. Ryrie keeps open both possibilities (*Biblical Theology of the New Testament* [Chicago, 1982], 194).

[7] This should not be understood as denying the reality of the working of the Holy Spirit in the modern charismatic movement. I gladly acknowledge that the Spirit of God is at work in striking ways in many such groups. All I am saying here is that we should be on our guard against a too-hasty identification of the gifts set out in the New Testament lists. It may be that they are being repeated exactly in our days. But it may also be that the Spirit of God is doing a new thing. We cannot solve our exegetical difficulties by appealing to contemporary experience.

the presence of the Spirit in believers is God's mark of ownership (like the seal that a first-century person might put on personal property). The Spirit teaches us (1 Cor. 2:13) and lives in us (2 Tim. 1:14). He empowers us (*hikanōsen*, 2 Cor. 3:6).

THE CHURCH

Life in the Spirit has a markedly corporate style. Those saved in Christ are brought into the fellowship of the church.[8] Paul assumes that all who put their trust in Christ become members of the church, and he has a great interest in that institution (62 of the 114 New Testament examples of *ekklēsia* are in Paul, more than half the total). Basically he thinks of the local church (cf. "as I teach in every church" [1 Cor. 4:17]; cf. also references to the church as assembled [1 Cor. 11:18; 14:19–28]). He speaks of "the church of God" (1 Cor. 1:2; Gal. 1:13), of "the churches of God" (1 Cor. 11:16; 1 Thess. 2:14), and of "the churches of Christ" (Rom. 16:16; cf. Gal. 1:22). He sometimes refers to churches of a specific region, e.g., "the churches of Galatia" (1 Cor. 16:1; Gal. 1:2; cf. 1 Cor. 16:19; 2 Cor. 8:1; Gal. 1:22; Col. 4:16; 1 Thess. 1:1; 2 Thess. 1:1).

Paul sometimes thinks of the smaller church unit—the "house church" (Rom. 16:5; 1 Cor. 16:19; Col. 4:15; Philem. 2). Precisely what this meant is not clear,[9] because there were no church buildings at that time and presumably all churches met in private houses. But house churches are spe-

cifically mentioned and they appear to refer to smaller groups than the main body. They were not schismatic, for greetings were sent to them in letters to the main church.

Sometimes Paul has in mind the universal church in distinction from the local church. Thus he speaks of God as having set the apostles "in the church" (1 Cor. 12:28; apostles were not local officials), and of himself as having persecuted "the church" (1 Cor. 15:9; Gal. 1:13). But especially is this the case in his view that the church is Christ's body (Col. 1:24), over which Christ is head (Eph. 1:22; 5:23; Col. 1:18). The church is subject to Christ (Eph. 5:24) and it is through the church that God's "manifold wisdom" is made known in the heavenly realms (Eph. 3:10). Christ loved the church and gave himself for it (Eph. 5:25), and he continues to nourish it (Eph. 5:29). Though there is emphasis on divine care, Paul also says that "the care of all the churches" falls on him (2 Cor. 11:28); there is an area of human responsibility.

Paul has a number of interesting pictures of the church. The church is a building with Christ as its foundation (1 Cor. 3:11). From another point of view it is built on the foundation of the apostles and prophets (Eph. 2:20). More specifically it is "God's temple" (1 Cor. 3:16; cf. Eph. 2:21), a term that agrees with the habitual description of believers as "the saints" (notice that this expression is always plural; Paul never speaks of an individual

---

[8] Michel Bouttier says of Paul, "What unites him with Christ unites him with the Corinthians, and what unites him with the Philippians unites him with Christ" (*Christianity According to Paul* [Naperville, Ill., 1966], 62).

[9] Wayne A. Meeks objects to the translation "the church in N.'s house," holding that ἐν οἴκῳ would be the natural way of saying this, whereas the expression is κατ' οἴκον. He sees it as "the 'basic cell' of the Christian movement, and its nucleus was often an existing household." But "it was not coterminous with the household." "Common trades" and new converts would be added (*The First Urban Christians* [New Haven and London, 1983], 75–76).

believer as a saint; he sees the group as holy). The church is a household (Eph. 2:19; Gal. 6:10; 1 Tim. 3:15). It is Christ's bride (2 Cor. 11:2; cf. Eph. 5:25–32). It is his body (Col. 1:18, 24; cf. Rom. 12:4–5). It is "the Israel of God" (Gal. 6:16; cf. its relationship to Abraham [Rom. 4:16; Gal. 3:29]).[10] It is a commonwealth made up of fellow citizens (Eph. 2:19; Phil. 3:20), the people of God (Rom. 9:25–26), the new humanity (Col. 3:10–11). There are other ways of viewing the church, but these are sufficient for us to see that for Paul the church is many-splendored.

SACRAMENTS

Paul does not often refer to the two sacramental ordinances that have meant so much to the church through the centuries, but what he says is important. Thus, he informs us that "in one Spirit we were all baptized into one body" (1 Cor. 12:13), making the point that the important thing is what the Spirit does. Indeed, so important is this that there are expositors who hold that Paul is not referring to baptism by water at all—he is using "baptized" in a metaphorical way (cf. Matt. 3:11).[11] They often contrast "Spirit baptism" with "water baptism," without giving consideration to the fact that this is a distinction the New Testament never makes. It seems more probable that he

has water baptism in mind and that he is saying that it is the Holy Spirit who makes the believer a member of the church, not the use of water.[12] It is the Spirit who makes us all one, and Paul goes on to show the scope of this unity: "whether Jews or Greeks, whether slaves or free"; it is the same Spirit of whom all "drink."

The note of unity is struck again when Paul says, "As many of you as were baptized into Christ have put on Christ. There is neither Jew nor Greek, there is neither slave nor free, there is neither male nor female, for you are all one in Christ Jesus" (Gal. 3:27–28). This time there is no mention of the Spirit, but the link with Christ means a link with one another. And it is unity with Christ that is stressed when the apostle says, "As many of us as were baptized into Christ Jesus were baptized into his death" (Rom. 6:3). Believers have died to a whole way of life. We have been buried; that old way has gone forever. Now we "walk in newness of life" with Christ (Rom. 6:4; cf. Col. 2:12 for the same combination of burial and rising to new life). We are one with Christ.

Holy Communion is not featured prominently in Paul's writings. But he asks the Corinthians, "The cup of blessing which we bless, is it not a participation in the blood of Christ? The bread which we break, is it not a participation in the body of Christ?"

---

[10] Cf. Paul S. Minear: "Paul did not fall back upon a concept of two Israels, the old and the new, or the false and the true. He defined God's Israel as one people, as measured qualitatively by God's mercy in the cross of Christ" (*Images of the Church in the New Testament* [Philadelphia, 1960], 72).

[11] Cf. Alan Redpath: "If we have been saved by God's grace, washed in the blood of Christ, at that moment we were baptized by the Holy Spirit into the body of the Lord Jesus" (*The Royal Route to Heaven* [Westwood, N.J., 1960], 149).

[12] Michael Green points out that six of the seven New Testament references to baptism in the Spirit contrast John the Baptist with Jesus. This is the only reference to such baptism without the contrast and here "it is made abundantly plain that not just the tongues speakers, not just the miracle workers, but *all* the Corinthian Christians had been baptised in the Holy Spirit and had drunk of his waters. Just as we are not to separate baptism from justification, so we are not to separate it from the gift of the Holy Spirit" (*To Corinth With Love* [London, 1982], 36).

(1 Cor. 10:16). He goes on to speak of the unity of believers: "We, the many, are one loaf, one body, for we all share in the one loaf" (v. 17). The passage is not without its difficulties, but Paul appears to mean that the faithful take Christ (his body and blood) into their innermost being as they participate in the communion and that their unity is furthered by their participation.

This makes it a very solemn and important act, and Paul accordingly castigates in strong terms those who take "their own supper" before others, so that one is hungry and another is drunken (1 Cor. 11:21); this is not "the Lord's Supper" (v. 20), but a caricature. He goes on to tell of Christ's institution of the Supper (vv. 23–26). He brings out its meaning (1) by referring to the new covenant Christ inaugurated, (2) by saying that we take part in it in remembrance of Christ, and (3) by saying that in the sacrament we "proclaim the death of the Lord, until he comes." To profane such a holy rite is to be "guilty of the body and blood of the Lord" (v. 27); anyone who does this is "not discerning the body" (v. 29). This seems to mean that the offender does not realize the sense in which the body of Christ is given, though some see a reference here to the church as the body of Christ.[13] Perhaps I should add that there is no good reason for accepting the view that some have put forward—namely, that Paul's view of the sacraments is substantially indebted to or even derived from the Hellenistic mystery religions. The differences are too many and the resemblances too superficial for such a view to retain any plausibility.[14]

THE WAY OF FAITH

Paul has made "faith" one of the great Christian words. He uses it constantly (142 times; he also has the verb "to believe" 54 times, and the adjective "faithful" 33 times). His usage is such as to leave his readers in no doubt that faith is fundamental for the Christian. There is an intellectual content to faith (it means "believing that—" ; e.g., Rom. 6:8; 10:9), but we should not think of it primarily in intellectual terms. For Paul faith means trust, wholehearted trust in Christ as the One who died to bring us salvation.[15] And it means commitment, a commitment of the whole life to the Savior.

It is by faith that we appropriate the gift of salvation. The "righteousness from God" comes to us through faith (Rom. 3:22; Phil. 3:9). We are justified by faith (Rom. 3:28, 30; 5:1; Gal. 3:24), and, of course, there is that great text from Habakkuk that Paul quotes twice and that we should probably understand in this sense: "He that is just by faith will live" (Rom. 1:17; Gal. 3:11; see Hab. 2:4). Similarly propitiation is "through faith" (Rom. 3:25), as is adoption (Gal. 3:26).

Paul devotes a whole chapter to

---

[13] Cf. Bouttier: "In this they show that they have not yet learnt to discern the Lord's Body, i.e. to recognize it in one another" (*Christianity According to Paul,* 69).

[14] "The differences between Pauline and Hellenistic sacramentalism are essential and not superficial" (A. D. Nock, *St. Paul* [New York, 1963], 77). Of 1 Corinthians 8:4–9, T. R. Glover says, "This was flat denial, and there could hardly be more abrupt denial, of the central idea of the sacramental religions" (*Paul of Tarsus* [London, 1925], 136). Martin Hengel calls the view that Paul depended on the mystery religions "this remarkable theory" (*Between Jesus and Paul* [Philadelphia, 1983], 160n.26).

[15] Werner Georg Kümmel defines faith in this way: "That is what believing means—to look away from self, disregard both one's wretchedness and one's merits, and trust in God's having settled the matter through Jesus Christ" (Martin Dibelius, *Paul,* ed. and comp. Werner George Kümmel [Philadelphia, 1966], 117).

Abraham, the great exemplar of faith: "Abraham believed God and it was reckoned to him as righteousness" (Rom. 4:3, 22–23; Gal. 3:6; see Gen. 15:6). This is a mark of Paul's originality, for the Jews tended to see Abraham as an outstanding keeper of the law (even though the law had not yet been given): "Abraham our father had performed the whole Law before it was given" (Mishnah, *Kidd.* 4:14).[16] But for Paul it was Abraham's faith that was important. The first independent action of the great patriarch was his astonishing act of obedience to God's call. He was seventy-five years old at the time, so it was no rash impulse of youth. He took his wife, his household, and their possessions and left his country, his kindred, and his father's house (Gen. 12:1–4). Why? Solely because God called him. He believed in God, so he went out without a clue as to his destination, a breathtaking example of whole-hearted commitment. Abraham knew no more than that God had called him. But that was enough.

Paul adds a reference to David to show that he too provides evidence that salvation comes from God's imputing of righteousness (Rom. 4:6–8), not from obedience to law. Then it is back to Abraham for the important point that his faith was reckoned as righteousness long before he was circumcised.[17] Circumcision was a sign of the covenant (Gen. 17:9–14); the Jew saw it as proof that he was within the covenant community, and "all Israelites have a share in the world to come" (Mishnah, *Sanh.* 10:1). But for Paul the timing is all-important. Abraham was accepted by God long before he was circumcised. Circumcision was a seal of the righteousness by faith that Abraham had in his uncircumcised state (Rom. 4:11), not, as the Jews thought, of the impossibility of any of their race suffering final rejection by God. The Jews were fond of referring to Abraham as their father, but Paul sees the patriarch as the father of the faithful, be they circumcised or uncircumcised (Rom. 4:11–12). The apostle connects the promise to Abraham with "the righteousness by faith" (Rom. 4:13). It is grace that is important, not law, and this means faith (Rom. 4:14–16) by which we appropriate grace. The argument is an impressive demonstration of the truth that God's way is grace and always has been grace, and further that the gift of grace is appropriated by faith. It is all the more impressive in that it centers on Abraham, the prime example for the Jews of a keeper of the law. But for Paul it is clear that it is "those who are characterized by faith" who are "sons of Abraham" and who "are blessed with faithful Abraham" (Gal. 3:7, 9).

Faith is characteristic of Christians. We "stand fast in faith" (or "the faith" 1 Cor. 16:13), we "abide" in it (Col.

---

[16] The Rabbis understood Genesis 15:6 as pointing to Abraham's merit rather than his trust. C. E. B. Cranfield cites two relevant passages from Mekhilta on Exodus 14:15, 31: "The faith with which your father Abraham believed in Me merits that I should divide the sea. . . . Our father Abraham became the heir of this and of the coming world simply by the merit of the faith with which he believed in the LORD" (*A Critical and Exegetical Commentary on the Epistle to the Romans* [Edinburgh, 1975], 1:229; both passages proceed to quote Gen. 15:6).

[17] The faith on the grounds of which he was accepted before God was exercised by Abraham long before the birth of Ishmael, and when Ishmael was born Abraham was 86 years old (Gen. 16:16). He was not circumcised until he was 99 (Gen. 17:24), so that the time must have been over thirteen years. According to Jewish chronology, it was longer still, for the Jews held that Abraham was seventy years old at the time of the dividing of the sacrifice (Gen. 15:10; Seder Olam R.1, cited in *SBK*, 3:203). This would mean a twenty-nine-year interval.

1:23), we "walk" in it (2 Cor. 5:7). It is "by faith" that we have open access to God (Rom. 5:2; "through faith" [Eph. 3:12]), and it is "through faith" that Christ dwells in our hearts (Eph. 3:17). Faith is not static, and Paul looks for it to grow (2 Cor. 10:15; 2 Thess. 1:3; cf. 1 Thess. 3:10). Paul quite often links it with love and has a magnificent description of the Christian life as "faith working by love" (Gal. 5:6). He can also speak of the Thessalonian Christians' "work of faith" (1 Thess. 1:3). In all this it would be a mistake to think of faith as a human product standing over against the divine act for our salvation. Faith itself comes from God, for to each believer God "has imparted a measure of faith" (Rom. 12:3).

Sometimes the apostle speaks of "the faith" (e.g., 2 Cor. 13:5; Gal. 1:23; 6:10; 1 Tim. 4:1, 6). Used in this way, the term stands for the whole system of Christian teaching, and some see in it a loss of early Christian spontaneity and a hardening into orthodoxy. But to understand Christianity as having teachings that must be believed does not necessarily mean the loss of the first fine flush of believing enthusiasm.[18] And it is significant that the name given to Christianity is not "the law" or "the teaching," but "the faith." Faith is something special. Paul can call Christians "believers" (Rom. 3:22; 1 Thess. 1:7); it is always faith that matters.

THE WAY OF LOVE

Paul keeps insisting that the Christian life is a life of love. It begins with love, for it is the love we see at Calvary that makes us Christians in the first place. And when we are Christians, we find ourselves members of the church, the beloved community. As members of this community we are called to live in love, in love for God, in love for one another, and in love for all. Whereas for the Jew the law was the divinely given instrument that molded the servant of God, for Paul "love is the fulfilling of the law" (Rom. 13:8–10; Gal. 5:14; 1 Tim. 1:5). Love is central, for love is what God is.

God not only has love for us; he also produces love in us. The believer does not work up love out of his own resources. As C. F. D. Moule has said, "*Agape* is not a virtue among other virtues so much as a totally new impulse, divinely implanted: it is God's love for us in Christ, reflected and responded to."[19] Love comes as we accept God's way. It is not that some people become rather good at loving; rather, God's love "is poured into our hearts through the Holy Spirit" (Rom. 5:5; Moffatt brings out the thought of abundance with "floods our hearts"). God gives us "a spirit of love" (2 Tim. 1:7). When Paul lists "the fruit of the Spirit," it is love that comes first (Gal. 5:22).

From another angle, we are taught by God to love one another (1 Thess. 4:9). It is the Lord who makes believers increase and abound in love one to another (1 Thess. 3:12; cf. 2 Thess. 1:3). Love is "in Christ Jesus" (1 Tim. 1:14), and love is "in the Spirit" (Col. 1:8); indeed, it is "the love of the Spirit" (Rom. 15:30), a phrase that

---

[18]"Believing that" is there from the beginning (1 Thess. 4:14; cf. Rom. 6:8; 10:9). The verb πιστεύω takes a variety of constructions, using the prepositions ἐπί (Rom. 9:33; 1 Tim 1:16), εἰς (Rom. 10:14; Gal. 2:16), and διά (1 Cor. 3:5); the dative (Rom. 10:16; 2 Thess. 2:12); it is also used absolutely (Rom. 13:11; 1 Cor. 1:21).

[19]*The Birth of the New Testament* (London, 1962), 140.

appears to mean "the love produced by the Spirit."[20] Paul is in no doubt that love is no human achievement but the result of God's working in the believer.

Believers "walk" in love (Eph. 5:2; we deserve severe criticism when we do not [Rom. 14:15]). Love by its very nature is habitual; we do "all things" in love (1 Cor. 16:14). In his matchless treatment of love (1 Corinthians 13) Paul indicates that no brilliance in eloquence, in spiritual perception, in faith, in works of charity, or in devotion can compensate for lack of love (1 Cor. 13:1–3). Love is persistent and kind, not boastful (v. 4). Love is unselfish, not given to anger or to keeping record of wrongs (v. 5); it is glad when truth prevails, not when iniquity is strong (v. 6). Love lasts forever (vv. 7, 13).[21]

Love is a quality the believer is to "pursue" avidly (1 Cor. 14:1; 2 Tim. 2:22); we must not think it will appear in us willy-nilly. Love is the foundation of the Christian life (Eph. 3:17); it is a wonderful thing to "be strong to comprehend, with all the saints, what is the breadth and length and height and depth and to know the love of Christ that passes knowledge" (Eph. 3:18–19). It is clear from this thread that runs right through the Pauline corpus that Paul saw love as the great distinguishing mark of Christians. In a world of people motivated by ambi-tion, greed, factiousness, selfishness, and the like, Paul expected Christians to be notable for their love, both as individuals and as a community. They are "knit together" in love (Col. 2:2), "the bond of perfection" (Col. 3:14). The body is built up "in love" (Eph. 4:16) and by love (1 Cor. 8:1). Paul often writes warmly about the love he sees in the churches (Eph. 1:15; Col. 1:8; 1 Thess. 3:6; Philem. 4). He expects people to show it (2 Cor. 2:8; 8:8; Gal. 5:13), and he prays for it to abound (Phil. 1:9).[22]

In view of the places he assigns to faith and love, we can appreciate his masterly summary: in Christ, ritual matters like circumcision or its absence do not matter at all, just "faith working through love" (Gal. 5:6).

Paul's overwhelming emphasis on love comes out in the way he uses some other words. Thus he habitually addresses fellow believers with the affectionate "brothers" (he uses *adelphos* 133 times). The warmth of love characterizes his relationship to church members. Perhaps we should notice here his emphasis on the "goodness" words.[23] For Paul, love is not a wishy-washy sentimentality. It has ethical content. Paul sees clearly that the very best for loved ones is that they be established in the way of goodness. Thus, he constantly rebukes vice and exhorts to that uprightness of conduct without which a satisfying way of life is impossible.

---

[20] So Cranfield, *Romans*, 2:776.

[21] See the fuller treatment in my *Testaments of Love: A Study of Love in the Bible* (Grand Rapids, 1981), 239–59.

[22] John Knox makes the point that Paul put this into practice and that he was himself loved: "Many moderns have so *disliked* Paul that they do not realize that many of his contemporaries *loved* him"; he speaks of being "amazed at the number and extent of the passages concerned entirely with expressing Paul's own feelings toward his churches—whether of tender solicitude when they were being tried, of grief over their failures or sufferings, or of joy over their triumphs" (*Chapters in a Life of Paul* [London, 1954], 95). He goes on to remark that no one could have written 1 Cor. 13 without having "walked in that 'more excellent way.' " Cf. also Wilfred Knox: "He was a man of intense affection. His love for his converts is always triumphing over his anger at their facile desertions and their failure to live up to the standards he expects of them" (*St. Paul* [New York, 1932], 54).

[23] Paul has ἀγαθός 47 times, ἀγαθωσύνη 4 times, καλός 40 times, δίκαιος 17 times, δικαιοσύνη 57 times, χρηστότης 10 times (only Paul uses it in the New Testament), χρηστός 3 times.

And it may not be amiss to point to his view of suffering. We commonly regard suffering as an unmitigated evil, and we do all we can to avoid it. We find the existence of suffering a difficulty in the way of seeing God as a good God. Now Paul was no stranger to suffering (recall his catalog of horrors [2 Cor. 11:22–29]); he was no armchair strategist, safe in his ivory tower. But he calls on his correspondents not only to put up with suffering, but to exult in it, an exhortation that launches him into a chain of reasoning leading right on to the love of God (Rom. 5:3–5). For Paul, suffering is the evidence, not that God does not love us, but that he does. He can speak of the constancy of the Thessalonians in their persecutions and troubles as "evidence of the righteous judgment of God" (2 Thess. 1:4–5).[24] There are qualities of character that are forged in the fires of affliction and that we never develop in days of careless ease. Paul sees it as part of God's love for us that he leads us through trials to make us the best we can be.

Suffering is also the means of setting forward God's purposes. Paul rejoiced in his sufferings, for he was able to say, "I fill up what is lacking in the afflictions of Christ in my flesh for the sake of his body, which is the church" (Col. 1:24). The suffering that was his lot was not meaningless; it was part of the way the purpose of God was set forward. Those same sufferings of Paul were also evidence of his own love. Bornkamm brings this out when he draws attention to the significance of Paul's emotions. He speaks of "pain that makes him weep, anger and indignation, complaints and accusations, bit-

ter irony, utter condemnation of the agitators and rebels, defenses and even commendations of himself, which though expressed against his own will and very out of character are nevertheless moving outbursts of his heart in which his wounded love woos those in danger and misled."[25] We must not be so wrapped up in Paul the controversialist that we do not see Paul the lover of his fellow Christians.

THE WAY OF HOPE

Paul is highly interested in the consummation of all things, and he mentions the end of this age in one way or another in every one of his letters except that to Philemon. An eschatological interest was, of course, not uncommon among the Jews of the time, but what was distinctive of Paul was the role he perceived Christ fulfilling. Paul sees Christ's work of salvation as of central importance: "The fullness of the time" was already come when God sent Christ into the world (Gal. 4:4). "The ends of the ages have come" (1 Cor. 10:11). The apocalyptists of that day despaired of this present world and looked for it to pass away and be replaced by God's new creation. But for Paul the new creation is a present reality (2 Cor. 5:17). In a very meaningful sense eschatology means "the first things" of the Christian way rather than "the last things." In Christ all things are made new. Already.

But that does not mean that the possibilities in Christ's salvation are all exhausted in the here and now. Paul looked for the final working out of God's plan in a return of Christ to this

---

[24] Commenting on the joy in affliction of 1 Thessalonians 1:6, A. D. Nock says, "This joy was for Paul a principal note of the Christian life: it is not *eudaimonia*, 'happiness', or *hedonē*, 'pleasure', terms absent from Paul's vocabulary" (*St. Paul*, 148).

[25] Günther Bornkamm, *Paul* (London, 1971), 167.

earth. Seven times he spoke of Christ's *parousia,* a term that meant "presence," then it came to mean "coming to be present," "arrival." It was the term used for the coming of a person of high rank, especially the emperor when he visited a province. Paul's most explicit account of what Christ's *parousia* means tells us that "the Lord himself will come down from heaven with a shout, with an archangel's voice and God's trumpet" (1 Thess. 4:16). He adds that the dead in Christ will be raised and that "we who are alive, who remain," will be caught up to meet the Lord in the air, and thus "we shall be always with the Lord" (v. 17). The resurrection of believers follows from that of the Lord: Paul refers to "Christ the firstfruits, then those who are Christ's at his coming" (1 Cor. 15:23).

So significant is the end time, so accepted in Christian teaching, that Paul refers simply to "the day of our Lord Jesus Christ" (1 Cor. 1:8); it does not require explanation. Paul can exult in it. At Christ's appearing he expects to find the Thessalonians as his "hope" and "joy" and "crown of glorying," his "glory and joy" (1 Thess. 2:19–20). There is a strong power of evil, but Christ will destroy it at his coming (2 Thess. 2:8); indeed he everywhere assumes that the coming of Christ means the final destruction of evil (Gal. 5:19–21; 2 Thess. 1:7–9) and the ushering in of the final state of blessedness (a truth that may be expressed in terms of judgment, though the believer may face the judgment with confidence [Rom 8:1; 1 Cor. 3:13–15; 2 Cor. 5:10]).[26] So we read of "the blessed hope" (Titus 2:13), and there are several passages that refer in

one way or another to the splendor and majesty of the occasion (Eph. 2:7; 2 Thess. 1:7–10; 2:8; 2 Tim. 4:1, 8) and to the blessing that the Lord will then give his servants (Col. 1:12; 2 Tim. 4:8). Paul prays for his converts to be "blameless in holiness" before God when our Lord Jesus comes "with all his holy ones" (1 Thess. 3:13; cf. 5:23). Sometimes he refers simply to "the kingdom of God" (Gal. 5:21).

God's sovereignty will be fully manifested (1 Cor. 15:24–28); death itself, "the last enemy," will be destroyed (1 Cor. 15:26). The "full number" (*plērōma*) of the Gentiles will be brought in (Rom. 11:25) and God's promises to Israel will be fulfilled (Rom. 11:26–31). Creation will be liberated from its bondage to corruption.

The glorious future is certainly in mind in Paul's use of other terms. Sometimes, for example, his use of "glory" is eschatological (e.g., Rom. 8:18, 21; 2 Cor. 4:17), and the same may be said of terms like "hope" (Col. 1:5). Some so extend this that they see Paul as being preoccupied with the nearness of the end of the age. His whole ministry is seen as little more than a preparation for the imminent *parousia.* But if it is true that often in the past the eschatological element in Paul has been minimized, it is also true that it is possible to exaggerate it. As we have seen, Paul has a good deal to say about life in the here and now. If he saw Christianity as an apocalyptic movement, it was apocalyptic with a difference. As Lucien Cerfaux puts it, "Instead of turning in on itself like the other forms of Judaism after the persecution of Antiochus Epiphanes, Chris-

---

[26] Many Evangelicals hold strong views on Christ's millennial reign and interpret these passages differently. But Paul never refers explicitly to the millennium, and it seems better to see his statements as referring simply to final triumph.

tianity undertook the duty of preparing for the birth of a new age for mankind by changing men's minds,"[27] and we might add, their hearts and lives. For Paul, there is a sense in which the new age has already come: "If anyone is in Christ, there is a new creation" (2 Cor. 5:17). What everyone agreed would take place at the end, Paul sees as already in operation: judgment, death, and resurrection. As a present reality, they give a distinctive note to Paul's view of the end, even though they do not negate the reality of the final consummation.[28]

It has become a dogma of critical orthodoxy that Paul expected the end of all things during his own lifetime. This is held to be obvious from words like "we who are alive" in a passage dealing with the Lord's coming (1 Thess. 4:17), and from the general tone of his references to the *parousia*. If he says "we" when speaking of the living at the time Christ comes again, then surely he includes himself! It is not usually noted that the application of the same method of exegesis to other passages would lead to the conclusion that he expected to be dead. He says, "God both raised the Lord and will raise us" (1 Cor. 6:14), and again, "He who raised the Lord Jesus will raise us with Jesus" (2 Cor. 4:14).[29] How could God raise Paul unless Paul had died?

But it is precarious to infer either that Paul means he will be alive or that he means he will be dead at the last great day. He has a habit of classing himself with those he is writing about, quite irrespective of whether the activity in question is one he would engage in or not. Indeed, quite often it is impossible to envisage Paul as engaging

---

[27] *The Christian in the Theology of St. Paul* (London, 1967), 133. Paul insisted on the right use of the present time (Eph. 5:16; Col. 4:5; cf. Gal. 6:9–10).

[28] Many argue strongly for the centrality of apocalyptic in Paul. Thus, J. Christiaan Beker holds that "the center of Paul's thought is to be located in his christologically determined future apocalyptic." "I contend that the center of Paul's gospel lies in his apocalyptic interpretation of the Christ-event" (*Paul's Apocalyptic Gospel* [Philadelphia, 1982], 76, 88). E. Käsemann speaks of "the fact that Paul's apostolic self-consciousness is only comprehensible on the basis of his apocalyptic, and that the same is true of the method and the goal of his mission" (*New Testament Questions of Today* [London, 1969], 131). But E. P. Sanders does not see Paul as an apocalyptist at all: "The similarity between Paul's view and apocalypticism is general rather than detailed. Paul did not . . . calculate the times and seasons, he did not couch his predictions of the end in visions involving beasts, and he observed none of the literary conventions of apocalyptic literature" (*Paul and Palestinian Judaism* [London, 1977], 543). Bornkamm maintains that Paul's thought is "totally opposed to that of apocalyptic" (*Paul*, 147). Cf. Hans Conzelmann: "[Paul] does not give an apocalyptic interpretation of the world situation, or calculate apocalyptic signs and periods" (*An Outline of the Theology of the New Testament* [London, 1969], 256). In my book *Apocalyptic* (London, 1973) I have pointed out that apocalyptic is not a suitable vehicle for the Christian gospel (see especially pp. 96–101). "We cannot have it both ways. Granted that both the incarnation and the End are important, both cannot be the really significant thing. For the apocalypses there is the concentration on the future. In Christianity there is the recognition that the incarnation, with the atonement as its high point, is the most important event of all time" (p. 97). Beker and others do try to have it both ways. Paul sometimes uses language borrowed from apocalyptic, but the meaning is not the same: "Apocalyptic's speculations, panoramas, and concepts fall away or even are expressly rejected (1 Thess. 5:1ff.)" (Bornkamm, *Paul*, 199).

[29] It is contended by some that in his earlier letters Paul expected an imminent *parousia*, but changed his mind by the time he wrote his later letters. But Paul was converted in the early 30s. He wrote 1 Thessalonians c. 50, and 1 Corinthians c. 54 (C. K. Barrett thinks early 54 or perhaps toward the end of 53 [*A Commentary on the First Epistle to the Corinthians* (London, 1978), 5]). No one seems to have explained why he should hold to an imminent *parousia* for about twenty years and lose it during the next three or four. The letters are too close together for any convincing argument for a major change. Beker holds that "the total Pauline correspondence took place within the space of no more than six years (A.D. 50–56)" and that "there is no clear evidence for a maturing in Paul during his letter-writing period" (*Paul the Apostle* [Edinburgh, 1980], 32–33).

in the activity of which he writes. For example, he wrote, "Let us not commit fornication" (1 Cor. 10:8)—"us," not "you." Again, he said, "Let us cast off the works of darkness" (Rom. 13:12), long after he had abandoned such evil ways. Mature in the Christian life as he was (cf. 1 Cor. 13:11), he could speak of God's good gifts being given "in order that," he said, "we be no longer babies" (Eph. 4:14). He could say, "If we deny him . . ." and "if we do not believe . . ." (2 Tim. 2:12–13). He asks, "Do we nullify the law?" (Rom. 3:31); "Shall we continue in sin?" and "Shall we sin?" (Rom. 6:1, 15). He speaks of "our unrighteousness" (Rom. 3:5) and asks, "Do we provoke the Lord to jealousy?" (1 Cor. 10:22). Sometimes he makes it even more personal by using the singular, as when he uses the phrase "through my lie" (Rom. 3:7) or asks, "Shall I take the members of Christ and make them members of a harlot?" (1 Cor. 6:15). He envisages action in which "food makes [one's] brother stumble" (8:13), though it would have been easy to leave it quite general: "a brother."

So we should not read too much into Paul's "we who are alive." It does not necessarily mean more than "Christians who are alive." Other "we" passages should similarly be examined with care.[30] We should also notice that Paul certainly contemplates the possibility of his death, for he has "the desire to depart and be with the Lord" (Phil. 1:23). His death is also implied in his desire "to attain the resurrection of the dead" (Phil. 3:11). He recognizes that his imprisonment may result in life or in death (Phil. 1:20), a phraseology that is similar to his "whether we live . . . or whether we die . . ." (Rom. 14:8), and his "whether in the body or out of the body" (2 Cor. 5:9; cf.1:9). There are difficulties with the opening part of 2 Corinthians 5, but it is hard to resist W. G. Kümmel's conclusion: "Paul is reckoning with the possibility, which he does not hope for, that Christians, himself included, can die before the Parousia."[31] His statement "I die daily" (1 Cor. 15:31) means constant danger of death and seems to show that he took seriously the possibility that he might die.

Paul may have expected that he would not die before the *parousia*. I do not know. All that I am saying is that the evidence of the New Testament gives more reason for thinking that he expected to be dead when his Lord came than that he expected to be alive. The common assumption is unjustified. In any case Paul concentrated on the tasks of the present as his letters amply attest. It is quite possible to "build for the future without necessarily knowing whether it is near or remote."[32] For Paul, it is the fact of the *parousia* that is important, not its precise time.

There is much more in Paul and much more that is important. I have said little about important concepts like truth, peace, freedom, hope, obedience, joy, and the like. This is meant to be a compact treatment, and not everything can be included. But what has been

[30] James D. G. Dunn holds that the expectation of an imminent *parousia* "was a prominent feature" in the Thessalonian correspondence. But he denies that such a *parousia* is expected in 1 Corinthians 15:51–52, Romans 13:11f. ("Near? yes; but how near?"), and Philippians 1:20ff. He sees no urgency in Colossians (the only reference being 3:4; cf. 1:13; 2:12; 2:20–3:3) and finds no reference to the *parousia* in Ephesians (*Unity and Diversity in the New Testament* [London, 1977], 325, 345–46). Although I cannot identify with all these positions, I appreciate Dunn's caution.
[31] *The Theology of the New Testament* (London, 1974), 240.
[32] Lucien Cerfaux, *The Christian in the Theology of St Paul*, 93.

included is enough to indicate a little of the depth and the breadth of Paul's understanding of the Christian way of life.

It is plain that Paul has a profound and well-thought-out theology. It is not given in a systematic form, and we all experience difficulty in trying to arrange it in a coherent system. But that is our problem, not Paul's. He was sure that God had done something wonderful in Christ, and the certainty of that pervaded all his thought. He was sure that God would bring what he had done to a magnificent climax in the world to come, when all evil would be destroyed and the triumph of God and of good would be manifest. He was sure that God in his love had provided for all the needs of his people in the intervening period and specifically that he had sent his Holy Spirit to guide them and to lead them in the way of love. The love of God is the great, dominating reality and calls forth a love in the hearts of God's people. There is nothing greater than love (1 Cor. 13:13).

pARt two

the synoptic Gospels and acts

e face a problem when we turn to the Gospels. If we concentrate on what Jesus did and said, we may overlook the fact that each of the Evangelists is a theologian. If we try to bring out the contribution of each, we may give the impression that Jesus said and did little.[1] Whichever procedure we adopt, we must bear in mind the disadvantages attendant on our choice and the advantages of the other way of considering the Gospels. I have opted for taking the Gospels one by one. This enables us to see not only what Jesus said and did, but also how each Evangelist understood what he said and did. In this section we look at the three Synoptic Gospels and include Acts because that is part of Luke's two-volume work. In doing the study in this way, I am mindful of the fact that without Jesus there would be no Christianity, no gospel—and no Gospels! It is a common teaching of all the New Testament writers that God did something unique in the life and death and resurrection of Jesus, and that that unique something is the most important thing that ever happened. I do not want us to lose sight of this.

Each of the Evangelists has his own theological perspective, but we are not to think of the theology of the individual writers as being all-important in the Gospels bearing their names. None of them is a theological genius propounding a unique set of original ideas for the edification of the faithful. Each is writing about Jesus. It is what Jesus said and what Jesus did that is the subject of each of the Gospels and it is the endeavor to bring this out that is the reason for the writing of the Gospels. When we study any one of the Gospels, it is legitimate to look at the selection of material the writer has made and ask why he made it and what he means by

---

[1] It is possible to exaggerate the differences between the Gospels, as in Willi Marxsen's classification: "Mark really writes a Gospel; in his book, Matthew offers a collection of gospels which are etiologically joined to the life of Jesus; Luke writes a *vita Jesu.*" "From *this* viewpoint we must simply state that *there are no 'Synoptic' Gospels*" (*Mark the Evangelist* [Nashville, 1969], 150n.106, 212; Marxsen's italics).

writing as he did. But it is Jesus who matters, not the Evangelist. Leonhard Goppelt brings out the importance of this in his two-volume *Theology of the New Testament*. His first volume is subtitled "The Ministry of Jesus in Its Theological Significance." That is our proper subject of study in the Gospels. We will look at the way that ministry is depicted by Mark and the others, but our concern is with Jesus.

A further presupposition of this study is that the Gospels present us with reliable information about Jesus. Some critics so stress the part of the church in handing on the tradition incorporated in the Gospels that Jesus is reduced to insignificance. That the part played by the church is important we need not doubt. Each of the Evangelists was a church member and each wrote with the needs of the church in mind. Each conveys to us, and could convey, only information that survived in the church. There is much in the life of Jesus that is unknown to us; clearly what is preserved survives because it was remembered in the church as important.

But for the church to be selective is one thing; to be creative is quite another. There are students who so stress the part played by the prophets in the early church that the prophets and those associated with them seem to produce the tradition. On this view, when a prophet passed on what he felt God was saying to and through him, he might well introduce it with some such

formula as "Jesus said." To us, it is said, this looks like a claim to factuality, to them it was a claim to inspiration. Then, when the prophet had done his work, the community passed on the tradition and, as it did so, it modified it and added to it. It may even be held that we know little about Jesus as he was. We know him only as the church remembered him through a holy haze. The memory, on this view, is largely shaped by the church's veneration for him as the one to be worshiped.[2]

I propose to take the Gospels as giving us essentially what Jesus said and did.[3] The part played by the prophets is unknown and I do not care to speculate. The part played by the church is shrouded in the mists of time, and I see no way of penetrating those mists. I am, of course, aware that there is much discussion concerning the authenticity of the sayings and deeds attributed to Jesus in all four Gospels and that scholars have evolved a variety of techniques to grapple with the problems. Even so, the scholars are a long way from being in agreement. Pursuant to the aim of surveying briefly the theology of the canonical New Testament, I do not propose to go into such discussions. To do so would lengthen the book beyond endurance and would in fact produce a different kind of book. My concern is with the theology of the Gospels as they stand, not with the hypothetical steps by which they reached their present form.

That this procedure is not unreason-

---

[2] Cf. Rudolf Bultmann: "The Christ who is preached is not the historic Jesus, but the Christ of the faith and the cult . . . the kerygma of Christ is cultic legend and the *Gospels are expanded cult legends*" (*The History of the Synoptic Tradition* [Oxford, 1963], 370–71; Bultmann's italics). This author's use of "legend" must be understood carefully, but clearly he is not ascribing a high historicity to the Gospels.

[3] Martin Hengel writes, "Given the tendency which is so popular in Germany today to eliminate the earthly Jesus because it is said to be impossible to grasp him and that he has no theological significance, it is necessary to stress the obvious fact that without the activity of the earthly Jesus it becomes absurd to speak of 'Jesus' concern', and the church founded by Easter which, for whatever reason, no longer dares to ask after the earthly Jesus, is separated from its starting point" (*Between Jesus and Paul* [Philadelphia, 1983], 61).

able is perhaps indicated by Morna D. Hooker's discussion of the relationship between Jesus and Paul.[4] She finds a link between Jesus' teaching of the kingdom—although there are uncertainties: "Are we dealing with future eschatology, realized eschatology, or perhaps inaugurated eschatology?"[5]—and Paul's justification by faith (which is both present and future). The two concepts are linked both in their view of the relationship between God and man and in their ethical aspects. There are differences, but there is also continuity. Dr. Hooker is not unduly handicapped by questions such as "Exactly what did Jesus teach?" Perhaps the same is true of the present study. While there certainly are questions in the criticism of the Gospels, some of which are at present unanswerable, there are also clear enough indications of the theology they teach for us to proceed in our quest.

It would have been possible to deal only with the four Gospels in this section and to put Acts in some other part of the book. But the Johannine writings have an individuality of their own and they are different enough from the Synoptic Gospels for us to put the three Synoptists together and assign the fourth Gospel, together with the other Johannine writings, to a later section. As for Acts, there can be no doubt that Luke and Acts are two volumes of a single work, and there is little to be said for splitting up our study of them.

There is some controversy about dating. Some scholars regard Mark as having been written later than Matthew or Luke or both,[6] but most see it as the earliest of the Gospels, and I will, therefore, treat it first. Not much depends on our choice, as the theology of the book is much the same whether it came first or last. Nevertheless, it is likely that it was first and that the production of the Gospel genre was begun by Mark.

There is some discussion as to just how novel this genre is. Mostly Christians have seen in it a new type of writing,[7] but in recent years some scholars have concluded that a Gospel is a form of biography.[8]

Though this has been strongly argued and some good points have been made, the differences between these two types of writing are too many and too significant. Thus, the Gospels tell us nothing about the formative influences on Jesus throughout his early years and nothing, apart from the birth narratives and one incident when he was about twelve years old, about his life prior to his public ministry. And when we come to the public ministry, we have only a small proportion of Jesus' teaching and his life[9] and a

[4] *A Preface to Paul* (New York, 1980), 32–35.

[5] Ibid., 32.

[6] See, for example, William R. Farmer, *The Synoptic Problem* (Dillsboro, 1976).

[7] Norman Perrin begins an article entitled, "The Literary *Gattung* 'Gospel'—Some Observations" (*ExpT* 82 [1970–71]: 4–7), with this statement: "The literary *Gattung* 'gospel' is the unique literary creation of early Christianity. This is a statement which I would make with confidence because for all that we may learn from Hellenistic or Jewish texts, none of them is adequate to provide the model for the Christian gospel."

[8] See, for example, Clyde Weber Votaw, *The Gospels and Contemporary Biographies in the Greco-Roman World* (Philadelphia, 1970); Charles H. Talbert, *What Is a Gospel?* (London, 1978). This view has been criticized by many, for example, Ralph P. Martin, *Mark: Evangelist and Theologian* (Exeter, 1972), 19ff.; D. E. Aune, "The Problem of the Genre of the Gospels," in R. T. France and David Wenham, eds., *Gospel Perspectives* (Sheffield, 1981), 2:9–60.

[9] "It has been calculated that three or four weeks would suffice for everything related in Mark, except 1:13" (D. E. Nineham, *The Gospel of St Mark* [Harmondsworth, 1963], 35).

disproportionate amount of information about his death and resurrection.

That is the critical point. A book that comes to its climax with a trial scene, the hero's death as a criminal, and then a resurrection is unique. This is not biography. It is "gospel," the good news of what God has done to bring salvation. A deep theological purpose has shaped the narrative.

5

the gospel of mark

Mark loses no time in telling us what he is about. His opening words are "The beginning of the gospel of Jesus Christ the Son of God."[1] Here is how it all started, he is saying, and what started he defines as "the gospel." The word was not in use as the title of a book (that usage appears to be no earlier than Justin, about the middle of the second century). It is the "good news" of whose beginning Mark writes.[2] He is more than usually interested in the gospel and indeed uses the term seven times (eight if we include 16:15). This is more often than anyone else in the New Testament except Paul. Here it is the good news "of Jesus Christ," which may mean "the good news about Jesus Christ" or "the good news that Jesus Christ preached." In Mark there seems little difference. A little later Mark speaks of Jesus as "preaching the gospel of God" (1:14), a statement that brings out the point that the gospel originated with God. Mark is writing about something that God himself has done. And

it is Jesus who tells us the good news from God. The gospel is not something obvious, part of the common knowledge of religious people. It is good news, Mark knows, because Jesus brought it from God.

Now if God has good news for us, it is important that we respond rightly. Jesus' initial proclamation is summed up in this way: "The time has been fulfilled and the kingdom of God has come near; repent and believe in the gospel" (1:15). The gospel came in God's good time (cf. Gal. 4:4; Eph. 1:10); we are not to think of it as brought about by the circumstances of first-century Palestine or any other human activity. It is determined by God alone. The good news concerns God's kingdom. God is sovereign. He rules in human lives and lays down what he demands from people. The concept of God's rule is found in one way or another in the Old Testament, in the intertestamental literature and in the rabbinical writings. Many who set it

---

[1] The words "Son of God" are lacking from some MSS (ℵ* Θ 28ᶜet al.), and some critics omit them accordingly. But the attestation is strong and it is supported by the fact that Mark has the expression at critical points throughout the Gospel, the baptism (1:11), the Transfiguration (9:7), and the Crucifixion (15:39). Most scholars are persuaded by such considerations and accept the reading.

[2] C. E. B. Cranfield lists ten possible ways of understanding the opening words (*The Gospel According to Saint Mark* [Cambridge, 1959], 34–35), so the meaning is not obvious. But Mark is fond of the term "gospel," and it seems best to understand him to say that he is telling us how all this "good news" that centered on Jesus began.

forth had a strong eschatological tendency, with vivid imagery describing what will happen when God intervenes at the end of the age to overthrow earthly systems and set up his own rule over all. Others, less eschatologically minded, see the rule of God at work when godly people take on themselves the yoke of the law of God and so hasten the time when God's rule will be universal.[3] Jesus taught the inwardness of the kingdom and its future coming, but he did not identify himself with earlier speculations. Hugh Anderson puts it this way: "With Jesus everything is subordinated to the one essential declaration: *God's reign is coming*. It is as direct and unadorned as that, and Mark has captured its directness in 1:15."[4]

In the light of what God has done and will do, Jesus challenges people to respond: they are to repent and believe. Repentance means facing up to the fact that we have done what we ought not to have done and have left undone what we should have done. Repentance means that we recognize that we have failed to live up to the highest and best we know. Repentance means that we abandon every evil way and opt to live radically new lives. Repentance means whole-hearted transformation. It is not the putting aside of a minor peccadillo or two. Jesus is calling for a reorientation of the whole of life.[5]

This is further brought out in the call to believe the gospel.[6] When God has spoken, those who hear must accept the divine word. This can be costly. Jesus later says that it is necessary to "lose" our life for Jesus' sake and the gospel's if we are to save it (8:35). He spells out something of what this means when he speaks of leaving "home or brothers or sisters or mother or father or children or lands" (10:29). Mark will make it clear that the "good news" is that God has acted decisively for our salvation and that it is because of the grace of God and not any human merit that we enter into life. But he is not writing about cheap grace. The gospel makes demands (it is significant that Mark records the call of the first disciples immediately after Jesus' challenge to repentance and faith, 1:14–20). When God has done so much for us, why should we not respond by giving all for him? We are not to see this as an extra demand made on leaders or outstanding saints. It is not a message for the chosen few. Jesus says that this gospel "must be preached to all the nations" (13:10). He also refers almost incidentally to its being preached "in all the world" (14:9). Mark is writing no miniscule Gospel, concerned with minor liturgical matters and the like. It is a Gospel that demands the transformation of the whole life, and this not only for a few outstanding saints: the gospel is the gospel for the whole world.

What God is doing in Jesus involves a conflict with evil. Immediately after

---

[3] The taking on oneself of "the yoke of the kingdom of heaven" is linked with that of "the yoke of the commandments" (Mishnah, *Ber.* 2:2). See also *SBK*, 1:172ff.

[4] Hugh Anderson, *The Gospel of Mark* (London, 1981), 85.

[5] Leonhard Goppelt puts strong emphasis on Jesus' call for repentance and says, for example, "Each of Jesus' demands was after nothing less than a transformation of the person from the very core, i.e., total repentance" (*Theology of the New Testament* [Grand Rapids, 1981], 1:118).

[6] The construction is πιστεύειν ἐν τῷ εὐαγγελίῳ. Vincent Taylor points out that this is the only place in the New Testament where this construction occurs (John 3:15; Eph. 1:13 are not real parallels); it "is best explained as translation Greek." He renders it "believe the Good News" (*The Gospel According to St. Mark* [London, 1959], 167). BAGD cite Hofmann for "on the basis of," Wohlenberg for "*bei*," Deissmann and Moulton for "in the sphere of" (which is also favored by Nigel Turner, *A Grammar of New Testament Greek*, ed. J. H. Moulton, iii [Edinburgh, 1963], 237). Bultmann sees it as "a linguistic variant" of εἰς (*TDNT*, 6:211n.271).

Jesus' baptism the Spirit drove him into the wilderness, where he was tempted by Satan (1:12–13). Mark draws attention to the initiative of the Spirit. The temptation was the work of the evil one, but Mark sees God as having his purpose in it too. The Spirit is in life's trials. Mark also tells us that the angels "were ministering" to Jesus, the tense of the verb apparently indicating that they did this throughout the temptation. We are not to think of this difficult time as one when Jesus was without the help his Father gives. Matthew and Luke tell us that Jesus was fasting throughout the forty days, but Mark says nothing about this. He concentrates on the temptation; it was the conflict with evil that mattered. He brings out some of the horror of it by his reference to the wilderness, which was seen as the place of demons and the like (cf. Luke 8:29; 11:24; SBk, iv:515–16), and to the wild beasts that were with Jesus (cf. Ps. 22:12–21; Isa. 13:21–22; for their absence was a sign of God's blessing [Isa. 35:9; Ezek. 34:23–28]).

Mark does not record any triumphant conclusion to the temptation— for him the opposition of evil did not cease.[7] Satan is not prominent in this Gospel, but Mark does emphasize Jesus' ongoing conflict with evil: eleven times he speaks of the "unclean spirits" who confronted Jesus (Matthew has the term three times, and Luke five). These spirits could recognize Jesus as God's Holy One (1:24) or as the Son of God (3:11), but they were invariably

in opposition to him. "What have I to do with you?" said one of them to Jesus and added, "I adjure you by God, don't torment me" (5:7). Again, the opposition may be said to come from "demons" (e.g., 1:34, 39); evil may take many forms. But always Mark has the thought that Jesus was triumphant. Constantly he cast the spirits out. The good news includes the present and final defeat of evil.

We should not pass lightly over the way Mark depicts discipleship. The rabbis had their disciples, but they did not select them; the would-be disciple sought out a teacher and attached himself to him. He did this so that he might learn and perhaps in time even surpass his teacher. In contrast to this, Jesus called his disciples; on occasion he sent those who wanted to be his disciples off to work elsewhere (5:18–19). The rabbis debated with their disciples; he did not with his. And, above all, he was Lord; being a disciple of Jesus meant leaving everything to follow him (1:16–20; 2:14; 10:28–30; 13:12–13). Jesus was not just another rabbi; he was unique, and being his disciple had a flavor all its own.

The gospel centers on Jesus, and in his portrayal of his Master Mark makes two points strongly: Jesus was completely human (he showed human limitations and was treated like a man), and he was the strong Son of God (he did miracles and possessed supernatural knowledge). Some studies of Mark's Gospel have so stressed one of these

---

[7] Ernest Best, however, argues from 3:27 that Mark means us to see that Jesus completely defeated Satan at the temptation; the rest was no more than mopping up operations (*The Temptation and the Passion* [Cambridge, 1965], 15). By contrast, James M. Robinson sees the conflict with evil as continuing throughout the Gospel, notably in the exorcisms (*The Problem of History in Mark* [London, 1957], 35). He sees the decisive victory in the resurrection (p. 53), though the conflict still continues in the history of the church (pp. 60, 67). Ulrich W. Mauser is another to see the conflict as continuing throughout Jesus' ministry: "The whole gospel is an explanation of how Jesus was tempted" (*Christ in the Wilderness* [London, 1963], 100).

aspects of the person of Jesus as to ignore the other. But both are important, and we miss something of what this Gospel is teaching unless we see this. It is essential for an understanding of what Mark is saying that we see Jesus as truly a man—as the strong Son of God become man.

JESUS THE MAN

There can be no doubt about the lowly humanity of Jesus in the second Gospel. We see this, for example, in the account of his reception at Nazareth (6:1–6). Local people, astonished at his wisdom and his "works of power" (*dynameis*), asked, "Is not this the carpenter, the son of Mary and brother of James and Joses and Judas and Simon? And are not his sisters here with us?" (v. 3). There are difficulties here; some manuscripts read "the son of the carpenter," and there is the problem of why Jesus is called "the son of Mary." But, as Anderson puts it, "The whole thrust of the question in verse 3 is to show that those who ask it *cannot believe because of the all-too-human connexion of Jesus with an ordinary family.*"[8] Mark says that Jesus could do no mighty work there except heal a few sick folk, and the account ends with Jesus' amazement at his townsfolk's unbelief (v. 6). This is a very human Jesus, knowing rejection as in some way all members of the human race do.

So, too, we should notice Jesus' reaction when the Pharisees asked him for a sign from heaven (8:11–12). Two things are significant: first the definite refusal ("No sign will be given to this generation"); Jesus did not want to appear as a divine worker of wonders. Second, there is the fact that Jesus "sighed deeply," a very human reaction. The attitude of the disciples to Jesus should not be overlooked either, for example, when they reproached him in their terror: "Teacher, don't you care that we are perishing?" (4:38). To talk to him in this way is certainly to treat him like a man. And Mark records some very human emotions of Jesus, emotions that include indignation (10:14) and anger and grief (3:5). Toward the end of his Gospel Mark says that Jesus was ignorant of the time of the *parousia* (13:32).

But most important of all is the emphasis he puts on the death of Jesus. For one thing, there are Jesus' prophecies; he spoke of his rejection by the elders, the chief priests, and the scribes, and he foretold his death (8:31; 9:31; 10:33–34, 45). And Mark devotes about a fifth of his Gospel to Christ's death and resurrection. He records the cry of dereliction: "My God, my God, why did you abandon me?" (15:34). There are mysteries in this saying, but it certainly points to a very human Jesus. Perhaps we should include here also the rather strange verbs used in reference to Jesus in Gethsemane (14:33), for they point to human limitation.[9] The words of Jesus show that his death and resurrection were central for him, and the structure of the whole book shows that they were central for Mark. We do not understand what Mark is doing unless we see that basically he is writing about the Cross. He is, in a sense, a theologian of the Cross. The center of gravity of his theology is the Cross.

---

[8] Anderson, *The Gospel of Mark*, 159 (Anderson's italics).

[9] The expression is ἐκθαμβεῖσθαι καὶ ἀδημονεῖν. Karl Barth sees ἐκθαμβεῖσθαι as signifying "a horror which gripped Him in face of the frightful event which confronted Him," and ἀδημονεῖν "a foreboding from which there was no escape, in which He could find no help or comfort" (*Church Dogmatics* 4:1 [Edinburgh, 1956]: 265).

The Cross was at the heart of Paul's gospel, as we have seen.[10] But Paul devotes very little space to the earthly life of Jesus (so little that some critics have thought that he had only a few scraps of information about it).[11] By contrast, Mark roots the Cross in history.[12] He says a good deal about what Jesus did, and his Gospel moves along at a lively pace. There is a vividness about his narrative, and his accounts tend to be fuller and more lifelike than their equivalents in Matthew or Luke, even though his Gospel is so much shorter than theirs.

Mark omits most of Jesus' teaching (chs. 4 and 13 are the only considerable stretches of teaching in his whole Gospel). But he puts emphasis on the fact that Jesus was a teacher; he uses the word "teacher" twelve times (the same number as the much longer Matthew), and the verb "to teach" seventeen times (a higher number than in any other book in the New Testament, except Luke, which also has seventeen; Matthew uses the verb only fourteen times). He seems to be avoiding giving the impression that Christianity means following a list of precepts given by an authoritative teacher, while yet retaining the authoritativeness. In the rabbinic literature there is emphasis on the importance of what is taught, not on the importance of the rabbi who taught

it. But for Mark it is the Teacher who is supremely important. It is who Jesus was and what he did that matters so much to him.

A number of scholars have speculated that some early Christians accepted the teaching of Paul, but, emphasizing the apostle's minimal treatment of the life of Jesus, thought of the Christ as a heavenly being who had little or no contact with earthly reality (like some of the "saviors" in the Hellenistic religions of that day). It is Mark's achievement to take the accounts of Jesus' life and teaching that were in circulation in the early church and unite them to the passion narrative in such a way as to show that the earthly life of Jesus is important in itself and is an integral part of the process whereby God intervened in human life to bring salvation to sinners.[13]

We need not accept the extreme position in order to see that there is a valuable truth here. Mark did bring out the importance of the earthly life of Jesus in a way that is not apparent in the Pauline writings, and for this the whole church has been grateful through the centuries.

THE SON OF GOD

Mark opens his Gospel with a reference to Jesus Christ as "Son of God"

---

[10] Ralph P. Martin brings out the link with Paul: "Mark appears as the Pauline theologian of the cross" (*Mark: Evangelist and Theologian* [Exeter, 1972], 13).

[11] Paul does in fact say more about the earthly life than is usually realized (see above pp. 41–42). But it is undeniable that in comparison with the Gospels he says little.

[12] Curiously Ernst Käsemann says, "The historical life of Jesus is no longer the focus of Mark's attention. It merely provides the stage on which the God-man enters the lists against his enemies. The history of Jesus has become mythicized" (*Essays on New Testament Themes* [London, 1964], 22). This is surely to miss a main emphasis of Mark.

[13] Willi Marxsen emphasizes this. "Mark's Gospel is the confluence of two streams coursing through primitive Christian preaching. One is conceptual-theological, represented, e.g., by Paul. The other is kerygmatic-visual, using the so-called material of synoptic tradition. Mark brings the two streams together. . . . This fusion is Mark's achievement and cannot be too highly prized" (*Mark the Evangelist* [Nashville, 1969], 147–48). This is surely a valid point. But I cannot accept other aspects of Marxsen's position—for example, his view that in this Gospel "Galilee is not primarily of historical but rather of theological significance as the locale of the imminent Parousia" (p. 92).

(1:1), and when he comes to the climax of his writing, he tells us that the centurion at the cross said at Jesus' death, "Truly, this man was God's Son" (15:39). "The Son of God" is thus the first and the last of the titles used of Jesus in this Gospel. As we saw in the section on Paul, the expression can mean much or little. It may be used of believers as members of the heavenly family, though Mark does not have this particular usage (but cf. 2:5). The centurion at the cross may have meant the expression in some such way, but Philip H. Bligh has a strong argument that he had in mind that "*this* man, not Caesar, is the Son of God."[14]

Mark surely recorded the words because he saw the fuller meaning. The term can point to one who stands in such a relationship to God as nobody else does. There can be little doubt that when he uses the expression of Jesus, Mark gives it all the meaning it can take.[15]

Twice only he records a divine voice, and both times God calls Jesus "Son." Mark is saying that God tells us how we should see Jesus. At his baptism the voice "from heaven" (clearly the voice of God) said, "You are my beloved Son; in you I am well pleased" (1:11). This cannot be understood as the accolade given to someone who is merely a good man; God's "beloved Son" is someone special. We see this again on the Mount of the Transfiguration,

when the voice from the cloud said, "This is my beloved Son, listen to him" (9:7). For a moment three chosen disciples—Peter, James, and John— had a glimpse of the glory of God's Son, a glory not manifested throughout his earthly life, but real for all that. Mark leaves us in no doubt about it.

Mark records this truth from another angle when he tells his readers that evil spirits recognized Jesus. When they saw him, evil spirits "used to fall down before him and cry out saying, 'You are the Son of God!'" (3:11; the tenses of the verbs point to continuing action). A particular case is that of the Gerasene demoniac, who addressed our Lord as "Jesus, Son of God most high" (5:7). He recognized the power of Jesus, for he disclaimed anything that linked him with Jesus and he realized that Jesus might deal sharply with him. Jesus had the power to do so.

The disciples do not use this title in Mark (nor in Luke; occasionally they do in Matthew). Nor does Jesus, though once he speaks of himself as "the Son," saying that no one knows the time of the *parousia*, "not even the angels in heaven, nor the Son. . ." (13:32). The article *the* puts him in a special relationship to the Father. Again, when the high priest questioned Jesus by asking, "Are you the Christ, the Son of the Blessed One?" he replied, "I am. . ." (14:61–62).[16] Clearly he saw himself as standing in a relation-

---

[14] *ExpT* 80 [1968–69]: 53. JB, NEB translate "a Son of God," but NIV, RSV have "the Son. . . ." If Colwell's rule that definite nouns that precede the verb normally lack the article (*JBL* 52 [1933]: 12–21) holds here, the correct translation is "the Son," not "a Son." Nigel Turner classes this passage among those where the predicate is definite (*A Grammar of New Testament Greek*, 183). We should understand the Greek to mean "the Son of God."

[15] Cf. William L. Lane: "[Mark] clearly intended his readers to recognize in the exclamation a genuine Christian confession, in the consciousness that these words are true in a higher sense than the centurion understood" (*The Gospel According to Mark* [Grand Rapids, 1974], 576).

[16] Instead of ἐγώ εἰμι, some MSS read σὺ εἶπας ὅτι ἐγώ εἰμι (Θ f13 565 700 Or). Taylor accepts this reading on the strength of its attestation and because it would also account for the text of Matthew and Luke, and it illustrates the note of reserve regarding Messiahship so frequently found in Mark (*The Gospel According to St. Mark*, 568). But the attestation of ἐγώ εἰμι is stronger and the other reading

ship to the Father that is shared by no one else. This is a distinctively Christian view; Jewish sources do not use "Son of God" when they speak of the Messiah.[17]

THE SON OF MAN

Throughout the four Gospels Jesus constantly referred to himself as "the Son of man." This expression occurs over eighty times and is, with two exceptions, used only by Jesus himself. The one exception in the Gospels is in John 12:34; the crowd, after Jesus had used the expression, echoed the phrase when they asked, "Who is this Son of man?" The only passage where it is used by anyone else is Acts 7:56; the dying Stephen saw the heaven opened and the Son of man standing at God's right hand. It is found in all four Gospels and in each of the sources that critics discern. There seems no doubt that Jesus used the expression and used it often.

What it means is not easy to determine. It is not a natural expression in Greek, but is a literal rendering of the Aramaic *bar-nasha,* which would normally be understood as "man." There are some passages where this meaning is possible, but not many. Jesus is clearly referring to himself when he uses the term. There is an enormous literature on the subject, and it cannot be said that there is anything approaching unanimity on the meaning of the term.[18] But many see it as originating ultimately from the scene described in Daniel 7, where "one like a son of man" came with the clouds of heaven, "approached the Ancient of Days and was led into his presence." To this significant figure "was given authority, glory and sovereign power; all peoples, nations and men of every language worshiped him. His dominion is an everlasting dominion that will not pass away, and his kingdom is one that will never be destroyed" (Dan. 7:13–14). The Son of man here is in close relationship to God, and his sovereignty over mankind is clear. There is not much evidence for seeing this figure as the Messiah, and what there is is disputed.[19]

---

may have arisen because of conformity to Matthew's reading. Lane accepts the shorter reading and comments, "The Sanhedrin would understand Jesus' words as an unqualified claim to messianic dignity. The prophecy and the clear response 'I am' are mutually supportive" (*The Gospel According to Mark,* 537).

[17] See J. D. Kingsbury, *The Christology of Mark's Gospel* (Philadelphia, 1983), 36–37; he notes a possible exception in some texts at Qumran. D. E. Nineham comments on this Gospel: "Anyone who reads the Gospel straight through will recognize that it is as Son of God rather than as teacher or prophet that St. Mark presents Our Lord" (*The Gospel of St. Mark* [Harmondsworth, 1963], 48).

[18] In a study like this it is not possible to survey the extensive literature. But perhaps we should notice Matthew Black's appraisal of the views of Barnabas Lindars (who denies that "Son of man" is a title and who sees only nine authentic occurrences of the term in sayings of Jesus) in *ExpT* 95 (1983–84): 200–206. Concerning Mark there is the important study by Morna D. Hooker, *The Son of Man in Mark* (London, 1967).

[19] The expression is used in the "Similitudes of Enoch" (chs. 37–71 of 1 Enoch), but the date and the relevance of this are disputed. C. H. Dodd is not certain of the precise meaning of the three Ethiopic expressions translated "Son of man," nor of whether they refer to "the Elect One" or to "the elect" in general, nor whether the Similitudes are pre-Christian or later. He concludes, "The Similitudes are in any case an isolated and probably eccentric authority for the association of the title 'Son of Man' with an 'apocalyptic Messiah,' and cannot be used with any confidence to elucidate the New Testament" (*According to the Scriptures* [London, 1957], 116–17). E. Isaac reports a consensus of "the members of the *SNTS* Pseudepigrapha Seminar" that "the Similitudes were Jewish and dated from the first century A.D." (James H. Charlesworth, ed., *The Old Testament Pseudepigrapha* [New York, 1983], 1:7). But Isaac sees 1 Enoch as "influential in molding New Testament doctrines concerning the nature of the Messiah, the Son of Man . . ." (p. 10).

It seems that Jesus used the expression to bring out certain aspects of the work he came to do. I have examined the term elsewhere, and it may suffice if I reproduce my conclusion:[20] "Why then did Jesus adopt this term? We might answer, firstly because it was a rare term and one without nationalistic associations. It would lead to no political complications. 'The public would . . . read into it as much as they apprehended of Jesus already, and no more.'[21] Secondly, because it had overtones of divinity. J. P. Hickinbotham goes as far as to say, 'The Son of Man is a title of divinity rather than humanity.'[22] Thirdly, because of its societary implications. The Son of man implies the redeemed people of God. Fourthly, because it had undertones of humanity. He took upon Him our weakness."

As the term is used in Mark, we may discern three groups of sayings. The first speak of Jesus' authority, as the Son of Man, in his public ministry. In these sayings, Jesus spoke with authority in areas where his hearers would not have expected him to say what he said. Thus, he told the paralyzed man lowered before him: "Your sins are forgiven." When people objected to this as blasphemy, Jesus said, "The Son of man has authority on earth to forgive sins" and then he did the miracle to demonstrate the fact (Mark 2:5, 10–12). The Son of man was performing a function that everyone recognized as divine, and this was, of course, the point of the objection. On another occasion Jesus declared that "the Son of man is Lord even of the sabbath" (Mark 2:28). The sabbath was insti-tuted by God (Gen. 2:3; Exod. 20:8); to claim authority over a divine institution was to make a high claim indeed.

A second group of passages looks to the end of this age and sees the Son of man as an authoritative figure then. Of the person who is ashamed of Christ and his words in this generation, Jesus said, "The Son of man will be ashamed of him when he comes in the glory of his Father with the holy angels" (8:38). Jesus also speaks of the Son of man as "coming in clouds with great power and glory" (13:26) and in response to a question from the high priest replies, "You will see the Son of man seated at the right hand of the power and coming with the clouds of heaven" (14:62), a saying that the high priest regarded as blasphemy and that led immediately to Jesus' condemnation by the Sanhedrin (vv. 63–64). Such passages express the certainty that Jesus would be vindicated in due course in the heavenly sphere even though he might be rejected by leaders here on earth.

There can be no doubt that the passages in these two groups ascribe to Jesus the highest imaginable place. But there is a third group, and the fascinating thing about the way Mark records the use of this title is that in this, the largest group (containing nine out of Mark's fourteen uses of the expression), it refers to lowliness and suffering. Thus immediately after Peter has made the memorable declaration, "You are the Christ," Jesus began to teach the disciples "that the Son of man must suffer many things . . ." (8:29–31). This marks a turning point.[23] Up till now Mark has had a good deal to say

---

[20]*The Lord From Heaven*[2] (Downers Grove, 1974), 28.

[21]Reginald H. Fuller, *The Mission and Achievement of Jesus* (London, 1954), 106.

[22]*Chmn* 58 (1943–44): 54.

[23]Oscar Cullmann speaks of "the unique significance" of Peter's confession in that "here for the *first* time the disciples speak with Jesus with regard to what he is in their eyes. Here it is seen that the arrangement of material, which of course is due to the evangelists, can become important in giving

about Jesus' miracles. There are at least fifteen of them, and in addition there are passages that refer in general to his healing sick people. But from this point on there are very few (the boy who had fits [9:14–27], blind Bartimaeus [10:46–52], the fig tree [11:13–14, 20–21]). Up till now Mark has used the title "the Son of man" twice; from this point on, however, he uses it twelve times. And it is especially significant that there is now an increasing emphasis on the instruction of the disciples and specifically on teaching about the death of Jesus.

Shortly after the Transfiguration we find Jesus teaching the disciples: "The Son of man is betrayed into the hands of men and they will kill him" (9:31). He will be "delivered up to the high priests and to the scribes, and they will condemn him to death" (10:33). Then there is this wonderful saying: "The Son of man did not come to be served but to serve, and to give his life a ransom for many" (10:45). The death of the Son of man is not a disaster, but an act of service in which he liberates his people from the bondage into which sin has brought them. The ransom is the price paid to deliver from slavery or the sentence of death; this is a saying that thrills one with the thought of the price Christ paid and of the freedom into which he bought us.

All this is in line with the will of God, for in the Upper Room Jesus could assure the disciples that "the Son of man goes as it is written of him." Prophecy showed that this was God's plan. That does not mean that Judas, the betrayer, was guiltless, for Jesus went on to say, "But woe to that man through whom the Son of man is betrayed" (14:21). Then in the Garden of Gethsemane, when Jesus came to the sleeping disciples for the third time, he said, "The hour has come; look, the Son of man is betrayed into the hands of sinners" (14:41).

From all this it is clear that Jesus' use of the expression in Mark's Gospel brings out two things: his majesty and his lowliness.[24] It is the genius of this Gospel to combine and emphasize these two things. Jesus is supremely great, and the Son of man sayings make this clear. But his greatness does not consist of power and majesty and the like; it is seen in his death to save sinners. That is the great truth that is at the heart of this Gospel and at the heart of the gospel.

THE CHRIST

As we saw when studying Paul, "Christ" means "anointed" and the term was used of the great One whom God would send in due course to be a deliverer in a very special sense. The term has become so much part of the Christian vocabulary (together with its Hebrew equivalent, "Messiah") that we would expect it to have been used often of Jesus during his lifetime.

---

significance to the individual narrative. It is, so to say, a commentary on the part of the evangelist" (*Peter: Disciple, Apostle, Martyr* [London, 1962], 180). Some scholars argue that Caesarea Philippi does not really mark a critical point in Jesus' ministry. But there can be no doubt that Mark writes of it as having great significance. For him it was a major turning point.

[24] Morna D. Hooker stresses the importance of authority in Mark's use of the term: "All are expressions of this authority, whether it is an authority which is exercised now, which is denied and so leads to suffering, or which will be acknowledged and vindicated in the future" (*The Son of Man in Mark* [London, 1967], 180). She sees Jesus' use of the term as expressing his certainty of future vindication, whereas for the early church the vindication had already taken place in the resurrection and exaltation. Thus the term is common in the speech of Jesus and almost totally absent outside the Gospels (pp. 190–91).

This proves not to have been the case. Mark has the term only seven times in his entire Gospel. We may conjecture that Jesus discouraged the use of the term during his lifetime because of the way it was used in the Palestine of his day. He was not the Messiah in the sense in which people generally understood the term, and to use the title would accordingly invite misunderstanding.[25] But he *was* the Christ, the Messiah, and it is apparent from the opening words of the Gospel of Mark, "The beginning of the gospel of Jesus Christ" (1:1). The whole book is about the good news of Jesus, and Jesus truly is God's Messiah.

Quite early Mark speaks of Jesus as expelling demons from certain sufferers and adds the interesting information that Jesus "did not allow the demons to speak because they knew him" (1:34). Some MSS add: "to be the Christ"; if this addition is genuine, we have an eighth occurrence of the term. But whether it is accepted or not, it gives us the sense of it. There was that about Jesus that was known to the denizens of the spirit world, evil though they might be, a reality that was not apparent to the people of Galilee. Had they heard the demons speaking of him as he really was, they would have misunderstood. It was better that they not be told.

Wilhelm Wrede pointed out this "Messianic secret," and it has been a matter for discussion ever since.[26] The demon-possessed recognized Jesus, but they were commanded to be silent (1:25, 34; 3:12; cf. 5:6-7). He often discouraged people from telling of the great things he did for them (e.g., 1:44; 5:43; 7:36), and there are occasions when he withdrew from public view, perhaps to conceal himself (1:35-38; 7:24; 9:30). Jesus gave the disciples special, private instruction (4:10-13; 7:17-23; 9:28-29; 10:32-34; 13:3ff.). Wrede saw the "secret" as a pattern imposed on the material by Mark. He held that Jesus never claimed to be the Messiah, the post-Easter church firmly believed he was, and Mark then justified the church by saying that Jesus really did claim to be the Messiah but kept it secret.

Very few accept Wrede's position these days, but most see it as the starting point for discussions of the secrecy motif. The subject is complicated by the fact that, while Jesus did sometimes enjoin secrecy, there were occasions when he demanded the opposite. Thus he commanded the healed Gerasene demoniac, "Go home to your friends and tell them what the Lord has done for you" (5:19). Again, the healing of a lame man was done in such a way as to invite publicity, for Jesus introduced the miracle with the words "in order that you may know that the Son of man has power on earth to forgive sins. . ." (2:10). It is not easy to see how miracles like the feeding of the multitudes could be anything other than public. Mark is describing a ministry of Jesus in which he "could not be hidden" (7:24). H. Räisänen speaks of

---

[25] Oscar Cullmann thinks that "according to the Gospel tradition Jesus saw the hand of Satan at work in the contemporary Jewish conception of the Messiah" (*The Christology of the New Testament* [London, 1959], 124). He sees this as the probable explanation of Wrede's "messianic secret" (see below), and holds that Jesus "showed extreme reserve toward the *title* Messiah" (p. 126).

[26] This is illustrated by the fact that Christopher Tuckett has gathered nine essays from recent writing on the topic, covering a wide range of opinion, and has furnished a comprehensive introduction in which he outlines many contributions to the subject (*The Messianic Secret* [London and Philadelphia, 1983]).

"the tension which exists in the Gospel between secrecy and openness,"[27] and he certainly points to a reality.

We should also bear in mind that the secrecy motif appears in other places besides the exorcisms and the healing miracles. Thus when Peter spoke of Jesus as the Christ, Jesus "seriously enjoined them that they tell no one about him" (8:30). Passing through Galilee, Jesus did not want anyone to know of it (9:30). And Mark makes it clear that even the disciples often did not understand the meaning of Jesus' teaching (e.g., 8:17–20, 33).

Clearly Mark's usage is complex. Wrede's view has been subjected to criticism from a variety of angles, but perhaps most important is the point made by Vincent Taylor: "Far from being an editorial device imposed upon tradition, it is an integral part of the material itself."[28] He sees "the clue to the 'Messianic Secret'" as "Jesus' own sense of His Messianic task. With that destiny unfulfilled, and to undiscerning minds, He could neither deny nor admit that He was the Messiah."[29] J. D. G. Dunn goes so far as to say, "We are now in a position to stand Wrede's line of reasoning on its head,

for our conclusion thus far is that certain elements of that motif are clearly *historical;* that is, that the Messianic character of the tradition is not the result of Mark's redaction, but of pre-Markan but postresurrection Christian theology—it belongs to the incidents themselves."[30] Some scholars continue to hold that Jesus did not think of himself as the Messiah, but the evidence is rather that he did claim messiahship but did not understand this in the same way as the Jews of the day did. To claim the title openly would have been to invite misunderstanding, since people would take the term in their way, not his.[31]

Jesus did not reject the title "Christ" when Peter used it of him (8:29). Indeed, he used it himself, as when he spoke of giving a cup of water "in the name because you are Christ's" (9:41).[32] But he did not do this often. Jesus did, however, discuss the scribal interpretation of the Christ as "the Son of David"; he posed a question as to how it was possible for the Christ to be both David's Son and his Lord (12:35–37; no answer is given). In the Olivet Discourse, Jesus said that people would be saying, "Here is the Christ,"

---

[27] Tuckett, *The Messianic Secret,* 138.

[28] *ExpT* 49 [1947–48]: 149.

[29] Ibid., p. 151. In a later article he writes, "Jesus is the Messiah all the days of His ministry, but He cannot accept popular acclamation because He knows that He is the Messiah only as He suffers, dies, rises again, and returns as Lord to His own" (*ExpT* 65 [1953–54]: 250).

[30] *TynBul* 21 [1970]: 110.

[31] Cf. Ulrich Luz: "The secrecy motif embraces different contents and indicates theologically two different things: the miracle secret points to the power of Jesus' miracles which cannot remain hidden because it is the sign of the messianic age; the messianic secret qualifies the nature of Jesus' messiahship which must be understood kerygmatically, i.e. from the perspective of the cross and resurrection, if it is to be really understood . . . the messianic secret warns against interpreting the historical Jesus independently of the cross and resurrection because any such understanding of Jesus' authority can only have the character of a satanic temptation" (Tuckett, *The Messianic Secret,* 87).

[32] The Greek means literally "in name that (or, because) you are Christ's." It is an unusual expression and has led to textual variants, with some scholars denying that Mark used the term "Christ" here. Thus Lane thinks Mark wrote "on the ground that you are mine" (*The Gospel According to Mark,* 342n.66). Anderson, however, accepts it and sees "considerable stress on the awkward Greek phrase." He holds that "Mark possibly thinks that the loyal Christian disciple must be completely satisfied with the most insignificant service, even as God himself is content with those who offer it" (*The Gospel of Mark,* 237).

or "There he is" (13:21). This points to messianic speculations as continuing, but Jesus sees those who engage in them as having the wrong approach.

The other two occurrences of "Christ" in Mark are on the lips of Jesus' opponents. The high priest asked Jesus, "Are you the Christ, the Son of the Blessed?" to which Jesus replied, "I am" and went on to refer to his appearance at the end of the age (14:61–62). Jesus' explicit acceptance of the title is not to be overlooked. The mockers called to the crucified Jesus, "Let the Christ, the King of Israel, come down now from the cross, so that we may see and believe" (15:32). Mark records no response.

From all this it is plain that Mark sees Jesus as indeed the Messiah. He does not emphasize it, but this truth is there. We understand neither Mark nor Jesus unless we see this.

THE KINGDOM OF GOD

It is clear from the Synoptists that Jesus' favorite topic in his teaching was the kingdom of God. This is much more prominent in Matthew and Luke than in Mark,[33] but Mark's treatment of the subject is not without interest. Quite early he tells us that Jesus came preaching the gospel of God and saying, "The time has been fulfilled and the kingdom of God has come near; repent and believe in the gospel" (1:14–15). The kingdom is thus closely bound up with the good news and with the coming of Jesus; it is when Jesus comes that the kingdom has come near. And this coming demands from people the response of repentance and faith.

The Greek term *basileia* (like the Hebrew *malkuth* or the Aramaic *malku*) means not so much a realm as a reign; it is not an area or a group so much as God in action. It points to God at work in people. The kingdom, Jesus says, belongs to children and those like them (10:14–15).[34] Only one who receives the kingdom as a child does will enter it. The qualities in children that invite the comparison appear to be those of helplessness and insignificance, perhaps also implicit trust and simplicity.[35] A little child is quite helpless and in the ancient world was seen as unimportant.[36] And a child trusts wholeheartedly. So must it be with those who commit themselves to the kingdom of

---

[33] Mark refers 14 times to the kingdom of God, Matthew speaks of "the kingdom of heaven," "the kingdom of God," and the like 46 times (plus twice of the kingdom of the Son and once of believers). Luke refers 34 times to God's kingdom, 4 times to that of Christ, and once to the kingdom given to his followers.

[34] The genitive τῶν τοιούτων denotes possession, "belongs to such as these" (NIV, RSV et al.), not "consists of such." Vincent Taylor comments further, "Of great interest and importance is the concurrence of the statement that the Kingdom belongs to children with the command ἄφετε τὰ παιδία ἔρχεσθαι πρός με. The implication is not far distant that in a true sense Jesus Himself is the Kingdom" (*The Gospel According to St. Mark*, 423).

[35] Sherman E. Johnson notes the view that "a normal child lives by grace, not works; he does not think that he must earn his parents' love and care by flattery or good behavior but accepts them naturally and responds spontaneously with his affection"; he adds the possibility "that Jesus thinks of the unsophistication and freshness of the child, whose world is new and filled with marvels" (*A Commentary on the Gospel According to St. Mark* [London, 1960], 172).

[36] Cf. F. Crawford Burkitt: "Apart from the Gospels, I cannot find that early Christian literature exhibits the slightest sympathy towards the young. . . . The young folk did well to shout, 'Hosanna to the Son of David!' in the Temple, for His voice is almost the only one for centuries that spoke of them with love and sympathy in the things of religion" (*The Gospel History and Its Transmission* [Edinburgh, 1907], 285–86). We should not take Jesus' attitude to children as a commonplace; it was revolutionary.

God. It is difficult for the rich to enter the kingdom (10:23–25), not so much because poverty is a virtue as because riches are always a temptation to materialism and self-reliance. The person who relies on his own strong right arm will never really trust God.

In the kingdom love is all-important. There was a scribe who recognized that the commandments to love God with all one's heart and one's neighbor as oneself are greater than all animal sacrifices, and of him Jesus said, "You are not far from the kingdom of God" (12:34).

There is a wholeheartedness about the service of Christ and of the kingdom (which amount to much the same thing) as we see from the teaching that it is better to remove hand or foot and so enter life than to go to hell. The same has been said about the eye: "It is better for you to enter the kingdom of God with one eye rather than having two eyes to be thrown into hell" (9:47). In addition to emphasizing the importance of a thoroughgoing commitment, these verses equate "life" with "the kingdom of God" and set both over against the eternal torment of hell. Jesus is speaking of something with eternal significance when he speaks of the kingdom.

Knowledge of the kingdom is not something obvious and open to all. Jesus explained his use of parables to "those around him with the Twelve" in these terms: "To you [you is emphatic] is given the mystery of the kingdom of God, but to those outside all things are in parables, so that seeing they may see and not understand. . ." (4:10–12).[37] Knowledge of the kingdom is a matter of revelation;[38] it is not at all obvious that in the Man from Nazareth we see the coming of God's own kingdom. This knowledge is "given"; it is not open to the natural man. The revelation comes to the childlike and the committed. The kingdom is not a matter of spectacular growth; Jesus went on to tell the parable of the seed growing secretly (4:26–29). That the kingdom is also like "a mustard seed" seems to mean that its beginnings are small, but its growth incomparably large (4:30–32). Mark tells us that Joseph of Arimathea was "awaiting" the kingdom (15:43), a statement we may take as revealing a typical attitude to the kingdom. It is quiet trust in God, not any spectacular achievement that brings about membership in the kingdom.

Mark sees the consummation of the kingdom as a future occurrence (14:25). But in some sense it is a present reality, for Jesus speaks of some standing by him who would not taste death "till they see the kingdom of God having come with power" (9:1). The precise meaning of these words has been hotly debated,[39] but Mark uses

---

[37] There has been a great deal of discussion of this passage. Some scholars think that "in parables" is not a reference to the parables Jesus told, but has a meaning like "in riddles"; some are perplexed by ἵνα ('so that') and suggest that it is equivalent to ὅτι or that it is used in an imperative sense, or that it is a mistranslation of an Aramaic term, and there are other views. For our present purpose it is not necessary to go into such questions. The meaning is surely something like that given by Taylor: "To the disciples it had been given to know the secret of the Kingdom, but to those without everything happened in riddles" (The Gospel According to St. Mark, 258).

[38] The word μυστήριον is used in the mystery religions of knowledge known only to the initiated, but in the New Testament it is knowledge that people cannot find out for themselves but that God has now made known.

[39] C. E. B. Cranfield finds the saying "one of the most puzzling in the gospels" (The Gospel According to Saint Mark, 285). He goes on to list seven possible interpretations in addition to the view that it shows that Jesus expected the parousia to take place very soon, and favors a reference to the Transfiguration.

them to lead into the account of the Transfiguration; and it seems that he wants us to see this as a preliminary manifestation of what the kingdom means.

The future consummation means a good deal to Mark. Teaching like that in the parables of the seed growing secretly and the mustard seed (4:26–32) emphasizes the glorious future. Perhaps one point of the parables is to contrast the small beginnings in the little group about Jesus with the world-wide church into which it would grow. But the main point is surely that the future consummation will far surpass anything seen on earth.

This main point is particularly clear in the eschatological discourse in chapter 13 in which Jesus speaks of his coming in due course "in clouds with great power and glory" (13:26). There will be signs preceding his coming (13:14ff.), but it will be unexpected for all that (13:35–37); even Jesus himself did not know when it would be (13:32). There is a problem in this statement of Jesus: "This generation will not pass away until all these things take place" (13:30). The best understanding of this language of imminence (both in Mark and elsewhere) is put succinctly by C. E. B. Cranfield: "In one sense the interval between the Ascension and the Parousia might be long or short; but there was a more important sense in which it could only be described as short; for this whole period is the 'last days'—the epilogue, so to speak, of history—since it comes after the decisive event of the life,

death, resurrection, and ascension of Christ."[40]

FAITH

What does Jesus look for in those who are prepared to follow him? We have already seen that his first demand was for repentance and faith (1:15), and this sets the pattern. Jesus did not ask for conventional conformity to codes of conduct. He demanded radical renewal, not the imitation of accepted models. His followers must repent— they must turn away from their sinful past; a few cosmetic alterations will not do. And in forsaking their past, they must trust Christ, they must believe. Faith becomes the habitual attitude, and it shines through all Jesus is saying. We should beware of taking this as obvious. It may well be the conventional thing after centuries of Christianity, but there seems to be no religion before Jesus that looked for faith in the deity.[41] The demand for faith in Jesus is a distinctive of the Christian way.

We see it in connection with the miracles of healing. Jesus could say, when healing was accomplished: "Your faith has saved you" (5:34; 10:52). Both noun and verb are important. Mark could have used a verb that simply meant "healed" (his vocabulary includes *therapeuō* [e.g., 1:34; 3:2] and *iaomai* [5:29]). Instead, he chose one that at least hints at a wider salvation. And, of course, faith is the fundamental Christian attitude. So we read that Jesus healed the paralytic in response to the faith his bearers showed (2:5), and

---

[40]*IB*, 3:275. He gives the meaning of the coming "in this generation" in these terms: "The meaning then is that the signs of the End which Jesus has described in *vv.* 5–23 will not be confined to a remote future: his hearers must themselves experience them, for they are characteristic of the whole period of the Last Times" (*The Gospel According to Saint Mark,* 409).

[41]Cf. Goppelt, "In the Hellenistic milieu of Jesus no religion did, in fact, solicit faith toward the deity" (*Theology of the New Testament,* 1:149); Gerhard Ebeling, "I know of no parallels to that in late Judaism" (*Word and Faith* [London, 1963], 238).

he encouraged Jairus with this reassurance: "Don't be afraid, only believe" (5:36). There is a noteworthy conversation with the father of the boy with "a dumb spirit" that threw him into fits. Jesus encouraged him by saying, "All things are possible to him who believes" (9:23), at which the man cried out, "I believe, help my unbelief" (v. 24). The healing shows that Jesus accepted this small faith and makes it clear that it is not spiritual giants for whom Christ looks, but humble people, people who will trust him, even though their faith is small.

Faith is the right attitude toward Jesus, but we should not misunderstand this, as though it meant that he was helpless when people did not believe in him. He could do no "mighty work" at Nazareth where the people did not believe in him, but Mark immediately adds that he healed a few sick people (6:5). The point is that Jesus was not a kind of "stunt man," continually compelling attention by spectacular works of wonder; he simply "could not" do miracles where this would be the interpretation put on his actions. But his power is not limited by people, for even in Nazareth he healed some. More commonly, however, he did his miracles in an atmosphere of faith, where people responded to who he was and would not see his miracles as the attempt to gain popularity by the use of the spectacular.

Jesus rebuked the disciples for their lack of faith (4:40; cf. 11:22). He makes it clear that the faith of "one of these little ones" is precious (9:42). This refers to children, but most agree that it also includes all the insignificant, the world's "little people." When such have faith in Jesus, that faith is to be respected. This has relevance for prayer, for in prayer faith is of the utmost importance (11:23–24).

But throughout this Gospel it is the faith that trusts the lowly Jesus in all of life that is desperately important. Mark is writing of a Jesus who did not conform to the specifications for a first-century hero.[42] He did not compel attention with spectacular achievements. He did miracles, it is true, but not to help the world's great ones, who would have given him wide publicity and would perhaps have heaped honors on him. Mostly he helped the poor and lowly and usually requested the healed to keep it quiet. The kind of miracle he did was not the kind that aroused wonder and stupefaction (like the miracles reported of Hellenistic wonder-workers). He did not frequent the corridors of power. Mark speaks of his ministry in Galilee and mentions his going to Jerusalem only at the time he was put to death. Mark sees Jesus as calling for a trust that persists in the face of rejection, danger, humiliation, and ultimately death.

Jesus is the strong Son of God, indeed, but he trod a lowly path. If we are to be his followers, we must see the glory in his lowly service and walk in the same way ourselves. People must trust; a "sign" will not be given (8:12). In Mark Jesus does "mighty works," but these are the outworking of what he is, not something extra thrown in to prove that he is divine. They do not compel belief. They did not do so at Nazareth, where the people recognized that he had done "such mighty works" (6:2) but rejected him. The people at the foot of the cross said that they would believe if Jesus came down (15:32). But that is not faith. That is

---

[42] Otto Borchert makes this very clear in his book *The Original Jesus* (London, 1933).

the way of the "false Christs" against whom Jesus warned his followers (13:21–22). For these false Christs, spectacular, glittering outward show was all-important. For Jesus it had no place. He looked for a faith that trusts him for what he is, no matter what the outward difficulties.

THE MEANING OF THE CROSS

We have seen that in this Gospel the Cross has the central place.[43] Here above all we see the truth behind Martin Kähler's frequently quoted statement that the Gospels are "passion narratives with extended introductions." By the way he structures his Gospel Mark leaves no doubt that it is the Cross that is central. He has given a good deal of space to it, and his whole book comes to its climax with this narrative. Mark sees the will of God as accomplished in the death of Jesus (cf. 14:36 and the use of *dei*, which shows that the death was "necessary" [8:31; 14:31]). This is so even though from another point of view that death was brought about by the malice of men.

Mark's arrangement of his material puts the account of the anointing at the beginning of the passion (14:3–9); Jesus went to his death as the Anointed One. Mark also puts the prophecy of the disciples' failure (14:26–31) immediately alongside the account of Gethsemane (14:32ff.); he contrasts the faithlessness of people with the faithfulness of Jesus—a faithfulness that cost a fearful price.

Throughout the narrative there is some emphasis on the theme of kingship (15:2, 9, 12, 17–18, 26, 32). This is a stronger emphasis than we find in Matthew or Luke and reminds us of a key thought of John. For Mark Jesus might be rejected and killed but in these events he was king; the readers must see him as such. Then as he hung on the cross there was a series of extraordinary happenings: the darkness (15:33), Jesus' two loud cries (15:34, 37), the tearing of the curtain in the temple (15:38), and the verdict of the centurion that Jesus was truly the Son of God (15:39). Mark makes it clear that this was not a normal death, not even a normal execution. On Calvary something very great and very significant took place. For the most part Mark is content simply to record what happened; he does not attempt to bring out what that significance was. But there are some sayings that bear further examination.

One is the "ransom" saying: "The Son of man did not come to be served but to serve, and to give his life a ransom for many" (10:45). I have examined this saying elsewhere, and it may be sufficient to refer to these discussions.[44] Jesus is saying that he will pay the price to set people free. "Ransom" was used of the price paid to free a prisoner of war or a slave or someone under sentence of death. He does not say from what he is freeing people, but in the context of this Gospel it is clearly freedom from sin and from a sinful way of life. Such freedom does not come easily or auto-

---

[43]"One of the most generally accepted axioms in the modern study of Mark's Gospel is that this evangelist is pre-eminently interested in Jesus' Passion. We may go further and claim that, in the light of a *redaktionsgeschichtlich* approach to Mark, this evangelist has imposed upon a mass of materials at his disposal a theological understanding of Jesus' ministry in terms of a preaching of the cross" (Martin, *Mark: Evangelist and Theologian,* 117).

[44]*The Apostolic Preaching of the Cross,* 3d ed. (London, 1965), 29–38; *The Cross in the New Testament* (Grand Rapids, 1965), 52–55.

matically. It demands a price, and that price Jesus paid. The ransom was paid "on behalf of [*anti*]" many, *anti* here having substitutionary force.[45]

Then there is the prayer in which Jesus accepts the will of the Father that he drink the "cup" (14:36). He does not explain what the cup is, but Old Testament passages show that the cup is "a metaphor for retributive punishment but here obviously implying suffering and death" (Anderson).[46] It is "the cup of the wrath of God" (Best).[47]

Mark's quotation (14:27) from Zechariah 13:7 is of interest, especially as Mark states, "I will smite the shepherd"—making it an act of God himself—whereas in the Old Testament the verb is imperative ("Strike the shepherd"). The emphasis is on the scattering of the disciples, but the divine action also speaks of judgment. We should probably see another expression of substitution: sinners should bear the judgment, but God places it on the Good Shepherd.

Mark tells us of the last meal Jesus had with his disciples. He says that Jesus took bread, broke it, and gave it to them, saying, "Take, this is my body." He gave thanks over a cup and gave it to them. They all drank from it, and Jesus said, "This is my blood of the [new] covenant that is poured out for many" (14:22–24). The Lord's Supper no doubt was familiar to all Mark's Christian readers, and he tells of its institution in a way that shows it commemorated the making of a covenant that fulfilled the prophecy of Jeremiah 31:31ff. It does not matter greatly whether we read the word "new" or not; any covenant that Jesus made was necessarily new. This covenant was brought into being by the blood of Jesus. The shedding of his blood was the means by which people would be brought into right relationship with God, and the means by which the new people of God would be brought into being.[48]

There is also the dreadful cry of dereliction, "My God, my God, why did you abandon me?" (15:34). As this is the only word from the cross that Mark records, it is evident that he saw it as important. In modern times the words have seemed so shocking that many have watered them down in one way or another. It has been suggested, for example, that Jesus was reciting Psalm 22 (of which they are the opening words), a psalm that ends on a note of trust. On this view he was simply commending himself to the Father.[49] Others agree that the words point to a breach with God, but see this as so unthinkable that they emend or reject the text altogether. But if we are to take Mark seriously, we must reckon with this saying.[50] Jürgen Moltmann insists on this. He holds that "the theology of

---

[45] *BAGD* gives the first meaning of ἀντί as "1. in order to indicate that one person or thing is, or is to be, replaced by another *instead of, in place of.*" Best quotes Barrett approvingly as seeing here "some idea of equivalence" (*The Temptation and the Passion*, 142–43). Cf. A. E. J. Rawlinson: "The phrase sums up the general thought of Is liii, and expresses the idea of a vicarious and voluntary giving of life" (*St Mark* [London, 1925], 147).

[46] *The Gospel of Mark*, 320.

[47] *The Temptation and the Passion*, 156.

[48] P. S. Minear sees this as essentially what the whole Gospel is about: "He tells the story of the inauguration of an eternal Covenant between Jesus and disciples of every generation. This story covered sixteen chapters, yet it also could be condensed into a dozen words: 'This is my blood of the covenant, which is poured out for many'" (*Saint Mark* [London, 1963], 35).

[49] See, for example, Nineham, *Saint Mark*, 428.

[50] Cf. Vincent Taylor: "It appears to be an inescapable inference that Jesus so closely identified Himself with sinners, and experienced the horror of sin to such a degree, that for a time the closeness

the cross must take up and think through to a conclusion this third dimension of the dying of Jesus in abandonment by God."[51]

I do not think that we can ever plumb the full meaning of this saying.[52] But at least we can say that the death of Jesus was a horror—a horror in which the close fellowship with the Father that had sustained him throughout his earthly life was broken. I do not know of any explanation that comes close to doing justice to these words other than one that insists that in his death Jesus was bearing the sins of the world. He was one with sinners. He took away their sin. He endured the separation from God that is the consequence of sin. And because he endured it, we who believe in him will never be abandoned by God.[53]

We should further notice the way Mark introduces his passion narrative and the way he rounds it off. Most discussions of chapter 13 take it as a more or less self-contained unit ("the little apocalypse") in which Mark gives expression to some significant eschatological teaching. But we should bear in mind that he has placed this chapter immediately before his passion narrative. The chapter is not a typical piece of Jewish apocalyptic as is often contended. It is true that it contains apocalyptic language, and this language is important. It makes it clear that the Jesus whose crucifixion Mark is about to narrate is the One who is to come in due course to usher in the end of all things. But the chapter contains many exhortations, and its main thrust concerns discipleship. As Cranfield has said, "Its purpose is not to impart esoteric information but to sustain faith and obedience."[54] Many things typical of apocalyptic are absent from this discourse, and many things that are present are not found in typical apocalypses.[55]

It seems that Mark has put this chapter in this place to make it clear that the One whose passion he is about to describe is the supremely great One, not some obscure nobody. As R. H. Lightfoot says, "Chapter 13 is undoubtedly designed by the evangelist as the immediate introduction to the Passion narrative, in the sense that as we read the story of the Passion in this gospel in its utter realism and unrelieved tragedy we are to remember always the person and office of Him of whom we read. He, who is now reviled, rejected, and condemned is none the less the supernatural Son of man."[56] The Jews did not understand who it was they were demanding be put to death; Mark will not let his readers make that mistake.

There has been much discussion of

of His communion with the Father was broken" (*Jesus and His Sacrifice* [London, 1939], 162). He thinks that we must ask what is implied by all this and goes on to say, "The implications are theological: the desolation is historic fact" (p. 163).

[51] *The Crucified God* (London, 1974), 162. Cf. Goppelt, "Jesus' death was vicarious atonement for all in terms of its essential structure because, by dying in accord with the will of God, he also took up for himself God's judgment decreed upon the wickedness of all" (*Theology of the New Testament*, 1:198).

[52] I have discussed the problem in *The Cross in the New Testament*, 42–49.

[53] Best sums up Mark's view of the passion in this way: "The Cross is judgment; this is seen in the rending of the veil and the darkness that came over the world at the time. The judgment is borne by Jesus, in that he drinks the cup of God's wrath, is the shepherd smitten, and is the one who is overwhelmed by the floods of baptism for men. His blood is shed for others as his life is given for them" (*The Temptation and the Passion*, 191).

[54] *The Gospel According to Saint Mark*, 388.

[55] I have examined this chapter in my *Apocalyptic* (London, 1973), 87–91.

[56] *The Gospel Message of St. Mark* (Oxford, 1962), 50–51.

whether this Gospel originally ended at 16:8. Some think that Mark wrote more but that his original ending has now been lost.[57] Even though verse 8 is a rather abrupt ending for a Gospel, most seem to agree that he intended to end his book at 16:8 (to which later writers have appended endings to make the Resurrection appearances clear-er).[58] William R. Farmer has argued that verses 9–20 belonged to the original Gospel, though they represent Mark's redactional use of older material.[59] Whatever the truth of the matter is, Mark leaves his readers in no doubt that the crucified[60] Lord has risen triumphant. For Mark the end is not stark tragedy, but strong triumph.

---

[57] W. L. Knox argues that 16:8 is an impossible ending for a book ('The Ending of St. Mark's Gospel," *HTR* 35 [1942]: 1–23).

[58] Ned B. Stonehouse points out that the opening of this Gospel is abrupt and reasons that we should not be surprised at something similar in the ending: "If Mark can be satisfied to narrate so little concerning the beginnings of the life of Jesus, there is nothing to compel him to treat the conclusion at length" (*The Witness of Matthew and Mark to Christ* [London, 1958], 117).

[59] *The Last Twelve Verses of Mark* (Cambridge, 1974).

[60] Kingsbury comments on the perfect tense: "Theologically, the truth Mark underscores by having the risen Jesus designated as the crucified one is that the resurrection does not 'undo' the crucifixion but, on the contrary, confirms the fact that Jesus' death on the cross is the decisive event of his ministry" (*The Christology of Mark's Gospel,* 134).

6

the gospel of matthew

Perhaps the first and most outstanding impression we get about the Gospel of Matthew when we turn to it from the Gospel of Mark is the very great increase in the amount of Jesus' teaching. Matthew has included almost all of the second Gospel in a writing one and a half times as long as Mark, and a good deal of the extra material is teaching. There are long sections: the Sermon on the Mount (chs. 5–7), the mission charge to the Twelve (ch. 10), the parables of the kingdom (ch. 13), life in the Christian community (ch. 18), and the *parousia* (chs. 24–25).[1] And whereas Mark has very few parables, Matthew has at least seventeen,[2] including a long connected section (ch. 13). Mark puts his emphasis on what Jesus did, but Matthew sees as very important also what Jesus said.[3]

There is also a difference in tone. Matthew is somewhat more reverential.

Thus he omits some references to Jesus' anger (Mark 3:5; 10:14), and he omits the accusation that Jesus was beside himself (Mark 3:21). Where Mark tells us that Jesus replied to the rich young ruler's "Good teacher" with "Why do you call me good? No one is good except one, namely God" (Mark 10:18), Matthew has "Why do you ask me about what is good? There is one who is good" (Matt. 19:17). Matthew is kinder to the Twelve, too. He sometimes omits references to their ignorance or bewilderment (e.g., Mark 9:6, 10, 32) and speaks of their privileged position (Matt. 13:16–17; cf. Mark 4:13). He includes incidents like the dreams of Joseph (1:20; 2:13, 19, 22), the Magi (2:12), Pilate's wife (27:19), the coin in the fish's mouth (17:27), Pilate's washing of his hands (27:24), the earthquake, the rending of the rocks, and the rising of dead saints at

---

[1] R. E. Nixon aptly remarks, "The first discourse is basically ethical, the second missionary, the third kerygmatic, the fourth ecclesiastical, and the last eschatological" (Donald Guthrie and J. A. Motyer, eds., *The New Bible Commentary Revised* [London, 1970], 813). At the end of each of these blocks of teaching Matthew has the formula "and it happened when Jesus finished these sayings" (7:28; 11:1; 13:53; 19:1; 26:1). This marks them out as significant divisions of his book.

[2] A good deal depends on what we class as parable; some include short parabolic sayings (for example, the blind leading the blind [15:14]), others insist on a story. A. M. Hunter notes varying totals ranging from thirty to sixty-two; his own answer is "about 60" (*Interpreting the Parables* [London, 1960], 11). Some will find more than seventeen in Matthew, but there cannot be any doubt about these.

[3] R. V. G. Tasker finds this Gospel "remarkable for the extent to which and the manner in which the ethical teaching of Jesus is presented" (*IBD*, 2:964).

the Crucifixion (27:51–53). How these are to be related to what we read in the other Gospels is a task for the exegete; here we simply notice their significance for what they reveal of Matthew's theological purpose. Matthew makes it clear that Jesus had an important place for the Twelve, that God guides people sometimes by dreams, and that God does things in this physical universe as he works out his purpose.

There is a "Jewishness" about this Gospel, as we see, for example, in Matthew's emphasis on the fulfillment of what is written in Scripture. So too Matthew refers to such Jewish matters as the temple tax (17:24) and phylacteries (23:5); he speaks of the validity of the law (5:18–19); and he says that the teaching (though not the example) of the scribes and Pharisees should be followed (23:2–3). His five great discourse sections invite comparison with the five books of Moses, though we must reject the inference sometimes drawn from this, that Matthew is depicting Jesus as the giver of a new law. For Matthew, as for the other Evangelists, it is gospel, not law, that is at the heart of the Christian way. But Matthew is certainly interested in the importance of Jesus' teaching; converts are not only to be baptized but to be taught to keep all Jesus' commands (28:20). From what he has written and the way he writes it, G. D. Kilpatrick

concludes that Matthew was "a Christian scribe,"[4] a conclusion with which most scholars agree. Matthew's "Jewishness" should not be stressed to the exclusion of another feature of this Gospel, its universalism (8:11–12; 12:21; 21:43; 28:16–20).

Throughout the long history of the church perhaps no Gospel has been more influential than Matthew. It was often thought to have been the first to be written, and its first place in the order when the Gospels were bound together gave it prominence. It was very widely used liturgically, and its careful arrangement, with groups of teachings put together (like the Sermon on the Mount) has been of great practical use.[5]

THE BEGINNING OF THE GOSPEL

Matthew's opening is unique; there is nothing like it in any of the other Gospels. With its cryptic heading and its long genealogy, it makes little appeal to the modern Westerner. But if we pass it by, we pass by something that Matthew clearly regarded as important. He begins with "Book of *genesis* of Jesus Christ, Son of David, son of Abraham." The meaning of *genesis* is not obvious. The word can mean "beginning" or "origin," and in 1:18 it clearly means "birth." But it can be used more or less in the sense of

---

[4] *The Origins of the Gospel According to St. Matthew* (Oxford, 1946), 135. Kilpatrick further says that Matthew's style "lacks the ruggedness of Mark or of St. Paul's Epistles, the brilliant mastery of Greek shown in the Epistle to the Hebrews, or the variety of imitation apparent in the Lucan writings. By comparison it is undistinguished, but neat, clear, and direct, possessing the character of serviceability rather than distinction" (pp. 136–37).

[5] Sherman E. Johnson speaks of Matthew as "this most influential of all Christian books." He adds, "The layman frequently says that John, or perhaps Luke, is his favorite of the four; yet it is probable that he will make actual use more often of Matthew, either for defence and controversy or for the upbuilding of his moral and spiritual life" (*IB*, 7:231). Krister Stendahl says of the prominence of this Gospel over seventeen centuries: "This fact may well have had deeper significance for the history and the theology of Christianity than will ever be properly assessed" (Matthew Black and H. H. Rowley, eds., *Peake's Commentary on the Bible* [London, 1980], 769).

"history" (as Gen. 2:4 LXX), and it can introduce a genealogy (Gen. 5:1). We could thus understand it here as a heading for chapter 1 ("the account of the birth of Jesus Christ"), or for the whole book ("the account or history of Jesus Christ"), or for the genealogy. Nothing much hinges on our decision, but, standing where it does, it looks like a heading for the whole book.

In this formal heading we should notice the formal title Jesus Christ, which occurs again in this whole Gospel only once (or perhaps twice); Matthew has "Jesus" 150 times and "Christ" 17 times, thus it is clear that he prefers the human name. We will look at the title "Son of David" in a later section; here it is enough to say that it points to the Davidic Messiah, the Messiah as King, while the reference to Abraham looks back to the origin of the Jewish nation, the people of God. Matthew is hinting at the new people of God, under the sovereignty of the Messiah, their King.

The genealogy that follows is structured into three divisions, each of fourteen generations. This is clearly symbolic, for some names are omitted to get the second group down to fourteen,[6] and there are only thirteen names in the third group (which covers a period of about five hundred years; it seems once more as though names have been omitted). It is not clear why the number fourteen was selected. Some have suggested that we should take fourteen (twice seven) as standing for two weeks; all told there would then be six weeks of people leading up to the seventh, the perfect age, the age of the

Messiah. We cannot rule this out altogether, for it was the sort of thing that some first-century writers did. But this does not seem to be Matthew's style. Elsewhere he has nothing of this sort.[7] What is clear is that he singles out certain high points in his genealogy, notably connected with Abraham, David, and the Exile. The name of Abraham will recall God's dealings with the patriarchs; that of David, all that "the Son of David" means; and the Exile is a significant reminder of judgment, a theme to which Matthew devotes considerable attention. The third group is interesting in that it consists of people who are largely unknown. While Matthew does not minimize the importance of Jesus' royalty, he is mindful of the fact that Jesus is "meek and lowly in heart" (11:29) and that he called many ordinary people to be his disciples. It is significant that the "little people" loom so large in this genealogy.

That Matthew includes four women is striking, for women were normally not included in genealogies. That there are four can probably be explained by the fact that in Jewish writings four women are often named as outstanding: Sarah, Rebecca, Rachel, and Leah. But it is not this quartet that Matthew names. Nor has he produced real or fictional names for wives for other members of his genealogy. We should see, then, that these four are important. Three of them were morally dubious. Tamar (v. 3) had a child by her father-in-law, Rahab (v. 5) was a prostitute, and Uriah's wife (v. 6) an adulteress. It is a sinful world we live in, and Matthew is writing about sin and salvation

---

[6] Three consecutive kings are missing from the second fourteen, Joash, Amaziah, Azariah (see 1 Chron. 3:11–12), as also is Jehoiakim (1 Chron. 3:15).

[7] Joachim Jeremias sees this as "very possible" but wonders why, if it is true, Matthew did not make his allusion clearer. He sees the symbolic meaning of the number rather in the fact that in Hebrew the letters of David's name have the numerical value of 14 (4 + 6 + 4). "In Jesus the number of David is completed for the third and last time" (*Jerusalem in the Time of Jesus* [London, 1969], 292, 292n.75).

and grace. He faces the fact that the Savior's ancestry included known sinners.

We should further notice that all four women were Gentiles, and this in a Jewish genealogy! Matthew is usually regarded as having written a rather Jewish Gospel, but he was well aware of the fact that the gospel of salvation is for all the world. The genealogy tells his readers that fact, if only they have eyes to see.

JOHN THE BAPTIST

Matthew tells us that John the Baptist came before Jesus and prepared the way for him. John was a stern ascetic (3:4; 11:18), and in accord with this his disciples practiced fasting (9:14). He was a prophet (11:9; 21:26), who called on people to repent (3:2). For John repentance meant not only sorrow over sins of the past but the producing of what he calls "fruit worthy of repentance" (3:8); those who responded in faith to his teaching were to live lives that accorded with repentance.[8] There is a strong ethical note in John's teaching.

But the main thrust of his preaching was that Another was to come. The first words Matthew records from this stern man of the desert are "Repent, for the kingdom of heaven has drawn near" (3:2). John was clear that he was to be followed by another, greater than he, "whose sandals," he said, "I am not worthy to carry. He will baptize you with the Holy Spirit and fire" (3:11). He speaks of preparing the way of the Lord, citing a prophecy that in the Old Testament referred to God and that he now uses of Jesus (3:3; cf. 11:10),

whose coming was the decisive happening. The same truth is brought out in Jesus' teaching that John was the Elijah of prophecy (11:14; 17:10–13; see Mal. 4:5).

John's was a significant function; Jesus later said of him that there was never a greater "among those born of women." Jesus went on, however, to say, "He that is least in the kingdom of heaven is greater than he" (11:11). The coming of Jesus marks the turning point. All the greatness of John mattered little alongside membership in the kingdom. Jesus made the same point when he said that "the Prophets and the Law prophesied until John" (11:13). Jesus does not belittle the magnificence and the depth of Old Testament religion. But that religion is simply the preliminary to something far greater. Now the kingdom of heaven replaces all the splendor of the former revelation. It is a breathtaking claim.

The theme of judgment runs through John's prophesying. He spoke of "the coming wrath" (3:7) and brought out its imminence with his reference to the axe at the root of the trees, a position indicating that the axe would shortly be used (3:10). He spoke of the One who would follow him as having his winnowing fan in his hand (to separate the wheat from the chaff), preparatory to putting the wheat into the barn, but burning up the chaff "with unquenchable fire" (3:12).

Judgment is an important feature of this Gospel, and it is fitting that this note be struck right at the beginning. Sin is a horrible evil, and the coming of the kingdom means the making of a way of salvation from sin through what Jesus would do, but it also means the punishment of unrepentant sinners.

---

[8]George E. Ladd sees the presence of an idea derived from the Old Testament. He says, " 'Conversion' expresses the idea better than repentance. 'Repentance' suggests primarily sorrow for sin; *metanoia* suggests a change of mind; the Hebrew idea involves the turning around of the whole man toward God" (*A Theology of the New Testament* [Grand Rapids, 1975], 38–39).

TEACHING ABOUT GOD

Matthew knows a mighty God, one who is ceaselessly active and who works his sovereign will—the living God (16:16; 26:63; cf. 22:32). More than sixty times this Evangelist appeals to the fulfillment of Scripture,[9] and every such fulfillment, of course, means that God has planned something, that he has spoken about it through his servants the prophets, and that he has now brought it to pass. It is a sufficient condemnation of the Sadducees that they did not know "the Scriptures nor the power of God" (22:29).

Right at the beginning of this Gospel we see something of the way God works. There is first the sending of the Christ, with some detail about the Virgin Birth. God acted in a special way to bring about a special purpose. When Joseph hesitated to marry Mary, God spoke to him in a dream (1:20). Matthew draws attention to the fulfillment of prophecy in this holy birth (1:22; see Isa. 7:14) and goes on to bring out the point that it all means "God with us" (1:23). The visit of the Magi is testimony both to the fact of the divine purpose and to God's willingness to reveal his purpose to Gentiles. Then, when Herod planned to kill the infant Christ, God intervened, sending the Magi home without their seeing the monarch again (2:12) and sending Joseph and Mary with the baby down to Egypt (2:13–15). In due course it was God who brought them back to Israel (2:19–21). And, just as he begins his Gospel with the activity of God, so Matthew ends it with the activity of God. God sent his angel to roll away the stone from Jesus' tomb (28:2). And disciples are to be baptized in the name of the Father, as well as of the Son and of the Spirit (28:19).

This sovereign God makes demands on his worshipers. People are warned that they cannot serve both God and mammon (6:24). The unity and indissolubility of marriage arises from the fact and order of God's creation (19:4–6). There are duties people owe to Caesar (governments), and there are duties they owe to God; let them not confuse the two (22:21). They are to do the will of God (7:21), to abandon the wide way that leads to destruction and enter through the narrow gate (7:13). They must not nullify the Word of God (15:6).

There are passages that point to the inevitability of judgment.[10] Judgment awaits the murderer (5:21), but also the person who is angry with his brother without good reason (5:22). To judge others is to invite judgment on oneself (7:1–2). There will be a recompense for all who do not forgive

---

[9] F. C. Grant has brief discussions of 61 Old Testament quotations in Matthew, "not counting innumerable echoes of single words and phrases which give Matthew's style its marked 'biblical'—i.e., OT—coloring" (*IDB*, 3:307–10).

[10] Sherman Johnson remarks, "The first impression made by Matthew is that judgment is the leading theme" (*The Theology of the Gospels* [London, 1966], 50; he immediately adds, "yet further attention will show that this is almost completely balanced by grace and mercy"). Matthew uses the verb κρίνω 6 times, and the nouns κρίμα and κρίσις one and 12 times respectively, a total of 19 uses of the judgment words. Mark's total is one, and Luke's 13. Matthew also has the thought of judgment without the specific "judgment" words, as in his great judgment scene in 25:31–46. G. Barth points also to his use of expressions like μισθός (10 times, Mark one, Luke 3), "outer darkness" (only in Matthew), "weeping and gnashing of teeth" (almost confined to Matthew). He also says, "Among the Gospels only Matthew contains detailed descriptions of the final judgment" (G. Bornkamm, G. Barth, and H. J. Held, *Tradition and Interpretation in Matthew* [Philadelphia, 1963], 58–59). And only Matthew in the whole New Testament "thinks of the work of Christ" as "the establishing of the judgment of God" (p. 149).

(18:35). We will be called on to give account of "every careless word" (12:36). Even in a passage concerned basically with comfort, the thought of judgment can appear, for not only will the Servant not break the bruised reed nor quench the smoldering wick, but "he will proclaim judgment to the nations" (12:18).[11] Judgment will be evenhanded: each person will be recompensed according to his deeds (16:27).

Matthew often looks to final judgment. Then people will be classed according to their deeds (25:31–46). The "weeds" will be gathered for destruction (13:40). A number of times Matthew refers to the outer darkness and to the weeping and gnashing of teeth that show that darkness to be so unpleasant (8:12; 13:42, 50; 22:13; 24:51; 25:30). In this spirit the scribes and Pharisees are castigated as "a generation of snakes" and warned that they will not escape "the judgment of hell" (23:33); this whole chapter thunders out the inevitable judgment that awaits the outwardly religious, who use their religion as a cover for their innate selfishness and wickedness. Cities that did not respond to God's mighty deeds will fare badly on the Day of Judgment (11:20–24), as will the city that does not receive God's messengers (10:15). In such passages the judgment on cities like Sodom, Tyre, and Sidon is taken for granted. It does not require demonstration. It is assumed also when we are told that "the men of Nineveh" and "the queen of the south" will rise up in the judgment to condemn the present generation (12:41–42). Final judgment is basic.

Matthew has a splendid picture of Judgment Day, with "the Son of man" as the central figure (25:31–46). But we are not to think of this as taking place independently of the Father. The Son of man will come "in the glory of his Father" (16:27). It accords with this that it is only the Father who knows when it will all happen (24:36). So too the saved on that day are those blessed by Jesus' Father (25:34).

But Matthew's central teaching about God is that he is gracious and loving. He keeps referring to God as "Father"; he does this 44 times, more than anyone else in the New Testament except John (122 times; Mark has this usage 5 times; Luke, 17; and Paul, 42). This brings a new element into religion. It is not that the epithet was never applied to God previously. It was, but it was used in a more distant fashion than with Jesus. There was always some addition, as in the phrase "our Father in heaven." God was thought of as a great Father over all the people, but there was a respectful distance between his worshipers and such a great Being. But Jesus spoke of God in terms of intimacy; he used the address "My Father" (7:21; 10:32, 33; 11:27; 12:50; 16:17; 18:10, 14, 19, 35; 20:23; 25:34; 26:29, 39, 42, 53). Clearly he lived on terms of intimacy with God, such as none other did.[12]

The command to love even our enemies has this purpose: that we may

---

[11] The verse is often understood of "justice" rather than judgment (so NIV, RSV), but we should bear in mind the comment of A. H. McNeile: "Κρίσις in Mt. has not the wide meaning of מִשְׁפָּט, almost 'religion'; he understands it of the fast approaching judgment" (*The Gospel According to St. Matthew* [London, 1915], 172).

[12] "A study of the implications of the sayings of Jesus, especially of those in which he speaks of his Father, leaves the reader of the New Testament with precisely the same impression that Jesus' opponents had; it is hard to avoid the conclusion that Jesus meant to convey the fact of a unique relationship which he had with God, a relationship moreover which implied deity" (Albright and Mann, *Matthew*, clviii). Gustav Dalman says of Jesus' use of the term "Father": "The usage of family

be children of the heavenly Father, "for he makes his sun rise on evil people and good, and he sends rain on just and unjust folk" (5:43–45).[13] Jesus goes on to point out that if we love those who love us, we are doing no more than the worldly do, and this is not enough for the servants of a loving God: we are to be perfect as the Father is perfect (v. 48). In this spirit Matthew reports Jesus' summary of the law in two commandments, that we love God with all our heart and our neighbor as ourself (22:34–40). It is the peacemakers who are to be called "God's sons" (5:9).

God's care extends throughout creation, for he feeds the birds and clothes the plants (6:26–30; cf. 15:13); not one sparrow falls to the ground apart from the will of the Father (10:29).[14] The Father gives good gifts to those who ask him (7:11; cf. 6:1–4, 6, 18). When they are in trouble, he tells them what to say; indeed, his Spirit speaks through them (10:19–20).

God is specially concerned for the world's little people. He has made his revelation, not to this world's great and wise ones, but to "babies" (11:25). People must take care not to despise one of these little people, because "their angels in heaven continually see the face of [the] Father who is in heaven" (18:10). There are mysteries in this saying, but not the slightest doubt that it regards the little ones as very impor-tant in God's sight. So it is that it is not God's will that one of the little ones should perish (18:14).

Matthew sees God as interested in people's prayers. When people agree in their praying, they may look with confidence to God to answer (18:19). And, of course, Jesus teaches the prayer we have come to know as "the Lord's Prayer" (6:9–13).

THE PERSON OF JESUS

It is the teaching of Jesus and the teaching about Jesus that dominate this Gospel. Matthew may mention other things and other people, but he is writing about Jesus, as his heading makes plain. He is concerned through-out with the greatness of his Lord. As W. D. Davies puts it, "It is the illumi-nation of Jesus as Lord of His commu-nity that Matthew has in mind, in their relation to the Law, Jesus being the new Moses of the new Sinai, and in relation to the world, His mission being henceforth to the Gentiles."[15] His opening emphasizes the unusual manner of Jesus' birth, and Matthew is concerned with Jesus right through to the Resurrection, with which the book concludes. We see it in the way he uses such expressions as "the Son of God," "the Son of man," and "the Christ."

---

life is transferred to God: it is the language of the child to its Father" (*The Words of Jesus* [Edinburgh, 1902], 192).

[13] Ladd denies that this means that God is "Father" to anyone other than Jesus' disciples. If we see a universal Fatherhood here, he thinks, we must by the same exegesis see God as Father of the birds (6:26). "It is not as Father that God cares for the birds, and it is not as Father that God bestows his creaturely blessings on those who are not his children" (*A Theology of the New Testament*, 86).

[14] The Greek is ἄνευ τοῦ πατρὸς ὑμῶν "without your Father." *BAGD* cites the equivalent expression "without the gods," meaning "without the will of the gods." David Hill notices the suggestion that Jesus means that "the death of sparrows and the deaths of apostles are not deprived of the *presence* of God, although he may not have willed their end." He rejected this in favor of RSV "without your Father's will" (*The Gospel of Matthew* [London, 1972], 193. This does seem the best interpretation.

[15] James Hastings, ed., *Dictionary of the Bible*, rev. ed., ed. F. C. Grant and H. H. Rowley (Edinburgh, 1963), 632.

Quite apart from details it is apparent in his whole picture of Jesus.[16]

Again and again Matthew records the fulfillment of prophecy in the life of Jesus.[17] This starts early (1:22–23) and sometimes takes unexpected forms as in the expression "He will be called a Nazarene" (2:23).[18] It carries on throughout the Gospel, and Matthew is still finding fulfillments of Scripture in the passion narrative (27:46). We are probably meant to discern the same basic understanding in passages that do not explicitly say so. Thus Robert Banks examines the passage in which Jesus says that he did not come to destroy the law or the prophets, but to fulfill them (5:17–20). He concludes "that it is not so much Jesus' stance towards the Law that he is concerned to depict; it is how the Law stands with regard to him, as the one who brings it to fulfillment and to whom all attention must now be directed. For Matthew, then, it is not the question of Jesus' relation to the Law that is in doubt but rather its relation to him!"[19] Jesus is not someone who stands in subjection to the law, but the One to whom all Scripture points.

Matthew sees Jesus as One who did "mighty works." All told, he records about twenty miracles, three quarters of them being works of healing (in addition to which on several occasions he tells us that Jesus healed many [4:23–25; 8:16; 14:36; 15:30–31; 19:2]). Almost invariably his accounts are shorter than the corresponding narratives in Mark; he omits picturesque details and concentrates on the bare facts. It seems that he is more interested in their theological meaning than in their possibilities as gripping accounts.[20] His miracles fulfilled prophecy (8:17; 12:15–21), and this means that they were more than spectacular wonders. They were in the plan of God, they showed that the One whom God had meant to come in due course had now made his appearance. Something greater than Jonah the prophet, greater than the magnificent king Solomon, greater than prophet or king or priest was here. Those who saw the miracles ought to have discerned the hand of God in them.

This is implied in Jesus' answer to John the Baptist. From prison John sent messengers who asked Jesus, "Are

---

[16] Cf. Georg Strecker: "The Gospel must be explained primarily in terms of Christology, not in terms of ecclesiology" (Graham Stanton, ed., *The Interpretation of Matthew* [Philadelphia and London, 1983], 77). Stanton notes that W. Trilling and E. Schweizer see the emphasis as ecclesiological, and comments, "Surely this is an unnecessary debate: both themes are important for the evangelist" (p. 8). This is true, but for Matthew nothing is quite as important as christology.

[17] There is a series of "fulfillment" passages in Matthew that introduces at least ten (and possibly as many as fourteen) quotations by using the verb *plēroō*, and in which the text differs from that of the LXX, which Matthew uses elsewhere (e.g., 1:22–23; 2:15). There has been a good deal of scholarly debate on these passages without a consensus. For our purpose it is sufficient to notice that they represent a distinctively Matthean way of emphasizing the importance of fulfilled prophecy.

[18] This is an enigma, for the words do not occur in the Old Testament. Some find a connection between the Hebrew רֵצֶנ ("branch," "shoot") and the word "Nazareth"; they see a reference to passages like Isaiah 11:1. Matthew has the plural, "the prophets," which may mean that he has in mind the general thrust of prophetic teaching rather than a specific passage. R. V. G. Tasker sees an allusion to "the contempt for Jesus shown by the religious authorities of Israel because of His association with what they regarded as a provincial backwater" (*The Gospel According to St. Matthew* [London, 1961], 45).

[19] *JBL* 93 [1974]: 242. Banks adds, "As this analysis has sought to show, however, such a way of posing the issue stems from the authentic words of Jesus which Matthew's account enshrines."

[20] Cf. Sherman Johnson, "Matthew, unlike Mark, does not dwell on the details of the miracles. He uses them for their theological purpose and abbreviates them to the essentials" (*The Theology of the Gospels*, 60n.1).

you 'the coming One' or do we await someone else?" Jesus pointed to the works he was doing (11:2–6); they showed who he was. It is implied also in the rebukes Jesus gave to the cities in which he had done so many wonderful things and who had not responded (11:20–24). This does not mean that Matthew depicts Jesus simply as a worker of wonders. Antiquity knew of such people, at least in times subsequent to Jesus,[21] and it is possible that some were earlier. These wonder-workers were concerned to astonish people (and often to make a good living out of doing so). But Jesus' miracles were not such as to compel belief. It was always open to people not to recognize the hand of God in what he was doing, and this happened, for example, in the case of the people of Nazareth. They recognized that Jesus did "mighty works," but, far from believing in him, they took offense at him (13:54–58). Herod the tetrarch was also in no doubt about the reality of Jesus' miracles. But neither did he respond with faith. He dismissed the miracles on the curious ground that Jesus was John the Baptist risen from the dead (14:1–2).

But another attitude was possible. When Jesus walked on the water and called Peter to come to him, the incident climaxes with the disciples worshiping him and saying, "Truly you are God's Son" (14:33). We should notice also that Jesus allowed Peter to share in his power; Peter walked on the water. On another occasion Jesus healed many people and the reaction of the crowd was to glorify the God of Israel (15:31). The spiritually perceptive would see that in the miracles of Jesus God was at work in a special way.[22]

This is evident also in Jesus' relationship to God throughout this Gospel. As we saw earlier, it is noteworthy that he constantly speaks of God as his Father, thus bringing something new into religion. He lived in the closest intimacy with God.

From another angle, the greatness of Jesus is seen in his saying that he will come in glory at the end of the age. We will see this as one of the important aspects of Jesus' use of the term "the Son of man." The Son of man would suffer, but he would also in due course come with his angels to bring this world to an end. Sometimes we get this thought without the use of the term "the Son of man," as when the disciples asked Jesus, "What will be the sign of your coming and of the end of the age?" (24:3).

We see this also in Jesus' performance of functions that belong to God. Thus he declared that he had power on earth to forgive sins, and he used a miracle to give evidence for the point (9:2–8). So with judgment (12:18; 25:31–46). Judgment is a divine function. The Jews did not expect it to be exercised by the Messiah. Strack-Billerbeck says, "According to the Rabbinic

---

[21] William F. Albright and C. S. Mann point out that "the Hellenistic wonder-workers in question are, so far as we know, post-Christian in date" (*The Anchor Bible: Matthew* [New York, 1971], cxxv). It seems that some writers are in error in appealing to such wonder-workers as though they were a well-known phenomenon in Jesus' day, so that the early church felt constrained to make Jesus fit the pattern. As far as we know, there was no such pattern at this time.

[22] Raymond E. Brown draws attention to the fact that Jesus "consistently refused to work a miracle simply as a proof. . . . The miracle was not primarily an external guarantee of the coming of the kingdom; it was one of the means by which the kingdom came" (*New Testament Essays* [Milwaukee, 1965], 171). As I put it some years ago, "The miracles are not something extra, something added to the revelation in order to accredit it. They are part of the revelation" (*The Lord From Heaven* [London, 1958], 20).

view it is exclusively God who will judge the world. . . . In Rabbinic literature there is no passage which unambiguously places the judgment of the world in the hand of the Messiah."[23]

More could be cited. But it is not so much from individual passages as from the thrust of the whole that Matthew's emphasis is to be discerned. For him there can be no doubt but that in Jesus Christ we see God come to effect our salvation.

THE SON OF GOD

Matthew makes more use of the "Son of God" concept than does Mark (though as we have seen, it is an important title for Mark and he uses it at critical points of his narrative). He has Mark's references at the baptism (3:17), the transfiguration (17:5), and the death of Jesus (27:54). Where Mark has a reference to the Son of God in his opening, Matthew refers to "Jesus Christ, the Son of David, the son of Abraham" (1:1). Matthew also omits a reference to the Son of God made by the unclean spirits (Mark 3:11), but he includes the words of the Gerasene demoniac (8:29).

Matthew uses the concept of Jesus' sonship often. He starts early with a prophecy from Hosea: "Out of Egypt did I call my Son" (2:15; the words come from Hos. 11:1). We might not have expected such an application of the prophecy, but it shows us two characteristics of Matthew: a readiness to see the fulfillment of prophecy and the deep conviction that Jesus has a special relationship to God. Sometimes he quotes expressions of doubt, as in

Satan's "If you are the Son of God . . ." (4:3, 6) or the words of the mockers who called to Jesus "Come down from the cross if you are the Son of God" (27:40) or the high priest's adjuration "Tell us whether you are the Christ, the Son of God" (26:63). But in all these cases there can be no doubt that Matthew sees the expression as fully applicable.

The disciples used the expression. At one time this happened after Jesus came to them walking on the stormy sea. Peter had tried to walk to Jesus and, after beginning to sink, had been saved by him and rebuked for his lack of faith. When they got into the boat, the wind dropped. The voyagers worshiped Jesus, saying, "Truly you are the Son of God" (14:33). And, of course, there is Peter's great confession of faith at Caesarea Philippi, "You are the Christ, the son of the living God" (16:16). There is no question but that the expression must here be given its fullest force.[24]

Jesus once claimed special intimacy with the Father in the use of this title. He thanked the Father for hiding certain truths from this world's wise ones and revealing them to "babies." He added, "All things were delivered to me by my Father, and no one knows the Son except the Father, nor does anyone know the Father except the Son and anyone to whom the Son wills to reveal him" (11:27). Jesus went on to say that he would refresh those who labor and are heavily burdened; if they take his "yoke" on them, they will find "rest for their souls" (11:28–29). This is to claim a very special relationship with the Father indeed. Jesus is saying

---

[23] *SBK*, 2:465.

[24] "Far from this being an explanatory gloss by Matthew, it is perfectly in order in the context of Messiahship" (Albright and Mann, *Matthew*, 194). Ladd begins his summing up of Jesus' use of the term "Son of God" by saying, "We conclude that Jesus thought of himself as the Son of God in a unique way" (*A Theology of the New Testament*, 168).

that he has the same intimate knowledge of the Father as the Father has of him. That is a relationship such as nobody else has, one that is fraught with the most significant consequences for those who come to Jesus.

We should draw much the same conclusion from Matthew's infancy narratives. He has the account of the "virgin birth" (though "virgin conception" would be a more accurate description of the event) and of the coming of the Magi to worship the Infant. Whatever his terminology, these accounts bring out the truth that Matthew was writing about One whose relationship to God is unique.

THE SON OF MAN

Matthew has his equivalent of almost all of Mark's uses of this expression, and he preserves Mark's threefold division—with sayings about Jesus' earthly ministry, those that speak of suffering, and those that refer to his coming in glory. He also has Mark's concentration of the title in the later period of the ministry. He recounts twelve miracles of healing before Peter's confession at Caesarea Philippi (as well as general statements about multiple healings [e.g., 4:23–25; 8:16]) and two afterwards; he has four "nature" miracles before and one afterwards. But once Peter has come to his understanding of the person of Christ, the Lord begins to teach the necessity of his suffering and death. There are nine occurrences of "the Son of man" before this point and twenty after it. The expression is bound up with Jesus' understanding of his mission as one that involved not only suffering for sinners but, in the end, exaltation.

Matthew has rather more of what we might call general references to his mission than has Mark. Thus he says

that the Son of man has nowhere to lay his head (8:20) and that he came "eating and drinking" (11:19). Sometimes these expressions point to a Being of great dignity, as in the statements that the Son of man has authority on earth to forgive sins (9:6) and that he is Lord of the Sabbath (12:8). In this world he is engaged in sowing "good seed" (13:37).

At Caesarea Philippi Jesus asked, "Whom do people say that the Son of man is?" (16:13). This saying, incidentally, shows that the title was not in common use as a messianic title; if it had been, Jesus would have given the answer in the way he asked his question. From this point on, every reference to "the Son of man" deals either with his rejection and suffering (eight times) or with his exaltation in glory (twelve times). Right after Peter's confession, Jesus "began to show his disciples that he must go off to Jerusalem and suffer many things . . ." (16:21; in Mark this is a "Son of man" saying). The prediction is repeated: "The Son of man will suffer"; "The Son of man will be delivered up into the hands of men, and they will kill him" (17:12, 22–23); "The Son of man will be delivered up to the high priests and scribes" (20:18); "The Son of man did not come to be served, but to serve, and to give his life a ransom for many" (20:28); "The Son of man is delivered up to be crucified" (26:2); "The Son of man goes as it is written of him" (26:24); "Alas for that man through whom the Son of man is delivered up" (26:24); "The Son of man is delivered into the hands of sinners" (26:45). There is a strong emphasis on suffering as that for which the Son of man came.

But we should not miss the other side of Matthew's emphasis. Not long after the prediction at Caesarea Philippi that Jesus would suffer, there is the prophecy that "the Son of man will come in the glory of his Father with his angels" (16:27). There is a reference to the Resurrection (17:9), and another to the time when "the Son of man will sit on the throne of his glory" (19:28). The coming of the Son of man will be like the lightning (24:27): his "sign" will be seen in heaven and "all the tribes of the earth will wail and they will see the Son of man coming on the clouds of heaven with power and great glory" (24:30). His coming will be like the days of Noah (24:37, 39). It will be unexpected (24:44); it will be in glory (25:31); Jesus assures the high priest: "You will see the Son of man seated at the right hand of the Power and coming on the clouds of heaven" (26:64).

This is a remarkable series of passages. Matthew leaves us in no doubt that the Crucifixion is of the very essence of the mission of Jesus. That is what he came for. But he leaves us in no doubt either that that is not the end of the story. There is the future coming of the Son of man. The time is quite unknown, even the Son himself does not know it (24:36). It is the certainty, not the time, that Matthew emphasizes.

THE CHRIST

Matthew reproduces almost all of Mark's references to the Christ. One that is missing is that of the giving of a cup of cold water because one belongs to Christ (Mark 9:41; Matthew has the water given "for the name of a disciple"); also missing is the invitation to "the Christ, the King of Israel" to come down from the cross (Mark 15:32; Matthew has "the King" but not "the Christ"). But he has more of his own. Five times in the opening of his Gospel he uses this title—first in his heading, "The book of the genesis of Jesus Christ"; then in a reference to "Mary,

of whom was born Jesus who is called 'Christ' " (1:16); then in a note of time, from the Babylonian exile to Christ (1:17); and in an announcement of the narrative of the birth of Jesus Christ (1:18); and an inquiry from Herod as to where the Christ would be born (2:4). Right from the beginning it is clear that Matthew is writing about the Christ, the Messiah. Later he tells us that John the Baptist while in prison heard of "the works of the Christ" (11:2).

After this, we come to Peter's great confession at Caesarea Philippi, which Matthew describes a little more fully than does Mark. Where Mark tells us that Peter said simply, "You are the Christ," Matthew has the fuller statement, "You are the Christ, the Son of the living God" (16:16). Jesus told him that this had been "revealed" to him— not by human agency, but by the heavenly Father (16:17). He added that he would build his church on this rock (16:18), that the "gates of Hades" would not prevail against it, and that he would give "the keys of the kingdom of heaven" to Peter. The incident closed with Jesus' direction that the disciples should tell no one that he was the Christ (16:20). The passage raises enormous difficulties, some of which will be discussed in a later section. Here it is enough to notice that the passage assigns to Peter a place of leadership on the basis of his confession. And it shows us that as the Christ, Jesus looked forward to a significant future for his followers.

Matthew records Jesus' questions to the Pharisees, "What do you think of the Christ? Whose Son is he?" (22:42)—questions that led into a discussion about the Son of David. The point being made is that the Christ, though the Son of David (and thus, in contemporary eyes, subordinate to David) is in fact David's Lord. Later we read that the disciples have one teacher, the Christ (23:10). Other sayings bring out the fact that in due time there would come claimants to the title of Christ (24:5, 23).

At Jesus' trial the high priest said to him, "I adjure you by the living God that you tell us whether you are the Christ, the Son of God" (26:63), to which Jesus replied, "You said it." He added that he would come on the clouds of heaven (26:64). Clearly the high priest did not take seriously the possibility that Jesus was the Christ. He asked the question, not as a quest for information, but because Jesus' claim to being the Christ could be made to look like an incipient rebellion against the Romans. Jesus' answer does not embrace the term. The way he puts it implies that it is the high priest's word, not his; in the sense in which the high priest understood the term, he was not the Christ. But if he could not affirm it, he could not deny it either, for in the sense in which he understood it he was in fact the Christ.

We should bear in mind that a claim to messiahship was not regarded as in itself blasphemous. The high priest was not trying to get Jesus to make a blasphemous statement, but to get him to say something that could be made into an accusation before Pilate. A "messiah," it could be argued, is a political figure, a leader of rebellion and thus a potential danger to Rome. Jesus' answer must have been unexpected, for he eschewed politics, but claimed a much more significant place. Evidently the high priest and his allies made use of the term, for we find the mockers hitting Jesus and commanding, "Prophesy for us, Christ, who is it who

hit you?" (26:68). And twice Pilate spoke of Jesus "who is called 'Christ'" (27:17, 22).

In this Gospel, then, "Christ" is clearly a title, with the possible exception of the opening where it may be a proper name. Elsewhere it lacks the article only when the mockers address Jesus as "Christ." For Matthew, the word means "the anointed One," "the Messiah." And Jesus fulfilled that role.

THE SON OF DAVID

David was the great king of Israel, the man after God's own heart. Of all the kings of Israel and Judah there was none to match him and it is plain that "Son of David" was in consequence a title of high honor,[25] as well as an indication that the person so designated could claim descent from the greatest of the kings. It was used as a messianic title and as such expressed a longing for a Messiah who would renew the kingdom of David and in general be to the people of his day what David had been to those of his. In the first century it seems to have been linked with militaristic expectation (was not David a mighty warrior?). To a subject nation it was an expression of hope, the hope of freedom under their own ruler instead of the hated conqueror. This was perhaps the reason that the title is not featured in the Gospels nearly as prominently as some of the other messianic titles. Mark and Luke both have it three times only, and it is not prominent in the later books of the New Testament. That is easily understood, for outside of Palestine who knew or cared about David? We should not overemphasize this, though, for these are occasional references to

---

[25] Gustav Dalman discusses the Davidic descent of Jesus (*The Words of Jesus*, 319–24). He thinks that when people called Jesus "Son of David," "they virtually appealed to Him as 'Messiah'" (p. 319).

Jesus' Davidic descent (cf. Acts 13:34; Rom. 1:3; 2 Tim. 2:8). But it is plain that David did not figure prominently in the early church's estimate of Jesus.

But Matthew has the expression "Son of David" nine times (including one reference to Joseph [1:20]). He begins his Gospel with a reference to Jesus Christ as "Son of David" (to which he adds "son of Abraham"). Right at the beginning he makes it clear that Jesus' relationship to David is important. He will indeed be all that is involved in being king in descent from the great ruler of Israel. But after this Matthew (like the other Synoptists) always has the expression as used by others, mostly in appeals to Jesus for help. Thus a couple of blind men called out to Jesus, "Have mercy on us, Son of David" (9:27). Curiously a Canaanite woman addressed him by this title as she appealed for help for her daughter: "Have mercy on me, O Lord, Son of David . . ." (15:22). Perhaps she thought it would be good politics for a Canaanite to appeal to Jewish national sentiment. At any rate, for whatever reason, she used the title. Notice further that she combined it with "Lord," and this was the case also in the repeated request from two blind men with their plea "Have mercy on us, O Lord, Son of David" (20:30–31). On another occasion Jesus healed a blind and dumb demoniac, causing people to wonder whether he could be "the Son of David" (12:23).

When Jesus' triumphal entry into Jerusalem took place, Matthew tells us that, among other things, the crowds cried out, "Hosanna to the Son of David" (21:9), a cry that the children took up later and repeated in the temple precincts (21:15); notice the presence of the lame and the blind as well (21:14); does Matthew wish us to see Jesus as King over the lowly? The precise meaning of "Hosanna" is unclear, but plainly it was an acclamation designed to give honor to the person being greeted. And it is interesting that when Jesus rode in triumph into Jerusalem, it was as "Son of David" that the crowds acclaimed him.

At the conclusion of an incident in which his enemies put a series of tricky questions to Jesus and were discomfited by his answers, he invited them to do some thinking. He asked whose son the Christ was and received the answer "David's." He cited Psalm 110, which speaks of the Messiah as "Lord" and proceeded to ask, "If then David calls him 'Lord,' how is he his son?" (22:41–45). People of the day usually held that there had been a golden age in the past; they deduced that the ancients were greater and wiser than the present generation. Thus it would be expected that David would be greater than his descendants. But was not the Messiah to be very great? And does not the psalm call him Lord? How could the Messiah (who would come later) possibly be greater than David (who was great in an earlier age)? The Pharisees could not answer. But for Matthew the fact that Jesus the Messiah is greater than David was not for a moment in doubt. That he was "Son of David" pointed to some important aspects of his person and his work; it indicated his greatness. But it did not imply that he was in any way inferior to David.

THE KINGDOM

As with Mark and Luke, Matthew has much to say about Jesus' teaching on the kingdom. But, whereas they tend to concentrate on "the kingdom of God," Matthew has that expression only five times. He prefers "the kingdom of heaven," a phrase he uses thirty-two times, and which most agree means much the same thing, being no more than a typical Jewish way of avoiding the use of the name of God. In addition he has expressions like "the kingdom" (six times [e.g., 4:23]), "your kingdom" (once, in prayer [6:10]). He refers to it as that of the Son of man (three times [13:41; 16:28; 20:21]). He has "the kingdom of their Father" (once [13:43]); also that of "my Father" (once [26:29]). All told, Matthew uses such expressions almost fifty times. He can also refer to "the throne of God" (23:22), which, of course, points to sovereignty.

Matthew has almost all of Mark's teaching on the subject of the kingdom (he omits the little parable about the seed growing secretly and the reference to the scribe who was not far from the kingdom), but he adds significant material to it. Like Mark, he tells us that Jesus taught that the kingdom had come near (4:17), but he also says that John the Baptist pointed to the same thing (3:2) and that the disciples were instructed to give the same message (10:7). Matthew will not let us miss the point that the kingdom has approached in the coming of Jesus. But this does not mean that Jesus would lead an army in rebellion against Rome. Throughout this Gospel, Jesus is a meek and lowly person and he speaks of people with corresponding qualities as those who will enter the kingdom: "the poor in spirit" (5:3), the persecuted (5:10), the childlike (18:1–4). More shocking was his warning to the religious people of his day that the tax collectors and prostitutes would go into the kingdom of God before they would (21:31). In view of the widely held opinion that wealth was a sign of God's blessing, we should connect this with Jesus' teaching that it is hard for a rich man to enter the kingdom—so hard, indeed, that it is easier for a camel to pass through the eye of a needle than for a rich man to enter the kingdom (19:23–24).

None of this means that Jesus took lightly the ethical implications of membership in the kingdom. He told his hearers that unless their righteousness exceeded that of the scribes and Pharisees they would certainly not enter the kingdom (5:20). It is not enough to greet him, "Lord, Lord"; they must do the will of God (7:21). He speaks of people being very much in earnest, such as those who made themselves eunuchs "for the kingdom of heaven's sake" (19:12). There are a number of parables that stress the infinite worth of the kingdom, such as that of the merchant who, looking for beautiful pearls, sold all he had to get one outstanding specimen and that of the man who sold all he had in order to acquire treasure hidden in a field (13:44–45). Such passages do not, of course, imply that people earn their place in the kingdom by their outstanding merit, but they simply emphasize the fact that we must be in earnest about the kingdom.

That the way into the kingdom is the way of grace is brought out in the parable of the laborers in the vineyard (20:1–16). It does not seem fair that those who had worked through the heat of the day and done most of the hard labor should be paid no more than those who did one hour's work in the cool of the late afternoon. But Jesus is bringing out in striking fashion the great truth that we do not merit our salvation by our hard work. God saves us because he loves us, not because we are good. T. W. Manson reminds us that there was a little coin called a pondion, which had the value of a twelfth part of a denarius, the wage for a day's work. The owner could have paid each worker for exactly the number of hours he had worked. But "there is no such thing as a twelfth part of the love of God."[26] God's love in all its fullness is lavished on the humblest of his children. But if the kingdom is not to be acquired by our own works, it is a gift that we should prize highly. John the Baptist was a great man, Jesus said, so great that there has not been a greater among those born of women, but the littlest in the kingdom is greater than John (11:11). And this great gift is not for some chosen few. In the end many will come from the east and west (from all over the world) to be with Abraham and Isaac and Jacob in the kingdom (8:11). The exact expression "the kingdom of God" (or "of heaven") does not occur before the New Testament, but something of the idea was certainly known among the Jews. The Old Testament prophets looked for the coming of "the Day of the Lord" from early times (cf. Amos 5:18) and the idea persisted that in due course God would intervene in the world. He would destroy all evil and set up a new order that accorded with his will. During the intertestamental period the idea flourished, and apocalyptic literature set forth in vivid language the writers' deep conviction that God would certainly overthrow evil, and that very soon. Thus Jesus' language about the kingdom would strike a chord in many faithful and patriotic hearts.

But Jesus' teaching did not fall into any of the patterns with which people were familiar. In particular his combination of the present[27] and the future was puzzling. For that matter it still is. There are people who put all their emphasis on the kingdom as a present reality ("realized eschatology") and there are others who think Jesus saw it

as entirely future, something yet to come. But rather than trying to force all his teaching into a mold of our own devising, it is better to recognize that sometimes Jesus spoke of the kingdom as present and sometimes as future. In a very important sense it came when Jesus came. God was present in Jesus, doing mighty works, teaching spiritual realities, reconciling the world to himself. That coming transformed everything. But in an important sense the kingdom is still future. It will come when Jesus comes back. In a very meaningful sense the kingdom has come because Jesus has come. But in an equally meaningful sense the kingdom will come when Jesus comes. It is present. It is future.

So Jesus can speak of the Son of man as coming in his glory with all his angels and sitting on his glorious throne (25:31), clearly a future event. He will then say to certain people, "Come, . . . inherit the kingdom prepared for you" (25:34). And such a future consummation is surely in mind when Jesus says he will not drink of the fruit of the vine until he drinks it new in the kingdom of his Father (26:29). So also the prayer "Your kingdom come" has both a present and a future reference (6:10).

There is a view that in this Gospel (and for that matter throughout the New Testament) the consummation of all things is viewed as imminent. The statements that the kingdom of heaven is near (3:2; 4:17; 10:7) are taken to mean that it will come in all its fullness very soon. If this could be demonstrated by other considerations, then Matthew's language would fit in, but it does not establish it by itself. What

---

[26] *The Sayings of Jesus* (London, 1949), 220.

[27] C. H. Dodd finds Jesus' sayings about the kingdom of God as a present reality distinctive: "They have no parallel in Jewish teaching or prayers of the period" (*The Parables of the Kingdom* [London, 1938], 49).

Matthew's language seems to mean is that the ministry of Jesus, which was about to start, in one sense signified the coming of the kingdom.

John the Baptist used the language of imminence (3:7, 10, 12), but again this appears to point to the ministry of Jesus. The mission charge to the Twelve includes a warning about the Day of Judgment but gives no indication when this will be (10:15). A little later Jesus assures the apostles, "You will not complete the cities of Israel until the Son of man comes" (10:23). This certainly looks like a statement that the *parousia* is at hand, but the saying is very puzzling. It is not completely clear what "completing" the cities means, nor in what sense the Son of man's coming is to be understood. Certainly the apostles finished that particular mission and returned to Jesus before the end of the age,[28] which Matthew well knew when he recorded the words. He must have understood them in some other sense. Albright and Mann say, "The second part of vs. 23 simply states a truth: *The Man's coming* will supervene before the mission to Israel has been fulfilled."[29]

There are references to "harvest" and "the end of the age" (13:30, 39), to the division between the good and the bad "fish" (13:47–50), to the Son of man as coming in the Father's glory to recompense each according to his deeds (16:27), and similar statements. These certainly attest Matthew's interest in what will happen at the end of the age, but they give no indication of how far

off that may be. The disciples might ask, "What will be the sign of your coming and of the completion of the age?" (24:3) but the answer comes in general terms and there is no indication that the end is imminent. The gospel will be preached in all the world before the end comes (24:14). Nobody except the Father knows when the end will be (24:36; cf. 25:13). Therefore, Jesus' followers are to watch (24:42); they cannot know when it will all happen and so must continually be on their guard. The implication is that it will all happen at an unexpected time. This is the teaching also of the parable of the ten girls (25:1–13). Five of them looked for the bridegroom to come back quickly and therefore had no reserves of oil. It was these believers in an imminent return who found themselves excluded from the feast. A delay is surely implied right at the end of this Gospel where Jesus speaks of making disciples, of baptizing them, and of his presence with his own "until the consummation of the age" (28:20).

All this surely means that Jesus' *parousia* is of the greatest importance. But it does not mean that either Jesus or his followers looked for the consummation of all things in the immediate future. There would be an interval, and it is nowhere said how long this will be.

THE PARABLES OF THE KINGDOM

A feature of the Synoptic Gospels is the use Jesus makes of the parable as a method of instruction (and most find

---

[28] Ladd holds that the view that the eschatological kingdom would come before the end of the apostles' mission is erroneous. "This interpretation does not reckon with the composite character of the chapter. This pericope clearly looks beyond the immediate mission of the twelve to their future mission in the world. The present verse says no more than that the mission of Jesus' disciples to Israel will last until the coming of the Son of Man. It indicates that in spite of her blindness, God has not given up Israel. The new people of God are to have a concern for Israel until the end comes" (*A Theology of the New Testament*, 200).

[29] *Matthew*, 125.

something like this in John as well). A. M. Hunter estimates that parables make up more than a third of Jesus' recorded teaching;[30] the sheer bulk of Jesus' parabolic teaching is impressive. For our present subject there is in Matthew a specially significant group of parables that are called "parables of the kingdom."[31] Eleven times Matthew has the formula "The kingdom of heaven is like . . ."[32] (Mark and Luke have it twice each).

These parables have been the subject of a good deal of discussion. C. H. Dodd maintained that they are to be understood of the crisis posed by the coming of Jesus and that they are not rightly understood as giving us general teaching about the Christian life.[33] He speaks of "ruling out any interpretation of the parables which gives them a general application, and insisting upon their intense particularity as comments upon an historical situation." The parables "use all the resources of dramatic illustration to help men to see that in the events before their eyes—in the miracles of Jesus, His appeal to men and its results, the blessedness that comes to those who follow Him, and the hardening of those who reject Him; in the tragic conflict of the Cross, and the tribulation of the disciples; in the fateful choice before the Jewish people, and the disasters that threaten—God is confronting them in His kingdom, power and glory. This world has be-

come the scene of a divine drama, in which the eternal issues are laid bare. It is the hour of decision. It is realized eschatology."[34] Though not arguing for realized eschatology, Colin Brown is similarly insistent on the necessity of decision: "For the truth about God and man cannot be learnt directly as if it were a series of mere facts which involved no personal commitment. The parables are language-events which challenge a personal response."[35]

Joachim Jeremias in his noteworthy examination of the parables (*The Parables of Jesus*) built on Dodd's work. Specifically he saw in the parables as we have them indications that changes were made during transmission. Parables originally directed to the crowds or to Jesus' opponents are made to form instruction for the disciples, and accounts that originally were meant to give eschatological teaching, or teaching about the crisis brought about by Jesus' coming, are now the vehicles of hortatory teaching.

But I. Howard Marshall's important monograph *Eschatology and the Parables* seems to have demonstrated that "the interpretation of the parables in terms of realized eschatology leads to forced explanations of many of them, and on the other hand the interpretation of the teaching of Jesus in terms of an imminent coming of the kingdom fails to do justice to the parables and leads to an

---

[30] *Interpreting the Parables,* 7.

[31] L. Mowry compares Jesus' parables with those of the rabbis and finds the latter, used "primarily to clarify or to prove a point of the Mosaic law," to be "usually characterized by scholastic pedantry, rather than vigor and originality. Jesus' parables, on the contrary, support the evangelists' claim that he taught and preached with authoritative power and with creative novelty" (*IDB,* 3:652).

[32] J. Jeremias objects to this traditional translation; he sees an underlying Aramaic *l* and prefers "It is the case with the Kingdom . . ." (*The Parables of Jesus* [London, 1954], 78–79). I. Howard Marshall accepts this (*Eschatology and the Parables* [London, 1963], 27–28).

[33] But C. H. Peisker says, "The message of the parables cannot be reduced to a single theme; each one must be examined individually" (*NIDNTT,* 2:749).

[34] *The Parables of the Kingdom,* 195, 197–98.

[35] *NIDNTT,* 2:753.

unnecessarily sceptical estimate of their authenticity."[36] This means that we should understand parables such as that of the seed growing secretly and the mustard seed as indicating the certainty of growth as God works out his purpose, and those of the net and the weeds as pointing to the response to which Jesus challenges people and to eventual judgment. Other parables teach that there is a crisis that threatens Jesus' hearers (the children at play, the barren fig tree), and yet others look for the *parousia* after an interval (the ten girls, the burglar, the watchman).

The parables form a vivid and fascinating study and present important aspects of the kingdom. Specifically they teach that the coming of the kingdom involves a note of crisis: it compels people to decision. It also inaugurates a process of great growth (the mustard seed and the yeast [13:31–33]).[37] The kingdom may have appeared insignificant in the time of Jesus, but that is not the whole story. It has vital power, and it will grow and grow. The parables also teach that the consummation of all that the kingdom means awaits the *parousia* of Jesus at some unknown future date.

THE PASSION

Matthew devotes a seventh of his Gospel to the account of the Crucifixion and the Resurrection. As with the other Evangelists, it is clear that it is this that is the most significant thing. It seems that Matthew's interest in this theme starts early, for he records Jesus' words to John the Baptist when that preacher of righteousness hesitated to baptize the one of whom he said, "I have need to be baptized by you, and you come to me?" Jesus replied, "Suffer it now, for thus it is fitting for us to fulfill all righteousness" (3:14–15). The meaning of this reply is not obvious, but those interpreters seem to be right who see a connection with Isaiah 53, where the "righteous" Servant is spoken of as "justifying" many (Isa. 53:11); he identifies with them and dies for them. Thus, C. E. B. Cranfield says, "The righteousness that Jesus was determined to fulfil to the uttermost was the role of the Suffering Servant of the Lord."[38] Jesus "enters the ranks of sinners. By this means he fulfils 'all righteousness.' "[39]

There is no explicit reference to the passion in the temptation narrative, but at least Matthew makes it clear that at the threshold of his public ministry Jesus looked at the possibilities of being a wonder-worker and of establishing a mighty empire with a sovereignty over all the world and rejected both as temptations of the devil. That was not the way for the Christ to fulfill the divine will. We may perhaps see some-

---

[36] *Eschatology and the Parables*, 48.

[37] Dodd finds the parables of growth "susceptible of a natural interpretation which makes them into a commentary on the actual situation during the ministry of Jesus"; he rules out "a long process of development" (*The Parables of the Kingdom*, 193). But this is surely not doing justice to what Jesus actually said.

[38] *SJT* 8 [1955]: 54. Similarly G. W. H. Lampe thinks that "It may not be too much to claim that this saying shows that Jesus is regarded by St. Matthew as interpreting His Sonship and Messianic anointing in such a way as to identify Himself with the righteous Remnant of Israel and, as its representative, to unite Himself with those who are undergoing John's baptism in order that they may be constituted a renewed community of the 'saints'. Perhaps we may go even further and see a deeper meaning in the words of Jesus; the Servant who is to suffer vicariously and 'bear the sin of many' will procure a general justification, or declaration of righteousness, for His people" (*The Seal of the Spirit* [London, 1951], 37–38).

[39] Barth, *Tradition and Interpretation in Matthew*, 138.

thing of this again when we approach the account of the Transfiguration. We usually take this as a manifestation of splendor, and so, of course, it is. But it may be significant that the two who talked with Jesus were Moses and Elijah, the law-giver and the prophet, both of whom had agonized over the sins of the people they identified with. And as they went down from the mountain, Jesus and his friends were talking about his death and his resurrection and the place of John the Baptist in these events.

Whether we are right in seeing a reference to Jesus' suffering in all this, there can be no doubt that Matthew repeatedly reports Jesus' predictions his passion. Joachim Jeremias sees Jesus' mention of the days when "the bridegroom will be taken away from them" (9:15) as "an open prophecy of the Messianic passion."[40] Jesus said that "the Son of man" would be "three days and three nights in the heart of the earth" (12:40). Like Mark, Matthew tells us that immediately after Peter's great confession at Caesarea Philippi, Jesus "began to show his disciples that he must go up to Jerusalem and suffer many things from the elders and high priests and scribes and be killed, and on the third day be raised" (16:21). The disciples' recognition of him as the Messiah was the signal for him to instruct them about the meaning of messiahship. For Jesus messiahship was not to be understood in terms of arms and victorious battles, of splendor and riches, but of lowliness and rejection and poverty. It meant in the end a death for sinners.

The Transfiguration was followed by a miracle of healing and that in turn by another prediction of betrayal and death and resurrection (17:22–23). Then when Jesus was going up to Jerusalem, he made a similar prediction, this time adding that he would be delivered up to the Gentiles who would mock and scourge and crucify him. And again, there is the assurance of resurrection on the third day (20:17–19).

Unlike the other Gospels, Matthew introduces his passion narrative with yet another prediction. Jesus said, "You know that after two days there is the Passover, and the Son of man is delivered up to be crucified" (26:2). Matthew goes on to emphasize the fulfillment of Scripture in all that was happening at that time (26:54, 56), specifically in a variety of details connected with Jesus' death. Thus, evidently with Zechariah 11:12 in mind, he refers to the money paid to Judas, for he explicitly mentions the thirty pieces of silver, as Mark and Luke do not (26:15). He quotes, from the same prophet, words about the smiting of the shepherd and the scattering of the sheep (26:31; see Zech. 13:7). His reference to being exceedingly sorrowful (26:38) is put in words reminiscent of the psalms (Ps. 42:6, 11; 43:5), while Jesus' words to the high priest about the Son of Man seated at the right hand of power and coming with the clouds of heaven (26:64) are also from the Old Testament (Ps. 110:1; Dan. 7:13). Matthew points to a fulfillment of prophecy in the purchase of the potter's field with the money paid to Judas (27:9; see Jer. 32:6–9; Zech. 11:12–13).

When Jesus was on the cross he was offered wine mixed with gall (27:34; see Ps. 69:21), and the casting of lots over Jesus' clothing is another passage

---

[40] *TDNT*, 4:1103; he says that many regard this as a community saying.

with Old Testament language (27:35; see Ps. 22:18). We see this also in the mockery by the passers-by who were wagging their heads (27:39; see Ps. 22:7; 109:25). The suggestion that Jesus' trust in God is misplaced (27:43) is another Old Testament motif (Ps. 22:8; the idea is found elsewhere, but not expressed in words so closely resembling Matthew's). Finally there is the cry of dereliction that Matthew shares with Mark: "My God, my God, why did you abandon me?" (27:46; see Ps. 22:1). This emphasizes the terrible cost to Jesus of his death for sinners. But because he endured that abandonment, sinners need never experience it. This is evidently important to Matthew, for this is the one saying from the cross that he records (see further the discussion in Mark).

All three Synoptists record Jesus' prayer in Gethsemane, but Matthew has the fullest account. Only he tells us, for example, that Jesus addressed God as "My Father" (Mark and Luke have simply "Father"). And Matthew alone records what Jesus prayed the second time and further that he prayed the same thing the third time. For Matthew what took place in the Garden was very important. All the more is this the case in view of the certainty that God could have prevented wicked men from arresting his Son. Matthew tells us of Jesus' confidence that his Father could provide "now more than twelve legions of angels" (26:53). His death did not occur because of the scheming of Caiaphas and the military might of Pilate; it happened by the will of God. This is seen also in the use of the exact words of the Lord's Prayer as Jesus

prayed in Gethsemane, "Your will be done" (26:42). Earlier Jesus had said, "My time [*kairos*] is near" (26:18; cf. 26:45); here his *kairos* is surely the time determined by God for the consummation of his saving work.[41] That the death of Jesus was an act of obedience to the Father is important for this Evangelist. Matthew may further be hinting at the element of voluntariness in Jesus' death with his unusual way of describing it: "He let go his spirit" (27:50).[42]

Matthew emphasizes the place of the elders in bringing about Jesus' death (26:3, 47, 57; 27:1, 3, 12, 20, 41; 28:12), whereas Mark mentions them only three times in this connection, and Luke once. He also refers to the high priest(s) quite often (as does Mark), but his inclusion of the elders seems to show that it was not only the ecclesiastics who rejected Jesus. The nation's elder statesmen in general were involved also. Matthew sees malevolence in the council; the council was "against Jesus to kill him" (27:1); its members took action to free Barabbas and destroy Jesus (27:20). And Matthew records the frightening cry of the crowd: "His blood be on us and on our children" (27:25).

It is to Matthew that we owe our information about Roman uneasiness about what was happening. He tells us of the dream of Pilate's wife and her suggestion that Pilate have nothing to do with "that righteous man" (27:19). In the same spirit he says that Pilate washed his hands before the people, saying that he was innocent of Jesus' blood (27:24). This led to the people's voluntary acceptance of responsibility

---

[41] David Hill says that time here, "like 'hour' in John's Gospel, refers to Jesus' death—not to the meal, nor to his return" (*The Gospel of Matthew* [London, 1972], 337).

[42] Ἀφῆκεν τὸ πνεῦμα; Mark and Luke say ἐξέπνευσεν, and John has παρέδωκεν τὸ πνεῦμα. None of these is a usual way of referring to death. Matthew's verb is sometimes used with τὴν ψυχήν (Gen. 35:18; Josephus *Ant.* 1.218, et al.), but his expression remains unusual.

for Jesus' death (27:25). This is the thrust of the whole Barabbas episode (27:15–26). Matthew makes it clear that the Romans considered Jesus innocent and did not want him executed. It was the Jews who clamored for Barabbas and insisted on Jesus' death.

He further tells us that when Jesus died, some strange things happened. Besides mentioning the tearing of the temple's curtain (stated also in Mark and Luke), he speaks of an earthquake, of rocks being broken, of tombs being opened and bodies of saints being raised, adding that after Jesus' resurrection these saints went into the Holy City and appeared to many (27:51–53). Clearly Matthew wants his readers to see that the death of Jesus was a cataclysmic event. He is writing about no petty happening, but something that destroyed the screening off of the presence of God in the temple, that shook the physical earth to its foundations, and that had profound effects even in the realms of the dead.

Matthew has an important saying that shows us the significance of Jesus' death. He records Jesus' explanation of the cup at the Last Supper: "This is my blood of the [new] covenant which is poured out for you for the forgiveness of sins" (26:28). It is not certain whether we should read the word "new" (it is absent from some of the most important manuscripts, and it may well have been imported into the text from Luke's narrative). But whether it is read or not, it is implied; any "covenant" that Jesus made at that time had to be a new one. Jesus is clearly referring to the great prophecy

in Jeremiah 31:31ff. The people had so consistently broken the covenant God had made with the nation that God spoke through his prophet of a new covenant that he would make, a covenant that would not depend on the people's ability to keep it, but on two things—inwardness and forgiveness. God would write his law on their hearts, meaning they would be so changed that they would be upright people (cf. 18:3), not people striving desperately to conform to an outward code that corresponded to nothing in their innermost being. And there would be forgiveness, which Matthew saw as stemming from the death that Jesus was about to die, not from the sacrifices offered on Jewish (or, for that matter, Gentile) altars. Jesus' death would really deal with sins and put them away forever. In the light of such facts as Jesus' identification of himself with sinners (3:15) and his giving of himself as a ransom for many (20:28), this surely means that he saved sinners by taking their place.[43]

Before we leave the passion narrative perhaps we should notice that Matthew has a particular interest in Judas. It is he who records that Judas asked the chief priests, "What will you give me?" as the prelude to the betrayal, and that they offered thirty pieces of silver (26:15). When Jesus prophesied that he would be betrayed by one of the Twelve and the apostles began to question who it would be, it is this Gospel that tells us that Judas asked, "Is it I?" (26:25). And it is only Matthew who tells us that when the traitor greeted Jesus in the garden, the Master addressed him

---

[43]G. Barth holds that Matthew "adopted the interpretation of the death of Jesus as an atoning sacrifice for sins from tradition"; this means that it is a very early and widespread view. He says further, "Matthew not only adopts the thought of the atoning sacrifice but at the same time he interprets it, and indeed in the sense that the forgiveness of sins through the substitutionary sacrifice of Jesus does not mean any invalidating of the will of God, of the law, but means precisely the establishing of it" (*Tradition and Interpretation in Matthew,* p. 147).

as "Friend." Matthew also has some words that might mean "Do what you have come for" or "Why have you come?" (26:50; Mark omits them and Luke has "Do you betray the Son of man with a kiss?"). And this is the only Gospel in which we read of Judas' remorse, of his attempt to return the money by hurling it into the sanctuary, and of his suicide (27:3–10). From Matthew's account it is clear that it is possible for one who appears to be close to Jesus to be a traitor, and he writes his passion narrative in such a way as to bring this out.

DISCIPLESHIP

Jesus called some of his disciples right at the beginning of his ministry (4:18–22), and sometime later he called Matthew (9:9–13). Each time the call is to a wholehearted following, as is shown by the fact that those called left their modes of livelihood to be with Jesus. Personal attachment to Jesus and loyalty to him and all he stood for are of the essence of the discipleship to which he called people.[44] This contrasts with the discipleship that was practiced in the rabbinical schools. There the disciple was a learner, engaged in constant debate with his leader. The disciple aimed to master the tradition and in the end to be a teacher himself. But Jesus' disciples were "witnesses to a Person, not guardians of a tradition."[45]

Jesus made it clear to would-be followers that it would cost them something to follow him (8:19–22), and

evidently they felt that the price was too high, for there is no indication that they ever became disciples. He spelled out the cost when he said that anyone who followed him must take up his cross, a vivid metaphor for a death to all self-centeredness. Anyone who wills to save his life will lose it, Jesus said, and the way to saving the life is to lose it for Christ's sake (16:24–25). The same truth is brought out in the incident in which the two sons of Zebedee and their mother approached Jesus for the principal places in his kingdom. He replied, "You don't know what you are asking" and went on to ask, "Can you drink the cup that I shall drink?" (20:20–22; for Jesus' cup see 26:39). Again it is self-sacrifice, not self-seeking that is the way of discipleship. It was this that deterred the rich young ruler (19:16–22). He clearly relished the thought of becoming a follower of Jesus. But he did not want to do so at the cost of his wealth. Jesus looked for an attachment to himself personally that transcended possessions and even family ties (12:48–50). Small wonder that though the harvest is great, the workers are few (9:37).

Matthew has words of comfort for the persecuted, who, surprisingly, are "blessed": the kingdom is theirs (5:9). The persecution of God's people is not a new phenomenon, for the prophets had known it (5:12). Disciples are to pray for their persecutors (5:44), for a right attitude is important if they are to be "sons" of the kingdom (5:45). When they are persecuted in one city, they should flee to another (10:33);

---

[44] Bornkamm examines the use of $\kappa\acute{u}\rho\iota o\varsigma$ by the disciples. He points out that in this Gospel the disciples do not address Jesus as "Teacher" or "Rabbi," except for Judas Iscariot (26:25, 49; contrast the other disciples [v. 22]), but as "Lord." The word $\kappa\acute{u}\rho\iota o\varsigma$ may be used simply as a term of respect, but Bornkamm finds that the disciples do not so use it. Rather, "the title and address of Jesus as $\kappa\acute{u}\rho\iota o\varsigma$ in Matthew have throughout the character of a divine Name of Majesty" (*Tradition and Interpretation in Matthew* [Philadelphia, 1963], 42–43).

[45] Albright and Mann, *Matthew,* cliv.

they must not let persecution divert them from their task.[46]

We see the radical nature of following Jesus in the incident in which the disciples of John the Baptist pointed out that both they and the Pharisees fasted, whereas Jesus' followers did not. But Jesus was not asking simply for the performance of conventional religious practices and conformity to conventional religious standards. He asked, "Can the sons of the bride chamber mourn as long as the bridegroom is with them?" and added, "but days will come when the bridegroom will be taken away from them, and then they will fast." When he went on to say, "No one puts a patch of undressed cloth on an old garment . . . nor do they pour new wine into old wineskins" (9:14–17), he was not inviting people to a patched-up Judaism, the old system with a few innovations. He was inviting them to a radically new way of life. It could not be contained within Judaism. Like the new patch on an old robe, it would pull away. Like the new wine in the old wineskins, it would burst the container. Those who follow him must face this fact.[47]

An example of the new outlook is Jesus' attitude to clean and unclean foods, a subject that climaxes a discussion sparked off by a complaint from Pharisees and scribes from Jerusalem about the fact that Jesus' disciples transgressed the tradition of the elders in not washing their hands ceremonially before eating (15:1–20). Jesus had more than one thing to say in reply, and he finished by pointing out that it is not what goes into the mouth that defiles, but what comes from within— the evil thoughts that lead to evil actions. This was radically new, for almost every religion had (and for that matter still has) food laws of one sort or another. But Jesus is interested in something that matters far more than such trivia. There is a marked emphasis in this Gospel on the unimportance of what is merely outward and the importance of the inward (e.g., 6:1–6, 16–18; 7:15–20; 12:33–37).

Matthew puts a good deal of emphasis on the role of Jesus as a teacher, as is evidenced by the large amount of teaching in his Gospel. Being a disciple means learning, and Matthew makes it clear that the disciples did learn many important teachings from Jesus. For example, when Jesus warned against the leaven of the Pharisees and Sadducees, and the disciples did not understand (they thought this had something to do with the fact that they had no bread), Jesus explained so that they did understand (16:11–12; cf. 13:51; 17:13).[48] Matthew often omits Mark's

---

[46]"All in all, Matthew writes his gospel to keep persecution of the church from stymieing evangelism" (Robert H. Gundry, *Matthew* [Grand Rapids, 1982], 9).

[47]Some scholars emphasize Matthew's kinship with Judaism; cf. Bornkamm: "Matthew understands the law in a way which does not differ in principle from that of Judaism—or better—which in principle 'does not' differ" (*Tradition and Interpretation in Matthew*, 31). It is true that Matthew has a certain kinship with the approach of the scribes, but we must not miss the fact that with all his stress on the law and demand for righteousness he is not saying the same thing as the scribes. He is looking for something radically new.

[48]Cf. Ulrich Luz, "Jesus is the teacher who leads his disciples to understanding. . . . The disciples are men of little faith, but they do understand" (Stanton, *The Interpretation of Matthew*, 103). A number of scholars see the disciple teaching in Matthew as "transparent"; they see it as addressed to the original followers of Jesus, but in such a way that the reader sees right through to what is expected of all Jesus' followers. Peter is often seen in this way as the ideal disciple. This can be argued too strongly, for Matthew is concerned with what Jesus taught. But he is certainly not engaging in an academic historical enterprise. He expects his readers to take Jesus' disciple teaching seriously and apply it to themselves.

references to a lack of understanding, and this is usually interpreted as a passing over of the faults of the disciples, but perhaps it should be seen rather as part of Matthew's concentration on Jesus' effectiveness as a teacher. Matthew does not depict the disciples as naturally perceptive, but as enlightened by what Jesus taught them. That he is not defensive toward them is seen in his faithful recording of their lack of faith (6:30; 8:26; 14:31; 16:8; 17:20; 28:17). The Gospel of Matthew has the fullest account of the episode where Jesus predicted his death, Peter rejected the prediction, and Jesus rebuked Peter (16:22–23). And Matthew alone tells us that that disciple denied Jesus "before them all" (26:70) and that he used an oath at the second denial (26:72). Matthew is concerned not so much to deny the faults of the disciples as to show the greatness of their Teacher.

Another important aspect of being Jesus' disciple is brought out in the discussion that followed the Pharisees' accusation that Jesus cast out demons only with the help of Beelzebul the ruler of the demons (12:24). Jesus pointed out that that would mean that the evil one's kingdom was divided, a kingdom that could not stand, and he went on to say that the sons of the Pharisees also cast out demons. Would the Pharisees say the same about them as they did about Jesus? Then he came to the critical point: "But if I cast out the demons with the Spirit of God, then there has come upon you the kingdom of God" (12:28). The presence of the kingdom is seen in the power that overthrows the demons. Only when the strong man is bound can his house be plundered, and this leads on to the forthright saying, "He who is not with me is against me" (12:30). There is no neutrality in the war Jesus is fighting. He is calling people to a life in which the power of the evil one has been broken. He is offering them a new power, a power not their own, so that Satan may exercise no sway in their lives. In that situation we either opt for Jesus or we do not. There is no middle way. Those who come to Jesus must be aware of what he is about and of the new power he has brought into life.

In the Beatitudes we see this absoluteness of Jesus and the reversal of values it involves (5:1–12). It is not those whom the official hierarchy in Judaism accounted blessed who were really blessed by God, but the people who were poor in spirit, the mourners, the meek people, those who hungered and thirsted for righteousness, the merciful, the pure in heart, the peacemakers, the persecuted. Contemporary religion would have agreed with some of these, but certainly not with the complete list. Jesus was far from accepting the conventional religious values of his day.

We see this further in the way he dealt with the transgression of the commandments. Judaism of the time took seriously the duty of obeying the law of God and went to great lengths to define exactly what was and what was not a transgression. The letter of the law was most important. Exactly what God prescribed must be done, nothing less. But if the letter was not transgressed, the worshiper was in the clear. Jesus, however, took commandment after commandment and showed that it is quite possible to remain within the letter of the law while breaking the spirit of it. It is not enough to refrain from the command not to murder. To be angry with one's brother without a cause is to embrace the kind of feeling that leads to murder. And that breaks the commandment. So does the angry and insulting word

(5:21–22). It is the same with the lustful look, with telling the truth only when on oath, and so on. Jesus' teaching is not a modified Judaism. It is a radical novelty, and it certainly needs inner power. Jesus taught that although fruit shows what the tree is like, the important thing is that the tree be good. If the tree is good, the fruit will also be good (7:15–20; 12:33). With a different metaphor he counseled building on a good foundation (7:24–27). If the foundation is right, the house will be secure; if the foundation is faulty, the house will fall.

Jesus' major demand is that people live in love. We have already noticed that he sees this as the way we are to be God's children (5:43–48) and that the whole law can be summed up in the commandments to love God and man (22:36–40; cf. also 19:19). The love commandment shows how the law is to be interpreted. We should also notice the Golden Rule (7:12) and the fact that it is a tragedy when love becomes cool (24:12). It is the way of the world to love the attractive and those who love us. It is the way of the followers of Jesus to love because they have been loved by God. In the Christian way it is the love of God that comes first, and our love is always a response to his. For that reason Christians cannot confine their love to those they find naturally attractive or those who love them or who can bring them some benefit. They love because they have been loved by the God of grace.

Love is practical. It leads to concern for others, specifically for the poor, who in first-century Palestine lived in dreadful hardship. Jesus' followers would help them financially, but they would do this unobtrusively, not sounding a trumpet before them in the ostentatious manner of some who sought a reputation for piety (6:2–4).

Jesus would not accept the ritual taboos of his contemporaries. Matthew records the controversy over the way the Sabbath was to be kept (12:1–14). Typically the religious Jew took the regulations for the day's observance with the utmost seriousness. The Sabbath was to be set apart from all the other days as God's holy day. One way to keep the day holy was to refrain from healing on that day. But Jesus insisted that it is no mark of holiness to refuse to meet genuine need, whether it be hunger (12:1) or sickness (12:10). Freely he met both.

Jesus emphasized the importance of children.[49] It is necessary to "turn" and become like children if we are to enter the kingdom (18:3). Specifically this calls for humility (18:4). But this teaching goes beyond the fact that adults are counseled to become like children in important qualities like humility and trust: it makes clear that children have value for their own sake. A dreadful fate awaits anyone who brings trouble to one of the least of those who believe in Christ (18:6). The "little ones" here includes lowly disciples,[50] but we should not overlook the importance of children in Jesus' eyes. When the disciples tried to stop people who were bringing children to him, Jesus forbade them. He received the children and laid

---

[49] Matthew has παιδίον 18 times, whereas Mark has it 12 times, and Luke 13; no one else has it more than 3 times. Matthew also has τέκνον 14 times (equal to the highest in any one book), θυγάτηρ 8 times (only Luke with nine has it more frequently), and υἱός 89 times (the most in any book). Matthew has an interest in children.

[50] Some indeed hold that the term simply means "disciples." Cf. E. Schweizer, "The most characteristic expression for the Matthean community, however, is 'one of these little ones' used to describe the disciple" (Stanton, *The Interpretation of Matthew,* 138).

his hands on them in blessing (19:13–15). The high priests and the scribes had no sympathy for children; they called on Jesus to bid the little ones who cried, "Hosanna to the Son of David" to be quiet. But Jesus reminded them of the Scripture: "Out of the mouths of babies and sucklings you have perfected praise" (21:15–16; the quotation is from Ps. 8:2). He welcomed children.

Jesus wanted people to trust God. He called on them not to be worried about the necessities of life, such as food and clothing. The birds do not worry, but God sees to it that they are fed. The plants do not worry, but God sees to it that they are clothed more gloriously than even the great King Solomon ever was. So there is no reason for worry, and Jesus expects us to trust (6:25–34).

The trusting person is a praying person. There is no ostentation about true prayer, unlike the "prayers" of some who prayed in order to be seen by other people (a reputation for piety helps!). Prayer is to be in secret; it is an affair between the disciple and God; it concerns no one else (6:5–6). Prayer is to be simple, without the empty repetitions some used. And Jesus gave the model that has helped so many Christians through the centuries—the Lord's Prayer (6:7–13).

We should not leave the section on discipleship without noticing that Matthew has a marked emphasis on ethical qualities. It is interesting that he uses the word *agathos*, "good," eighteen times (Romans, with twenty-one, is the only New Testament book to use it more often), and *kalos*, which also means "good," twenty-one times (more than any other book; 1 Timothy is next with sixteen). He also has *dikaios*, "righteous," more than any other book (seventeen times; next is Luke with

eleven; he has *dikaiosynē*, "righteousness," seven times, the most in any book outside of Paul's writings (Mark does not use it, and Luke has it once). At the other end of the scale, though there is no preponderance among the words for sin, he does use *ponēros*, "evil," twenty-six times, exactly twice as often as Luke, whose use is next most frequent, and *hypokritēs*, "hypocrite," thirteen times out of seventeen in the whole New Testament. Word counts do not prove everything, but at least these show that Matthew is interested in people who manifest (or fail to manifest) these qualities.

THE MISSION OF THE TWELVE

On one occasion Jesus sent the Twelve on a preaching tour. The tour was confined to Israel. Jesus specifically told his disciples not to go to the Gentiles or even to the Samaritans (10:5); this mission was to "the lost sheep of the house of Israel" (v. 6). Some features of his charge seem to apply only to that mission, whereas others are of wider application. Be that as it may, on this occasion Jesus gave the disciples authority over demons and disease (10:1, 8). He sent them without material resources; God would look after them. The burden of their message was "The kingdom of heaven has drawn near" (10:7). They went thus with a message of peace, and Jesus gave directions as to what their reactions should be when they were received peacefully and when they were not (10:11–15).

But they were not to expect to be received well; they went as sheep among wolves (10:16). This statement leads to a section on persecution, a section that deals not only with the commission to the Twelve but also with the events that would befall the followers of Jesus in later times. Those who follow him are to rely on God when they stand before hostile tribunals; in such circumstances the Spirit of their Father will be speaking in them (10:20). They must not be afraid (10:26). God cares for them (10:30–31). They will doubtless be tempted to turn away from such a difficult task, but they are warned that eternal issues hang on their reaction. If they are ashamed of Christ before men, he will be ashamed of them before his heavenly Father; to deny him before men is to invite his denial of them before the Father (10:32–33). No earthly affection can be allowed to compete with the love his followers have for him. They must take up their cross in following him and lose their life for him in order to find it (10:37–39).

This leads to the affirmation that anyone who receives Christ receives the Father who sent him (10:40). This is a profound and important truth, and it leads to a corresponding dignity being given to the followers of Christ. Even the smallest service that any one of them does in the name of Christ will not go unrewarded.

THE CHURCH

Matthew is usually thought to be more interested in the church than are the other Evangelists.[51] He seems to assume a community of Jesus' people

throughout his Gospel. He is the only one of the four Gospel writers to use the word "church" (*ekklēsia*), and he does so in two important passages (16:16–19; 18:15–18).[52] The first comes from the occasion at Caesarea Philippi when Peter confessed his faith in Jesus as "the Christ, the Son of the living God." To this Jesus replied, "You are blessed, Simon bar-Jona, for flesh and blood did not reveal this to you, but my Father who is in heaven. And I say to you, 'You are Peter [*petros*], and on this rock [*petra*] I will build my church, and the gates of Hades will not overthrow it. I will give you the keys of the kingdom of heaven, and whatever you bind on earth will be bound in heaven, and whatever you loose on earth will be loosed in heaven'" (16:16–19).

We notice first that this is not a human discovery. It came by revelation. This does not necessarily mean that there was a blinding flash of illumination; there may have been a slow process as Peter watched his Master—a process during which God led him to a right understanding Jesus. What matters is the revelation, not how it came.

The church is to be built on the rock. The play on words and the address to Peter makes it clear that that apostle is assigned a special place. Roman Catholics have traditionally thought that Jesus here appointed Peter as the head of the church, that Peter became bishop of Rome, that he passed on his position to his successors at Rome,[53] and that

---

[51] Cf. F. C. Grant: "Matthew is sometimes described as the 'ecclesiastical' gospel, and appropriately, for its interests are far more thoroughly centered in the church than are those of any other gospel—or any other writing of the NT" (*IDB*, 3:311).

[52] These are often regarded as unauthentic, as for example by Eduard Schweizer for the first (*The Good News According to Matthew* [London, 1976], 336ff.), and Rudolf Bultmann for both: "These are sayings created independently by the Church" (*The History of the Synoptic Tradition* [Oxford, 1963], 146; cf. also 138–41). They are accepted as genuine by K. L. Schmidt, *TDNT*, 3:518–26; Oscar Cullmann, *Peter: Disciple, Apostle, Martyr* (London, 1962), 164ff.

[53] This position was reaffirmed by Vatican II. The Council proclaimed that "the role that the Lord gave individually to Peter, the first among the apostles, is permanent and was meant to be transmitted

all those outside the communion thus established cannot claim to be certainly members of the true church. But this is to go very far and very fast. Jesus did not say that he would build on Peter (*petros*), but on the rock (*petra*), and the small difference in the two words is important.[54] It is possible to understand the Greek to mean that the rock is not so much the man as the confession he has just made. It is on the basis of confessing Jesus as the Christ, the Son of God, that the church is to be built. Many think we do justice to the language most completely if we combine the two ideas and see the rock as Peter in the act of confessing his faith in Jesus.[55]

The keys of the kingdom may symbolize the teaching office. In 23:13 we read of the scribes and Pharisees as shutting the kingdom of heaven to people, preventing them from entering; their teaching was such as to keep people out. If this is what Jesus means, then with this teaching authority goes the power of binding and of loosing,

i.e., of declaring forbidden or permitted; it is an extension of the teaching function of the leaders of the church of Jesus Christ.[56] The teacher who has the mind of Christ will present teaching that is ratified in heaven. In any case, we should not think that the power of binding and loosing is confined to Peter; it is expressly assigned to others as well, apparently "the church" (18:18).

The passage clearly looks forward to the continuing existence of Jesus' followers as a worshiping group. It assigns a special place to confessing Jesus as Christ and Son of God and sees Peter as important and as a leading apostle because he made this confession before all of the others did. And it anticipates the teaching that was to open up the kingdom of heaven to people in future days.

The other passage concerning the church speaks of the procedure to be followed when one member sins against another. The offended brother should first speak to the offender in the

---

to his successors" (*The Documents of Vatican II,* ed. Walter M. Abbott [London, 1966], 40); "After Peter's profession of faith, [Jesus] decreed that on him He would build His Church; to Peter He promised the keys of the kingdom of heaven" (p. 344).

[54] Aramaic does not have this difference. But we are dealing with a Greek text, and the postulated Aramaic original was such that it was rendered into Greek with two different words.

[55] The subject was, of course, vigorously debated at the Vatican Council of 1870. W. H. Griffith Thomas gives an interesting summary of a speech prepared by Archbishop Kenrick to be delivered at that Council; it was not in fact delivered there, but it was subsequently published. Kenrick noted five interpretations of the passage that were held in antiquity: "(1) The first declared that the Church was built on Peter, an interpretation endorsed by seventeen Fathers. (2) The second understood the words as referring to all the Apostles, Peter being simply the Primate. This was the opinion of eight Fathers. (3) The third interpretation asserted that the words applied to the faith which Peter professed, a view held by no less than forty-four Fathers, including some of the most important and representative. (4) The fourth interpretation declared that the words were to be understood of Jesus Christ, the Church being built on Him. This was the view of sixteen writers. (5) The fifth interpretation understood the term 'rock' to apply to the faithful themselves, who, by believing on Christ, were made living stones in the temple of His body. This, however, was the opinion of very few" (*The Principles of Theology* [London, 1930], 470–71). The interpretation that became normative in the Roman church is far from certain, and it was a long way from being the usual view in the early church.

[56] Cf. George E. Ladd: "As a matter of fact, the disciples had already exercised this authority of binding and loosing when they visited the cities of Israel proclaiming the kingdom of God. Wherever they and their message were accepted, peace rested upon that house; but wherever they and their message were rejected, the judgment of God was sealed to that house (Mt. 10:14, 15)" (*A Theology of the New Testament,* 118). Günther Bornkamm sees the binding and loosing as referring "primarily to teaching authority" (Stanton, *The Interpretation of Matthew,* 93).

hope that they can settle the matter between them. The important thing is to try to win back the offender and restore him to fellowship.[57] If that approach does not work, the offended one should tell one or two others; perhaps they will be able to succeed. If the offender refuses to listen to them, the brother is to "tell it to the church"; if he does not obey the church, he is to be considered the same as "the heathen and the tax-collector" (18:15–18). This is a purely disciplinary procedure and tells us little about the essence of the church.[58] It is clearly expected that the church will try to preserve peace among its members, but the expulsion of the obdurate shows that there are limits to what can be tolerated within the membership.

A further mark of ecclesiastical interest is seen in the command to baptize. The very last thing Matthew tells us about the risen Christ is that he told his followers to make disciples from all the nations "baptizing them in the name of the Father, and of the Son, and of the Holy Spirit" (28:19). They were to teach these new disciples to keep all that Jesus commanded. Obedience is an important part of being a disciple. He added a promise that he would be with them "through all the days until the consummation of the age" (28:20).

Much of the teaching in this Gospel is seen as "disciple teaching," and this strengthens the hands of those who emphasize the community. "Matthew does not work in a vacuum, but within the life of a church for whose needs he is catering; his Gospel more than the others is a product of a community and for a community."[59] In agreement with this is the fact that he is unusually interested in the brothers: he uses the word "brother" thirty-nine times (as does Paul in 1 Corinthians), more than in any other book except Acts, which has it fifty-seven times.

[57] Cf. Schweizer: "The straying one's honor is to be maintained by an initial conversation without witnesses, and the expression 'win back' shows that what matters is the sinner, not a 'pure community'" (*The Good News According to Matthew*, 370).

[58] A number of writers draw attention to the similar regulation at Qumran—for example, A. R. C. Leaney, *The Rule of Qumran and Its Meaning* [London, 1966], 178, 180.

[59] Krister Stendahl, in *Peake's Commentary on the Bible*, 769.

the Gospel of Luke and acts: the doctrine of God

It is generally agreed that it is one and the same author who wrote the Gospel of Luke and the Acts of the Apostles. This makes him a very important figure in any study of the New Testament, for the two writings together form more than a quarter of the whole. This author has contributed more than any other, and, even aside from the fact of divine inspiration, the sheer volume of his work would make it necessary for us to give serious attention to what he has written.

Throughout the history of the church it has usually been held that the author of both of these works was Luke, and there is no serious reason for disputing this. We will assume that Luke wrote both volumes, though not a great deal depends on the precise identity of the writer. Luke has generally been thought of as a historian, and most discussion about him has turned on the question of how good a historian he was.

In recent times it has been realized more clearly that, whatever merits he may have had as a historian, he must be thought of as a significant theologian. This is not universally held, and Vin-

cent Taylor, for example, says that Luke "is not primarily a theologian."[1] Over against that we could set the verdict of J. Christiaan Beker that Luke is "a master theologian"[2] and that of J. D. G. Dunn that he is one of "the three major New Testament theologians."[3] The spate of books on Luke–Acts in recent years makes it difficult to overlook the very real theological emphasis in this part of the New Testament. While it is true that Luke is important for the history he has written, it is also true that all that he writes has a serious theological purpose behind it. He is not writing a history of Jesus of Nazareth and following that with a sketch of the history of the early church; he is writing about what God did in Jesus and what God did in the early church. It is theology rather than history that is his basic concern, no matter how much he has put us in his debt for the historical information he has conveyed to us.

Perhaps we can see something of the situation with the help of Eduard Schweizer. In studying Luke and writing a commentary on this Gospel, he found himself "constantly harassed by

---

[1] *IDB*, 3:181.
[2] *Paul the Apostle* (Edinburgh, 1980), 162.
[3] *IT* 84 (1972–73): 7. He sees Paul and John as the other two.

the problems of christology or soteriology for which Luke seems to have no clear answer." But on the other hand, he says, "I detected in an ever-increasing way, to my own surprise, how much his approach helped me to a new theological understanding of the meaning of the Christ event." He found in Luke "a full load of stories about Jesus, of parables, many of them not known to the other Evangelists, and of descriptions of different life situations, like that of Jesus' journey to Jerusalem which provided a theologically important new setting of many incidents or sayings."[4] Luke does not engage in long and obviously theological discussions, but he does write about the events he has chosen from the life of Christ and from what happened in the early church in such a way that he helps us considerably in our theological quest. He is not professing to write a work of theology, but what he writes is theologically informed and contributes significantly to our understanding of New Testament theology.

A MIGHTY GOD

There are many possible starting points, for Luke's theology is many-sided. But let us begin with his thought that God is a mighty God, one who is able to work out his purpose and who does so. Very early we learn that it was "the power of the Most High" that would overshadow Mary, as a result of which the One who would be born of her would "be called holy, Son of God" (1:35).[5] We are not to think of Jesus as a good man who because of his goodness was given special favor by God, or even, as the adoptionists held,

was adopted into the Godhead. He was born because of the special exercise of the power of God. Mary could sing of "the Mighty One" who had "done great things" for her (1:49).

His earthly ministry was carried out in that same power. God "anointed him with power" (A10:38), and it was in this power that his public ministry was carried out; it was when "the power of the Lord" was present that Jesus did his works of healing (5:17). And if we look right through to the last things, Luke thinks of the Son of man as "seated at the right hand," not simply of God, but "of the power of God" (22:69). Matthew and Mark report the saying in the shorter form: "sitting at the right hand of the power" (Matt. 26:64; Mark 14:62). But the way Luke puts it it is made clear that the power is the power "of God." And it is the same power of God that is meant in the statement that the Son of man will come on a cloud "with power and great glory" (21:27).

The general position is that "the things that are impossible with men are possible with God" (18:27). Luke sees no limit to the power of God and rejoices that that power has been put forth in the work of salvation in Christ. So he reports that Paul commends certain people "to God and to the word of his grace which is able to build up and give the inheritance among all the sanctified ones" (A20:32). The power of God is mighty to bring salvation. And he does this where he chooses. In the face of God's giving his good gift to Gentiles, Peter could defend his action in preaching to them by asking, "Who was *I* to be able to resist God?" (A11:17).

---

[4] *Luke: A Challenge to Present Theology* (Atlanta, 1982), 1.
[5] Throughout these chapters references to Luke's Gospel are given simply with chapter and verse. References to Acts are preceded by A.

But showing the mightiness of God is not a matter of quoting individual texts. As the passages I have quoted show, there are such texts. But it is more than that. The whole spirit in which Luke writes makes it clear that for him God is the supremely great Being, One who does whatever he wills, and whom no one can hinder.[6]

THE KINGDOM OF GOD

As we have seen, the kingdom of God is an important concept in both Matthew and Mark. It is also very significant in Luke (who uses the phrase thirty-two times, with another six in Acts). And it fits in well with his emphasis on power, for it means the sovereign will of God in operation. Where God is King, his will is done. Much of what Luke says on the subject of the kingdom he has in common with Matthew or Mark or both, but he has also a considerable number of statements about the kingdom that are peculiar to his writings.

As an example of the way he makes his point consider the following saying of Jesus: "I must preach the kingdom of God in the other cities also, for this was I sent" (4:43). Mark reports Jesus as saying, "Let us go somewhere else, to the next towns so that I may preach there too" (Mark 1:38). The essence of the two reports is the same, but the way Luke puts it brings out the necessity ("I must") that stems from the sovereignty of God, for he speaks of the kingdom (as Mark does not), and

the divine mission ("I was sent"). Luke makes it clear that the kingdom was the constant theme of Jesus' preaching, for as he went on "from one town and village to another" he was "proclaiming the good news of the kingdom of God" (8:1).[7]

We see Luke's interest in the kingdom again in the way the account of the feeding of the five thousand is introduced. Matthew speaks of Jesus' compassion and of his healing the people (Matt. 14:13–14). Mark also tells us of Jesus' compassion on those "sheep not having a shepherd," and he says that "he began to teach them many things" (Mark 6:34). Luke tells us that Jesus welcomed the people. He mentions the healings, but in addition he tells us that Jesus was speaking to them "about the kingdom of God" (9:11). This is an important concept for him; he inserts it even when the other Evangelists do not see it as necessary.

He also brings out the urgency of the kingdom, as when he tells us that Jesus said to the potential disciple who wanted first to bury his father: "Let the dead bury their dead, but as for you, you go and preach the kingdom of God" (9:60). To another, who wanted first to bid farewell to his household, Jesus said, "No one who puts his hand to the plow and looks back is fit for the kingdom of God" (9:59–62). Matthew records Jesus' words about the dead burying their dead (Matt. 8:22), but he does not have the reference to the kingdom, nor the following passage about putting the hand to the plow.

---

[6] Luke's interest in power is illustrated by the fact that he uses the noun δύναμις 15 times in the Gospel and 10 times in Acts, (elsewhere, 1 Corinthians is the highest with 15); the verb δύναμαι 26 times in the Gospel, 21 in Acts (John has it 36 times); and the adjective δυνατός 4 times in the Gospel and 6 in Acts (Mark and Romans each have 5). Luke is concerned to make clear what people can or cannot do, and throughout his assumption is that God is supreme over all and none can resist his will.

[7] I. Howard Marshall says that Schurmann "finds here a pattern of missionary work intended to be followed by the early church" and he compares 13:22 and Acts 16:4 (*The Gospel of Luke* [Grand Rapids, 1978], 316). Whether we accept this or not, plainly Luke wants us to see that this was the pattern of Jesus' preaching ministry.

We should not miss Luke's interest in the kingdom and his realization of the demands it makes on those who receive it. It is in this way that we should understand Jesus' reference to the kingdom in his charge to the seventy before they went out on their mission. Among other things they were to proclaim the nearness of the kingdom (10:9; cf. Matt. 10:7). If any city did not receive them when they gave this message, they were to go out into its streets and say, "Even the dust of your city that sticks to our feet we wipe off against you; nevertheless know this: The kingdom of God has come near" (10:11; Matthew has the former words about the kingdom, but not these). The approach of the kingdom is a very serious matter. To reject it is a calamity. This is the point also of Jesus' warning to some complacent types that there would be wailing and gnashing of teeth when they saw the great patriarchs and the prophets in the kingdom while they themselves were thrown out. This does not mean that there will be no more than an exclusive minority in the kingdom; people will come from east and west and north and south and recline in the kingdom. But, although there will be many there, it is unwise to presume on one's position (13:28–30).

Something of this is apparent even in Jesus' speaking of the blessings that come to those in the kingdom. Peter once drew attention to the fact that he and the others near to Jesus had left their possessions and followed Christ. The implied question is something like this: "Does this mean that we have entry into the kingdom?" Jesus' reply speaks of the many blessings that they would receive, but he introduces it with a promise: "There is no one who has left house or wife or brothers or parents or children for the sake of the kingdom of God who will not receive manifold

more . . ." (18:28–30). To enter the kingdom is a costly affair. But it is abundantly worthwhile: there will be manifold blessings here and now and eternal life in the hereafter. And it is a fellow diner's recognition of the blessings in the kingdom that triggered Jesus' telling of the parable of the great supper (14:15).

There has been a good deal of discussion of the passage in which some Pharisees asked Jesus when the kingdom of God would come. They may have been genuine seekers or they may simply have been trying to discover Jesus' opinion with a view to making use of it against him at some time. Be that as it may, Jesus replied, "The kingdom of God does not come with observation, neither will they say 'Look, here it is' or 'There'; for look, the kingdom of God is in the midst of you" (17:20–21).

This certainly indicates that the Pharisees had the wrong idea of what the kingdom of God was like. They were looking for a kingdom very different from that of which Jesus taught. It would not come "with observation," i.e., "in such a way that its rise can be observed" (BAGD). It would not appear after they saw this or that kind of sign that they were anticipating.

The meaning of "in the midst of you" (*entos hymōn*) is disputed. Some suggest that Jesus is saying that the kingdom is an inward and spiritual affair; it takes place in the hearts of believers and thus cannot be observed. Of course, that is true (cf. Rom. 14:17), but that is not what Jesus is saying. There are many statements about the kingdom in the New Testament, and no statement besides this one lends support to a view that it is essentially inward. Others suggest that the words point to a sudden appearance. It will come so swiftly that there will be no question of seeing signs that enable the observer to predict its approach. But if this is what is meant, the words are used in a very unusual way. A further suggestion is that the meaning is "within your grasp": you may have the kingdom if only you reach out for it. The objection to this is that the kingdom is normally seen as God's gift rather than as the result of human endeavor. All in all it seems that we should accept the fourth suggestion, that the meaning is "among you." In the person of Jesus the kingdom has come into their very midst. It is he who brings in the kingdom.

Luke also lets us see that there is an important future aspect to the kingdom. That will depend on Jesus' coming again. In that sense there will be signs that will enable the perceptive to know that the kingdom is near (21:31; Matthew and Mark both have "it is near"; again we have Luke's tendency to make it clear that it is the kingdom that is in mind). But people must not exaggerate the nearness of the kingdom. The parable of the pounds is addressed to a situation in which some people thought that the kingdom would come "immediately" (19:11). That is not so, and Jesus made this clear.

There are two references to the kingdom of God in Jesus' statements in the Upper Room. In speaking of the Passover he had desired to eat with the disciples, Jesus said, "I will not eat it until it be fulfilled in the kingdom of God" (22:16).[8] The Passover was a festival of deliverance; it looked back to God's great action in freeing his people from their bondage in Egypt. Jesus was saying that this has typological

significance; the mighty deliverance in olden times pointed forward to the greater deliverance that would take place at the consummation of all things, the coming of the kingdom. And this eager looking forward to the final deliverance is apparent again when Jesus said that he would not drink of the fruit of the vine "until the kingdom of God comes" (22:18).

It is noteworthy that Luke continues to refer to "the kingdom of God" when he writes the Acts. He tells us that during the forty days between the Resurrection and the Ascension Jesus was speaking of "the things concerning the kingdom of God" (A1:3). Then the Christian preachers got busy. At Samaria Philip was "evangelizing about the kingdom of God and the name of Jesus Christ" (A8:12), and at Ephesus the kingdom was the burden of Paul's preaching for three months (A19:8). Right to the end, this was his message, for he testified to the kingdom of God when the Jews came to his lodging in Rome (A28:23). The very last sentence in Acts tells us that Paul in Rome preached the kingdom of God and taught about the Lord Jesus Christ, boldly and unhindered (A28:31). Paul did not make the kingdom an easy gospel, for he taught the people in Lystra, Iconium, and Antioch that "through many afflictions we must enter the kingdom of God" (A14:22).

From all this we see that Luke took the sovereignty of God very seriously. Clearly he deeply appreciated what Jesus had said about the kingdom, and he makes it clear both that Jesus taught about it often and significantly, and that this preaching continued in the early church. That God rules and that

---

[8]"The reference to fulfilment *in the kingdom of God* indicates that the Passover had typological significance. It commemorated a deliverance indeed, but it pointed forward to a greater deliverance, which would be seen in the kingdom of God" (Leon Morris, *The Gospel According to St. Luke* [London, 1974], 305).

in the fullness of time he will bring in his kingdom in the fullest sense are important parts of the Christian understanding of things.

GOD ACTED IN CHRIST

It is, of course, central to the Christian understanding of things that in the life and death and resurrection and ascension of Jesus we see nothing less than the action of God. We are not to think of Jesus as no more than a great man. God was at work in a very special way in Jesus. We have already noticed that Luke makes it clear that the birth of Jesus took place because of divine intervention. God is active throughout the ministry of Jesus. Luke tells us, for example, that Jesus told the former Gerasene demoniac to go back home and tell the people what God had done for him (8:39), not what he himself had done. It was God who was at work in Jesus. Luke's recording the man's commission to tell the people what God had done and then telling what Jesus had done seems to be a way of emphasizing the deity of Christ. But we should not miss the fact that God was active in Jesus' works of healing. Jesus did good works and healed those oppressed by the devil "because God was with him" (A10:38).

Like the other Evangelists, Luke speaks of Jesus as "the Son of God" (e.g., 1:35; 4:3, 9, 41; 8:28; A9:20). He was also the Christ "of God" (9:20; 23:35). Luke also tells us that "the grace of God" was on the boy Jesus (2:40; cf. 2:52), indicating that from Jesus' earliest years God was at work in and with him. Early in Jesus' ministry a demon-possessed man recognized him as "the holy one of God" (4:34), thus

pointing to his close connection with the Father. And Jesus gave evidence of his own recognition of his dependence on God when he spent a whole night in prayer before choosing the Twelve (6:12). It was important that this group of close associates be the right people. Jesus sought God's guidance before he made his selection.

The two on the road to Emmaus recognized that Jesus was "mighty in deed and word before God and all the people" (24:19). Even when they thought of Jesus as finally defeated and killed by his enemies, they recognized that his work and his words had had the approval of God.[9] But Peter put it better when on the day of Pentecost he told the crowds, "Jesus of Nazareth was a man attested to you by God in mighty works and wonders and signs that God did through him in your midst, as you yourselves know" (A2:22). There is emphasis here on the fact that the people themselves knew what Jesus had done. It had all taken place "in their midst"; "they themselves" knew what had happened. But they had seen no more than the miracles; they had not recognized what was really happening. Now Peter informed them that these miraculous happenings were God's attestation of Jesus. More than that, it was none less than God himself who did the mighty works.

Luke's account of the first days of the infant church makes it clear that what gripped those first believers was the fact and the wonder of the Resurrection. When Jesus died, the bottom dropped out of their world. When they found that he had risen, that he had conquered death, their whole outlook was revolutionized. The thrill of the Resurrection runs through all that Luke

---

[9]"This phrase conveys the thought that God himself approved of this powerful prophet" (R. C. H. Lenski, *The Interpretation of St. Luke's Gospel* [Minneapolis, 1946], 1184).

records of what was said and done in those exhilarating days. And constantly he brings out the truth that it was God who had brought about the Resurrection. Peter spoke simply of Jesus "whom God raised" (A2:24), and in the same sermon he came back to this thought by saying, "This Jesus did God raise, of which we all are witnesses" (A2:32). In his next sermon he complained that his hearers had killed "the Prince of life" but he added, "whom God raised from the dead," once more adding that he and his comrades were witnesses of what God had done (A3:15). He said that God "raised his child" (A3:26)—a thought that keeps finding expression (A4:10; 5:30; 10:40). When Paul came on the scene, Luke records that in Paul's sermon in the synagogue in Antioch of Pisidia he spoke of the Resurrection as God's act and did so repeatedly (A13:30, 33, 37). Clearly it was a dominant theme in early Christian preaching. God had acted in Christ, and it was God who had overcome death in raising Jesus.

The early preachers emphasized the way God had given honor and dignity to Jesus. Jesus "was exalted to the right hand of God" (A2:33). God made him "both Lord and Christ" (A2:36; Peter goes on to bring out the enormity of the crime of his hearers by adding, "This Jesus, whom *you* crucified . . ."). In accordance with a prophecy of Moses, God had raised up Jesus as a prophet (A3:22; 7:37). God exalted him to his right hand "as Prince and Savior" (A5:31) and appointed him "Judge of living and dead" (A10:42). God "anointed him with the Holy Spirit" (10:38). We should probably include here also the fact that it was in Jesus that God fulfilled his oath to David that he would raise up one of his descendants to sit on his throne (A2:30) and that of this king's

posterity he brought to Israel "a Savior, Jesus" (A13:23).

In all this we see one of Luke's major emphases. It was obvious to all when he wrote that the Christian movement was a reality. It could not be denied that there were people who owed their inspiration to Jesus and who claimed that he was the One who had brought universal salvation. One of the things Luke is making abundantly clear is that this is not to be regarded as just another human movement. We are not to think that some garrulous Galileans managed to persuade people to throw in their lot with them. Rather there was a great divine act: *God* sent Jesus to be the Savior. We do not understand this movement unless we see that God is in it. All that Jesus did he did because God was acting in and through him.

GOD ACTS IN BELIEVERS

Not only did God act in Jesus, but he continues to act in the followers of Jesus. No New Testament writer is more sure that God acts now than is Luke, as the miracles he records in Acts attest. He lists quite a number of them, such as the healing of the lame man in Acts 3, and he also has statements like "God kept doing [*epoiei*, continuous action] extraordinary miracles through the hands of Paul" (A19:11). The God of whom Luke writes is no powerless nonentity but a mighty God, interested in his people and ready to act among them to set forward his purpose.

Luke is sure that God speaks to people. Thus the Spirit spoke to Peter (A10:19; 11:12), and Paul and Barnabas went off on their missionary journey because the Spirit instructed certain teachers in Antioch to set them apart for the work to which they were called (A13:2). God did not leave himself without witness, something that is shown in his doing good for people, like sending rain and fruitful seasons (A14:17).

When in due course Paul and Barnabas returned to Antioch at the end of their first missionary journey and reported to the church that had sent them out, they told their hearers "what things God had done with them and that he had opened a door of faith to the Gentiles" (A14:27). It was not the apostles who had done the work, but God. They repeated this at the Council of Jerusalem (15:4), and Peter said in similar fashion that God had decreed that the Gentiles should hear the gospel through him (A15:7). At a later time Paul again reported to the church in Jerusalem what God had done among the Gentiles through his ministry (A21:19). So also we read that God "testified" through the preachers (A15:8) and that he "did signs and wonders among the Gentiles" through them (A15:12). It was he who called the preachers to the work of evangelism in Macedonia (A16:10). Paul could plan his movements, but, properly, he included a "God willing" clause (A18:21); it was God, not the apostle, who determined where he would work. When he recounts the facts of his conversion, he tells his hearers that Ananias said to him, "The God of our fathers foreordained you" (A22:14). On a similar occasion he made the point that the promise of God was very important: he was on trial because of his firm adherence to a belief in the fulfillment of the promise (A26:6).

Paul saw God as active in the day-to-day activities of his mission. God spoke to him at Corinth and encouraged him in his work there (A18:9–10). God spoke to him again in the barracks at Jerusalem and assured him that he would bear witness in Rome (A23:11). During the terrible storm on the voyage God's angel stood by Paul and gave him the assurance that he would indeed stand before Caesar and further that God had "given" him all those on board the ship (A27:23–24). Paul was conscious always of the power of the God who "raises the dead" (A26:8). But he did not confine the activities of God to great things at the end of the age. He saw him as active now, in the affairs of daily life, and as doing things for his servants now.

This, of course, was nothing new. God had spoken in the prophets (A2:17; 3:21; 7:6). He had judged a nation (A7:7). When the people turned away from him and worshiped idols, somehow the hand of God was in that, too, for he "gave them over" to their false worship; his punishment included their very idolatry when they might have enjoyed a more satisfying way of life (A7:42; cf. 23:3). In the political life of the nation God gave the people Saul as their first king (A13:21). And, of course, in the beginning God made the world (A17:24), and people are known as "the offspring of God" (A17:29).

GOD MY SAVIOR

Like all the other Gospel writers, Luke gives quite a lot of space to the passion narrative. It is his climax, and he narrates it with care. One feature of his writing is that he makes it clear that God was active in the work of salvation accomplished on the Cross. It was "by the predetermined purpose and foreknowledge of God" that Jesus was crucified (A2:23). God did not simply know what would happen; he planned it. The death of Jesus was his way of bringing salvation.

This is brought out with references to predictions of the passion, both in prophecy and in the sayings of Jesus.

Take, for example, Jesus' prophecy as he and his disciples made their way to Jerusalem: "All the things that are written through the prophets with respect to the Son of man will be fulfilled" (18:31). He then made particular mention of his being delivered to the Gentiles and of the mockery, the insults, the spitting, the scourging, the death, and the resurrection. Even down to the details, God had planned what would happen to his Son.

This prophecy of Jesus is often called his third prediction of the passion.[10] This is rather curious, for in fact it is not the third, but the seventh prediction in this Gospel (see 5:35; 9:22, 43–45; 12:50; 13:32–33; 17:25). The first of these lacks detail and simply says, "Days will come, and when the bridegroom is taken away from them. . . ." But there can scarcely be doubt that Jesus is referring to his violent death.[11]

He spoke of the necessity of his death: "The Son of man must suffer many things and be rejected by the elders and chief priests and scribes and be killed and on the third day be raised" (9:22). The word "must" (*dei*) points to a compelling divine necessity. It was not just that that was the way things would happen to turn out. It was God's plan, and it had to be fulfilled.

The third prediction came about when people were marveling at the wonderful things Jesus was doing. Evidently they were thinking that it must all lead to something wonderful, for Jesus began with a solemn injunction:

"*You* [the pronoun is emphatic: you who are so impressed by these marvels] put these words into your ears." They should not have their eyes fixed on some glorious outcome, for God had planned something very different. The prediction is quite general: "The Son of man will be betrayed into the hands of men." But the words surely point to the betrayal that led to the Crucifixion. Luke concludes this section by saying that the hearers did not understand and that they were afraid to ask (9:43–45).[12]

Jesus' statement "I came to cast fire on the earth" appears to be a reference to the judgment that his coming brought on all forms of unbelief. He went on to say, "I have a baptism with which to be baptized, and how I am constrained until it is accomplished" (12:49–50; NEB renders the last words in this way: "what constraint I am under until the ordeal is over!"). The imagery is unusual, but baptism here plainly points to death. We often see baptism as symbolizing cleansing, and on occasion it can have this meaning. But the more fundamental significance is death, as J. Ysebaert has shown.[13] The thought of judgment on sin leads to that of the death of Christ for sin. The passage gives us a glimpse of what it cost Jesus to see the Cross as inevitable and to move steadfastly toward it.

On one occasion some Pharisees warned Jesus that Herod was going to kill him. (The Pharisees were usually opposed to Jesus, so it is unusual to find them trying to help him.) His

---

[10] For example, Wilfrid J. Harrington has the heading "Third Prediction of the Passion" (*The Gospel According to St Luke* [London, 1968], 218).

[11] Marshall comments, "It refers clearly enough to the way in which Jesus was taken away from the disciples by death" (*The Gospel of Luke*, 226). Harrington, too, sees a reference to Jesus' death (*The Gospel According to St Luke*, 96).

[12] "The fear of the disciples suggests that the passion predictions may have been dramatic oracular utterances upon which Jesus did not elaborate" (E. Earle Ellis, *The Gospel of Luke* [London, 1966], 144).

[13] *Greek Baptismal Terminology* (Nijmegen, 1962), ch. 3.

response was "Go and say to that fox, 'Look, I cast out demons and accomplish cures today and tomorrow and on the third day I am perfected [or, reach my goal]'" (13:32). Although this is an unusual way of putting it, there is no doubt that Jesus was referring to his death and saying that it would take place in the way and time that God had chosen, not when Herod wanted it. Jesus went on to say, "It is necessary [*dei*] for me to go on my way today and tomorrow and the next day, for it is not possible that a prophet perish outside Jerusalem" (v. 33). Clearly he had his death in mind and equally clearly he was saying that it would take place in accordance with the will of God, not that of Herod.

The central place of his death comes out in another "must" saying. Jesus was talking with the Pharisees about the coming of the kingdom of God and said that his coming will be like the lightning, evidently a reference to the brilliance and the unexpectedness of his coming.[14] We might anticipate that he would go on to speak of his majesty or of his judgment of the people or the like, but instead we read, "But first he must [*dei*] suffer many things and be rejected by this generation" (17:25). There is no detail, but it is clear that once again it is his death that is in mind. That has been determined by God, and it will inevitably take place.

Predictions of Jesus like these agree with what the prophets had said long before. Luke tells us that Jesus referred to the fulfillment of "all the things written through the prophets" and again of "all the things written in the law of Moses and the prophets and the psalms" (18:31; 24:44). The conversa-

tion on the road to Emmaus was sparked off by the disciples' incomprehension of the death of Jesus and by our Lord's question, "Was it not necessary that the Christ should suffer these things and enter his glory?" (24:26). Then, "beginning from Moses and from all the prophets, he expounded to them the things about himself in all the scriptures." These things certainly included the fact that he must suffer and rise again (24:46). Sometimes there are references to specific prophecies, such as that regarding the stone the builders rejected (20:17) and Isaiah's words about being numbered with the transgressors (22:37).

It is plain, then, that Luke saw that what happened to Jesus was the action of God, foretold long before and recognized by Jesus throughout his ministry. Sometimes Luke simply speaks of God as acting, a feature of the songs in the early chapters. Thus, in the *Magnificat* Mary speaks of "God my Savior" (1:47) and goes on to refer to his scattering of the haughty, putting down potentates and exalting lowly people, and the like. The Song of Zechariah was likewise full of the great deeds of the Lord, who had "wrought redemption for his people" (1:68). We might have expected that the aged priest would have concentrated on the role of his new son, but, while he was not unmindful of the greatness of little John (1:76ff.), he first concentrated on the great work of redemption that God was bringing about. The Baptist also quoted prophecy when he said that "all flesh will see God's salvation" (3:6).

In the early history of the church there is a strong emphasis on the way God saves. Daily the Lord added to the

---

14 "The kingdom and the Son of man alike will come with the unpredictable ubiquity of a lightning flash, defying all calculation, so that no sentries can be posted to give warning of their approach" (G. B. Caird, *The Gospel of St Luke* [Harmondsworth, 1963], 197).

church those who were being saved (A2:47). They did not save themselves, nor did the preachers do the essential work. Salvation was the work of God. People who wanted salvation could "call on the name of the Lord" (A2:21), but calling was all they could do. The salvation they received was the gift of God. Paul commends people "to God and to the word of his grace, which is able to build up and to give the inheritance . . ." (A20:32); he also refers to the gospel as "the gospel of the grace of God" (A20:24). It was God who "brought to Israel the Savior Jesus" (A13:23). It was God who "raised up his child and sent him to bless" his people (A3:26). An interesting part of the teaching of Acts is that repentance, which we generally see as something we do, is regarded as a gift of God (5:31; 11:18).

We should notice Luke's references to the sacraments. He tells us of Christ's institution of the Holy Communion (22:17–20) and of the early church as continuing "in the breaking of the bread" (A2:42). He says that after his first sermon Peter called on people to be baptized and that many did so (A2:38, 41). There are many references to people's undergoing baptism (e.g., 8:12, 38; 10:48; 16:15, 33; 18:8). There have been and still are strong disagreements among Christians as to the precise significance of these ordinances. But there is no doubt that if people are saved by their own merit they are meaningless. Both point to a work of salvation that God has already done.[15]

More could be added from Acts.

Judas's treachery, which led to the Crucifixion, had been prophesied long before (A1:16). Evil people brought Jesus to the Cross, but they succeeded in doing only what God had determined should be done (A4:27–28). That Christ should suffer was a matter of prophecy (A3:18; 26:22–23; 28:23).

An interesting example of the way that this was accepted in the early church comes from the account of Philip and the Ethiopian. Philip found this man sitting in his chariot and puzzling over Isaiah 53. There is no indication that Philip had any indication beforehand that this passage would be coming up, but "beginning from this scripture, he preached to him Jesus" (A8:35). Another significant saying is one that Paul received in a vision in Corinth. God said to him, "I have many people in this city" (A18:10). They had not yet done anything about being saved; many of them had not even heard the gospel. But they were God's. Clearly it is he who would bring them to salvation in due course.

Thus in a variety of ways Luke brings out the truth that it is God who brings salvation. He saw this as having been predestined from eternity and foretold in the prophets. Then it was accomplished in the sufferings and death and resurrection of Jesus and preached by a variety of people in the early church. God is a mighty God, and he has wrought a mighty salvation.

---

[15] Cf. James Denney, "There is nothing in Christianity more primitive than the Sacraments, and the Sacraments, wherever they exist, are witnesses to the connection between the death of Christ and the forgiveness of sins. . . . It is not due to any sacramentarian tendency in Luke, but only brings out the place which the death of Christ had at the basis of the Christian religion, as the condition of the forgiveness of sins, when he gives the sacramental side of Christianity the prominence it has in the early chapters of Acts" (*The Death of Christ* [London, 1905], 84–85).

THE LOVINGKINDNESS OF GOD

Luke's reference to the "tender mercy" of God (1:78) is unusual. Literally it means something like "entrails of mercy." In Greek writings generally the word for "entrails" refers not only to the inward parts of the human body but also, often, to deeply felt emotions. But the interesting thing is that when the Greeks used the term, they meant something like anger. To them, when anyone was deeply stirred, that person was angry. But to Christians, to be deeply stirred is to be compassionate (cf. the old-fashioned expression "bowels of compassion"). It is a striking term to use of God; it brings out vividly the truth that God acts compassionately.[16]

God's compassion is seen in the attitude he has to all his creation. Not one sparrow is forgotten by him (12:6). God feeds the ravens (12:24) and clothes the plants (12:27–28). The followers of Jesus are thus taught a lesson: the God who cares for all he has created will certainly care for them.

God forgives. The scribes and Pharisees reasoned that God is the only one who can forgive (5:21). Luke is not disagreeing with their basic conviction; their error is that they do not see that Jesus shares in the nature of deity as he asserts his right to forgive by working a miracle. God's readiness to forgive comes out in the parable of the Pharisee and the tax collector when the latter prayed, "God, be propitiated to me, the sinner" (18:13).[17] The man was a sinner and could not justify himself in any way. But he could appeal to God for mercy and find it.[18]

The sinful woman who wept over Jesus' feet and poured precious perfume on them also found mercy. Jesus said, "Her sins, many as they are, have been forgiven," and he went on to cite her love as evidence that she had indeed been forgiven (7:47).[19]

Luke makes it clear that forgiveness is to be proclaimed. This starts early, for he tells us that Zechariah said of his infant son John: "You will go before the Lord to prepare his ways, to give knowledge of salvation to his people by the forgiveness of their sins" (1:76–77). And in due course this is what he did, for he preached a baptism of repentance for the forgiveness of sins (3:3). Luke tells us that the risen Lord told his followers to preach forgiveness (24:47), and we find Peter immediately doing just that (A2:38) and explaining to the Sanhedrin that God had acted in Jesus "to give repentance to Israel and forgiveness of sins" (A5:31). Peter proclaimed forgiveness again to Cornelius and his friends (A10:43), and Paul did likewise in the synagogue in

---

[16] See the discussion in Nigel Turner, *Christian Words* (Edinburgh, 1980), 78–80. The Christian usage is not entirely new, for it is to be found in LXX and in *The Testaments of the Twelve Patriarchs*. But it is noteworthy for all that.

[17] The Greek word ἱλάσθητι is normally translated "be merciful" or the like, and there is no need to cavil at the translation. But we should bear in mind that the idea in this word is the putting away of anger (see above, pp. 34–35). "Even as he looks for forgiveness he recognizes what he deserves" (Morris, *The Gospel According to St. Luke*, 265); this recognition is "the cry to God for mercy" (Büchsel, *TDNT*, 3:315).

[18] Cf. T. W. Manson, "This publican was a rotter; and he knew it. He asked for God's mercy because mercy was the only thing he dared ask for" (*The Sayings of Jesus* [London, 1949], 312).

[19] C. F. D. Moule gives the meaning as "I can say with confidence that her sins are forgiven, *because* her love is evidence of it." The view that her love is "the ground of her *forgiveness,* not of the *assurance* that she has been forgiven," he says, is "a non-Christian conclusion which throws the sentence into complete opposition both to the preceding parable and to the second half of this very verse" (*IBNTG,* 147).

Antioch in Pisidia (A13:38) and before king Agrippa (A26:18). Forgiveness is an important part of the outworking of the divine compassion.

Sometimes Luke tells us that God "visits" his people. Now a visit from God might be an uncomfortable thing for sinners, and there are occasions when the verb "visit" is used to teach that God will surely punish evildoers (e.g., Exod. 32:34; Jer. 14:10; NIV translates the word as "punish" in these passages, but see KJV). When Luke uses the verb, however, it is always with the idea that God is visiting in order to bless. He can link "visit" with redemption (1:68), and he tells us that on one occasion the people who saw a miracle of Jesus recognized that God had "visited his people" (7:16). Later, when God brought Gentiles within the scope of salvation, James described it in terms of a visitation (A15:14). For God to visit is for him to show compassion.

Luke also wrote of "joy in heaven" over one sinner who repents (15:7, 10). Joy had been prophesied in connection with the birth of John the Baptist. In view of the way most people see this man as a stern and almost forbidding figure, this should not be overlooked (1:14). And when the angel of the Lord came to the shepherds, it was with the "good news of great joy" that the Savior had been born (2:10). There is joy for some who received the word like seed sown in a rocky place (8:13), but this is a shallow emotion and not to be compared to the joy of those who preached faithfully and found even the demons subject to them (10:17). And Luke tells us that the disciples returned to Jerusalem "with great joy" after Jesus had ascended to heaven (24:52). Then when the gospel was preached and others were won to Christ, there were more occasions of joy (A8:8; 13:52; 15:3).

We should also bear in mind that Luke is fond of referring to "the word of God" (e.g., 5:1; 8:11, 21; 11:28; A4:29, 31; 6:2, 7; 8:14; 11:1; 12:24). Every instance of the use of this phrase is a witness to God's willingness to make some revelation. Luke does not see God as remote and hidden, unwilling to meet the need of his people. He is compassionate and makes known to sinners what they need to know to enter salvation.

Grace is, of course, one of the great Christian words, one that is markedly Pauline (Paul uses it 100 times out of its 155 New Testament occurrences). We do not usually notice that Luke is the next most frequent user (8 times in the Gospel, and 17 in Acts). Sometimes he uses the term in the sense of "credit": "What credit is that to you?" (6:32–34), and sometimes he uses it in much the same way as Paul does (e.g., A15:11). But Luke does not simply repeat Paul. He is the only one in the New Testament who has the expression "the word of his grace" (A14:3; 20:32), and James Moffatt sees in this and in "the gospel of the grace of God" (A20:24) evidence of Luke's originality in using the concept of grace.[20] Although it is true that we must look to Paul for the distinctive Christian concept of grace, it is also true that Luke has an importance of his own for our understanding of the concept.

---

[20]*Grace in the New Testament* (London, 1931), 362–63.

8

the gospel of luke and acts: the doctrine of christ

The Gospel of Luke has been called "the most beautiful book there is."[1] Whether we endorse this evaluation or not, we cannot doubt that Luke has given us a wonderfully attractive account of the ministry of Jesus and, for that matter, when he moves on to Acts, of the life of the early church. In this Gospel we see Jesus as a warm and winsome figure, and it comes as no surprise that he was the "friend of tax collectors and sinners" (7:34). Jesus often addressed people as "friend" (the word "friend" [*philos*] occurring 15 times in Luke and another 3 times in Acts—of a New Testament total of 29). The Jesus of the third Gospel is certainly one of us, a very human (though sinless) figure.

Luke tells us that Peter spoke of Jesus as "a man attested . . . by God with powerful deeds and wonders and signs, which God did through him" (A2:22). There is no doubt about the great things that God did through Jesus. But there is no doubt either that Jesus was "a man." Luke, of course, has some incidents from Jesus' infancy, and

he records the fact that "the child grew and became strong, full of wisdom, and God's grace [or favor] was upon him" (2:40). He rounds off his account of the visit to Jerusalem and the child's adventure in the temple by mentioning the return to Nazareth and the information that "Jesus increased in wisdom and in stature and in favor with God and with men" (2:52). Such passages point to the normal human process of growth and development.

Jesus had the usual physical needs; for example, he could be hungry (4:2). He had human emotions: he was astonished at the faith of the centurion (7:9). He wept over the city of Jerusalem (19:41), and there is moving human pathos in his lament, "Jerusalem, Jerusalem, who kills the prophets and stones those sent to her, how often did I wish to gather your children together in the way a hen gathers her brood under her wings and you would not!" (13:34). Luke makes clear that Jesus was a religious person,[2] and it is to him that we owe the information that it was Jesus' custom to worship in the syna-

---

[1] So E. Renan, *Les Évangiles* (Paris, 1877), 283. F. C. Grant sees Luke as "the most valuable of our four," and Luke-Acts as "the most valuable writing in the New Testament" (*The Gospels* [London, 1957], 133).

[2] "Jesus was the most religious man who ever lived; He did nothing and said nothing and thought nothing without the thought of God. If His example means anything at all it means that a human life without the conscious presence of God—even though it be a life of humanitarian service outwardly

gogue on the Sabbath (4:16). Luke also tells us a number of times that Jesus prayed (e.g., 3:21; 5:16; 6:12; 9:18, 28–29); on one occasion he prayed all night (6:12). He underwent the human experience of temptation (4:1–13), and Luke ends his account of the temptation by saying that the devil left Jesus for a while; in other words, Jesus endured temptation throughout his life in the same way as the rest of mankind.

People certainly treated Jesus like a man. Thus they laughed at him when he refused to agree that Jairus's daughter was dead (8:53), and the criticism of some that he was "a glutton and a drunkard" (7:34) shows that his opponents had no doubt of his kinship with other human beings. The same saying shows that Jesus was no ascetic; he certainly enjoyed life. This does not mean that he lived self-indulgently. He said on one occasion, "I am among you as the servant" (22:27); this is a statement that further points to a genuine humanity. After his arrest he was mocked and beaten by people who apparently saw no reason why they could not get away with their infamy; the object of their scorn was a real man, but only a man (22:63). And at the end of it all Jesus died with this prayer on his lips: "Father, into your hands I commend my spirit" (23:46), a prayer that, as Joseph A. Fitzmyer says, "is a mark of supreme human dedication."[3]

It is true that Luke does not depict Jesus' humanity as starkly as does Mark, but it is also true that he is in no doubt about his Lord's genuine humanity. This comes through not so much in isolated passages that may be quoted (though I have noted some of these) as in Jesus' general manner of life. He obeyed, and he gave commands that might be obeyed or disobeyed. He asked questions and sought information. He died a human death.

But perhaps we should notice one or two points about Jesus' death. We read that as he faced death, Jesus prayed earnestly in the garden of Gethsemane and came to accept God's will (22:42). Most manuscripts add the words about the angel who strengthened him and about his agony and his sweat that was like great drops of blood falling down to the ground (22:43–44). It seems likely that we should accept these words, despite the hesitation of some to do so.[4] They reveal something of the horror that death meant for him, the death in which he became one with sinners and died their death.

But the humanity of Jesus is not the whole story. Just as plainly as Matthew and Mark, Luke sees more in Jesus than just another Galilean. Jesus taught with an authority that the Evangelist did not see in other teachers, and he lived a life that was a revelation of none less than God. We turn to the way Luke brought out this other aspect of Jesus.

---

like the ministry of Jesus—is a monstrous perversion. If we would follow truly in Jesus' steps, we must obey the first commandment as well as the second that is like unto it; we must love the Lord our God with all our heart and soul and mind and strength" (J. Gresham Machen, *Christianity and Liberalism* [New York, 1934], 94).

[3] Joseph A. Fitzmyer, *The Gospel According to Luke (I–IX)* [New York, 1983], 193.

[4] The textual problem is a difficult one. Bruce M. Metzger says that the committee producing the UBS text felt the words to be unauthentic but decided to retain them in the text, but print them within double square brackets (*A Textual Commentary on the Greek New Testament* [London, 1971], 177). I. Howard Marshall finds the problem difficult but "with very considerable hesitation" accepts the passage (*The Gospel of Luke* [Grand Rapids, 1978], 832). The words are rejected in an article by Bart D. Ehrman and Mark A. Plunkett, "The Angel and the Agony: The Textual Problem of Luke 22:43–44" (*CBQ* 45 [1983]: 401–16).

SON OF GOD AND
SON OF MAN

Luke makes use of a number of the titles we have seen in Matthew and Mark. Thus, he sometimes refers to Jesus as "the Son of God." This begins quite early. The angel Gabriel came to Mary and told her that she would bear a son, whom she was to call "Jesus." Gabriel went on to say, "He will be great and will be called 'Son of the Most High.'" This is followed by some information about his royal greatness, which led Mary to ask, "How will this be, since I do not know a man?" Gabriel answered, "The Holy Spirit will come upon you, and the power of the Most High will overshadow you; therefore that which is born will be called 'Holy, Son of God'" (1:30–34). There has been a good deal of discussion of the virginal conception—a teaching that is rejected by many modern scholars.[5] But clearly Luke accepted it, and it was important for him. It governed his understanding of the term "the Son of God" and makes it clear that he did not use the expression with a minimal meaning. For Luke "the Son of God" meant that Jesus' relationship to the Father is unique. He could on occasion refer to disciples as "sons of the Most High" (6:35), but he did not see Jesus as simply another such son. The words of Gabriel make it quite plain that Jesus was God's Son in a way that nobody else was or ever could be.

Luke has this title in the temptation narrative in much the same way as Matthew has it (4:3, 9; cf. Matt. 4:3, 6), and the same may be said of a number of other passages. But perhaps we should also notice that at the Transfiguration, the voice from the cloud declares, "My Son, the Chosen One" (9:35; Matthew and Mark have "my beloved Son"). And there are two places where Luke alone has the expression. One of these is at a time when the demons came out of many people, saying as they did so, "You are the Son of God" (4:41). Luke sees the demons as being well aware of this long before the disciples realized who Jesus was. The other occasion is in the trial scene, where this Evangelist says that the members of the Sanhedrin asked Jesus "Are you the Son of God?" (22:70).

Luke also relates a couple of occasions when Paul used the expression. Soon after Ananias came and laid hands on him and baptized him, Paul became active. "In the synagogues he preached Jesus, that he is the Son of God" (A9:20). In a later sermon the apostle quoted Psalm 2:7 and applied to Jesus the words "You are my Son" (A13:33). But clearly this title did not play a big role in the preaching of the early church.

It is much the same with "the Son of man." Luke has quite a number of passages in which he shares with Matthew or Mark or both some sayings in which Jesus uses this expression of himself. In this Gospel we see the same threefold use of the term: it refers to Jesus (1) in the exercise of his public ministry, (2) in his suffering, and (3) in his coming again in glory. But we should also notice that Luke sometimes has the expression in places where the other Evangelists do not have it, and there are a few completely new sayings.

---

[5]There is an enormous literature on the virgin birth. Let me simply refer to a few of the books. J. Gresham Machen, *The Virgin Birth of Christ* (London, 1958); Thomas Boslooper, *The Virgin Birth* (London, 1962); Hans von Campenhausen, *The Virgin Birth in the Theology of the Ancient Church* (London, 1964); Raymond E. Brown, *The Virginal Conception and Bodily Resurrection of Jesus* (London, 1973).

An example of the former type is the statement in which Jesus mentions a variety of evils that people will do to his followers "for the Son of man's sake" (6:22). Matthew has a similar saying but it ends with "for my sake" (Matt. 5:11). We could see something of the same thing in 12:8 (Matt. 10:32). Again, in the arrest narrative Jesus asked the traitor, "Judas, with a kiss are you betraying the Son of man?" (22:48; cf. Matt. 26:49; Mark 14:45).

But there are some "Son of man" sayings that appear only in Luke. One of these is that people will want to see "one of the days of the Son of man" (17:22). There are problems in the interpretation of this saying. It may refer to the times of the Messiah, though it is not a usual way of referring to it. Some think that "one of the days" means "the first of the days," and if so, the reference is to the opening of the messianic reign. Another opinion is that the disciples will at some unspecified time in the future wish they could be back in the days when Jesus was with them; still another view is that they will wish they were with him in heaven. We cannot be certain, but it seems that the first explanation is the best. People will want to see the Messiah, but his coming cannot be hastened.

Jesus asked, "When the Son of man comes, will he find faith [or, the faith] on the earth?" (18:8). This points to widespread apostasy before the return of the Lord, and such apostasy is attested elsewhere. Another saying urges the hearers to be watchful so that they will be able to "stand before the Son of man" (21:36), meaning that they will enter into the fullness of salvation. A third was spoken at the end of the Zacchaeus incident: "The Son of man came to seek and to save the lost" (19:10; some MSS have similar words in Matt. 18:11, but usually the words are not seen as authentic there). The final passage is that in which the angel at the tomb reminded the women that Jesus had said, "The Son of man must be betrayed into the hands of sinful men and be crucified and rise on the third day" (24:7). Right to the end there is the thought that the Son of man must fulfill his vocation, and that this vocation means suffering for others.

Luke records the one occasion on which "the Son of man" occurs on the lips of someone other than Jesus. He tells us that at the end of his speech to the Sanhedrin Stephen said, "Look, I see the heavens opened and the Son of man standing at the right hand of God" (A7:56). This assures Luke's readers of the permanent place in glory occupied by the Son of man. His vocation on earth involved suffering, but his place in heaven is the supreme place. There is no doubting his splendor.

SON OF DAVID

We have seen that the title "Son of David" is important for Matthew. We cannot say that the title itself is an important formula for Luke, for he has it only three times (twice as blind Bartimaeus called to Jesus, asking for his sight [18:38–39], and again when Jesus asked, "How do they say that the Christ is David's Son?" [20:41]).

But it is otherwise with the connection with David (Luke has the name "David" 13 times in his Gospel and another 11 times in Acts). Luke tells us that before the birth of Jesus Mary "was betrothed to a man whose name was Joseph, of the house of David" (1:27). Here there is dispute as to whether he is saying that it was Joseph or Mary who was of David's house.[6] Not much turns on our decision, because Luke seems to indicate that Mary was of Davidic descent (1:32, 69), as was Joseph (2:4). Here he may be referring to Jesus' legal descent or to his actual descent, and he is claiming that he was of the royal line. Verse 32 adds the point that he has a glorious destiny: none less than God will give him the royal throne.

The Song of Zechariah declares, "[God] has raised a horn of salvation for us in the house of David his child" (1:69). A horn is a symbol of strength (cf. Ps. 18:2), and there is a prophecy that God will "make a horn grow for David" (Ps. 132:17). The meaning thus is that God will bring about a mighty salvation through a descendant of David (or, perhaps, salvation through some mighty descendant of David). There is a further link with David in the reference to "the city of David," where Jesus was born (2:4, 11), and a reminder that Joseph was "of the house and lineage of David" (2:4). Not much can be made of the mention of David in the genealogy (3:31), though we should notice that it adds to the evidence that Luke saw Jesus as a descendant of David. There is a reference to one incident in David's life—namely, his eating the "bread of the Presence" (6:4). Jesus saw this as a kind of precedent for his disciples' action in plucking and eating kernels of wheat on the Sabbath.

Luke cites Scripture a number of times with such phrases as "the Holy Spirit foretold through the mouth of David" (A1:16), "David says" (A2:25), or the like (A2:31, 34; 4:25). He sees it as the utterance of God, as the reference to the Holy Spirit shows, but he sees it also as the utterance of a man and thus makes his references to David.

He evidently sees David's prophecy of the Resurrection as important. He tells us that in his sermon on the day of Pentecost Peter quoted Psalm 16:8–11 with its promise that God would not give his "holy one" over to corruption. This could not refer to David himself, because David died and was buried and his tomb was there among them. Thus, David spoke the words with reference to the Messiah. Being a prophet, he foretold that the Messiah would rise from the dead (A2:29–32). Peter has a similar piece of reasoning when he proceeds to argue that Psalm 110:1 does not mean that David ascended to heaven, but that Jesus did (A2:34–36). Yet another psalm is quoted to show that the raging and the plotting of the people prophesy the actions of Herod and Pontius Pilate in conjunction with Gentiles and Israelites as they acted against Jesus but succeeded only in doing what God had foreordained (A4:25–28, quoting Ps. 2:1–2).

There is a brief mention of David in Stephen's speech. Stephen informed his accusers that David "found favor" with God and that he wanted to build a temple (A7:45–46; the word here is *skēnōma*, which really means a tent, a tabernacle; the word may be intended

---

[6] Marshall opts for a reference to Joseph: "Had the phrase been meant to refer to Mary, it would have had to be differently constructed" (*The Gospel of Luke,* 64). R. C. H. Lenski thinks differently: "It is rather superficial to think that the main person to be introduced is Joseph, and that we must know about his Davidic descent. The main person is this maiden, and Joseph is introduced only as the man to whom she is betrothed, and it is about her descent that we must know. . . . We construe: 'to a maiden . . . out of David's house' " (*The Interpretation of St. Luke's Gospel* [Minneapolis, 1961], 61). Alfred Plummer finds it "unnecessary, and indeed impossible, to decide" (*A Critical and Exegetical Commentary on the Gospel According to S. Luke* [Edinburgh, 1928], 21).

to evoke associations with the tent of meeting in the wilderness). He did not build it, but his intentions were good.

There are further references to David in Paul's first sermon. Paul saw that God had raised up David to be king—"a man after my own heart, who will do all my will." It is from this man's descendants that God has now raised up Jesus as Savior, according to his promise (A13:22–23). Paul sees the Resurrection as a fulfillment of prophecy (A13:33; see Ps. 2:7). He goes on to some words in Isaiah: "I will give you the sure, holy things of David" (A13:34; Isa. 55:3), and to a psalm that Peter had used earlier: "You will not give your Holy One to see corruption" (A13:35; see Ps. 16:10). There are problems about the precise meaning of this passage, but the main thrust is clearly that Paul finds justification in Scripture, and specifically in passages that go back to David, for seeing the resurrection of Jesus as the object of prophecy. David served his generation according to the will of God. But that did not stop him from dying and seeing corruption. It was Jesus, whom God raised, who saw no corruption.

At the Council of Jerusalem James quoted from Amos: "I will raise up again the tent of David that has fallen down" (A15:16; see Amos 9:11). There are problems with parts of this quotation (where it appears to depend on the LXX rather than the Hebrew text). But the words about David seem fairly clear; the meaning is that God has raised up the church as the place where worship is to be carried on.[7]

From all this it seems that Luke finds Jesus' relationship to David of some significance. He does not use the expression "Son of David" very often, but he uses it enough to show that he was aware of its significance for messiahship.[8] God had always planned to do great things through a descendant of the great king, and these things he did in Jesus.

It is interesting to find some emphasis on the Resurrection in words Luke finds in David. The early chapters of Acts in particular make it clear that the Resurrection gripped the early Christian preachers. And they found part of its significance in that it had been foretold in what David wrote; that is, it was the fulfillment of a definite plan, not some ad hoc solution improvised when Jesus fell foul of the Jewish authorities. Luke sees God's plan clearly foreshadowed in what David said.

THE CHRIST

Luke finds the title "Christ" important for his understanding of what God did in Jesus. It is not his most frequently used title, but some see it as most significant. And Luke alone tells us that it was from this title that the followers of Jesus were given their distinctive name "Christians" (A11:26; cf. 26:28). He uses the term twelve times in his Gospel and twenty-five times in Acts. Almost invariably he has the article with it: he refers to "the Christ"—i.e., "the Messiah"—and

---

[7]"Probably the rebuilding of the tabernacle is to be understood as a reference to the raising up of the church as the new place of divine worship which replaced the temple. . . . The church is then the means by which the Gentiles may come to know the Lord" (I. Howard Marshall, *The Acts of the Apostles* [Leicester, 1980], 252). F. F. Bruce, however, prefers to see a reference to "the resurrection and exaltation of Christ, the Son of David, and the reconstitution of His disciples as the new Israel" (*Commentary on the Book of the Acts* [London, 1954], 310).

[8]"Luke understands fully the Jewish meaning of Messiah son of David. Evidently he holds that this concept, so far as it goes, is appropriately applied to Jesus" (Sherman Johnson, *The Theology of the Gospels* [London, 1966], 42).

does not use "Christ" as a proper name as does Paul. Sometimes he links it with "Jesus" ("Jesus Christ" or "Christ Jesus") or with "Lord."

Luke uses the title early in his writing, telling his readers that the angel spoke to the shepherds of the birth of "a Savior who is Christ the Lord" (2:11). The expression has no article (it is literally "Christ Lord"), and this has led to diverse interpretations. Some see the meaning as "an anointed Lord"; others go along with a few manuscripts that read "the Lord's Christ" (taking "Lord" to refer to God the Father). But it is better to take it as applying the two categories "Christ" and "Lord" to the baby Jesus.[9]

There is a slightly different expression when Luke tells us of Simeon, who had the divine assurance that he would not die before he had seen "the Lord's Christ" (2:26), the Messiah whom God had promised centuries before, the One whom the pious in Israel had so long awaited. Some thought perhaps John the Baptist was this Messiah, but Luke makes it clear that he was not (3:15–17). We are probably meant to get some understanding of what this means from Jesus' sermon in the synagogue at Nazareth, which Luke alone reports. He tells us that Jesus began by reading some words from the prophet Isaiah: "The Spirit of the Lord is upon me, because he has anointed me . . ." (4:18; the quotation is from Isa. 61:1). "Christ" means "anointed," and thus the passage presents the anointing in terms of the

gift of the Holy Spirit. Being "Christ" means having a special connection with the Father ("the Lord's Christ") and also with the Spirit (as we see from the virginal conception and the coming of the Spirit at the baptism of Jesus (3:21–22).

In our study of Mark we saw that the demons knew who Jesus was, long before this was known by others. Luke has this, too, but he expresses it in terms of "Christ," as Mark does not. Mark tells us that Jesus did not allow the demons to speak "because they knew him" (Mark 1:34; on another occasion they called him "the Son of God" [3:11]), whereas Luke puts it this way: "Demons came out of many, crying out and saying, 'You are the Son of God.' And he rebuked them and did not allow them to speak, because they knew that he was the Christ" (4:41). Perhaps the demons' use of the expression "Son of God" points us back to the temptation narrative when Satan had said, "If you are the Son of God . . ." (4:3, 9). The demons knew all too well that he really was the Son of God, and his expulsion of them shows him acting as the Son of God should. But Luke goes on to the thought that he was the Christ. This shows him to be not only the strong Son of God but also the anointed One, the One with the very Spirit of God.[10]

Jesus' silencing of the demons is not to be understood in terms of a "messianic secret." The way Jesus' ministry was carried out it was impossible for his messiahship to be kept secret. It is

---

[9] W. Grundmann points out that this saying "combines the Jewish Christian confession of Jesus as the Messiah with the Gentile Christian confession of Jesus as the Lord. This is an ecumenically important statement in both Lk. and Ac." (*TDNT*, 9:533).

[10] Cf. Marshall: "The term 'Messiah' is seen to be applicable to a more-than-earthly figure, able to exorcise demons, and on a different level from political saviours. At the same time, Luke's purpose may be to indicate that 'Son of God' must not be understood in purely Hellenistic categories as a reference to a charismatic, semi-divine figure, but must be seen in the light of Jewish messianic expectation" (*The Gospel of Luke*, 197).

rather that he did not wish the demons to be those who spoke about it. It was better that people should come to understand for themselves that the One who did what he did, taught what he taught, and lived as he lived was indeed the Christ of God.

It is interesting that the three Synoptics have three different versions of Peter's great confession at Caesarea Philippi. Matthew wrote, "You are the Christ, the Son of the living God" (Matt. 16:16), and Mark's Gospel declares simply, "You are the Christ" (Mark 8:29). Luke has "the Christ of God" (9:20). It is characteristic of Luke that he thinks of Jesus as the Lord's Christ (cf. 2:26). It is the fact that God anointed him and sent him that is important. This way of describing Christ's Person and work is unique to Luke in the New Testament, and it indicates Luke's firm conviction that the Messiah is One who is called by God, equipped by God, and sent by God. He is no independent figure, but belongs to God.

All three Synoptic Gospels include the discussion of the Christ as David's Son (20:41), and there is no need to repeat what was said earlier. But only Luke tells us that when Jesus was brought before Pilate, his enemies accused him of perverting the nation, forbidding to give tribute to Caesar, and saying that "he himself is Christ, a king" (23:2). Pilate would not be expected to understand all that is involved in the title Christ, so they explained it in terms that he could comprehend. It is perhaps also the way they understood it, but it is tendentious for them to put it this way. In their examination of Jesus, while they had clearly tried to get him to say something like this, he had refused to do so (22:67–71). There is a truth in what they said, but it is not in the sense that they understood it. Luke wants us to see that there was a royalty about Jesus, though Jesus in no way made the political claim that his enemies said the title Christ implied.

The mockers at the Crucifixion said, "Let him save himself if he is the Christ of God, the chosen one" (23:35), and a similar understanding is implied in the words of the impenitent thief "Are you not the Christ? Save yourself—and us!" (23:39). They saw Christ in terms of splendor and mighty power; it was quite unthinkable that he would die on a cross, accursed by God. Suffering and messiahship were mutually exclusive. But Luke makes it clear that this is a misunderstanding. The risen Lord asked the two on the road to Emmaus, "Must not the Christ suffer these things and enter into his glory?" (24:26). Here "must" is significant: there is no room for any other possibility. Suffering, as well as resurrection, is assigned in prophecy to the Messiah (24:46), and therefore it is unthinkable that he would have any other lot.

This line continues in Acts. That the Christ would suffer is foretold, not by some obscure and unimportant seer, but by "all the prophets" (A3:18). "Times of refreshing" depend on repentance and on sin's being blotted out, and this leads on to the thought that God would send the Christ (A3:19–20), an evident reference to the *parousia*. Luke tells us that when Paul preached in the synagogue in Thessalonica, he told his hearers that "the Christ must suffer and rise from the dead and that this is the Christ— Jesus whom I proclaim to you" (A17:3). We should not run these two too close together. He first makes the unexpected point that the Christ must suffer and rise from the dead, this having been foretold in Scripture. Then he goes on to the second point, that the

Christ Scripture describes in this way is Jesus.[11] The suffering Christ is presented in Paul's words before Agrippa (A26:23), this time with the additional information that he was the first to rise from the dead and that he would proclaim "light" to both Jews and Gentiles. That Jesus is the Christ is Paul's message on other occasions also (A18:5, 28), as it was in his earliest preaching right after his conversion (A9:22).

It is a distinctive message of Luke that the Christ must suffer. As we have seen, from the time that Peter came to understand that Jesus was the Christ, Jesus taught his disciples the necessity of his suffering. But he expressed this teaching in terms of "the Son of man," not the Messiah. For Luke, however, suffering is an integral part of being *Christ,* and he finds this in Scripture. This does not mean that he starts with the Scriptures and finds that they prophesy that Christ will suffer. He starts with Jesus and his sufferings for others and then finds that the Scriptures foretell this. It is Jesus who is the standard, not Luke's individual approach to his Bible.

That the Christ was to suffer to bring about salvation calls for a response, and Luke tells us of a number of occasions when the preachers called for faith in Christ. Paul reminds the Ephesian elders that this kind of preaching is what he had done among them (A20:21). He had also spoken to Governor Felix about the need for this faith (A24:24).

Earlier Peter spoke of God as having given to Cornelius and those in his house the same gift as to those early Christians "who believed on the Lord Jesus Christ" (A11:17). Clearly it was accepted that the way to receive the blessings Christ made available through his sufferings and his rising from the dead was the way of faith. There is no distinction between original Christians and later converts or between Jews and Gentiles. For all, it is trust in Christ that is the important thing.

The centrality of trust in Christ is crucial because in him we see nothing less than the action of God. In his first sermon Peter said, "Let all the house of Israel know for certain that God has made both Lord and Christ this Jesus whom you crucified" (A2:36). This statement has sometimes been interpreted as expressing an adoptionist christology, the idea that Jesus was a man and no more but that, after the Crucifixion, God raised him from the dead and gave him a new position, that of Lord and Christ. Now it may well be that there were some in the early church who had such an idea, for we are speaking of the first days, a time before there had been any opportunity for reflection and for thinking through what the life and death and the resurrection and ascension of Jesus of Nazareth meant. But it is not what Luke meant. For him Jesus was Savior, Christ, and Lord at the time of his birth (2:11).[12] It is because of what God is doing in Christ that his salvation is so important and so secure.

---

[11] Grundmann writes, "This statement shows that Paul presented a new Messianic doctrine in the synagogue and that he supported it from Scripture. At the end of his presentation, which was based on the facts about Jesus, he said that this Messiah whom Scripture expects is Jesus, whom I proclaim. The witness of Scripture is fulfilled. Here Ac. preserves an essential methodological element in Paul's missionary witness which makes it clear, as Luke never tires of showing, that the reality of Jesus has produced a new understanding of what the Messiah is, and hence of what Scripture says about him" (*TDNT,* 9:536).

[12] Grundmann reasons that since Luke speaks of Jesus as Lord and Christ from the beginning, "the statement cannot be taken to imply adoptionist christology" though he notes that Luke "might well be using a formulation that derives from adoptionist christology and relates to Jesus' resurrection and

Luke makes a good deal of "the name" of Christ. In antiquity the name meant far more than it usually does with us. In some way it summed up all that the person was, and this gives "the name of Christ" a far-reaching significance. When people were baptized in this name (A2:38; 10:48; 19:5), it meant at the least that the baptized were firmly committed to all that Christ was. It was an expression of faith and loyalty. When a man was commanded in the name of Christ to get up and walk, it meant that Christ was being invoked in all the fullness of his being to bring healing to the man (A3:6–8). In telling what had happened Peter said, "In the name of Jesus Christ of Nazareth, whom *you* crucified, whom God raised from the dead, in him this man stands before you healthy" (A4:10). Here we see that "the name" includes some understanding of the death and resurrection of Christ and that it also includes a power that can make the lame whole people. So it is not surprising that Paul was able to command an unclean spirit to come out of a possessed girl in the name of Jesus Christ and that the spirit obeyed (A16:18). This name is a powerful name.

The early preachers preached in the name of Christ (A5:40; 8:12), which is not so very different from preaching Christ (A8:5). This sometimes led them into danger as the letter sent from the Council of Jerusalem to the church at Antioch shows: it recognizes that Barnabas and Paul were men "who had hazarded their lives for the name of our Lord Jesus Christ" (A15:26).

There is a striking passage in the account of Peter's preaching in the house of Cornelius. Among other things, Peter referred to the word that God sent to the children of Israel, "preaching peace through Jesus Christ—he is Lord of all . . ." (A10:36). Peace is, of course, peace between God and man, but in the context of a message given in the house of a pious Gentile to whom God had given a vision there can be little doubt that there is also the thought of peace between people as widely divided as were Jew and Gentile. There is a comprehensive peace. And it is brought about by Jesus Christ, who is spoken of in this connection as "Lord of all."

From all this it is clear that Luke sees "Christ," the title of the Jewish Messiah, as highly significant. We expect the title to be used in a Jewish setting, but this Evangelist keeps using it in Gentile environments. It was too important a title to be ignored when the church spread to lands beyond Israel and to people not accustomed to thinking in Jewish categories. For all of us Jesus is the Christ of God, as well as the Lord.

THE LORD

Luke's most frequent title for Jesus is "the Lord" (103 occurrences in his Gospel and 107 in Acts). The title is, of course, a very general one and was used in a wide variety of senses. It was used of the owner of anything, such as a donkey (19:33) or a vineyard (20:13). It was often used as a polite form of address as when a servant addressed his master (13:8; 14:22). Such usages could readily lead to its becoming a normal way of addressing or speaking of a superior, and so the term came to

---

exaltation. But he reconstructs it as a statement about all God's work in relation to Jesus Christ" (*TDNT*, 9:535, 535n.285).

be used for people of high rank. Not only were people in high place "lords," but the term was applied also to gods. This did not mean that the term ceased to be used of men. It did not. But this scarcely presents a problem, other than the precise interpretation of individual texts. It has never been insuperably difficult to distinguish between a human "lord" and a divine one.

The word was used in the Septuagint, the translation of the Hebrew Old Testament into Greek, as a periphrasis for the divine name Yahweh.[13] Luke retains this usage; we find it twenty-five times in the opening two chapters of his Gospel; he speaks of "the commandments and ordinances of the Lord" (1:6), "the temple of the Lord" (1:9), and so on. He uses also the word in Acts, especially in references to "the angel of the Lord" (e.g., A5:19; 8:26; 10:3). To speak of Jesus as "the Lord," then, is to give him a very significant title. Fitzmyer writes, "In using *kyrios* of both Yahweh and Jesus in his writings Luke continues the sense of the title already being used in the early Christian community, which in some sense regarded Jesus as on a level with Yahweh."[14]

It is a mark of the exalted meaning of the term "the Lord" as the early Christians used it that it is not always easy to see whether they meant Jesus or the Father. Thus Peter exhorted Simon Magus to repent and "pray to the Lord" (A8:22; cf. the reference to "the Lord Jesus" in v. 16). And it is not clear whether "the word of the Lord" is that of Christ or of the Father (e.g., A8:25; 19:10). The perplexity is evidently ancient, for in quite a number of cases the manuscripts are divided, with some reading "the word of God" and others "the word of the Lord." There is a similar perplexity about the statement "The will of the Lord be done" (A21:14). In each such case the passage gives an equally good sense if we understand the reference to be to the Father or to Christ.

In Luke the term is often used as a form of address to Jesus. Thus one of the disciples said, "Lord, teach us to pray" (11:1; cf. 12:41 et al.). This could well be no more than a polite form of address. Is this true also of requests for healing (as in 18:41)? Or is the use of the term in such a request a recognition of Christ's superior status? In view of the way "Lord" was used in addressing people we should not make too much of this. Yet there are some passages where the fuller meaning is at least a possibility. Thus, for example, when Peter sees himself as a sinner at the time of the miraculous catch of fish, he exclaims, "Go away from me, for I am a sinful man, Lord" (5:8). Again, a potential disciple says, "I will follow you, Lord" (9:61). This usage shades off into that in which prayer is made to Jesus (A7:59–60).

A noteworthy feature of Luke's use of the term is the way he uses it in

---

[13] There are some ancient MSS that do not translate but have the divine name in Hebrew letters, evidently out of reverence for the name of God. Some argue that this was the pre-Christian practice and that "the Lord" was never used of God. Thus R. Bultmann says, "The unmodified expression 'the Lord' is unthinkable in Jewish usage" (*Theology of the New Testament* [London, 1952], 1:51). From this an argument is developed that "Lord" was never applied to Jesus on Palestinian soil; it developed in the Hellenistic world. But Fitzmyer argues compellingly that the usage is Palestinian (*The Gospel According to Luke (I–IX)*, 201–2). He gives the significance of the usage in this way: "The use of *kyrios* for Jesus would have meant putting him on the same level as Yahweh, without, however, identifying him" (p. 202). See also 40n.7 above.

[14] *The Gospel According to Luke (I–IX)*, 203. He adds, "This is not yet to be regarded as an expression of divinity, but it speaks at least of his otherness, his transcendent character."

narrative, as in the statement "The Lord had compassion on her" (7:13). This is rare in the other Gospels (Mark, for example, has it only once, in 11:3). But Luke uses it often and this both in his Gospel and in Acts. Clearly it was a recognized title of Jesus at the time he wrote, and he unhesitatingly used it as such. His usage is natural enough, but we should not gather that this way of speaking was much used before the Resurrection. During Jesus' earthly life other titles were used.

At the Resurrection the women were able to get into the tomb because the stone had been rolled away, "but they did not find the body of the Lord Jesus" (24:3). Later that day the disciples in Jerusalem were able to tell the two who had walked back from Emmaus: "Truly the Lord has been raised" (24:34). And it was this that was the burden of the preaching of the early church: "With great power the apostles used to give testimony of the resurrection of the Lord Jesus" (A4:33). But quite apart from the quotation of individual passages, it is clear from all that Luke writes about the early church that the Resurrection was of critical importance. As W. Foerster puts it, "The resurrection of Jesus is decisive. Without this the disciples might at any time have defined their relation to Jesus retrospectively by saying that He had been their Lord. But the real point now is that He still is the Lord."[15] To see Jesus who died as still the Lord transforms everything, including the way the disciples thought about Jesus. Once they were convinced that he had risen from the dead, they saw him in a new light, a new light that led them to speak quite naturally of him as "Lord." Could they put anything less than the fullest

meaning into calling the risen One "Lord"?

Because he is the Lord, the Lord who died and rose, the burden of the apostolic preaching was that sinners should put their trust in him. So it was that "believers were added to the Lord, a multitude of both men and women" (A5:14). People "turned to the Lord" (A9:35; 11:21). Again, "many believed in the Lord" (A9:42; cf. 11:17, 21; 14:23; 16:31 et al.). Paul summed up his message as one of "repentance toward God and faith in our Lord Jesus" (A20:21).

Clearly the risen Lord was the center of the movement, a truth that is brought out in a number of ways. Its adherents were "disciples of the Lord" (A9:1); they were baptized "in the name of the Lord Jesus" (A8:16); they spoke in his name (A9:28). The last thing Luke tells us about Paul is that in Rome he was "teaching the things about the Lord Jesus Christ" (A28:31). An interesting way of referring to their preaching was to say that they "preached the Lord Jesus" or simply that they "preached Jesus" or the like (e.g., A8:35; 11:20). This is to say that the good news they had from God is good news about Jesus Christ the Lord.

Those who responded were called to lives of wholehearted service. They were not complacent, for the church walked "in the fear of the Lord" (A9:31). Paul said he was ready to die "for the name of the Lord Jesus" (A21:13). We should not think that discipleship in the first century was safe or easy. It was neither. As the Lord had died for believers, they were called to a wholehearted commitment, one that was ready to face very real sacrifice.

We should notice a difficult passage

---

[15] *TDNT*, 3:1094.

where Luke says that Paul spoke of "the church of God [or, of the Lord], which he purchased with his own blood [or, the blood of his own]" (A20:28). Most authorities accept "God" as the correct reading, largely because it is the more difficult and thus more likely to be altered by the scribes (though NEB has "the church of the Lord, which he won for himself by his own blood").[16] The blood referred to must be the blood of Christ. If we understand the end of the verse as "the blood of his own,"[17] the meaning will be that God purchased the church with the blood of Christ, and this is generally accepted. But it is possible to take the text to read "the church of God, which he purchased with his own blood," in which case this is a reference to Christ as God. We cannot say that this is likely, but we should notice that Luke is ready to use language that at least comes close to calling Christ God.[18]

OTHER TITLES

Luke uses other titles. Thus he frequently calls Jesus "Teacher" (e.g., 9:38; 10:25). But this is such an obvious way of referring to one who taught as much as Jesus did that it scarcely calls for comment. Apparently a related term and one that Luke alone uses in the New Testament is "Master" (*epistatēs*, 5:5; 8:24, 45; 9:33, 49; 17:13). A. Oepke points out that in secular Greek this term is used in a wide variety of ways (such as for one who watches over herds, the driver of an elephant, an inspector of public works, and so on). But he thinks that in Luke it is a translation of "Rabbi" and thus is akin to "Teacher." In this Gospel it is a form of address and, with one exception, is used by disciples.[19]

Three times Luke calls Jesus "Savior" (2:11; A5:31;13:23; in addition he once has "God my Savior" [1:47]). The word was widely used in the ancient world and could refer to the salvation brought about by gods, physicians, philosophers, statesmen, and others. It was used of rulers and applied to the emperor (who might be called "the savior of the world").[20] When used of Jesus, it does not refer to him as the bringer of the temporal kind of salva-

---

[16] See the excellent discussion in Bruce M. Metzger, *A Textual Commentary on the Greek New Testament* [London, 1971], 480–81). He says that his committee thought the reading "God" more likely than "Lord."

[17] A number of authorities follow J. H. Moulton, who says of ἴδιος: "In the papyri we find the singular used thus as a term of endearment to near relations" and who approves the translation "the blood of one who was his own" (*A Grammar of New Testament Greek*, i, *Prolegomena* [Edinburgh, 1906], 90). Taken this way the passage is saying that God bought the church with the blood of one who was very dear to him.

[18] Fitzmyer sees this as one of three passages in which Luke may be calling Jesus God (the other two are Luke 8:39; 9:43). He apparently does not regard any as definitely doing this, but says, "What should be noted here . . . is that by the time Luke wrote his Gospel and Acts it would not have been impossible for a Christian author to refer to Jesus as God" (*The Gospel According to Luke (I–IX)*, 218–19). R. B. Rackham looks hard at the problem and, while he does not think we have a definite reference to Christ as God, he thinks Paul has moved very quickly from the Father to the Son, and says, "Now he unmistakably implies his equality and unity in divine prerogatives with the FATHER" (*The Acts of the Apostles* [London, 1909], 393).

[19] *TDNT*, 2:622–23.

[20] See *TDNT*, 7:1003–21. Foerster points to the limited use of σωτήρ in the New Testament (other than in the Pastoral Epistles and 2 Peter), which forms a contrast to the much more frequent use of σώζω and σωτηρία. He explains it in this way: "One can only say that there is a restraint in the use of σωτήρ which is to be explained by the fact that in the Jewish sphere σωτήρ could easily be linked with the expectation of a liberator from national bondage . . . while in the pagan world it suggested the idea of an earthly benefactor, especially in the figure of the emperor" (pp. 1020–21).

tion that was so widely understood in the ancient world, but as the bringer of salvation from sin and its consequences. He was called "Savior" at his birth (2:11), while his exaltation to the right hand of God is connected with his giving of repentance and forgiveness of sins (A5:31). The Savior came in fulfillment of God's promise (A13:23).

With "Savior," Peter and the other apostles link *archēgos* (A5:31), a word that is not easy to translate (NIV has "Prince"). It denotes "firstness" and thus may mean a prince, a ruler. But it is also possible to see it as a reference to one who begins anything ("as first in a series and thus supplies the impetus" [BAGD]). Moffatt takes it this way when he translates it "pioneer."[21] The word may also mean "originator, founder." On the whole it seems likely that we should understand it here in the sense "Leader" or "Prince." This meaning makes good sense also when Peter says, "You killed the *archēgos* of life" (A3:15). But it is also possible to see here the third meaning of the word, as Bruce does with his comment "You put the very Author of life to death— an amazing paradox!"[22] Whether Peter means "Prince" or "Author" he is saying that Jesus has a relationship to life such as nobody else has.

Sometimes Luke brings out the royalty of Jesus by referring to him as "King." He has it in the acclamation at the triumphal entry: "Blessed is the King who comes in the name of the Lord" (19:38; the other Synoptists do not have "King" in this place). He has it also in Pilate's question "Are *you* the King of the Jews?" (23:3; this question in this identical form is found in all four

Gospels), in the Jews' accusation (23:2; cf. A17:7), in the words of the mockers (23:37), and in the inscription on the cross (23:38). This recognition of Jesus as a King is seen also in the prayer of the penitent thief: "Jesus, remember me when you come into your kingdom" (23:42).

In addition, Luke sees Jesus as the "servant" of God (A3:13, 26) and as a "holy servant" (4:27, 30; the same word is used in 2:43, but there it means "child"). What was said about the servant in Isaiah finds its fulfillment in Jesus. J. Jeremias points out that this way of referring to Jesus is very old and that it never became "a commonly accepted term for the Messiah" among Gentile Christians.[23] We find it here in the very early Jewish church and not again in the New Testament.

We have seen that Jesus is the "holy servant," and sometimes he is simply "the holy One" (A3:14; cf. 1:35). Similarly Paul applies to Jesus a psalm that has the phrase "your holy One" (A13:35, citing Ps. 16:10), as Peter had done earlier (A2:27). Two different words for "holy" are used, but all these passages point to the consecration to God that is so characteristic of Jesus. He is linked to God in a special way.

With this we should notice the similar term "the Righteous One" (A3:14; 7:52; 22:14; cf. the verdict of the centurion at the cross [23:47]). The word is used in general of people who are upright (cf. Zechariah and Elizabeth, 1:6), and it may be used of God, who is perfectly righteous (cf. 2 Tim. 4:8). When used of Jesus, it sees him as "the ideal of righteousness" (BAGD). Peter speaks of him as appointed by

---

[21] William Neil favors this: the word is "used here rather as in Heb. 2:10; 12:2 ('pioneer')" (*The Acts of the Apostles* [London, 1973], 98).

[22] *Commentary on the Book of the Acts*, 89.

[23] *TDNT*, 5:703. He further says, "To the Gentile Church it was offensive from the very first because it did not seem to bring out the full significance of the majesty of the glorified Lord."

God to be the "Judge of the living and the dead" (A10:42), and to this we should add Paul's statement that God has appointed a day in which he will judge the world through him (A17:31). Final judgment is a significant reality, and it is important throughout the New Testament that our Judge at that time will be none other than our Savior.

In common with a number of other New Testament writers, Luke has the "rejected stone" theme. He reports Peter's statement that Jesus is "the stone that was despised by . . . the builders" but has become "the head of the corner" (A4:11). There is a strong contrast between the folly of Israel's rejection of Jesus and his vindication by God.

A title that clearly meant a great deal to Luke is "prophet." The people at Nain declared of him: "A great prophet has been raised up among us" (7:16), though a Pharisee with whom Jesus dined had serious doubts about that (7:39). People speculated that he was a prophet, perhaps Elijah (9:8, 19). Luke alone records the following words of Jesus with reference to his death: "It cannot be that a prophet perish outside Jerusalem" (13:33), combining the thoughts that he was indeed a prophet and that his rejection and death were certain. The two on the road to Emmaus told the "stranger" that Jesus had been "a prophet mighty in deed and word before God and all the people" (24:19). An interesting feature of the early preaching is that Jesus was identified with the "prophet like Moses" (Deut. 18:15–20; see A3:22–23; 7:37), whereas among the Jews this prophet was distinguished from the Messiah (cf. John 1:20–21). For the Christians, Jesus was both. In the fullest possible sense, he was a prophet. He was *the* prophet. The essence of the prophetic function was the prophet's speaking directly from God; he could say, "Thus saith the Lord. . . ." Jesus was the very mouthpiece of God. He spoke God's truth with the fullest authority.

the Gospel of luke and acts: the salvation of our god

Like all the other Evangelists, and for that matter all the other New Testament writers, Luke is concerned with bringing out the great truth that God has brought about salvation for people who did not deserve it. But he has his own way of dealing with the subject. He is the only one who wrote both a Gospel and an Acts, and we should overlook neither.

The Gospel tells us of what Jesus did and what he taught. It goes on to recount how he was betrayed and handed over to the Romans by the leaders of his own nation, how he was crucified and buried, how he rose and gave instructions to his followers. Matthew and Mark and John all seem to be content to end the account there. Not Luke. He goes on to tell about events that occurred after the Ascension—the coming of the Holy Spirit, the excited preaching of the early church, and the spread of the gospel, until he has Paul, one of his heroes, preaching in Rome boldly and without hindrance. It is a magnificent panorama, and it does not stop even there. Throughout both of his volumes he has references to the fulfillment of prophecy, so that he looks back to the age-old plan of God. And in both he has references to the final consummation when Christ will return and usher in all that is involved in the world to come.

It is true, of course, that the other Gospel writers also declare that God planned the history of the church from eternity past and, further, that in due course, God will bring in his perfect kingdom at the return of Christ. This is standard New Testament teaching. However, Luke has a unique way of handling it all, and his two-volume work gives him scope to make some points of his own. He tells a wonderful narrative, and he does it in his own way. Let us see what he has to say about salvation.

THE PLAN OF GOD

Luke tells us that in Gethsemane Jesus prayed, "Not my will, but yours be done" (22:42; so also Matt. 26:42). The Cross was not the defeat of God but the carrying out of what he had planned. Luke earlier referred to people who resisted the purpose of God (7:30), and he comes back to the thought of that purpose when he reports Peter's reference to "the set purpose and foreknowledge of God" (A2:23), which was manifested when the Jews handed Jesus over to be crucified. It was what God's "hand and purpose foreordained to happen" that

Herod and Pontius Pilate, together with Gentiles and Israelites, had done in crucifying Jesus (A4:28). The unconscious cooperation of all these actors underlines Luke's point that nothing human, no matter how mighty, can interfere with God's plan. Gamaliel recognized this: a plan of men can be overthrown, but not that of God (A5:38–39). God's purpose reached its high point in the death of Jesus for the salvation of sinners, but it did not begin only with the coming of Jesus. It was there already in the life of David (A13:22). It was in operation from ancient times, even if it reached its consummation when Jesus came.

Paul told the Jerusalem mob that at the time of his conversion Ananias had said to him, "The God of our fathers chose you to know his will . . ." (A22:14). From the beginning of his Christian experience he recognized that God was working his plan out in the world and that it was not like anything he had imagined in his pre-Christian days. Not surprisingly this became the theme of Paul's preaching, and he reminded the elders of Ephesus that he had not shrunk from declaring to them "all the purpose of God" (A20:27). On a smaller canvas Luke tells of a time when friends tried to turn Paul away from a course they saw as dangerous, only to be met by the apostle's stubborn refusal to turn away. In the end they desisted, saying, "The Lord's will be done" (A21:14). The God who was working out a great purpose in sending his Son to die for us had also a plan for Paul, whose trip to Jerusalem became the means of his reaching Rome with the gospel message. We should not miss Luke's point that a little group of unnamed Christians could recognize that God was working his purpose out in the movements of his servant Paul.

By using the verb that we translate "must" (or, "it is necessary"; *dei*), Luke brings out the thought that God is doing his will in the world. He uses this verb eighteen times in his Gospel and another twenty-two times in Acts. We may see something of the force of this by reflecting that the highest total in any other New Testament book is ten (in John). Luke uses *dei* in a way that brings out the thought of a compelling divine necessity. It is not simply that, considering all the circumstances, such-and-such is highly desirable. This verb means that the action is absolutely necessary. We should be clear that the necessity arises, not from circumstances, but from the will of God.[1]

Luke uses the verb in connection with a number of facets of Jesus' ministry. It appears in regard to the boy Jesus finding it necessary to be in his Father's house (2:49). It also comes out in connection with his preaching: it was necessary for him to go on to other cities (4:43). There is an interesting example of different values when a synagogue ruler says, "There are six days in which you must be healed" and Jesus asks, "Was it not necessary that this woman, being a daughter of Abraham, whom Satan bound for eighteen years, be loosed on the sabbath?" (13:14, 16). Both saw a necessity, but whereas the synagogue official was concerned with legal niceties, Jesus was concerned with the fulfillment of his

---

[1] Walter Grundmann points out that among the Greeks generally "behind the term stands the thought of a neutral deity," a kind of impersonal fate. He sees Luke as familiar with the verb from his Hellenistic background, but as using it in a different way. In Luke "Jesus sees His whole life and activity and passion under this will of God comprehended in a δεῖ. . . . It has its basis in the will of God concerning Him which is laid down in Scripture and which He unconditionally follows" (*TDNT*, 2:22).

divine mission, and took notice of people's needs. A similar necessity compelled him to go to Zacchaeus's house (19:5). There were other houses in Jericho. But his mission of salvation brought him to this one.

Most frequently connected with this necessity in the plan of God is the necessity for Jesus to have suffered (9:22; 17:25; 24:7, 26, 44; A17:3). This may be seen in the light of the prophecy that he would be numbered with transgressors (22:37). Scripture must be fulfilled (A1:16). Jesus says that he "must" be on his way "today and tomorrow and the next day," for a prophet cannot perish outside Jerusalem (13:33). And, though the language is different, we should see much the same thought in the immediately preceding words, which refer to his "bringing to completion" his works of healing "today and tomorrow," while "on the third day" he would reach his goal (13:32).[2] This is one of Luke's major thoughts and we should not miss the way he emphasizes it. The death of Jesus was right at the heart of God's plan of salvation.

We see this necessity also in the fact that "heaven must receive him until the time of the restoration of all things" (A3:21; it was a time foretold in the prophets). The interval between the Ascension and the *parousia* is part of God's plan. And we see the divine necessity in the salvation that is brought to people during this interval: "There is no salvation in any other, neither is there any other name given under heaven among men in which we must be saved" (4:12). The plan of God is clear. The way of salvation has come through Jesus, and it is nonsense to suggest that there is any other way.

We see this also in the words of Paul to the Philippian jailer, who had asked Paul and Silas, "Sirs, what must I do to be saved?" and received the answer, "Believe on the Lord Jesus and you will be saved" (A16:30–31). The purpose of God in salvation is clear enough, and Luke records the words that show this.

Sometimes Luke has the thought that there is divine necessity in the service that ordinary Christians are bound to render. Thus people must always pray and not grow faint (18:1). On a somewhat different level is the comforting information for those who face hostile tribunals that in such a time the Holy Spirit will teach them what they "must say" (12:12). We should not in our relief at the comfort overlook the obligation. In such circumstances there are certain things that *must* be said. God plans it that way. Peter brings this out with his forthright words to the high priest: "We must obey God rather than men" (A5:29). For Luke it is important that the humblest Christian see that in daily living for Christ there are some necessities thrust on each of us. Christian service is not optional.

Luke sees Paul as a special example of the way God works his plan out through human agents. He uses the word "must" quite often in connection with Paul's activities. The voice on the Damascus road told him to go into the city, where it would be told him what he "must do" (A9:6). The service to which he was called was something he *had to* do. That this would not always be comfortable is seen in the Lord's words to Ananias: "I will show him what things he must suffer for my name's sake" (A9:16). Paul certainly learned this well, and we find him

---

[2]The verbs are ἀποτελέω and τελειόω, both of which hint at reaching one's end or aim (τέλος).

telling converts: "Through many afflictions . . . we must enter the kingdom of God" (A14:22). He reminded the Ephesian elders that he had showed them by his hard work that they "must help the weak" (20:35). We see a little of the divine purpose also in the use of "must" with regard to Paul's going to Rome (A19:21; 23:11) and of his being tried before Caesar (A25:10; 27:24). The purpose does not stop with the ascension of Christ, but carries right on in the life of the church.

Sometimes Luke makes use of the verb *horizō* ("to mark off the boundary, determine"), as when he reports these words of Jesus: "The Son of man is going, according as it has been determined" (22:22). The same verb is used in the expression "the set purpose," linked with the foreknowledge of God as the basic reason for Jesus' being delivered up to death (A2:23). Looking further ahead, we see that Jesus has been "determined by God to be the Judge of living and dead" (A10:42; so also in A17:31). The same verb is used of God's determining the times and boundaries of human habitation (A17:26). God is concerned with all the nations and their way of life, not only with the great work of redemption. And a different verb is used of Christ's having been "appointed" (A3:20) and of God's appointment of Paul (A22:14; 26:16). With yet another verb Luke tells of witnesses of the resurrection who had been appointed by God (A10:41).

In common with other New Testa-

ment writers Luke draws attention to the fulfillment of Scripture in the life and death of Jesus (e.g., 4:21; cf. 1:70; 18:31; 21:22; A3:18; 26:22–23). Luke sees not only the broad sweep of Christ's atoning death as foretold but also some of the details, such as the fact that he was "numbered with transgressors" (22:37) or the words with which he commended himself to the Father at the moment of death (23:46).[3]

But it is not only the fulfillment of specific passages of Scripture to which Luke points. It is significant that he starts his Gospel by referring to "the matters that have been fulfilled among us" (1:1); the whole unfolding panorama is a fulfillment of what God has set in motion.[4] Luke quite often refers to what is fulfilled (e.g., 1:20; 9:31; 21:24; 22:16; 24:44; A3:18; 12:25; 13:27). There is often a sense of purpose in the verb *teleō*, which Luke uses significantly of the baptism that Jesus had to accomplish (12:50) and of the fulfillment of Scripture (18:31; 22:37).

We see something of Luke's deep interest in God's way of salvation in a couple of touches in his Transfiguration narrative. That account tells of Jesus' appearance in glory, but Luke manages to connect it with the Passion. Immediately before this narrative he has some sayings of Jesus, including a prediction of the Passion (9:22–27), and he introduces the Transfiguration account with the note that it was about eight days "after these sayings" that it took place (9:28). Then when the

---

[3]Cf. W. Barclay: "It was to the Cross that all the scriptures looked forward. The Cross was not forced on God; it was not an emergency measure when all else had failed and when the scheme of things had gone wrong. It was part of the plan of God, for the Cross is the one place on earth, where in a moment of time, we see the eternal love of God" (*The Gospel of Luke* [Edinburgh, 1967], 312).

[4]N. Geldenhuys comments, "The perfect participle passive is used here to indicate the permanent state after the completed action. The expression also points to the fact that in Jesus the divine promises of the Old Dispensation have been fulfilled and that a new era has been inaugurated. The fullness of the saving purpose of God has been revealed and the glad tidings must be proclaimed" (*Commentary on the Gospel of Luke* [London, 1952], 56).

transfigured Jesus was talking with the heavenly visitants, it was his coming death that was the subject of the conversation (9:31).[5] Luke makes it clear that Jesus appeared in glory, but these touches (not found in the other Gospels) show how the Cross dominated his thinking, so that it crops up in unexpected places.

SALVATION HISTORY

Writers on Luke often use the German term *Heilsgeschichte* to denote what his Gospel is about. The word is not easy to translate into English,[6] but it at least directs attention to Luke's concern for history and his conviction that what God did in Jesus took place against a broad historical background. In this he differs from the other Evangelists. They tell us something of what Jesus said and did, but they refer to secular history only where this directly impinges on the Gospel record, as when Jesus was brought before Pilate. Luke begins by referring to many who have written "a narrative,"[7] and by using this term he characterizes his book as one concerned with history.

Luke speaks of a decree of Caesar Augustus that all the world should be enrolled (2:1). This is not mentioned in the other Gospels, and it poses a historical problem for us today, for such a decree is not extant. But whatever our problems, there is no doubt that the point was important for Luke. He sees the purpose of God as set forward not only by what happened in Judea and Galilee, but also by what the emperor in far-off Rome did. That emperor may have known nothing about the God of Israel, but what he did set forward God's purposes nonetheless. Luke goes on to present further problems for us in his mention of Quirinius, governor of Syria. But, however we solve them, this further mention of a secular official locates these events firmly in the context of historical happenings.

The process is repeated in the complicated date in 3:1–2. Again there are problems for the modern historian, but again Luke is setting forward his theological purpose. All history finds its place in God's plan and no matter how great a person such as the emperor may be, his real significance is his part in the great plan that God is working out. We must not be indifferent to the historical process, for in it God is doing important things.

Notice that what Luke is describing relates to both Roman and Palestinian history. He has references to the emperors Augustus and Tiberius but also to Herod (1:5), Herod Antipas, Philip, and Lysanius (3:1) and to Annas and Caiaphas (3:2). He refers to a famine in the days of Claudius (A11:28) and to a decree of that monarch that brought Aquila and Priscilla to Corinth

---

[5]The word used is ἔξοδος, which may mean no more than "departure" but which here surely means "departure from this life." Cf. Conzelmann: "The purpose behind the heavenly manifestation is the announcement of the Passion, and by this means the proof is given that the Passion is something decreed by God" (*The Theology of St Luke* [London, 1961], 57).

[6]C. K. Barrett objects to some common translations: " 'Redemptive history' suggests that history redeems, and 'history of salvation' suggests that salvation is an institution" (*From First Adam to Last* [London, 1962], 4n.).

[7]The word is διήγησις, on which Fitzmyer remarks that Luke "adopts for his work a term current among Hellenistic litterateurs and historians. The frequency with which the word occurs in both classical and Hellenistic Greek writers, especially by those who profess to write history or about history and the way it should be written, makes it impossible to miss the intention with which Luke proposes his account of the Christ-event" (*The Gospel According to Luke (I–IX)*, 173).

(A18:2). He tells us of Gallio the proconsul (A18:12) and of the two Roman procurators Felix and Festus (A23:24; 24:27). He even names two Roman officers, the chiliarch Claudius Lysias and Julius a centurion of the Augustan cohort (A23:26; 27:1). And, although all the Evangelists speak of Jesus as being brought before Pontius Pilate, only Luke tells of Herod's part in the affair (23:6–12).

Luke then sets what God has done in Christ firmly in the history of the day. Salvation is not concerned with some mystical and mythical religion, with no relation to reality. It is something that God worked out—in this life, with real people. We should notice further that Luke did not stop his account when the earthly history of Jesus of Nazareth reached its conclusion. He went on to tell of the early days of the church, to the time in fact when the outstanding preacher Paul came to Rome. Luke ends with Paul preaching openly and unhindered in the world's capital. Salvation goes on and on in the church, salvation, not in the sense that anything more is done to put away sins, because for Luke what Jesus did was decisive, but rather in the sense that what Jesus died to bring about is made actual in those who respond to the preaching. History is the stage on which God works out his plan, and for Luke Jesus is right at the center.

H. Conzelmann entitled his important book on Lucan theology *Die Mitte der Zeit*, "The Middle of Time," and the title points to an important truth for this Evangelist. Much happened before Jesus came, but it was all preliminary. Much happened after his ascension, but it was all the working out of what he did in his atoning death. Although it is not unrelated to history, either before or after Jesus' life on earth, the life and death and resurrection and ascension of Jesus are for Luke the very center of history—the center, not in the sense that there is exactly the same amount before as after, but in the sense that this is the pivot on which everything else turns. We do not understand Luke unless we see the central importance of Jesus.

The history of the early church is important for him too, even if it does not have the central importance of Jesus. It was a time when the gospel was offered to Jews, and "the hope of Israel" is Luke's theme to the end (A28:20). But when the Jews as a whole did not respond, that did not mean that God's plan was defeated. It meant that the extension of that plan to the Gentiles became apparent. Luke brings this out in his record of Paul's address in the synagogue in Antioch of Pisidia (the first sermon of Paul's that he records). Paul says that it was "necessary" that the preachers speak "the word of God" to the Jews first. But when the Jews rejected it, the preachers turned to the Gentiles (A13:46–47).

The important thing is that the coming of Jesus means the coming of the new age. He did not come to mend a badly worn Judaism with a new patch.[8] His new wine could not be contained within the old wineskins of

---

[8] Matthew and Mark both have this saying in this form: "No one puts a patch of unshrunk cloth on an old garment," where the thought is that of the greater strength of the patch; it tears away from the old, thus making a worse tear. Luke is rather saying, "To patch an old garment with a piece torn from a new one is to spoil both, the new by being torn and the old by having a patch that does not match" (Leon Morris, *The Gospel According to St. Luke* [London, 1974], 121). Evidently the idea of the patch was used more than once, with different force on different occasions. There is strength in Jesus' way, as Matthew and Mark put it, certainly. But the point in Luke is that it does not agree with the old.

conventional Judaism (5:36–37). He was teaching something radically new, and we do not understand Jesus (or Luke) unless we see that. He recognizes that not all will be happy with what he is doing. There are those who say, "The old is good" (5:39) and refuse even to try the new.[9]

Luke makes a good deal of the importance of a radical change in the whole way of life. Early in his Gospel he tells us that an angel announced that it would be the work of John the Baptist "to turn the hearts of the fathers to the children" (1:17). The fathers may be the great patriarchs of old, and the angel may be saying that the conduct of Zechariah's contemporaries is such that the patriarchs would be displeased. John would call on them to live very differently so that they would be acceptable to the patriarchs. In this way he would turn the hearts of these great ones, so that they would now approve of their descendants. Or he may have in mind the families of his day, divided by the evil they do. When they are persuaded to do what is right, there will be harmony between fathers and sons. However we interpret the passage, there is a call for wholehearted change in conduct, a change reflected in the words "to make ready for the Lord a prepared people" (1:17). As they were, the people were not prepared for the Lord. To make them ready required a very big change.

The *Magnificat* gives eloquent expression to the reversal of accepted values that mattered so much, for it spoke of the exaltation of the lowly and the putting down of the people of high estate (1:51–55).[10] This accords with the Sermon on the Plain—with its blessings for the poor, the hungry, those who wail, and those who are hated, together with corresponding woes for the rich, the full, those who laugh, and those who are well spoken of (6:20–26). These words are often made into a plank for social reform and of course they do shock us out of our complacent acceptance of conventional values. But they are more than that. This entire Gospel makes it plain that Jesus was much more than a social reformer. He was interested in the kingdom of God—with all that that means. His words express a thoroughgoing repudiation of accepted standards and values. Luke's Gospel shows in many ways that "what is exalted among men is an abomination before God" (16:15). People are on the wrong track and have wrong values. They have very little in the way of achievement, for when they are through, the verdict must be that they are "unprofitable servants" (17:10). It is not natural for people to see themselves in this way, and yet once again we see how this Gospel calls for a complete reversal of human values, a radical revolution in the whole way of life.

ACCOUNTABILITY

Luke sees all people as accountable to God and continually coming short of what they ought to be. He does not have statements about the universality of sin, but he brings out the point in his own way. Thus he tells of a time when Jesus used contemporary happenings to hammer home the lesson. There

---

[9] Some MSS read, "the old is better," but the true text is rather "the old is good." Jesus is not picturing people who compare the two ways and decide for the older, but those who are so set in their old ways that they do not even consider the new. They will not budge.

[10] Cf. William Barclay: "There is loveliness in the *Magnificat* but in that loveliness there is dynamite. Christianity begets a revolution in each man, and a revolution in the world" (*The Gospel of Luke* [Edinburgh, 1961], 10).

were some Galileans whom Pilate had killed apparently while they were in the act of worship, for he mixed their blood with that of their sacrifices. And a tower collapsed in Siloam, resulting in the deaths of eighteen people. Were these people killed because they were greater sinners than other people? Jesus vigorously repudiates that thought and drives home the lesson they should be learning: "Unless you repent, you will all likewise perish" (13:1–5). The clear implication is that they were sinners, every one of them (cf. "No one is good except God" [18:19]), and because they were sinners, they were liable to the judgment of God.

Much the same point is made by the parable of the barren fig tree (13:6–9). The gardener pleaded for a stay of execution for the tree so that he could dig around it and manure it. But both he and the owner were clear that if it did not bear fruit, it should go. Sinners be warned!

The lesson keeps coming out in the parables. The account of the rich man and Lazarus is not primarily about sin and judgment, but it makes no sense unless we see these realities for what they are (16:19–31). The parable of the rich fool (12:16–21), with its "this night your soul will be required of you," stresses accountability. So does the parable of the pounds (19:12–27), where each servant is called on to give account of himself and where the delinquent faces punishment. The parable of the wicked farmers (20:9–18) is a forceful setting out of the truth that evil people face an inevitable retribution. They may get away with their sin for a time, but they are accountable and eventually will reap the due reward of their deeds.

Luke brings out the same point in other ways. Thus, he records Jesus' instructive and emphatic teaching re-

garding proper fear: "I will show you whom you should fear; fear him who after he has killed has power to throw into Gehenna. Yes, I say to you, fear him" (12:5). It is not death that is the significant thing, and God is not to be feared because he can bring this earthly life to a conclusion. He is to be feared because of what he can do in the hereafter. Clearly Jesus is referring to the punishment of sin, and once again we see the note of accountability made the more serious because of the way we all sin. So Jesus says that Capernaum will be "brought down to Hades" (10:15). Certain sinners will be "denied in the presence of God's angels" (12:9). Blasphemy against the Holy Spirit will never be forgiven (12:10). Those who "devour widows' houses" will in due course receive a severe condemnation (20:47).

A striking note in the early preaching in Acts is the way the preachers keep insisting on the awful responsibility of their hearers for the death of Jesus. That death fulfilled the plan of God but nevertheless Peter says to the people of Jerusalem, "You crucified and slew" him (A2:23). Later he goes on to say, "This Jesus whom *you* crucified . . ." (A2:36; the pronoun is emphatic). In his second sermon Peter speaks of Jesus as the One whom the Jews "delivered up and denied in the presence of Pilate, when he had decided to release him" (A3:14). He carries right on, "But *you* denied the Holy and Righteous One and asked for a murderer to be released to you; you killed the Prince of life . . ." (A3:14–15). These words are addressed to the ordinary people of Jerusalem, but Peter said the same thing before the highest authorities among the Jews: "Jesus Christ of Nazareth, whom *you* crucified . . ." (4:10; see vv. 5–6 for his audience). Peter repeats the charge again and again

(A5:28–30; 10:39), as do Stephen (A7:52) and Paul (A13:27-28). It is abundantly plain that the early preachers put emphasis on people's accountability to God.

We should not leave this aspect of our subject without reflecting that we too are accountable. It is easy to say that Caiaphas and Pilate and their associates were the ones responsible for the crucifixion of Jesus. But if we take seriously the point that the New Testament writers are making that Jesus died for the sins of the world, then we share in that guilt. We are not studying something academic that leaves us unscathed.[11]

With guilt goes the thought of judgment. In his Gospel, as we have seen, Luke records words about hell and being denied before the angels of God. Accountability means judgment— judgment by the highest of standards and before the highest of tribunals. In Acts we find that Jesus is to be the Judge on the last great day (A10:42; 17:31). From one point of view this is a comfort, because no one can conceivably be as considerate of us as the One who loved us so much that he died for us. But from another point of view, his being the Judge makes the judgment serious. If he came to earth and lived and died to put away sins and make a way of salvation, we cannot expect him to regard as of no consequence the actions of people who continue in sin.

REPENTANCE

All the New Testament writers in one way or another call for sinners to turn from their sin. But these writers have their distinctives, and we should notice that Luke stresses more than the others the need for repentance.[12] Like Matthew and Mark he tells his readers that John the Baptist called people to a "baptism of repentance" (3:3; A13:24; 19:4) and invited people to produce "fruits worthy of repentance" (3:8). But, as they do not, he goes on to John's filling out of his message by explaining what this meant: those who had plenty should share with those who have little, the tax collectors should collect no more than they were entitled to, and soldiers should be content with their wages and make no attempt at violence and extortion (3:10–14).

All three Synoptics have this saying of Jesus: "I did not come to call righteous people but sinners"; only Luke adds "to repentance" (5:32). It might be argued that this is implicit in Matthew and Mark, but the point is that it is explicit in Luke. He will not let us escape the demand for repentance. He tells us that Jesus uses the repentance of Nineveh as a rebuke to the present unrepentant generation (11:32) and that he even uses the failure of Tyre and Sidon for the same purpose (10:13; they would not have resisted the evidence of the "mighty works" as this generation did). We have

---

[11] D. R. Davies makes the point that evil deeds like the crucifixion of Jesus always need the action of "good" men, for the evil left to themselves cannot bring such things about (*The Art of Dodging Repentance* [London, 1952], 34–35). He brings this home to people of our day. He speaks of "the generation of our blood-soaked, cruelty-ridden world" and adds, "Of all the men who have lived and died since Calvary, we men of today can least pretend to the possession of superior virtue, of a deeper, finer, more responsible morality. The unnumbered millions done to death and the millions condemned to a living death in remote spaces scream denial of any such pretension. No century has more clearly recrucified Christ than the twentieth" (p. 41).

[12] Luke has μετάνοια 5 times in his Gospel and 6 times in Acts (he thus has 11 of the 22 New Testament occurrences of the word). He has the verb μετανοέω 9 times in the Gospel and 5 times in Acts (it occurs 34 times in the New Testament, 12 being in Revelation).

already noticed that Jesus invited his hearers to reflect on Pilate's killing of the Galileans and on the deaths of those on whom the tower in Siloam fell; here I add that he said, "Unless you repent you will all perish likewise" (13:3, 5).

But when there is repentance, there is joy in heaven—a truth repeated in successive parables (15:7, 10). Repentance means an end to sinning, and Jesus teaches that repentance causes a joy that extends beyond this earth. Matthew has a parable about a shepherd looking for a lost sheep, a shepherd who rejoices over the one that was found more than over the ninety-nine that were not lost (Matt. 18:12–14). There is nothing about repentance, as there is with Luke.

With this emphasis on repentance in the teaching of Jesus, it is not surprising that from the first the preachers of the early church looked for this attitude. After the first Christian sermon, Peter said to his hearers, "Repent, and be baptized, every one of you . . ." (A2:38). He did it again in his next sermon: "Repent then and turn . . ." (A3:19). Peter urged Simon Magus to repent (A8:22), as Paul did the Athenians (A17:30). Indeed, before King Agrippa Paul said that he had not been disobedient to the heavenly vision, but that "first to those at Damascus, then in Jerusalem and in all the country of the Jews, and to the Gentiles" he had proclaimed "repentance and that they should turn to God and produce works worthy of repentance" (A26:20). This statement, coming at the end of his career as it does, and covering such a wide range of those among whom he had worked, makes it clear that repentance was central to his preaching.

Some statements make it clear that we are not to think of repentance as a human virtue, worked up out of human resources. It is in some sense a gift of God. God exalted Christ in order "to give repentance to Israel and forgiveness of sins" (A5:31). And it was God who gave to the Gentiles "repentance unto life" (A11:18).

All this fits with the great basic Christian stress on grace. It is a gracious God who gives the gift of repentance and thus admits to life those whose sinful lives would otherwise have led them to death. We should notice further that this demand for radical repentance and complete change of life arises from the fact that the Christian way is a way of grace. In a religion of law what matters is to keep one's account in credit, to have a healthy surplus of good deeds over bad. But in the way of salvation by grace it is not enough to have done a certain number of good deeds. One must turn away, not from some evil, but from every evil. Repentance is to be wholehearted, and the demand for such a repentance springs from the wholehearted salvation that Christ has won for his people.

THE CENTRALITY OF THE PASSION

Like the other Evangelists, Luke makes the Passion the high point of his Gospel. It is as clear for him, as it is for them, that Jesus' death and resurrection were the very heart and center of God's way of saving us. We have already seen some of the evidence for this in such things as the predictions of the Passion, Luke's concept of the suffering Messiah, and the working out of the plan of God, for, as this Evangelist sees it, that plan put the death of Jesus at the heart of the way of salvation. Luke's Gospel has been structured in such a way as to make the Passion the climax of it all.

Luke's infancy narrative is a significant opening. There is nothing like it in any of the other Gospels. We must not be so taken with the beauty of the accounts that we do not notice that Luke is setting forth some of the important motifs that run through his book. There we find, for example, that the baby Jesus is both Christ and Lord; he is the Savior. He is set for the fall and the rising of many in Israel, while the sword that would pass through Mary's soul points to sadness and rejection.

When Jesus delivered his programmatic sermon at Nazareth, he indicated that his concerns would not be those usual to messianic claimants. As he proclaimed "the Lord's acceptable year" (4:18–19), he would be concerned with good news for the poor, with the release of captives, with the giving of sight to the blind, with freedom for the crushed. The people were astonished at Jesus' "words of grace," but the account ends on a note of rejection (4:29–30), a note Luke strikes in other places as well (7:33–35). Luke has this in mind from the first.

We have seen that Luke's account of the Transfiguration mentions that Moses and Elijah talked about Jesus' death (9:31), and later in the same chapter we find another of Jesus' predictions of his coming suffering (9:44–45). Jesus spoke of the "baptism" that lay before him and added, "What constraint I am under until the ordeal is over!" (12:50 NEB).[13] Consistently he moves toward the Cross.

A noteworthy feature of Luke is the travel document (9:51–19:44; some end this section elsewhere, such as at 19:27). There has been a good deal of scholarly discussion and disagreement on this section. Some see more than one journey, others believe that Luke was using different traditions of the one journey, still others say that, in reality, there never was a journey but that Luke has used the motif for his own theological purposes in writing.[14] W. G. Kümmel finds so much confusion in this part of the Gospel that he decides we can scarcely say more than that "the Lord, who goes to suffer according to God's will, equips his disciples for the mission of preaching after his death."[15]

But we *can* say this, and it is important. It means that from 9:51 on, Luke has the Cross in view. It is not something that cropped up somehow at the last minute, when things went wrong. It is something to which Jesus moved with deliberate steps as he fulfilled the purpose of God. And though there is a good deal of disciple teaching in this part of the Gospel, Kümmel reminds us that it is teaching in view of the impending death of the Lord. This whole section stresses the centrality of the Passion. Right at the outset, Luke says that Jesus "set his face to go to Jerusalem" (9:51).

The thought of the progress to Jerusalem is repeated a number of times in the travel narrative (9:51, 53; 13:22;

---

[13] G. B. Caird thinks that Jesus "was consciously echoing the teaching of John the Baptist, and incidentally demonstrating how great a gulf lay between him and the greatest of his predecessors. John had prophesied the coming of one who should baptize with the fire of divine judgment: it had never occurred to him that the Coming One might be the first to undergo that baptism" (*The Gospel of St Luke* [Harmondsworth, 1963], 167).

[14] W. G. Kümmel lists the opinions of seven scholars holding six different opinions about the significance of the travel narrative (*Introduction to the New Testament* [London, 1966], 99). There is agreement that the passage has theological significance, but clearly there is no agreement as to precisely what that significance is.

[15] Ibid.

17:11; 18:31; 19:28). Indeed Luke has a deep interest in that city[16] and mentions the name "Jerusalem" thirty-seven times in his Gospel (Matthew has it thirteen times; Mark, ten; and John, twelve). Like Matthew and Mark, Luke has most of the action outside of the capital city, so it is all the more striking that he mentions it so often. John includes a good deal of the action that occurred in Jerusalem, but Luke uses the name of the city three times as often as John does. It seems that for Luke Jerusalem is the city of destiny, the place where God was to accomplish the work of redemption in the passion of the Lord, the place where the Spirit would be given, the place where the church would have its beginning. So when he has the passion in mind, it is quite in keeping with this approach that he repeatedly speaks of Jesus as going to Jerusalem. In another writer this might mean no more than that the capital city was his destination. In Luke it means that he was making his way to the place where God's plan would come to its climax.

Luke devotes a good deal of space to his record of the Passion itself, as, of course, do the other Evangelists. The seriousness with which he treats this part of his Gospel shows that for him it had the greatest significance. Generally the narrative follows the same lines as those in the other Gospels but Luke has some pieces of information that the others do not. Thus, he tells us of the questioning among the disciples in the Upper Room as to which of them would be the greatest (22:23), of Jesus' desire to eat the Passover with them (22:15–18), and of Jesus' words to Peter that Satan wanted to sift him like wheat (22:31–32). Only Luke tells us about the two swords (22:35–38), about the angel who strengthened Jesus in Gethsemane, and about the bloody sweat (22:43–44; there is textual doubt about this passage). He tells us of the question whether the disciples should use the sword (23:49), of Jesus' healing of the wounded ear (22:51), of the accusation of Jesus' enemies (23:2), and of Jesus' appearance before Herod (23:6–12). He tells us of Pilate's declaration that Jesus was innocent (23:13–16), and he has in a fuller form than we find in the other accounts the mob's calling for Barabbas to be delivered to them. It is in Luke that we read of the "daughters of Jerusalem" (23:27–31), of the prayer "Father, forgive them . . ." (23:34), of the penitent thief (23:40–43), and of Jesus' prayer as he was dying: "Father, into your hands I commend my spirit" (23:46). There are some other Lucan touches. I have not tried to be exhaustive in this list.[17]

Luke is not simply repeating what the others have said. He is deeply interested in the passion, and, although he does not hesitate to use material the others have (an account of crucifixion requires a good deal of common material), he has gathered information that the other Evangelists do not have. He leaves us in no doubt that this is the great central thing. This is what Christ came for. There is evil here—the malice of Jesus' enemies, the readiness of one of his followers to betray him, the mob baying for the blood of a man they

---

[16]There are two forms of the name of the city. Luke prefers Ἰερουσαλήμ, which he uses 27 times in the Gospel and 36 in Acts, a total of 63 of 76 in the whole New Testament. He also has Ἱεροσόλυμα 10 times, with another 23 in Acts, making a total of 33 of 63 in the New Testament.

[17]Vincent Taylor devotes a book to the passion narrative in Luke in which he argues that this Evangelist does not basically depend on Mark but has his own sources of information about the passion (*The Passion Narrative of St Luke* [Cambridge, 1972]).

knew had committed no offense, the failure of the Roman governor to liberate a man he recognized as innocent. But there is also the hand of God. And because God is at work, the last word is not tragedy but triumph.

THE TRIUMPH OF GOD

Throughout his Gospel Luke tells of a struggle between good and evil, between God and the devil—a struggle that comes to its climax at the Cross. He is in no doubt that the last word is not with evil. It is with God and with good.

As the other Synoptists do, Luke tells us several times that Jesus expelled demons (4:33–37, 41; 6:18; 8:2, 27–39; 9:37–43; 11:14; 13:11–16). We should bear in mind that, while demon-possession was widely recognized in the ancient world, and while there were people who purported to cast demons out, the phenomenon plays little part in the Bible other than in the Synoptists' accounts of Jesus' ministry.

Luke gives us something of the significance of it in his account of the exorcism in 11:14. The expulsion of the demon led some critics to ascribe to Beelzebul what Jesus had done. Jesus pointed out that this would mean that Satan was divided against himself. It also raised the question of how their sons did their exorcisms; if his enemies were right, they had Satan's minions in their own households! The crunch comes when Jesus says, "But if it is with the finger of God that I cast out the demons, then there has come upon you [nothing less than] the kingdom of God" (11:20). He goes on to the parable of the strong-armed man who is overcome by someone stronger than he and concludes with "He who is not with me is against me, and he who does

not gather with me scatters" (11:23). There is no neutrality in the struggle in which Jesus is involved.

The conflict with the demons continues in Acts, though there are not as many exorcisms there. But when people tended to find demons everywhere, it must have been a very significant part of the Christian message that all the forces of hell had been defeated. Peter said that Jesus "went about doing good and healing all who were oppressed by the devil" (A10:38), and he himself rid certain people of unclean spirits as did Philip and Paul (A5:16; 8:7; 16:18).

Luke makes it clear that there was nothing magical about this. The exorcists of antiquity apparently loved to come up with new and potent spells. The seven sons of Sceva tried to cast out an evil spirit by using the name of "Jesus, whom Paul preaches." But the man leaped on them and drove them out of the house naked and wounded (A19:13–16). We are not to see the name of Jesus as the latest technique for practitioners of magic. In that name the apostles did indeed do wonderful things, and through it they exercised power over the demons. But this power is open only to those who come humbly, committing themselves by faith to the service of Jesus Christ and seeking to set forward the purposes of God, not to advance their own reputations for magical prowess.

Throughout his Gospel, Luke has the note of conflict with evil. Jesus is constantly opposed by evil forces, and Luke is clear where the victory lies. Jesus expels the demons. They cannot withstand him. Nor can they withstand those who come in Jesus' name. On one occasion, Jesus sent the Twelve out on a preaching mission and gave them authority over the demons (9:1). On another occasion he sent out seventy (or seventy-two; the MSS are divided) of his followers, and while there is no specific mention of the demons in their commission, when they came back they said with joy "Even the demons are subject to us in your name" (10:17). Jesus' reply begins, "I saw Satan fallen from heaven like the lightning" (10:18). The words are difficult, but this seems to be the best way of taking them: "To the casual observer all that had happened was that a few mendicant preachers had spoken in a few small towns and healed a few sick folk. But in that gospel triumph Satan had suffered a notable defeat."[18] Notice that there is no mention of Satan in Jesus' charge to the preachers. But their victory over evil is a victory over Satan.

Conzelmann denies that there is any activity of Satan in this Gospel between the temptation and the passion: "When Jesus was alive, was the time of salvation; Satan was far away, it was a time without temptation. . . . The Temptation is finished decisively ($\pi \acute{\alpha} \nu \tau \alpha$), and the devil departs. A question of principle is involved here, for it means that where Jesus is from now on, there Satan is no more—$\ddot{\alpha} \chi \rho \iota \kappa \alpha \iota \rho o \tilde{\upsilon}$."[19] It is difficult to square Conzelmann's repeated statements with what Luke actually says. As we have seen, he has a picture of an ongoing contest between Jesus and the forces of evil. He sees Satan as defeated when the disciples have success (10:18). He refutes an accusation of his enemies on the ground that if what they said were true, Satan would be divided against himself (11:18). This is in the activities of his mission; it refers to the time that Jesus was on earth and active. He talks about "a daughter of Abraham" whom Satan had kept bound for eighteen years (13:16) and whom Jesus released. In the parable of the sower Jesus speaks of the devil coming and taking the Word from people's hearts lest they believe and be saved. If we are going to take our theology from what Luke says rather than from theories of the way he writes, we must surely see that Satan was active throughout Jesus' ministry and that it is one of Luke's major thrusts that Jesus constantly defeated the forces of evil.

Satan was especially active in the Passion. He participated in the Betrayal by entering into Judas (22:3). He wanted to sift Peter like wheat (22:31). This is a mysterious saying, but one that leaves us in no doubt but that he wanted to disrupt Jesus' work and that a great trial lay ahead of Peter. Jesus, when he was arrested, said, "This is your hour, and the dark Power has its way" (22:53 MOFFATT). It is clear that this is the critical moment in the conflict between Christ and the powers of evil.[20]

And, of course, the Cross leads on to the Resurrection, the resounding triumph of Christ over the evil one. The end of Luke's Gospel and the opening

---

[18] Leon Morris, *The Gospel According to St. Luke* (London, 1974), 185. Cf. Marshall: "This evidence suggests that the mythological idea of the fall and defeat of Satan is here being utilized by Jesus to express symbolically the significance of the exorcism of the demons. The exorcisms are a sign of the defeat of Satan" (*The Gospel of Luke*, 429). J. M. Creed sees it differently: "An ecstatic vision on the part of Jesus is suggested, but it is not clear when we are to understand it to have taken place" (*The Gospel According to St. Luke* [London, 1950], 147).

[19] *The Theology of St Luke*, 16, 28; see also 156, 188, et al.

[20] Cf. Karl Heim: "According to Jesus' own assertion it is the final battle, terrible and decisive, of the war that fills the whole of His life, against the satanic power that wants to dethrone God . . . the thought of an anti-godly power against which this war is waged cannot be eliminated from the mind of Jesus as an unimportant concept to be attributed to popular ideas of His time. On the contrary: this is the fundamental conviction that makes His whole life-work from the beginning to the terrible end into a fierce war with an invisible enemy" (*Jesus the Lord* [Edinburgh and London, 1959], 90–91).

of Acts are full of the thrill of that triumph. It is clear that it took the followers of Jesus completely by surprise. They had expected nothing like this and were plunged into the depths of gloom by what happened on Good Friday. But the Resurrection changed everything. It showed that Jesus had not been defeated by the worst that his enemies could do. Nothing seems as final as death, and Jesus had died. But for him it was not final. He rose victorious.

All this, of course, is common to the other Evangelists and, for that matter, to all the New Testament writers. They were thrilled by the Resurrection message. But Luke has his own way of bringing out the triumph. His Resurrection narratives, for example, are his own, except that he shares with Mark and Matthew the account of the visit of the women to the tomb. How much we owe to him for the unforgettable account of the two who walked with Jesus on the road to Emmaus and for that scene in the Upper Room when they told the others that Jesus really had risen!

When we have this cue, we find significant themes in the earlier part of this Gospel. There are prophecies in which Jesus declared that he would rise (9:22; 11:29–30; 18:33). At the time they were uttered, such words must have seemed mysterious. The disciples would have reasoned, "Obviously we must take these words metaphorically, but what meaning can we give them?" Now we can see that Jesus was simply forecasting his ultimate triumph. And we should reflect that Luke records that Jesus raised from the dead the daughter of Jairus (8:41–56) and the son of the widow of Nain (7:11–15). Jesus never did stand in the same relationship to death as do the children of men. He was "the Prince of life" (A3:15); "it

was not possible for him to be held" by death (A2:24). Jesus' resurrection was foretold in Scripture and thus God willed it to happen. Paul saw the same necessity about Jesus' resurrection as about his death: he found both in Scripture and therefore both had to occur (A17:3).

Luke is certain of the Resurrection. He begins Acts by telling his readers that after his passion Jesus showed himself to be alive "with many sure proofs" (A1:3). The early chapters of Acts are full of the joy of the Resurrection, as indeed we might expect. It is plain, however, that the disciples were thoroughly dejected when Jesus died. He had been central to their thinking and their living and now he was a corpse. What should they do? Where should they go? Then suddenly, all that pessimism was dispelled. The gloom vanished in the profound conviction that the impossible had happened. Jesus had triumphed over death. He was not dead, but alive. Small wonder that the Resurrection gripped them and that they made it the center of their message.

In his first sermon, Peter has a long section about this (A2:24–36), even though the sermon was called forth by the extraordinary happenings that accompanied the coming of the Holy Spirit. It cannot be said that the preacher skimped on the importance of the coming of the Spirit, but it is significant that at such a time he spoke so fully of the Resurrection. That was the great thing that God had so recently done and that must be clearly set forth. Thus, the Resurrection finds a prominent place in most of the preaching of the early church.

It is repeated again and again that God raised Jesus, not just that Jesus rose (2:32; 3:15, 26; 4:10; 5:30; 10:40; 13:30, 33, 34, 37; 17:31). As

Luke saw it and as the early preachers saw it, the Resurrection means that God himself had acted to reverse what evil men did at Calvary and to accomplish his purpose. Thus the Resurrection was not simply one of the many things the preachers mentioned; it could be said that "with great power the apostles kept testifying to the resurrection of the Lord Jesus" (A4:33). They "preached in Jesus the resurrection of the dead" (A4:2).[21] The function of an apostle was to be "a witness . . . of his resurrection" (A1:22). Even where it was likely to be unpopular, as in intellectual Athens, the Resurrection was preached (see A17:18).

Luke does not stop at the Resurrection. He finishes his Gospel and begins Acts with accounts of the ascension. The Resurrection was wonderful, but, after all, it took place here on earth. But Jesus' place was in heaven, and Luke leaves us in no doubt that he returned there. We have seen that he put a good deal of emphasis on Jesus' passion, and his resurrection and his ascension were in some sense one with his death. Right at the beginning of his travel document as he looks forward to Jesus' journey to Jerusalem to be crucified, he speaks of the days coming, not when Jesus would die, but when he would be "taken up to heaven" (9:51 NIV).[22] In the Upper Room, with the Cross in immediate prospect, Jesus speaks to the disciples of the "kingdom" he appointed for them; there is glory as well as suffering ahead (22:29–30).

So it is that sometimes Peter speaks of exaltation as well as of resurrection. He can say, ". . . having been exalted therefore to the right hand of God" (A2:33), and again, "Him did God exalt to his right hand" (A5:31).[23] This probably means much the same as that "God glorified his servant Jesus" (A3:13) and that God "made" Jesus both Lord and Christ (A2:36). The thrust of such passages is that Jesus is in the supreme place. The Resurrection did not mean that he was simply returned to the life on earth that he had before (as was true with people like the daughter of Jairus, the son of the widow of Nain, and Jesus' friend Lazarus). It meant that God set him in the highest place in heaven. It meant that he was in a position to do things like send the Holy Spirit with the spectacular results described in Acts 2. It meant that the lowly, rejected One was now the supreme, exalted One. It meant the triumph of God.

THE MEANING OF THE CROSS

How does the death of Jesus bring salvation? Granted that Luke puts a good deal of emphasis on the passion and the exaltation of Jesus, what significance does he see in all this? An answer is not easy, for Luke rarely addresses himself to such questions. He proclaims the fact without going deeply into the way it all works out. But now

---

[21] F. F. Bruce comments, "The meaning seems to be that they proved from the fact of Jesus' resurrection (ἐν τῷ Ἰησοῦ, 'in the case of Jesus') the general principle of resurrection, which the Sadducees denied" (*The Acts of the Apostles* [London, 1951], 116).

[22] Some take the word ἀνάλημψις to refer to Jesus' death (e.g., Gerhard Delling, *TDNT*, 4:9; though "possibly" the term includes the Ascension). Better is the position of G. B. Caird: "Luke packs a whole theology into the word *analempsis*, which means an assumption, a reception up into heaven. The word contains a strong echo of the Elijah motif which has already figured so prominently in the Gospel (cf. 2 Kings 2:9–11). But Luke uses the word here in a thoroughly Johannine fashion to cover the whole complex of events by which Jesus made the transit from earth to heaven—crucifixion, resurrection, and ascension" (*The Gospel of St Luke* [Harmondsworth, 1963], 140).

[23] In both passages τῇ δεξιᾷ could mean "by" or "at" or "to" the right hand.

and then he does make statements that bear on the problem.

It is probably significant that he sees Jesus as "the Servant of the Lord" (A3:13, 26; 4:27, 30). Although the Servant is not mentioned in Peter's first sermon, it may be that Peter is thinking of him. Vincent Taylor could write, "Already in this discourse [i.e., A2:22–36] it is clear that the dominating conception is that of the Servant, humiliated in death and exalted by God in the fulfilment of his supreme service for men. This claim is valid even though the Servant has not yet been mentioned."[24] J. Jeremias sees the use of the term "Servant" as belonging to "a very ancient stratum of the tradition," and he further holds that the references to Jesus as "the Righteous One" (A3:14; 7:52; 22:14) may derive from Isaiah 53:11.[25] In that case they are probably meant to remind us of the righteous Servant of the Lord. Certainly when Philip spoke to the man from Ethiopia, he started from Isaiah 53:7–8 and "preached Jesus to him" (A8:35).

Such passages make it clear that Luke understood Isaiah 53 to refer to the sufferings of Jesus, and he once explicitly tells us that Jesus applied words from that chapter to himself (22:37). That chapter certainly speaks of atoning sufferings, and Jeremias says, "Because he goes to his death innocently, voluntarily, patiently and in accordance with the will of God (Isa. 53) his dying has boundless atoning virtue. It is life flowing from God, and life in God which he outpours."[26] We can say this at least. And because Isaiah 53 is full of the thought of substitution, there is at least the possibility that Luke saw something of this in the way Jesus wrought atonement.

Sometimes he hints at ways of understanding the atonement. We see this in his account of the institution of the Lord's Supper. It is only Luke among the Evangelists who tells us that Jesus said his body was "given" for his followers and that they should "do this in remembrance" of him. It is only Luke who writes that the cup was "the new covenant" in Jesus' blood (22:19–20; the adjective "new" is absent from the better MSS in the first two Gospels but should be read in Luke). That Jesus' death was vicarious, that he established the new covenant in his death, and that his people are to have this constantly before them in a solemn liturgical ordinance are not unimportant pointers to the saving efficacy of his death.

Again, Luke speaks of "the church of God, which he purchased with his own blood [or the blood of his own]" (A20:28). This is not far from the imagery of redemption (which means the payment of a price to liberate from captivity). In recording this, Luke is at least saying that God saved us at great cost; he is also saying that the price was the death of Christ. In the history of the church, this way of looking at the atonement has attracted many; and it has sometimes led to excessive literalism, when people have asked and answered the question, "To whom was the price paid?" Luke cannot be faulted in this matter, for he does not develop the thought. But at least he sees our salvation as the result of an act of purchase, where the price was the blood of the Savior.

Three times Luke records the fact

---

[24] *The Atonement in New Testament Teaching* (London, 1946), 18.
[25] W. Zimmerli and J. Jeremias, *The Servant of God* (London, 1957), 91.
[26] Ibid., 104.

that Jesus died "on a tree" (A5:30; 10:39; 13:29). This is a curious way of referring to crucifixion, for the word is not a very natural one to use of a cross. It means literally "wood" and is used of a variety of objects made of wood, such as cudgels (Matt. 26:47), the stocks in a prison (A16:24), and timber for purposes of building (1 Cor. 3:12). It sometimes refers to a tree (Rev. 2:7; 22:2), hence the common translation. But the word was not usually used to denote a cross, and we should not be misled by the frequency of its appearance in Christian hymns. As G. B. Caird says, it "is not a description of the Crucifixion which would naturally occur to a bystander."[27] The expression would have aroused horror in the average first-century Jew, because it reminded him of the words "anyone who is hung on a tree is under God's curse" (Deut. 21:23). For some Jews it was impossible that Jesus could be God's Messiah, because he died in a way that showed he was under God's curse. The form of expression is Jewish (many draw attention to relevant passages in LXX and in Hebrew writings).

Why, then, did Luke choose to include these passages, so unusual in the way they refer to crucifixion and carrying such a dreadful freight of meaning for those acquainted with Jewish ways of thinking? It seems that he wanted to bring out the point that Jesus bore our curse.[28] Paul refers to the curse once (Gal. 3:13), and Peter to the tree once also (1 Peter 2:24). This way of looking at the Cross is confined in the New Testament to these three passages in Acts and the two in Gala-tians and 1 Peter. That Christ bore our curse is not a commonplace of New Testament teaching, but it is one way Luke looks at the Cross, and a way that he uses more than anyone else.

Sometimes theologians emphasize the fact that Luke has no equivalent of Mark 10:45—the statement that Jesus came to give his life as a ransom for many—and that his extensive writings do not develop any particular theory of atonement. It is suggested that Luke is interested in Jesus' sufferings not as atoning but as the path to glory. Men treated Jesus badly, but he bore his sufferings patiently and entered glory. Thus, Conzelmann thinks that in Luke there is no "direct soteriological significance drawn from Jesus' suffering or death."[29] Some conclude that Luke was typical of many early Christians—having a deep gratitude to God for sending Jesus but without any real idea that Jesus' death brought salvation. That idea, it is said, is the result of the work of thinkers like Paul.

It may be granted that Luke did not have the lively theological penetration that Paul had. But then who does? This is no reason for dismissing the points Luke makes. It is true that students of the atonement will always spend more time with Paul than with Luke, but that does not mean they may ignore Luke. After all, he explicitly says that the body of Jesus was given for us, that the cup at the Last Supper was the new covenant in his blood poured out for us, and that we are to keep remembering all this in the Holy Communion. He says that the death of Christ purchased sinners, that the prophecy of

---

[27] *The Apostolic Age* (London, 1955), 40.

[28] Cf. Marshall: "One may wonder whether there is a hint of the idea, developed by Paul, that a person who so died was regarded as being under the curse of God" (*The Acts of the Apostles* [Leicester, 1980], 120). Neil, however, has no doubts, but says of the hanging of Christ on the tree: ". . . thus making him accursed according to the Law" (*The Acts of the Apostles*, 97).

[29] *The Theology of St Luke*, 201.

Isaiah 53 with its vicarious suffering was fulfilled, and that Christ bore the curse of God.

Why does he put a good deal of emphasis on the sufferings and death of Jesus? He certainly puts no meaning on them other than that they were soteriological. He does not speak of Jesus as a martyr, for example. When he makes a number of statements about the meaning of Christ's death and when he devotes such a large amount of space to setting it forth, we may well accept that for him, as for other New Testament writers, Calvary meant more than the rejection of a good and godly man. It was God's way of providing salvation for sinners.

the Gospel of Luke and acts: the holy spirit

Luke has a good deal to say about the Holy Spirit. He uses the word *pneuma* 36 times in his Gospel and 70 times in Acts, the latter number being the most in any New Testament book (1 Corinthians with 40 is next; but Paul's total of 146 exceeds that of Luke). Sometimes he uses the word in referring to the unclean spirits, who were so constantly in opposition to Jesus (e.g., 4:33; 9:39; A5:16; 8:7), but mostly he uses it of the Holy Spirit.

We see in Paul's writings that the early Christians had a distinctive view of the work of the Spirit. Whereas other religions saw a divine spirit as coming on only a few especially important people, Christians realized that God's Spirit comes on all believers. And whereas pagans thought that the presence of the divine spirit was to be known by various forms of ecstatic behavior, Christians knew his presence by his "fruit" in ethical conduct. Luke does not enunciate these points the same way Paul does, but they are just as important to him.

He begins this theme quite early, with the message of the angel to Zechariah that the son that would be born to him would be "filled with the Holy Spirit from his mother's womb" (1:15). No part of John's life would be lived apart from the presence of the Spirit. Both of John's parents are said to have been "filled with the Holy Spirit"— Elizabeth, when Mary came to see her during her pregnancy (1:41), and Zechariah, when he was about to utter his great Song (1:67). These seem to be simply infillings of the Holy Spirit for those special occasions. It looks more like a continuing state when we read of Simeon that "the Holy Spirit was upon him" (2:25). The Spirit revealed to him that he would see the Lord's Christ before he died (v. 26), and at the right moment he came to the temple "in the Spirit" (v. 27);[1] the Spirit guided him to be there when Mary and Joseph brought Jesus there. Clearly, Luke presents this man as one in whom God's Spirit lived in a special way.

JESUS AND THE HOLY SPIRIT

There are some important statements connecting the Holy Spirit and Jesus,

---

[1] J. Reiling and J. L. Swellengrebel give the meaning of the expression as " 'in the Spirit', i.e. 'guided by the Spirit' (NEB), not on his own account or initiative" (*A Translator's Handbook on the Gospel of Luke* [Leiden, 1971], 132).

especially during the early part of the Gospel. Thus, the angel Gabriel explained to Mary how his words would be fulfilled: "The Holy Spirit will come upon you and the power of the Most High will overshadow you; therefore that which will be born will be called holy, Son of God" (1:35). This means that the Holy Spirit was involved in bringing about the Incarnation.

Before Jesus began his public ministry John the Baptist contrasted his work with that of the great One who would follow by saying that, whereas he, John, baptized with water, that Other "will baptize you with the Holy Spirit and with fire" (3:16). The meaning of baptizing with fire is not obvious, and a number of suggestions have been made.[2] It seems to be referring to purification, the fitting complement of baptism with the Spirit. This is not mentioned again in Luke, but Acts records that Jesus told the disciples to wait in Jerusalem for "the promise of the Father," after which he said, "John indeed baptized with water, but you will be baptized with the Holy Spirit not many days from now" (A1:4–5). Clearly he is referring to the experience on the Day of Pentecost. This is confirmed by Peter's use of the same prophecy in his defense of his action in baptizing Cornelius and his associates. The Holy Spirit, he says, fell on them "just as on us at the beginning," and then he remembered what the Lord had said: "John indeed baptized with water but you will be baptized with the Holy Spirit" (A11:15–16). God gave to them "the same gift as to us" (v. 17). Baptism in the Holy Spirit means receiving the Spirit as at Pentecost (A2:33).

When Jesus was baptized by John, the Holy Spirit came down on him in visible form like a dove[3] (3:22 [Luke says that Jesus was praying; that is, the Spirit came on him not during the baptism but immediately after it]). It is clear that the baptism, together with the descent of the Spirit and the voice from heaven, marked the beginning of Jesus' ministry, and it is significant that the Spirit is associated with this beginning. We may fairly deduce that the human Jesus needed the equipment of the Spirit for the work that he would now begin. It was not a work to be taken in hand in purely human strength and wisdom.

Luke stresses the place of the Spirit in the temptation narrative. Jesus was "full of the Holy Spirit" and "was led in the Spirit in the wilderness" (4:1). Jesus had been called by the Father and given the Holy Spirit; plainly this was the start of the ministry for which he had come. But what sort of Messiah was he to be? There is a sense in which Satan tempted him to be the wrong sort of Messiah, one who turned stones into bread for his own sustenance, one who did spectacular but pointless miracles, one who would establish a mighty world empire. But that is not the whole

---

[2] I have summed them up in this way: "The reference to *fire* is taken by some to be in apposition with *Spirit*, 'the fire of the Spirit' (Harrington), by some to mean testing (Creed), by others to point to judgment. The context favours the last-mentioned, and W. H. Brownlee has drawn attention to a passage in the Dead Sea scrolls referring to an eschatological fire of judgment which he thinks supports this interpretation. But it is the same people who are baptized with the Holy Spirit as with fire (and the two are governed by one *en* in the Greek). It seems best to see John as thinking of positive and negative aspects of Messiah's message. Those who accept Him will be purified as by fire (*cf.* Mal. 3:1ff.) and strengthened by the Holy Spirit" (*The Gospel According to St. Luke* [London, 1974], 97–98).

[3] The symbolism of the dove is puzzling, as in Jewish writings this bird was a symbol of Israel, rather than of the Holy Spirit. But there can be no doubt about its meaning here. It is a piece of Christian symbolism, not something taken over from Jewish sources (or for that matter Gentile sources).

story. The Holy Spirit was in it too. The Spirit led him and was with him throughout that time when he faced the question of what sort of Messiah he would be.

When the temptation was over, Jesus "returned to Galilee in the power of the Spirit" (4:14). Luke says little about Jesus teaching in the synagogues, and then he begins the account of Jesus' visit to Nazareth by mentioning the sermon in the synagogue there. After reading a passage from Isaiah that began with "The Spirit of the Lord is upon me," Jesus started his address with these stirring words: "Today this Scripture has been fulfilled . . ." (4:18, 21).

The program laid down in the passage from Isaiah is important, as is the way Jesus fulfilled it. But here our concern is to notice that it was not something that could be fulfilled without divine aid. The Holy Spirit was upon Jesus, and it is impossible to confine Luke's meaning to the duration of the sermon at Nazareth. The Spirit of the Lord was upon Jesus throughout his ministry, even though Luke does not often refer to this (but cf. his reference to Jesus' rejoicing "in the Holy Spirit" [10:21]). Luke records Peter's summary of what Jesus did: God "anointed him with the Holy Spirit and with power, [and he] went about doing good and healing all who were oppressed by the devil, for God was with him" (A10:38). The Spirit was on Jesus at all times, and his whole ministry was the result of the presence of the Spirit. Indeed, at the end of Jesus' earthly ministry, just before the Ascension, Jesus gave commandments to the apostles "through the Holy Spirit" (A1:2).

PENTECOST

For Luke what happened on the day of Pentecost was of critical importance. He has recorded the words of Jesus that the heavenly Father will "give the Holy Spirit to those who ask him" (11:13). But during the time Jesus was on earth the gift was apparently not given (or not given widely; there were a few people such as Zechariah and Elizabeth and Simeon who had received the gift). As we have seen, Jesus saw the fulfillment of the prophecy of John the Baptist that he would baptize with the Holy Spirit, not in what he did during the days of his flesh but in the outpouring of the Spirit narrated in Acts 2. There were unusual physical phenomena: a sound like a mighty wind and tongues like fire (A2:2–3). But the significant thing was that they were all filled with the Holy Spirit (v. 4).

This transformed the whole situation for the little group of believers. They had been hiding in an upper room, apparently still somewhat fearful, though the Crucifixion was now some weeks in the past. But with the Holy Spirit within them, they went out into the most public place and preached boldly. And we never again read in the New Testament of Christians being afraid to speak for Christ. The coming of the Spirit transformed them.

There are various ways in which this is described. The initial report says that they "were filled with the Holy Spirit" (A2:4; cf. 4:8, 31; 9:17; 13:9, 52), and presumably this means much the same as being "full of the Holy Spirit" (the use of the adjective instead of the verb [A6:3, 5; 7:55; 11:24]). Other passages speak of the Holy Spirit as "coming" on disciples (A1:8; 19:6) or falling on them (A10:44; 11:15). Again, God poured out the Spirit on people (A2:17–18; 10:45) or "gave" the Spirit (A15:8; cf. 8:18). From the human point of view it can be said that people "received" the Spirit (A2:38; 8:15, 17; 10:47; 19:2). It does not appear to matter greatly how it is expressed. Peter says that the Spirit "fell" on Cornelius and those with him "just as also on us at the beginning" (A11:15), although the "falling" terminology is not used in Acts 2. Whatever the words, the great truth is that God in Christ has given the Spirit to those who put their trust in him, and this gift of the Holy Spirit is the necessary equipment for Christian service. From this point on, Acts is full of what people did when the Holy Spirit was at work in and through them.

There is a good deal about the guidance the Holy Spirit gave God's servants. Jesus told his followers not to be anxious when they were brought before hostile tribunals, because the Holy Spirit would teach them what to say (12:11–12). The impression the early Christians made on their judges (e.g., A4:13) shows how this worked out. They found the voice of the Spirit also in Scripture; the Spirit spoke through David (A1:16; 4:25) and through Isaiah (A28:25). He also spoke to people of that day, such as Simeon (2:26), Philip (A8:29), and Peter (A10:19; 11:12). The Spirit spoke to the church at Antioch (A13:2) and initiated the first missionary journey of Paul and Barnabas.

There is a firm consciousness both of the presence of the Spirit and of their ability to discern his leading in the wording of the decision of the Council of Jerusalem: "It seemed good to the Holy Spirit and to us . . ." (A15:28). Similar to this are the words of Peter and the other apostles: "We are wit-

nesses of these things and so is the Holy Spirit . . ." (A5:32).

The Spirit is very much in evidence in the account of Paul's going up to Jerusalem. When Paul had completed his work in Ephesus, he "purposed in the Spirit" to go to Jerusalem (A19:21). That he went "bound in the Spirit" (A20:22) appears to mean that he was under the constraint of the Spirit to make the journey, though he did not know what the outcome would be. But he did know something of the difficulties that lay ahead, for he said, "The Holy Spirit testifies to me in every city, saying that bonds and afflictions await me" (v. 23). At Tyre there were Christians "who said to Paul through the Spirit that he should not go on to Jerusalem" (A21:4); this is a perplexing statement, since it was by the Spirit's compulsion that Paul was on his way there. Probably the Spirit revealed to them that Paul would suffer in Jerusalem, and, appalled at this, they added their own urging that he should not go. As Marshall puts it, "The disciples at Tyre may not have been well-informed on the finer points of predestination, and could have thought it possible to say to Paul, 'If this is what is going to happen to you, don't go.'"[4] We see something of the same situation at Caesarea, for when the prophet Agabus took Paul's girdle, bound himself with it, and said, "Thus says the Holy Spirit, 'The man whose girdle this is the Jews will bind thus in Jerusalem and they will give him over into the hands of Gentiles'" (A21:11), the local Christians urged Paul not to go. But, of course, he felt that he must obey the Spirit's leading, even though it might mean suffering. Incidentally, we meet Agabus on one other occasion and

---

[4]I. Howard Marshall, *The Acts of the Apostles* (Leicester, 1980), 339.

there, as here, he is accurately forecasting the future "through the Spirit" (A11:28).

In the ministry of Paul and Silas there is a most interesting example of the way the Spirit guided believers. After Paul and Silas had gone through "the region of Phrygia and Galatia," the Spirit forbade them to preach in the province of Asia, so they headed for Bithynia, but again the Spirit would not allow them to go there. Then Paul had a vision in which he saw a Macedonian asking for help, and the Christians all agreed that this was the way the Spirit was leading them (A16:6–10). We are not told how they knew that the Spirit was forbidding them to go into Asia and Bithynia, but the missionaries were sure of this. Guidance did not come to them all at once. They tried more than one avenue before discovering where it was the Spirit wanted them to go.

The Spirit, then, is very active in guiding and directing the early believers. He also "snatched up" Philip after the baptism of the Ethiopian eunuch (A8:39). He "sent out" the missionaries (A13:4). He gave "encouragement" to the church (A9:31), and "appointed overseers [or bishops]" in it (A20:28).

It follows from all this that the Spirit is a very important being, One who is not to be despised or taken lightly. Jesus said that a word spoken against the Son of man may be forgiven, whereas anyone who blasphemes the Holy Spirit will not be forgiven (12:10). This sin is more than the utterance of a form of words; it is a way of thinking and living that refuses to treat the Spirit as holy, that disregards and rejects him. Ananias and Sapphira lied to the Holy Spirit (A5:3) and "agreed to put the Spirit of the Lord to the test" (v. 9). Their exemplary punishment was not for one lie, but for their attitude to the Holy Spirit. And Stephen complained that his accusers always resisted the Spirit in the same way as did their fathers (A7:51). For Luke it is important to have a right attitude toward the Spirit.

Acts records an exciting period in the church's life. It is plain that Luke saw the Spirit as living and active, as One whose presence illuminated and inspired the church. To blur or overlook this teaching is to miss that which alone enables the church of God to do the work to which it is called and be the church it ought to be.

11

the gospel of luke and acts: discipleship

The action of God in Christ demands a response, and Luke is just as clear as the other Evangelists that a response must be made. He has his own way of making the point. We have already noticed his emphasis on repentance. The contemplation of what God has done for sinners should lead them to see the error of their ways and to turn from them. This must be done wholeheartedly. No one can undergo the repentance that Luke writes about and still remain much the same person. Repentance means a complete change of mind, the appropriation of a new attitude to life. It is probably significant that Luke speaks a number of times of Christianity as "the Way" (A9:2; 19:9, 23; 22:4; 24:14, 22); sometimes also he refers to it as "the way of the Lord" (A18:25) and "the way of God" (A18:26). Interestingly all the references in Acts are in some way linked with Paul, who does not use the expression in his epistles. Luke apparently is fond of the term. It draws attention to Christianity as a whole way of life, not simply as a means of satisfying religious impulses.[1] And Luke does not speak of "a" way, but "the" way; the expression points to a deep conviction of the rightness of Christianity[2] and of the impossibility of any other way of leading people to God.

In the material that Luke shares with the other Evangelists he sometimes brings out more than they do the wholeheartedness that the call to follow Christ demands. For example, all three Synoptists record Jesus' call of Matthew and tell us that Matthew responded to his call and followed him. But only Luke says that he "left everything" (5:28). Matthew and Mark tell us that Simon and his brother left their nets and followed Jesus (Matt. 4:20; Mark 1:18). Luke has a different incident at the climax of which Peter and others "left everything" (5:11), not just the nets. Matthew shares with Luke the account of the potential disciples, one of whom was warned that foxes and birds have places of rest, but the Son of man (and thus his disciples) had nowhere to lay his head, while another was told to let the dead bury their dead (Matt. 8:18–22). There Matthew

---

[1] The origin of the term is unknown (cf. E. Haenchen, *The Acts of the Apostles* [Oxford, 1971], 320), though something like it is known from earlier Jewish usage including the Qumran scrolls (cf. Günther Ebel, *NIDNTT*, 3:938–39). It is apparently a name the Christians applied to themselves, and it is one of the earliest designations of the church.

[2] Cf. Wilhelm Michaelis, "Christians, however, believe that they are in the right, and this is expressed by the use of ὁδός" (*TDNT*, 5:89).

stops. But Luke adds a third: the man who wanted to say good-bye to those of his household, only to have Jesus say to him, "No one who puts his hand to the plow and looks back is fit for the kingdom of God" (9:61–62).[3] All three Synoptists have the saying about denying oneself and taking up the cross, but only Luke says this must be done "daily" (9:23). Luke is not suggesting that discipleship is tougher than Matthew and Mark see it, but in some places he brings out more strongly than they do what is implied.

Some of Jesus' teaching about discipleship is for the most part preserved only in Luke (14:25–33; Matt. 10:37–38 is parallel to vv. 26–27). Here we find the difficult words about the impossibility of being a disciple unless one hates one's closest relatives, "one of the most uncompromising statements of the claims of the Kingdom in the New Testament."[4] Sometimes "hate" and "love" are used in such a way as to make it clear that "to hate" can mean "to love less." This is clearly the meaning when we read that Leah was "hated" by her husband (Gen. 29:31, 33, as is its reading in Deut. 21:15–17). It is such a meaning that we should give to the present expression. Jesus demanded that people should love even their enemies (6:27); so it is impossible to think that he is now calling for a literal hatred of one's intimate family. He is saying that being his disciple means loving him in such a way that the best of earthly loves seem like hatred in comparison.

Luke then records two parables that stress the importance of counting the cost (14:28–33). A farmer who decides to build a tower will look a fool if he starts to build and then finds that he does not have the money to finish the job. A king going to war must reckon whether he has the army to defeat the enemy; if he does not have such an army, he does not fight but seeks peace before battle is joined. The two accounts make similar points (we must count the cost) but they are not identical. The farmer may build or not, as he chooses, but the king is in danger. He is being invaded; the other king is "coming against him" and he must take action. In the former case the question posed for the would-be disciple is, "Can you afford to be a disciple?" In the second it is, "Can you afford not to?"[5] Both points were important for Luke.

People live their lives "before God." Luke tells us that Zechariah and Elizabeth were righteous "before God" (1:6). The same expression comes into the priest's liturgical activity (1:8), and a similar one into Mary's finding of favor with God (1:30). Even the smallest thing, the fall of a sparrow is not forgotten "before God" (12:6), while some things that seem all right to people are abomination "before God" (16:15). Peter and John asked whether a certain action was right before God (A4:19), and Stephen asserted that David found favor before God (A7:46). The almsgiving of Cornelius was remembered before God (A10:31), and he and his friends were met "before God" when Peter came (v. 33). Clearly Luke saw varied activities as taking place in the very presence of God. This means at least two things: (1) we are warned that all that we do is done in the presence of God so that we are accountable people and (2) the disciple

---

[3] Cf. E. Earle Ellis, "Service for the kingdom requires an undivided loyalty" (*The Gospel of Luke* [London, 1966], 152).

[4] T. W. Manson, *The Sayings of Jesus* (London, 1949), 131.

[5] A. M. Hunter makes this point in *Interpreting the Parables* (London, 1960), 65.

must realize that discipleship is concerned with the whole of life, not simply with some parts of it. Christians through the centuries have often been tempted to compartmentalize life, setting some of it apart as "religious," and seeing other aspects as having little or nothing to do with their religious profession. Luke warns us that all of life is lived in the sight of God.

A PATTERN OF LIFE

We may see something of the Christian pattern of life if we look at some of the things Luke tells us about Paul. He speaks of Paul's spectacular conversion, which can scarcely be our model, for he tells of no other such Christian conversion. But Paul's response to Christ can show us what our own response should be. He was obedient (A26:19), and that meant being baptized and proclaiming Christ (A9:18, 20). It meant being zealous for God, as indeed he always had been, even when he was a persecuting Pharisee (A22:3–4); he had always served God with a good conscience (A23:1; 24:16). The God he served as a Christian was "the God of our fathers" (A24:14), the same God he had served as a Pharisee. It was not God who had changed; it was Paul. He could say that his hope was in God (A24:15) and that he looked for help from God (A26:22). Paul believed God (A27:25), and faith, of course, mattered very much to Luke (he uses the noun *faith* 26 times in Luke–Acts and the verb *to believe* 46 times).

It is this kind of response Luke looks for from those who would call themselves the followers of Christ. He speaks of turning to the Lord (A3:19; 9:35; 11:21; 15:19; 26:18, 20; 28:27). People are to be God's "servants" (A16:17), to seek him (A17:27), and to fear him (A10:2, 22; 13:16; cf. 16:14; 18:7). Luke often speaks of praising God (e.g., 1:64; 2:20; 5:25; 13:13; A2:47; 3:8–9) and glorifying him (7:16; 17:15; A4:21; 21:20); it is a serious matter when anyone does not give glory to God (A12:23).

Faith is especially important. During Jesus' lifetime faith was often connected with healing miracles, and frequently we find the refrain "Your faith has saved you" (7:50; 8:48; 17:19; 18:42). In such passages there is obviously a concentration on healing, but it is hard to think that the faith of which Jesus approves in such cases means no more than a conviction that a miracle could be worked. It seems much more likely that there is also an attitude to Jesus and that this goes beyond the miracle. In the boat in the middle of the storm Jesus asked the disciples, "Where is your faith?" (8:25); he also spoke about those of little faith (12:28). The disciples asked him to increase their faith, and this led him to speak of what can be done when there is faith even as small as a mustard seed (17:5–6).

In Acts, faith is still connected with healing (A14:9); faith "in the name" means faith in all that Jesus is (A3:16).[6] However, the description of Stephen as a man "full of faith and of the Holy Spirit" (A6:5) has nothing to do with healing; it means that Stephen had a special degree of faith. There is a similar statement about Barnabas

---

[6]The Greek construction is far from straightforward, but the meaning seems to be that the miracle took place in response to the man's faith and that his faith was brought about "through Jesus." Cf. E. Haenchen: "The name is ineffective unless faith in it is present, but on the other hand it is the name preached by Peter which enables the faith to come into being. The significance of faith is stressed, of course, because the content is that of an 'appeal preached with missionary intent' (Bauernfeind . . .)" (*The Acts of the Apostles* [Oxford, 1971], 207).

(A11:24). In these passages, nothing is said about the object of faith, but other places speak specifically of faith in Jesus (A20:21; 24:24; 26:18). Some references are to "the faith" (A6:7; 13:8; 14:22; 16:5), probably indicating that faith was of the essence of the Christian way. Gentiles came to be included in the church because God had opened "a door of faith" (A14:27).

When Luke uses the verb *to believe,* he may do so in reference to particular people, like Mary (1:45), or he may make it general as in the interpretation of the parable of the sower: "The devil takes away the word from people's hearts lest they believe and be saved" (8:12). He may speak of believing someone's words (1:20), but of course the verb is most often used of believing people.

Luke uses a variety of constructions with this verb. Sometimes it is the simple dative (which has the meaning "give credence to"), as when he refers to those who did not believe John the Baptist (20:5) or those who did believe Philip (A8:12) or the prophets (A26:27). Sometimes he uses it in regard to believing God; in this use it may indicate saving faith (A16:34; 5:14; 18:8) or accepting the guidance God gives (A27:25). It is saving faith when it is faith in the Lord—that is, the Lord Jesus.

Sometimes Luke has the verb followed by the preposition *epi,* "upon," showing that faith has a solid basis, it rests "on" something or someone. Thus Jesus referred to believing "on" the things the prophets had spoken (24:25). But mostly Luke uses this construction when people believe "on"

Jesus (A9:42; 11:17; 16:31; 22:19). Believing *eis,* "into," is similar; faith takes one out of oneself and into Christ. "All the prophets" bear their witness, said Peter, "that everyone who believes into him will receive forgiveness of sins through his name" (A10:43; cf. A14:23; 19:4).[7]

Luke also uses the verb intransitively: people are said simply to believe. Or again, the participle may be used to mean "believers." As Luke saw it, it is not necessary to say what they believe or in whom they believe. In a Christian context faith in Christ is so basic that it is enough to use the verb without qualification. We find this usage in Jesus' interpretation of the parable of the Sower. The devil takes the word away from people's hearts lest they believe and be saved (8:12), while there are others who believe only for a time (8:13). Neither of these references to faith is found in the parallel passages, but it is characteristic of Luke to refer to it. Again, Jesus encourages Jairus by saying, "Only believe, and she will be saved" (8:50). In this statement faith appears to be connected with healing. Luke makes most use of this construction in Acts, where it is the characteristic expression for coming to be a Christian or for being a Christian. At the end of Peter's first sermon Luke refers to "all those who believed" (A2:44), and a little later he said that "many believed" (A4:4). Similar expressions are found again and again (e.g., A4:32; 11:21; 13:12, 39, 48; 18:27; 21:20). It is clear that for Luke faith was fundamental. It is the necessary way of entering into the salvation Christ died to bring.

---

[7] It is possible that he also once follows the verb with ὅτι "that," indicating that faith has content; it is not a vague optimism, but a firm belief that God had done or will do certain things. Elizabeth pronounced a blessing on Mary who "believed ὅτι there will be a fulfilment . . ." (1:45). But ὅτι here probably means "because." The construction is used of the followers of Jesus in Jerusalem who did not believe that Saul of Tarsus was a disciple (A9:26).

UNIVERSALISM

Luke was probably a Gentile. That may account for his demonstrating that salvation in Christ is open to people from all races. There were those in the early church who saw the new way as indeed open to all, but only on the condition that they in effect became Jews: they had to be circumcised and comply with the law of Moses (A15:1, 5). Paul spent his life combating such views, and Luke was squarely on the side of Paul on this matter.

It is not that Luke denigrates the Jews. He quotes Simeon's song in which that aged saint spoke of God's salvation as "a light for revelation to Gentiles" but immediately adds "and for glory to your people Israel" (2:32). It is interesting that Matthew, the "Jewish" Gospel, has the visit of the Magi in its opening and closes with the commission to preach the gospel to all the world. Luke, the Gentile Gospel, begins and ends with the temple at Jerusalem! And it is Luke who tells us of the presentation of the baby Jesus in the temple (2:22ff.) and of his visit there when he was twelve years old (2:41–51). As we noted earlier, Luke has many more references to Jerusalem than any of the other Evangelists has. It is in Jerusalem that God determined to bring to a climax the work of salvation that he would accomplish in Jesus. There cannot be the slightest doubt about Luke's emphasis on the place of Jerusalem and indeed of all things Jewish in the background to Christianity.

But for all that, Luke has a wide vision. He sees people of all races as included in the scope of salvation. The message of the angels to the shepherds is one of "peace on earth" (2:14), not simply peace in Israel. It is significant that both he and Matthew quote from Isaiah 40 in connection with the ministry of John the Baptist. But where Matthew has three lines of the prophecy, enough to tell of the voice calling on people to prepare the way of the Lord, Luke adds another five until he comes to the words "all flesh will see God's salvation" (3:4–6). Luke shares Matthew's interest in the voice in the wilderness and in preparing the way of the Lord, but he also makes it clear that the salvation that the Lord will bring is a salvation for the whole world. He tells us of Jesus' astonishment at the faith of the centurion, a faith greater than any found in Israel (7:9), and he records the words about people coming from the east and the west, from the north and the south to recline in the kingdom of God (13:29). Matthew has both passages, but he speaks only of those from the east and the west; Luke's interest in the whole world is perhaps seen in his addition of the other two points of the compass. Matthew and Luke both have genealogies of the Lord, but whereas Matthew begins with Abraham, Luke goes right back to Adam (3:38), the father of all and not simply of the Jewish nation.

There are also the Samaritans. Matthew mentions them once: when Jesus sent the Twelve on a mission he told them not to go into any city of the Samaritans (Matt. 10:5). Mark says nothing at all about them. But Luke is interested in them (as is John). He has the wonderful parable of the good man from Samaria (10:30–37), and he tells us also about the Samaritan leper, who, among the ten who were healed, was the only one to return and give thanks to Jesus (17:15–16). But Samaritans were not always attractive people. Once Jesus sent disciples to a Samaritan village to prepare a place for him to stay, but the villagers rejected them when they found that they were going to Jerusalem (9:52–53). But whatever the hostility of the villagers (and of James and John, who wanted to call down fire on them [v. 54]), it is noteworthy that Jesus wanted to stay among them. Many Jews would not have wanted to do so.

The risen Jesus commanded his followers to be witnesses to him in Jerusalem and all Judea. So far, so good. But—and this may have come as a mild surprise to his Jewish followers—he adds Samaria and then "the end of the earth" (A1:8). The interest in Samaria continues, for when a persecution scattered the little group of Christians, Philip went to Samaria, where he had a notable success. In due course Peter and John came down and laid hands on the new believers there (A8:1–25). This was the first expansion of the church to the peoples outside Judaism, and from that time on it seems that the church in Samaria could be ranked with those in Judea and Galilee (9:31). It is interesting that when Paul and Barnabas were on their way to the Council of Jerusalem, they passed through Phoenicia and Samaria and brought joy to the brothers as they told of the conversion of the Gentiles (A15:3).

We can see how revolutionary this inclusiveness was when we consider Jesus' sermon at Nazareth. When he spoke of God's blessing the widow of Zarephath and Naaman the Syrian (4:26–27), the villagers became so angry that they rose up and took Jesus to a place where they planned to throw him over a cliff. Their attitude to non-Israelites was plainly not his.

Jesus refers to the Gentiles in his eschatological discourse. Luke includes the words about the Jerusalemites being led captive among all nations, and about Jerusalem being "trodden under foot by the Gentiles until the times of the Gentiles are fulfilled" (21:24). The words do not, of course, concern the salvation of the Gentiles, but they are further proof of Luke's interest in them (they are not mentioned in the parallel passages).

Acts is almost a demonstration of this interest in itself. It begins with the church in Jerusalem, and, despite the definite command of Jesus that his followers take the gospel to other places, the believers were content to stay where they were. But in due course persecution arose and scattered them (A8:1). That led to the evangelization of the Samaritans. Then came Peter's vision, his visit to Cornelius, and the baptism of Gentiles in his household after the Holy Spirit came upon them.

Luke goes on to Paul's missionary journeys with Barnabas and Silas, journeys that brought many Gentiles into the Christian church. But we should not miss the point that when Paul and Barnabas preached at Antioch of Pisidia, they explained to the Jews that "it was necessary that the word of God be spoken to [them] first" (A13:46). It was only when the Jews rejected the message that the disciples turned to the Gentiles. Luke safeguards the place of the Jews (as Paul does with his "to the Jew first but also to the Greek" [e.g., Rom. 1:16]). However, the natural result of bringing the gospel to Gentiles was that the church became increasingly Gentile, and Luke describes the progress of the gospel in many lands until he brings his account to its close with Paul preaching in Rome. There is no question for Luke but that Christianity was no tiny Jewish sect; instead, it was a religion in which people from every nation would have their place.

Luke's interest in the universal scope of the gospel is not confined to national and geographical extension. It was important to him that people from all nations come within the scope of

Christ's saving activity, but it was also important that the gospel be brought to groups of people that were deprived in some way. Thus he shows an interest in women and children and in society's outcasts. The ancient world in general accepted divisions in society without question and gave privileges to some classes above others. But Luke was clear that Christ had broken down barriers. Let us proceed to look at some of the far-reaching changes Jesus made in cultural patterns.

WOMEN

It was a man's world, and, though there were differences from time to time and from place to place, it was all but universally held that women were inferior to men. Daniel Rops says of women among the Jews:

> The wife owed her husband total fidelity, but she might not claim it in return. Her husband could not sell her, but he could repudiate her without any difficulty: the cases in which the wife could ask for a divorce, on the other hand, were exceedingly rare. The rank which society assigned her was inferior, from every point of view. . . . Women did not eat with the men, but stood while they ate, serving them at the table. In the streets and in the courts of the Temple they kept at a distance from the men. Their life was in the house. . . .[8]

The *Jewish Encyclopedia* points out that there was no great difference in the place of Jewish women from that of others in antiquity: "The woman was held of less account than man."[9] Jewish women could not give evidence in court,[10] and they were apt to find themselves in strange company, as

when they were excluded from those eligible to lay hands on an animal to be offered for sacrifice along with deaf mutes, imbeciles, minors, the blind, Gentiles and slaves (Mishnah, *Menahoth* 9:8).

The rabbis did not include women among their disciples. They not only did not teach women, but regarded it as a sin to do so. R. Eliezer said, "If any man gives his daughter a knowledge of the Law it is as though he taught her lechery" (Mishnah, *Sotah* 3:4). There is a very old prayer that a man might pray: "Blessed art thou, O Lord . . . who hast not made me a woman." This prayer gives religious evidence of the prevailing point of view. It is interesting that the corresponding prayer for a woman is, "Blessed art thou, O Lord, who hast fashioned me according to thy will." We may well feel that the women had the better of it (it is better to be made according to the will of God than simply not to be of the other sex). But that is a modern and Christian view, not one that the Jews of New Testament times would have accepted.

The lot of women outside Palestine was much the same. M. Cary and T. J. Haarhoff say that in the Greek and Roman world women

> never escaped the bond of tutelage. So long as a woman remained unmarried, she stood under the authority of her father or some other male relative. A married woman passed into the power (Lat. *manus*) of her husband; a widow might "belong" to her son. The match was arranged over her head between her father or guardian and the bridegroom (or his parent), and in consideration of a sum paid to her family to compensate for the loss of her services, she was conveyed

---

[8] Daniel Rops, *Daily Life in Palestine at the Time of Christ* (London, 1962), 128.

[9] *The Jewish Encyclopedia* 12 (New York, n.d.): 557.

[10] In certain restricted circumstances women were allowed to bear witness, but even so it could be said, "Women, even a hundred of them, are legally equal to one witness" (Talmud, *Yebamoth* 115a).

from one household to another. She owned no property save her strictly personal outfit. . . . If she did not satisfy her husband, she might be returned to her family, or transferred to another husband.[11]

There was more freedom for women in Rome, especially upper-class women, than in other places, and through the years there was a tendency for women's lot to improve. But there is no denying that generally speaking they were in a subordinate position and that they were severely limited in all sorts of ways.

The Christian attitude was revolutionary. Take, for example, the fact that Jesus taught women from the first. There is the well-known example of Mary and Martha. When Martha complained about her sister because "she sat at the Lord's feet and listened to his teaching," Jesus commended Mary. He told Martha that only one thing is really needful and that Mary had chosen "the good part which will not be taken away from her" (10:38–42). Clearly Jesus accepted it as the normal thing that women should receive his instruction, a far cry indeed from the attitude of the rabbis.

There were women in his entourage, among whom Luke names Mary Magdalene, Joanna, and Susanna (8:1–3). Fitzmyer finds here "a recollection about Jesus which differed radically from the usual understanding of women's role in contemporary Judaism. His cure of women, his association with them, his tolerating them among his followers (as here) clearly dissociates him from such ideas as that reflected in John 4:27 or early rabbinical writings."[12] It was not surprising that Jesus received support from women who could afford to help (the rabbis gladly received help from pious women). But it was surprising that he included them among those who traveled with him. In passing we notice that, while most of Jesus' followers were from the poorer people, the fact that there were women who helped the apostolic band "from their means" indicates that there were some who were well off (as is shown also by the information that Joanna was the wife of one of Herod's officials).

The Gospel of Luke begins with a fairly long narrative on the infancy of John the Baptist and of Jesus. As we might expect, women are the subject of much of this narrative. Here we meet Elizabeth and Mary, and notice their piety. Luke includes the Song of Mary (1:46–55) and in general gives a picture of two attractive personalities. When Jesus was presented in the temple, Anna, a prophetess, was there to greet the holy child and to speak of him to "all who awaited the redemption of Jerusalem" (2:38).

Luke also includes accounts that

---

[11] *Life and Thought in the Greek and Roman World* (London, 1961), 142. They further point out that in neither Greece nor Rome could a woman transact business without a male guarantor (p. 145), though in some cases he was no more than a man of straw. There were restrictions on the movements of women, and, for example, in Athens and presumably in other places in Greece they were not allowed to go into the theatre (ibid.). Of course there were differences. In well-off families women often had a better lot than in poorer ones, and through the years the lot of women varied; at some times restrictions were fewer than at others. But it is clear that on the whole women in the ancient world suffered many restrictions and faced many difficulties.

[12] *The Gospel According to Luke (I–IX),* 696. Fitzmyer cites Mishnah *Aboth* 1:5 as an example of the rabbinic teaching he has in mind. This reads: "Jose b. Johanan of Jerusalem said: Let thy house be opened wide and let the needy be members of thy household; and talk not much with womankind. They said this of a man's own wife: how much more of his fellow's wife! Hence the Sages have said: He that talks much with womankind brings evil upon himself and neglects the study of the Law and at the last will inherit Gehenna."

involve women, such as the widow at Nain whose only son Jesus raised from the dead (7:11–17). Luke expressly mentions Jesus' compassion for the woman and his gentle words, "Don't cry." He tells of the bent woman who was unable to straighten herself and who got an unexpected blessing when she went to synagogue one Sabbath and Jesus healed her (13:10–13). The ruler of the synagogue was indignant because the healing had occurred on the Sabbath; for him that quite overshadowed the relieving of the woman's distress. The attitude of Jesus is in sharp contrast to his and those of the other Pharisees.

The account of the bent woman is in Luke alone. Probably exclusively his also is the account of the woman who wept over Jesus' feet as he reclined at a meal in the house of a Pharisee, wiped his feet dry with her hair, and anointed them (7:36–50).[13] It is impossible to imagine a woman doing this to a rabbi. The general attitude is well expressed in the disapproval of the host, who thought that Jesus could not be a prophet, for if he had been he would have known "who and what sort of woman" was touching him (v. 39). He did not have to add that a prophet would have had nothing to do with a woman like this. But Jesus did not look at women, even sinful ones, as the Pharisee did; he preferred to forgive her and remark about her love and her faith (vv. 47–50).

Luke shares with Mark the account of the widow's mite, but we should notice it as part of his interest in women (21:1–4)—an interest that is shown also in the account of the woman with a hemorrhage and the account of Jairus's daughter. The other Gospel writers have parallels to much of the discourse in 17:22–37, but not to Luke's "Remember Lot's wife" (17:32). And it is only Luke who tells us of the woman who interjected as Jesus was teaching: "Blessed is the womb that carried you and the breasts that you sucked," leading Jesus to pronounce a blessing rather on those who hear and keep God's word (11:27–28). Only Luke tells us that Jesus commended the widow of Zarephath (4:26), and again it is only Luke who tells us of the great crowd of the people "and of women" who followed Jesus as he was taken out to be executed (23:27–31). He tells of their bewailing him and lamenting for him, of Jesus telling them not to weep for him. These women were probably not his followers ("Daughters of Jerusalem"), but he had compassion on them and tried to turn their thoughts into more beneficial channels than mourning for him. Unless there was repentance, great horrors would come on the city.

Women are often mentioned in parables, such as the woman who put some yeast in three measures of flour (13:21). Luke shares this parable with Matthew. But he also has exclusive accounts: those of the man who married and therefore could not come to the banquet (14:20), the woman who lost a coin (15:8–10), and the widow who pestered the unjust judge (18:1–5).

The apostles ran away when Jesus was arrested, but some women were still there when Jesus was crucified (23:49). Women followed Joseph of Arimathea and helped with the burial (23:55–56). Luke's unique Resurrec-

---

[13] Many regard this as the same incident as those recounted in Matthew 26:6–13, Mark 14:3–9, and John 12:1–8. I have discussed the problem in my book *The Gospel According to John* (Grand Rapids, 1971), 571–74, and come to the conclusion that, while the other three describe the same incident, that in Luke is different.

tion passages, like those of the other Gospels, tell much about the activities of women (24:1–11). Luke names Mary Magdalene, Joanna, and Mary the mother of James and says there were others. After Jesus ascended, Luke lists the apostles who assembled in Jerusalem and tells us that they were gathered with "the women" (the mother of Jesus is specifically named) and the brothers of Jesus (A1:14).

Evidently women played a significant part in the life of the early church. On the day of Pentecost Peter quoted Joel's prophecy, which, he said, was being fulfilled in the gift of the Spirit, and he specifically included the references to the daughters as well as the sons who would prophesy and to the female servants of God as well as the males on whom the Spirit would come and who would prophesy (A2:17–18). As the church grew, there was "a multitude of both men and women" (A5:14), and women are specifically mentioned among those baptized at Samaria (A8:12). Three times we are told that Saul the persecutor arrested women as well as men (A8:3; 9:2; 22:4). We get a little glimpse into the life of the church in the complaint of the "Hellenists" against the "Hebrews" that their widows were being neglected in the daily assistance (A6:1). This shows that there were poor people in the church, that those who were able to help did so, and that particular attention was given to the widows (who in antiquity were proverbial for vulnerability). On the more affluent side, Sapphira was as guilty as her husband in keeping back part of the price of the possession they sold for the benefit of the church (A5:1–2).

Among the believers was Tabitha (or Dorcas), who was "full of good works and almsdeeds" (A9:36) and whom Peter brought back to life. Then there was Mary, John Mark's mother, in whose house believers gathered to pray for Peter during his imprisonment (A12:12). Luke's interests come out in the amusing incident of the door-keeper, a slave girl called Rhoda, leaving the apostle standing at the gate while she raced in to tell the gathering that Peter was there and argued with those who said she had seen a ghost (A12:13–17). Luke also tells us of another slave girl, the fortune-teller in Philippi out of whom Paul expelled a spirit (A16:16–18).[14]

As the church spread, it met opposition from some devout women (A13:50),[15] but more commonly women were in the forefront of the advance. At Thessalonica "a great multitude" of devout Greeks believed, and Luke adds, ". . . and of the leading women not a few" (A17:4). At Berea there was further success: a large number "of prominent Greek women and of men" believed (A17:12).[16] The role of women was perhaps even more impor-

---

[14] Cf. F. F. Bruce: "She is described by Luke as a 'pythoness', *i.e.* as a person inspired by Apollo, the god particularly associated with the giving of oracles, who was worshipped as the 'Pythian' god at the oracular shrine of Delphi (otherwise called Pytho) in central Greece. Her involuntary utterances were regarded as the voice of the god, and she was thus much in demand by people who wished to have their fortunes told" (*Commentary on the Book of the Acts* [London, 1954], 332). In a footnote he cites Plutarch, who called such people ventriloquists and adds, "ventriloquists, that is to say, whose utterances were really and not only apparently beyond their conscious control."

[15] Bruce comments, "The wives of many of these leading citizens—like well-to-do women in many another city of the Roman world—were loosely attached to the synagogue as God-fearers, and it was probably through them that their husbands were influenced to the disadvantage of Paul and Barnabas" (*Commentary on the Book of the Acts,* 284).

[16] I. Howard Marshall points out that "the order of the words suggests that the women are particularly prominent in the new Christian group" (*The Acts of the Apostles* [Leicester, 1980], 280).

tant at Philippi, for when Paul and his companions went to the place of prayer by the riverside on the Sabbath (evidently there was no synagogue in this Roman colony), they spoke "to the women who had gathered" (A16:13). The woman Lydia, whose heart the Lord opened and who was baptized, invited Paul to make her home his base (A16:14–15). No man is mentioned as the church made its beginning, though later the jailor believed.

The account of the visit to Lystra mentions Timothy's mother, as well as the fact that she had married a Greek (A16:1). Paul's preaching in Athens produced no spectacular results, but Luke mentions that among the converts was "a woman named Damaris" (A17:34). He gives us a little information about Priscilla (A18:2, 18, 26); she took part in instructing the redoubtable Apollos, and was therefore evidently a woman of some ability. Luke tells us also of Philip the evangelist, who had four daughters who prophesied (A21:9). Also mentioned are the women of Tyre who went out with their children to see Paul off when he set out for Jerusalem (A21:5). Clearly Luke was appreciative of the great contribution women made in the early days of the church.

He also speaks of some who were not Christians, such as Candace, queen of the Ethiopians (A8:27); Drusilla, wife of Felix the governor (A24:24); and Bernice, wife of King Agrippa (A25:13, 23; 26:30). He also records Stephen's words about "Pharaoh's daughter" (A7:21), and he has a tantalizing reference to Paul's sister, whose son informed the apostle that there was a plot to kill him (A23:16). Did the

family still live in Tarsus? Was she married to a Jerusalemite? Had she become a believer? There are no answers to these questions. But it seems fitting that it is Luke alone who mentions her.

Luke, then, helps us see the tremendous change in status that Christianity brought to women. He did not go along with the accepted standards of his day, relegating women to an inferior place and treating them as of small account. He had learned something better than that from his Master, and no one in the New Testament makes the new place for women clearer than does Luke.

CHILDREN

As we saw in the study of Mark, Jesus took an unusual interest in children.[17] For the ancient world in general and for great religious teachers in particular, children were of small importance. But Jesus took a great interest in them, and Luke chronicles some of this interest. Like Matthew and Mark, he tells of the raising of the daughter of Jairus from the dead (8:41–56), but he alone says that the little girl was Jairus' only child (v. 42).[18] We see the same thing in his treatment of the man whose son had fits (9:38–43). Again Luke shares the account with the other Synoptists, and again only he has the detail that the boy was an only child (v. 38). He has this detail again in the raising of the son of the widow of Nain (7:12). Clearly Luke appreciated the way parents felt about an only child.

He tells us, as the other synoptists do, of the child whom Jesus took to teach the disciples a lesson in humility

---

[17] See above, p. 106.

[18] She was μονογενής. Fitzmyer comments on this passage: "The Greek text does not imply that the man had sons but was concerned about an only daughter. His anguish is rather about a sole descendant" (*The Gospel According to Luke (I–IX)*, 745).

(9:47). Mark and Luke both say that Jesus "took" a little child; he did not have to send for one, there was one there. It seems that there was often a child or children where Jesus was. He was attractive to children. Luke shares with Matthew Jesus' teaching about people's rejection of John the Baptist as well as himself, and he illustrated this by the games children played (7:32). Did any other great religious teacher watch children at play? And, of course, Jesus forbade the disciples to send away those who wanted to bring children to him (18:15–17): "Whoever does not receive the kingdom of God like a little child will certainly never enter it" (v. 17).

Luke slips in one reference to children, which he alone has, when he recounts the episode of the man whose friend came at midnight to borrow some bread. The reluctant lender pointed to the difficulties: the door was locked, and his children were with him in bed (11:7). And in real life we see Luke's interest at a later time when he tells of the children of Tyre who went out with their mothers to see Paul on his way (A21:5).

This aspect of the way Luke looked at the Christian scene receives its emphasis in the infancy accounts in the opening two chapters of his Gospel. Were it not for this, we would know nothing of the home and family of John the Baptist. But Luke lets us see something of what it meant to the childless old couple that God sent them the gift of a baby. There is a good deal of detail about how this came about, and it is interesting to know that the Holy Spirit was on John, not only during the days of his public ministry, but all his days ("from his mother's womb" [1:15]). At the time of his circumcision "the hand of the Lord was with him" (1:66). He "became strong in spirit" and "was in the deserts until the day of his manifestation to Israel" (1:80).[19]

And, of course, Luke has the beautiful accounts of the coming of the angel to Mary with his message that she would be the mother of the Savior (1:26–38) and of the birth of the child (2:1–7). He tells us of the coming of the shepherds (2:8–20). He says that the child was circumcised (2:21) and that he was presented to the Lord in the temple (2:22–24). He gives us information about the reactions of Simeon and of Anna when they encountered the child (2:25–38). He tells us something of the way the boy developed (2:40, 52) and has the interesting account of the twelve-year-old Jesus in the temple listening to the teachers and asking them questions (2:41–51).

With his unusual interest in children Luke draws attention to another aspect of the universalism inherent in the Christian message. The whole of life is important, and children as well as adults matter to God. It is a lesson that the church has not always kept in mind as much as it should. But if we ever forget the importance of children, it is not Luke's fault.

---

[19] It is possible that John was brought up in some such community as Qumran. It is known that the Essenes brought up other people's children, and that the men of Qumran had a deep respect for priests. John's parents were old and almost certainly died while he was quite young. The Qumran community was strongly opposed to what went on in the temple at Jerusalem, and it is interesting that there is no record of John's taking part in the temple worship as there is of his father. It is no more than a hypothesis, but it is interesting that so much fits together. And, of course, if that was the way of things, in due course John rebelled against the teaching in which he had been brought up, which may be the meaning of "the word of the Lord came to John the son of Zechariah in the wilderness" (3:2).

THE POOR

Luke has a special interest in the poor. He uses the word *ptōchos,* "poor," ten times, whereas Matthew and Mark both have it five times. He further has the word *plousios* eleven times, while Matthew has it three times, and Mark twice. Mostly his use of the word "rich" is to warn against the dangers of riches, so that it is fitly considered alongside "poor."

Luke records a sermon of Jesus in the synagogue at Nazareth early in his mission (4:16–30). He does not regard it as the beginning of it all, for he has recorded earlier work (4:14–15). But he chooses this as the first incident in Jesus' public ministry that he describes in full. It seems that he is giving us an outline of Jesus' program. These are the things the Messiah would accomplish, and this is the message the Messiah would bring. It is noteworthy that Luke begins with Jesus' reading from the prophet Isaiah: "The Spirit of the Lord is upon me, because he has anointed me to preach the gospel to poor people . . ." (4:18; the words are from Isa. 61:1). The first thing mentioned here about Jesus' ministry is that it was a ministry to the poor. This comes out also in Jesus' reply to the messengers from John the Baptist. John from his prison had sent his followers to ask, "Are you 'He who comes'? Or do we look for another?" (7:19). To this Jesus replied by directing attention to his works of mercy in giving sight to the blind and the like, and he comes to his climax by saying, "The good news is preached to the poor" (7:22). It is that that brings home the truth that God's Messiah has indeed come.

The first Beatitude in Luke is "Blessed are you poor people" (6:20). In this, as in the Nazareth sermon, other unfortunates are linked with the poor, and in both it is said by some exegetes that we should take "poor" in strict literalness. It is pointed out that Matthew spiritualizes by recording the words as "Blessed are the poor in spirit" (Matt. 5:3), and the suggestion is made that Luke, by contrast, is referring to poverty as such.

But this overlooks some key facts. Luke precedes the Beatitudes with the information that Jesus "lifted up his eyes to his disciples and said . . ." (6:20), and he gives Jesus' words as "Blessed are you poor, for yours is the kingdom of God." It is also to overlook the fact that people are not poor from choice. An occasional eccentric chooses poverty, and there are people who, in revolt against a materialistic society, choose poorer circumstances than those to which they could readily attain. But such people are not poor in the sense Jesus intended. The poor as a class are poor because circumstances have forced poverty on them. It is not easy to think that Jesus calls people blessed because of something they did not choose and would very much like to avoid. We should bear in mind some words of G. Gutierrez. He said that saying Luke 6:20 refers to material poverty "would lead to the canonization of a social class. The poor would be the privileged of the Kingdom, even to the point of having their access to it assured, not by any choice on their part but by a socio-economic situation which had been imposed on them."[20]

Jesus' words are not a benediction on poverty as such (only the comfortable and those beyond the reach of penury

---

[20]*A Theology of Liberation* (London, 1974), 297. Similarly Leonhard Goppelt rejects a reference to literal riches and poverty; rather "life was lost for the one who thought he could live on that which he had provided for himself!" (*Theology of the New Testament* [Grand Rapids, 1982], 2:281).

would make such a claim!). They are words of encouragement to those who have given up all to follow him. Poor they undoubtedly were as this world counts riches, but that is not the most important consideration. Poor though they were, they were richly blessed. It was to such poor people that Jesus' whole ministry was directed.

We are reminded of the frequent use of "the poor" in the Old Testament as a designation of God's pious ones: "This poor man called, and the LORD heard him" (Ps. 34:6); "the poor have hope" (Job 5:16); and there are many more such references. Again, it is not poverty as such that is commended, but God's people are those who recognize that they have no power of themselves to help themselves and who trust in God and not in any human power. Putting it another way, the rich in this world are subject to great temptations to put their trust in their riches. Their wealth and their position enable them to do so many things that those with fewer resources cannot do that they are all too strongly tempted to carry this over into the spiritual realm. They forget that "whoever trusts in his riches will fall" (Prov. 11:28). Such an attitude cuts people off from the blessing of the Lord. But the poor are not so readily prone to yield to this temptation. They have other temptations that the rich escape, but that is not the point. The point is rather that God's people are those who have learned to put their trust in him and not in their own strong right arm. The paucity of their material resources is a symbol of this.

Perhaps this gives Luke his deep concern for the poor as such. Whether this is the reason or not, it cannot be denied that Luke is unusually interested in the poor. They turn up in his parables: the host at the great supper sending his servants to bring in the poor of the city (14:21) and the rich man ignoring the poor Lazarus (the only person in Jesus' parables to be given a name). At a banquet Jesus advised his host not to invite rich people to a meal "lest they invite you in turn and you be repaid" (14:12). Rather he should invite the poor—they cannot repay him, and he will be recompensed at the resurrection.

Jesus noticed the widow who put two tiny coins into the collection in the temple and commended her (21:1–4). Luke records Jesus' words to the rich young ruler that he should sell all he had and give it to the poor (18:22). And he notices that when Zacchaeus responded to the presence of Jesus, he decided to give half his fortune to poor people (19:8).

This last example shows that Luke does not invariably condemn riches. Zacchaeus may well have compiled his fortune in evil ways (he was a tax collector [19:2], and members of his fraternity were notorious for using their position to extort money wrongfully). But his meeting with Jesus changed all that. "Today salvation has come to this house," said Jesus (19:9), and that salvation meant a different attitude to money, among other things. Luke tells us also of rich people who were giving their gifts for the work of God in the temple (21:1). Jesus said that the poor woman with her two little coins gave more than they did, but there is nothing wrong with the fact that they were giving. It is possible that we should see the rich man in the parable of the unjust steward as another whose wealth is not a matter for criticism; but if J. M. L. Derrett is correct in his understanding of this passage, the man was party to the illegal levying of interest,[21] and thus he was guilty of succumbing to the temptations that beset the wealthy.

In other cases there can be no reasonable doubt. Luke records Jesus' warning to the rich: "Woe to you who are rich, for you have received your comfort" (6:24).[22] These words stand over against the blessing on the poor, those who do not rely on their own achievement but rely wholly on God. The rich so often do not do this. "It is easier for a camel to go through the eye of a needle," Jesus said, "than for a rich man to enter the kingdom of God" (18:25). This saying follows hard on the incident of the rich young ruler, the man who thought he had kept the commandments, but who in the last resort kept his riches rather than obeying the call of God (18:18–23).

We should also notice that the rich do not come out well in the parables. The account of the rich man and Lazarus is a vivid illustration of the way a man can be so taken up with his wealth and the advantages it gives him that he can be completely insensitive to the plight of the poor at his very gate, and he may well finish up in hell. The rich fool, who had many goods laid up for many years and wanted to build bigger barns to hold them, was another person so taken up with his wealth that he was unable to perceive the larger picture (12:16–21).

Luke's treatment of the poor, then, is a significant feature of his work. It underlines the importance of a right attitude toward God and of the ease with which material prosperity can lead people away from God.

THE DISREPUTABLE

We see Luke's universalism in the way he brings out the truth that Christ brings salvation to people whom the world esteems but lightly. He starts this quite early, for he tells of the shepherds receiving the message from the angels at the birth of the Christ child (2:8–20). Shepherds were a despised class. They were considered unreliable and were not allowed to give evidence in a court of law (Talmud, *Sanhedrin*, 25b). Their wandering mode of life meant that they allowed their flocks to graze on others people's pastures. It also meant that their "Here today, gone tomorrow" attitude led them to be adept at petty pilfering. Their manner of life kept them from observing the ceremonial law, so religious people looked down on them. Yet it would not be fair to deduce that the particular shepherds of whom Luke wrote were anything other than godly men. We cannot think that the message about the Savior would be given to them unless this was so. But there is no denying that they came from a class that was widely despised.

Another despised class was the tax collectors, and it is worth noting that Luke has ten of the twenty-one times tax collectors are mentioned in the New Testament (Matthew has eight). The Romans did not bother to set up a complicated bureaucracy to collect their taxes from the conquered peoples. They preferred to put the taxing rights up for auction, and they assigned them to the highest bidders. The successful bidders proceeded to collect the taxes, plus something extra as their legitimate charge for doing the work. And, human nature being what it is, they

---

[21] See his *Law in the New Testament* (London, 1970), 48–77.

[22] *MM* points out that in the papyri the verb ἀπέχω "is constantly found in the sense of 'I have received,' as a technical expression in drawing up a receipt."

normally collected more than Roman law provided. This habit of taking more than was due led, of course, to their being hated by those who paid the money, and this in turn led to the collectors being even harsher. Usually the tax farmers were from outside Palestine, but perhaps Zacchaeus had the rights for Jericho, for he is called a "chief tax collector."[23] In their work they were in constant contact with the Gentiles, making themselves ceremonially unclean, a fact that would not endear them to the religious. They were probably required to work on the Sabbath—another count against them. And they were collaborators with the hated Romans, helping them in their sovereignty over Israel instead of trying to overthrow them. Therefore, they were held in low esteem. It is significant that we often read of "tax collectors and sinners."

Luke speaks of some of these men as coming to John the Baptist for advice and being told that they should collect no more than they were entitled to. It is significant that this is the one piece of advice that John gave them. Their extortions were widely known. But some at least responded to what John said and accepted his baptism (7:29).

Jesus called one of their number, a man named Levi, from his toll booth, and Levi held a large reception that was attended by many of his former associates. This caused the religious to question the disciples as to why Jesus did such a thing, and it elicited the saying "The well have no need of the doctor, but those who are sick; I have not come to call righteous people, but sinners to repentance" (5:31–32). They accused Jesus of being "a friend of tax collectors and sinners" (7:34), an accusation that apparently did not worry either Jesus or Luke.

Luke introduces his three parables about the lost—the lost sheep, the lost coin, and the lost son—by saying, "All the tax collectors and the sinners were drawing near to listen to [Jesus]" (15:1). The continuous tense may imply that this was a repeated practice; certainly Luke gives the impression that this was the case. In one very significant passage in Luke—namely, the parable of the tax collector and the Pharisee—a tax collector is the very central figure (18:9–14).

We should also notice that Luke has the account about the sinner who wept over Jesus' feet, wiped them with her hair, and afterward anointed them with perfumed oil (7:37–50). This appears to be a different incident from similar incidents in the other Gospels, and it is significant that Luke expressly tells us that the woman was a sinner.[24] Finally, in this section we should notice that disreputable people are found in quite a number of parables in this Gospel (7:41–42; 12:13–21; 15:11–32; 16:1–12; 18:1–8).

Clearly Luke is not concerned with conventional patterns of righteousness. He was well aware that Jesus was concerned with saving sinful people from their sins and that he was often found with those whom the religious leaders of his day would have condemned and rejected. But that is not the Christian way. Luke lets us see that there is hope for the worst and most despised of people. The followers of Jesus should despair of no one.

---

[23] The word is ἀρχιτελώνης. It occurs only here, but it is difficult to see what else it could mean.
[24] The word is ἁμαρτωλός, on which Marshall comments, ". . . probably a prostitute" (*The Gospel of Luke*, 308).

INDIVIDUALS

The gospel is a great message, one with a universal application. As we have seen, Luke is interested in its universal scope and has a number of ways of bringing this out. But he does not see all this in terms of a mighty movement affecting nations and swaying multitudes. With all his vision of the greatness of the Christian way, Luke never loses sight of the importance of the individual. He tells us about a great number of individuals, often people of whom we do not read elsewhere. Thus, he begins his Gospel with Zechariah and Elizabeth, and he goes on to tell us of Simeon and Anna. He tells us of the widow of Nain whose only child died and of the sinful woman who anointed Jesus' feet. It is in this Gospel that we find that Mary sat at Jesus' feet while Martha got the meal ready. It is Luke who tells of the bent woman whom Jesus healed one Sabbath in the synagogue and of the man with the dropsy whom he healed in the house of a Pharisee on another Sabbath. Luke tells of the ten lepers and relates the gratitude of the Samaritan among them; Zacchaeus, also, is found only in Luke. Again, the two who walked with Jesus to Emmaus are obscure folk, known to us only because Luke has recorded their Sunday stroll.

We learn a good deal about the early church from the letters of Paul. But again, it is Luke who tells us about many people of whom we would know nothing apart from him. He tells us who were gathered in the Upper Room praying after Jesus ascended, and it is from this that we know that Jesus' brothers were linked with the Christians. He tells us of Joseph called Barsabbas and of Matthias, the two from whom would be selected the replacement for Judas in the apostolic band. He writes of Barnabas who sold a field and laid the proceeds at the apostles' feet. We read of faulty Christians like Ananias and Sapphira; of people who needed healing, like Aeneas and Tabitha, who was also called Dorcas; of people converted in unusual ways, like Cornelius and the Philippian jailer; of John Mark, who went to the work with great associates but did not measure up; and of Eutychus, who could not stay awake during a long sermon.

Luke tells us of some of the people who opposed the Christians. He speaks of the high priestly family, Annas and Caiaphas, whom we know from the Gospels, but also John and Alexander. He writes of Simon Magus, who misunderstood the way the Holy Spirit is given. He speaks of those in high place who were involved in Paul's arrest and what followed: Claudius Lysias the tribune; Felix the governor, who was not averse to being bribed; Tertullus the orator; and Festus, the energetic successor of Felix.

There is much more. To detail all those that Luke mentions would be to make a very long list and would scarcely add to the point already made. It is clear that Luke was more than a little interested in people, whether they were supporters of the Christian faith or its vigorous opponents. He is well aware that in God's sight the humblest of his people matters.

PRAYER

Prayer is plainly a very important activity for the believer depicted in Luke's writings. This Evangelist has one word for "prayer," *proseuchē*, that appears three times in his Gospel and nine times in Acts and the corresponding verb "to pray" nineteen and sixteen times respectively. He has another word for prayer, *deēsis,* three times in the Gospel, and its corresponding verb eight times, with another seven in Acts. Nobody else matches him in this interest. We have already seen that he puts emphasis on the fact that we are saved by God in Christ, and it follows for him that we are constantly dependent on God for the strength and the wisdom we need to live out the Christian life. So he emphasizes the importance of prayer.

It is not only the prayer of the believer that preoccupies him; he lets us see Jesus at prayer often (3:21; 5:16; 6:12; 9:18, 28–29; 10:21–22; 11:1; 22:41–45; 23:46). Some of the instances when Jesus prayed are found in the other Gospels, but seven times it is Luke alone who recorded that he prayed. He makes it clear that Jesus prayed extensively when face to face with every crisis of his life. The example of the Master is very clear in this Gospel.

Jesus' teaching about prayer is also very clear. He taught by giving the pattern prayer: "When you pray say, 'Father, hallowed be your name'" (11:1–4) and by exhorting the disciples to pray (22:40, 46). So with some of his parables. The friend who came at midnight (11:5–8) encourages persistence in prayer, while the parable of the unjust judge is expressly told so that people might always "pray and not be weary" (18:1). The parable of the Pharisee and the tax collector is not strictly a parable about prayer, but it certainly teaches us important truths about the right and the wrong sorts of prayer. Jesus warned that some "in pretense make long prayers"; they will receive the greater condemnation accordingly (20:47).

The verb *deomai* is used a number of times of people asking Jesus to do things (5:12; 8:28, 38; 9:38), which may or may not be prayer as we understand the term, depending on how they regarded Jesus. But there can be no doubt when Jesus uses the term to tell the disciples to "pray the Lord of the harvest that he may send out workers into his harvest" (10:2), a prayer that directs the attention of those praying away from themselves and their own needs. But Jesus is aware of those needs and on another occasion tells the disciples to pray that they may escape disasters that will come on earth (21:36). It is this verb that Jesus uses when he prays for Peter that his faith will not fail (22:32).

We see how well some of his followers had learned the lesson with the way they prayed in the days after his ascension. On one occasion when they had prayed, the place where they were was shaken and they were all filled with the Spirit (A4:31). Cornelius was a man who prayed constantly (A10:2), and Philip urged Simon Magus to pray for forgiveness, upon which Simon asked Philip to pray for him (A8:22, 24).

No one who reads Luke with attention can fail to be impressed with his teaching on prayer. Believers are not able to lead the Christian life in their own strength, so they must constantly look to God for the strength they need. And that means they must pray. But Luke does not encourage us to pray simply for our own needs. He makes it clear that we are to pray for one another and for the setting forward of God's purposes. Real prayer cannot be selfish.

JOY TO THE WORLD

Sometimes Christianity has been presented as a very serious faith, solemn to the point of being gloomy. People have been so set on attaining the joys of heaven that they have forgotten the joys of earth. Luke would not have recognized such a way as truly Christian. Joy runs through his two volumes, and it is clear that he understood Christianity as a faith that filled the whole of life with joy, whatever else it did.[25]

People sing in Luke's writings. Early in his Gospel we have some of the great hymns in Scripture—the Song of Mary (1:46–55), the Song of Zechariah (1:68–79), and the Song of Simeon (2:29–32). There is the song of the angels as they announced the birth of the Savior (2:14). An interesting piece of music where we would not expect it is the song of Paul and Silas when they were put in prison at Philippi (A16:25). A typical first-century jail was not the place where we would have expected to find rejoicing, but then Paul and Silas were not typical first-century prisoners. Despite their outward circumstances, they could rejoice because of what God had done and was doing and would do for them and through them.

"Blessed are you who wail now, because you will laugh" said Jesus, and Luke records the saying (6:21). Rejoicing starts early in this Gospel, with the angel's message to Zechariah about the baby that would be born to him and Elizabeth: "You will have joy and gladness and many will rejoice at his birth" (1:14). Elizabeth told Mary that the baby in her womb "leaped in gladness" at the coming of "the mother of my Lord" (1:43–44), and Mary's song includes the words "my spirit

rejoiced in God my Savior" (1:47). When Zechariah got back his speech after his spell of dumbness, his first words were words of praise to God (1:64). Simeon blessed God when he took the baby Jesus into his arms (2:28). In such ways Luke makes it clear that the coming of the Savior is cause for great rejoicing as well as for deep thankfulness.

People "glorified" or "praised" God for his salvation and his goodness to them. It began with the angels (2:13) and continued with the shepherds (2:20), and we see it in the blessing that came during the ministry of Jesus. When Jesus healed the lame man brought to him on a stretcher carried by friends, the man responded by glorifying God, and the people who saw it also glorified God (5:25–26). People glorified God when Jesus raised the son of the widow of Nain from the dead (7:16), as did the bent woman whom Jesus healed in the synagogue on a Sabbath (13:13), the grateful leper whom Jesus had cleansed (17:15), and the blind man to whom Jesus gave sight near Jericho (18:43; here again all the people joined in). Then as this Gospel begins to come to its climax we find great joy at Jesus' triumphal entry into Jerusalem, with all the crowd praising God (19:37). And Luke ends his Gospel not on a note of sadness because Jesus had ascended and been separated from his followers, but on a note of joy and praise (24:52–53).

Jesus "rejoiced [perhaps exulted] in the Holy Spirit" (10:21).[26] And in his

---

[25] Cf. Bo Reicke: "No other Evangelist or writer in the New Testament deals so often with the idea of joy as Luke." He sometimes parallels the other synoptists, but he "also speaks of joy, however, in many other passages and far surpasses every other New Testament writer in the *frequency* with which he refers to the word 'joy' " (*The Gospel of Luke* [London, 1965], 77).

[26] The word is ἠγαλλιάσατο, on which F. W. Farrar comments, " 'Exulted,' a much stronger word than the 'rejoiced' of the A.V.; and most valuable as recording one element—the element of exultant joy—in the life of our Lord" (*The Gospel According to St Luke*, [Cambridge, 1893], 251–52). He goes on to refer to the legend that, while Jesus wept often, no one ever saw him smile. Whoever originated that libel had not read Luke attentively.

parables he tells of rejoicing—rejoicing of people here on earth when a lost sheep or a lost coin is found (15:6, 9) and rejoicing "in heaven" (15:7) and "before the angels of God" (15:10) over a repenting sinner. Many religions have a concept of a God who is so high and holy that sinners scarcely come to his attention; the Christian picture of God is distinctive: though God is infinitely great, nevertheless he rejoices over one sinner who repents. It is wonderful that he accepts the repenting sinner, but it is surpassingly wonderful that he, the mighty God, rejoices at this. The sinner, of course, rejoices at this too, and Luke gives us a picture of one such in Zacchaeus (19:6). There was a good deal of rejoicing also in the city of Samaria, which Philip evangelized (A8:8). There was rejoicing too by the Ethiopian eunuch who had Jesus preached to him (A8:39), by the Gentiles who believed in Antioch of Pisidia (A13:48), and by the household of the Philippian jailer (A16:34).

It is hard to read Acts without coming to see that the early church was a very joyful group of people. This comes out in express statements, but it was a part of the general atmosphere of that church. The power of the Holy Spirit was manifest, and there were people being brought to faith in Christ constantly. This produced a continuing joy among the believers. Peter quoted a psalm to bring out the truth that Christ rose from the dead in accordance with Scripture, but the psalm's stress on joy reflected the experience of the believers as well as the point the apostle was making (A2:26–28, quoting Ps. 16:8–11). Luke gives a short summary of the Christians' daily life: "Daily they continued with one accord in the temple, and, breaking bread in homes,[27] they partook of food with rejoicing . . ." (A2:46; there is another link between food and joy as good gifts of God in Paul's preaching at Lystra [A14:17]).

When Barnabas came to Antioch, "he saw the grace of God and rejoiced" (A11:23), and this joy was spread widely when he and Paul visited a number of churches after their first missionary journey and told the Christians how the Gentiles had been converted (A15:3). Then when the delegates from the Council of Jerusalem came to Antioch and gave their report on the Council's findings, there was even more joy in the church (A15:31).

The mission to Pisidian Antioch ended in persecution, which we might have thought would quench the joy of the young converts. But no, "the disciples were filled with joy and with the Holy Spirit" (A13:52). Earlier the apostles in Jerusalem were arrested on account of their preaching. They were beaten and, before they were released, were told not to preach again. But "they went out from the Sanhedrin rejoicing because they were deemed worthy to suffer for the sake of the name" (A5:41). People do not normally rejoice when they suffer, but such was the deep joy of the early church that outward circumstances could not take it away. Their Savior had suffered to bring them salvation, and they were content to suffer in bringing that salvation to other people.

When we consider the circumstances of the early church, with its difficulties from within and without, with its daunting task of evangelizing the world

---

[27] The expression is κατ' οἶκον. Cf. F. F. Bruce: "They ate 'by households', as we translate the Greek phrase (AV 'from house to house' gives the sense fairly well)" (*Commentary on the Book of the Acts* [London, 1954], 81). *MM* gives evidence from the papyri for the meaning "according to households" (contrasted with "according to individuals").

with such slender resources, with its membership consisting so largely of insignificant and unimportant people, it would not have been surprising if there had been gloom and pessimism. However, the note of joy that Luke stresses is unmistakable and significant. The early church was surely a joyful church, as authentic Christianity must cause us to be to this day.

EARLY CATHOLICISM

In recent discussions a good deal of attention is paid to Luke's part in the beginnings of institutionalism in the church. Some hold that initially the Christian way brought people a great sense of liberation, a life characterized by charismatic freedom (cf. 1 Cor. 14). In due course, believers settled down into the ordered life of the catholic church, with its ordained ministry, its sacramental life, its administration of discipline, its moralism, and all the rest. The full development took time, but in the later parts of the New Testament, it is said, there are the first steps toward what scholars have come to call "early Catholicism."[28] These scholars claim Luke was a prime mover in bringing about the change and sometimes in distorting or losing important teachings of primitive Christianity in the process.

Eschatology looms large in the discussions. Käsemann sees early catholicism as complete when the expectation of a speedy *parousia* disappears.[29] The first believers are thought to have lived in the constant expectation that Jesus might come back at any time, an expectation that did away with any need of the church as an institution. But for Luke the idea that Jesus' return was imminent had faded away; he was much more interested in the settled life of the church as his writing of a history of its early days shows.[30] In this view salvation was a distant hope; it was postponed to the time of the remote *parousia*.

We may say a number of things in reply to this. The idea that the primitive church lived in the daily expectation of the return of Christ is not as well grounded as many of its exponents would have us believe. There is no evidence whatever that any believer ever held that the preaching should stop when Jesus ascended. There was always the thought of an interval, and the length of that interval was not known. If the return was expected at any moment, why did Paul embark on his preaching journeys? Why did Philip have to go to Samaria and Azotus? Why did the Council of Jerusalem meet, and why did it lay down terms of Gentile acceptance into the church? I have no doubt that some of the early Christians did in fact expect the Lord

---

[28] John H. Elliot lists the following as pointers in the direction of early catholicism: "the organization of the Church according to hierarchical in contrast to charismatic ministry; the development of the monarchical episcopate; an objectification of the proclamation and an emphasis upon a strictly formulated rule of faith; a stress upon 'orthodoxy' or 'sound doctrine' in opposition to false teaching; moralization of the faith and conception of the gospel as new law; an understanding of faith in objective rather than subjective, in static rather than dynamic, terms, as *fides quae creditur* in contrast to *fides qua creditur*; a development of the principle of apostolic succession and transmitted authority; a distinction between laity and clergy; a conception of an authoritative interpretation of the scriptures; a trend toward 'sacramentalism'; the formulation of a 'natural theology'; a concern for ecclesiastical unity and consolidation; and an interest in the collecting of the apostolic writings" (*CBQ* 31 [1969]: 214).

[29] *New Testament Questions of Today* (London, 1969), 237.

[30] "You do not write the history of the Church, if you are expecting the end of the world to come any day" (Käsemann, *Essays on New Testament Themes* [London, 1964], 28).

to return at any moment, but I see little evidence that such a belief governed the actions of a majority of the first believers.[31]

A second thing is that, as Luke depicts it, the church did not relegate salvation to a remote future but saw it as a present reality. The Holy Spirit was active among believers, and Acts thrills with the wonder of what that activity meant. No doubt there was more to salvation than the church experienced at that time, but the *parousia* was simply understood to be the culmination of all the good that the church was presently experiencing.

And the church always looked back to Calvary. For the New Testament writers the message of the cross was central. It is a fallacy to think that the church ever looked so wholeheartedly to the realization of salvation at the *parousia* that it forgot that salvation was accomplished at Calvary.

ESCHATOLOGY

Luke's interest in eschatology is not fully taken into consideration by some who see him as an exponent of early catholicism.[32] He has the thought of the eschatological judgment in his account of John the Baptist with his "axe laid toward the root of the trees" (3:9), and with his reference to the process of winnowing and of burning the chaff with unquenchable fire (3:17). He tells us that Jesus told the seventy to say, "The kingdom of God has come near to you" (10:9) and, when people did not receive their message, to wipe the dust of the town off their feet against them and say, "Nevertheless know this, 'The kingdom of God has come near'" (10:11). Matthew has his equivalent of the first reference to the kingdom and the words about wiping the dust from the feet, but he does not have the second reference to the approach of the kingdom. It is to Luke that we owe the words "Let your loins be girded and your lamps burning, and you be like men awaiting their master . . ." (12:35ff.). Verse 39 has a parallel in Matthew, but clearly Luke's inclusion of so much that Matthew does not have shows that he has his own eschatological interest. He did not simply pass on what everybody else said.

It may be that we are meant to see an eschatological reference in the table discourses in Luke 14. We must bear in mind that in Jewish thought the messianic banquet was an integral part of the eschatological scene, and it may be that when Jesus spoke of banquets he had this in mind, whatever contemporary application there may have been. There can scarcely be any doubt about the passage concerning the great feast, for Jesus spoke these words in response to some words from a fellow diner: "Blessed is he who eats bread in the kingdom of God" (14:15). With particular reference to v. 10, Bo Reicke says, "The meal serves only as a starting point for eschatological reflection."[33] It is not easy to read this chapter and

---

[31] Cf. Leonhard Goppelt: "The question about the expectation of an end was seldom raised by the church and was discussed only marginally" (William Klassen and Graydon F. Snyder, eds., *Current Issues in New Testament Interpretation* [London, 1962], 198).

[32] Käsemann holds that Luke's attempt to write the history of the Christian religion as secular history "only becomes possible where primitive Christian eschatology, the dynamic force of New Testament preaching, is in eclipse" (*New Testament Questions of Today,* 21).

[33] *The Gospel of Luke,* 80. Reicke concludes his discussion of the table discourses by saying, "It is puzzling how prominent exegetes can hold that Luke has de-eschatologized the gospel. Every word in the passages quoted presupposes a connection between the preaching of Jesus in the past, the present missionary situation, and the future consummation of the kingdom of God" (p. 81).

conclude that Luke does not have an eschatological interest.

Luke 17 has some unique and some shared material. To Luke we owe the saying that the kingdom of God is "among you" (*entos hymōn* [17:21]).[34] Matthew has the saying about Noah (v. 27), but not that about Lot (vv. 28–29). Luke has the reference to two being in one bed, one of whom will be taken and the other left (v. 34). Matthew shares with Luke the statement about two women grinding at a mill. The two men in a field are mentioned by Matthew only, whereas the two in a bed are mentioned in Luke only. Some scholars draw attention to eschatological sayings that Luke has omitted and conclude that he has no interest in the subject. But by overlooking the eschatological sayings that Luke alone has, they miss the point that this Evangelist has his own way of doing things. He would not have the touches that are peculiar to his Gospel if he did not have an eschatological interest.

In our Lord's great eschatological discourse it is not easy to see what statements refer to the *parousia* and what to the destruction of Jerusalem. There is no doubt that Luke knows that Jesus refers to the *parousia,* for he includes words like "then they will see the Son of man coming in a cloud with power and great glory" (21:27); he adds some words that he alone records: "When these things begin to happen look up and lift up your heads, because your redemption is drawing near" (v. 28). In the discourse as a whole Luke makes clearer than the other

writers do that the destruction of Jerusalem is quite separate from the *parousia;* G. B. Caird sees this as Luke's "own peculiar contribution to New Testament eschatology."[35] Once again we must notice that the fact that Luke does it his own way does not mean that he does not see eschatology as important. He does. And he does not want his readers to confuse it with any other event in human history.

Some early Christians may have done just that. Charles H. Talbert holds that some confused the *parousia* with the Ascension, and others with what happened at Pentecost. He sees Luke as opposing all such views and he finds two dominant emphases in the eschatology of Luke–Acts: "One is the proclamation that the End is near," the other "is the attempt to prevent a misinterpretation of the Jesus-tradition by someone in the Lucan sphere of influence to the effect that the eschaton had been and could be fully experienced in the present."[36]

Whatever the case with the details in Talbert's argument, I do not see how it can be disputed that Luke is refuting erroneous ideas about the End, not denying that the End will come. He is not even denying that the End may be soon. It is too often overlooked that he has included these words of Jesus: "This generation will not pass away until all things have taken place" (21:32). There are problems with this verse, but it certainly raises the question of why Luke should have included it if he rejected the imminence of the *parousia.* He is not so much denying the

---

[34] George E. Ladd has a long note on this verse in which he states the principal views. He gives the meaning of the words as "the Kingdom was already in their midst, but in an unexpected form" and notes that the passage goes on to the thought that "There remains in the future a coming of the Kingdom with apocalyptic power" (*Jesus and the Kingdom* [London, 1966], 224n.25). See further the discussion on pp. 147–48 above.

[35] *The Gospel of St Luke* (Harmondsworth, 1963), 229.

[36] *Jesus and Man's Hope* (Pittsburgh, 1970), 191.

reality of the *parousia* as making it clear that there are stages in God's plan and there are events that must happen before the *parousia*.

Thus, it seems that Luke has his own way of looking at eschatology and that many of the criticisms leveled at him amount to no more than that he expresses his eschatology in his own way. He is not simply repeating what other members of the early church said. But that is no reason for denying his eschatological interest, or for seeing him as removing the *parousia* to the remote future. On the grounds of eschatology there is no reason to see him as trying to establish a form of catholicism.

THE WORD

Luke's emphasis on "the word" is distinctive. He begins his Gospel with a reference to "eyewitnesses and ministers of the word" (1:1)—a most unusual way of putting emphasis on "the word." He goes on to refer four times to "the word of God" and three times more to "the word" in the interpretation of the parable of the sower, in each instance clearly meaning the Word of God. Once he has "the word of the Lord." When we turn to Acts, we find this tendency greatly increased. In Acts "the word of God" is referred to thirteen times, "the word of the Lord" ten times, while "the word" is used absolutely thirteen times. There are also two references to "the word of his grace," and one each to "the word of this salvation" and "the word of the gospel." This gives a total in Acts of forty references to the Word in one way or another. Clearly it is very important to Luke.

It agrees with this that Luke's atti-

tude to the ministry is not "catholic." The most that can be said is that in Acts he tells of the appointment of elders. But he never mentions ordination. Some passages might be interpreted as referring to ordination, but Luke never says this explicitly, and a "catholic" could never leave such an important part of the life of the church in doubt. It is the same with the sacrament of the Lord's Supper. There are passages in Acts where "the breaking of bread" may indicate the sacrament, but every one can be understood also as indicating an ordinary meal. I am not saying that all of those instances should be so understood, but that a "catholic" could not leave such an interpretation to chance. A catholicism without valid orders or regular sacraments is a very curious catholicism indeed.

Luke told his readers that he was writing so that they might "know the certainty of the things in which [they] had] been instructed" (1:4). He makes it clear that he has followed all things closely, and he speaks of "eyewitnesses" (v. 2). In other words he is claiming that he is giving an authentic and reliable account of what must be believed about Jesus.

He seems to be doing much the same in Acts. There has been a good deal of discussion of the speeches in that volume, but it appears that Luke is setting out what the apostles preached. He is not doing this in stereotyped form, as though the repetition of the exact form of words was important. James Dunn says, "The sermons are by no means repeated stereotypes: not one is parallel to another throughout, each has its own distinctive elements . . . and the speeches of Acts 7 and 17 are quite unlike any of the rest."[37] Luke is not

---

[37] *Unity and Diversity in the New Testament* (London, 1977), 362.

saying, "This is the form of words that must be accepted." But he is saying, "This is what the apostles preached." With this before them, Christian teachers will not be in the position to set out their own views as authentic Christianity. They must adhere to the traditional teachings if they are to be accepted as genuinely setting out Christian teaching. As Talbert puts it, "It is clear that in the Lucan succession the elders are appointed in order to serve the tradition. The church and its ministry are brought under the judgment of the apostolic word. It is the Word which legitimizes the church and its ministry and not *vice versa*."[38]

We must bear in mind that, while the enunciation of the gospel message is important, its preservation is also a significant activity. Luke may not be the kind of creative theologian that Paul was; we do not find in his writings the exciting new ways of understanding the Christian message that are so constantly cropping up in Paul. But we do find an insistence on the retention of the great truths that the creative minds have put forward. I. Howard Marshall reminds us that "the preservation of the truth of the Gospel by the appeal to tradition and by the establishment of the ministry is an integral part of the whole. While its function is a subordinate one, it is nevertheless an important one in assisting the proclamation of the Word of grace revealed in Christ, which is the center of the NT revelation." To reject this is to run the risk of losing one's "hold on the central Gospel itself, since there are no safeguards to protect the truth of the faith once for all handed down to the saints."[39]

Luke's emphasis on "the Word" is not always noticed, but it is important. He uses the term "word" (*logos*) ninety-eight times, of which sixty-five are in Acts. Many of these have little relevance to our study, but some are significant. Thus in his account of the early church in Acts Luke has "the word of God" and "the word of the Lord" ten times each, while he has simply "the word" fourteen times. In addition he uses expressions like "the word of his grace" (twice), "the word of the gospel," "the word of this salvation," and "a word of exhortation." Add to this a series of words for proclamation,[40] and it is clear that Luke saw the Word as very important for the life and growth of the church.

It is difficult to reconcile the idea that Luke is advocating some form of institutionalism with his strong emphasis on the work of the Holy Spirit. To read Acts is to get a glimpse of the life of a dynamic group that is the very antithesis of a concern for an institution. When people are concerned basically to respond to the Spirit, there is an element of unpredictability that is not easy to square with what "catholicism" stands for.

Once again it seems that some critics are too ready to blame Luke for not being another Paul or John. He is his own man, and he writes in his own

[38] *Jesus and Man's Hope*, 206. Cf. C. K. Barrett, "Luke's stress on the proclamation of the Word . . . shows that the Word itself was the decisive factor"; the church is an agency of salvation "only in so far as it provides the framework within which the preaching of the Word takes place" (*Luke the Historian in Recent Study* [London, 1961], 72, 74).

[39] Richard N. Longenecker and Merrill C. Tenney, eds., *New Dimensions in New Testament Study* (Grand Rapids, 1974), 230.

[40] In Acts Luke uses εὐαγγελίζω fifteen times, καταγγέλλω eleven times, διαμαρτύρομαι nine times (all three more often than in any other New Testament writing), and κηρύσσω eight times. There is an important article on the subject by Dr. Meinarth H. Grumm, "Another Look at Acts" (*ExpT* 96 (1984–85): 333–37).

way. His concern for the preservation of what the apostles preached shows his vital interest in the truth of the Christian gospel. That must not be lost sight of. Talbert points out that "the Lucan brand of Early Catholicism . . . in character is 'proto-Protestant.' *Sola Scriptura* is a major plank in the Lucan theological platform."[41] I do not think that either "catholicism" or "protestantism" is a good term to apply to Luke (even if we prefix it with "early"). But, if we had to choose, "protestantism" fits better with what he has done.[42]

---

[41] *Jesus and Man's Hope,* 39.

[42] I have examined the topic at greater length in an article, "Luke and Early Catholicism," in *WTJ* 35 [1973]: 121–36.

part three

the johannine writings

ome of the most difficult problems in the New Testament are posed by John's writings—the Gospel of John, his three epistles, and Revelation. Traditionally they have all been ascribed to one author, and that author is the apostle John. In modern times this position has been abandoned by many. Very few scholars these days hold to the apostolic authorship of any of these books; there is a strong tendency to think of a "Johannine" school, a group of early Christians who held a number of positions in common, in distinction from, say, Paul and those who thought like him, or those whose position is summed up in the ideas in the Synoptic Gospels. This has to be seen as quite probable; whoever wrote these books wrote for people who would be interested in them, and there is no reason why we should not think of a community of like-minded people of a "Johannine" stamp.

Whether we should divide up the authorship of the Johannine writings among the membership of the group is another matter. Many see Revelation as so different in style from the other Johannine books that they find it impossible to think of common authorship. Others agree with the difference in style but point out that we do not know how big a part an amanuensis played in the composition of first-century writings.[1]

If we grant that it is improbable that the apostle John (who had been by trade a fisherman) wrote anything extensive without having a scribe to take it all down, we are left with the possibility that that scribe may well have shaped what was written. This could conceivably have involved quite an extensive process, for John and Peter were described as "unlettered and ignorant men" (Acts 4:13). It must always be kept in mind also that, apart from Revelation, all of these books are anonymous and that, while Revelation gives the name of its author as John, it does

---

[1] For the role of amanuenses in the composition of documents in antiquity, see the article by E. Earle Ellis referred to above (21n.6).

not say which John. All this means that the question of authorship is a confused and difficult one. There are those who hold to the conservative view,[2] while others regard a number of authors as a necessary hypothesis.

It would require a good deal of space to go into questions like these, and that seems scarcely profitable in such a treatment as this. So I simply note that there are problems and leave it at that. My concern here as elsewhere is not with who it was who wrote the books, but with what the books contain. I propose accordingly to look at the Gospel first, then the epistles (there is surely sufficient homogeneity to take the three together), then Revelation.

---

[2] Thus, E. Stauffer can say, "We have sufficient ground to ascribe these five writings to a common author of remarkable individuality and great significance, and to identify him with the apostle John." But he notes that objections are urged, so suggests "the cautious thesis: the Johannine writings of the NT are to be ascribed to the apostle John or to his influence" (*New Testament Theology* [London, 1955], 41).

12

the Gospel of John: the doctrine of christ

The Fourth Gospel is by common consent one of the most important books that has ever been written. Its influence in the Christian church and beyond it has been incalculable. It has evoked an enormous literature, and the problems it raises are nowhere near a final solution. One of the intriguing things about Johannine studies is the fact that, while the scholars learnedly pursue their abstruse quests, ordinary men and women—yes, and boys and girls too—read the book without asking questions and find not only that they can understand it, but that they learn to their souls' health. All this means that it is not easy to know where to begin our study of it.

But as good a starting point as any is that of the Gospel itself—Jesus. The book opens with "In the beginning was the Word . . ." (1:1), and toward the end the author tells us why he wrote: "These are written that you may believe that Jesus is the Christ, the Son of God . . ." (20:31). It is a book about Jesus. This is underlined by the fact that John uses the name "Jesus" 237 times, far and away the most in any New Testament book (next is Matthew with 150; Luke has 89; and Mark, 81; Paul's total is 213 spread over his entire correspondence, the most in any one of

his letters is 37 in Romans). John is absorbed in Jesus, and, while it is true that he gives attention to other topics, he also sees everything in the light of who and what Jesus is and the importance of Jesus' coming to earth to live and to die for us.

THE WORD

In his prologue, John four times calls Jesus "the Word," a designation he does not use again in the entire Gospel. We use the term *word* for a unit of language, whether spoken or written, but the Greeks gave it a much wider usage. They distinguished between what they called the *logos prophorikos,* the word going forth from a person (that is the way we use "word"), and the *logos endiathetos,* the word remaining within a person. The *logos endiathetos* meant something very like our "reason"; it pointed to the thinking, rational part of our nature. As they looked at this mighty universe, some of the philosophers discerned a principle of rationality. The sun and the moon rise and set with regularity; the planets move in their orbits; the seasons follow each other in regular sequence. So they thought of a *Logos,* a Word, that runs right through the universe, something like a "world soul."

The Jews did not have this usage, but there are some not unimportant Jewish usages that form part of the background to the way John uses the term. There are passages in the Old Testament that use concepts like "wisdom" or "word." Thus in Proverbs 8 wisdom is personified and says, "The Lord possessed me at the beginning of his work, before his deeds of old; I was appointed from eternity, from the beginning, before the world began. . . . I was there when he set the heavens in place. . . . Then I was the craftsman at his side . . ." (Prov. 8:22–30). It is not easy to be sure how literally people took such passages, but it is beyond doubt that in the first century Jewish thinkers speculated about such a heavenly being as Wisdom.

There were similar speculations about the Word, based on such biblical passages as that in which we read "By the word of the LORD were the heavens made" (Ps. 33:6). This reminds us that in the account of creation in Genesis 1 we read repeatedly that God spoke; that was all that was needed for him to create. There is power in the Word of God. The Word is given almost an existence of its own when we find that "the Word of the Lord came" to this or that prophet (e.g., Jer. 1:2, 4; Ezek. 1:3; Hos. 1:1), while in Isaiah we read, "So is my word that goes out from my mouth: It will not return to me empty, but will accomplish what I desire and achieve the purpose for which I sent it" (Isa. 55:11).

To this we could add personifications of the Law. That the Law and the Word meant much the same is seen in the way the two may be used in

parallel: "The law will go out from Zion, the word of the Lord from Jerusalem" (Isa. 2:3; Mic. 4:2). The Law occupied a very significant place in the discussions of the rabbis.

We should also give some consideration to the Targums. These were translations of the Old Testament into the language of the people (readings in the synagogues were in Hebrew, a language not necessarily understood by the congregation). At first this was done only orally, but in time some of the Targums were written and these give significant information about how the Jews of the time understood Scripture. The name of God, we find, was not pronounced, and when the reader came to it he substituted some reverent periphrasis, such as "the Lord," or "the Holy One." And sometimes the reader would say "the Word." This was a common practice. William Barclay says that in the Targum of Jonathan[1] the expression is used about 320 times.[2] This is not exactly the usage we have seen in John or in the Old Testament, because the expression here means God himself, not someone close to him. But the point is that where people were used to the Targums, they were familiar with the use of *memra,* "word," to point to deity.

Many find Philo an important part of the background of John's use of the term. This great Jew of Alexandria made extensive use of the term *Logos* in his unusual combination of Old Testament thought and Greek philosophy.[3] He could speak of the *Logos* as a "second God," but he sometimes uses the term of the one God in action. C. H. Dodd sees Philo as very impor-

---

[1] This is a Targum on the Former and the Latter Prophets, the books in our Bibles from Joshua to 2 Kings (excluding Ruth) and the books of the prophets (excluding Daniel).

[2] *The Gospel of John* (Edinburgh, 1956), 1:7.

[3] According to W. F. Howard, Philo used the term "no fewer than thirteen hundred times" (*Christianity According to St. John* [London, 1943], 36–37).

tant if we are to understand John and holds, for example, that John's opening words "are clearly intelligible only when we admit that λόγος, though it carries with it the associations of the Old Testament Word of the Lord, has also a meaning similar to that which it bears in Stoicism as modified by Philo, and parallel to the idea of Wisdom in other Jewish writers."[4]

More could be said. But this is not an exhaustive discussion, and it is sufficient to point out that "Word" was an important concept for John's first readers, whether their background was Jewish or Greek. William Temple said that the *Logos*

> alike for Jew and Gentile represents the ruling fact of the universe, and represents that fact as the self-expression of God. The Jew will remember that "by the Word of the Lord were the heavens made"; the Greek will think of the rational principle of which all natural laws are particular expressions. Both will agree that this Logos is the starting point of all things.[5]

John says that this *Logos* was "in the beginning," that he was with God and that he was God (1:1). There has been much discussion about this last point; some agree with Moffatt that "the Logos was divine," understanding this as meaning something less than deity. But this can scarcely be derived from the Greek, which seems to mean that the Word was nothing less than God,[6] however hard or easy that is to fit that meaning into our theologies. John is giving the *Logos* the highest possible place.

He proceeds to a number of things the *Logos* does that show him to be a most exalted personage, but then we come to this surprising statement: "The Word became flesh and lived among us" (1:14). This is a strong statement of the Incarnation. "The Word" is that being who has been described as "God" (v. 1). "Became" means more than "showed himself in" or "appeared as"; the aorist tense means action at a point of time. Thus John is not referring to some timeless manifestation but to a definite happening at a definite time. And "flesh" is a very strong term. John has just used it (v. 13) for what is human as opposed to what is divine (cf. 3:6; 6:63; 8:15). John could have softened what he had to say by using some such form of words as "the Word took a body" or "the Word became man"; instead, he chose words that were almost offensive. James D. G. Dunn speaks of "the shocking nature of his assertion,"[7] and we should not miss the point.

When John calls Jesus the Word, then, he is drawing attention to Jesus' greatness. The Word is mentioned with

---

[4] *The Interpretation of the Fourth Gospel* (Cambridge, 1953), 280. A. W. Argyle is another to emphasize the importance of Philo. He doubts whether there has been put forward "any fully satisfactory alternative interpretation" of John's Gospel to that which sees it in the light of Philo (*ExpT* 63 [1951–52]: 385–86).

[5] *Readings in St. John's Gospel* (London, 1947), 4.

[6] E. C. Colwell produces evidence to show that in the New Testament definite nouns preceding the verb lack the article (*JBL* 52 [1933]: 12–21). We should understand the expression as "the Word was God."

[7] *Unity and Diversity in the New Testament* (London, 1977), 300–301. He goes on to bring out the "scandalous claim" that "to believe in Jesus is to crunch or chew his flesh and drink his blood" (6:51–63). He speaks of this as "otherwise needlessly offensive language" which "can only be understood as deliberately and provocatively directed against any docetic spiritualization of Jesus' humanity, *an attempt to exclude docetism by emphasizing the reality of the incarnation in all its offensiveness*" (p. 301; Dunn's italics). We should not miss the strength of the language with which John asserts the reality of the Incarnation.

deity, and the Word is himself God. It is a strong note to sound in his opening section. But with that he joins the thought of incarnation. High though the Word undoubtedly is, he came right where we are. These are thoughts that recur throughout John's Gospel.

JESUS IS THE CHRIST

John tells us expressly that he wrote his book that we "may believe that Jesus is the Christ" (20:31). This plan he works out right through his Gospel. It starts with the beginning of the narrative proper, right after the prologue. He speaks of the witness of John the Baptist and says that John's first words to the delegation sent from Jerusalem to inquire into his activities were "*I* am not the Christ" (1:20). The Baptist's "*I*" is emphatic, giving this implication to his statement: "It is not I, but another already in your midst who is the Messiah."[8] John has quite a dialogue with the delegation, but the thrust of what he says is that he himself is not important; the important one is to come after him (cf. vv. 26–27).

He takes the thought a stage further when he comes to Philip's attempts to persuade Nathanael to come to Jesus. Philip assures his friend that he and others had found the One to whom the Old Testament bore witness, the One of whom Moses wrote in the law, as did the prophets in their writings (1:45). That the messianic prophecies of the whole Old Testament are fulfilled in Jesus is part of the case John is making. We are to see this also in the words of Nathanael when he exclaimed to Jesus, "*You* are the Son of God, *you* are the King of Israel" (v. 49). The emphatic personal pronouns and the conjunction of "Son of God" and "King of Israel" show that John has the Messiah in mind.

In his next chapter, John has the account of Jesus driving the traders from the temple. In commenting on this event many draw attention to the prophecy of Malachi: "Suddenly the Lord you are seeking will come to his temple; the messenger of the covenant, whom you desire, will come" (Mal. 3:1). The act of temple cleansing was, as Sir Edwyn Hoskyns put it, "not merely that of a Jewish reformer: It is a sign of the advent of the Messiah."[9]

We are back with John the Baptist after Jesus' conversation with Nicodemus. Some of his followers were displeased with the success of Jesus, but the Baptist reminded them that he had said earlier that he was not the Christ, but only that he had been sent before him (3:28). He goes on to the analogy of the bridegroom and his friend. The bridegroom, not his best man, has the bride, but that does not diminish the joy of the best man. The point is plain that John the Baptist did not have the first place, but that Jesus had it, and that John was happy that it be so. It is a different way of bringing out Jesus' messiahship, but it makes essentially the same point.

The account of Jesus' meeting with the woman at the well is a fascinating one, and this is the only place in this Gospel (and one of very few places anywhere) where before his trial Jesus claimed to be the Messiah. The woman declared that certain matters were a question for the Messiah when he would come, and to this Jesus replied, "I am he, I who speak to you" (4:26).

---

[8] R. Schnackenburg, *The Gospel According to St John* (New York, 1968), 1:288.
[9] Edwyn Clement Hoskyns, *The Fourth Gospel,* ed. Francis Noel Davey (London, 1948), 194.

His "I am" is what Schnackenburg calls "the formula of revelation";[10] the unusual Greek is the language of deity, language that Jesus uses often in this Gospel. Perhaps Jesus could reveal his messiahship to this Samaritan woman when he did not do so to the Jews, because the term did not have the political associations it had among the Jews. The Samaritans thought of the Messiah (whom they called the *Taheb*) primarily as a teacher. For whatever reason, John tells us that Jesus claimed messiahship in this conversation.

The woman was clear on Jesus' claim. She went into the village and invited people, telling them, "Come, see a man who told me all the things I ever did. Could this be the Christ?" (v. 29). In due course the people were able to declare their adherence to Jesus, not because of the woman's testimony, for they said, "We have heard for ourselves and know that this is truly the Savior of the world" (v. 42). The language is different, but once again it is the messianic significance of Jesus to which it points.

In chapter 5 John recounts a healing and a sermon, toward the end of which come the words of Jesus to his opponents: "If you believed Moses you would believe me" (5:46). Jesus is the One of whom Moses wrote—another way of saying that he is the Messiah (cf. 1:45).[11] John consistently brings out the truth that the Old Testament points forward to the coming of the Christ.

There are probably messianic ideas behind the desire of some of the people to make Jesus a king in the wake of his feeding of the five thousand (6:15).

Jesus decisively rejected this and withdrew into the mountain to escape the people's enthusiasm in a wrong cause. John is interested in bringing out Jesus' rejection of wrong ideas of messiahship as well as in fulfilling what the Messiah really was. We see this again in Jesus' reference to the manna (6:30–31) when his opponents challenged him to do what Moses did. Jesus had just fed five thousand people with a few loaves and fishes, but apparently they were reasoning that this was not really very much when one thinks of what Moses did. He fed a whole nation (not a mere five thousand), and he did it for forty years (not just for one meal). And he gave manna, bread from heaven (not ordinary bread and fish). There was a Jewish expectation that when the Messiah would come, the miracle of the manna would be renewed: "And it will happen at that time that the treasury of manna will come down again from on high, and they will eat of it in those years because these are they who will have arrived at the consummation of time" (2 Baruch 29:8). The demand for a sign, made in the way it was, is clearly a demand that if Jesus was indeed the Messiah he should accredit himself by bringing down the manna. So Jesus pointed out some errors in their position. First, it was not Moses who gave the manna, but God. Second, God did not simply give the bread in days of old; he gives it continually, and that bread is "he who comes down from heaven and gives life to the world" (6:33). Again there is the thought that Jesus is the Messiah, but not in the way they thought. They were wrong about

---

[10] Schnackenburg, *The Gospel According to St John*, 1:442.

[11] R. C. H. Lenski sees this in all that Moses wrote: "Great things he touches slightly, and little things, dry genealogies, small occurrences in the lives of the patriarchs, he describes at length, because these have a bearing on the Messiah. From the story of creation onward, through all the following history, ceremony, prophecy, and promise, he is ever in the mind of Moses" (*The Interpretation of St. John's Gospel* [Columbus, 1956], 426).

what the Messiah would be and do, and because of this they could not recognize him when he was among them.

There is messianic speculation again at the Feast of Tabernacles. Some of the people wondered whether the rulers had come to the conclusion that Jesus was indeed the Christ, because they said nothing when Jesus taught openly (7:26). But the people objected that when the Christ came, nobody would know where he came from. On this reasoning Jesus could not be the Christ because it was well known where he came from. Some of the Jews clearly held that the place of origin of the Messiah was known, for the chief priests and the scribes told Herod that he would be born in Bethlehem (Matt. 2:4–5). But others held that the Messiah's coming would be totally unexpected: "Three come unawares: Messiah, a found article and a scorpion" (Talmud, *Sanh.* 97a). Sometimes it is said that the Messiah will be "revealed" (e.g., 4 Ezra 7:28; 13:32), which, of course, means much the same thing. The Jews thought that the Messiah would be a man and he might well be living among them, quite unknown until the time of revelation.

This is a good example of John's irony. Had these objectors really known Jesus' origin as they said they did, they would have had the refutation of their objection. They thought he was just a man from Nazareth. But this was not the whole story nor even the most important part of it. He is "from above" (3:31; 8:23). John does not state this truth in refutation of the objectors; he leaves it for his informed readers to infer. And in doing so he brings out another aspect of Jesus' messiahship.

Subsequently there were people who saw Jesus as the Messiah on account of his miracles (7:31), and there were others who objected to his messiahship on the grounds that he came from Galilee, whereas they thought the Messiah would come from Bethlehem (vv. 41–42; clearly they differed from those mentioned earlier who did not know where the Messiah would come from, v. 27). Again we have John's irony. He did not stop to refute the objection, but those who knew the facts knew that Jesus was born in Bethlehem.[12] The very objection they brought forth was itself a proof that he is God's Messiah.

When Jesus called himself "the light of the world" (8:12), it seems that he was making another claim to messiahship, for the rabbis could say, "Light is the name of the Messiah."[13] Throughout this Gospel, light is an important concept, and it is not seen as a natural human possession. It is something that Jesus alone brings, he who is the Light of the world. Thus from yet another point of view we see him depicted as God's Messiah.

The light imagery persists, of course, in the account of the giving of sight to the man born blind (ch. 9). But at one point the question of the Christ comes before us specifically. The parents of the blind man "were afraid of the Jews, for the Jews had already agreed that if anyone confessed him to be Christ he should be put out of the synagogue" (9:22). A good deal of discussion has taken place over precisely what "excom-

---

[12] Cf. C. K. Barrett: "John's irony goes far deeper than this. The birth place of Jesus is a trivial matter in comparison with the question whether he is ἐκ τῶν ἄνω or ἐκ τῶν κάτω (8.23), whether he is or is not from God" (*The Gospel According to St. John* [Philadelphia, 1978], 330–31). A little later he says, "All disputes about the birth place of the Messiah, the heavenly Man, are far wide of the point."

[13] Cited from John Lightfoot, *A Commentary on the New Testament from the Talmud and Hebraica,* 3 (Grand Rapids, 1979): 330.

munication" meant at this time and whether it could have been used against the followers of Jesus. In some form the practice is very old (Ezra 10:8), and there are statements about it in the Mishnah, for example, in a saying attributed to Simeon b. Shetah, *c.* 80 B.C. (*Taan.* 3:8). But it is not known how it was carried out in New Testament times or for what offenses.

This makes the dogmatism of some writers difficult to understand.[14] It is particularly curious that some hold that John was simply reading back into the time of Jesus what happened in his own day. But we have no more information about excommunication at any date feasible for the writing of this Gospel than we do for the time of Jesus. C. F. D. Moule questions "whether there is any inherent reason for declaring this to be unhistorical,"[15] and this seems to be the position we should adopt. The Jewish authorities used excommunication in some form, and as they were strongly opposed to Jesus, why should they not use this weapon against him? For our present purpose the point is that the authorities were prepared to take strong action against anyone who acknowledged Jesus as the Messiah.

The matter surfaced again at the Feast of Dedication when the Jews met Jesus in Solomon's colonnade in the temple. Their question is not clear. It may mean (as NIV and most other translations) "How long will you keep us in suspense? If you are the Christ, tell us plainly" (10:24). But the first question might be understood as "Why do you plague us?" or even "Why do you take away our life?" (in which case they would seem to mean that they thought Jesus would do away with Judaism). Fortunately, the second question is clear, and that is our present interest. They demanded a plain answer to the question whether Jesus was the Christ. To this Jesus replied, "I told you and you do not believe. The works that I do in the name of my Father bear witness about me." His "I told you" may mean that, although he had not said specifically, "I am the Christ," the general thrust of his teaching makes this clear. Or he may mean that his "works" accredit him. They show that he is indeed the Christ. But the Pharisees lacked the spiritual perception to understand the significance of what Jesus did.

Martha is a striking example of one who had spiritual perception. It is unfortunate that she is usually remembered for her words on a bad day when she was worried about getting a proper meal for a distinguished guest. But when Jesus came to the family after Lazarus had died, she made a notable confession: "I believe that you are the Christ, the Son of God, he who should come into the world" (11:27). Her "I believe" is in the perfect tense, signifying that she had come to believe and that this belief remained permanently. And her confession is practically in the terms in which John gives the aim of his book (20:31). Is he saying that Martha had made the kind of confession he aimed at?

There is a somewhat curious episode toward the end of Jesus' public ministry. Jesus predicted his death in these words: "I, if I be lifted up from the earth, will draw all men to myself"

---

[14] Barrett doubts whether there is an accurate reference to excommunication here. He points to the twelfth of the Eighteen Benedictions, which he thinks, was probably meant to exclude Christians from the synagogue community (*The Gospel According to St. John,* 361–62). But this is later, and John can scarcely be referring to it.

[15] *The Birth of the New Testament* (London, 1962), 107.

(12:32). John explains that "he said this, signifying by what death he would die" (v. 33). This puzzled some of the crowd, and they said, "*We* [the emphatic pronoun] have heard out of the law that the Christ abides for ever, and how do *you* [the emphatic pronoun again] say that the Son of man must be lifted up?" (v. 34).

It is interesting that they speak of the Christ at all. The term was not used in the preceding discussion (not since 11:27, in fact). The questioners implied that Jesus claimed to be the Christ, but there is no evidence in this Gospel that he made such a claim in Jerusalem at any time. Perhaps they were reasoning from the triumphal entry, which was described earlier in the chapter. They would infer that this pointed to a triumphant conqueror, and it was not easy to reconcile this with Jesus' death.

Why they thought the Christ would live for ever is not easy to explain, for they appealed to the law, and there is no such definite statement in that part of Scripture. The view was, however, held within Judaism (e.g., 1 Enoch 49:1; 62:14), though not universally (some thought that the Messiah would die). What John is letting us see is that, without any definite claim being put forward by Jesus, the crowd at Jerusalem had the idea that he saw himself as the Messiah, and they could not reconcile that with his death.

This examination has not been exhaustive, but we have been able to see that in every chapter of this Gospel that deals with Jesus' public ministry, the subject of messiahship comes up. A claim may be made or denied, or events may show who Jesus is. But John never lets his readers go for long without some aspect of messiahship coming forward. This is by no means John's only category for interpreting Jesus, but it is a very important one. We cannot understand what his Gospel is aiming at unless we see this.

THE SON OF GOD

With "the Christ" John links "the Son of God" in his statement of the aim of his Gospel (20:31). As we have seen in our earlier studies, this term could mean much or little. It could be used of a pious man and show that he stood in a special relationship to God. But it could also be used of deity. There is no doubting that when John uses it of Jesus, he uses it with the fullest meaning. John uses the word *huios*, "son," of sonship within a human family; that is a normal usage and needs no comment. But when he speaks of the heavenly family, he prefers to use "children" rather than "sons" for believers. When he uses the term *son* with reference to God, it is always Jesus he has in mind. In other words, he sees Jesus' sonship as special, as distinctively different from that of pious people.

He brings this out with the use of the term *monogenēs,* which he uses of Jesus four times. The word is translated "only-begotten" in KJV, but it really means "only," "unique"; the word has nothing to do with begetting.[16] It certainly indicates that Jesus stands in such a relation to God as no one else does. John speaks of seeing his glory, "glory as of the only one from a Father" (1:14), and he apparently calls him

---

[16] Μονογενής is connected with γίνομαι (stem γεν-), not γεννάω. It is used in reference to the legendary bird the phoenix, the only one of its kind. It is used in Hebrews of Isaac (Heb. 11:17), though Isaac was not Abraham's only son. But he was "unique," the son of promise.

"uniquely God who is in the bosom of the Father" (1:18).[17] It is this "only" Son whom God sent into the world to bring salvation (3:16), and on whom people must believe if they are to receive that salvation. If they fail to believe in him, they are under condemnation (3:18).

The Gospel of John often speaks of "the Son" without qualification and without significant difference from the fuller expression "the Son of God." This absolute use is another way of bringing out Jesus' unique place. We may be "children of God," but he is "the Son." The Father "loves the Son" (3:35; 5:20), and the two are so bound up with each other that "the Son can do nothing of himself, only what he sees the Father doing" (5:19). In his prologue, John spoke in such a way as to indicate that the *Logos* existed from eternity; he complements this with some words of Jesus: "The Son abides for ever" (8:35). His being is eternal. He has life "in himself" in the same way as the Father does (5:26; this is the Father's gift to him).

Witness is a very significant category in John, as we will see later. Here we notice that, from the beginning, witness was borne to the Son of God. John the Baptist bore witness "that this is the Son of God" (1:34),[18] and Nathanael spoke of Jesus as "the Son of God" and "the King of Israel" (1:49). Some contend that it is unlikely that Jesus would have been greeted in such terms so early in his ministry, but Dom John Howton has argued convincingly that John and Nathanael did use the term, though without fully understanding its significance. It is part of the apostle John's aim to bring out its fuller meaning.[19] It is a title to which Jesus himself laid claim (10:36).

Some have argued that Jesus is here claiming to be "Son of God" only in the sense in which godly human beings can claim the title, but this is surely erroneous. In the first place, in this Gospel the title is never applied to human beings, and, in the second place, Jesus explains it: he is speaking of himself as "him whom the Father sanctified and sent into the world." It is this kind of claim to which the Jews objected before Pilate; they said that Jesus "made himself the Son of God" (19:7).

People are expected to "honor the Son as they honor the Father" (5:23); to withhold honor from one is to withhold honor from the other. In a variety of ways John gives expression to the thought that the Father and the Son are so intimately related that what anyone does (or does not do) to the one he does (or fails to do) to the other. He links the two in terms of glory; the sickness of Lazarus was "for the glory of God, that the Son may be glorified through it" (11:4). The Father is "glorified" in the Son (14:13), and Jesus prays that each may glorify the other (17:1). John has an interesting idea of glory, as we see from this statement in the prologue: "The Word became flesh and lived among us and we saw his glory" (1:14). What did people see? They saw the lowly man

---

[17] Many good MSS read μονογενὴς Θεός, including P66 P75 ℵ BC*L33 and much patristic evidence. Scribes would more readily tend to write μονογενὴς υἱός, which is supported by AC³KΘ et al. Both the evidence of the MSS and transcriptional probability favor the former. See further the note in Bruce M. Metzger, *A Textual Commentary on the Greek New Testament* (London, 1971), 198.

[18] This is the reading of most MSS and is accepted by many scholars. But some good MSS read "God's Chosen One" and this is read by, for example, NEB. Transcriptional probability favors it, for there would be every reason for scribes to alter another reading to the familiar "the Son of God," but it is hard to see why they would substitute "Chosen One" for "Son."

[19] See his article, " 'Son of God' in the Fourth Gospel" in *NTS* 10 (1963–64): 227–37.

from Nazareth, who spent his life in humble service and died a felon's death to save his people. When he speaks of seeing "glory," he can scarcely mean the kind of glory that was manifested in the Transfiguration, for he does not record it. For John, real glory consists in the willing acceptance of a lowly place in order to bless others. Especially is this true of the Crucifixion, and when John is writing about the Cross, he says that Jesus is "glorified" (e.g., 12:23; 13:31). Vincent Taylor, speaking of certain Johannine passages (3:14; 8:28; 12:32), comments, "There could be no vainer controversy than the dispute whether in these passages the crucifixion or the exaltation is meant. The death *is* the exaltation."[20]

The Son of God brings salvation. John tells us that God so loved the world that he gave his Son (3:16); he sent his Son to save the world (3:17). We should probably understand the Son's gift of life (5:21) in the same way, though some take this to mean his raising of people at the last great day. John certainly gives expression to that thought (5:28–29), but it is also a Johannine thought that God gives life now. His gift of salvation means setting people free (8:36). The offer of salvation looks for a response in faith, and for this reason John speaks of believing in Jesus (3:18, 36; 6:40; 11:27; 20:31). To refuse in disobedience to make that response is to invite the wrath of God (3:36).

The Son of God has eschatological functions. John is often said to concentrate on life as a present gift and to overlook the *parousia* that meant so much to other New Testament writers.

But we should not miss the fact that John tells us that "an hour is coming in which all who are in the tombs will hear his voice [i.e., the voice of the Son of God] and will come out, those who have done good things to the resurrection of life and those who have done evil things to the resurrection of condemnation" (5:28–29). It is interesting that "the Father judges no man, but he has given all judgment to the Son" (5:22). This is distinctive Christian teaching. Among the Jews it was firmly held that judgment is a function that belongs to God alone; the Jews did not see the Messiah as Judge.[21] John sees Jesus as the Messiah of Jewish expectation, but he does not limit him to what the Jews thought the Messiah would do. The Son of God is a grander figure by far than the Messiah as the Jews saw him, and his function as Judge of the world brings this out.

THE SON OF MAN

In John's Gospel, Jesus often calls himself "the Son of man," though less frequently (13 times) than in the Synoptics, and the title is always linked in some way either to the salvation Christ brought or to his connection with heaven. Thus, Jesus tells Nathanael that he and others will see "heaven opened and the angels of God going up and going down on the Son of man" (1:51). This appears to be a clear reference to Jacob's vision (Gen. 28:10–15), but in place of Jacob's ladder it is the Son of man who is the bridge between earth and heaven; he is the one who will bring the realities of heaven to people on earth. He is the

[20] *The Atonement in New Testament Teaching* (London, 1946), 147.
[21] Cf. *SBK* cited on p. 123 above. S. Mowinckel says that in Jewish writings "we never find a clear and emphatic statement that the Son of Man will raise the dead" (*He that Cometh* [Oxford, 1959], 401). To say that Jesus will both raise the dead and sit in judgment is to assign to him functions reserved for God in Jewish thinking.

only one who has gone up to heaven (3:13), and Jesus spoke of himself as "going up where he was formerly" (6:62).

Jesus says the Son of man will be "lifted up" (3:14; 8:28; 12:32; cf. the response of the crowd [12:34]). The verb in these passages (*hypsoō*) is often used of exaltation in the sense of being given a place of high honor (e.g., Acts 2:33; cf. Phil. 2:9). John uses it of Jesus' being lifted up on a cross to die, as we see from his explanation in 12:33. But for John the Cross is the supreme glory, as this way of referring to it shows. To the ordinary first-century Palestinian the cross was a symbol of shame; to John it was a symbol of glory. Indeed he uses the verb "glorify" when he is referring to the Cross (12:23; 13:31).

In some of the sayings he records, John combines the thoughts of Jesus' death for our salvation and of the spiritual nourishment he brings. Thus in the discourse about the living bread we find that the Son of man gives the food that abides for ever (6:27) and that people have no life in them unless they eat the flesh of the Son of man and drink his blood (6:53). Clearly in such sayings Jesus had in mind his death and the salvation he brings. Sometimes the emphasis may fall on one of them, as with Jesus' question to the formerly blind man whether he believed in the Son of man (9:35). That clearly referred to salvation, and other passages just as clearly point to Jesus' death (12:23; 13:31).

THE "I AM" SAYINGS

In John's Gospel there is a distinctive use of "I am" in sayings of Jesus. The expression can, of course, be used in very ordinary affirmations. But when the Old Testament was translated into Greek, the translators evidently felt that divine speech should be treated in a special way. So, when God is the speaker, instead of using the normal way of translating "I am," they often used the emphatic pronoun. It is this solemn, emphatic form of speech that John ascribes to Jesus on several occasions. There are seven passages in which "I am" has a predicate, and these are one of the well-loved features of this Gospel.

Thus, Jesus says, "I am the bread of life" (6:35, 48). There are variants in the same discourse: "I am the bread that came down from heaven" (v. 41); "this is the bread that comes down from heaven" (v. 50); "I am the living bread that came down from heaven" (v. 51); cf. "the bread of God is he who [or that which] comes down from heaven" (v. 33). In first-century Palestine, bread was the basic food; it was necessary for life. Jesus is saying that he is the supplier of what is necessary for spiritual life. It is not that he gives this bread; he *is* this bread. To come to him is to enter a really satisfying life, a life in which there is no longer a deep, unsatisfied longing (6:35). Moreover, the gift of life is at the cost of Jesus' death, for "the bread that I will give is my flesh, for the life of the world" (6:51; cf. the references to eating the flesh and drinking the blood of the Lord Jesus [vv. 53–56]). The bread imagery obviously is very meaningful, thus Jesus makes a declaration of eternal importance by the use of one small but immensely significant phrase.

Jesus also says that he is "the light of the world" (8:12; there is a similar saying but without the emphatic pronoun in 9:5, while the giving of sight to the man born blind is surely to be seen as a demonstration of Jesus' power to bring light to those in darkness). Some derive the saying from pagan sources, but this seems unnecessary. Light is a common enough piece of imagery, and it turns up in all sorts of places. If we are looking for a background to Jesus' saying, we may well find it in the Feast of Tabernacles, a feature of which was brilliant lighting in the Court of the Women in the temple. But the lights were not lit at the end of the Feast, and against that darkness to say that Jesus is the Light of the world is meaningful indeed. There may be also a reference to the pillar of fire in the wanderings of the Jews in the wilderness. Chapter 6 has a reference to the manna, and apparently chapter 7 has a reference to the rock from which the water flowed, so it would fit to have this as a reference to the pillar of fire. Whichever way we take it, Jesus is the source of the world's illumination.

"I am the door of the sheep" (10:7), Jesus said, and again, "I am the door" (v. 9). In the discourse the door is primarily the door into the sheepfold, but clearly Jesus means more than that. The door is the way into the presence of God, and Jesus is the one way people may come into that presence. There is something exclusive about *the* door; it is the one way. But in the passage Jesus uses the imagery in two ways. In the first, he is the door by which the shepherds enter; those who do not come through this door are not true shepherds; they do not love the sheep. In the second, he is the door through which the sheep enter; those who come through this door enter salvation.

Jesus goes on to say, "I am the good shepherd; the good shepherd lays down his life for the sheep" (10:11), and again, "I am the good shepherd and I know my own and my own know me" (10:14). The first thing he says about the good[22] shepherd is that he lays down his life for the sheep. This immediately sets him apart from the ordinary run of Palestinian shepherds. Such men lived with an element of danger, and doubtless some of them perished in carrying out their work. But death was always unintentional for them. In the last resort they would regard their own lives as more important than those of their sheep. But for Jesus the essential thing was that he died for his own. His saving death is central.

That deep concern implies a personal knowledge of the sheep. In modern times, when flocks of sheep are huge, it is nonsense to speak of the individuality of a particular sheep. The animal is simply one of a large undifferentiated mass. Not so with the Palestinian shepherd and his small flock. And not so with Jesus. However many his people may be, he knows each of them as an individual, and they know him—a precious part of salvation.

The next of the "I am" sayings was spoken to Martha after the death of her brother Lazarus. "I am the resurrection and the life," Jesus assured her. "He who believes in me will live though he should die" (11:25). Jesus not only brings resurrection and life, he *is* these things. The joining of resurrection and life perhaps is meant to show that it is the life of the world to come that Jesus has primarily in mind. The life that is associated with Jesus is no fragile, perishable thing, but a life that endures. And it puts physical death in perspec-

---

[22] Καλός means "beautiful" as well as "good," and some think we should see this meaning here. This overlooks John's habit of making little difference between synonyms, and "the good shepherd" is the way we should understand the expression. But we should also notice the comment of William Temple: "We must not forget that our vocation is so to practise virtue that men are won to it; it is possible to be morally upright repulsively!" (*Readings in St. John's Gospel,* 166).

tive. For people immersed in this present physical life, death seems the end of everything. But, though a person may die, if he believes in Christ, he will live. Jesus is the life that triumphs over death.

Life is in the next saying, too: "I am the way and the truth and the life" (14:6), and again it is eternal life that is meant. The way (cf. Heb. 10:20) is the way to God; it receives emphasis here by repetition (vv. 4–5). As with the door, there is something exclusive about "the" way, and this is further brought out with the additional statement "No one comes to the Father except through me." The truth is surely the truth of the gospel, the truth that alone brings people to God, and here it is coupled with the thought that Jesus may be relied on absolutely.[23]

The last of these sayings is "I am the true vine" (15:1), repeated as "I am the vine" (v. 5). What is emphasized here is the importance of vital connection with Christ. When the vine cane is separated from the vine, it dies. Again we see that real life is bound up with Christ. It means living in him and having him live in us (15:4). We should also bear in mind that the vine is sometimes a symbol of Israel, the people of God, and often of Israel as

faithless (Ps. 80:8–16; Isa. 5:1–7; Jer. 2:21; Ezck. 15; 19:10–14; Hos. 10:1). In place of faithless Israel we now have the true vine. We should notice also that the passage conveys the message that fruitfulness is important and is the necessary and, I must add, natural consequence of abiding in the vine (15:2, 4, 8).

There are also passages in which Jesus uses the "I am" formula but without adding a predicate. Thus he calls on people: "Believe that I am" (8:24; 13:19) and says to the Jews, "When you have lifted up the Son of man, then you will know that I am" (8:28). "Lifted up" means "lifted up on the cross" and Jesus is saying that there is a revelatory aspect of the crucifixion; when he has been crucified, those who reflect on what has been done will come to know something of who he really is. Jesus also outrages his opponents by saying, "Before Abraham was, I am" (8:58). It is not easy to see this as anything less than the language of deity, for Jesus is affirming that he has timeless existence.[24]

There is something of this also in his words of reassurance when the storm-tossed sailors saw him walking on the sea: "I am; don't be afraid" (6:20). Although the saying is primarily a

---

[23] The use of three nouns causes some to suggest that we should use adjectives instead—e.g., Moffatt: "I am the real and living way." But "truth" and "life" are too important in this Gospel for this to carry conviction. That each noun has an article is curious and causes Moule to wonder whether this is simply the use with the abstract noun, whether the second and third are simply accommodation to the first (which is required by the context), or whether we should take it to mean "I am the Way, I am Truth, I am Life" (*IBNTG*, 112). Better is Turner's acceptance of Zerwick's suggestion that the reference "is to Christ as the real truth, life, light, etc.; all other truths, lives, lights, being transitory" (Moulton-Howard-Turner, 3:178).

[24] ἐγώ εἰμι in LXX renders the Hebrew אֲנִי הוּא, which is the way God speaks (*cf.* Deut. 32:39; Isa. 41:4; 43:10; 46:4, *etc.*). The Hebrew may carry a reference to the meaning of the divine name יהוה (*cf.* Exod. 3:14). We should almost certainly understand John's use of the term to reflect that in the LXX. It is the style of deity, and it points to the eternity of God according to the strictest understanding of the continuous nature of the present εἰμι. He continually IS" (Leon Morris, *The Gospel According to John* [Grand Rapids, 1981], 473n.116). Barnabas Lindars is doubtful whether John intends "to convey a hint of the divine name I AM" and sees the point of the saying as "that Jesus 'continues for ever' (verse 34), and therefore is the eternal Son of God"; the expression denotes "timeless pre- existence" (*The Gospel of John* [London, 1972], 336).

means of self-identification, the way in which it is expressed seems to hint at deity. So also when Jesus identifies himself in Gethsemane (18:5–6, 8).[25] Other passages may have a similar nuance (4:26; 7:34, 36; 8:16, 18). It is possible, of course, to explain several of these passages in a natural "human" fashion, yet the large number of them calls for notice. John has many more than any of the other Evangelists, and it is difficult to resist the impression that he has something special to tell his readers by the use of this form of speech. The Jesus who uses it so often stands in a very special relationship to the Father.

Another unusual feature of Jesus' speech is his habit of prefixing solemn and important statements with "Amen." Matthew has this "Amen" thirty-one times; Mark, thirteen; Luke, six; and John, fifty. A curious feature is that in John the expression is invariably repeated ("Amen, amen I say. . ."), whereas in the Synoptics it is single. Perhaps John has retained a form of speech Jesus used (he seems to have repeated names at times, as with "Martha, Martha" and "Simon, Simon" [Luke 10:41; 22:31]). "Amen" was normally used as the response of a congregation to something uttered by the leader on the people's behalf; by saying, "Amen," they acknowledged that the words were their own (the word is the participle of a verb meaning "to confirm").

But Jesus put "Amen" before his own words and not at the end of those of someone else. It marks them out as being specially solemn and as carrying his attestation. We may be all the more certain that they are true because he solemnly validates them. There is in his use of the word the implication that God supports him in what he says, so that the expression has important christological implications. In effect Jesus is saying that God accepts these words and that he will see that they are fulfilled.[26] To speak like this is to say that God is in him in a way that he is not in any other.

WITNESS

One of the distinctive categories of the Fourth Gospel is witness. John has the noun fourteen times compared to three times in Mark and once in Luke (it does not occur in Matthew); he also has the verb thirty-three times, while Matthew and Luke have it once each and Mark does not have it at all. John in fact uses both noun and verb more often than anyone else in the New Testament. Thus we can clearly see how important it is to him that there is ample testimony to the central truths he is writing about.

In his prologue, John says of John the Baptist that "he came for witness, that he might bear witness of the light so that all might believe through him" (1:7). Then in the next verse he comes

---

[25] C. H. Dodd sees the repetition as resembling that in 5:50, 51, 53, and says, "In each place an expression entirely natural in the circumstances is given a special importance by a repetition which is sufficiently unnatural to draw the reader's attention" (*Historical Tradition in the Fourth Gospel* [Cambridge, 1963], 75n.2).

[26] Gerhard Ebeling thinks that Jesus' use of "Amen" gives expression "to the fact that Jesus identifies himself entirely with his words, that in the identification with these words he surrenders himself to the reality of God, and that he lets his existence be grounded on God's making these words true and real" (*Word and Faith* [London, 1963], 237). H. Schlier holds that in the way Jesus used the expression "we have the whole of Christology *in nuce*. The one who accepts His word as true and certain is also the one who acknowledges and affirms it in his own life and thus causes it, as fulfilled by him, to become a demand to others" (*TDNT*, 1:338).

back to it. John was not the light but came "in order to bear witness of the light" (v. 8). Later John bears witness (v. 15; the use of the present tense seems to mean that the testimony was of continuing force). And as far as the Fourth Evangelist is concerned that is all that the Baptist does. When he comes to John's ministry he starts with these words: "And this is the witness of John . . ." (1:19). The Baptist tells people that he is not the Christ, nor for that matter a prophet, he is only a voice (1:19–23). And that voice continues to bear witness to Jesus. John is not worthy even to loose the sandal thong of the One who comes after him (v. 27), and Jesus is shown to be the great One because of the sign of the Spirit coming down on him like a dove (v. 32). So John puts it on record that "This is the Son of God" (v. 34).

John comes before us again in chapter 3, and while the word "witness" is not used of him there, he was witnessing. Some of John's followers were concerned because Jesus had a greater following than he, but John reminded them that he had always said that he was not the Christ, only the one who went before him (3:28–29). Then when Jesus spoke of the Baptist, it was in terms of witness: "You sent to John," he told the Jews, "and he bore witness to the truth" (5:33). He praised John as "the lamp that burns and shines" and went on to say that he has witness greater than that of John (5:35–36; this implies that he did have that witness, but he had more). Long afterward there were people who remembered that, while John did no miracle, "all the things John said about this man were true" (10:41).

But John is far from being the only one who bore witness in this Gospel. There is a sevenfold witness: in addition to the witness of John, there is that

of the Father, of the Son, of the Holy Spirit, of Scripture, of Jesus' works, and of people who responded to Jesus' ministry. That is an impressive list and shows that the Evangelist saw ample testimony to Jesus. There is no excuse for not believing.

The witness of the Father is introduced with the words "There is another who bears witness of me, and I know that the witness that he witnesses about me is true" (5:32; notice a typical Johannine emphasis with the repetition of the word "witness"). Jesus says further, "The Father who sent me, he has borne witness about me" (5:37; cf. 8:18). The testimony of the Father was not obvious to the Jewish opponents of Jesus, but that was because they did not hear his voice, nor see his form, nor have his word abiding in them (5:37–38). But it was this testimony, shown in Jesus' works (5:36), that carried conviction to Jesus.

There is a great deal about the witness of Jesus, and this is of central importance, for in this Gospel the truth is emphasized that Jesus is the Revealer. It is in him that we see what God is like. He is "from above"; he is not "of this world" (8:23). He lets us see what God demands of us; he reveals the truth of God and what that means in our lives on earth and in our hopes for the life to come. His place is central and his witness brings this out.

On the first occasion on which the witness of Jesus is mentioned he associates his followers with him in assuring Nicodemus, "We speak what we know and bear witness to what we have seen and you people do not receive our witness" (3:11). Jesus had been speaking of the new birth and now assured his hearer that what he has said is soundly based. Jesus is not teaching airy fantasies with no basis. A little later he said that people did not receive the testimony of him "who comes from above," and again there is the affirmation that he spoke out of knowledge (vv. 31–32). This failure of the people to believe him is a sad fact to which John comes back again and again. Jesus came from God, was the revelation of God, and had been sent by God, but people would not listen.

On this occasion, however, he adds, "He who receives his witness has set his seal that God is true" (v. 33). To attach oneself to Jesus is different from becoming a follower of a man (such as John the Baptist). It means that one recognizes that God has sent Jesus, that in a special sense God is present in Jesus. It means to accept the truth of the revelation that God has made in Jesus and thus to set one's seal to the truth of God.

We have already noticed some parts of an important passage on witness in John 5. There Jesus spoke of the witness of the Father and also of that of the Baptist. But he spoke of his own witness, too, and began with the words "If I bear witness about myself my witness is not true" (5:31). It was basic to Jewish law that a person's testimony to himself is not to be accepted, and two or more witnesses were required to establish a case (Deut. 19:15).[27] Some think that this is the point here, and use the word "valid" rather than "true" (so Rieu, Moffatt). But Jesus seems to be saying more than that. His testimony about himself is such that if it stood by itself, it could not be true. The things he said had to be supported by the Father; if they were not, they could not be true.[28] And, of course, what this whole Gospel is saying is that they are supported by the Father. The supreme revelation of the Father is given in Christ. God, so to speak, has gone on record in Christ.

There is objective evidence for this in the "works" Jesus did (5:36; 10:25; cf. 14:11; 15:24). The miracles could be misinterpreted, and the Jews persisted in misinterpreting them. But if they were considered rightly, the hand of God could be seen in them. This is not unlike the witness of Scripture (5:39; cf. vv. 45–47). Rightly read, the ancient Scriptures pointed to Christ, as the many fulfillments of prophecy recorded in the Gospels show. But the Jews read them wrongly and did not discern what God was doing in their midst.

An accusation of the Pharisees gives another slant on unsupported testimony: "You are bearing witness about yourself; your witness is not true" (8:13). Jesus had more than one answer to this. The first is that his witness was true because he was qualified to bear it: he knew where he came from and where he was going (v. 14). The Pharisees with their purely human judgment ("according to the flesh") could never reach a just appraisal of Jesus. They did not have the necessary spiritual perception. The second answer is that Jesus was not in fact alone in his witness: the Father joined him, thus giving the two witnesses their law required (vv. 16–18). The Pharisees' lack of spiritual perception meant that they could not recognize this either. But the failings of the spiritually blind do not invalidate spiritual truth.

---

[27] The rabbis said things like, "None may be believed when he testifies of himself. . . . None may testify of himself" (Mishnah, *Ket.* 2:9).

[28] Temple makes an important point when he says, "If His word stood alone, it would not be true at all. For divine revelation did not begin and end in Him, though it reached its crown and finds its criterion in Him. There must be other evidence, not only to support His own, but because the nature of His claim is such that it can only be true if all the work of God—the entire universe so far as it is not vitiated by sin—attests it" (*Readings in St. John's Gospel*, 116).

Before Pilate Jesus summed up his whole mission in terms of witness: "For this I[29] was born and for this I came into the world,[30] that I might bear witness to the truth" (18:37; he adds, "Everyone who is of the truth hears my voice"). Truth here is, of course, not simply the truth that stands over against falsehood, but truth in a deep, religious sense, the truth of God, a truth that is so closely connected with all that Jesus stood for that he could say, "I am . . . the truth" (14:6).[31] Those who are committed to the truth of God recognize him, while others, like Pilate, do not understand him. It was in the pursuit of this truth that Jesus earlier said to his brothers, "The world cannot hate you, but me it hates, because I bear witness about it that its works are evil" (7:7). Part of being a witness for the good is to make clear what is evil.

Jesus bore witness that "a prophet has no honor in his own country" (4:44), a truth that he knew from bitter personal experience and not simply as an intellectual proposition. And there is another glimpse of what it cost him to bring about our salvation when he "was troubled in spirit and bore witness and said, 'Truly, truly, I tell you that one of you will betray me'" (13:21). We are not to think that the Son of God went through life serenely above all the troubles that plague lesser folk. He suffered too, and it hurt him that one of his intimates was going to betray him.

The witness *of* Jesus is very significant, but for John it is also important to notice the witness *to* Jesus. Of prime importance here is the witness of the Holy Spirit (15:26; cf. 16:14). Jesus' departure from the earth would not mean the end of all he had come to do and teach. The Spirit would come, and his witness would continue the same great divine work. The Spirit in the church is not doing something different from or alien to the work of Christ. He is bearing his witness to the same great work and the same great person.

John is also mindful of the fact that there is a place for human witness. This is not by way of giving Jesus information that he would not have apart from us, for "he had no need that anyone should testify about man, for he himself knew what was in man" (2:25). Human witness is rather for human benefit; it is a testifying to the facts of the gospel, to what God has done in Christ. John puts emphasis, for example, on the reality of the death of Jesus. There was someone who saw it, and "he who has seen has borne his witness, and true is his witness, and that one knows that he speaks truth . . ." (19:35). There are some difficult problems here (see the commentaries), but what is clear is that there was a witness who could testify to what was done at

---

[29]"I" is the emphatic pronoun on which Lenski comments: "The pronoun ἐγώ is full of majesty; 'I for my part' in contrast with all others who ever have been termed kings" (*The Interpretation of St. John's Gospel*, 1232).

[30]"What he asserts about himself puts into the strongest relief the fact that he originates from another world, and has no other purpose in this world than to bear witness to that other world and its reality. Hence the pleonasm, that he 'was born for this' and has 'come into the world for this' to bear witness to the truth. Pre-existence and incarnation are the precondition for, but not the point of this way of speaking" (R. Schnackenburg, *The Gospel According to St John*, 3:249–50).

[31]According to Raymond E. Brown, John has portrayed Jesus "as the unique revealer who alone can speak and show the truth about God. Jesus has no real subjects as would be true if his kingdom were like other kingdoms; rather he has followers who hear his voice as truth. Only those who belong to the truth can understand in what sense Jesus has a kingdom and is a king" (*The Gospel According to John*, *XIII–XXI* [New York, 1970], 869).

the Crucifixion. John attaches considerable importance to this.

So, too, with the narrative as a whole. At the end of this Gospel we read, "This is the disciple who bears witness about these things and who wrote these things, and we know that his witness is true" (21:24). Again there are problems (who are "we"?), but again it is clear that the writer regards what he has written as "witness"; he has not made a strikingly original composition out of his head, but has borne witness to what was done. That is to be a continuing function for the followers of Jesus after the coming of the Spirit (15:27).

We see something of what witness should be and what it can effect in the case of the woman at the well. When she had come to know Jesus, she told the people of her village about it and brought them to him. The result was that many believed "on account of the word of the woman as she witnessed . . ." (4:39). And at a later time there were those who had been present when Jesus raised Lazarus from the dead who bore their witness and thus caused the Jerusalem mob to go out to see him (12:17–18).

It is in the nature of witness that the person who witnesses is a committed person.[32] As long as I remain silent I keep all my options open. But the moment I bear my witness that changes. Then I can no longer say anything different without branding myself a liar. Witness necessarily involves commitment. John makes it clear

that there are committed people, people who bear their witness to Jesus. And he has the breathtaking thought that God has committed himself, for he has borne witness to Jesus. He has said in effect, "This is what I am like." God has gone on record in Christ.[33]

SIGNS

John has his own distinctive terminology when he speaks of the miracles of Jesus. The synoptists generally use the word *dynamis* ("deed of power," "mighty work") when they refer to them, but John never uses this term. John has two words: *sēmeion* ("sign") and *ergon* ("work"), words that the Synoptists use but not in referring to the miracles of Jesus. They perhaps come close, as when they record the people's asking Jesus for a "sign" (Matt. 12:38; Luke 11:16), a request he persistently refused (Matt. 12:39; 16:4). There is also "the sign of the Son of man" (Matt. 24:30). But as applied to what Jesus actually did, the word is John's own.

"Sign" occurs seventeen times in John. Once we find that John the Baptist did no sign (10:41), and twice Jesus' opponents asked what sign he showed (2:18; 6:30), and again they wondered whether the Messiah would do more signs than Jesus (7:31).

Jesus himself used the word when he spoke of those who would not believe unless they saw "signs and wonders" (4:48). At least once he said that his hearers sought him out not because they "saw signs" but because they "ate

---

[32] Cf. Gabriel Marcel: "To be a witness is to act as a guarantor. Every testimony is based on a commitment and to be incapable of committing oneself is to be incapable of bearing witness" (*The Philosophy of Existence* [London, 1948], 68).

[33] A. A. Trites sums up what all this means today: "First, witnesses are passionately involved in the case they seek to present. . . . Secondly, witnesses are held accountable for the truthfulness of their testimony. . . . Thirdly, witnesses must be faithful not only to the bare facts of the Christ-event, but also to their meaning. This entails presenting Christ and his message in the significance which genuinely belongs to them" (*NIDNTT*, 3:1049–50).

of the loaves and were filled" (6:26). It is a sobering thought that these people saw a miracle performed but did not realize they were in the presence of the Son of God. As Hans Conzelmann puts it, "They have experienced the miracle, but have not understood it as a sign."[34] Jesus, then, did not make much use of this term for his miracles.

But John did. He saw the miracles, not simply as wonderful and inexplicable, but as meaningful. In the literal sense of the term they were "significant." When he concludes the account of the first of Jesus' signs, the changing of the water into wine in Cana of Galilee, John tells us that the disciples "believed in" Jesus (2:11). It was a meaningful happening, and they discerned enough of the meaning to enable them to see the "glory" of Jesus. In due course others came to believe on account of the signs (2:23). Nicodemus gave expression to his conviction when he said to Jesus, "No one can do the signs you are doing unless God be with him" (3:2), a conviction not so very different from that of those Pharisees who interrogated the blind beggar to whom Jesus gave sight and who asked, "How could a man that is a sinner do such signs?" (9:16).

The difference of opinion on that occasion over whether Jesus was "from God" or not shows that it was not enough to see the sign and its result. There had to be spiritual perception. Where this was lacking people simply did not believe. It was not that they denied the miracle; they just refused to see the hand of God in it. Of this kind were those who saw signs and did not believe (12:37). They might say that if they saw "signs and wonders," they would believe (cf. 4:48), but this did not happen. It was always possible for them to look at the miracle with a critical eye. There is an instructive passage at the end of the account of the raising of Lazarus. The chief priests and the Pharisees did not deny that a stupendous miracle had taken place; indeed, they said, "This man does many signs" (11:47). But this did not lead them to faith; it led them to plot the death of both Jesus and Lazarus (11:53; 12:10–11), so far were they from understanding the meaning of the sign they were discussing.

But there were others. Some people followed Jesus on account of the signs (6:2; cf. 12:18). When Jesus fed the multitude with the loaves and fishes, those who saw it hailed him as a prophet (6:14). And we must remember that John wrote about the signs in order that people might believe (20:31). It is, of course, possible to misinterpret them but it is also possible to profit from them.

WORKS

John's favorite word for the miracles is not "signs" but "works." This is not always noticed and, for example, Alan Richardson says of this Evangelist, "Occasionally he uses the relatively colorless word 'works'."[35] But this is to miss something important that John is saying to us. The word is not confined to the miracles, and John uses it for the things people do, whether good (e.g., 3:21; 8:39) or bad (e.g., 3:19–20; 7:7). Good deeds may be spoken of as "the works of God" (6:28); this points to the truth that we do not do good deeds of ourselves; God is in them. There is an important saying of Jesus about the good deeds the believer will

---

[34] An Outline of the Theology of the New Testament (London, 1969), 346.
[35] The Miracle Stories of the Gospels (London, 1959), 30.

do: "The works that I do he will do too, and he will do greater works than these because I am going to the Father" (14:12). The departure of Jesus does not mean that his people will be left to themselves; on the contrary, they will be helped to such an extent that they will do these "greater works."

But, although John thus uses the term "work" for what people do, his characteristic use of the term is for what Jesus does. In eighteen of his twenty-seven uses of the word it means the works of Jesus. Sometimes it refers to the miraculous, as when Jesus says, "I did one work, and you are all astonished" (7:21). More commonly it lumps the miraculous and the nonmiraculous together as when Jesus refers to "the works" that he did in the name of his Father (10:25). This word refers especially to his miracles, but the expression is general enough to include all the good deeds that Jesus did, miraculous or not. The point is that Jesus' life was all of a piece; it cannot be said that he did some things as God and some things as man. He was one person. The whole of his life was the fulfillment of one overriding divine purpose.[36] We are not to limit the divine to the miraculous. We should probably also reason that what for us is a miracle was for him simply a "work"; being who and what he was, he did these things naturally. We are not to think of the miracles as being something extra, so to speak, a divine addition to accredit the teaching. They are part of the revelation; they are the consequence of Jesus' being who he was.

The works are distinctive, "the works that no other person did" (15:24).

They are not the unaided works of the man Jesus: he said, "The Father abiding in me does his works" (14:10). "[They are] works that the Father has given me to do" (5:36). Thus it is that at the end Jesus could say, "I have glorified you on the earth, having completed the work that you gave me to do" (17:4).

The works Jesus did have a revelatory function: they teach people about God. Jesus says that his works "bear witness" about him (5:36; 10:25), and he calls on people to believe in him because of the works: "If I do not do the works of my Father, do not believe me. But if I do, even if you do not believe me, believe the works, so that you may come to know and continue to know that the Father is in me and I am in the Father" (10:37–38). Similarly he says, "Believe on account of the works themselves" (14:11). This is to ascribe a very significant place indeed to "the works."

For John, then, this is a very important term. It is the word Jesus usually used; twice he spoke of "signs" but on every other occasion he referred to the miracles as "works." We may perhaps see in this some evidence of an Old Testament background, for there we often read of the works of God, especially in creation and in delivering his people. The God who did such wonderful works in Old Testament days continued to do them in the life of Jesus.

JESUS THE MAN

Regarding Jesus' teaching and his wonderful deeds, John makes it clear that God was doing something extraordinary. The realities of heaven have been brought to people here on earth.

---

[36] B. F. Westcott sees "the works" as referring to "the whole outward manifestation of Christ's activity, both those acts which we call supernatural and those which we call natural. All alike are wrought in fulfilment of one plan and by one power" (*The Gospel According to St. John* [Grand Rapids, 1954], 199).

This has led some to think that John saw Jesus as not really human, but as, in Käsemann's phrase, "the God who goes about on earth".[37] That scholar speaks of John's "naïve docetism,"[38] and refers to "my key word, unreflected docetism."[39] Clearly he holds that John has given us a portrait of One who was not really human, but deity striding the earth. On this view there was no incarnation, but a descent of deity to this earth in the manner of the legends of the Greek gods. In the *Festschrift* for G. E. Ladd I have argued that Käsemann's position is not supported by the evidence.[40]

John in fact depicts a very human Jesus. Repeatedly he speaks of him as a man (e.g., 4:29; 5:12; 7:46; 9:16; 11:47). Jesus spoke of himself as a man: "Now you are seeking to kill me, a man who has spoken the truth to you" (8:40). So did his enemies: "We are not stoning you for a good deed but for blasphemy, and because you, being a man, make yourself God" (10:33). The interesting thing about this latter passage is that at the same time as they recognize that Jesus claims to be more than man they plainly regard him as man. Thus, both Jesus and those about him had no doubt about his real humanity.

And John describes him as human. He tells us, for example, that Jesus sat by the well "wearied" (*kekopiakōs*) from his journey (4:6). That he suffered from thirst seems clear from his request for a drink (v. 7); he was thirsty also on the cross (19:28). By the well the disciples tried to get Jesus to eat something, only to be greeted with the rejoinder, "I have food to eat that you do not know of" (4:32). Käsemann thinks this shows that Jesus' food was different from the food that sustains other people, but this is surely untenable. Everett F. Harrison explains the words in this way: "Christ had lost for the time the desire for food in the consuming joy of pointing a needy soul to the place of forgiveness and rest."[41] Is not this the natural way to understand the words? Do not all God's servants at some time know something of the same thing? At any rate the disciples did not think of some different and supernatural source of nourishment, for they asked whether anyone had given him something to eat (v. 33). They thought of him as eating the same kind of food as everyone else. And they lived with him.

Jesus' whole way of life is human. He went to a wedding with his mother (2:1), and at the end of his life as he was hanging on the cross, he thought of her and made provision for her (19:26–27). He seems to have had a normal family life (2:12). His brothers told him how to behave in a way that anyone who has brothers will recognize (7:3–5). When his death loomed before him, he was troubled and asked whether he should pray to be delivered from it (12:27). He loved his friends (11:5) and shed tears at Lazarus's tomb (11:35; this expresses grief at the misunderstanding of the people, not at the bereavement, for he was about to raise Lazarus). He was troubled in spirit at that time (11:33) and again when he told the disciples that one of them would betray him (13:21).

---

[37] *The Testament of Jesus* (London, 1968), 27.
[38] For example, *The Testament of Jesus*, 26, 45, 70.
[39] *The Testament of Jesus*, 66.
[40] "The Jesus of Saint John" in Robert A. Guelich, ed., *Unity and Diversity in New Testament Theology* (Grand Rapids, 1978), 37–53.
[41] *John: The Gospel of Faith* (Chicago, 1962), 34.

There is something of a problem with Jesus' knowledge. Those who see a docetic Christ emphasize the fact that Jesus knew many things that are beyond the knowledge of ordinary mortals. Jesus certainly had some unusual knowledge (cf. 2:24–25; 5:42; 6:61; 7:29; 10:15). But it is also true that he had to find things out. Thus, he "found" the man he cured of lameness (5:14) and the blind man to whom he gave sight (9:35). He "came to know" (*gnous*) that the man by the pool had been lame for a long time (5:6), and the same verb is used of his getting to know that people wanted to make him a king (6:15).

Often he asked questions. Sometimes these are the kinds of question that any teacher asks when the answer is known; they are simply a method of making a point (e.g., 8:43, where Jesus not only asks a question, but answers it). But on other occasions he seems to have asked questions because he did not know and wanted to find out. Thus, he asked where the tomb of Lazarus was (11:34), and he put a question to Pilate about the source of the governor's information (18:34). Such questions make it difficult to hold that here on earth Jesus was omniscient.

It is much better to hold that where special knowledge was required for the fulfillment of his mission God gave him that special knowledge. Such knowledge arose out of his close relationship to the Father (see 8:28, 38; 14:10 et al.). But ignorance in some things is part of normal human experience, and the evidence is that John saw Jesus as sharing in this kind of limitation.

Those who deny that the Jesus of the Fourth Gospel was human can certainly draw attention to his greatness. But this is to be understood carefully. We saw earlier that John uses the idea of "glory" in a very unusual way—what Origen called "humble glory."[42] It is the glory of one who walks in a lowly path when he could have had a splendid one. This lowliness is a much more significant feature of this Gospel than people usually realize.

This is brought out by J. Ernest Davey's important study, "The Dependence of Christ as presented in *John*."[43] This is far and away the longest chapter in his treatment of the Johannine portrait of Jesus, and in it he shows that Jesus depended on the Father for all sorts of things: power (5:30), knowledge (8:16), his mission and message (4:34), his being, nature, and destiny (5:26; 6:57; 18:11), his authority and office (17:2; 5:22, 27; 10:18), love (3:16; 17:24–26), glory (13:32; 17:24), his disciples (6:37), his testimony (5:31, 37), the Spirit (1:33), guidance (11:9). Davey sees Jesus' dependence in his obeying the Father (4:34) and in passages such as this: "He who sent me is with me; he did not leave me alone" (8:29). He finds twenty-two titles of Jesus in the Gospel and 1 John, most implying dependence ("Son," for example, implies dependence on the Father).

Davey agrees that there are some aspects of John's Gospel that might be held to support docetic views, but he denies that these are typical. That Jesus was dependent on the Father is typical. "Few persons who have not studied the Fourth Gospel with care in this regard can have any conception of the extent to which this idea of dependence is emphasized in it as the chief constituent in Christ's experience of God the Father; one might indeed call this

---

[42] See M. F. Wiles, *The Spiritual Gospel* (Cambridge, 1969), 82.
[43] This is a chapter in his book, *The Jesus of St. John* (London, 1958), 90–157.

dependence the ruling element in John's portrait of Christ."[44]

It seems, then, that John makes it just as clear as any of the Synoptists that Jesus was fully man. The evidence that Jesus was also fully God should not blind us to Jesus' humanity. He trod the lowly way, and that meant both living a genuine human life in humility and obscurity and, in the end, dying the death of a criminal, death on a cross. The place John gives to the Passion should not be overlooked. All four Gospels display it as the culmination of Jesus' ministry. And, of course, this is further evidence of Jesus' very real humanity. It is human to die. The humanity of Jesus is important for an understanding of the purpose of what John includes in his Gospel.

[44] *The Jesus of St. John*, 77. He holds that, while all four Gospels bring out both the humanity and the deity of Christ, theologically the synoptists stress the deity and John the humanity (p. 170). A. M. Hunter is persuaded by this argument (*According to John* [London, 1968], 115).

13

the Gospel of John: God the father

John sees God as Father, and, indeed, dwells on this concept. He uses the term "Father" 137 times, the greatest number in any one book in the New Testament. Matthew has the word 64 times (the next most frequent); Mark has it 18 times, and Luke 56 times. Thus John uses the term more than twice as often as the next most frequent user of the word. And he uses the word mostly of God (122 times). It is Johannine usage that has led the church to speak of God as "Father" so characteristically. Other writers have this usage, but it is not dominant for them as it is for John. He uses the word "God" 83 times, a rather high number. But his characteristic word is "Father."

THE FATHER AND THE SON

In a large number of cases the Father and the Son are linked in some way. John may speak of what the Father is doing or of what he is in himself, or he may refer to the Father's relationship to people. But what gives the term "Father" its depth of meaning is what

we learn from its association with Christ. It was in sending the Son and in what he accomplished through the Son that we see what it means that God is Father.

John's association of the Father and the Son begins in the prologue. There we find that the *Logos* was in the beginning, was with God, and was God (1:1; cf. v. 18). At the end of the Gospel Thomas says to Jesus, "My Lord and my God" (20:28). Jesus was accused of making himself equal with God (5:18) and of making himself God (10:33). He is uniquely from the Father (1:14; cf. 16:27–28), he "is in the bosom of the Father," and he has revealed the Father (1:18). The word "bosom" denotes intimacy and affection, and here it indicates that he comes to us from the very heart of God. It is because of this close relationship that he can reveal God to us in the way he does. He gives us genuine and intimate knowledge of the Father because of his relationship to the Father.[1] He "came out from God" (8:42).

Jesus has a special relationship to

---

[1] The verb is ἐξηγέομαι, on which John Marsh says, "John has chosen a Greek word which is at once the technical term for the Jew in making known the Rabbinic interpretations of the Law, or for the revelation of divine secrets; and a term characteristic of Greek religion for the publication of divine truths. So to Jew and Greek, the evangelist would say, the incarnate Word brings from the very heart of God a full revelation of what is in his heart and mind for man and for his world" (*The Gospel of St John* [Harmondsworth, 1968], 112).

God, for it is only he who has seen the Father (6:46). The Jews recognized that he regarded God as his Father in a special sense; they saw this as blasphemy and tried to kill him for it (5:18), and they asked Jesus where his Father was (8:19). When Jesus said, I am ascending to "my Father and your Father and to my God and your God" (20:17), he indicated that there is a difference between his relationship to the Father and ours.

It is a persistent strand of Johannine teaching that the Father and the Son are in some sense one (10:30). This must be understood carefully, for there is also a sense in which Jesus could say, "The Father is greater than I" (14:28). This is probably to be understood in terms of the Incarnation, which means a voluntary acceptance of certain limitations. But that the two are very close is clear throughout this Gospel. Jesus came "in the name" of his Father (5:43). He repeatedly ascribed his teaching to the Father (8:38, 40; 12:49–50; 14:24) and spoke of receiving commands from him (10:18; 14:31; 15:10). The deeds he did were "the works the Father" had given him to do (5:36; cf. 10:32, 37); they were done "in the name" of the Father (10:25), indeed it was the Father dwelling in Christ who did the works (14:10). "Of God" characterizes his relationships: he is "the Son of God" (1:34 and many other references), "the Lamb of God" (1:29, 36), "the bread of God" (6:33), "the holy one of God" (6:69).

To know the Son is to know the Father (8:19; 14:7; 16:3); neither the Father nor the Son it seems can be known apart from the other. God is with Jesus, who is "a teacher come from God" (3:2). To see the Son is to see the Father (14:9). There were people who had both seen and hated both the Son and the Father (15:23–24). So it is that Christ knows the Father, and the Father knows him (10:15), the Father is in him and he is in the Father (10:38). All that the Father has is the Son's (16:15), and vice versa (17:10). Each is "in" the other (17:21), and the two are a unity (17:11, 22). Small wonder that Christ says, "No one comes to the Father except through me" (14:6).

In keeping with all of this is the fact that the Father has "sealed" the Son (6:27), marked him for his own. He glorifies him (8:54) and sanctifies him (10:36). There are also several references to what the Father gives the Son (6:37; 10:29; 13:3; 17:24). It is clear that the Father was active throughout the earthly life of the Son. We are not to think of Jesus as acting independently of the Father. In all he said and did there is the action of none less than God the Father himself.

We see this in Jesus' constant reference to the Father. For example, when he was contemplating his death, Jesus said, "Now my soul has been troubled, and what shall I say? 'Father, save me from this hour'? But for this I came to this hour. Father, glorify your name" (12:27–28). His suggested prayer[2]

---

[2] It is possible to take the passage in the sense that Jesus really prayed that God would save him from this hour (as do commentators such as Bernard, Hendriksen). But if this is the case, Jesus immediately changes his mind and says, "But for this reason I came to this hour." The strong adversative ἀλλά that introduces this addition also favors the view that Jesus has posed a question and that he now goes on to a decisive reason against the proposed course. We should also notice that the suggested prayer is preceded by a deliberative subjunctive "What shall I say?" which naturally would introduce a suggested rather than a definite prayer. The view that a hypothetical prayer is meant is favored by R. H. Lightfoot, Strachan, and others.

faces the possibility of his avoiding the death that lay before him and hints at laying this possibility before the Father. Jesus himself rejected this because it was for this reason that he had come into the world. For our present purpose the important thing is that the whole matter is referred to the Father. It was to do his will that Jesus had come. If he was to avoid death, it would be only because that was what the Father willed, and he would have to seek it in prayer. We should understand other references to prayers of Jesus in much the same way (e.g., 11:41; 14:16). And when Jesus lifted up his eyes to heaven and said, "Father, the hour has come" (17:1), he was giving expression to the truth that the Father had planned the saving work and was now bringing it to its consummation. In the Garden Jesus spoke of his death as the cup that the Father had given him (18:11). It is along much the same lines that throughout the Upper Room discourse he so often referred to "going to the Father" (e.g., 13:1; 14:12, 28; 16:10, 17). After the Resurrection he spoke of ascending to the Father (20:17).

We see this activity of the Father in references to the followers of Jesus. The Father will honor one who serves Jesus (12:26), and from another point of view it is what he had heard from the Father that Jesus taught his disciples (15:15). It is hardly surprising, then, that when he contemplated his departure from the world he commended them to his Father's care (17:11).

As we would expect, the bond between the Father and the Son is love. The Father loves the Son (3:35; 5:20; 10:17), and the Son loves the Father (14:31). Curiously John 14:31 is the one place in the entire New Testament where the love of the Son for the Father is explicitly mentioned. We may fairly say that his love for the Father underlies much of what is said and that it is presupposed everywhere. But only in John do we find it set forth explicitly.

THE FATHER IS ACTIVE

The Greeks thought of their gods as far too great to be disturbed by the activities of petty mankind. John saw the Father as far too great to neglect the needs of those he had made. He tells us that Jesus said, "My Father is working right up till now" (5:17), and again that he referred to what he saw the Father doing and said that he himself did the same things (v. 19). This is an important way of bringing out the fact that Jesus was very close to the Father: he did not do similar things, but the same things. But it also brings out the fact that the Father is ceaselessly active in the world he created. God, it is true, rested after the six days of creation, but this must be understood in the sense that he rested from creation. Unless he continued to be active in sustaining what he had made, it would cease to exist.[3] Jesus is referring to his continuing activity.

Sometimes this activity is concerned with glory related in some way to the incarnate Son. Jesus prayed, "I glorified you on the earth" (17:4), where the context makes it plain that the glory came because Jesus had done the work the Father gave him. Similarly he assures his followers that he will answer their prayers "in order that the Father may be glorified in the Son" (14:13). He himself prayed that the Father would glorify his name (12:28), and

---

[3]C. H. Dodd cites a saying from the Hermetic writings: "God is not idle, else all things would be idle, for all things are full of God" (*The Interpretation of the Fourth Gospel* [Cambridge, 1953], 20).

that he would glorify the Son (17:5). The Father's glory may be seen in the "fruit" the disciples would bear (15:8). Just what is meant by "fruit" is not explained here, but we find from other passages in the New Testament that the term is used of the good qualities that Christians are expected to show in their lives (e.g., Matt. 3:8; 7:20; Gal. 5:22; Phil. 1:11). When the saving work of Christ transforms the lives of sinners, God is glorified.

The activity of the Father can be seen in the way he helps in the production of this fruit. Just as Christ is the vine, so the Father is the vine-dresser (15:1).[4] Left to itself, a grape vine will produce little fruit. For maximum fruitfulness careful pruning is necessary, and Jesus is saying that this is true in the spiritual realm. The Father is constantly active, pruning away all that hinders fruitfulness; Christian character is not produced by letting our natural forces run riot. Another aspect of the care of God for his people is shown in this promise: "No one can snatch them from the hand of the Father" (10:29). God will never let go of the believer. Our confidence rests not on our feeble hold on God, but on his firm grip on us.

THE MISSION OF THE SON

John very often speaks of the Father's sending the Son, a fact that brings out both the unity of the two and the divine compassion for sinners. God did this even for sinful people. There are two Greek words for "to send" and each occurs in John more often than in any other book in the New Testament.[5]

All told there are forty-one references to the sending of the Son, and "the Father who sent me" is a common expression on the lips of Jesus throughout this Gospel. For John it is of fundamental importance that Jesus did not simply "appear." We are not to think of him as simply a religious man with a special insight into the ways of God, such that he was able to instruct his contemporaries in the right way of serving God. He was not just a gifted Galilean who got the idea of gathering people around him and instructing them in things that seemed good or useful or even necessary. He said, "I did not come of my own volition, but he sent me" (8:42; see also 7:28; 8:26). His teaching was not self-originated, for he spoke "the words of God" (3:34; cf. 7:16; 12:49; 14:24). His knowledge of God was connected with the fact that God sent him (7:29).

It is the will of him who sent Christ that he should lose none of those he had given him (6:39). The will of God is for them to continue in salvation. They were saved in the first instance, not because they chose to come to God but because the Father who sent Christ drew them (6:44), and, having begun a good work, he will see it through to the end.

The very concept of mission, of being "sent," contains within it the thought of doing what the Sender wills, and Jesus says that his food is to do the will of him who sent him (4:34); he did not seek to do his own will but that of him who sent him (5:30); he came from heaven for that very purpose (6:38). He found it neces-

---

[4]The word is γεωργός, which means "farmer"; it is a more general term than "vine dresser." Some translators prefer to bring this out with terms like "gardener." This is defensible, but here it is clearly someone who looks after grape vines who is meant.

[5]He uses ἀποστέλλω 28 times (Matthew has it 22 times, Mark 20, Luke 25), and πέμπω 32 times (Matthew 4, Mark 1, Luke 10). Some have tried to find a difference in meaning, but it is not easy to see this in John. See further my book *The Gospel According to John* (Grand Rapids, 1971), 230n.78.

sary to "work the works of him who sent" him, and he associated others with him in doing this (9:4).

The closeness of the Father and the Son is brought out with the concept of mission. It means that Jesus is not alone; he said, "He that sent me is with me" (8:29; cf. 16:32). This is applied specifically to judgment; when Christ judges, he is not alone, but the Father who sent him is with him (8:16). In a number of places an action with regard to the one is that action toward the other. To believe in Christ is to believe in him who sent him (12:44); to see him is to see him who sent him (12:45); to receive him is to receive him who sent him (13:20; on this occasion there is also the thought that to receive a believer is to receive Christ). People who do harm to the followers of Jesus do so because they do not know him who sent him (15:21). The Father "sanctified and sent" Jesus "into the world" (10:36), and this points to a very special mission. If people fail to honor the Son, they thereby also fail to honor "the Father who sent him" (5:23).

He was the Son of God, sent by God to bring salvation to the world (3:17). It was important, therefore, that the world should come to believe (5:24). It was clear that the Jews who opposed Jesus did not have God's word abiding in them, because they did not believe "him whom [God] sent" (5:38). The crowd asked Jesus what they should do to "work the works of God," and were told, "This is the work of God, that you believe in him whom he sent" (6:28–29). The "works of God" reduce to one—believing in him whom God sent. Faith is connected with the sending of the Son in other verses also (e.g., 11:42; 17:8, 21). Eternal life is knowing God and "him whom [he] sent, Jesus Christ" (17:3). Sometimes it

is knowledge that is important, and the unity of believers should cause the world to know that God had sent Jesus (17:23).

Two other points should be made. The one is that as the Son had been sent, so in due course he was to return to him who sent him (7:33; 16:5, 7). The idea of mission involves the thought of the completion of the mission and that is followed by the return of him who was sent. The other point is that Jesus said to his followers, "As the Father sent me, I, too, send you" (20:21; cf. 17:18). That the Father sent the Son has implications for the way of life of those who follow the Son.

That God is a sending God is seen also in his sending of the Holy Spirit (14:26). But we will consider that fact when we consider John's teaching about the Spirit. Here it is enough to notice that John certainly thinks of God as a sending God. He sent the Son. He sent the Spirit. He sends disciples.

A GREAT GOD

John thinks of God as an almighty Being, One who is well able to bring his purposes to pass. John does not give "the kingdom of God" (3:3, 5) anything like the prominence it has in the Synoptic Gospels. But that God is supreme is just as clear to him as it is to them; he chose to bring it out in different ways. Thus he makes it clear that it is the will of God that is done. It is God's will that people believe on the Son and so have life eternal (6:40). To that end God "draws" people (6:44). There is a strongly predestinarian strain in such sayings and we see it again when Jesus says, "No one can come to me except it be given him from the Father" (6:65). John makes it clear again and again that the initiative in our salvation is with God. He accomplishes it all.

This can be spoken of in terms of love. "God so loved the world that he gave his only Son" (3:16)[6] and in that way brought about salvation. Those so loved are expected to respond with an answering love, and Jesus said, "He who has my commandments and keeps them" is "the one who loves me" (14:21). He also refers to those who "do not have the love of God in" them (5:42).[7] It is possible for people to reject the most wonderful of loves when it is offered to them. John makes it clear that love for Christ is not divorced from ethical behavior. It is nonsense to say that we love him if we do not obey him. The apostle goes on to say that the one who loves Christ will be loved by the Father. We must not miss the love of God when we think about the way our salvation is brought about. John repeats the thought (14:23), and again he tells us that Jesus told his followers, "I am not saying that I will ask the Father on your behalf, for the Father himself loves you" (16:26–27). The way is open for them to approach God themselves. They are not coming to a stern tyrant who must be placated by someone else, but to a Father who loves them. This is the intent also when Jesus spoke of "the free gift of God" (4:10).

This love does not mean that people may be complacent, reasoning that since God is loving, all will come out well in the end. There is that terrible "wrath of God," and John says that this wrath remains on the disobedient (3:36). He does not mention "wrath" again, but his references to judgment and to the place the Jews who opposed Jesus found themselves in before God shows that he is not unmindful of the reality the term denotes, nor of the truth that it must ultimately be reckoned with.

That the Father "has life in himself" (5:26) means more than that he is alive. We are alive, but there is nothing necessary about our lives. The world would be going on even if any one of us had never existed. If we were to live, we had to be given life in some way. Not so with God. His life is inherent in his being; it is necessary life.[8] Without his life there could be no other life. With him is "the fountain of life" (Ps. 36:9).

Another aspect of the Father is revealed in Jesus' statement that no one had ever seen the Father except "him who is from God" (6:46; cf. 1:18). Consistently John teaches that no one knows God other than through the revelation that Jesus brings. The world does not know the Father (17:25). The greatness of the Father is seen in Jesus' words "the Father is greater than I" (14:28). All through this Gospel the greatness of Jesus is stressed, so this statement, which evidently applies to him as the incarnate Christ, shows that the Father is supremely great. With that

---

[6] John says ὥστε ἔδωκεν, not ὥστε δοῦναι, as might have been expected. The construction with the infinitive is found only 21 times in 84 New Testament occurrences of ὥστε, so it is far from usual (especially when we remember that 15 of the 21 are in Paul). It seems that John is putting some emphasis on the fact of God's giving: it is not only that he loved "enough to give," but he loved "so that in fact he gave."

[7] This probably means that they do not love God, but some see a reference to people who have rejected the love God gives. Perhaps in the Johannine manner both thoughts are in mind, for, as B. F. Westcott reminds us, "God is at once the Author and the Object of this love" (*The Gospel According to St. John* [Grand Rapids, 1954], 202).

[8] Barnabas Lindars sees a reference to "the self-subsistent being of God" (*The Gospel of John* [London, 1972], 225).

we should take the two forms of address in Jesus' great prayer—"holy Father" and "righteous Father" (17:11, 15). Neither is used anywhere else in the New Testament. They remind us of ethical aspects of God's being; the Father's greatness is not unrestrained power. God always uses his power righteously.

THE FATHER'S CHILDREN

John records a number of sayings that bring out what it is to be God's children. God gave those who received the *Logos* the right to become "the children of God"; these people were born, not of any human activity, but "of God" (1:12–13). This does not mean some tiny, exclusive group, because the children of God extend far beyond the nation Israel and it is part of Jesus' function to gather the scattered ones (11:52). Nor does it mean that all who claim to be God's children in fact belong to the heavenly family. There were people who claimed to have God as their Father, but their attitude to Jesus and their bondage to sin showed that they were not God's people at all (8:41–42); they were the Devil's children (8:44).

God's children show their lineage with works "done in God" (3:21). And in response to a misunderstanding of the Jews about "the works of God," Jesus said that the work of God is to believe in God (6:28–29). Such belief is important and is linked with believing in Christ (14:1).

The temple is the "Father's house" (2:16; cf. 14:2), and it is in accordance with this that John gives attention to worship. The Samaritans and many Jews thought that God had to be worshiped in a special place, be it Samaria or Jerusalem. Jesus, however, pointed to a time when worship would be offered in neither place (4:21).

But place does not matter. What matters is the way people worship. "God is spirit" (4:24); his essential being is such that he is not to be thought of as confined to any place. Because he is the kind of God he is, people are to worship "in spirit and truth" (4:23). Jesus adds that the Father seeks such people to be his worshipers. In other words, not all types of worship are acceptable to God. Those people who do worship properly will honor the Father, and they will honor the Son as they honor the Father (5:23).

John's Gospel also records some teaching about coming to God in prayer. In the Upper Room Discourse, Jesus tells the apostles that they have been chosen to bear fruit, fruit that would remain, in order that whatever they ask the Father in Jesus' name he will give them (15:16). Many people today think of prayer as the prerequisite for bearing fruit: if we are praying people, we will have fruitful lives. But here Jesus says that for his apostles it is the other way around: fruitful lives will enable prayer to be more effective. This is to regard prayer as very significant indeed. Jesus repeats the command to pray in his name (16:23, 26), "name" here meaning the whole character. Thus, the disciples were supposed to be praying, pleading on the basis of all that Jesus was and had done for them.

In the synagogue at Capernaum, Jesus quoted from Scripture, "They will all be taught by God" (6:45; see Isa. 54:13; Jer. 31:34). And he taught that the genuine seeker would know whether his teaching came from God (7:17). In other words, God gives people the teaching they need. Those who respond to what he is saying to them acknowledge his presence in the ministry of Jesus.

ESCHATOLOGY

The emphasis in John is on the present. The *Logos* has come to be among us, meaning that God is revealed and that he is present with us. The love of God has been made known, and in the death of Jesus salvation has become a present reality. "Eternal life" is a present possession. It is possible to emphasize all this to such an extent that we lose sight of the common New Testament position that, in due course, Christ will return and bring this life to an end and set up the final state of affairs.

But this is too simple. It is true that John puts a great deal of emphasis on the present, but it is also true that he knows that this is not everything, for he includes Jesus' words about the resurrection: "The Father raises the dead and gives life" (5:21). John emphasizes the place of Christ in all that will happen at the end, and he records Jesus' declaration that the Father judges no one; he has committed all judgment to the Son (5:22). But Jesus warned his adversaries that it is Moses, not he, who will accuse them to the Father (5:45). The Father's place in judgment is as clear in this Gospel as anywhere else.

There is a refrain that runs through Jesus' discourse in the synagogue in Capernaum: "I will raise him up in the last day" (6:39, 40, 44, 54). We should take this with the plain words of Jesus when he said, "An hour is coming in which all who are in the tombs will hear his [i.e., the Son's] voice and will come out, those who have done good things to the resurrection of life and those who have done bad things to the resurrection of judgment" (5:28–29). In the Upper Room, Jesus spoke of his going from the disciples and added, "And if I go and prepare a place for you, I will come again" (14:3). Such words leave us in no doubt that John looked for the return of Christ, for the resurrection of all the dead, and for final judgment.

14

the gospel of john: god the holy spirit

John has some very significant teaching about the Holy Spirit. He begins with the testimony of John the Baptist, who saw the Spirit "coming down out of heaven like a dove and it stayed on him" (1:32). The Synoptists all record Jesus' baptism, but only the Fourth Gospel tells what John the Baptist said about it. He has, however, one detail not in the Synoptics, namely, that the Spirit remained on Jesus. Jesus' public ministry was not only inaugurated in the power of the Holy Spirit, but the Spirit remained on him throughout that ministry.

John goes on to tell us that the Baptist had not known Jesus, but that this was the sign that had been given him so that he would know him who would baptize with the Holy Spirit (1:33). It is not clear whether this means that the Baptist had never met Jesus (it is quite possible that he had not; he had grown up in the wilderness [Luke 1:80]) or that he did not know that Jesus was the Messiah. The latter possibility is more likely. Either way we learn that the coming of the Spirit was a sign at the beginning of Jesus' ministry. The statement "He does not give the Spirit by measure" (3:34) probably refers to the Father's gift of the Spirit to the Son.[1]

BORN OF THE SPIRIT

In response to Nicodemus' polite conversation opener, Jesus said, "Truly, truly, I tell you, unless one is born anew [or, from above], he cannot see the kingdom of God" (3:3). He went on to speak of being born "of water and Spirit" (v. 5), of "that which is born of the Spirit" (v. 6), and of being born "of the Spirit" (v. 8). Clearly, the Spirit's work is important in the renewal of lives.

It is impossible to be certain whether one should translate "anew" or "from above."[2] The adverb could mean either, but in every other place where it occurs in this Gospel it means "from above."

---

[1] The expression might alternatively be understood in the sense that the Son gives the Spirit to believers without measure. But believers do not have the Spirit in anything like the way the Son has, and in any case, as both Augustine and Calvin pointed out, grace is given to each of us "according to the measure of the gift of Christ" (Eph. 4:7). Grammatically it is possible to take "the Spirit" as the subject rather than the object of the verb, and the meaning would then be that the Spirit makes his gifts without stint. But not many accept this way of understanding it.

[2] The word is ἄνωθεν, which means "from above" in 3:31; 19:11, 23. But John is fond of using words that may be taken in more than one sense, and some think that he intends his readers to see both meanings here (cf. Barclay, "reborn from above").

Against this is the fact that Nicodemus took it to refer to a second physical birth, for he spoke of entering his mother's womb again. But this is a misunderstanding; we should take the word in the sense of "anew" rather than "again." Jesus is speaking of something completely new. Many expressions in the Fourth Gospel may be taken in more ways than one. In any case, the birth of which Jesus is speaking is a rebirth, but it is also from on high. We should neglect neither fact.

There are many ideas about how we should understand birth "of water and Spirit,"[3] but they tend to fall into one or another of three groups. First, there are those who see water as referring to purification. It is natural to see water as pointing to a washing clean. Some make this precise, referring to the baptism of John as a "baptism of repentance" (Mark 1:4). The thought would then be that one must accept John's baptism and repent, then go on to the "baptism with the Holy Spirit" that Jesus brings. Or it may be left more general: there must first be cleansing from evil, a putting away of all that is wrong. But this negative must then be supplemented by the positive—the Spirit's work that enables believers to walk in the ways of God.

A second way of looking at "water" is to see it as connected with physical birth. If it refers to the release of the amniotic fluid at the birth of a baby, Jesus is alluding to ordinary, normal physical birth and saying that this must be followed by a spiritual birth along the lines of "that which is born of the flesh is flesh and that which is born of

the Spirit is spirit" (v. 6). The natural man cannot enter the kingdom; there must be a work of the Holy Spirit before than can take place.

One may also connect water with physical birth in a way quite foreign to our usage of *water*. H. Odeberg has shown that in rabbinic and other ancient sources words that denoted something wet ("water," "dew," "rain," "drop," etc.) were often used as a euphemism for semen.[4] This could yield a meaning close to the one we have just discussed—born in the usual, natural way and also born of the Spirit.

But we may take "water" and "Spirit" very closely together to yield the sense "spiritual water" or "spiritual seed" (supported by the fact that in the Greek there is one "of," *ek,* that governs both nouns). In this case, Jesus is saying that one must be born spiritually if one is to enter the kingdom; the expression would mean much the same as being born "of the Spirit." This view is all the more probable in that John very frequently uses slight variations in saying the same thing. So "born of water and the Spirit" could convey much the same meaning as "born of the Spirit."

The third major way of viewing the passage is to see a reference to Christian baptism. The conjunction of water, used as a new believer was initiated into the Christian church, and being "born," as the beginning of spiritual life, seems to some students to point irresistibly to baptism. It is urged in support of this view that at the time John's Gospel was written this would have been the way the words would most naturally have been understood and the writer must

---

[3] Bultmann and others regard ὕδατος καί as a later insertion and reject the words. But this is not a judgment made on textual grounds; the MSS evidence for them is convincing. The argument is basically theological, and the considerations urged do not carry conviction. The words should be read.

[4] *The Fourth Gospel* (Uppsala, 1929), 48–71. Perhaps we should notice also that the mystery religions use the idea of rebirth. But they are thinking of some magical renewal, not the transformation of the whole life that characterizes the birth of which Jesus is speaking.

have known what his readers would take him to mean. There is quite obviously a large subjective element in this argument, for we have no means of knowing how "natural" this interpretation would have seemed at the time.

There is one very strong argument against it, the impossibility of Nicodemus' understanding Jesus if this was what was meant. At the time of the conversation the institution of the Christian church lay some years in the future and Nicodemus could not possibly have grasped an allusion to a not-yet-existing sacrament. We can hold this view only if we totally abandon the historicity of the account.

The best way of understanding the passage seems to me to be the second one and in the sense that water points to semen. Jesus is then emphasizing that the way into life is not by human striving (however that be understood) but by a work of the Spirit of God. It is a truth that John insists on throughout his Gospel (cf. 1:13). Jesus did not come simply to tell people to try harder but to bring them new life by the Spirit. This is what Jesus is telling Nicodemus. The repetition gives emphasis: birth from above, of water and Spirit, of the Spirit.[5] And Jesus goes on to speak to Nicodemus of being "lifted up" so that everyone who believes in him may have eternal life (3:14–15). It needs the work of the Spirit before we can see the Cross for what it is and enter by faith into the life Christ died to bring us.[6]

There is a contrast between flesh and the Spirit and a connection between the Spirit and life in a discussion after the synagogue sermon at Capernaum. People found what Jesus had said "a hard saying" (6:60), and he responded by telling them that it is the Spirit who gives life, whereas the flesh is unprofitable; his own words are "spirit and they are life" (6:63). The thought is complex. There is surely a contrast between the perverse, fleshly interpretation the Jews were giving Jesus' words and the understanding of them that would come to the person under the convicting work of the Spirit. There is also the thought that no adherence to the letter will bring life, as Jewish teachers seem to have held. "Great is the Law," said the fathers, "for it gives life to them that practice it both in this world and in the world to come" (Mishnah, *Aboth* 6:7). Jesus is not teaching such an adherence to any law; rather, he is emphasizing the freedom of the life the Spirit brings. His words are "spirit" and they are "life," not because they form a new and more authoritative law, but because they are creative: they bring people into touch with the life-giving Holy Spirit. This means not just a striking saying here or there; all his words presume that only the Holy Spirit work produces spiritual life. There is an inseparable connection between life and the Holy Spirit.

THE TIME OF THE SPIRIT

Another of this Gospel's difficult sayings occurs in John's account of

---

[5] It is possible that we should see a reference to the Spirit in the first part of v. 8, where most translators and commentators understand the meaning to be "The wind blows where it wills. . . ." But πνεῦμα is the usual word for "spirit" in the New Testament, and we could translate the clause in this way: "The Spirit breathes where he wills. . . ." It seems to me that "wind" is probably the meaning here, but we should not overlook the possibility that John has both meanings in mind.

[6] E. Schweizer notes that the disciples will do "greater works" than Jesus (14:12) and dismisses the idea that this means miracles like healing (the pagans had stories like that). "For John the supreme miracle is when a person is brought to faith. When that happens a new world dawns, a new kind of life begins . . . it is the Creator-Spirit that summons us into life" (*The Holy Spirit* [London, 1981], 71).

what Jesus said as he taught on the last day of the Feast of Tabernacles. Traditionally the first part of the saying has been understood as in the RSV, "If any one thirst, let him come to me and drink. He who believes in me, as the scripture has said, 'Out of his heart shall flow rivers of living water'" (7:37–38). There is a problem in finding an Old Testament passage that says this, and many these days put the stop after "me" rather than after "drink," as NEB: "'If anyone is thirsty let him come to me; whoever believes in me, let him drink.' As Scripture says. . . ." The words about living water flowing from his heart may then be taken to refer to Christ rather than the believer. Actually not much is gained, because it is more difficult to find an Old Testament passage that speaks of Christ as giving the living water than one that says this of the believer. At least for the latter there are passages that refer to God's blessing in terms of water, with the implication that it be passed on (cf. Isa. 58:11; Ezek. 47:1ff.). While Christ must be seen as the ultimate source, it is also true that the believer passes on the blessing to others, and it appears to be this that Jesus is saying.[7]

But the big problem arises from what John says next. Jesus was speaking of the Spirit, says John, whom those who believe on him would receive, and then he adds words that are variously understood as "Up to that time the Spirit had not been given, since Jesus had not yet been glorified" (NIV and most translations), or "There was no Spirit as yet" (JB; so MOFFATT). Literally John says, "It was not yet Spirit. . . ." The difficulty with JB is that the whole of

Scripture shows that there was a Holy Spirit and that there always had been. The difficulty with "the Spirit had not been given" is twofold: (1) there is no word corresponding to "given" in the Greek text and (2) in fact there are people who were filled with the Spirit in earlier days, such as Elizabeth and Zechariah (Luke 1:41, 67).

We should take seriously the literal meaning of the words. John is saying that "it was not yet Spirit" in the sense in which we see the Spirit as active from the day of Pentecost on. There were manifestations of the Spirit, but in all his fullness the Spirit was not at work and would not be until Jesus was "glorified." In the divine economy the work of the Son preceded that of the Spirit; it was necessary that the atoning sacrifice be offered before the Pentecostal outpouring took place. We are not told why this should be. But clearly this is what happened. There is a little about what the Spirit was doing in the Gospels, but there is a mighty torrent of the Spirit's activity in Acts, and this continues throughout the Epistles.

THE SPIRIT OF TRUTH

In the Upper Room, on the night before the Crucifixion, Jesus gave significant teaching about the Holy Spirit. There are five important passages: 14:16–17; 14:26; 15:26; 16:7–11; 16:12–15. Jesus calls him "the Spirit of truth" (14:17; 15:26; 16:13), a phrase that points to one of the great concepts of this Gospel. John refers to truth often, and he makes it clear that in its deepest sense truth is closely involved with Jesus and what he was doing (14:6). The Spirit then is connected

---

[7]The linguistics appear to be against NEB. Gramatically "his" should refer to "he" not to "me." Further, it is the thirsty who need drink rather than the believing. In this metaphorical sense to believe is to drink.

with the truth of God that we see in the work of Jesus. He is "the Spirit who communicates truth,"[8] the Spirit who brings home to people the truth of the gospel, the truth that is in Jesus.

The Qumran scrolls also have this terminology, when they refer to "the spirits of truth and of error" (1 QS iii 18–19). But this is a striking example of the way identity in terminology goes with fundamental difference in teaching. The men of Qumran thought of "the spirit of truth" as one of two spirits striving within people for the mastery. It would seem that "the spirit of error" is on a par with "the spirit of truth"; there is not the grandeur that John associates with the Holy Spirit. Those who worship the Father are to do so "in truth" (4:23–24), and Jesus is "the truth" (14:6); "the Spirit of truth" thus associates the Spirit with the Father and the Son.

As the Spirit of truth, the Spirit will lead the disciples in (or into)[9] all the truth (16:13). This is not truth as a philosophical concept, but the truth that has been revealed in Jesus; the Spirit will lead them into an ever fuller understanding of what that truth means. It is as the Spirit leads us and not by the way of worldly wisdom that we come to see what the truth of God is. But the Spirit is not making some new revelation of his own that will do away with what Jesus said. Jesus says expressly, "He will not speak of himself, but whatever he hears he will speak"; there is to be no new Spirit-originated revelation. The Spirit will carry on with the teaching Jesus has given.

We should probably understand the words that follow in much the same way: "The things that are to come he will declare to you." We can scarcely take this to mean that the shape of the future will be made clear to Christians, for (1) the words do not necessarily mean this, and (2) through the centuries Christians have been just as puzzled as anyone else as to what lies ahead. Rather the words mean that the Spirit will lead believers to understand what the Christian way means. At the time Jesus spoke there were no Christian theologians who had evolved an understanding of what Christianity means. But through the centuries, the Spirit has been at work in the church and has led the people of God into a fuller understanding of what their faith means.

THE TEACHER OF THE CHURCH

There is quite an emphasis on the teaching function of the Spirit in these discourses. Jesus said that he would teach the disciples "all things" (*panta* [14:26]). This is expanded with the addition of these words: "and bring to your remembrance all the things I told you." Thus, what the Spirit teaches is what has been revealed in Christ. What Jesus taught is not destined to be superseded in due course by some new "dispensation of the Spirit." The Spirit teaches what Jesus taught. The definitive Christian revelation was made in Christ, and, while the full implications of that revelation are yet to be unfolded, it is that revelation and not something else that is the proper subject of Christian teaching.

The Spirit will "testify" of Christ (15:26). The idea of bearing witness is

---

[8] C. K. Barrett, *The Gospel According to St. John* (Philadelphia, 1978), 463.

[9] Some MSS read ἐν and some εἰς. But these two prepositions are not always sharply distinguished in New Testament usage, and we should perhaps not make too much of the difference.

an important one in this Gospel, and it points to something that is given, not a possibility that may well be replaced by something better. When the Spirit "testifies," then, he is pointing people to who Jesus was and what Jesus did. It is significant that Jesus immediately goes on to say, "You, too, testify." The apostles were not required to improve on what their Master had taught them and done for them; they were simply to tell others about it all. But they will do this only as the Spirit guides them.

Jesus says, "[The Spirit] will glorify me, because he will take of mine and declare it to you" (16:14). The Spirit is not there to take attention away from Jesus any more than to modify his teaching. So what he does will bring glory to Christ, and here once more there is the thought that it is the teaching of Jesus and not some novelty that the Spirit will impress on the apostles. This time there is an addition: "All things that the Father has are mine; that is why I told you that he will take of mine and declare it to you" (16:15). Jesus is talking about the things of no one less than God, and these things are not to be trifled with.

THE DIVINE PRESENCE

The Spirit would be with the apostles forever (14:16). Jesus explains that, far from having the Spirit forever, the world cannot even receive the Spirit of truth (14:17); it does not see him, it does not know him. Throughout all of church history, those outside the church have considered Christianity to be folly. It makes no sense to those who are insensible to the promptings of the Spirit of truth. To those who receive him it is another story. Nothing in all this whole wide world can compare to the knowledge of God and the indwelling of the Spirit of God, with the peace and the power and the dynamic that they bring.

"It is expedient for you that I go away," said the Master, "because if I do not go away the Paraclete will not come to you. But if I go away I will send him to you" (16:7). To those with him in the Upper Room this must have been a hard saying. They had left everything— homes, family, friends, and jobs—to be with him.

Now he says that it is better *for them* if he leaves them. He is telling them that his physical presence, while helpful to them during the time of his ministry, was not the best thing for them. Obviously it was limited in time and space, and their need would not always occur when they were physically with him. But the coming of the Spirit was different. That would be a presence that would never be taken away. It was better for them, as it is better for us, that the divine Spirit be permanently present.

This presence is something that belongs to the people of God and to them only. Jesus said plainly of the Spirit that the world not only does not but "cannot" receive him; it neither sees nor knows him (14:17). There are those who are spiritually blind and spiritually ignorant. Lacking sight and knowledge, they cannot, of course, pronounce on the activities of the Spirit. To them this is completely unknown territory. By contrast, Jesus told the apostles that the Spirit would abide with and be in them (14:17). That which the world is unable even to perceive is for them one of God's good gifts. Triumph over evil is not a human achievement; it is the result of the Holy Spirit's work in and on behalf of his people.

CONVICTING THE WORLD

But, though the world does not recognize the Spirit of God, and though most of the work of the Spirit is done within those who are God's, one important work is done in unbelievers. It is the Spirit who "convicts" the world of sin and of righteousness and of judgment (16:8). The verb is used in several senses, but one meaning is clearly "to show to be in the wrong" (e.g., when James speaks of being "convicted by the law" [James 2:9]).[10] Büchsel says that in the New Testament the verb means "to show someone his sin and to summon him to repentance."[11]

It is natural to us all to put the best construction on what we have done. We do not naturally see ourselves as sinners. There are always extenuating circumstances, and we are not really wicked; we were tried beyond measure or caught in a weak moment or overwhelmed by unusual temptations. It takes a work of the Holy Spirit in our hearts for us to see ourselves for what we really are—sinners, people who have broken God's law and are guilty before him, those who must say, "We have left undone what we ought to have done and done what we ought not to have done."

To the statement that the Spirit will convict the world of sin Jesus adds, "of sin, because they do not believe in me" (16:9). This might mean that their sin consists in the fact that they do not believe in Jesus, and, however we take the words, in the last resort the failure to believe is fatal. The words might, however, be understood in the sense that unbelief is an outstanding example of sin, or perhaps that the unbelief shows that the world has completely wrong ideas of what sin in fact is. None of these is impossible. I have written elsewhere that the basic sin is the sin that puts self at the center of things and consequently refuses to believe. This is the world's characteristic sin. It received classic expression when God sent His Son into the world and the world refused to believe in Him. The world is guilty, but it requires the Spirit to bring this home.[12]

The Spirit will also convict the world "of righteousness," because Jesus was going to the Father and the disciples would no longer see him (v. 10). The conviction that arises because of Jesus' departure is clearly connected with what happened on Calvary. The language of justification, with its emphasis on righteousness, is typically Pauline, but this passage shows that Jesus used it during his earthly ministry. In his death, Jesus was fully obedient to the will of God and thus acted in righteousness. And it is this death that enables sinners to stand before God as righteous. But the truth about righteousness is not a human discovery; if we come to know it, it is because the Holy Spirit has done his work of convicting.[13]

The third part of the Spirit's convicting work concerns "judgment, because the ruler of this world has been judged"

---

[10]The verb is ἐλέγχω. *MM* gives examples of its use in the papyri, including one where the participle is used in the sense of "the prosecutor." They see the meaning in the fourth Gospel and specifically in this passage as to "bring to light the true character of a man and his conduct."

[11]*TDNT*, 2:474.

[12]*The Gospel According to John* (Grand Rapids, 1971), 698.

[13]Cf. William Barclay, "When you think of it, it is an amazing thing that men should put their trust for all eternity in a crucified Jewish criminal. What *convinces* men that this crucified Jew is the Son of God? *That is the work of the Holy Spirit.* It is the Holy Spirit who convinces men of the sheer righteousness of Christ" (*The Gospel of John* [Edinburgh, 1956], 2:225).

(v. 11). "The ruler of this world" is, of course, Satan (cf. 12:31), and the Cross meant his overthrow. Much modern writing contains a strong emphasis on the defeat of the Evil One, and this is an important part of the Atonement. But we should not overlook the fact that the Atonement is not simply a work of power. It is a work of judgment. Christ acted in accordance with right, and thus Satan was not simply dethroned because he was not powerful enough to resist God. He was overthrown because that was the right thing. In the Cross, justice was done, but it takes a work of the Holy Spirit before any of us can see that. From this world's point of view the Cross was a miscarriage of justice, the wrongful slaying of an innocent man. But that is only part of what happened there. The Spirit makes it clear to God's people that it was a just judgment that overthrew the Evil One.

THE PARACLETE

In the Upper Room Discourse, Jesus' references to the Spirit use the Greek term *paraklētos*, a word very difficult to translate and accordingly often simply transliterated "Paraclete." It is not the translation of any Hebrew term, and the Jews, in fact, transliterated it, too. Thus, we must look for its meaning in Greek sources.

It means "called to the side of," with the implication that one has called for help. The standard Greek lexicon of Liddell and Scott defines the word in these terms: *"called to one's aid,* in a court of justice: as Subst., *legal assistant, advocate. . . ."* The word could, therefore, denote someone like the counsel for the defense in our modern courts, which is the reasoning behind translations like "Counselor" (RSV), or "Advocate" (NEB). Johannes Behm denies that the word is the technical term for the professional legal person who conducts the defense, but he does agree that it is to be understood "in the light of legal assistance in court, the pleading of another's case."[14] The point is that the word could be used of anyone who helps the accused in court, not only for the professional who leads the defense. But at least we can say that the word is used for someone who helps and that it has a legal background.

In its five occurrences in the New Testament (all in John's writings—four times in the Fourth Gospel and once in 1 John) there is no great emphasis on the legal meaning (other than in 1 John 2:2). Thus, whereas the legal person had the task of instructing the court, the Gospel of John portrays the Paraclete as teaching the apostles (14:26), being with them constantly (14:16), and bearing witness to Jesus (15:26). He is the One who "convicts" the world; that is, he has a prosecuting function, not one on behalf of the defense.

What comes through in all the passages where the Paraclete is mentioned is that he is active in helping people (MOFFATT and GNB translate this word as "Helper"). We may well discern the legal background to the term in that sinners will be in trouble when they are accused in the heavenly court, and it would be true to say that all the assistance the Paraclete provides (teaching and bringing to the apostles' minds what Jesus said, as well as bearing witness to Jesus and convicting the

---

[14] *TDNT*, 5:801. He says, "There is no instance of παράκλητος, like its Lat. equivalent *advocatus*, being used as a tt. for the professional legal adviser or defender of an accused person in the same sense as σύνδικος or συνήγορος," which, he says, is "still the word for a legal advocate in modern Gk." (ibid., 801n.8).

world of sin) is intended to help prepare people for the day when they will meet God. The Spirit is concerned with ultimate issues as well as with those things that matter here and now.

There is a legal background, then, to what the Paraclete does, but no legal term quite covers his work. We can use a term like "Friend" or "Helper," but this fails to draw attention to the legal background. We are reduced to using the transliteration "Paraclete" or else a translation that does not do justice to some aspect of the Spirit's work. But what matters is that we see what the term means, not that we find an English equivalent that draws attention to every aspect of his work.

THE SPIRIT IN THE CHURCH

On the evening following the Resurrection, Jesus met his disciples as they were gathered behind closed doors. Among other things, Jesus breathed on them and said, "Receive [the] Holy Spirit" (20:22). His next words might be understood as "If you forgive the sins of any, they have been forgiven them; if you retain those of any, those have been retained," or "Of whomsoever you forgive the sins they have been forgiven them; of whomsoever you retain [them] they have been retained."[15] There is not a great difference in meaning, and the problem is not here. The problem is rather whether Jesus is conferring on the church the power to forgive people's sins through its authorized ministers. The Roman Catholic Church, for example, sees the power of absolution here and regards the verse as applying to individual priests.

There are difficulties with this view. One is the fact that the verb "breathed" has no object. We must insert one in English, for we cannot say, "He breathed and said. . . ." But we should be clear that there is not a series of breathings on the individuals there gathered; John is speaking about a single expulsion of breath on the company. It is a gift to the disciples as a whole, not to individuals among them.

Then there is the problem of the composition of the group. Those who see the power of absolution do not usually regard it as given to any and every Christian (though R. H. Strachan takes this point of view[16]) but confine it to the priesthood. They believe that only the apostles were present on this occasion. But such a view is scarcely warranted. John is surely describing the same assembly as that in Luke 24:33ff., and that included Cleopas and an unknown companion of his. There may well have been other disciples; we have no warrant for confining the gathering to the apostles.

Further, "any" (or "whomsoever") is plural in both clauses. Jesus is not speaking of individuals but of groups, of classes of people. When the church is led by the Spirit, it will be able to declare authoritatively what are the sins that are forgiven and what are the sins that are not. The declaration is to be made not by the priest to the individual penitent but by the church to the world. It is not unlike the rabbinic "binding" and "loosing" that pointed to forbidden and permitted actions.

We should bear in mind also that the power of retaining sins is on a par with that of forgiving. Bearing in mind human fallibility, it is impossible to

---

[15] The problem is the meaning of ἄν. This could be the conjunction "if" or it could be the suffix "-ever." Most recent translations opt for the former. JB, however, has "for those whose sins you forgive . . . ," taking it the latter way.
[16] R. H. Strachan, *The Fourth Gospel* (London, 1955), 329.

think that God would confer on any person (or group of people) the absolute right to retain sins in the sense of withholding forgiveness. We might perhaps be able to think that when a priest made a mistake and forgave someone he should not have forgiven, God would nevertheless endorse the action. What we cannot think is that when a priest makes a mistake and retains a sin he should have forgiven, God will withhold forgiveness. But in this passage the one goes with the other.

In any case the verbs (according to the best text) are both in the perfect tense. Jesus is saying that when the Spirit-filled church pronounces that such and such sins are forgiven, it will be found that forgiveness has already taken place. He is not giving the church the power to do it then and there. The Spirit enables the church to declare authoritatively what God has done in the matter of forgiving or withholding forgiveness.[17]

John, then, has an exceedingly rich and full amount of teaching about the Holy Spirit, considering the small amount of space he devotes to the subject. The way the gift of the Spirit is related to the glorification of Christ is of the utmost importance and gives us our best insight into why we have so little about the Holy Spirit before the events on the day of Pentecost and so much about him afterwards. In every age, too, it is vital to make clear the central importance and absolute necessity of rebirth by the Spirit. It is a continuing temptation for us to think that we enter eternal life by our own efforts, and we must always be reminded that we no more accomplish our spiritual birth than we do our natural one. The place of the Spirit is given an emphasis in John's Gospel that Christians must never neglect.[18]

---

[17] Some see another reference to the Spirit in the words usually taken as John's way of describing the death of Jesus: "and having bowed his head, he gave up the spirit" (19:30). Most understand the article as equivalent to "his" and see the meaning as that Jesus yielded up his spirit in death. But Hoskyns thinks it possible to take the words as meaning "He handed over the Spirit," words "directed to the faithful believers who stand below." He concludes his discussion by speaking of this interpretation as "not only possible, but necessary" (E. C. Hoskyns in *The Fourth Gospel*, ed. F. N. Davey, [London, 1950], 532). His argument is not convincing, however, and we should see here a reference to the way Jesus died and not to any gift of the Spirit.

[18] We should notice that the most serious split in the Christian church took place at least nominally over the interpretation of "proceeds" in 15:26. The Eastern Church maintains that this means that the Spirit takes his origin from the Father whom it sees as the one "fountain" of deity. The Easterners recite the Nicene Creed using the phrase "proceedeth from the Father," whereas in the West the words are "proceedeth from the Father and the Son." There can be no doubt that the words were inserted into the Creed in the West without proper authority. But that does not mean that the East is right. The point for our present study is that $\pi o \rho \varepsilon \acute{\upsilon} \varepsilon \tau \alpha \iota$ in the verse in question is not describing the eternal relations between the Persons of the Trinity, but referring to the sending of the Spirit into the world after the departure of the Son. The passage is irrelevant to the controversy.

15

the Gospel of John: the Christian life

John is more than a little interested in the way we enter the new life that has been made possible by what God has done in Christ. He is equally interested in what is involved when we set out to live the Christian life. Life is an important category throughout the Johannine writings. The word itself occurs thirty-six times in the Fourth Gospel, thirteen times in the Epistles, and seventeen times in Revelation. The greatest number of times it appears in any non-Johannine book is fourteen in Romans; next is seven times in Matthew.

John also has the verb "to live" seventeen times. It is clear that John is more than usually interested in life as a Christian concept. Seventeen times in his Gospel he speaks of "life eternal," but he does not seem to make a consistent distinction between "life" and "life eternal"; the fuller content given by the adjective makes the Christian life so distinctive that whenever he speaks of it, it is life eternal that he has in mind, whether he uses the adjective or not. And, of course, he has many things to say about the Christian life when he does not use the specific term "life." But it is convenient to begin our discussion with that term.

LIFE ETERNAL

Much is said in the Old Testament about life, but there it is mostly this present life in which the blessing of God is to be enjoyed. Life is connected with prosperity (Deut. 30:15), living for a long time (Ps. 91:16), joy in the presence of God (Ps. 16:11). This last may be understood of more than this life, for the writer goes on to speak of "eternal pleasures at [God's] right hand." Evil people have their reward only in this life (Ps. 17:14), a statement that implies that there is more than this present life. The dead will in due course be raised (Isa. 26:19), some of them to "everlasting life" (Dan. 12:2). This is not a subject that receives a great deal of attention in the Old Testament, but it is there and it is part of the background of the New Testament.

The idea that God's people will be with him in a life that never ends developed among the Jews in the period between the Testaments. People came to think of the age to come in contrast to this age, and "everlasting life" is the life of the age to come, life that will be experienced after the resurrection.

The terminology of the Synoptic Gospels is much the same, except, of course, that they do not use the concept so often. When the lawyer tested Jesus with the question, "What shall I do to inherit life eternal?" (Luke 10:25) and when the rich young ruler put the same question, they had in mind life with God in the age to come. So when Jesus speaks of people who make sacrifices for him as inheriting life eternal (Matt. 19:29), he is speaking of the life to come, not of this present life.

John has this idea, but when he uses the terminology of eternal life, he has more. The word we translate as "eternal" (*aiōnios*) means literally "pertaining to an age [*aiōn*]." Theoretically the age could mean the age before creation or this present age, but in practice the word was used of the age to come. Since that age is the culmination of everything and since it has no end, the word could mean "everlasting"; it is used in this way (e.g., Matt. 18:8; Mark 3:29; Luke 16:9). It may well be that sometimes John has this in mind when he uses the adjective, but it seems that basically he means "life proper to the age to come." He is speaking of the life that others looked for in the coming age as being present now. Here and now believers experience what that life is. They do not need to wait until they pass through death to know what life in this most meaningful sense is.

John has not lost sight of the importance of the end of this age. He has a futurist eschatology, and he records Jesus' statement about people in the tombs hearing the voice of the Son of man and coming out, some "to the resurrection of life," others to "the resurrection of judgment" (5:28–29). So, too, he refers to those Jesus will raise "on the last day" (6:39–40, 44, 54).

But his great thought is that life eternal is a present possession of those who come to Christ. He who hears Jesus' word and believes him who sent him "has life eternal and does not come into condemnation, but he has passed out of death into the life" (5:24). The present tense ("has") is significant; he has it now. So is the perfect ("has passed"); he has already passed right out of death into life, the eternal life. But is it not a matter of quoting this or that passage. Throughout his Gospel, John presupposes that those who have come to believe in Christ no longer live the old life. The Spirit has brought about a new birth within them. Their essential being is "not from the world" just as is the case with Christ (17:16).

This is central for John. Jesus came "that they might have life and have it abundantly" (10:10). Life is not a peripheral interest but the aim of the Incarnation. The Son of man would be "lifted up in order that everyone who believes may have eternal life in him" (3:14–15); "God so loved the world that he gave his only Son, in order that everyone who believes in him should not perish but have life eternal" (3:16). We see it again in the purpose of the writing of this Gospel, so that people might believe and have life in Christ's name (20:31). John leaves his readers in not the slightest doubt about the centrality of life eternal.

John repeatedly associates this life with Christ. In his prologue he tells us that life was "in him," and he goes on to point out that "the light was the life of men" (1:4). The former expression links life with him in the closest possible fashion and prepares us for later statements that he is the life (11:25; 14:6). Life, of course, is in the last resort linked to the one God and Father, but, just as the Father "has life in himself," so he has "given to the Son to have life in himself" (5:26). The Son has the same kind of life as the Father has. People must come to Christ if they would have life (5:40); they must believe in him (3:16, 36; 6:40); they must eat his flesh and drink his blood (6:53–54). Such passages mean that there is no other way to life; life is ineluctably bound up with him.

This thought is emphasized in the discourse about "the bread of life." When Jesus identifies himself with this bread (6:33, 35, 41, 48, 51), he claims a special relationship to life and to the way life is given to people. People should not spend their labor for the food that perishes; they should seek that which the Son of man gives, the food that remains to eternal life (6:27). That this is closely linked with his death comes out in the references to eating his flesh and drinking his blood (6:53, 54, 56, 57, 58). The words are often taken to refer to the Holy Communion, but there are difficulties with this view. The strength of the language is one of these difficulties. Jesus says plainly that unless we eat that flesh and drink that blood, we have no life (6:53). It is impossible to apply these words to any liturgical observance. Flesh and blood, when they are separated, point to death. Jesus is surely saying that the way to life is by appropriating what his death brought about. Our life comes through his death. This is no tiny salvation, for the bread Christ gives is his flesh "for the life of the world" (6:51).

We have seen that the way we appropriate the life he makes available is by faith. It can also be linked with "seeing" the Son of man (6:40), or with his words (6:63, 68). It is his gift (10:28; 17:2). It is also the gift of the Father, who gave his Son so that whoever believes in him may have life eternal (3:16). Or it may be said that whoever believes the Father ("him that

sent me") has life eternal and does not come into judgment (5:24). If we understand the "living water" to point to the Holy Spirit (7:38–39), then life is connected with him, too, for the water that Jesus gives will be in him who receives it "a fountain of water leaping up into life eternal" (4:14; the water Jesus gives is "living water" [v. 10]). We should perhaps notice also the conviction of the Jews that they had life eternal in the Scriptures, a conviction that Jesus did not refute altogether, because he said, "They are they that testify of me" (5:39). The point here is that the Jews certainly associated life with the study of the Bible,[1] but their wooden reverence for the letter prevented them from seeing its true meaning. Had they read it rightly, they would have come to Christ and entered into life.

John has thus a variety of ways of putting the truth that eternal life comes as God's free gift and that it is associated with the work of Christ. Father, Son, or Holy Spirit may be said to be the source of that life and even Scripture comes close. But however it is put, the thought is always that life eternal is the gift of God and further that it comes to us because of Christ's atoning work.

The adjective "eternal" associates it with the world to come, and this is brought out in other ways. Thus we read of the "resurrection of life" into which some of those raised at the last day will come (5:29). This is probably to be understood also in Jesus' words to Martha: "I am the resurrection and the life. He who believes in me, even if he dies, will live, and everyone who lives and believes in me will never die" (11:25–26). In other words, there is a

---

[1] Rabbi Hillel said, "The more study of the Law, the more life . . . if he had gained for himself words of the Law he has gained for himself life in the world to come" (Mishnah, *Aboth* 2:7).

strong eschatological aspect to this life. Jesus is not speaking of a life that has relevance only for the here and now. This is put another way when he says, "He who loves his life loses it, and he who hates his life in this world will keep it to life eternal" (12:25). To concentrate on this world is to lose the next, with all that that means both now and after death.

Sometimes John brings out important truths about life by speaking of its opposite, death. He uses the word "death" eight times—slightly more than any of the other Gospels. He uses it to assure his readers that the believer "has passed out of death into life" (5:24). If anyone keeps Jesus' word, "he will not see death. . . . He will not taste death" (8:51–52). There are also expressions that speak of the death of Jesus (12:33; 18:32) and make it clear that the manner of his death (on a cross) was important. John does not explain why this was important, but it seems clear that the reason is that death on a cross meant the bearing of the curse (Deut. 21:23; cf. Gal. 3:13).[2] It was through the death of Jesus, a death in which he bore the curse that sinners had incurred, that life comes to those who believe.

THE PASSION

Each of the Evangelists has his own way of impressing on his readers the importance of the passion narrative.

John introduces the passion with his long narrative of what happened in the Upper Room on the night before the Crucifixion. The disciples did not know what lay immediately ahead, but Jesus did, and John tells of that evening with this very much in mind.[3] There are twelve chapters of this Gospel devoted to the public ministry of Jesus and then nine to the events surrounding the passion and Resurrection. Indeed, it is possible to reverse those figures as, for example, P. Gardner-Smith does: he regards the account of the raising of Lazarus as the beginning of the Passion narrative. He goes as far as to say, "In a sense the whole Gospel is a passion narrative, for the Fourth Evangelist has the great consummation always in mind."[4]

The Cross is not mentioned in John's prologue, but, as John's Gospel proceeds, the Cross is clearly implied in his speaking of others rejecting Jesus and of the life that Jesus would bring believers. Early in Jesus ministry, John the Baptist speaks of him as "the Lamb of God" (1:29, 36). This expression is not found before this passage and is not altogether clear. It is often understood as a reference to the Passover sacrifice, but against that is the fact that the Passover victim was not necessarily a lamb (sometimes it was a kid); besides, in the usage of the time the sacrifice was referred to simply as "the Passover" (*to pascha*, as in 1 Cor. 5:7). Other suggestions are that "the Lamb of

[2] Cf. Raymond E. Brown: "In Jewish eyes the execution of Jesus on a cross would bring him into disrepute. It was considered the same as hanging (Acts v 30, x 39), and Deut xxi 23 enunciates the principle: 'A hanged man is accursed by God' (see Gal iii 13)" (*The Gospel According to John (XIII–XXI)* [New York, 1970], 851).

[3] C. H. Dodd points out that in the section 13:31–14:31 "the longest passage without direct reference to going and coming is no more than five verses. This dialogue in fact is occupied with the interpretation of the death and resurrection of Christ" (*The Interpretation of the Fourth Gospel* [Cambridge, 1953], 403). And while the "going and coming" theme is not so prominent after 14:31, the Cross is in view throughout. The whole of the Upper Room discourse is clearly designed to bring out the meaning of the Cross.

[4] *Saint John and the Synoptic Gospels* (Cambridge, 1938), 42.

God" may refer to the lamb led to the slaughter (Isa. 53:7), to the Servant of the Lord (Isa. 53), to the gentle lamb (Jer. 11:19), to the triumphant lamb of the apocalypses, to the lamb God provided for Abraham and Isaac (Gen. 22), to the guilt offering (Lev. 14:12ff.), to the scapegoat, and others. There is no shortage of suggestions, but neither is there conclusive evidence of what John had in mind.

However, he says that the Lamb of God "takes away the sin of the world" (1:29), and a lamb that takes away sin must be a sacrificed lamb. The fact that is is impossible to tie down the reference with any exactness but that it is possible to see it as pointing to any one of a number of sacrifices (as the above list shows) perhaps gives us the clue. The expression points to all that the sacrifices were meant to achieve and could not, and assures us that what the sacrifices dimly foreshadowed Christ would perfectly perform. He really would take away sin by his death.

John tells us that at the marriage in Cana of Galilee when Jesus' mother told him there was no wine, Jesus said, among other things: "My hour has not yet come" (2:4). According to the context we may take this to mean no more than "It is not yet time for me to act." But this turns out to be the first in a series of statements that Jesus' "hour" or "time" had not yet come (7:6, 8, 30; 8:20). Then when the Cross is immediately before Jesus, he said, "The hour has come" (12:23, 27; 13:1; 16:32; 17:1). John does not draw attention to the expression, but the sequence is impressive. In a quite unobtrusive way John makes his point that everything was moving to the intended climax. Jesus had come for a purpose, and that purpose was to be seen in the Cross.

There is a well-known problem about the cleansing of the temple. Did it take place twice? Did John move the account from the end of the ministry to the beginning? Did the synoptists move it from the beginning to the end? Such questions need not detain us,[5] but we should notice that John has it early and links it with a prophecy that had to do with the Crucifixion and the Resurrection. The Jews challenged Jesus with this question: "What sign do you show us because you do these things?" to which Jesus replied, "Destroy this temple, and in three days I will raise it" (2:18–19). They took the saying to refer to the destruction of the temple in which they worshiped, but John explains that Jesus was speaking of the temple of his body (v. 21). This discussion is peculiar to John; the synoptists relate a cleansing of the temple, but they have nothing like these words of Jesus.

The meaning of Jesus' reply to the Jews has been the subject of vigorous dispute. Some see in it a reference to the church (the "body of Christ"), others think of the abolition of the sacrifices or the destruction of the physical temple.[6] Such views depend on the supposition that either John had a distorted version of the saying or that he misunderstood it. For our present purpose, the important thing is that John plainly understood the words to refer to Jesus' death and resurrection and that he has put this very early in his Gospel. Again we see that from the beginning the Cross was in view.

There are also references to Jesus' being "lifted up" (3:14; 8:28; 12:32–34). There can be do doubt that John takes the verb to mean "lifted up on a cross," and in the last of the

---

[5] I have discussed the problems in *The Gospel According to John* (Grand Rapids, 1971), 188–96.
[6] See my book *The Gospel According to John*, 198–205.

passages he adds his own explanation: "He said this, signifying by what death he would die" (12:33). But this is not the way the verb was usually used. We see it, for example, in Acts 2:33 of Jesus' exaltation to heaven (it is also used in Phil. 2:9 in a compound form in reference to his exaltation). The very word that the early church used for Jesus' exaltation John uses for his crucifixion.

With this we should take John's concept of glory. He says in the prologue: "We saw his glory, glory as of the only One with the Father, full of grace and truth" (1:14). What was it they saw? They saw the lowly Man from Nazareth, moving among ordinary people in a backwater of the Roman Empire. They saw him teach ordinary people, do some miracles, live uprightly and courageously, and die on a cross. Some suggest that John has in mind the glory revealed at the Transfiguration, but that is to overlook the fact that he does not record this. And it overlooks his profound understanding of glory. For John glory, real glory, is to be seen when someone who could occupy a majestic and exalted place accepts instead a place of lowly service. Supremely is glory to be seen in the Cross, for there One who had no need to die suffered on behalf of others. So when John says that Jesus was "glorified," he often means that he was crucified (7:39; 12:16, 23; 13:31; cf. 21:19). To understand glory as John did is to see the Cross casting its shadow over the whole of the life of Jesus.

Some of the "I am" sayings point us to the Cross. Thus although the bread-of-life sayings (6:35, 48 et al.) in themselves have no necessary connection with death, they acquire it when Jesus goes on to speak of people eating his flesh and drinking his blood (6:51,

53ff.). Life comes from appropriating his death. So with the Good Shepherd (10:11, 14). The essence of his activity is that "the Good Shepherd lays down his life for the sheep." We perhaps discern something of the same in the saying "I am the resurrection and the life" (11:25), though some argue that it is the resurrection and the life of the believer to which the words refer. But what cannot be denied is that consistently in this Gospel it is the death of Jesus that brings life to the believer.

John makes it clear that the salvation Jesus died to bring has a universal scope. Jesus is "the Savior of the world" (4:42; the expression is found again in 1 John 4:14 and nowhere else in the New Testament). This does not mean that everyone in the world will necessarily be saved, but it does mean that the salvation Christ brings is no parochial deliverance, but is available for people everywhere, no matter what their race or nation. It is significant that the words were spoken by new Samaritan believers; they formed the firstfruits of the extension of salvation beyond the Jews. Their statement is not isolated. God sent his Son so that the world might be saved through him (3:17), and Jesus gave his flesh "on behalf of the life of the world" (6:51). Jesus looked beyond the flock of Israel for his sheep (10:15–16). When Caiaphas gave his cynical advice that one man should die rather than that the nation perish (11:50), John interpreted this to mean that Jesus would die, not only for the nation, but also "so that he might gather into one God's children that were scattered abroad" (v. 52). Jesus saw that the purpose of his being "lifted up" was to draw "all men" to himself (12:32). And the reference to "all flesh" in Jesus' prayer in the Upper Room (17:2) is probably to be understood as another indication that his concern extended to all mankind.

There are extensive indications of hostility to Jesus—for example, in chapters 7 and 8. Here John appears to have concentrated his account of the kind of opposition Jesus encountered throughout his ministry. He introduces this section of his Gospel by telling his readers that the Jews were trying to kill Jesus (7:1), a theme that is repeated (7:19, 20, 25; 8:37, 40; cf. 5:18); there were attempts to arrest him (7:30, 32, 44; cf. also 11:57) and to stone him (8:59; cf. 10:31). None of these attempts was successful. John is insistent that they took place before Jesus' "hour" had come, and until then he was quite "safe." But they show that in this world the Son of God was not welcome and so reveal the atmosphere of hostility. They are part of the way John makes the point that in the end the death of Jesus was inevitable.

I said above that John interpreted some words of Caiaphas in a universal sense. It is worth looking at those words more closely. The high priestly party and the Pharisees agreed that after the raising of Lazarus there was danger for them. Everyone would believe in Jesus, they thought, if he continued to do his "signs," and this would provoke the Romans to take action to remove what liberties they enjoyed. But they went no further than grumbling about it. Caiaphas rudely told them that they were ignorant ("You don't know nothing," he said, with an emphatic double negative— wholly proper in Greek) and went on, "Nor do you work it out that it is expedient that one man should die instead of the people and that the whole nation should not perish" (11:49–50). This was sheer political expediency: it did not matter whether the man was innocent or not. "Let us kill him so that the rest of us do not perish" is the thought. But John

records the words because he saw a deeper truth in them. As high priest, Caiaphas was prophesying. God had him utter the words because they were true, but true in a very different sense from that intended by Caiaphas. Jesus would die "instead of [or, in place of] the people"; John adds that this meant not the Jewish nation alone, but all "the scattered children of God." The words of Caiaphas point to substitution. Jesus was to die *hyper* the people; he was to be in their stead so that they were to be delivered. This is an important indication of how John understood the Atonement.

In chapter 12, John draws his account of Jesus' public ministry to a close and makes some important statements that lead in to his account of the passion. Some Greeks came to Philip asking to see Jesus, and presently Philip and Andrew brought them to Jesus. John says nothing more about them, but clearly Jesus saw their coming as significant, for immediately he said, "The hour has come" (12:23). The presence of these Greeks turned Jesus' thoughts to the death he would die to bring sinners to God. He does not see his death as defeat but as triumph, for he speaks of being "glorified." He goes on to point out that a grain of wheat remains as it is unless it falls into the ground and dies. Only when it "dies" (i.e., ceases to exist as a grain) does it produce fruit. This points to a general truth about fruitfulness. The person who loves his life loses it, and only the one who loses it in this world keeps it for life eternal (12:24–25). Jesus looks at the possibility of praying, "Father, save me from this hour" (the Johannine equivalent of Gethsemane?) and rejects it, praying instead that the Father's name be glorified (12:27–28). This leads on to the passage about Jesus being "lifted up."

All this shows us plainly that the thought that Jesus would die to bring salvation runs right through this Gospel. It is not that John thinks of a teacher who suddenly lost popularity and contrary to all expectation was handed over by his own people to the Romans and put to death. He sees that the Cross was before Jesus from the very first. He came to die for others.

His account of the actual Passion is individual. He has much in common with the synoptists, but he puts his own stamp on it all. He puts some emphasis on the fact that the will of God was done and, for example, shows Jesus as master of the situation. When the posse came to arrest him, Jesus ("knowing all the things that were coming upon him" [18:4]) made no attempt to hide or escape but went out to meet the soldiers. He asked them, "Who are you looking for?" and twice made them say that they wanted "Jesus of Nazareth" (18:5, 7), and this meant that the disciples were free. His care for them at this difficult hour is significant. So is the majesty with which he met the enemy with the emphatic "I am," the language of deity. The result was that they went backward and fell to the ground (18:6). Jesus is not a helpless fugitive, hounded to death by a too-powerful enemy. He goes forward to his "hour" and faithfully fulfills the will of God. We speak of his "arrest," but in John this is not strictly accurate. The soldiers do not "arrest" Jesus; Jesus gives himself up.

John omits the account of the agony in Gethsemane. It has been conjectured that he wished to concentrate on Jesus' mastery of the situation at this point and that the agony might have been misunderstood. At any rate, he has already given his equivalent in the questioning in 12:27ff., following as it does on his meditation on the grain of wheat falling into the ground and dying. He has depicted Jesus' lowliness throughout his Gospel, and it may be that he does not wish to concentrate it in one incident. Whatever his reason, he omits the agony, and thus we see from another angle that John relates the facts in his own way.

John gives a number of details that are absent from the other accounts. It is only he who tells us that Jesus was first taken before Annas and that when he was taken out to be crucified, he carried his cross. We owe to John the information that the inscription on the cross was in three languages and that the Jews queried the wording. He has three of Jesus' "words" from the cross that are not found elsewhere—his words to Mary: "Behold, your son"; those to the beloved disciple: "Behold, your mother" (19:26–27); and those words of final triumph: "It is finished" (19:30). He alone tells us of the piercing of Jesus' side and of the part Nicodemus played in the burial.

One of John's most significant contributions is what he tells us about the trial before Pilate. It is clear from all the Gospels that Jesus' trial was in two stages: the proceedings before the Jewish authorities and those before Pilate. John has little to say about what took place before Caiaphas but a great deal about what happened when Jesus was brought to Pilate.

With great dramatic power John portrays the confrontation between Christ and Pilate, the representatives of God and of Caesar. All the other actors fall into the background—Annas, Caiaphas, the soldiers, impulsive Peter and his companions, and the Jerusalem mob—and we are left with Jesus and Pilate talking about kingship (18:33–38). With the mob in the background, there is perhaps a hint that the state is swayed by forces that we do not see, but the basic thing John is telling us is that in the last resort it is either Christ or Caesar who rules. Christ is king, but not as Caesar understands the term; he is king in that he bears witness to the truth (18:37). But Pilate did not even understand what truth is (v. 38).

It is truth that is important, not power. Pilate declared three times that Jesus was innocent (18:38; 19:4, 6). But the Jews raised the question of "Caesar's friend" (19:12), bringing a not-too-subtle pressure to bear on Pilate's decision. That was their use of power. And Pilate succumbed. He gave the word for Jesus to be put to death. That was his use of power. Power corrupts.

But the truth of God is not defeated. The Resurrection brings out John's point that real sovereignty is with God, not with the grubby purveyors of earthly power. Judas had done his bit, as had Annas and Caiaphas and their companions who had kept themselves undefiled so that they might take their part in the feast. The mob might have called for Jesus' release but instead were pulled this way and that by the high priests so that they called for Barabbas to be released and, concerning Jesus, yelled "Crucify!" The soldiers were vastly amused by the comedians among them who devised ways of mocking a helpless prisoner. And there was Pilate, who wanted to do what was right, but not if it inconvenienced him. It was an astonishing conglomeration of people who were not particularly evil, but who could say, "We have no king but Caesar" (19:15). Their confession was true in a deeper sense than they realized. John vividly makes these points: in the end there is no king other than Christ or Caesar and that, despite the delusions of worldly people, in the end it is Christ who is supreme.

FAITH

So John makes it clear that life comes through death, eternal life for the people of God through the death of the Son of God. How do people appropriate that gift of God? John's answer is, "Through believing."

John uses the verb "to believe" (*pisteuein*) ninety-eight times—a very large number in a book of twenty-one chapters. He never uses the corresponding noun "faith," a fact that has never been satisfactorily explained. Perhaps the point is that the verb is more dynamic than the noun. It is convenient for us to use the word "faith," since it occupies such a large place in the Christian understanding of things, but we should bear in mind John's terminology.

John uses this verb in four ways. His most frequent construction is to use it with the preposition "into" (*eis*); the phrase is then normally translated "believe in [or on]" and may be meant to convey something of the meaning of coming to be "in Christ," to use the Pauline phrase.[7] Bultmann sees a reference to the missionary preaching of the early church, whereby a believer was "converted from (Jewish or) pagan belief to Chr. faith."[8] We are to see faith, as John understood it, as a wholehearted commitment so that the believer became one with Christ and came to be within Christ. John says a

---

[7] J. H. Moulton says that "εἰς recalls at once the bringing of the soul *into* that mystical union which Paul loved to express by ἐν χριστῷ" (*A Grammar of New Testament Greek,* i, *Prolegomena* [Edinburgh, 1906], 68). He does not see much difference between πιστεύειν εἰς and πιστεύειν ἐπί but stresses the difference between both and the dative.

[8] *TDNT,* 6:204.

good deal about "abiding in" Christ (15:4 et al.), and it is this state into which believing introduces us. John does not explicitly connect the concepts of believing and abiding, though he sometimes comes close to doing so (12:46).

The "believe in" construction is occasionally used of believing in God (14:1; so also 12:44), but in the overwhelming majority of cases it refers to believing in Jesus. Sometimes John has the expression "believe in the name [of Jesus]," in which "name" stands for the whole person (2:23), and there are references to believing in the Son (3:36), in the Son of man (9:35), in Jesus (12:11), "in him" (e.g., 3:16), "in me" (e.g., 6:35), and in the light (12:36). Plainly the construction is a way of bringing out the importance of trust in Jesus, and this may be done from any one of a number of angles.

It is often said that faith means trust in a person, not an intellectual adherence to a set of propositions. There is truth in this, of course, and the frequent references to believing in Christ certainly brings it out. But there is an intellectual content in faith, and we do not grasp what John is saying unless we see that. Thus Peter spoke of believing that Jesus is "God's Holy One" (6:69); this, taken along with the truth that Jesus had "words of life eternal," made it unthinkable that the apostles should cease to follow Jesus. Martha declared her belief that Jesus was the Christ (11:27), and John's whole book was written so that people would come to believe this (20:31). Several times Jesus used this construction. People should believe "that I am" (8:24; 13:19), where the overtones of divinity should not be missed.[9] Jesus' relationship to

the Father is involved in other uses. "Believe me that I am in the Father and the Father is in me," Jesus said (14:11). The disciples were commended for believing that he came out from God (16:27; cf. 16:30). Faith that the Father sent Jesus is mentioned a number of times (11:42; 17:8, 21). Faith as John understood it means more than trusting Jesus as a good teacher and a good man. It involves the acceptance of certain truths about his person. We cannot really believe unless we see him as he is.

The construction with the dative means to accept as true, to give credence to someone. John uses this of God (5:24); it is important to believe what he has said. Characteristically he uses it also of Christ (e.g., 4:21; 8:45–46). It may refer to Christ's word (4:50) or his words (5:47) or his works (10:38); they are all bound up with his person. And, of course, people are expected to believe Scripture (2:22), which may be particularized with the author's name, such as Moses (5:46–47) or Isaiah (12:38).

Believing is highly important to John; he used the verb so often that he could use it absolutely, simply speaking of "believing"; it is not necessary to say always in whom one believes (e.g., 1:50; 4:41). John's thirty examples of this construction make it plain that for him believing is of great importance.

But we should not think that each of these constructions is so distinctive that the use of one excludes the others. If we understand faith as John did, it is plain that it does not matter greatly how we express it; all that faith involves is implied. If we really trust in Christ, then, of course we accept what he says

---

[9]Cf. R. Schnackenburg: "It is the Old Testament revelation formula which the Johannine Jesus, as the revealer of the New Testament, claims for himself. In him, he is saying, God is present to reveal his eschatological salvation and offer it to men" (*The Gospel According to St John* [New York, 1982], 2:200).

as true, we also accept certain truths about his person and his relationship to the Father, we believe the Father and the revelation made in Scripture, and all this is so fundamental that it can simply be said that we believe. We see this in passages where more than one of the constructions is used. Thus, Jesus asked the man born blind, "Do you believe in the Son of man?" and a little later the man said, "I believe" (9:35–38). Again we read, "He who believes on him . . . he who does not believe . . ." (3:18), and in this juxtaposition of statements, it is impossible to put a difference of meaning between the two constructions. So also John wrote his Gospel that we "may believe that Jesus is the Christ, the Son of God, and that believing [we] may have life . . ." (20:31). Here we cannot put a difference between "believing that" and "believing." But wherever and however it is expressed, the important thing is that we believe.[10]

LOVE

The basic truth is that God loved the world so much that he gave his Son to bring salvation (3:16). It is clear that in this statement in John 3:16 sinners are in mind. John is not talking about a love drawn out from God by outstanding human merit or attractiveness. The wonderful thing about God's love is that it is poured out on those who have no merit and are undeserving. And it is a costly love. It meant the Cross. It is in this spirit that Jesus told the disciples that he did not say that he would pray for them, "for," he said, "the Father himself loves you" (16:27).[11] Indeed, in his great high-priestly prayer, Jesus said to the Father, "You loved them as you loved me" (17:23). It is with a very great love indeed that the Father loves us, a love determined by his loving nature, not by any merit of ours. He does love those who love Jesus and obey him (14:21, 23), but the foregoing passages show that this is not to be understood as a love for the deserving. The student of this Gospel should be in no doubt about the greatness of God's love or about the fact that it is lavished on us irrespective of our deserving.

John often speaks of the love of the Father for the Son (e.g., 3:35; 5:20; 10:17), and clearly this is one of the great truths that underlie this Gospel. In Jesus we see not only a heavenly visitant, but the Son on whom God's love rests in all its fullness. The love of the Son for the Father is everywhere presupposed, but it comes to expression only once, when Jesus speaks of the world knowing that he loves the Father (14:31).

His love for people is spoken of more often. To die for one's friends as Jesus did is to show a love greater than any other (15:13). He loved them intensely. The cross shows that, as does also the fact that he loved them as the Father loved him (15:9), and that he loved them "utterly" (13:1; the expression could also mean "to the end"; in the Johannine manner, both meanings may be intended, but it is on the quality of the love that the emphasis

---

[10] Occasionally we find other constructions with the verb, such as the accusative (11:26), $\pi\epsilon\rho\acute{\iota}$ "about" (9:18), and perhaps $\dot{\epsilon}\nu$ (3:15), though this latter is better taken as an example of the absolute use, with $\dot{\epsilon}\nu$ going with $\ddot{\epsilon}\chi\eta$.

[11] His verb here is $\theta\iota\lambda\acute{\epsilon}\omega$, whereas it is $\dot{\alpha}\gamma\alpha\pi\acute{\alpha}\omega$ in 3:16. Some see a marked difference between the two verbs, especially in Jesus' conversation with Peter by the lakeside (21:15–17). But it is impossible to find a clear distinction in the way John uses the two verbs over all, and it is better to see no more than a stylistic variation.

falls). Jesus exhorts his followers to "abide" in his love (15:9–10). Nothing, of course, can stop him from loving us, but we can so live as to hinder the operation of that love. By keeping his commandments we foster the closeness of the fellowship. John often tells us that Jesus loved the disciples as a group (13:34; 15:9), and sometimes he mentions Jesus' love for individuals, for example, for Martha and for Mary and for Lazarus (11:5; Lazarus is also identified to Jesus as "he whom you love" [v. 3]). And, of course, there are references to "the disciple whom Jesus loved" (13:23; 19:26; 20:2; 21:7, 20).

The love of God and Christ for us invites an answering love. Jesus speaks of those who love him (14:15, 23, 28; 16:27), often linking the keeping of his commandments with this love. Clearly if we really love Christ, we will want to do the things that are pleasing to him, whereas if we consistently disregard his directions, doubt is cast on the reality of our love (cf. 14:24). Jesus gave his disciples what he called "a new commandment": "that you love one another as I have loved you" (13:34; cf. 15:12, 17). There is a very old commandment that believers love one another (Lev. 19:18), so it is not love in itself that is new. What is new is that we are to love as Christ has loved us, and his is a love that gives and gives—and that for unworthy people. He loves because he is a loving Person, not because of attractiveness in the beloved. And the more we have absorbed the love of God in Christ for our unworthy selves, the more we will respond by becoming loving people. It is this kind of love that will enable people to know that we are disciples of Jesus (13:35).

The importance of love is seen in the threefold question that Jesus put to Peter (21:15–17). Peter had three times denied that he knew Jesus, and his place of leadership in the group must have been called into question. His threefold affirmation of his love for the Lord, coupled with Jesus' threefold commissioning of Peter to feed the flock, surely restored him to his place. It is interesting that in such a situation Jesus did not ask him about his courage or his resourcefulness or his readiness to give good leadership. He asked him about his love, and only about his love. There is nothing more important in the Christian's life than love.

John sometimes refers to lesser loves that people have. He speaks of some who loved darkness rather than light (3:19), and of those who loved the praise of men (12:43). He reminds us that the world loves its own (15:19) and warns that anyone who loves his life will lose it (12:25; the present tense points to the truth that the very fact of loving this life means losing it).

SIN

John's interest in such topics as the Incarnation, eternal life, faith, and love is very obvious, and some students go on from there to say that he had little interest in sin. It comes thus as something of a surprise to find that he has the word *hamartia,* "sin," seventeen times, which is the same number as in 1 John and more than is found in any other book except Romans (forty-eight times) and Hebrews (twenty-five times). For John sin is an important concept. Quite early he records the words of the Baptist: "Look, the Lamb of God who takes away the sin of the world" (1:29), and toward the end of his book he records Jesus' saying about the forgiveness of sin (20:23). The eternal life that means so much to him can be thought of in terms of the forgiveness of sin.

Sin is a very serious matter. Jesus said to the man he had just cured of lameness that had lasted thirty-eight years: "Sin no longer, lest something worse happen to you" (5:14). Several times Jesus referred to people "dying in sin [or sins]" (8:21, 24), obviously a horror that is all the worse for not being defined. He spoke of the sinner as "sin's slave" (8:34). Not all sins are on the same level, for Jesus said that the one who delivered him up to Pilate had "a greater sin" than that of Pilate (19:11). This does not mean that Pilate did not sin in the matter. The term "greater sin" implies that there is "lesser sin"; Jesus was not saying that Pilate was guiltless. All sin is a dreadful evil, but the nation that had the word of God and still delivered up the Son of God to be killed was committing a particularly dreadful sin.

Jesus rejected some erroneous ideas of sin. Thus, John tells us of an occasion when, confronted with a man blind from birth, the disciples asked Jesus, "Who sinned, this man or his parents, that he should be born blind?" (9:2). They were asking their question in view of a Jewish conviction expressed neatly by R. Ammi: "There is no death without sin, and there is no suffering without iniquity."[12]

It was not easy to see how a person could, before he was born, sin so terribly that his punishment was lifelong blindness. Nor was it any less difficult to see how a sin of his parents, no matter how dreadful it was, should result in the lifelong punishment, not of them, but of their son. The rabbis

did not find such problems completely insurmountable,[13] but the disciples found it difficult to account for the man's blindness. Jesus told them that sin was not responsible for the man's plight. His statement must have brought a deep feeling of relief to people accustomed to thinking that all suffering was due to prior sin.

At the end of that incident there is an important teaching about sin. Jesus spoke of his coming into the world for judgment, "so that those who do not see might see and those who see might become blind" (9:39). The statement about giving sight, whether physical or spiritual, is not difficult to understand, but the statement that follows is difficult. Probably Jesus meant that his coming shows up people like the Pharisees who claimed to have sight but were spiritually blind: now they were seen for the blind men they were. These Pharisees asked, "Are *we* blind, too?" to which Jesus replied, "If you were blind, you would not have sin; but now you say, 'We see'; your sin remains" (9:41). They claimed spiritual sight but acted like blind men. That was their sin.

The coming of Jesus brought out the sin of the world that opposed him. In the Upper Room Jesus told his followers that the people in question would not have "had" sin had he not come and taught them. But as it was they had no excuse for their sin (15:22). He had a similar saying about his works. They had seen what he did and still rejected him; that means they had seen and hated both Jesus and the Father (15:24).

---

[12] Talmud, *Shab.* 55a.

[13] They held that a baby could sin while still in the womb, a view based on Genesis 25:22 (see *SBK*, 2:528–29). There is some evidence of a view that the soul is preexistent (Wisdom 8:20), and it was thought that it could sin then. But such views do not seem to have been widely held. On occasion children were believed to have been born leprous or epileptic on account of parental sin (*SBK*, 2:529). The death of a young scholar was put down to his mother's idolatry while she had been pregnant with him (Ruth R. VI. 4).

It is the rejection of what God was doing in Christ that shows people to be sinners. Even religious people opposed Jesus and thus opposed God, yet they had no consciousness of doing wrong. It takes the work of the Holy Spirit within us to make us conscious of our sinfulness (16:8), but if people reject the work of the Spirit within them, they cannot know their sin. That sin is connected with failure to believe in Jesus (16:9).

John mostly has the word "sin" in the singular—that is, not so much individual acts of evil, but the principle that moves one to a wrong course. It is that that is our basic problem, and "the Lamb of God" in his sacrificial death puts away that sin (as well, of course, as the individual sins people do). The people of the day, and especially the religious people of the day, may have been conscious of the fact that now and then they did wrong things. But they did not realize their innate sinfulness, nor did they know that that sinfulness led them into sin and made them sin's slaves. John saw this clearly and he saw equally clearly that Jesus provided the answer to the human plight. Jesus took away the sin of the world.

THE WORLD

John has a great deal to say about "the world." He uses the word *kosmos*, "world," seventy-eight times, whereas no non-Johannine writing has it more often than twenty-one times (1 Corinthians; 1 John has it twenty-three times). The concept of "the world" in John's writing is important for our understanding of what Jesus came to do.

The term basically means something like "order" (LSJ), from which it came to be used of an ornament, a decoration (as in 1 Pet. 3:3). But the ancients found no ornament, no jewel that could rival this universe in which we live, with all its order and beauty. So *the* ornament, *the* jewel, is the *kosmos*. We see this usage in the prayer of Jesus when he referred to the glory he had with the Father "before the world was" (17:5; cf. v. 24; 21:25 et al.). But as people see it, the most significant part of the universe is this part in which we live, so the term came to be used of this earth. The Word was "in the world" (1:10); Jesus came out from the Father and "came into the world" (16:28). Such usages are quite natural and scarcely call for comment.

In a further natural development the term is used for what is most significant for dwellers on earth: the inhabitants of earth themselves. Thus Jesus speaks of himself as "the light of the world" (8:12; 9:5) and refers to the judgment of the world (12:47). The Pharisees said despairingly, "Look, the world has gone off after him" (12:19).

But the world in this sense is not homogeneous. Some people in the world respond favorably to the message of Jesus, and some do not. The term is sometimes used with reference to those who do so respond, though this is not common. Jesus is called "the Savior of the world" (4:42); he says that he came to save the world (3:17; 12:47). He is "the Lamb of God who takes away the sins of the world" (1:29). Behind this work of salvation is the love of God, for "God so loved the world that he gave his only Son, so that every one who believes in him should not perish but have life eternal" (3:16). Christ "gives life to the world" (6:33, 51). Such passages do not mean that every individual in the world will be saved, but they point to the universal scope of the salvation Jesus brings. It is not confined to the Jews or any other nation nor to the pious or the intellectuals or the rich or the poor or any restricted group. It is a salvation that is open to all, whoever they may be. This is an important part of our understanding of John's view of what Christ has done.

Most commonly, however, John sees the world as opposed to Christ and Christ's people. In the Upper Room Judas (not Iscariot) wondered how Jesus would manifest himself to them "and not to the world" (14:22). The two groups of people are distinct. This is brought out also when Jesus distinguished himself from "the Jews" by saying, "You are from below, I am from above; you are of this world, I am not of this world" (8:23). His essential being is heavenly; it does not belong to this world as does that of his adversaries. The distinction between being "of this world" and not being of it is thus much the same as being "from below" and being "from above." Jesus repeated the distinction and linked the disciples with himself (17:14, 16). From another angle Christ's kingdom is not of this world (18:36). He is supreme as king, but that does not mean he had the same kind of sovereignty as Pilate. His whole aim and outlook was different.

The disciples were given to Jesus "out of the world" (17:6), and their nonworldly being means that the world hated them. Jesus said to his unbelieving brothers, "The world cannot hate you." By contrast, it did hate him because he testified of it that "its works were evil" (7:7). There is bound to be opposition between the world that loves its evil and those who belong to God and who therefore oppose that evil. If the disciples had been "of the world," the world would have loved them, but Jesus had chosen them "out of the world" and this incurred the world's hatred (15:19). But the world hated Jesus before it hated them (15:18); it is not surprising that the hatred it had for the Master passed over to the disciples. The world hated them because they did not belong to it (17:14). It rejoiced when they were grieved (16:20).

The opposition of the world is seen at the very beginning of this Gospel, for in the prologue we read that the *Logos* was in the world, the world that was made through him, "and the world did not know him" (1:10). The light came into the world, and men loved darkness rather than light because of the evil they did (3:19). The world did not know God (17:25). This is not surprising, for Satan is its ruler (12:31; 14:30; 16:11). The world cannot receive the Spirit of truth (14:17), though that Spirit convicts it of sin and of righteousness and of judgment (16:8).

All of this leads to the thought that the world is still the object of God's love (cf. 3:16). The Father sent the Son into the world (10:36; 17:18; cf. Martha's words: "he who comes into the world" [11:27]). Jesus spoke to the world (8:26; 17:13; 18:20), thus indicating a readiness to teach those who would listen. And he prayed, not for the world as such (how could he possibly pray that the world continue in its worldliness?), but that the world might believe and might know that the Father sent him (17:21, 23). And, although Jesus did not pray for the world (17:9), he did not pray either that the disciples should be taken from the world (17:15). They had a role there, and just as the Father sent the Son into the world, so the Son sent them into the world (17:18). That role is not spelled out, but from this whole Gospel it is clear that they were to live for God and proclaim the message Jesus had given them so as to win people for God.

With the Cross in immediate prospect, and with the tiny band of disciples about to forsake him and flee, Jesus could say, "I have overcome the world" (16:33). The world did its worst to him, and it would continue to bring troubles to his people (16:33). But the victory is not with the world. It is with Christ, and this is for John the significant truth. Let not his readers be despondent or mistaken. It is Jesus who has overcome.

LIGHT

The conflict between light and darkness is a natural piece of symbolism and is found in many religions. John wrote of the *Logos* as creating all things and added, "In him was life, and the life was the light of men" (1:4). This probably refers to Old Testament passages linking life and light with God, for example: "With you is the fountain of life; in your light we see light" (Ps. 36:9). The light and the life the Jews saw in God John sees in the *Logos*. Whoever follows him will have "the light of life" (8:12). Without him we are in darkness, but he brings the light that illuminates all of life.

"The light shines in the darkness," John wrote, "and the darkness did not overcome it" (1:5). It is precisely the function of light to shine in the darkness. There is no point in striking a match for illumination in broad daylight, whereas in the dead of night even a small source of light gives welcome illumination. The people of God are sent to shine in the darkness. It is easier and more pleasant to add our little quota of light to the light that like-minded people are shedding. But the darkness of the world needs illumination. That, John says, is what it received when Jesus came. The light keeps shining, and the darkness does not defeat it.[14]

John keeps hammering away at his major theme that in Jesus we see the Son of God who was sent into the world to bring us salvation at the cost of his life. He sees this in terms of light and darkness. The *Logos*, he says, "was the true light who gives light to every man" and he was "coming into the world" (1:9). "The light has come into the world," says Jesus (3:19), and again, "Yet a little while the light is among you" (12:35). He said, "I am the light of the world" (8:12; 9:5), and again, "I have come, a light, into the world" (12:46). All such sayings reveal that the world's illumination is to be found in Jesus, with the opposite always implied and sometimes stated: that to reject Jesus is to reject the light and to grope in darkness.

John the Baptist was one who knew the light for what it was. He was sent from God in order to bear witness about the light (1:6–7). John was not himself the light (1:8), but came to bear witness to it. His contemporaries had a dim perception of what was going on, for they were willing to rejoice for a little time in his light (5:35). But by and large they came under condemnation for loving darkness rather than light because of the evil of their deeds (3:19). Their doing wrong meant that they hated the

---

[14] The NIV has "the darkness has not understood it" (cf. KJV). The verb καταλαμβάνω has the idea of holding on to something so that it becomes one's own, and this can on occasion be used of mental perception. The translation can thus be defended. But darkness does not try to understand light; the two are rather in continual opposition. A less common meaning of the verb is "overcome," and this seems to be the meaning here. John is picturing the conflict and saying that darkness did not win. The aorist tense perhaps refers to the single event of the climax of the conflict at Calvary. But even there darkness was not the winner.

light and did not come to it lest their deeds be exposed for what they were (3:20). Like men walking in the dark, they stumbled because the light was not in them (11:10). Notice the change of imagery: Jesus talked about light as something within us, not an external aid. It is, of course, both; everything depends on which point is being emphasized. Passages like these give a strong condemnation of the evil thing that darkness is.

But there are those who, like the Baptist, respond to the light. They "do the truth" and come to the light (3:21); they walk as they have light, and the darkness does not overtake them (12:35). They believe in the light (this makes it clear that the light is closely connected with Jesus), so that they may become "sons of light" (12:36). Clearly John sees the concept of light as an important way of viewing Christ and his salvation.

TRUTH

The concept of truth in Greek writings generally is very much like our own. Truth is a quality of speech (truth as opposed to falsehood), or it is a quality of being (truth as opposed to mere appearance). But the concept is richer and more varied in the Old Testament; for example, God can be called "the God of truth" (Ps. 31:5; Isa. 65:16). We know ultimate truth only as we know God. This has consequences for who we are and the way we live. The psalmist refers to speaking the truth not only with the lips but also in the heart (Ps. 15:2); he "walks" (i.e., lives) in the truth of God (Ps. 26:3). "O LORD, do not your eyes look for truth?" asked Jeremiah (Jer. 5:3). There are many more references to truth; in the Old Testament truth is a rich and full concept.

The New Testament writers had this Old Testament concept as their background, and they too saw truth as having a wide meaning. As in the Old Testament, so in John truth is associated with God, whose word "is truth" (17:17). Those who worship a God like this must worship "in spirit and truth" (4:23–24).

Truth is especially associated with Jesus. Jesus assured Pilate in the most solemn terms that truth was his basic concern: "For this reason was I born and for this reason I came into the world that I might bear witness to the truth" (18:37). The *Logos* is "full of grace and truth" (1:14) and further "grace and truth were through Jesus Christ" (1:17). Notice the link with grace. John does not use the word "grace" in his Gospel after the prologue, but it is to be understood along with truth, and "truth" he uses often. It seems that the truth that is associated so strongly with Christ brings salvation. Grace and truth come to people only because Christ brings them.

Pilate asked the question, "What is truth?" (18:38) at a very significant point in this Gospel. Jesus was before him, the disciples had fled, the Jewish leaders had handed him over, the governor had to make his decision. He had spoken to Jesus about being king and Jesus told him that the whole reason for his coming to this earth was connected with truth. Well, what is truth? John gives no answer in words, not from Jesus nor Pilate nor anyone else. But there is an answer in deeds, for John goes on immediately to his account of the Crucifixion. "There can only be one meaning of $\dot{\alpha}\lambda\acute{\eta}\theta\epsilon\iota\alpha$ in the Fourth Gospel: it is the truth about the death and resurrection of Jesus, to which witness is borne in 16:7 and 17:19. This is in accordance with the whole theology of the Fourth Gospel, the central point of which is the 'lifting-up' of Jesus."[15]

So it is that Jesus could say, "I am . . . the Truth" (14:6). In this full sense, truth is not something apart from Jesus such that he can point people away from himself to the truth. Rather, in the deepest sense of the word, he *is* the truth. Constantly he spoke the truth (8:40, 45–46; 16:7). In this Gospel the one thing John the Baptist did was bear witness to Jesus, and this is described as bearing witness to the truth (5:33). Perhaps we can see this also when the devil, the opposition to Jesus, is said not to take his stance in the truth, because the truth is not in him (8:44). As John sees it, there cannot be the slightest doubt that ultimate truth is attainable through Jesus, and only through Jesus.

Sometimes Jesus spoke of "the Spirit of truth" (14:17; 15:26; 16:13), one of whose functions is to lead Jesus' followers "in" or "into" all the truth (16:13). Truth has its application to them. Those who "abide" in Jesus' teaching, those who are truly his disciples, know the truth, and the truth sets them free (8:32). Jesus was not speaking primarily of intellectual freedom, though there is a sense in which those who have been set free by Christ are freer in their thinking and in every other way. He was referring to the freedom from false ways, from sin's delusion, that his salvation brings. Evil always means bondage, and those so bound are (among other things) ignorant of their real position. It is only the truth that can set them free. And when the truth has done its work, it becomes so characteristic of them that they can be said to be "of the truth" (18:37; cf. the reference to him who is "of God"

[8:47]). They can be said to "do the truth" (3:21); truth is a quality of their actions as well as of their speech. They are sanctified "in the truth" (17:17), a statement that probably contains another reference to Christ's saving work, for he goes on to say that he sanctifies himself so that they may be sanctified in truth (17:19). His sanctification of himself surely is associated with his saving death.

JUDGMENT

John has a lot to say about judgment. He uses the noun *krisis*, "judgment," eleven times (only Matthew, using it 12 times, has it more often) and the verb *krinein*, "to judge," nineteen times (only Acts, with 21, exceeds this; if we total the uses of both noun and verb, Matthew has 18; Acts, 22; and John, 30). We sometimes translate the judgment words as "condemnation" and "condemn," for John sometimes uses these words of a negative judgment (as we sometimes do, too, though perhaps not as often as John does).

It is perplexing that sometimes John wrote that Jesus did not come for judgment (3:17; 8:15; 12:47) and sometimes he said he did (9:39; cf. 3:19; 5:20, 30; 8:16; 12:48). We should be clear that Jesus' mission was a mission of salvation. He did not come to judge anyone, but to save people. He died on the cross to bring salvation, and his death was in prospect from the beginning (1:29; 3:16). But salvation is not automatic: "He who believes" is not judged; but "he who does not believe has been judged already because he has not believed" (3:18).

Judgment is the reverse side of salvation. Jesus died to bring us salvation,

---

[15] A. Corell, *Consummatum Est* (London, 1958), 161.

but that does not mean we are forced into salvation. The way is open wide, and every believer enters in. But anyone who refuses to believe, who prefers to go his own self-centered way rather than to accept the changes that are involved in being Christ's, brings down judgment on himself. The offer of salvation means judgment on the person who rejects the gift. It is impossible to separate the two. So, from one point of view, Jesus did not come to judge people, but to bring them salvation, and believers are saved. But from another point of view the offer of salvation necessarily means judgment for those who reject it: "If I had not come and spoken to them," Jesus said, "they would not have had sin; but now they have no excuse for their sin" (15:22; a similar statement is made about the works Jesus did among them [v. 24]). We are responsible people. We cannot avoid the responsibility for our actions, and part of the reason for Jesus' coming was to make us face up to that responsibility—in other words, to bring us to judgment.

We see this also in passages that tell us something about the nature of the judgment. Immediately after the great words about God's giving his Son in love so that believers may be saved (3:16), we are told that God's purpose was salvation, not judgment (v. 17). Then comes a statement about what happens to the person who believes and what happens to the one who does not (v. 18). This latter person "has been judged already.... And this is the judgment that the light has come into the world and the men loved darkness rather than the light because their deeds were evil" (vv. 18–19). This is a very important passage for our understanding of John's view of judgment. He does not say that people will be judged *because* they loved darkness rather than light. He says that the fact that they loved darkness rather than light *is* their judgment.

Picture a person endlessly shut up in a dark room. The room has no window, the walls are black, the ceiling is black, the floor is black, and the door is shut. There is no light whatever. That person has an impoverished existence, an existence that is scarcely worth calling an existence. But he need not stay there. The door is not locked. He can open it and walk out into God's good sunshine. But he does not. He loves darkness. It is his love for darkness that confines him to his cramped and narrow existence.

John is saying that people who choose to follow a life of sin and refuse to believe in Jesus Christ are like that. It is not so much that God is saying, "I'll punish you!" as that they are punishing themselves. Their love for darkness, their rejection of light, is itself their punishment, and they have chosen it for themselves.

Judgment is thus a present reality, just as eternal life is a present reality. But there is to be a fuller experience of eternal life in the hereafter, and the same is true of judgment. The present judgment that means so much to John is not the only judgment. Judgment day at the end of the world is a reality. And the criterion on that day is still what people have done with the teaching of Jesus: "The word that I have spoken, that will judge him in the last day" (12:48). John emphasizes the fact that the Judge on that great day will be none other than Jesus. We noticed earlier that this is distinctive Christian teaching. The Jews did not think of the Messiah as judging men; they were sure that final judgment will be in the hands of God alone. John does not really alter that, but he sees God as doing his judgment through the Son. The Father in person "judges no one, but he has given all judgment to the Son" (5:22); "he has given him authority to do judgment, because he is the Son of man" (5:27). So it is that at the last day those in the tombs will hear the voice of the Son of man and will come out, "those who have done evil things to the resurrection of judgment [or condemnation]" (5:28–29).

John sometimes speaks of the quality of judgment. Jesus objected to the judgment of his opponents because they judged "according to appearance" (7:24) and "according to the flesh" (8:15). His own judgment is not like that. Indeed, that may be part of the reason he said he does not judge (8:15); what Jesus does is so different from what they did that it can scarcely be called by the same name. His judgment is "righteous" or "just" (*dikaia;* 5:30); it is "true" (*alēthinē;* 8:16). This arises because of his close fellowship with the Father: he does not seek to do his own will but that of the Father (5:30); he is not alone, for the Father who sent him is with him (8:16).

What he says about judgment is not at all obvious to the natural person, and Jesus teaches that it needs the work of the Holy Spirit to convict anyone of judgment (16:8). This basically concerns the judgment of "the prince of this world" (16:11), for it is far from obvious that in the Cross a judgment has been passed on the evil one. It needs the insight the Spirit gives to discern this. It is important to see that right is done in the way we are saved as well as in the fact that we are saved. Satan is not simply defeated, but judged.

SACRAMENTS

There is a wide diversity of views about the importance John attaches to baptism and the holy communion. He does not mention either, and from this some have drawn the conclusion that he does not regard them as having any importance. Others, however, hold that, while he does not mention them by name, John gives important teaching about baptism in chapter 3 and about holy communion in chapter 6. One can extend this, as, for example, Oscar Cullmann does, by seeing references to baptism in passages where John speaks of water and to holy communion where he refers to blood.

It is not easy to dismiss the fact that John mentions neither sacrament. This is all the more remarkable in regard to holy communion because his account of what happened in the Upper Room is far and away the longest of the four accounts. We would have expected some mention of it. That John does not mention it there surely indicates that he did not give it the same central position as some scholars do.

The language of 6:51–58 seems to some exegetes so self-evidently eucharistic that they regard as special pleading any understanding that does not see a reference to the communion. But there are four strong arguments against it.

One is the *context.* John tells us that the words were spoken, not to a group of committed disciples, but to a crowd of people who included opponents of Jesus and people who were interested in him but not really committed. No one has satisfactorily explained why John should want us to believe that it was to such an audience that Jesus gave his teaching about a sacrament that was to be observed by committed Christians only. Nor has anyone explained why Jesus should have taught that audience about a sacrament that had not yet been instituted. They could not possibly have understood him.

A second is the *language.* Jesus said,

"Unless you eat the flesh of the Son of man and drink his blood you have no life in you" (6:53). The language is absolute. Without the eating and drinking of which Jesus speaks, there is no life at all. But it is impossible to hold that the one thing necessary for eternal life is the performance of a liturgical observance. We should also notice that the language is not, in fact, the language of the eucharist. Jesus spoke of eating his "flesh," not his "body," but it is the word "body" that is used when the ancient church spoke of the communion. The difference may not be great, but it is there. This is not the way the early Christians referred to communion.

The third point is that the blessings that are said to flow from eating the flesh and drinking the blood of Christ are said in this very passage to flow from receiving Christ or from believing in him (vv. 35, 40, 47). If eternal life comes from believing in Christ, then it is not tied to a liturgical observance.

Fourth, the Jews often used the metaphor of eating and drinking to mean taking something within one's innermost being. It did not necessarily refer to the physical act of ingesting nourishment. It often refers to receiving the Law, for example, or for "celestial food." We ought not to think that words like these must be understood to indicate the reception of something physical; they refer to the gift of spiritual blessing.[16]

While, however, the passage is concerned to teach us that we receive Christ in a spiritual manner, once we have learned this, we may say, "This, too, is how we receive him when we take the bread and the wine."[17] But this is very different from seeing the words as primarily concerned with a sacramental act.

It is some such attitude that we should take to John's sacramental teaching in general. He says nothing directly about these observances. But he does teach about the spiritual realities to which they point, and an understanding of what he says enables us to observe them more meaningfully.

---

[16] H. Odeberg amply documents this use (*The Fourth Gospel* [Amsterdam, 1968], 235–69). Of the view that John 6 refers to the holy communion, he says, "One who understands the words of the eating and drinking of the flesh and blood to refer to the bread and wine of the Eucharist takes exactly the mistaken view of which Nicodemus in ch 3 and the 'Jews' here are made the exponents, viz. that J's realistic expressions refer to objects of the terrestrial world instead of to objects of the celestial world" (p. 239).

[17] Cf. F. D. Maurice: "If you ask me, then, whether he is speaking of the Eucharist here, I should say, 'No.' If you ask me where I can learn the meaning of the Eucharist, I should say, 'Nowhere so well as here'" (cited in C. J. Wright, *Jesus the Revelation of God* [London, 1950], 180).

16

the epistles of john

Traditionally these three letters have been attributed to the writer who wrote the Gospel of John. There is a great variety of opinion about this, but it is agreed that, even if they were not written by the same man, they came from the same circle. There are many of the same ideas, though they are sometimes developed differently. The basic position is the same. The Johannine writings belong together.

GOD THE FATHER

There is an enormous concentration on God in these epistles. The word "God" is used sixty-seven times, and "Father" eighteen, of which sixteen refer to God. So many references to God in such a short space is unmatched anywhere else in the New Testament. And there are some striking statements, such as "God is light" (1 John 1:5) and "God is love" (4:8, 16).

Two things are particularly stressed: the connection of God with Jesus Christ and the connection of God with his people. There are repeated references to "the Son of God" (e.g., 1 John 3:8; 4:9, 15; 5:5, 10). For this writer it is desperately important that we see the relationship of Jesus to the Father. He speaks of "the testimony that God testified about his Son"

(5:10). In the foregoing treatment of the Gospel we saw that the bearing of witness commits a person and that John has the daring thought that God has committed himself in Jesus. In 1 John the thought is, if anything, even clearer. To deny the Son means that we do not have the Father, whereas to confess the Son is to have the Father (2:23). Abiding in the Son and in the Father go together (2:24). To go on our own, so that we no longer have the teaching of the Son means that we do not have God, whereas to abide in the teaching is to have both the Father and the Son (2 John 9), for the Father sent the Son (1 John 4:9–10, 14).

The recipients of 1 John were evidently perplexed about "spirits." People claimed to be "inspired" and therefore that their teaching must be accepted. The readers are told not to take "spirits" at their own evaluation. They are to be tested, for "every spirit that confesses that Jesus Christ has come in the flesh is from God" (1 John 4:2; cf. 2 John 7). Any spirit that does not make this confession thereby shows itself to be "antichrist" (v. 3).

John emphatically declares the love of God throughout these writings (e.g., 1 John 2:5; 3:17) and, indeed, "God is love" (4:8, 16). We know love, not from our love for God but from his for us in sending his Son as the propitiation for our sins (4:10). It is this action of God that admits us into the heavenly family (3:1–2, 10), and there are several references to being "begotten of God" (3:9; 4:7; 5:1, 4, 18). We are reminded of the teaching of the new birth in John 3 (and cf. John 1:13). Another reminiscence of the Gospel is the teaching that people may be "of God" (*ek tou theou,* 1 John 4:4, 6; 5:19; 3 John 11; cf. John 8:47). An important teaching is that we are to "abide" in God (1 John 4:16). This is probably much the same as "fellowship" with God (1:3, 6); fellowship is not mentioned in the Gospel).

JESUS CHRIST

The place assigned to Jesus Christ is critical. It is clear that the writer was faced by strong opponents, some of whom had left the group (1 John 2:19), though some remained (3 John 9), among whom some claimed to be inspired (1 John 4:1–3). How were Christians to know who were right and who were wrong? John is clear—the critical thing is the attitude to Jesus. There were apparently some people who had a highly "spiritual" view of the divine nature and a very low view of matter. They felt that deity could not have any contact with matter, and thus there could be no incarnation. For them the man Jesus could not possibly have been the divine Christ.

It is against such a background that we must understand words like "Who is the liar except he who denies that Jesus is the Christ? This is the antichrist, who denies both the Father and Son" (1 John 2:22). Notice that the enemy is not denying Jesus alone when he says he is not the Christ. He is denying the Father, too, because he viewed God as someone other than the God who sent *his Son* to be our Savior. A god who might send a man to be his messenger is a very different being from the loving Father who sent his Son to be our Savior. To deny that Jesus is God's Christ or God's Son is to reject the God who loved with the love we see on Calvary. This is so fundamental that of those who "do not confess Jesus Christ come in the flesh," John says, "this is the deceiver and the antichrist" (2 John 7). Such a person is not simply making an honest mistake; he is deceiving people.

"Everyone who denies the Son does not have the Father; he who confesses the Son has the Father too" (1 John 2:23). The Father and the Son are inseparable. No prophet is really "inspired" unless he confesses that Jesus Christ has come in the flesh (4:2). Not to confess Jesus means not to be one of God's people, but rather to belong to antichrist (4:3; this term is found in these writings only in the New Testament). It is important to confess that Jesus is the Son of God (4:15), to believe that he is the Christ (5:1) and the Son of God (5:5), and to believe in his name (3:23; 5:13).

1 John has some important things to say about the atonement Christ wrought. It is more explicit than the Gospel of John on this subject. Thus, "the blood of Jesus his Son cleanses us from every sin" (1 John 1:7). Clearly it is the death that is significant. This is the point also of the writer's insistence that Jesus Christ came "through water and blood, not in the water only but in the water and in the blood" (5:6). There has been much discussion of this passage, but it seems that we should understand the water to point to Jesus' baptism, and the blood to his death. There were some people in the early

church who could not accept the thought of the Christ being crucified. They held that the divine Christ came on the man Jesus at his baptism, but left him before his crucifixion. John is insisting that not only the baptism but also the cross of Christ is important. It was the death, not the baptism, that took away sin.

So, too, Jesus Christ is our Advocate with the Father (1 John 2:1), the One who pleads for us when we sin. And he is "the propitiation for our sins" (v. 2); again God "loved us and sent his Son to be the propitiation for our sins" (4:10). Like Paul, John is saying that there is that terrible thing, the wrath of God, exercised toward sinners, and that Christ's death was the means of turning that wrath from us. So too Christ was manifested "that he might take away sins" (3:5).

Another way of putting it is to speak of Christ as "the Savior of the world" (1 John 4:14; this is an expression found only here and in John 4:42). This is not the view that in the end everyone will be saved, but that salvation is not limited to any one group (such as the Jews) and that it is adequate for the needs of all people everywhere. John also said, "For this reason the Son of God was manifested, that he might destroy the works of the devil" (1 John 3:8). Life is one of his great concepts: "God has given us life eternal and this life is in his Son" (5:11). To have the Son is to have the life; from another angle we see that all our hopes of salvation rest on Christ and what he has done for us. John also speaks of forgiveness (1:9; 2:12). Salvation is many-sided, and, although John does not set out to give a comprehensive account of it, he leaves us in no doubt that whatever had to be done Jesus did.

That Jesus deals with sin is important because we are all sinners. "If we say that we have no sin we deceive ourselves and the truth is not in us. . . . If we say that we have not sinned we make him a liar and his word is not in us" (1:8–10). The point of this is that all God's dealings with people proceed on the basis of their being sinners. Centuries before, God sent his prophets and lawgivers to urge people to turn from sin, and the climax of everything was the coming of God's Son to put sin away. To deny that we have sinned is thus to deny the truth of the whole revelation God has made. "Sin is lawlessness" (3:4), the refusal to submit to the law of God and the assertion of the individual's own will. This is seen for the dreadful thing it is when we put it against the background of the love of God so forcefully brought out in this letter. God's love is seen in the giving of his Son; the Cross speaks eloquently of his care for others. To insist on one's own way and one's own benefit in the light of that self-sacrifice is the most horrible thing there is. Truly "he who does sin is of the devil" (3:8).

THE CHRISTIAN LIFE

The Christian life is, as would be expected in the light of all that Christ has done, a wholehearted affair. It means a complete renunciation of sin: "Everyone who abides in him does not sin," and again, "Everyone who sins has neither seen nor known him" (1 John 3:6). This can be put very forcefully: "Everyone who has been begotten of God does not sin, because his seed remains in him, and he cannot sin because he has been begotten of God" (v. 9). It is probably important that the tenses of the verbs here are continuous. The writer is not saying that a Christian can never do any wrong thing; he is saying that he cannot continue in ways of evil. To sin habitually is not possible for someone who has been reborn by the power of God. If he sins, that is out of character. His habit is to serve God and to do what is right (v. 7).[1]

But it is love that receives the emphasis (*agapē* occurs 21 times in these epistles; *agapaō*, 31; and *agapētos*, 10). In one of the most important passages in the whole New Testament John says, "In this is love, not that we have loved God, but that he loved us and sent his Son to be the propitiation for our sins" (1 John 4:10). And again, "In this we know love that he laid down his life for us" (3:16).

We will never find what love means if we start from the human end. We must start from the cross, where we see the love of God, not for the attractive or the devout or the meritorious, but for sinners, those who, apart from the Son's propitiatory act, would experience only the wrath of God, the ill desert of their sin. It is this that is behind the repeated statement "God is love" (4:8, 16). God loves because it is his nature to love, not because our attractiveness has drawn love out of him or our merits have won him. As we have seen, we are all sinners and thus unattractive to God. He loves us, not because of what we are, but because of what he is.[2]

Our love, then, is a response to God's love: "We love, because he first loved us" (1 John 4:19). "Love is of God" (v. 7). Only because we have experienced the love we see in the Cross do we love in the distinctively Christian way. Sometimes John speaks of Christians loving but does not specify the objects of their love, as when he says, "Everyone who loves has been begotten of God" (4:7; see also 3:14, 18; 4:8, 19). The new-born have a new capacity to be loving people. In some measure they have come to love as God does; they love not only the attractive, the beautiful, and the good, but all who are the objects of God's love. They love God (4:20–21; 5:2), and they love one another (e.g., 3:23; 4:7); they love "the brothers" (e.g., 2:10; 3:14; 3 John 1).[3] In this way God's love is "perfected" in them (1 John 4:12). Indeed, love is concerned to keep God's commandments (5:3). It is striking that these letters, which put such stress on love, have more references to God's commandments than any other New Testament book (*entolē*, "command," occurs 18 times, whereas Paul has the word only 14 times in all his epistles). Again, love and fear are incompatible, for perfect love casts fear out (4:17–18).

The believer has passed out of death into life (1 John 3:14); he has eternal life (e.g., 1:2; 2:17; 5:11). Characteristic is the thought of "abiding" (the verb *menō* occurs 27 times). Mostly this abiding is in God (e.g., 2:6; 3:6), but it may be in the light (2:10), in the Son and the Father (2:24), or in the teaching (2 John 9). Again, the word of God may abide in us (1 John 2:14; cf. 2:24), or an "anointing" (2:27), or life

---

[1] I. Howard Marshall sees this view as "perhaps the most popular understanding of the passage among British commentators" (*The Epistles of John* [Grand Rapids, 1979], 180). He himself prefers to see the passage as meaning "the eschatological reality, the possibility that is open to believers, which is both a fact ('he cannot sin') and conditional ('[if he] lives in him')" (p. 182). It is, however, not easy to see what this means nor how it is any more satisfactory than the view Marshall rejects.

[2] I have developed this more fully in *Testaments of Love* (Grand Rapids, 1981).

[3] Some have deduced from the emphasis on love for the brothers that the writer is concerned only with brotherly love; he has no love for those outside the Christian community. But this is to ignore the fact that he expects Christians to love with a love like that of God for sinners (1 John 4:10). This is not incompatible with a love for the brothers. But it is broader.

(3:15), or love (v. 17), or truth (2 John 2). And God abides in us (1 John 3:24; 4:12) and so does his "seed" (3:9).

The Christian life may be thought of as the negation of "the world." This term may be used in a neutral sense (1 John 2:2; 4:9), but more often it refers to the world as opposed to God and the people of God. The world in this sense did not know Christ, and it does not know the children of God (3:1)—how can it? Worse, it hates God's people (3:13). This is not surprising, for the world is linked with false prophets, the antichrist, and deceivers (4:1, 3; 2 John 7); indeed, the whole world lies in the power of the evil one (1 John 5:19). But believers need not fear, for "Greater is he that is in you than he that is in the world" (1 John 4:4).

We are not to love the world nor the things that are in it (1 John 2:15). God loved the world (John 3:16), but, of course, that does not mean the world in the sense of "worldliness." Rather it means the world's people; God loved them and sent his Son to be their Savior. The thought in 1 John 2:15 is rather that we must not set our love on this present world, we must not be preoccupied with worldliness. The emptiness of worldliness means that those who are seduced by its attractiveness suffer irreparable loss. John warns against its superficiality and its transitoriness (2:16–17). It is tragic to forsake the solid for the superficial, the eternal for the temporal.[4]

[4] An old lexicon gives this definition of κόσμος in its "worldly" aspect: "The whole circle of earthly goods, endowments, riches, advantages, pleasures, etc., which, although hollow and frail and fleeting, stir desire, seduce from God and are obstacles to the cause of Christ" (*A Greek-English Lexicon of the New Testament,* being *Grimm's Wilke's Clavis Novi Testamenti,* trans., rev., and enl. Joseph Henry Thayer [Edinburgh, 1888], 357).

17

the Revelation
of John

Most Christians find Revelation a difficult book because of its vivid visions, its curious beasts, its series of seals and trumpets and bowls, and its unusual symbolism. It represents a kind of literature that was common enough at the time the Christian movement began but is not produced today. It thus requires a special effort if we are to understand what the writer is saying to us.

John begins with "Revelation [*apokalypsis*] of Jesus Christ," and from this we get the word "apocalyptic"—a word we use to describe a whole class of literature. But this book differs from many apocalypses,[1] and several times John calls it a prophecy (1:3; 22:7, 10, 18–19). He is using the apocalyptic format to convey "the word of God" (1:2) for his day. There are some who deny that John had a serious theological purpose, and others who suggest that he lacks important parts of the Christian message. Against the first contention, in the early church the author was called *ho theologos,* "the theologian"; those nearest him in time recognized what he was about. And if he does not have the complete Christian message, this means only that he

brings out vividly in an apocalyptic approach those aspects of the Christian message that he felt were needed in his day.

John wrote to a little, persecuted church that was in danger of becoming disillusioned. When the gospel was preached in their area, people were told that God had sent his Son, who died on a cross to put away their sins and open up the way to everlasting life. The Son had risen from the dead and had ascended to heaven. In due course he would come back and then he would reign over all the earth. All earthly empires (like that of Rome) would be subject to him, and believers would enter into the glorious kingdom. For little people who had been pushed around by the Romans, this was a great encouragement. They were glad to become Christians, and they looked and longed for the return of the Lord.

But nothing happened. The Romans were as oppressive as ever. Some of the believers were killed or imprisoned. Evil prospered as it had always done. Had it all been a mistake? Was Caesar too strong for Christ? Would wrong always prevail over right?

Revelation was written to a little

---

[1] See my *Revelation of St. John* (London, 1969), 23–25.

group of Christians puzzled by questions like these. Basically it presents a theology of power. The writer is saying in effect: "You are seeing only part of the picture. If you could look behind the scenes, you would see that God is working his purpose out and that in his own good time he will completely overthrow all evil. The salvation he worked out at Calvary will not fail to achieve its final aim." We must keep John's purpose in mind. We will not find here a full statement of all that Christianity teaches, but we will find a concentration on those aspects of the faith that would bring home to his readers the truths they needed to know.

THE GLORIOUS LORD

John has greetings "from Jesus Christ, the faithful witness [or, the witness, the faithful one], the firstborn of the dead and the ruler of the kings of the earth" (1:5). His first vision is one of the Lord in all his glory (1:12–20). Unless we see the Lord for what he is, we will not see anything in its true perspective. Having made his point that Jesus is the supreme Lord, John reveals a series of titles as the book unfolds. He is "the first and the last and the living one" (1:17–18); he is the One who has the keys of death and Hades (1:18). He is "the Son of God" (2:18), One who is "holy" and "true," "who has the key of David, who opens and no one shuts, who shuts and no one opens" (3:7), "the ruler of God's creation" (3:14 NIV). He is "the Lion of the tribe of Judah, the root of David" (5:5). Then he is "a lamb standing, as though slain" (5:6). This is part of a vision in which the praise of the Lamb is taken up by the four living ones and the twenty-four elders around the throne of God, from whom it passes to myriads and myriads of angels, and, as

though this is not enough, to the whole of creation. Everything in heaven and earth and under the earth joins in a great chorus of praise to the Lamb.

The chorus of praise arises because the Lamb is seen as worthy to open the seven seals, and this he proceeds to do (e.g., 6:1, 3). As the narrative unfolds, it is seen that the book is the book of human destiny, and the vision means that the Lamb is in control of it all. It is clear that Christians, far from being an insignificant and unimportant group, are the followers of One in whose hands is the destiny of all people and all nations.

The greatness of the Lamb is indicated in the way he is joined with God. Thus there are references to "the throne of God and of the Lamb" (22:1, 3) and to people standing before the throne and before the Lamb (7:9). The one hundred and forty-four thousand are described as "first-fruits to God and to the Lamb" (14:4). Again and again the writer puts the Lamb on a level with God.

John makes it clear right at the beginning that Jesus is the supreme One. He may be lightly esteemed in parts of the Roman Empire, but he is given highest honor in heaven. Throughout the entire writing Jesus is seen as Lord of all. He does what he wills, and angels move at his direction. John wants his readers not to be in the slightest doubt about the greatness of Jesus.

Jesus' greatness makes his saving work possible. As early as verse 5 we read that Jesus Christ "loves us and loosed us from our sins in his blood." Later we read that he was killed and that with his blood he purchased for God people "from every tribe and tongue and people and nation" (5:9). A paradoxical piece of imagery informs us that the saved have whitened their robes "in the blood of the Lamb" (7:14); in another vision we find that the victory of the saved came "through the blood of the Lamb" (12:11). The Lamb imagery of this book is striking. It begins when one of the elders tells John that "the Lion of the tribe of Judah" has prevailed to open the closely sealed book. So John looks to see the lion—and sees the Lamb (5:5–6)! It is interesting that the Lamb is a constant symbol for Christ, for the symbols earthlings normally choose are of predatory birds and beasts.[2] But the things of God do not go by the rules of men. In the end it is not predatory might that matters, but very different qualities. The Lamb is a symbol of this heavenly difference.

But when John uses the Lamb imagery, he often has the idea of the death of the Lamb in mind. The shedding of the blood of Jesus is central. Indeed that is implicit in the concept of "the Lamb as though slain" (5:6; cf. 5:9, 12). He was slain "from the foundation of the world" (13:8). The very term "Lamb" (which John uses twenty-nine times of its thirty New Testament occurrences[3]) points to a sacrificial offering, and the triumph that is linked with the Lamb in this book surely means triumph through death.

This book thrills with the strong note of victory, of victory linked with Christ. For example, in the letters to the churches there is a refrain referring to "him that overcomes." This is not to be understood as though it meant that Christians in their own strength are able to get the victory. Rather, Christ brings victory to his people. They simply stand firm against all odds, strong in the divine enablement (cf. 12:11). This will be implied also in the thought that he made his people "a kingdom, priests to God" (1:6; 5:10). He has opened up for them a glorious destiny.

GOD OVER ALL

John has a deep reverence for God. His book is full of vivid imagery, and he does not hesitate to go into some detail when he speaks of Christ, as the vision in chapter 1 makes clear. But when he speaks of God in heaven he uses great reserve: "He who sat [on the throne] was like in appearance to jasper stone and carnelian, and there was a rainbow around the throne like in appearance to an emerald" (4:3). God cannot be described; we can only bow before him in awe. Smoke from the glory of God keeps people out of the temple (15:8); again and again there are references to the glory of God. Perhaps this comes to its climax with the information that it is God's glory that is the light of the heavenly city (21:23).

The living ones near the throne never cease to worship day or night as they cry, "Holy, holy, holy is the Lord God the Almighty, who was and is and is to come" (4:8). Although this book puts strong emphasis on power, the first thing the inhabitants of heaven say about God is that he is holy. Physical

---

[2] J. P. Love comments, "This is perhaps the most important figure of the Book of Revelation. None but an inspired composer of heavenly visions would ever have thought of it. When earth-bound men want symbols of power they conjure up mighty beasts and birds of prey. Russia elevates the bear, Britain the lion, France the tiger, the United States the spread eagle—all of them ravenous. It is only the Kingdom of Heaven that would dare to use as its symbol of might, not the Lion for which John was looking, but the helpless Lamb, and at that, a slain Lamb" (*John. Jude. Revelation* [London, 1960], 65).

[3] His word is ἀρνίον. He does not use the word ἀμνός, another word for "lamb," which is found four times in the New Testament.

power is important, but moral strength is more significant.

God is the living God (7:2); he lives for ever and ever (4:9–10; 10:6). "The breath of life from God" gives life to the dead (11:11). His works are marvelous, and with this fact is linked the thought that his ways are just and true (15:3). John's thoughts about God are various. But the thing that keeps coming out is the power of God. The little church is to be in no doubt at all that God is a mighty God and that he will do his will, whatever the tyrants of the earth may plan. Again and again—nine times in all—we read that he is almighty (e.g., 1:8; 4:8; 11:17). Those in heaven ascribe power and might to him (e.g., 7:12; cf. 11:17; 12:10).

God's great power means that, basically and finally, the tyrants of earth are helpless. Sometimes there is the thought that God works out his plan and they must simply do what he wants them to do. Thus in a vision that includes ten kings and the beast John says, "God has given into their hearts that they should do his purpose" (17:17). More often God is simply too strong for them, and he overthrows them in his own time. "Strong is the Lord God who judges" (18:8). But we should notice the word "judges"; John is not writing about a God who as it happens is stronger than the kings of the earth. His God has a strong moral purpose, and the pains that come on evil people are not simply so much suffering; they are judgments, the due reward for the evil they have done.

The triumph of God is not described without a realistic sense of the power of evil. The leader of the forces of wrong is seen in a number of guises; he is "the great dragon, the ancient serpent, who is called 'Devil' and 'Satan,' who deceives the entire inhabited world" (12:9). We read of the beast that came up out of the sea and of his henchman, the beast that came up out of the earth (13:1, 11). There are unclean spirits (16:13; 18:2), demons (9:20; 18:2), spirits of demons (16:14), and the devil's angels (12:7). John is sure that there are evil people, too, and he writes vividly of "the great harlot" (17:1) and of "Babylon the great" (17:5; 18:2). He speaks often of "the great city," by which he seems to mean every city and no city; it is man in organized community, and this he sees as hostile to God. All this means that John is clear about the opposition there is to the cause of God in both human and superhuman forces. He sees evil around him, but does not think of human malevolence as the worst of it all. Behind all human evil is the malign visage of Satan. There is war between the forces of good and evil here on earth, but that is only part of a greater conflict, for John speaks of war in heaven (12:7). We are caught up in a conflict greater by far than anything we see here on earth. John is no starry-eyed optimist, unable to perceive the strength of the opposition. He well knows that evil is strong.

But John is quite sure of victory. Just as realistically as he sees the strength of evil, he sees the power of almighty God. Throughout his book he stresses the sovereignty of God, and as he comes to the climax he looks for the final defeat of all the forces of evil. He speaks of the battle "on the great day of God, the almighty One" (16:14), and gives space to tell of the way all that is wrong will be routed (chs. 17–20). This includes evil people, for the vision vividly portrays the overthrow of the great city (ch. 18) and of Satan and his close associates (20:7–10). In the end John can say, "the kingdom of the world has become that of our Lord and his Christ, and he will reign for ever and ever" (11:15).

GOD AND HIS PEOPLE

The God who is so great and who wages a ceaseless war against the strong forces of wrong is great enough to take a loving interest in his people. The love terminology is not frequent in this book (but cf. 3:9; 20:9); however, the thought that God cares for his own runs through it all. He has spoken to his people, and we hear of "the word [or words] of God" a number of times (e.g., 1:2; 17:17; 19:9). Indeed this whole book is a revelation "that God gave" (1:1). Sometimes we read of God's speaking (1:8), but more usually (perhaps more reverently) there is a voice from heaven (10:4) or an intermediary (7:13ff.). Whichever way John puts it, there is the thought that God cares for his people and gives them the revelation they need to see them through their difficulties.

In the messages to the seven churches in chapters 2–3 there is the constant thought that God is interested in all that his people are doing; he knows their failures and their successes and will give them his blessing (cf. 2:7; 3:12). Those Christ has redeemed are redeemed "to God" (5:9); they are his forever. Salvation is ascribed to God (7:10; 12:10; 19:1), and the holy city, the place of the saved, comes from God (21:2, 10). In a beautiful and unexpected gesture, God himself, not some intermediary, "will wipe every tear from their eyes" (7:17; cf. Isa. 25:8).

Those who are saved are expected to respond. They are "a kingdom, priests to God" (1:6; 5:10). A kingdom presupposes a king, so that the saved are brought under the sovereignty of God; they are not saved for a life of idleness, but of service. And being priests also means service, even if of a different kind. Notice that this word is applied to believers generally, not to people in the ministry or any other restricted group. Together we are a group of priests, speaking to the world on behalf of God and to God on behalf of the world to whom we bring the gospel message.

Much is said about worship in Revelation (the verb *proskyneō* being used in this book 24 times of its 59 New Testament occurrences, the next most frequent use [13] being in Matthew). Mostly this is worship in heaven (e.g., 4:10; 7:11) but is it not true that what God's servants are doing in heaven, God's earthly people should be doing on earth? There are also references to the worship of evil deities (13:4; 14:11), so that readers are reminded to be careful whom they worship. This comes out with the twofold instruction to John that he is not to worship an angel, but God only (19:10; 22:8–9).

The reference to "the Lord's day" (1:10) is the only time Sunday is referred to in this way in the New Testament, though we have other references to worship on the first day of the week (Acts 20:7; 1 Cor. 16:2; cf. John 20:19). There are many songs throughout this book, a fact that points to a musical aspect to worship, and there are references to giving thanks to God (11:17) and praising God (19:5)—actions that are apt in worship, though they are also capable of a much wider use.

John emphasizes the value of prayer. He speaks of the four living ones and the twenty-four elders, those nearest to the throne of God, as holding bowls full of incense, "which are the prayers of the saints" (5:8). On earth prayer often seems a lonely and valueless thing, but in heaven those closest to God are interested in the prayers of God's people: the bowls are golden— of the greatest value. A little later John tells of a period of silence in heaven before the prayers are offered. This time there is an angel involved and a golden censer, and the offering is made on a golden altar (8:1–3). And when the offering has been made, the censer is hurled to the earth, "and there were thunders and voices and lightnings and an earthquake" (v. 5). John is surely saying that prayer is both valuable and effective.

Much more could be said about this interesting and exciting book. It is written in an individual style; it says nothing about some things to which other New Testament writings devote considerable attention. Even so, John has some important things to say. He sees God enthroned in heaven and working out his purposes on earth. The prayers of God's people are heard and valued. Those people have been redeemed by Christ's atoning death, and those who trust him will find salvation in heaven in due course. Jesus has finished his work on earth and has returned to heaven, from where he will return at the appointed time to deliver his people and to defeat all evil forces. The things of which John writes have permanent value for God's people.[4]

---

[4]This is a compact treatment, and I have not attempted to deal with the difficult question of the millennium. This is partly because of limitations of space (in this book I have had to omit much that I consider important and would like to have included) and partly because of the fact that all discussions of this difficult and divisive question must in the end remain inconclusive. Proponents of premillennialism, postmillennialism, and amillennialism hold their positions with arguments that seem to them convincing but that do not persuade those outside their circle.

PART FOUR

the general epistles

e consider now the group of writings usually called the Catholic Epistles or General Epistles. Unlike the epistles of Paul, they are not addressed to particular churches, and we are left to guess at their probable destinations from their contents. Apart from the fact that they are not addressed to specified recipients, there is little that unites them. Yet they have always been valued in the church and will all repay study.

Hebrews is the largest of these writings and must rank as one of the most weighty in the New Testament. Second Peter and Jude are usually not ranked so highly. Yet all these books are part of the canonical New Testament, and if we are to take seriously the idea of a theology of the New Testament, we must give consideration to what they say. At the least they remind us that not everyone in the New Testament church was a Paul or a John. And at best nobody can neglect them without suffering loss.

These are all individual writings. They are not all written by the same author, nor do they have the same theme. So it is best to study them individually. The Johannine epistles, of course, belong to this group, but they have an obvious community with the other Johannine writings, so we have considered them in part 3. It remains for us to see what the other General Epistles contribute to the subject of New Testament theology.

the epistle
to the hebrews

This letter is distinctively different from all the other New Testament writings. It moves consistently in the areas of Jewish interests, and its view of Christ as a great high priest is its own. There are disputes as to its author (who, after all conjectures, remains unknown) and its original recipients (who were being tempted to relapse from their Christian profession and, it seems, to go back into Judaism). But we can study its teaching without going deeply into these difficult questions.

A GREAT GOD

The author of Hebrews has a deep interest in God, whom he mentions sixty-eight times (averaging once every seventy-three words). He knows a great God, One who made all that there is (1:2; 3:4; 4:3–4; 11:3). It is a fearful thing to fall into his hands (10:31), for he is "a consuming fire" (12:29; cf. the awe-inspiring description of his coming down on Mount Sinai, 12:18–21) and his wrath is real (3:11; 4:3). He is the Judge of all (12:23), specifically of certain evildoers (13:4), but also of "his people" (10:30). Indeed, teaching about "eternal judgment" is part of the "elementary teaching" about Christ (6:1–2). Judgment is as certain as death (9:27). We are reminded that

there are "angels of God" who all worship him (1:6) and there are numerous references to "the living God" (e.g., 3:12; 9:14). He is "the most high God" (7:1), and he is active in the affairs of people so that they can do things only "if God permits" (6:3). In his plan of salvation the ancients are not "perfected" apart from Christians (11:40). His will is done in the coming of Christ (10:7). He is able to raise the dead (11:19).

The author of Hebrews, thus, is in no doubt as to the greatness of God. But his emphasis is not on God's greatness. It is rather on God's grace, which he mentions from time to time (2:9; 12:15) and which underlies a great deal of what he sees that God is doing. Thus he is sure of God's revelation; he begins by telling us that God spoke in various ways and at various times in former days and that he has now spoken in his Son (1:1–2); he assures us that God spoke "in David" (4:7); he refers to "the word of God" (4:12; 6:5; 13:7); he speaks of "the oracles of God" (5:12) and of the testimony God gave in signs and the like (2:4). God is so interested in his people that he gives them all the guidance they need. There are people who are "the people of God" (4:9;

11:25), also referred to as "the house of God" (10:21).

In days of old God made a promise to Abraham and backed it up with an oath (6:13). There is a concern for the patriarch in the making of such a promise and there is an indication of God's greatness in that he had to swear by himself, for there is none greater by whom to swear. There is the thought also of his reliability: God cannot lie (6:18). The idea that God has promised blessing means a great deal to this author. He uses the word "promise" more than anyone else in the New Testament—a total of fourteen times (next is Galatians with ten). And in each instance he is referring to what God has promised. He may concentrate on one promise (4:1) or use the plural of the many promises of God (6:12), but either way he is bringing out the thought that God acts in grace. God's blessing comes, not because of human deservings but because of his will to bless. He makes his promises and fulfills them.

God is active in the salvation Christ brought about. The author is very interested in salvation, a term he uses seven times, which is more than anyone else in the New Testament. He does not always specify who brought it about, but it is clearly God the Father or Christ or both. Again, Christ's priesthood is "in the things of God" (2:17; 5:1; cf. 5:4, 10; 9:14), and it is God we approach through him (7:19, 25); he appears before the face of God for us (9:24). Throughout the epistle it is clear that it is this saving work of Christ that is central for the writer, so we turn to what he has to say about it, bearing in mind that for him God, none less, is active in bringing it about.

THE INCOMPARABLE CHRIST

The epistle begins with a sustained treatment of the person of Christ. Here the writer makes it clear that Jesus is a very wonderful person, one far above all creation and to be ranked with God. He speaks of him as a "Son" (e.g., 1:2—he uses this term a dozen times) in contrast to the prophets; immediately we are aware that he is on a different level from the most wonderful of men. The writer goes on to inform us that Christ is "the heir of all things," meaning that in relation to all this mighty creation he has the position of heir, the Son of the Owner. It was through him that God made all that there is.[1] He is the outshining (or perhaps, reflection) of God's glory and "the exact representation of his being" (1:3 NIV). Not only was he active in creation, but he also sustains the universe continually. The verb "to sustain" is *pherō*, which conveys the thought of carrying creation along, perhaps taking it to its goal; it is a dynamic concept (not a static one, like the Greek thought of Atlas holding everything on his shoulders). He made a cleansing of our sins and sat down at the right hand of God (a thought that recurs [1:13; 8:1; 10:12; 12:2]).

He is superior to the angels because "he has inherited a more excellent name than theirs" (1:4); his essential being is of a different order. The writer proceeds to bring this out with a series of quotations from Scripture, which speak of the Son, a form of address not used of angels (1:5), of the angels as worshiping him (1:6) and being his servants (1:7). He goes on to his royalty (1:8), to his work in creation and his eternity (1:10–12). God never invited an angel to sit at his right hand (as he

---

[1] He made τοὺς αἰῶνας, "the worlds" (KJV), or "the universe," as in most modern translations. The word is the usual word for "age," and some commentators see the meaning here as "the ages." "The universe" makes better sense, though the Greek word reminds us that things pass away.

did the Son [1:3]) till all his enemies were defeated (1:13). It is an impressive argument that, important as the angels are, they are far inferior to God's Son.

Having made this point, the writer goes on to the "so great salvation" that Christ worked out. Jesus appeared on earth as a man, inferior to angels, but that was only in the pursuit of his securing of salvation for sinners (2:9). The writer emphasizes the genuineness of Christ's humanity (2:10–18), but this is not by way of modifying what he has said about his greatness. Rather, he is saying that Christ was great enough to take the lowly place in order to secure salvation.

That brings him to the further point that "the high priest of our confession" is superior to Moses (3:1–6). This strikes us as something of an anticlimax, for we have already had an argument that Christ was greater than the angels. But for the Jews Moses was also seen as greater than the angels.[2] He was the man through whom God had given the law, and for the Jews that was the greatest thing that had happened in the history of the world. It was inconceivable to them that anyone could be greater than Moses. But the author points out that Moses was faithful as a servant in God's house, but Christ was faithful as Son over that house (3:5–6).

Having made his point that Christ is incomparably greater than anyone else and anything in all creation, the writer goes on to develop the thought that Christ brought salvation for all, and he uses concepts such as those of the great high priest, the priest like Melchizedek, and the new covenant to bring out his meaning. Through it all the greatness

of Christ is emphasized: he could never fulfill what is meant by "high priest" and other titles were he not so great. The writer's putting of Christ alongside God the Father is the necessary presupposition for all that he has to say about our Savior.

TRUE MAN

We have noticed that part of the author's understanding of Christ is that he was great enough to become man for our salvation. One of the fascinating things about this epistle is the way as high a christology as is conceivable is combined with the most realistic view of the weakness of human flesh. Thus the writer tells us that "in the days of his flesh" Jesus "offered prayers and supplications with loud crying and tears" (5:7). This is evidently a reference to Gethsemane, but in no other account do we have such a strong expression of Jesus' distress. He was then heard, we are told, for his "godly fear," another indication of real humanity. He "learned obedience" from what he suffered, and he was "made perfect" (5:8–9), "through sufferings" (2:10). The priesthood of the Son differs from that of earthly high priests, for he has been "made perfect for ever" (7:28). There are of course different kinds of perfection. The perfection of the bud is different from that of the flower; there is a difference between being perfectly ready to suffer and in actually having suffered. We may well say that Christ was always perfect in the sense of being ready to suffer and that in due course he attained the perfection of having suffered. But it remains that the writer to the Hebrews has used some striking expressions in bringing out this aspect of Jesus' humanity.

---

[2] For passages in the rabbinic writings that show that Moses was thought to be greater than the angels, cf. *SBK*, 3:683.

According to Hebrews, Jesus had to be[3] made like his brothers (2:17). He "suffered, being tempted" (2:18); indeed, he was "tempted in all respects as we are, apart from sin" (4:15). This may mean that, though he was tempted, he did not sin, or that he knows all temptation except that which arises from having sinned. Either way, there is emphasis on the reality of the temptation.

As far as Jesus' human origin is concerned, the Book of Hebrews tells us that he belonged to the tribe of Judah (7:14). Jesus put up with opposition from sinful human beings (12:3) and was put to death outside Jerusalem (13:12). All this points to a genuinely human life and death. We should notice also that the writer uses the simple human name "Jesus" nine times, and each time there seems to be emphasis on the humanity (he also has "Jesus Christ" three times and "our Lord Jesus" once, as well as "Christ" nine times). The author insists that Jesus' place is with God and at the same time that Jesus shared, and continues to share, in human nature to the full.

A PRIEST LIKE MELCHIZEDEK

The writer of this letter has his own way of writing, and nothing is more distinctive than his view of Christ as a priest or a high priest.[4] This proves to be a unique and very illuminating way of looking at the saving work of Christ. The author of Hebrews uses the term "priest" fourteen times (no other New Testament writer has it more often than Luke's five times) and "high priest" seventeen times (a term found elsewhere only in the Gospels and Acts—and that in reference to the contemporary Jewish holders of the office). He does not appear to put any great difference of meaning between the two.

He has a highly individual treatment of Melchizedek. He says three times that Christ is a priest or high priest like this man (5:6, 10; 6:20),[5] and later gives a full-scale treatment of the topic in chapter 7. Melchizedek appears in one incident in Genesis 14:18–20. We are told that he was king of Salem and priest of God Most High, that he brought out bread and wine to Abraham as Abraham returned from victory in battle, that he blessed him, and that he received from him a tenth part of the spoil. That is all. Nothing is said about Melchizedek's lineage or posterity. Nothing is said about him anywhere else in the Old Testament except for one reference to a priest like Melchizedek in Psalm 110:4.

This man's name means "king of righteousness," and his title means "king of peace." Both point to Christ's work, but these thoughts are not developed. Melchizedek was "without father, without mother, without genealogy, having neither beginning of days nor end of life" (7:3). This is probably following a Jewish way of reasoning,

---

[3] The verb is ὤφειλεν, "he owed it." As I have written elsewhere, "There is the sense of moral obligation. The nature of the work Jesus came to accomplish demanded the Incarnation. In view of this work, he ought to become like the 'brothers'" (Frank E. Gaebelein, ed., *The Expositor's Bible Commentary* [Grand Rapids, 1981], 12:29).

[4] O. Cullmann has a valuable discussion of the concept in his *Christology of the New Testament* (London, 1959), ch. 4.

[5] Translations often have "a (high) priest after the order of Melchizedek." But we should bear in mind that there is no other priest like this man. There is no "order"; there is just the solitary figure of Melchizedek who in several ways prefigures the Messiah.

which finds the silences of Scripture important.[6] The Bible says nothing about Melchizedek's parents, nor do we have his genealogy or information about his descendants. All this points to an important truth about Christ. What was true of Melchizedek in the sense that his record disclosed nothing else, was true of Christ in the most factual sense. He had no origin nor end. His life was of a different order from that of others. We should not overlook the fact that Melchizedek was "made like" the Son of God. We are not to take Melchizedek's priesthood as the standard and think of Christ as conforming to that pattern. It is the other way around: it is Christ's priesthood that is definitive, and Melchizedek simply helps us to understand it a little better. Christ's life is "indissoluble" (7:16); it is not that it happens not to end; it cannot end. There is a distinctive quality about his life to which the statements about Melchizedek point. Other priests die and are replaced, but there is no ending to Christ's priesthood (7:23–25).

The permanence of his priesthood is brought out by taking seriously what Psalm 110:4 says: "The Lord has sworn and will not change his mind: You are a priest forever" (7:20–22). God swore no oath when he established the Levitical priesthood, and thus there was no guarantee that there would not one day be a change. But with the priest who is like Melchizedek things are different. The fact that God has called Christ to be a priest like this and has sworn that he will be a priest "forever" means that Christ's priesthood cannot be superseded. It is absolutely permanent.

The payment of tithes to Melchizedek and the blessing given by him are arguments for the superiority of Christ to the Levitical priests. Levi, from whom those priests descended, was not yet born. He was "in the loins" of his ancestor Abraham when the tithe was paid; symbolically Levi paid it (7:9–10). And Melchizedek's blessing of Abraham is significant because there is no doubt at all that the less is blessed by the greater (7:7). Both facts point to the truth that the priesthood exercised by Christ is greater than that exercised by the Jerusalem priests.

Melchizedek then helps us to see that Christ's work as priest is far greater than that of any earthly priest. His is the permanent priesthood, which is eternal in its efficacy and which accordingly must replace all lesser priesthoods.

A GREAT HIGH PRIEST

Quite apart from Melchizedek, the concept of priesthood has much to tell us about the work of Christ. Christ is "a merciful and faithful high priest in the things of God" (2:17). Christ's qualities are important and so is the fact that his priesthood is exercised toward God.

Now the essence of priesthood is representative offering. The priest must be a genuine representative of those for whom he is a priest, and he must exercise his priesthood by making an offering to God (5:1). Earthly high priests had no problem with being genuine representatives. The priest was a human being like those he represented and, what is more, he was sinful, so that he had to offer sacrifices for his

---

[6]There is an example of this in Philo's application of the term ἀμήτωρ, "without mother," to Sarah because her mother is not mentioned in Genesis 20:12 (*On Drunkenness*, 59–61). This enables him to draw an edifying allegorical meaning.

own sins as well as theirs (5:3). To offer sacrifice was a holy thing, and nobody was permitted to do so unless called by God. This was true of the Levitical priests, and it is true of Christ (5:4–5). His genuine humanity is very important; as we have seen, the author insists on this. Now we see that it is part of Jesus' qualification to be a high priest. Without it he would not be a genuine representative, but he is really one with us; he is "not unable to sympathize with our weakness" (4:15).

Further, a priest offers the sacrifices. Earthly priests day by day offer sacrifices even though these offerings can never take away sins (10:11). "Every high priest is appointed to offer gifts and sacrifices" (8:3). So if we are to take priesthood seriously as a category for interpreting the work of Christ, we must see him offering a sacrifice. If he were on earth, he would not have been a priest, for there was already a priesthood that offered gifts and sacrifices (8:4).

A major emphasis in Hebrews is that Christ made one offering, an offering of himself, and that offering is perfectly and permanently efficacious. In contrast to the Levitical priests with their daily offering of sacrifices, he made one offering of himself once for all (7:27). This is a very important thought; it is repeated again and again. "Now he has appeared once at the consummation of the ages to put away sin through the sacrifice of himself" (9:26); he has been offered once to bear the sins of many (9:28); he offered one sacrifice for sins (10:12); by one offering he has perfected forever those who are sanctified (10:14); "through the eternal Spirit he offered himself without spot to God" (9:14). So he can say with complete finality, "There is no more offering for sin" (10:18).

The offering Christ makes is the offering of his body (10:10). There are those who interpret this part of the epistle as though the writer were arguing that it is the yielded will, not the offering of a material sacrifice, that is important. The old sacrifices of animals were of no value, they reason, because the will of the victim was not involved. But Christ willingly offered himself. There is, of course, truth in this. But we should not overlook the fact that the will of God was that we be sanctified "through the offering of the body of Jesus Christ once for all" (10:10). We are not being faithful interpreters of Hebrews unless we see that for the author the offering of the body was significant.

The repetition of the Levitical sacrifices shows their inefficacy. If they really took away sins, as the worshipers thought, then would they not have ceased to be offered (10:2)? If sin had gone, there would have been no more need of sacrifice. In any case it is impossible for the blood of bulls and goats to take sins away (10:4). The sacrifices cannot perfect the conscience of the worshiper (9:9).

It is important to realize that the sacrifice of Christ is not simply *a* way to God, but *the* way. The sacrifices of the old religion did not take away sin. The sacrifice of Jesus did. That difference meant that no matter how attractive some features of Judaism might be, it was not and could not be the final religion. The coming of the Son of God made all things new. The way of salvation that he inaugurated has both efficacy and finality.

THE NEW COVENANT

The idea that Christ's death meant the inauguration of the new covenant foretold by Jeremiah is not confined to the writer to the Hebrews. We have found it in Paul and in the accounts of the Last Supper in the Synoptics. But no one else makes nearly as much of it as does this writer. More than half of the total New Testament occurrences (seventeen out of thirty-three) of the word "covenant" (*diathēkē*) are found in his writings, and most of these refer to the new covenant.

We should notice first that there is something unusual about the terminology. The ordinary Greek word for "covenant" is *synthēkē*, but this does not occur in the New Testament. The word *diathēkē* is the normal word for a last will and testament. It is used in this way constantly, and outside the Bible it is very difficult to find an example of its being used with any other meaning. The idea of the covenant God made with Israel is, of course, one of the major concepts of the Old Testament. The translators perhaps felt that *synthēkē*, with its notion of two parties working out the terms of an agreement and then assenting to it, was not a good word to describe what happened when God made a covenant. There was no bargaining involved. God laid down the terms; all that Israel did was accept them. Whether this was the reason or not, the fact is clear: the translators chose *diathēkē*, the usual word for a will, as their normal rendering of the Hebrew word for "covenant." This was not an occasional rendering: they used it 277 times.

In the New Testament we are thus presented with a first-class problem. Do the New Testament writers (and does the writer to the Hebrews in particular)

use the word *diathēkē* in the way it was used in Greek writings generally (i.e., as "testament," "will") or in the way in which it was used in their holy Scripture ("covenant")? Traditionally it has been understood as "testament," and for this reason our Bibles bear on their title pages the wording "The Old Testament" and "The New Testament." Some recent scholars hold that the term should always be understood in the sense "covenant." A more balanced view is that while in the Bible the meaning "covenant" is the normal one, there are some passages in which the term should be understood as "testament" (e.g., 9:17).

On the first two occasions that he uses the term, the writer speaks of Jesus as the mediator of "a better covenant" (7:22; 8:6), adding the second time that it was enacted on better promises.[7] We see something of what he means when he proceeds to quote Jeremiah 31:31–34 at length—the prophecy of a new covenant in which God would write his law on the hearts of his people and in which he would remember their sins no more. He quotes this prophecy again in 10:16–17, but this time after the introductory words he goes straight to those about forgiveness. That is what matters to him. The way to God that Jesus inaugurated did not depend on obedience to an external code. God's law was written on the hearts of his people. It was inward. And in the end it was not their merits that brought them salvation, but the forgiveness that Jesus obtained by the shedding of his blood. The sacrifices offered under the

---

[7]The writer makes a good deal of use of the idea that in the Christian way things are "better" than in the way to which the readers may have been tempted to revert. The covenant, of course, is better, but notice also that there are a better Mediator (1:4), a better priesthood (7:7), better sacrifices (9:23), better things that accompany salvation (6:9), better promises (8:6), a better hope (7:19), a better possession (10:34), a better resurrection (11:35), the better thing that God has provided (11:40), a better country (11:16), and blood that speaks something better than that of Abel (12:24). He may also have a similar thought with other terminology as with the more excellent ministry (8:6).

old covenant could not take away sin; they could do no more than make a remembrance of it (10:3). But Christ has put sin away decisively (9:26). The old covenant, to which it seems some of his readers were clinging, was obsolete (8:13).

The writer points out that Jesus' death enables those who are called to receive "the promise of the eternal inheritance" (9:15), and he makes the important point that it is this death that gives redemption for the transgressions under the first covenant. The Levitical sacrifices did not take away sins; only the death of Christ could do that. But the Old Testament saints were truly saved, for the death of Jesus dealt with their sins as well as with those of people who would come later.

In his magnificent benediction at the end of the letter, the writer refers to "the blood of the eternal covenant" (13:20). It is clear that Jesus' priesthood was permanent; it would never be superseded as the Levitical priesthood had been. Now we see that this is true also of the covenant. The old covenant had served its purpose and been done away in Christ. But the new covenant was eternal. It would never be replaced.

DEALING WITH SIN

An interesting feature of Hebrews is the variety of ways in which the writer brings out the meaning of Jesus' saving work. In his opening sentence he tells us that Jesus "made a cleansing of sins" (1:3). Sin is defiling, but Jesus has completely removed the defilement. He is a merciful and faithful high priest in the things of God "so that he may make propitiation for the sins of the people" (2:17). Many translations use the concept of "expiation" here, but this word belongs to the word group that, as we have seen before, refers to the removal

of wrath. The death of Christ has removed the wrath of God.

Sometimes sin is thought of as being carried away, as when Hebrews says that Christ was offered "to bear the sins of many" (9:28). The idea of "bearing" sins is one that in the Old Testament means bearing the consequence or the penalty of sins (e.g., Num. 14:33–34; Ezek. 18:20). So Christ has taken on himself that which sinners ought to have borne.

The writer uses the terminology of sacrifice and speaks of Christ as having "offered one sacrifice for [*hyper*] sins for ever" (10:12; he uses "sacrifice" again in 9:26; 10:26; in the last passage "for" is *peri*, not *hyper* as in v. 12, another slight change in the way the sacrifice is viewed). Or he may speak of Jesus' "offering" (*prosphora*) of himself (10:10, 14, 18).

Sometimes the author prefers to use the terminology of forgiveness (10:18; cf. 9:22). Sin is "nullified" by Christ's sacrifice (9:26), and Jesus brought redemption (9:15). Twice the writer quotes the prophecy of the new covenant to show that God no longer remembers the sins of those in that covenant (8:12; 10:17).

We might also reflect that Hebrews speaks often of what the old way could not do, each time with the implication that Christ has now made good that deficiency. This has to do with offering for sin (5:3), with meeting the need of the worshiper's conscience (10:2), with the offering of gifts and sacrifices (5:1), with taking away sins (*aphairein* [10:4], *perielein* [10:11]), and with burnt offerings and sin offerings (10:6). The old way was unable to deal with the problem of sin, but Christ has dealt with it decisively and permanently.

The variety in his ways of looking at the work of Christ is an indication of the author's deep conviction that that work was many-sided and that it was the thoroughly effective, divine way of meeting our deepest need.

THE SHADOW AND THE SUBSTANCE

Sometimes the writer makes a distinction between heavenly realities and the imperfect copies we see on earth (e.g., 9:23), and there has been a good deal of discussion as to how far he is indebted to Platonism for his thoughts. Plato thought of the perfect "idea" of anything as being in heaven, so that what we see on earth is no more than an imperfect actualization of the heavenly archetype. Some have felt that the writer is making use of this distinction.

But it has been fairly countered that the epistle as a whole gives no indication that its author was a learned philosopher. It is pointed out that the Old Testament informs us that Moses was instructed to make everything for the tabernacle "according to the pattern" shown him on the mountain (Exod. 25:40); accordingly, some feel that we need nothing else to account for the author's usage.

There are statements in Jewish writings that say much the same thing as Exodus does—for example: "Thou hast given command to build a temple on thy holy mountain, and an altar in the city of thy habitation, a copy of the holy tent which thou didst prepare from the beginning" (Wisd. Sol. 9:8). The difficulty with this is that the emphasis in Jewish writings is on the earthly as an exact copy of the heavenly, and that is not what the author of Hebrews is saying.

We should probably see him as making use of a popular Alexandrian form of Platonism. His main thought agrees with the Old Testament, but he also declares that the heavenly far surpasses the earthly; in some passages this is very important. Thus, he thinks of the Levitical priests as serving in a sanctuary that was no more than "a copy and shadow" of the heavenly (8:5), the antitype of the true (9:24). The law itself has no more than a shadow of the good things to come; it is not itself the reality (10:1). Christ's ministry was not exercised in the temple, the earthly sanctuary, but in "the greater and more perfect tabernacle" (9:11), and his sacrifice was better than anything in the "copies of heavenly things" (9:23). Perhaps we should add (1) Moses' judgment that "reproach for Christ's sake" was of greater value than "the treasures of Egypt" (11:26) and (2) the contrast between Mount Sinai and Mount Zion (12:18ff.), with its added warning that contrasts the voice from heaven with that on earth (12:25).

All such passages help our author make his point that what has happened in Christ is far superior to what is to be found in any religion on earth, including Judaism. The way he puts it varies; the conviction that Christ and Christ's way are to be esteemed above all else is constant.

OUR RESPONSE TO CHRIST'S WORK

One of the jewels of the New Testament is the portrait gallery of men and women of faith in Hebrews 11. This is representative of a class of literature praising the heroes of the past, of which a well-known example is that beginning "Let us now praise famous men" (Sirach 44:1–50:21). But those others seem all to choose people with a variety of desirable qualities; Hebrews speaks only of faith. In this respect it is unique.

Some New Testament students are

critical of what the writer of Hebrews says because it is not the warm personal faith in Christ that we see in Paul. They see it as a cool confidence in unseen realities. But it is scarcely fair to demand that every writer reproduce the thought of Paul, great thinker though that apostle was. And the fact is that Hebrews has something important to tell us, even if it is not the sort of thing that Paul would have written. It is not unfair to say that in Paul, faith refers primarily to the past, to what God has done in Christ, to the justification that begins our Christian life. In Hebrews, however, faith looks to the future; it is the trust that launches out boldly into the unseen and the unknown, being fully assured that God will see his servant through. Both kinds of faith are demanded of us. But it is no criticism of Hebrews to say that its view of faith is its own.

Actually Hebrews sometimes has a usage not so very different from that of Paul; we are to have faith "to the saving of the soul" (10:39). We look to Jesus who is "the author and perfecter of faith" (12:2); we come to God through him (7:25). It is because we have such a great priest over the house of God that we "approach with a true heart in full assurance of faith" (10:22). This surely means that for this writer salvation is understood in much the same way as it is by other New Testament writers. Hebrews characteristically has its own way of putting it. But it is not a different way that is being advocated.

Faith is demanding. Abraham is commended for the fact that when God called him, "he went out by faith, not knowing where he was going" (11:8). That was a hard test as was the demand that he sacrifice his son Isaac. The way

Hebrews puts it, Abraham "offered Isaac" (11:17), the perfect tense envisaging the sacrifice as completed. Abraham believed that God was able to raise the dead (11:19) and evidently relied on resurrection to follow the sacrifice of his son.

Right through chapter 11, people are called on to trust God when everything is against them and they have no way of seeing a successful outcome of whatever it is that they are beginning. But it is through faith and steadfastness that we inherit the promises of God (6:12); contrariwise, those who lack faith do not profit; it is those who believe who enter God's rest (4:5–6).

Again, the Christian way may be expressed in terms of the enduring of chastening or the like. The writer invites his readers to remember the troubles they had had to endure when they became Christians (10:32–36), and he reminds them of the hardships that the people of God had suffered through the centuries (11:33–38). Christ suffered outside the camp, and they should go to him there and bear the consequent abuse (13:13).

In a classic treatment of the subject, he points out that discipline is a necessary part of being sons. The sufferings Christians endure are not nameless horrors, but the meaningful discipline of a loving Father. They are evidence, not that God does not love them, but that he does (12:5–11).

Obedience is important, for Christ saves "all those who obey him" (5:9). In old time, those who heard the good news but disobeyed failed to enter the blessing (4:6), and the readers are warned not to fall by their own disobedience (4:11). Rather, they should hold on to the grace[8] they had been

---

[8]Many translations have "Let us be thankful" or the like for ἔχωμεν χάριν, and this translation can certainly be defended. But in this epistle χάρις means "grace" not "gratitude." Further "Let us be

given and offer well-pleasing service to God "with reverence and awe" (12:28). Nothing in this letter can be held to teach that the Christian life is easy. The author will have nothing to do with cheap grace. But he does insist that grace is a reality. We may look to God for what we need to lead the kind of life that those ransomed by Christ ought to live.

---

thankful" does not really suit the context; it is more than difficult to construe it with the following "through which." It is grace, not gratitude that enables us to offer service to God (which should not be understood as a belittling of gratitude; it is very important, but it does not appear to be what the author is talking about here).

19

the epistle of james

The Epistle of James is marked by a robust emphasis on upright living, and this has led some to think that the writer had little theological interest. This is a mistaken inference. James is in no doubt about the importance of living out to the full the implications of one's Christian profession, but this is based not on some general philosophical principle, but on theological convictions. Although his letter is short, he gives evidence of knowing a surprising number of Old Testament books[1] and of a wide acquaintance with the teachings of Jesus. What he writes proceeds from this background.

James is a monotheist (2:19) and sees God as active. We should pray for wisdom, for God gives liberally (1:5). God has "chosen the poor in this world rich in faith" (2:5), which speaks both of God's care for the poor and of faith as his gift. People are made in God's likeness (3:9), a fact that, of course, has implications for the way they should live; it is not fitting that anyone should curse people, for example. God is con-sistently righteous and demands righteousness of his people. He is not tempted with evil, and he tempts no one (1:13). He looks for us to be "slow to wrath, for man's wrath does not work God's righteousness" (1:19–20). He picks out the visiting of widows and orphans in their troubles as an example of the kind of religion that God accepts; this is to be linked with keeping oneself from being stained by the world (1:27). James sees the world as being in opposition to God so that to be a friend of the world is to be an enemy of God (4:4). God resists proud people but gives grace to humble folk (4:6); "be in subjection, therefore, to God" (4:7). God responds to the right attitude in us: "Draw near to God," James says, "and he will draw near to you" (4:8). We see this in the case of Abraham. That patriarch trusted God, with the result that this was reckoned to him as righteousness and he was called the friend of God (2:23).

"Lord" sometimes refers to Christ (1:1; 2:1; 5:7–8), but more often it

[1] J. B. Mayor in his standard work on this epistle finds references or allusions to several Old Testament books: Genesis, Exodus, Leviticus, Numbers, Deuteronomy, Joshua, 1 Kings, Job, Psalms, Proverbs, Ecclesiastes, Isaiah, Jeremiah, Ezekiel, Daniel, Hosea, Joel, Amos, Jonah, Micah, Zechariah, and Malachi (*The Epistle of St. James* [London, 1897], cx–cxvi). Charles C. Ryrie, concurring with W. Graham Scroggie, states that "the Book of James reflects the teachings of Jesus more than any other book in the New Testament apart from the record of them in the Gospels" (*Biblical Theology of the New Testament* [Chicago, 1982], 137).

means God the Father; indeed James can refer to "the Lord and Father" (3:9). Perhaps this title reminds us that God has requirements we must keep and that failure to do so has consequences. The inconstant must not think that they will receive God's good gift (1:7). Again, the cries of poor reapers who have been defrauded are heard by the Lord (5:4).

The Lord is compassionate and merciful (5:11), though he will deal firmly with evildoers. His readiness to heal the sick who have been anointed with oil in the name of the Lord (5:14–15) shows this. James has much to say about prayer, and he obviously sees it as efficacious. But this can be only because the Lord is gracious and is ready to hear and respond.

FAITH AND WORKS

James's strong emphasis on being active in the service of the Lord comes out in his treatment of faith and works. Evidently he had been confronted by some Christians who maintained that it was necessary only to believe. As long as they had faith, they must have said, it did not matter how they lived. James rejects this in the most forthright fashion, and his "faith without works is dead" approach has led some to think that he is in conflict with Paul. They suggest that this part of the epistle opposes the Pauline teaching of justification by faith alone. Paul, they say, stresses faith, and James works.

But this is scarcely fair to either. If one of these writers is opposing the other, he has not done a very good job, because neither tackles the central point of the argument of the other. Paul certainly stresses the importance of faith and has some forthright statements such as "A man is justified by faith without works of the law" (Rom.

3:28); these are not easy to equate with, for example, "A man is justified by works and not by faith alone" (2:24). If we concentrate on one or two statements like this, we are left with an irreconcilable contradiction. And whatever conclusion we come to in the end, it is clear that the two writers are not saying the same thing. It would probably be true to say that Paul would not have expressed himself like James, nor James like Paul. But they are not contradicting each other.

We should notice first that James is not belittling faith. He accepts faith as the normal Christian attitude and, for example, speaks of "faith in our Lord Jesus Christ, the Lord of glory" (2:1); he sees the poor in this world as "rich in faith" (2:5); and he links faith with prayer (1:6; 5:15). In the controversial passage in which he stresses the importance of works, he still refers to his "faith" (2:18), which he will demonstrate by his works. He assumes that faith is important, and his question is not "Should a person have faith?" but rather "When is faith dead and when is it alive?"

The kind of faith he objects to is the kind of faith the devils have (2:19). They believe in God, but that does nothing more than produce a shudder. A faith that does not transform the believer so that his life is given over to doing good works is not faith as James understands it. That is a dead faith. It is the kind of faith that says to the needy, "Go in peace, be warm and filled," but does nothing about meeting either need (2:15–16).

That James is not teaching salvation by works is shown by his plain teaching on universal sinfulness. "All of us often go wrong" (3:2 NEB), he says, and he urges Christians, "Confess your sins to one another" (5:16). Sin is not only a matter of active wrongdoing; to know what is right and not to do it is also a sin (4:17). Snobbery is another sin (2:9); it is not a harmless peccadillo. To fail in only one point of the law is to be guilty of all (2:10). A person with standards like these does not expect people to save themselves. He looks for salvation through mercy, not judgment (2:13).

James, then, is not denying that faith is important, but he is insisting that faith is more than a barren intellectualism. In fact what he is looking for with his agreement that he has faith and works as well is suspiciously like Paul's "faith working through love" (Gal. 5:6). Despite their very different terminologies, the two are agreed that salvation comes as a result of a divine action, not human merit; that it is appropriated by faith; and that it must be lived out in consecrated lives.

We should notice further that when Paul and James speak of justification, they are speaking of different stages in the life of the servant of God. They both appeal to Abraham, but Paul is talking about the time of his initial step of faith, that faith that was reckoned to him for righteousness (Rom. 4:3, 9–10; cf. Gen. 15:6), while James speaks of a time years later when Abraham was called on to offer his son Isaac (not yet born at the time of which Paul was speaking) in sacrifice (2:21; cf. Gen. 22:2–18). It is fair to point out that when anyone first comes to God it must be in simple faith, but that after years in the service of God it is unreasonable to expect divine approval if one has no works to show for it (cf. 1 Cor. 3:12–15). Douglas Moo argues in his commentary on James[2] that where Paul uses justification of the initial step of becoming a Christian,

James, like Matthew and others, uses it of final justification, the kind of justification we will see on Judgment Day. It is common to the New Testament writers that judgment is on the basis of works, a conviction to which they hold without compromising the truth that salvation is all a gift of God and that we receive it by faith.

CHRISTIAN SERVICE

James has much to say about the way Christians should serve God, and if we were to look at it all, we would have to reproduce the entire epistle. But some things may be singled out. One of them is his treatment of the poor and the rich. Evidently there were some rich Christians among the believers he knew, though not many. Most believers were poor, and many of them were oppressed by those with more of this world's goods. But James is in no doubt as to where the blessing of God lies. "Has not God chosen the poor in this world rich in faith and heirs of the kingdom that he promised to those who love him?" (2:5). The rich dishonor and oppress the poor, but that is a blasphemy on "the good name that was called over [them]" (2:6–7). James counsels his readers to show no favoritism toward the rich in the manner accepted among worldly people. This might be done by giving preferential treatment and a better place to the rich (2:2–4). While the poor may well rejoice in his high position as a Christian, the rich should do so in his lowliness (1:9–10). The Christian way reverses usually accepted standards. James has a biting criticism of the rich who oppress the poor; he is sure that they will come into judgment (5:1–6).

---

[2] Douglas J. Moo, *The Letter of James: An Introduction and Commentary* (Grand Rapids, 1985).

In this eminently practical writing there is a large section on the use of the tongue (3:1–12). James is aware that we all sin and that it is particularly easy to sin with the tongue. Anyone who never sins that way would be perfect (3:2). James points out that we often control quite large things like horses or ships with quite small things like bits or rudders and that with a little fire we can burn up a whole forest. He adds that we can tame all sorts of beasts and birds but not the tongue. He warns us to be careful.

The law is important, and James speaks paradoxically of "the perfect law of liberty" (1:25); it is through that law that we will be judged (2:12). He speaks also of "the royal law" (2:8), which he goes on to explain in terms of love. It is clear that James sees the law as critically important, but it is equally clear that he does not understand it in the same way as Jews normally did. Leonhard Goppelt comments, "The Law was not perfect because it was the ideal type of law but because it claimed man entirely for his Creator, grasped him entirely from within, and made him free!"[3] Real liberty comes only from being the servant of God.

James wants to see Christians with staying power. Right at the beginning he points to the varied trials that beset the servant of God and sees them as the means of developing perseverance (1:2–4). Perseverance is the way to "the crown of life," which is nonetheless a good gift of God (1:12). He reminds us of the patience of the prophets and of Job (5:10–11). Believers have another incentive, namely, the coming of the Lord (5:7), which is near (5:8). We have here the familiar eschatological tension, found throughout the New Testament. The Lord is near, and we must await him expectantly. But we must also persist in working out our faith in ordinary, day-by-day living.

Prayer is a most important part of the Christian's life, and James looks for us to make full use of it, especially in cases of sickness. But he does not confine it to this; it should be used in any time of trouble. He remembers Elijah as a mighty man of prayer and looks to his readers to profit from this example (5:13–18).

There is more that I could say. But at least this brief study of the epistle should make it clear that James was certainly a theologically minded person, sure that God is active in all of life and that we must answer to him for all that we do. But basically he sees God as the compassionate Deity who has provided for our salvation. Now James looks to us to respond wholeheartedly.

---

[3] *Theology of the New Testament* (Grand Rapids, 1982), 2:205.

the first epistle
of peter

Being a Christian in the first century could never have been easy, but there were times when it was especially difficult, and this letter was written at such a time. Its recipients were in danger of suffering simply because they were Christians (4:16). They had undergone some suffering already, for the writer tells them not to be surprised at the "fiery trial" they were undergoing (4:12). Clearly he thought that many more such troubles were about to come upon them.

Christians may suffer for simply doing good. There is no credit, however, in putting up with deserved suffering; it is when people do good and suffer for it that they have God's approval (2:20). But there is an excellent motive for bearing unjust suffering well; believers are called to do this, for in this way they are following the example of their Savior, who did no wrong, but was crucified (2:21–23). They are to have the same attitude as he had (4:1); indeed they share his sufferings (4:13). Those who suffer according to the will of God should "commend their souls to their faithful Creator in well-doing" (4:19). It is better, if that is God's will, to suffer for doing good than for doing evil (3:17). There is blessing in suffering for doing right (3:14; 4:14). Peter

holds out hope that the believers' suffering would be only for "a little while" and that God would strengthen them (5:10).

We are not to think of 1 Peter, then, as a casual writing addressed to carefree citizens who might appreciate a few well-chosen platitudes. The writer was well aware that his readers were in danger, and he wrote his letter to them with a full awareness of their plight. He chose his words carefully, knowing that only what was eternally true would do here. He packed an extraordinary amount of basic Christian teaching into the small compass of his five chapters.

THE LIVING GOD

Once Peter refers to God as the "living God" (1:23), and the thought that God is vitally concerned with all that happens runs through his letter. God has chosen his people, and the thought of election recurs (1:1; 2:9; 5:10). God's will is done (2:15; 3:17; 4:2, 19). He has foreknowledge of who are his (1:2), and his Word abides forever (1:25). He is the Creator (4:19), and he is powerful (1:5; 5:11). In the end we must all reckon with this, for judgment is a reality for the dead (4:6), for God's people and for those who disobey the gospel (4:17). God resists the proud (5:5).

But we are also to think of God in terms of love and grace and kindness. He is the Father (1:2–3, 17) and "the God of all grace" (5:10). The whole letter was written to encourage the readers by testifying that "this is the true grace of God" in which they were standing (5:12). This is not unlike the exhortation to set their hope "on the grace being brought to [them] in the revelation of Jesus Christ" (1:13), where the meaning may be that grace will reach its consummation at the *parousia,* or that grace is a present reality. Both are true, and there seems little point in trying to decide between them. The prophets prophesied of the grace that was to come (1:10), which certainly refers to the grace God gave through Christ. Man and wife are joint heirs of "the grace of life" (3:7), and all Christians are to be good ministers of "God's multicolored grace" (4:10). God gives grace to lowly people (5:5). Clearly grace is a concept that matters a good deal; it is God's good gift to his people.

The Christian life is all a gift of God, for in his abundant mercy he has caused us to be born again (1:3); our spiritual life is sheer miracle. So it is that we have a living hope and look forward to an inheritance in heaven that is "incorruptible and undefiled and unending" (1:3–4). Our faith and our hope are in God (1:21; cf. 3:5), as is our strength for service (4:11). Christian service can be described as offering spiritual sacrifices to God (2:5), and it is interesting to see the variety of ways in which Peter relates the church to God. The church is "the people of God" (2:10), "the household of God" (4:17), and "the flock of God" (5:2), and its members are "God's slaves" (2:16).

All in all this is a very satisfying concept of a God who is ceaselessly active in his creation and particularly concerned for those for whom his Son died. He is constantly watching over them and, though they may be called on to suffer for his sake, they must know that his purpose is worked out even in that and in due course he will deliver them and bring them into glory.

THE CHIEF SHEPHERD

Peter has much to say about our Lord and about his saving work. He calls him "the shepherd and guardian of our souls" (2:25), where his word for "guardian" (*episkopos*) is that used for a bishop in the church. It is probably a little too early for us to understand it in this sense, but it certainly points to oversight and care. This is true also of "Chief Shepherd" (5:4), used only here in the New Testament. The writer is sure of Christ's superior place but also of his love for his people and his constant looking after them. He calls him "Lord" (1:3) and urges his readers to "sanctify" Christ in their hearts as Lord (3:15). Christ was predestined before the foundation of the world, though revealed only "at the end of the times" (1:20). He had a special place in God's scheme of things and a special relationship to God. That is, he was chosen by God and precious (2:4). Peter has a lot to say about Christ's saving work, as we will see in a moment, but he speaks also of his resurrection (1:3; 3:21) and of his high place in heaven at the right hand of God, where the heavenly hosts are in subjection to him (3:22). We are not to lose sight of his greatness.

There is a notable passage about the redemption that Christ brought about (1:18ff.). Strictly speaking, redemption means release on payment of a price, and Peter rejects the idea that valuable commodities like gold and silver might bring about such liberation. Instead, the redemption of which he writes was purchased with the price of "precious blood as of a lamb without blemish and without stain."

Peter introduces this with the words "Pass the time of your sojourning in fear, knowing that you were redeemed . . ." (1:17–18). Why does Peter write, "in fear"? Perhaps because it was a terrible price that Christ paid, and we must not take the thought of our redemption calmly, as though it were a natural thing. Sinners were in a plight from which there appeared to be no escape. It is extraordinary that a price has been found. There are consequences of this redemption. We are now delivered from the "empty manner of life handed down from our fathers" (1:18). God delivered us so that we should engage, not in futility, but in meaningful service.

The mention of a lamb moves us into the imagery of sacrifice. Christ's death was both a ransom and a sacrifice, and everything that was foreshadowed in the sacrifices of old is fully brought to pass in Christ. The sacrifices are no doubt also in the thought of Peter when he refers to the "sprinkling of the blood of Jesus Christ" (1:2).

Another noteworthy passage sees Christ's sufferings as both an example and a bearing of sin (2:21–25). Jesus was not put to death because of his wrongdoing, for "he did no sin." His sufferings were thus an example to the readers who were also liable to suffer for no wrongdoing but simply for their Christian profession. It was a comfort to know that their Savior had set them the example of how such suffering should be borne.

Peter goes on to say that Jesus "himself bore our sins in his body on the tree." Some have seen these words to mean that Jesus patiently endured all the ill-treatment he received right up to and including the Cross; they see it as a continuation of the thought that he set an example of how to endure suffering. But this is to overlook the language used. Peter is not talking about the sins of those who put Jesus to death, but of Peter's sins and those of his readers. Moreover he says, "in his body"; he is not writing about the attitude of spirit that endures ill-treatment in the right way (cf. also his reference to Christ as suffering "in the flesh" [4:1]). And he refers to "the tree," not to life as a whole. Similarly "by whose wound you were healed" looks to the Cross, not the endurance of insult.

The bearing of sins is not a common New Testament expression (elsewhere only in Heb. 9:28). But it is frequent in the Old Testament where it clearly means bearing the penalty of sins (e.g., Lev. 22:9; Num. 9:13, where NIV paraphrases). There is no reason for thinking that Peter is using the expression in any other than this Old Testament way. He is saying that Christ in his death bore the penalty for our sins.[1] We should also bear in mind that the passage has several coincidences of language with Isaiah 53 ("who did no sin"; "neither was guile found in his mouth"; "who bore our sins"; "by

---

[1] Cf. C. E. B. Cranfield, "The bearing of our sins means suffering the punishment of them in our place (cf. Num. 14:33). On the cross He bore not merely physical pain and sorrow that men could be so blind and wicked, but, what was much more dreadful, that separation from His Father ('My God, my God, why hast thou forsaken me?') that was the due reward of our sins" (*The First Epistle of Peter* [London, 1950], 67–68). F. W. Beare comments, "The best meaning for the verb here seems to be 'bear the consequences'" (*The First Epistle of Peter* [Oxford, 1947], 124).

whose wound you were healed"; "as sheep going astray"). Clearly the writer sees Jesus as the Suffering Servant.[2] Jesus died for us; he has taken our place.

Peter had this in mind again when he wrote that Christ "suffered for sins once for all, the just for the unjust, in order to bring us to God" (3:18). We are clearly moving in the same circle of ideas. Christ deals with our sins by suffering, specifically by dying in our place, "the just for the unjust." For the preposition "for" he uses *hyper,* which sometimes has a meaning like "on behalf of" but sometimes also "in place of,"[3] and it seems that it is the latter meaning we should see here.

Peter uses the rejected-stone motif (Ps. 118:22; Isa. 8:14; 28:16), Christ being the stone rejected by men but chosen by God for the most significant place (2:4–8). We are not to understand the cross of Christ from the way it appeared to people; God had his own purpose in it and the rejected One is the supremely important One, for in him God's salvation is worked out. The passage must have been a great encouragement to those who were suffering because of their faith, for it made clear the difference between the view persecutors took of them and the way God worked out his purpose in them.

The sufferings of Christ were predicted by the prophets (1:12); clearly these sufferings were in the purpose of

God. But so were the subsequent glories, which were also prophesied by the same prophets. God has called the readers of this letter "into his eternal glory in Christ" (5:10).

Peter has no doubt about the greatness of Christ and about the wonderful salvation he won for us. He has some of the most noteworthy statements in the New Testament about the atoning value of Christ's sufferings and about the glory that these sufferings bring believers.

THE HOLY SPIRIT

Peter does not say much about the Holy Spirit in this epistle, but he does make some significant statements about him. He begins with a statement linking "the sanctification of the Spirit" with the foreknowledge of God and the sprinkling of the blood of Christ (1:2), so it is clear that he has a high view of the person of the Spirit. The Spirit's work of sanctifying, setting people apart, and making them fit for the service of God is an integral part of the Christian salvation. The Spirit may be called "the Spirit of Christ" (1:11; cf. Rom. 8:9),[4] and this shows something of his importance in the Christian scheme of things and also links him closely with Jesus as the Author of our salvation.

The Holy Spirit is active in the work of proclamation, for the gospel was

[2] A. F. Walls points out that the Suffering Servant motif is to be found in Mark (which he thinks may with good reason be connected with Peter) and in the Petrine speeches in Acts as well as this letter. He adds, "Other New Testament writings, of course, are indebted to Isaiah liii, but it is surely not coincidental that these writings connected with Peter's name all bear the impress of the Servant so deeply that, diverse in form as they are, it can be described as their central thought about Christ" (A. M. Stibbs and A. F. Walls, *The First Epistle General of Peter* [London, 1959], 33).

[3] Harald Riesenfeld sees the preposition as having the meaning "in the place of" in passages like 1 Corinthians 15:29 (*TDNT,* 8:512–13), and it seems that this is the meaning required here. I have a note on the meaning of this preposition in *The Apostolic Preaching of the Cross* (London, 1965), 62–64.

[4] Some hold that the expression here means "the Spirit who is Christ" and see a reference to a preincarnate activity of Christ. This is not impossible, but a reference to the Holy Spirit seems more likely.

preached to these readers "in the Holy Spirit sent from heaven" (1:12). Preaching the gospel is no merely human achievement; unless the Holy Spirit is at work, there is no effectiveness. The conversion of souls is a divine, not a human, achievement. And the ongoing life of the Christian is under the influence of the Spirit for "the Spirit of glory, even the Spirit of God rests on you" (4:14). The readers were being ill-treated and insulted on account of their connection with Christ, but let them not be upset by this. None less than the Spirit of glory, the Spirit of God himself, is with them. What, then, do the reproaches of the world matter?

THE LIFE OF
THE CHRISTIAN

As the work of the Spirit within them indicates, believers are already enjoying salvation. Already they are receiving the salvation of their souls (1:9). (It is concerning this salvation that the prophets spoke in days of old [1:10]). There is much ahead of them but, like newborn babies, they are growing up in their salvation (2:2). The whole epistle makes it clear that believers already in this life possess salvation.

But in Peter's writings we see again the familiar eschatological tension between the already and the not yet. Salvation is a present possession, certainly. But it is also something that will be "revealed in the last time" (1:5). The readers should "gird up the loins" of their understanding; they should be sober and set their hope on the grace that will be brought to them at the revelation of Jesus Christ (1:13). Another exhortation to sobriety arises from the fact that "the end of all things is at hand" (4:7), and this surely cannot

be much different from the "day of visitation" (2:12), the day when the Chief Shepherd will appear (5:4). It cannot be said that Peter favors either side of the paradox. He gives due emphasis to both present and future salvation. We should forget neither.

The apostle has something to say about a variety of Christian virtues and experiences such as faith (1:7–9, 21), love (for Christ [1:8] and for the brothers [1:22; 2:17; 3:8; 4:8]; cf. the greeting with "a kiss of love" [5:14]), joy (1:8; cf. 4:13), hope (1:3, 13, 21; 3:15), and the like. But his emphasis is on the changed lives that should characterize Christians. We are born again, not of corruptible seed, but of incorruptible (1:23), which means a clean break with evil. We have been instructed not to do evil things such as being conformed to the lusts of our previous existence (1:14). We are to put away all malice, craftiness, hypocrisy, envy, and slander (2:1). We are to abstain from fleshly lusts (2:11). The readers had evidently known a good deal of this sort of living before their conversion, and Peter tells them they have lived long enough in evil ways (4:3).

But Peter is not engaging in some negative philosophy. The Christian life is gloriously positive, and he looks for his readers to be holy in all they do (1:15–16). They are to be obedient (1:14), to live good lives (2:12), to live in unity and love (3:8), to be self-controlled and to pray (4:7), to use whatever gift God has given them (4:10), to be humble (5:5–6). Christ takes the most unpromising of people and transforms them into the saints of God. Peter wants his readers to be absolutely certain that this transformation is not simply something to make them glad when they see it in others, but something that must take place in them too. It is a message that is still relevant.

The apostle values very highly the corporate life of Christians. He never uses the word "church," but he writes about it, as when he tells his readers that they are "a chosen race, a royal priesthood, a holy nation, a people for God's own possession" (2:9). They are like living stones to be built up into a "spiritual house," a holy priesthood, and as such they are to offer "spiritual sacrifices acceptable to God through Jesus Christ" (2:5). At one time they were not a people at all; now they are the people of God (2:10). This means that here they are aliens and exiles; they do not belong to this world (1:1; 2:11). The apostle's interest in the church is perhaps behind his references to baptism (3:21) and to the elders (5:1–4).

the second epistle of peter

In this epistle, Peter concentrates on a few points. He begins with the salvation God has given in Christ and the kind of living that should characterize those who have experienced this salvation. Then he goes on to the testimony of the prophets and of Scripture, to the problem posed by the appearance of certain false teachers, and finally to a section on the *parousia* and its delay.

Peter addresses his readers as "those who have obtained faith as precious as ours in the righteousness of our God and Savior Jesus Christ" (1:1). He writes of the initiative of Christ in bringing about faith and presents the work of Christ in terms of righteousness, somewhat in the Pauline manner. But there is a difference. In Paul righteousness is the right standing believers have; here the thought is that it is the justice, or the rightness, of Christ that brings about salvation.[1] Salvation does not proceed from any human endeavor but from what Christ has done, and we receive it by faith. Peter repeatedly says that Christ is Savior (1:11; 2:20; 3:2, 18). This is not expressed in the way other New Testament writers would

have put it, but it is essentially the same thought. The phrase "as precious as ours" expresses the equality between the apostles and other believers. Salvation comes in the same way for all.

Peter refers to Jesus as "our God and Savior Jesus Christ" (1:1). In this statement he is almost certainly calling him "God." It is possible that the meaning is "our God and the Savior Jesus Christ," but this is unlikely.[2] The author is giving the highest possible place to Christ. Incidentally he almost always uses the compound name "Jesus Christ" and frequently combines it with "Lord."

To him salvation means that "all things that belong to life and godliness" have been given to us (1:3). We have been "called" (1:3, 10), we have received "precious and very great promises" (1:4), and we have been "established in the present truth" (1:12). Clearly salvation is a wonderful gift and is to be highly prized. Peter makes this just as clear as anyone else in the New Testament does. And he emphasizes that we do not earn it; it is the gift of God in Christ.

---

[1] Cf. J. N. D. Kelly, who says that in this letter "*dikaiosunē* regularly connotes justice or fair dealing, and that provides an excellent sense here" (*A Commentary on the Epistles of Peter and of Jude* [London, 1969], 297).

[2] C. F. D. Moule sees it as probable that here and in Titus 2:13 "the article has been correctly omitted and that τοῦ (μεγάλου) Θεοῦ is intended to apply to Jesus" (*IBNTG*, 110).

He brings this out by speaking of our being "partakers of the divine nature" (1:4). Linked as it is with the thought of escaping the corruption that is in the world in lust, this comes close to the thought of some Hellenistic writers, who see the body as imprisoning us with our lusts and who see salvation as a release from the body. This is not Peter's meaning; he is using language that will be meaningful to his readers to bring out the thought that Christian salvation means the power of God working within the believer so that he is no longer subject to the power of evil (cf. John 1:12–13; Rom. 8:9).

Thus, the Christian life is to be lived in the power of God, not in the ways of this evil world. To faith believers must add virtue, knowledge, self-control, perseverance, godliness, brotherly love, and love (1:5–7). They are not to be ineffective and unfruitful, blind and shortsighted, forgetful that they have been cleansed from sin (1:8–9). They are to live lives of holiness and godliness as they await Christ's return (3:11–12). They are to grow in grace and the knowledge of Christ (3:18).

The writer urges all this because of the certainty of the facts on which their faith is based. They did not follow clever myths; there were people who, on the mount of the Transfiguration, heard the heavenly voice say of Jesus Christ: "This is my beloved Son" (1:17). Peter also points to inspired prophecy (1:19–21). He is sure that God has revealed himself and that a perfect salvation has been worked out on the basis of the shed blood of Jesus Christ. Let the readers live in the light of this fact.

FALSE TEACHERS

In Old Testament times God had sent great prophets to Israel, and false prophets tried to lead the people astray. It should come as no surprise, then, that New Testament believers would be confronted with false teachers.

Peter does not say much about the form of the false teaching; he is evidently not in the business of helping the error by repeating it. But he does say that they denied "the Master who bought them" (2:1). This clearly refers to the Cross as an act of redemption: Christ bought all believers with his blood. In what way the teachers denied this is not clear. It may be that their conduct was incompatible with a genuine belief in redemption, or they may have had some other view of the significance of the Cross. What really matters is that these teachers were astray at the heart of the faith.

22

the epistle of jude

There is considerable duplication of material between 2 Peter and Jude, and scholars have discussed the relationship between the two writings. Generally scholars think that Jude was written first and that 2 Peter depends on it. None of this matters much for our present purpose. Whoever wrote these two writings and whenever they were written, they are part of the New Testament and are to be considered when we look at New Testament theology as a whole. But there is no need to say a great deal about Jude because of the overlap with 2 Peter and the fact that in other points also the two writers are saying many of the same things.

There are close parallels in 2 Peter to all of Jude except the first three verses and the last seven. Both writers were confronted by busy heretics who were trying to subvert the orthodox, and both wrote to redress the situation. Jude would have liked to write about salvation (v. 3), but the pressing needs of the moment meant that he had to deal with the current situation. So he went on to speak of God's judgments on sinners (those who perished in the wilderness, sinning angels, Sodom and Gomorrah [vv. 5–7]). In rebuking the pride of the heretics, he spoke of the archangel Michael and of the way he called on God to rebuke the devil; he did not presume to do it himself (vv. 8–9). Jude saw the false teachers as failing to understand, as countenancing error for the sake of gain (as Balaam did), as being without substance, and therefore as coming under severe judgment (vv. 10–13).

But God is not defeated. Enoch prophesied about the judgment of these people (vv. 14–16), and later Jesus' apostles also prophesied of them (v. 17). Believers should thus not be greatly perturbed but continue in their "most holy faith" (v. 20) and keep on with their evangelistic and pastoral work (vv. 21–23).

There are problems with this short writing, but it is perhaps enough to notice that it says much the same as 2 Peter does. It emphasizes the importance of a right faith and of upright living. In the end Jude looks to God in Christ to keep us from falling and at last to present us faultless before him (vv. 24–25).

conclusion

One thing that emerges from this survey is that the writers of the New Testament books were all individuals. None was trying to keep to a "party line," but each wrote out of his own Christian experience to meet the needs of his readers as he saw them, and he wrote from the deep conviction that what God had done in Christ was of fundamental importance. But the way each expressed that is his own.

Paul is both strikingly early and strikingly original. His writings show that less than twenty years after the Crucifixion the main outlines of the Christian message were clear. He is usually seen as the man who emphasized the centrality of justification by faith, and there is good reason for this, for Paul set forth that doctrine with authority.

But we should not overlook the fact that he had other ways of viewing Christ's saving work and that he emphasized the Cross, reconciliation, deliverance from a variety of tyrants, and the turning away of the wrath of God. He was sure of the inability of people to overcome evil in their own strength, and he saw evil forces in many places. There is the power of sin, of the flesh (the enemy within), and of the evil one and other wicked spirits. We are under the sway of death. There were people who saw the law of God as vitally connected with the way people are to please God, but, from another angle, Paul could see it as another of the tyrants that keep us in bondage. He also saw it as holy and just and good, so his idea is complex.

But what is beyond doubt is that Paul saw God as active in Christ, delivering those who trust him. It is not the plight of sinners that is central to Paul's thinking but the wonderful deliverance that God has brought about in Christ. He has a number of vivid word pictures that bring out what God has done—redemption, reconciliation, propitiation, nailing the "handwriting that was against us" to the cross, and others. Whatever needed to be done Christ did, and there is no imperfection in the salvation he accomplished.

So we are called on to live in love for him who loved us so much. It is somewhat surprising that in much modern writing the extent to which Paul stresses the love of God, the love of Christ, and the love that should characterize believers is overlooked. But no one in the New Testament stresses love as Paul does—no one. Love is of central significance. Sometimes he brings out the place of love with other terminology as when he speaks of grace, which is nothing less than love in action. The love that Christians are to show is not a human achievement, and thus Paul stresses the place of the Holy Spirit, who indeed pours love into our hearts. The Spirit is active in energizing believers, and Paul speaks both of what he does in all of us and of his special "gifts" to chosen servants of God.

One could go on. The things that Paul contributes to our understanding of the Christian way seem never to end. But other writers have their own way of putting things. We saw that Mark presents his combination of Jesus' lowliness and majesty, his genuine humanity and his position as the strong Son of God.

Mark did something that nobody else had done before him, it seems: he wrote a Gospel and thus produced a new genre. He wrote in a way that is not to be seen simply as history, though there is history in his book. But he was well aware that he was not writing history as such, and in his opening statements he informs the reader that this is "gospel." He is conveying the "good news" of what God has done in Christ and for Mark that means showing that the Son of God came right where we are. He lived our life, with the exception that we make a hash of it with our evil deeds, whereas he showed what a human life can be like if it is lived as it ought to be lived. So Mark brings out Jesus' deeds of compassion, but also his deeds of power. He is to be seen as God as well as perfect man.

And Mark puts emphasis on Jesus' death on the cross; the Passion dominates his book. Mark is no Paul, of course. He has none of the apostle's rich imagery, and his thought is not as profound as that of Paul. But he is just

as clear as Paul in declaring that what God did in Christ was the really important thing. And, writing with this conviction, he has produced a new literary form, the Gospel. Mark has done something profound that has influenced Christians ever since.

It is interesting that it is Mark who brings out the failings of the Twelve more clearly than does anyone else. He makes it clear that they did not understand Jesus as we might have expected they would and that again and again they came short of being ideal disciples. At the critical point they all forsook Jesus and fled. It is important for us to see that the church was not established because of the coming together of a group of outstanding and holy men. On the contrary, the church was built on the preaching of discredited men. It was the power of God and not the courage or the saintliness of the first disciples that led to the appearance of the church of God, a truth that has meant much to weak and feeble followers of the Christ ever since.

Matthew also wrote a Gospel but did not say the same thing as Mark. He puts emphasis on the teaching of Jesus, and no one in the New Testament gives us as full information about what the Master said as Matthew does. Our knowledge of many of the parables we owe to him, and records of such teachings as the Sermon on the Mount have put all subsequent generations of Christians deeply in his debt.

Regarding the thematic emphases of this Gospel, what stands out clearly is that Matthew was deeply interested in the kingdom of heaven, and it is because of him that we have so much information about what Jesus said concerning the kingdom. It is not that he alone refers to the kingdom, for others do also. But he has brought out its force more fully and more clearly than anyone else. He was interested in the person of Jesus, too, and made much of the meaning of the title "Son of David," for example. Moreover, Matthew is the only Evangelist to use the word "church"; he was interested in the body of Christians.

Luke has traditionally been seen as a historian, and his interest in history is obvious. He is the only one of the New Testament writers to give us information about the history of the early church. And he locates the saving deeds in the framework of secular history in a way that the other Evangelists do not. Clearly Luke saw God as active in all of life, in the affairs of the pagan rulers as well as in the service that Christians render to God.

But we should be clear that he is not just another historian, giving information about first-century times. He too is an Evangelist. He wrote a Gospel, and Acts is simply the continuance of his Gospel. In a sense these two make up one book, a book in two volumes. We misunderstand if we see it simply as a history; it is rather the record of the gospel in action. Luke is telling us how God in Christ brought salvation to many and how the message came to Rome, the capital of the world.

Luke is unique; his writing two volumes alone shows that, but his uniqueness comes out in other ways also. We do not usually observe that Luke links suffering with the Christ and that he does so often. Other writers see suffering as integral to Jesus' ministry but link this with some such title as "Son of man." Luke emphasizes that Jesus suffered because he was the Christ. He does not bring out the meaning of the Cross in Paul's multivariegated way, but he lets his readers see that it was important, and indeed in his use of the term "tree" he brings out the truth that Jesus bore the curse that was due sinners.

Luke is clear that God is active in human affairs and shows in a fascinating way the truth that God guides his people. Luke loves a good miracle and in his account shows that God intervened again and again. He shows us how the Holy Spirit has guided Christians from the beginning. For the practical living of the Christian life it is important to know that we are not alone, and Luke makes this clearer than anyone else.

But perhaps he has put us most in his debt with the way he has brought out God's interest in and care for those whom the society of his day regarded with scant respect. Luke finds a special place for the poor, for women, for children, and for the disreputable. Through the centuries Christians have all too frequently been content to go along with the estimate of the people that were usually accepted in the society of their day. They have practiced a kind of "society ethic," doing the things that most people would do and avoiding those evils that society in general reproved. They have not seen that Christians are called on to be distinctive: to take what God has taught them in Christ as the standard, not what they see in the traditional values they see around them. And if they fail in this, it is not Luke's fault. He has made it clear that Jesus did not go along with the traditional values of the society of his day and that he expects from his people more than this.

For many people it is John who is the high point of the Bible, and this is understandable. We can only stand in awe and reverence for the understanding of the Christian way set out for us in the fourth Gospel. John has possibly seen more, and he has seen more clearly, than any other Christian and has put us all deeply in his debt by what he has written. He has some unusual ways of putting this, such as his opening reference to the Savior as "the Word." We may not be able to plumb the depths of all that he says, but we can appreciate that he is saying something important. And all that he says centers on Christ. Throughout his book it is our Lord who is right at the heart of things.

John preserves for us deeds and words that nobody else has recorded, and all the Christian generations have profited from this. It is John who has recorded the teaching that it is only as we are born of the Holy Spirit that we can enter the kingdom of God. And it is to John that we owe the "I am" sayings, the teachings about the bread of life, the light of the world, the good Shepherd, and much more.

What we do not notice as often as we should is that John brings out Jesus' constant dependence on the Father. The Jesus of the fourth Gospel can do nothing of himself; it is only because the Father is with him that he is able to do the things he does. John has the magnificent concept of "humble glory" (in Origen's phrase). He sees the glory of Jesus not in majesty and splendor but in lowly service. It is real glory when One who is so high and who could claim so much for himself instead leaves his place of privilege and serves others in the humblest capacity. And John brings this to its climax by including Jesus' reference to his being "lifted up," exalted, in the Cross. What to men and women seemed the ultimate in degradation John saw as the supreme exaltation.

Revelation, whether it was written by the same author as that of the Gospel and the epistles or not, is a work of a markedly different character. The techniques of apocalyptic with its vivid imagery are used with striking effect. Much puzzles us who were not brought up on the meaning of this genre and who must come to it from without. But no one can escape the force of the demonstration that, powerful though the forces of evil may be, they are no match for the power of the Lord God Almighty. Evil may seem to us to be so strong that we are quite unable to defeat it, but we must not go on from there to conclude that it is unstoppable. In the end it is the power of God and of good that will prevail, not the strength of the evil one and those who consort with him. And we would be much the poorer if we did not have the magnificent pictures of "the Lamb as it had been slain," and of the multitude who have washed their robes and made them white in the blood of the Lamb. John finishes with his picture of the new heaven and the new earth, which have been the inspiration of so many through the centuries. The servants of God in any age may find it difficult to make headway against evil, and it is easy to yield to the temptation to think we can never win and may just as well abandon the struggle and go over to the enemy. Revelation will help us regain God's perspective. The final visions are a compelling demonstration that God has wonderful things in store for his people.

Hebrews is another writing that moves in a world that is not ours. But this writer's picture of Jesus as a great High Priest, or as a priest like Melchizedek, or simply as a priest, brings out something important for our understanding of our Savior and our salvation. He was able to take a part of the ancient Scripture that had not meant much to other expositors and show that the incident in which Melchizedek met Abraham had important teaching for later generations.

He takes also the idea of covenant,

one that is found sporadically elsewhere in the New Testament, and shows that the new covenant that Christ made through his shed blood is of central importance. The Jewish people knew their covenant with God was highly significant. It made them the people of God in a special way. When that covenant is regarded as obsolete and as now replaced by "the new covenant," the writer is making an emphatic point that the Christian way is not a modified Judaism but something radically new. The terminology is different, but it is like the statement "I make all things new" in Revelation.

The author uses a considerable variety of ways of looking at the effects of Christ's atoning death. Few writers bring out the many-sidedness of the Atonement as he does. He particularly emphasizes sacrifices, as we might expect from his use of the priesthood concept, and he stresses the facts that Christ's sacrifice is of permanent validity and that there is no other sacrifice that really does take away sins. He thinks of Christ's work as performed in a heavenly sanctuary in the presence of God, whereas earthly priests necessarily work in a temple made with hands. A contrast between the earthly and the heavenly is made from time to time in this epistle.

A striking feature is the treatment of faith in Hebrews 11. The author of Hebrews does not use the concept of faith in the same way as Paul does, though he sometimes comes close to the Pauline use. But whereas Paul concentrates largely on faith as the means by which we are accepted by God, in Hebrews the emphasis is on faith as the means by which we serve God acceptably. The heroes of faith were people who trusted God to accomplish his purpose when there was nothing in their outward circumstances

to give them hope. This is an important part of living out the faith.

James is usually known from his emphatic statements about faith and works. There is no necessary contradiction between what he says and Paul's view of justification by faith, but James certainly does not express himself in the way Paul would. His insistence on a live faith in contrast to a faith without works remains an important part of the New Testament understanding of service to God. So does his insistence that the tongue is important and that it is easy to sin in the things we say. The church can always do with the robust emphasis on practical Christianity that is so much a feature of this writing.

The First Epistle of Peter was clearly written to a suffering church, and the writer's insistence that believers may sometimes be called on to suffer for their faith—to suffer when they do well—has always been very important for Christians. At countless times and in many places believers have been called on to suffer for their faith, as, of course, they still are in some parts of the world. Peter's insistence on a right attitude on the part of the sufferer and his assurance of God's sustaining hand are of continuing importance.

This epistle does deal with other important aspects of Christianity. Peter brings out something of the importance of the church with his teaching about a royal priesthood, a holy people, and the like. The corporate life of believers is integral to the Christian way. Moreover, this writer has some important teaching about Christ; for example, he is the only New Testament writer to call him the "Chief Shepherd." He also speaks of him as bearing our sins (a concept he shares with Hebrews). In another passage he denies that our redemption has anything to do with earth's precious things like gold or silver, but declares emphatically that it results from the precious blood of Jesus.

Many are inclined to take lightly the contributions of 2 Peter and Jude, but there is no reason for doing so. Both writers were faced with false teachers and remind us that not everything that claims to be Christian should be accepted at face value. It is possible to invoke the name of Christ for purposes very different from his. Second Peter speaks of Christ as "God and Savior" (according to our best understanding of the text); so the author has a very high view indeed of the Lord. And he has the interesting concept that the saved are partakers of the divine nature. This concept is akin to John's thought of being born of the Spirit, but it is not exactly the same. It would have been of great force in some parts of the Greek world, and this reminds us that each part of Scripture has its own force and its own usefulness. Being partakers of the divine nature affects daily living, and this letter stresses the virtues that are to characterize the walk of the believer. It has also a notable stress on the transitoriness of the world and the certainty of its ultimate destruction. That the *parousia* has not occurred as yet does not mean that it will not occur, a teaching that is still not without its value.

Jude is a small writing, but it has a notable emphasis on the reality of judgment. We are responsible people and that we will one day give account of ourselves is an important part of New Testament teaching. Jude shows that those who misrepresent Christian teaching are guilty people and must give account of themselves to God. He leaves us in no doubt as to the seriousness of engaging in false teaching. His final benediction has been loved by Christians through the centuries.

This short survey is not intended to give a potted summary of all the teaching of the various writers. It is simply a way of showing that they are all individuals. Of none of their writings can it be said, "There would be no great loss if we were without this." We may all have our favorite New Testament author, but that does not give us license to neglect the other writings. Nor should we twist what one writer is saying to make it come out the same as what another is saying. It is possible for two (or more) of them to convey the same truth in different language. But it is also possible for two (or more) of them to stress different aspects of the faith. Even this brief survey is enough to show that each of the writers has his own selection of Christian teaching and each expresses himself in his own characteristic way.

But with all their differences there is impressive agreement on certain fundamental truths. They are all "Christians," even if they do not all use that word. And that means they found a special place for Jesus Christ. Some put greater emphasis on Jesus' genuine manhood than others, and some speak of his Godhead more plainly than do others. The writers of the Gospels obviously pay much more attention to the details of Jesus' earthly life than the writers of the Epistles do, but it is the same Jesus they are writing about. And, although not all the writers have such a succinct way of putting it as John ("the Word was God"; "My Lord and my God"), all see Jesus as more than a mere man. In due course, when the theologians of the church came to characterize Jesus Christ as true God and true man, they were simply expressing in their own language a truth that they discerned throughout the New Testament. What modern scholars often call "the Christ event" was central for all the New Testament writers.

This means that these writers had a concept of God that was radically different from most of the thinking of antiquity. The Greeks typically located the gods in remote Mount Olympus. These gods were too great to be concerned with the petty affairs of puny man. So the sins of men and women were not as serious as the Christians thought (unless one was unfortunate enough or foolish enough to sin in such a way as to come before the notice of deity). It also meant that people must not look to the gods for affection and help. People might at times hope that they would merit the approbation of some deity, but they could not expect anyone as great as a god to take much notice of them.

The Christians did not see any reality in this kind of god, and so they radically rejected all such concepts. The God they knew was a very different being. He had made all this universe and all mankind, and he retained an interest in those he had made; indeed, he loved them. Throughout the New Testament the love of God and his concern for his people are constantly emphasized. This is given a greater emphasis by some writers than by others, but it is a reality to them all. Their God is an involved God. He is constantly at work in the world. One day he will bring the world to an end, and all the race will be judged. He is concerned for the way we live, and in his grace and his mercy he has fully provided for our need. The New Testament writers make it clear that he acted savingly in the death of Christ.

When they speak of what Christ has done for us, they emphasize the Crucifixion. There is not the slightest doubt that throughout the New Testament in the literal sense it is the Cross that is "crucial." There is an endless variety of ways of looking at it, pressing into service such concepts as redemption, covenant, sacrifice, particular sacrifices such as the Passover or the Day of Atonement or the sin offering, cleansing from sin, bearing sin, and much more. When we consider that in the ancient world death by crucifixion was regarded as a shameful thing, it is astonishing that believers should agree that Christ's crucifixion was so important and so glorious.

With it, of course, we must take the Resurrection, the importance of which is especially emphasized at certain periods, such as immediately after Pentecost. At that time the preachers gave it enormous emphasis. But throughout the New Testament it is invariably seen as one of the great facts about Jesus. Death could not hold him. He is superior to death, and he rose triumphant.

All this means that believers enter a new life. There is considerable emphasis on this from a number of angles. Sometimes there is the thought of eternal life, with the idea that the Christian life is life proper to the age to come. The age to come has broken into the world of time and sense and has brought about an entirely new situation.

The New Testament writers are pessimistic about the ability of the natural man to live in accordance with the will of God. They see us as slaves to sin, as dominated by the flesh, as yielding to the temptations of the evil one, but none of the New Testament writers sees us as able to live lives fit for the kingdom of God in our own strength. We are liable to the judgment of God, and we face the certainty of loss because of our sin. The wrath of God is real. What is clear is that, understand the human predicament as we will, Christ has fully met our need.

Thus, Christians live on a higher

level than they did before they came to know Christ. Nothing is more characteristic of the New Testament than its insistence that those who have been saved by Christ should live in accordance with their salvation. Sometimes lists of evil deeds are given with the reminder that this was the kind of thing believers did before they became Christians. We are not to think that the early church was made up of the most honorable and upright citizens. In one life after another the gospel transformed what must have seemed the most unpromising material.

God gave his Holy Spirit to those who trusted him, and the Spirit provided a strength that enabled believers to rise far above the best level they could reach with their natural endowment. The indwelling of the Spirit in believers is a fascinating part of New Testament teaching, fascinating because so many of the early Christians were people with little capacity for profound metaphysical thinking and whose previous way of life had not prepared them for the high standards required of Christians. The interesting thing is not that some of them fell, but that so many welcomed the Spirit and lived in his strength. The Christian church not only demanded but got a standard of living unique in antiquity.

In one way or another, all the New Testament writers stress the importance of love. That God is love is a statement that we find explicitly only in 1 John, but the truth of it pervades every book and chapter. It is basic that God is a God of love and that the salvation wrought in Christ is the outworking of the love of God.

Love as the New Testament knows it was a new thing. There was, of course, love of various kinds in the ancient world. But Jesus' "new" commandment was a commandment to love as he loved. And his love was a love not only for the attractive, but for sinners. Jesus taught his followers to be loving people. God loves us because he is a loving God, because it is his nature to love. Thus, he loves everybody, not only those who are charming or pious or upright or who have any other form of attractiveness. That is the kind of love that is demanded of the followers of Jesus—the kind of love that the Spirit produces in them. To live in love for others, in the spirit of the love that Christ had when he died for us while we were still sinners, is to show that a revolution has taken place within us. Because Christ has done so much for us, the only suitable response that we can make is to be ready to love as he loved.

The New Testament writers make it clear that Christ's departure from this earth is only temporary. They looked for him to return in due course, and the *parousia* was a constant expectation. There are disputes among the scholars as to how soon Christians in general thought all this would be, but that it was a precious expectation of the early church is beyond all doubt. The coming of Christ had altered everything. Now believers are living in "the last days," days of a different quality because of what Christ has done.

I could go on. I am not outlining all that the early church believed or even the theological points that seem to me necessarily the most important. I am simply making the point that in the New Testament it is plain that there are some permanently valid facts about God, about Christ, about the Holy Spirit, about sinful mankind, about the church of God, and about the kind of service the redeemed should render. Such teachings are the common stock of the Christian church: they are not the private views of this or that teacher.

All the points I have made in this summary are representative. They may fairly be said to be "New Testament teaching."

The point of all this is that there is such a thing as authentic Christian teaching. The followers of Christ have all too often read back their own ideas into Scripture and have demanded that their own private understanding should be binding on others. This attitude has led many to be suspicious of dogma and to be firmly convinced that an undogmatic Christianity is needed. It is easy to see why some hold such views and it is impossible not to be sympathetic with them. Narrow dogmatism is an ugly thing. Yet there are some great teachings that are a necessary part of authentic Christianity, and these teachings must be held as firmly in this century as in any other.

index of persons

Abbot, Walter M.   142n.53
Albright, W. F.   119n.12, 122n.21, 123n.24, 130, 136n.45
Ammi, R.   278
Anderson, Hugh   96, 98, 105n.32, 111
Argyle, A. W.   38n.29, 227n.4
Athanasius   12
Augustine   256n.1
Aulen, G.   61n.23
Aune, David E.   67n.34, 93n.8

Banks, Robert   121
Barclay, William   58n.5, 71n.43, 175n.3, 178n.10, 226, 256n.2, 262n.13
Barrett, C. K.   30n.14, 37n.28, 44n.19, 50n.39, 88n.29, 111n.45, 176n.6, 220n.38, 230n.12, 231n.14, 260n.8
Barth, G.   118n.10, 132n.39, 135n.43
Barth, Karl   44n.16, 98n.9
Barth, Markus   21n.6, 46n.29
Beare, F. W.   43n.14, 318n.1
Beasly-Murray, Paul   46n.29
Behm, Johannes   43n.13, 263
Beker, J. Christiaan   23n.10, 88nn.28,29, 144
Best, Ernest   21n.6, 31n.17, 97n.7, 111
Billerbeck, Paul   122
Black, Matthew   101n.18, 115n.5
Blass-Debrunner,   37n.28
Bligh, Philip H.   100
Boers, Hendrikus   10n.5, 14n.21
Bonsirven, J.   13n.18
Borchert, Otto   109n.42
Bornkamm, Günther   58n.8, 60nn.12,14, 69n.39, 70n.40, 86n.25, 88n.28, 136n.44, 137n.46, 142n.56
Boslooper, Thomas   159n.5
Bouttier, Michel   67, 80n.8, 82n.13

Bromiley, Geoffrey W.   10, 10n.4
Brown, Colin   131
Brown, Raymond E.   122n.22, 159n.5, 241n.31, 269n.2
Brownlee, W. H.   192n.2
Bruce, F. F.   11n.8, 20n.3, 28n.9, 65n.29, 162n.7, 170, 187n.21, 205nn.14,15, 215n.27
Brunner, Emil   72n.48
Büchsel, Friedrich   262
Bultmann, Rudolf   9, 25n.2, 31n.16, 92n.2, 96n.6, 141n.52, 167n.13, 257n.3, 274
Burkitt, F. Crawford   106n.36
Burnaby, John   58n.7

Caesar (Augustus)   21, 176
Caird, G. B.   153n.14, 182n.13, 187n.22, 189, 218
Calvin, John   256n.1
Cary, M.   202
Casey, Maurice   40n.7
Cerfaux, Lucien   68n.35, 87, 89n.32
Charlesworth, James H.   101n.19
Cole, R. A.   65n.30
Colwell, E. C.   227n.6
Conzelmann, Hans   9, 13n.17, 14n.24, 36n.26, 88n.28, 176n.5, 177, 185, 189, 243
Cranfield, C. E. B.   30n.14, 31n.15, 39, 48n.33, 53n.43, 57, 61, 83n.16, 85n.20, 95n.2, 107n.39, 108, 132, 318n.1
Creed, J. M.   185n.18
Cullmann, Oscar   39n.1, 43n.12, 44n.19, 49n.33, 102n.23, 104n.25, 141n.52, 304n.4

Dahl, Nils Alstruys   23nn.9,10, 61n.18
Dalman, Gustav   119n.12, 126n.25
Daube, David   20n.4

335

index of subjects

index of scripture references